The Attractions of the Moving Image

THE ATTRACTIONS OF THE MOVING IMAGE

Essays on History, Theory, and the Avant-Garde

TOM GUNNING

Edited and with an introduction by Daniel Morgan

The University of Chicago Press

Chicago and London

The University of Chicago Press, Chicago 60637
The University of Chicago Press, Ltd., London

Published 2025
Printed in the United States of America

34 33 32 31 30 29 28 27 26 25   1 2 3 4 5

ISBN-13: 978-0-226-47979-8 (cloth)
ISBN-13: 978-0-226-47982-8 (paper)
ISBN-13: 978-0-226-47996-5 (e-book)
DOI: https://doi.org/10.7208/chicago/9780226479965.001.0001

Library of Congress Cataloging-in-Publication Data

Names: Gunning, Tom, 1949– author. | Morgan, Daniel, 1977– editor.
Title: The attractions of the moving image : essays on history, theory, and the avant-garde / Tom Gunning ; edited and with an introduction by Daniel Morgan.
Description: Chicago : The University of Chicago Press, 2025. | Includes bibliographical references and index.
Identifiers: LCCN 2024038375 | ISBN 9780226479798 (cloth) | ISBN 9780226479828 (paperback) | ISBN 9780226479965 (ebook)
Subjects: LCHS: Motion pictures—History. | LCGFT: Essays.
Classification: LCC PN1995 .G86 2025 | DDC 791.4309—dc23/eng/20241010
LC record available at https://lccn.loc.gov/2024038375

♾ This paper meets the requirements of ANSI/NISO Z39.48-1992 (Permanence of Paper).

Contents

Preface: Pulling Pieces Together
Tom Gunning
ix

Introduction
The Energies of Cinema: On the Methods of Tom Gunning
Daniel Morgan
1

PART I. HISTORY

1 The Cinema of Attractions: Early Film, Its Spectator, and the Avant-Garde (1986/1990)
41

2 What I Saw from the Rear Window of the Hôtel des Folies-Dramatiques, or the Story Point-of-View Films Told (1988)
50

3 An Aesthetic of Astonishment: Early Film and the (In)Credulous Spectator (1989)
67

4 In Your Face: Physiognomy, Photography, and the Gnostic Mission of Early Film (1997)
83

5 Landscape and the Fantasy of Moving Pictures: Early Cinema's Phantom Rides (2010)
114

6 The Play between Still and Moving Images: Nineteenth-Century "Philosophical Toys" and Their Discourse (2011)
154

PART II. THEORY

7 The Exterior as *Intérieur*: Benjamin's Optical Detective (2003)
175

8 Systematizing the Electric Message: Narrative Form, Gender, and Modernity in *The Lonedale Operator* (2004)
193

9 Moving Away from the Index: Cinema and the Impression of Reality (2007)
227

10 To Scan a Ghost: The Ontology of Mediated Vision (2007)
246

11 The Long and the Short of It: Centuries of Projecting Shadows, from Natural Magic to the Avant-Garde (2009)
275

12 Chaplin and the Body of Modernity (2010)
289

13 The Language of Motion: Moving Images within the Evolution of Human Technology (2011; unpublished)
302

14 Moving through Friedberg's Properly Adjusted Virtual Window (2019)
314

PART III. AVANT-GARDE

15 Dr. Jacobs's Dream Work: Ken Jacobs's *The Doctor's Dream* (1981–1982)
335

16 The Critique of Seeing with One's Own Eyes: Ernie Gehr's *Untitled (1977)* (1982–1983)
346

17 "Films That Tell Time": The Paradoxes of the Cinema of Ken Jacobs (1989)
349

18 Towards a Minor Cinema: Fonoroff, Herwitz, Ahwesh, LaPore, Klahr, and Solomon (1989–1990)
363

19 Perspective and Retrospective: The Films of Ernie Gehr (1993)
372

20 Bodies Rest and Motion: The Films of Mark LaPore (2006)
392

21 From Fossils of Time to a Cinematic Genesis: Gustav Deutsch's *Film ist.* (2009)
399

22 Flaming Images: Burning through the Celluloid Closet (2009/2020; unpublished)
408

23 Abigail Child: The Pulse of the Last Machine (2011)
420

24 The Secret Language of the Traces of Light: David Gatten's *Dividing Line* (2011)
437

25 The Grain of the Scratch: The Precarity of Transparency in Cinema (2015; unpublished)
451

26 Transport of Joy: A Meditation on the Medium of Stan Brakhage (2013/2021; unpublished)
464

Acknowledgments
495

Notes
497

Index
539

Preface: Pulling Pieces Together

TOM GUNNING

While researching my dissertation in the late 1970s, I was trawling through microfilm reels of the early film trade journal *The Moving Picture World*, looking at issues for 1912. One day I came across a letter from a Fred Gunning, the manager of a nickelodeon in Chillicothe, Ohio. The name was familiar to me: it was that of my father's uncle, better known by his nickname, "Wid." I knew that in the 1910s Wid Gunning had moved from movie theater manager to publicity agent for the American branch of the French production company Éclair, then become a film critic for New York newspapers and later still worked in the industry, writing subtitles for the Lon Chaney film *The Miracle Man* and producing films as an executive for First National. Eventually he became the editor of another film trade journal, *Wid's*, the ancestor of *Film Daily*.

I begin this preface by invoking my film ancestor less to validate my filmic genealogy than to signal a recognition that the history I was researching (and, in fact, writing) reached back to the decade when my father was born—but not much further. Cinema has been around for only a bit more than a century; at the point I was reeling through *Moving Picture World*, its origins still lay very much within living memory. I was still encountering its fading embers. Indeed, while working on my dissertation on the films D. W. Griffith made for the Biograph Company, I was able to meet and speak with two of the extraordinary stars of those films, Blanche Sweet and Lillian Gish. And while still an undergraduate, I had spent an unforgettable evening with Fritz Lang (on whom I would later write a monograph).

My doctoral advisor, the legendary Jay Leyda, once told me he could recall watching an early Vitagraph film in a nickelodeon as a child. Indeed, Leyda embodied film history in his life as much as in his writing, from his time studying with Sergei Eisenstein in the USSR, to his work with leftist documentarians in the USA during the 1930s, to his brief stay in Hollywood in the 1940s, to his probing of film archives in China in the 1950s. History is measured in people's lives as much as in events and dates.

The essays collected in this volume span decades of my career as a film historian, critic, and academic. During that period cinema transformed radically, moving from being primarily an image on film to an electronic one, and from a medium consumed mainly in theaters or on broadcast TV to one viewable on a wide variety of platforms. But as a film historian, it has been a fundamental discovery and principle that there was no era in which cinema had not been undergoing major transformations, including its viewing experiences. It is my hope that these essays, reflecting my own passage through the terrain of film studies, reflect also the range and variety of cinematic experience. I have published two books, monographs on two major film directors: D. W. Griffith and Fritz Lang. The book on Lang surveyed his decades-long career, while the one on Griffith focused on only a few years, the very beginning of his work as a filmmaker. But each analyzed recurring elements of an evolving style. These books are precious to me, but as the introduction to the present anthology points out, I am probably best known for my essays; well over a hundred have been published, and a number of others remain in my drawer.

I confess to a love of this form, and the sense of experiment, attempt, and even evaluation contained in the term "essay." But I take even greater pleasure in this assembly of essays, so carefully compiled and commented on by my friend and colleague Daniel Morgan. Together, I hope, they convey a sense of the variety and multiplicity that lie at the core of my attraction to cinema. Cinema's century-plus history offers an amazing range in genres and intended audiences. It became not only the most popular of media (at least in the twentieth century) but also the most modern, both technologically and aesthetically. While it can present powerful stories or shape opinions and attitudes, I maintain that the primal attraction to cinema lies deeper, in the very nature of the moving virtual image. I believe each of these attributes, "moving" and "virtual," needs to be probed to give a full sense of what cinema is, has been, and perhaps will be. While the essays that follow do that in great detail, I want to sketch some of the parameters here.

My best-known essay, "The Cinema of Attractions," described an aspect shared by very early cinema—films made before approximately 1906—and the avant-garde cinema of later decades. The ground common to these rather different forms lies in an address to the spectator focused neither on following a story nor on grasping information: cinema's first job, I believe, is to attract the viewer. As a historian and critic, I sought to probe the means by which viewers have been attracted and held by the cinematic image. While I was inspired by looking at what films did besides telling a story, I confess a deep love of cinematic narrative. As I rejected the claim that cinema is by nature destined to tell stories, it also became clear to me that attractions and narrative are not mutually exclusive. Both narrative and nonnarrative films construct images and sound in such a manner as to create a cinematic experience, through which the viewer becomes absorbed in and transformed by what appears on the screen. I have tried to trace that involvement through the formal play of cinema, the way it creates new forms of attractions and narration.

As a historian, I find it vital to stress that cinema offered something new. Grasping that sense of innovation remains a challenge today. Indeed, the history of film theory shows that this process involves a balancing act. Film theory arose in the late 1910s and 1920s from two seemingly contradictory projects. First, it launched a polemic to establish film as an art form, to place it in relation to the already canonical visual and narrative arts: painting, sculpture, architecture, and the various forms of literature, such as drama, novels, poetry. But this project sometimes generated an apparently opposite argument—that film was something altogether *new*, fundamentally different from the older art forms. I strive to avoid shipwreck on either of these shoals: aligning cinema too closely with traditional arts, as merely another iteration, or making it too unique, a freak exiled from engagement with what my friend Yuri Tsivian often called its "sister arts."

Part of what I see as cinema's aesthetic mission lies precisely in articulating a dialogue with the other arts. Adapting works of literature or invoking works of visual art should not be scorned as slavish imitation; these encounters can engender new cinematic forms. Cinema's novelty should not be a barrier sealing it off from other arts but should instead create a contact zone where transactions and transformations can take place. The act of border crossing dissolves fixed identities. Nonetheless, the sort of inventory of film's expressive means created by early film theorists, culminating in Rudolph Arnheim's magisterial *Film als Kunst* (1932; translated as *Film as Art* in 1933), remains invaluable, both as historical documents of the emerging definition of film and as pedagogical aids to film analysis. Film (and media) analysts need to stay aware of such cinematic devices as editing, camera movement, framing, slow motion, lighting, camera angle, and so on. We must add to this inventory as technology develops and recognize their subtle variations, as elucidated in such textbooks as David Bordwell and Kristin Thompson's classic *Film Art: An Introduction.* In my work, however, I have increasingly decided that two broad aspects of cinema play defining roles: that of the moving image and that of the projected or virtual image. These are not individual formal devices but overarching elements that have shaped the history and aesthetics of the medium.

I have described the *moving image* as essential to the effects of cinema. This is hardly a novel observation (they are, after all, called "movies"). Cinema's reliance on motion is in fact so widely acknowledged as to be easily ignored. But I have tried to rouse us, as cinema viewers, from the slumber that habit and the commonplace induces, and to recognize what a revolution in imagery the moving image introduced. From the dawn of culture, humankind has produced images. While one can claim that certain images or pictorial technics are widely used to portray movement, it is incontestable that pictorial images remained static for millennia. The possibility of an image whose movement was actually perceivable (not simply symbolized or imagined) appears only in the modern era, with a scientific understanding of the visual perception of motion and the invention of devices that explore or trigger it. As pedagogical demonstrations of scientific phenomenon, such late eighteenth- and nineteenth-century devices as the phenakistiscope, flipbook, zoetrope, and praxinoscope were often referred to as "philosophical toys"—and retrospectively described as "proto-cinema." While I find the constructed genealogies of cinemas sometimes too simplistic, there is no question that cinema as a technology derived from these experiments with the perception of motion that could create a moving image. The motion picture apparatuses of Reynaud, Marey, Demenÿ, Muybridge, Edison, and Lumière all drew on these devices to present moving images. Cinema can be defined precisely as the art of moving images technologically achieved.

The moving image has often been approached as a stage in the perfection of the realistic image. But raising the specter of realism in cinema theory risks introducing a metaphysical quagmire, which I want to avoid for the moment. Of course, the association between cinema and realism is deep, pervasive, and ultimately unavoidable. But in highlighting the moving image of cinema I am more interested in its perceptual and aesthetic effects, which can exist outside of concerns for realism—in abstract films, such as those of Oskar Fischinger, as well as in Disney fantasies. Developing a sensitivity to various sorts of visual movement constitutes a central task not only of film aesthetics but of the history of film style. In addition to the perception of cinematic movement, the moving image necessarily introduces a temporal dimension: movement takes time but also marks it. The temporality of the moving image becomes one of its most innovative elements. The moving image adds the dimension of duration to the image, allowing the portrayal or recording of time, but it can also create structures of rhythm and measure that unite cinema to the arts of music and dance.

Some theorists have suggested that "moving image" should replace older words such as "cinema" or "film" as the term for the medium I am describing. I agree that an image that moves causes a redefinition of the image so radical that it could serve as the defining characteristic of a new medium. For my part, I retain the term "cinema" largely because of its historical use. In addition, the word's root in the idea of movement, the Greek κίνημα (*kínēma*, "movement"), avoids tying the image to a specific physical base (as the term "film" does).

There is also the other aspect of cinema besides the moving image, one we can conceive of broadly, beyond a specific device, yet one of unquestionable complexity. I have sometimes called this the "projected image," but the term may suggest an unduly narrow meaning, constrained to a particular technology. I will try here to render it specific yet indicate its varied forms. The virtual image refers to the way the moving image is presented, the manner of its appearance before an audience. The presentation (or exhibition) of cinema changes over its history and even varies within specific periods. In its origins, with devices such as Edison's Kinetoscope, moving images were back-projected onto a small glass screen viewed by a single spectator. With the Lumière Cinématographe the images, using the technology developed centuries before for the magic lantern, were projected onto a fairly large screen viewable by an audience. This of course became the dominant mode of cinema for some time. If we include the electronic video image in my category of cinema (a counterintuitive, if not heretical, move for many, but one I am not sure we can avoid, especially if we think in terms of the moving image), we have an image linearly beamed onto a glass screen, while with projected video the electronic image is projected as a beam of light onto a surface. My concern here is not to thoroughly describe the many platforms of moving image delivery but to stress that however various these forms may be, all display an image as a somewhat ephemeral and ungraspable phenomenon cast onto some sort of screen. This phantom image, never simply adhering to its support with any fixity, is, I think, best described as a virtual image. It seems to be a characteristic of cinema that its images are virtual in this sense: immaterial products of technologically processed light. I have sometimes described it with the somewhat poetic phrase "light-born[e] images." This immaterial image (in the sense of being ungraspable, nontactile), produced by an apparatus and shown on a screen, defines what I have called cinema's virtual image.

I have also sometimes referred to this as a "technological image." Of course, every image produced involves some degree of technology—production by means, not only of human hands, but of instruments and materials, *techne*. By "technological" I refer to what has often been described (pejoratively, in the early years of the twentieth century) as cinema's mechanical nature (a quality shared with photography and other processes of mechanical reproduction such as chromolithography). It is vital to my understanding of cinema that the appearance of its virtual moving image depends upon a technical apparatus, whether the Kinetoscope, a movie projector, or a video monitor. The physical proximity of this apparatus to the viewer may be masked (the projection booth, for instance, hides the projector from view and deadens its sound) but can rarely be irrevocably removed from the spectator's awareness (even if asserting itself only in moments of technical malfunction).

If I argue for the innovation that cinema introduced into the history of images (and continues to extend and explore), it is not to mark off a restricted reservation of media specificity, but rather to open a zone of interaction with other elements of culture. This somewhat tortured detour into definition and description is less an attempt at film theory (although I don't think I can entirely absolve myself of that) than an explanation of why I see a certain formalism as foundational for both my film history and my criticism. I have claimed that the technological nature of the cinematic image has an aesthetic effect even when elements of cinematic style and practice labor to limit a viewer's awareness of its process. My interest in cinema as an instance of modernism, while absolutely part of my historical investigation of the medium, remains rooted in its formal practice and aesthetic experience. As I examined films and their modes of exhibition during its first decades, I found that they supported claims made by Walter Benjamin that cinema had worked to mediate the multiple experiences of modernity (urbanism, new technologies of communication and transportation, modern systems of social control of identity) for twentieth-century audiences. As a medium of culture, cinema mediates not only the scenes it represents but the modern mode of experience, and tracing these mediations through the way films were made and talked about has been one of my ambitions.

I often invoke the statement by Roland Barthes that while a little formalism may remove an artwork from history, a lot will bring it back in. This has been a guiding principle for me, and my sense of the importance of cinema as a modern medium cannot be divorced from its formal devices. To immerse oneself in the forms of cinema ultimately entails following its history (as a technological device and as a social practice), while writing its history ultimately demands a full understanding of how these forms operate. Although particular essays may privilege one approach or the other, I hope that the effect of an anthology such as this demonstrates the intricacy of their intertwining. It has been a guiding principle of my work.

I began this preface with a fairly obscure instance of my family history intersecting with my larger project of film history. I close now with a bit of personal history, as it determined the course of both my work and this book. Around 1970 I took the step of turning my childhood and especially young adult obsession with the movies into a professional pursuit by entering the graduate program in cinema studies at New York University, which would soon offer the first academic PhDs in this field. Frankly, I did this less as a considered career move or educational venture than as a way to explain and excuse my constant moviegoing to parents and friends. But studying at NYU with such faculty as Annette Michelson, Ted Perry, and P. Adams Sitney, and eventually my thesis adviser Jay Leyda (as well as visiting faculty, notably Peter Kubelka, Noël Burch, and, toward the end of my prolonged time there, David Bordwell), not only opened my eyes to new critical and intellectual perspectives but convinced me that studying film could provide me with more than an alibi. Finally coming to roost as a professor in the Department of Cinema and Media Studies at the University of Chicago, with its initial faculty of Miriam Hansen, Yuri Tsivian, James Lastra, and James Chandler, not only formed the final stage of my academic career but, I believe, culminated my education. Helping to establish its graduate program meant, of course, learning as much from my students as from my faculty colleagues. An elegant symmetry lies in the fact that Daniel Morgan, one of my first doctoral students, eventually became not only a colleague but the editor of this collection. For years people had asked me about putting together an anthology of my essays (and I deeply appreciate that such a book was recently published in Japan), but this only became a reality through Dan's efforts. Besides being an extraordinary scholar and critic in his own right, Dan's insight into and care for the work of others has allowed him to assume the role of midwife not only for this work but for Miriam Hansen's culminating work, *Cinema and Experience: Siegfried*

Kracauer, Walter Benjamin, and Theodor W. Adorno, and the posthumous publication by our (un)common student, Hannah Frank, *Frame by Frame: A Materialist Aesthetic of Animated Cartoons*. In closing, I not only acknowledge a debt here but indicate my pride in finding a place in an ongoing legacy of cinema scholarship.

INTRODUCTION

The Energies of Cinema: On the Methods of Tom Gunning

DANIEL MORGAN

Of course an introduction to the work of Tom Gunning has to begin with attractions. Gunning was by no means an unknown scholar when he published "The Cinema of Attraction" in 1986. He had already written a number of essays on what he was then calling "the non-continuous style" of early cinema, and would soon complete his dissertation, a monumental study of the emergence of the "narrator system" in D. W. Griffith's Biograph films.[1] Gunning had also become an important critic and theorist of the avant-garde, with published essays on Ken Jacobs, Ernie Gehr, and others.[2] But "The Cinema of Attractions" was of an entirely different magnitude: perhaps only Laura Mulvey's "Visual Pleasure and Narrative Cinema" has had a comparable impact. Seemingly on its own, the essay transformed the study of early cinema—and of film history more broadly—and it continues to be treated as vital to historical and theoretical studies of the medium. So we need to begin there.

The argument of "The Cinema of Attractions" is relatively straightforward. Gunning begins by noting that previous accounts of early cinema had been written under "the hegemony of narrative films": early films were largely described as "primitive," inept precursors of more assured and sophisticated narrative forms to come. Rather than a kind of "primitive cinema," Gunning argues that early films functioned according to a logic of their own, and demand understanding on their own terms. He thus describes this period as "an exhibitionist cinema," one that he sees "less as a way of telling stories than as a way of presenting a series of views to an audience." Drawing on early writings of Sergei Eisenstein that advance a vision of the cinema based on the appeals of the circus (rather than high art), Gunning terms these views "attractions."[3] Attractions, he says, work by "inciting visual curiosity and supplying pleasure through an exciting spectacle—a unique event, whether fictional or documentary, that is of interest in itself." Most anything could be made into an attraction; even the film camera itself served "as an attraction in its own right."

And the impact of the essay has not been limited to the study of early cinema. Much like "the male gaze," the concept of "attractions" has moved beyond its original context and become central to multiple debates: special effects; the history of technology; genre; race and media; experimental and avant-garde cinema; the relation between cinema and the arts; digital media forms; and more. The concept has also made popular appearances, as when, for example, the *New York Times* marked an "emphasis on spectacle over narrative" in films such as Alfonso Cuarón's *Gravity* (2013).[4]

Such extensions of the concept of attractions are explicitly licensed by Gunning in the essay itself. As a period of film history, the cinema of attractions comes to an end fairly quickly. Then, Gunning argues in a far-reaching gesture, attractions themselves go underground, generating an "unexhausted resource" for later cinemas and cinematic practices. They are a subterranean energy lurking beneath the dominant cinematic modes that will emerge with, on the one hand, the "Spielberg-Lucas-Coppola cinema of effects" and, on the other, an avant-garde legacy that "can be traced from Méliès through Keaton, through *Un Chien Andalou* (1928), and Jack Smith."

This dual orientation of "The Cinema of Attractions"—at once deeply rooted in historical case studies and wildly open-ended—is central to the essay's success. It allows readers to grasp a coherent revaluation of film history in a single swoop, while also adapting and appropriating the logic of attractions for their own projects, whatever those might be. The dual orientation also characterizes Gunning's work more broadly. Like the essay, his thinking exceeds any strict category into which he is put. A historian, but also a theorist; a scholar of early cinema, but also a critic of the avant-garde; an analyst of classical Hollywood film, but also an archaeologist of contemporary media—and seemingly everything in between. Tom Gunning is an extraordinarily scholar who is difficult to pin down, and that is part of his work's enduring strength.

Of course I start with attractions—how could I do otherwise? But we can't just stay in history, whether of film or of film studies. Read carefully, "The Cinema of Attractions" provides the terms for an entire theory of cinema, from an account of the power and pleasures of cinematic images to the logic of cinematic history. In what follows, I trace the contours of this vision of cinema, showing not only how it is present in Gunning's early, canonical essay but how it reverberates and develops across his entire career.

THE CINEMA OF ATTRACTIONS

Attractions in and out of History

"The Cinema of Attraction" was first published in the now-defunct journal *Wide Angle* in 1986, then revised into its canonical form—and an *s* added, for "attractions"—in 1990 for Thomas Elsaesser's collection *Early Cinema: Space, Frame, Narrative.*[5] Emerging out of sustained conversations with André Gaudreault and others, the concept of attractions, it was immediately clear, challenged long-held assumptions about film theory as well as history, from the transhistorical appeal of narrative to the idea that early films operated on an opposition between recording the world (Lumière) and creating fictional spectacles (Méliès). Attractions flatten the difference, so that Lumière and Méliès, in this example, come to be united by a common aesthetic strategy—that of showing, of display. Such was the essay's success that "the cinema of attractions" became shorthand for the terms on which we understand early cinema, and for why early cinema matters as an area of study.

Interest in the study of early cinema had been growing through the 1970s and received a major impetus from the 1978 meeting of the Federation of International Film Archives (FIAF) in Brighton, England, where an astonishing array of films from 1900–1906 were screened (often for the first time in many decades). Supported by the work of archivists across the globe (especially the annual *Giornate del cinema muto*, a silent-film festival that began in 1982), by increasing research and speculation on "pre-Griffith" cinema, and by the availability of material in institutions such as the Library of Congress and the Museum of Modern Art (where Eileen Bowser was the film curator), a substantial body of scholarship began to emerge. John Fell's 1983 collection *Film before Griffith* provided a summation of much of this research, and more established scholars such as Noël Burch evinced increasing interest.[6] At the same time, avant-garde filmmakers such as Hollis Frampton, Ernie Gehr, and Ken Jacobs had begun using early films in their work.

As it achieved widespread recognition, Gunning's essay came to stand in for a broader disciplinary transformation, away from theory and toward history: from abstract speculation about the nature of the spectator to empirically driven accounts of the habits and practices of spectators; from cinema as an inherently ideological form to cinema as a historically diverse set of modes and tendencies. The role assigned to "The Cinema of Attractions" in this story is that of dethroning French theory, largely oriented around psychoanalysis, and in so doing instituting a new paradigm of historical research within the field.

The essay's broad appeal, then, owes not to its founding a field but rather to the way it crystallized broader shifts that were already—inexorably—under way. It gives a name, a cover concept, to a set of arguments and historical research that had been emerging for a decade. Indeed, part of the essay's success lies in the simplicity of the concept itself. Burch had previously discussed the uniqueness of early cinema, and even connected it to the avant-garde, but his definition worked around four separate and interlocking criteria.[7] By contrast, "attractions" is a single term that easily became a metonym for the entire period, and for a new way of thinking about film shaped by historical research.

Of course the story is more complicated. "The Cinema of Attractions" has a decided edge, a polemical force; it functions as a rhetorically driven wedge that will open space to allow a new way of proceeding. In this aspect, Gunning's essay is not so different from Mulvey's feminist manifesto. Mulvey is more obviously writing a polemic: the rhetorical intensity of her position is part of what makes it so memorable (e.g., "It is said that analyzing pleasure, or beauty, destroys it. That is the purpose of this essay"). And her work opened the door to theory, especially psychoanalytic theory, that would define the early years of film studies as an academic discipline. One might expect a competition between the two projects: theory versus history; psychoanalytic speculation versus archival research. Yet when Gunning mentions Mulvey in "The Cinema of Attractions," it is not, as one might expect, to challenge its psychoanalytic methodology but rather to use it as support for his own project to excavate "the dialectic between spectacle and narrative" (1:48). For Gunning, "Visual Pleasure and Narrative Cinema" furnishes evidence—in the form of its analysis of the spectacular display of the female body—that nonnarrative forms do not disappear with early cinema but remain present at the heart of narrative cinema.[8] Indeed, that affinity is one of the reasons "The Cinema of Attractions" has been important to feminist scholarship on early cinema.[9]

Mulvey and Gunning's essays have had their effect because they are not simply pitched at a theoretical level. Both make direct appeals to our experience with and knowledge of cinema, and that appeal is central to each essay. Once they make us look in a certain way, and think differently—or newly—about what we thought we already knew, we invariably come to see what they are describing. Gunning would later remark, discussing his claim that the close-up of the woman's ankle in *The Gay Shoe Clerk* (1903) is a source of visual pleasure—and not narrative information—that the point "should be evident for any one [*sic*] who actually watches the film."[10] It's a striking thing to say, not least because it is not about what a historical spectator said they saw but rather what the contemporary spectator sees. Gunning makes such perceptual claims part of a general argument that historical investigations must also be phenomenological, that his goal is "to describe our perception as we experience it" (6:168; also see 5:144).[11] Direct experience must support, complement, and augment historical considerations.

We see it for ourselves, and we know it is there. This is how "The Cinema of Attractions" extends beyond early cinema, functioning as a kind of instruction manual, teaching us what an attraction is and how to spot it. Gunning invites us to do our own work, to look for other attractions, and to use the term to rethink other principles of film history and practices. Once we learn to spot attractions, we see them everywhere across the history of cinema. It is for this reason that the essay ends not with a catalogue of attractions but with a model for how to go on finding them. What he elsewhere labels a "brief dose of scopic pleasure" (3:75) can easily be found in musicals and music videos, in short video formats such as Vine and TikTok, in special effects, and in the very dynamics of stardom. The use of "attractions" to describe these media is neither coincidence nor misappropriation. Gunning explicitly invites these uses, and they have not been reticent in their appearance.

Yet it is not all about teaching viewers to see. A theory of history, of how early cinema relates to later cinemas, underlies the essay. The fact of this connection is, again, not unique to Gunning. Burch, for example, will describe how films refer back to early cinema in order to capture something of its energies.[12] It's a common enough gesture, after all, with cases such as Hollis Frampton's use of an early film in *Gloria!* (1979) or Jean-Luc Godard's evocation of early film viewers in *Les carabiniers* (1963)—or the same scenario in Orson Welles's unfinished *Don Quixote*, during the sequence that Giorgio Agamben described as "the most beautiful six minutes in the history of cinema"—or the sheer visceral pleasure of *This Is Cinerama* (Merian Cooper, 1952), which portrays itself as a reinvention of cinema. Nor has the desire to return halted: Martin Scorsese's *Hugo* (2011) is a more recent example. There's an enduring fascination with the moment everything began, and one of the ways filmmakers demonstrate their desire to do new things is by returning to cinema's primal scenes. Echoing Burch and others, Gunning argued that contemporary filmmakers reach back to early cinema to draw out the force of newness it contained. It is an active relation, consciously striven for and achieved, a project Gunning describes as "awakening energies slumbering in old material" (21:405).

For Gunning, though, the place of attractions in film history is deeper. Attractions, he says, function independently of any conscious act of engagement; they are an undercurrent of sorts that emerges from time to time, as if filmmakers had no say as to whether they appear in their work or not. When, in the final paragraphs of "The Cinema of Attractions," he isolates "the Spielberg-Lucas-Coppola cinema of effects," it is not because *Star Wars* (1977) or *Close Encounters of the Third Kind* (1977) explicitly reach back to Méliès to articulate their logic of spectacle.[13] In a later essay, he talks about attractions as an "underground current flowing beneath narrative logic and diegetic realism." Attractions simply appear, unbidden, as a constitutive feature of the films' appeal—as if it were natural for cinema to forgo narrative (at times) in favor of visual delight. In this light, attractions function as what Stanley Cavell would identify as an "automatism," a part of a film that is experienced as "happening of itself."[14] An automatism carries with it meanings shared by filmmakers and viewers alike; in it the power and force of an aspect of a film is derived from outside itself. In a sense, then, attractions function as an automatism that shapes the unfolding of cinema's history, perhaps even something like a law of the medium.

Gunning, though, isn't mainly interested (as Cavell is) in the appearance of such automatisms in the current state of cinema. He is, after all, a historian. But his version of historical investigation is also not like that of Burch, starting from discussions of the present, then looking back to find the origins of a given feature. What he provides is more like a genealogical investigation, a study of origins as a means to understand how attractions move out and across the history of cinema. Gunning tries to situate attractions in their moment, but his argument is projective rather than simply contextualizing.

Part of this has to do with where he locates the stirrings that lead to cinema. At different moments in his career, Gunning has laid out different timelines behind the emergence of cinema. Some focus on the cultural situation of the late nineteenth and early twentieth centuries, ranging from popular entertainment to the emergence of the modern metropolis. Others take in more of the long nineteenth century, especially the prominence of optical toys such as the zoetrope and the phenakistoscope. At times he goes back even further, to the phantasmagoria of the eighteenth century or even to models of perception in Greek and Roman contexts. But the further the origin of attractions stretches back, the more it becomes a kind of transhistorical principle that cannot be bound to a single moment—and the more plausible it seems that attractions stretch out beyond the specific moment of film history in which they are dominant.

Later in his career, Gunning sometimes offers a more explicitly mystical model for thinking of the historical logic of attractions. In his writings on the avant-garde, he sometimes talks about the Kabbalah of Isaac Luria, in which "creation began with a disaster, as the vessels of the cosmos shattered when divine energy streamed into them. This divine tragedy caused fragments of the transcendent energy to fall into a world of matter, seeding it with sparks from the heavenly realm."[15] Through proper rituals or practices, that energy can be released again. "This process," Gunning writes, in an essay on Gustav Deutsch, "stands as an ideal metaphor for [his] transformation of found footage, reworking archival material, seeking to release and gather the energy contained within it." We could say the same thing about attractions. Gunning's writing suggests the presence of a kind of purity in early cinema: it is a cinema with no conception of what cinema ought to be. This purity may be lost with the emergence of narrative cinema, but the right activities can reenergize and revitalize that submerged charge of attractions. In this case, it seems the secret of "The Cinema of Attractions" is that it purports to be about early film history but is actually a metaphysics of cinema—one that is historically grounded or specified but cannot be contained to a historical moment.

From History to Theory (and Back Again)

I said at the outset that "The Cinema of Attractions" could suggest a broader theory of cinema. We can now start to see what that might entail. Recall that one of the key features of the afterlife of attractions is the downplaying of active intentionality on the part of later filmmakers; attractions are simply there, reemerging on their own terms and in their own time. Implicit in this model is a curious sense of passivity: held in thrall by moving images projected on a screen before us, we simply accept the powers and pleasures they have over us. It's a model that runs through the history of thinking about film, especially in a broadly realist tradition. Bazin, for example, speaks of "the irrational power of the photograph to bear away our belief."[16] Or there is Cavell's remark about the spectator's inherent "passiveness before the exhibition of the world."[17] Such rhetoric runs through Gunning's writings as well: "we are swept along with the motion itself" (9:240); "phantom rides substitute sensation for contemplation, overcoming effects of distance in a rush of visual motion" (5:143); cinema involves "a direct and overwhelming appeal to the senses" (11:282).

This "fascination" with the image in motion underlies many of Gunning's objects of analysis, from nineteenth-century philosophical toys that play between still and moving images to Griffith's construction of a parallel montage that moves us rapidly between spaces to what Gunning describes, in reference to Ernie Gehr's work, as "a laboratory of perception." There is something like a transhistorical principle in this view, an argument about how we perceive motion that is grounded in physiology. For Gunning, the crucial point is phenomenological: technologies and techniques "do not represent motion; they produce it." Representation of motion is the domain, we might say, of painting and drawing, as when comic artists draw a series of lines behind a character to indicate speed; with cinema, by contrast, we see movement itself. The result is a kind of automatic absorption on the part of the spectator: the moving image *is* motion, and we cannot help but be caught up by it.[18]

This basic fact, Gunning argues, is often overlooked in film theory. He criticizes Deleuze, for example, for dismissing the experience of cinematic motion (in favor of the "movement-image"). Such a refusal, Gunning argues, involves a reluctance to surrender to the powers of cinematic movement, even to the basic way movement can generate an impression of life—an anxiety involving "a fear of the machine" that, with worries about the visceral pleasures cinema provides, "poses a constricting inheritance for film theory."[19] But it seems, more directly, as though Gunning's appeal to the viewer's fascination with the image is a direct rebuke to a strand of film theory that emerged out of debates in the 1970s. This model of film theory held that what we see, what is given to us through our senses, is suspect at both an epistemic and a political level. Jean-Louis Baudry, for example, argued that the spectator's perceptual identification with the cinematic image precludes the possibility of a "knowledge-effect" taking place, securing the intensity of cinema's ideological force.[20] And Serge Daney criticized the immediacy of cinematic effects as "the accumulation of images, hysteria, carefully-measured effects, retention, discharge, happy ending: catharsis."[21] As a result, cinema was to be countered by an exercise of critical reason and judgment. Gunning's position, then, would be in line with a widespread rejection of this theoretical model, a broadly phenomenological approach that drew attention to the subjective experience of the viewer rather than a critique. Indeed, he sometimes speaks as if that fully accounted for his position, whether praising the writings of Maurice Merleau-Ponty, giving an overtly phenomenological account of the phantasmagoria ("First, imagine darkness"), or simply stating that "my task here is to describe our perception as we experience it"—a position he labels as "obviously phenomenological."

But that is not where his argument ends. Gunning does not give a critique of viewer-focused theoretical models, at least not in the way that Eugenie Brinkema will mock the tendencies in affect theory to focus on "personal accounts of any theorist's tremulous pleasures and shudderings."[22] For Gunning, knowledge effects and spectatorial fascination go together—they are in a sense inseparable, a dialectic fundamental to the history of moving images, what he describes as the "long existing game of fooling the senses and the uncanny pleasures it evoked."[23] It is never the case that we forget about the technologies used to produce moving images, that we think we are in the presence of natural phenomena. The very pleasures of the production of motion, in all its various guises, are predicated on our knowledge that our perception is being toyed with or deceived in some way. He thus describes the entire experience as "a direct and overwhelming appeal to the senses on the one hand, and the critique of illusion on the other" (11:282; see also 6:161). It is a dialectic that unfolds in different guises across the history of culture, from shadow plays to virtual reality, capturing an elemental feature of the way spectators engage the changing moving image.[24]

We can sense a methodological pattern here. Attractions come and go. Fascination ebbs and flows. For Gunning, there is no constant state to any aspect of cinema, no basic condition that remains regardless of what goes on around it. What is absent might become present at any time: realism might turn into spectacle; the pleasure of being fooled might turn into a knowledge of how that deception takes place. It is a model that Gunning captures in the title of an essay, " 'Now You See It, Now You Don't': The Temporality of the Cinema of Attractions." There, he describes a game of hide-and-seek in which attractions are always present as a shaping force of cinema—even if only in negation. As with the logic of passivity, it is a way of thinking that allows him to move effortlessly from microcosm to macrocosm, drawing together a range of disparate cinematic phenomena.

Perhaps the most striking example of this kind of thinking is Gunning's use of the metaphor of weaving. In one of his first essays on narrative and style, early in the 1980s, he describes parallel editing as a form of weaving, forming a fabric through the patterned intercrossing of threads.[25] In an essay on attractions cowritten with Gaudreault, Gunning quotes Jacques

Aumont's comment that " 'Griffith does nothing to hide the white threads which sew the frames together.' "[26] Later, in his analysis of *The Lonedale Operator*, weaving serves as an emblem for the creation of a single narrative out of a series of stories. Still elsewhere, in an essay on the avant-garde filmmaker Abigail Child, and with reference back to Griffith, Gunning unfolds the metaphor: "As in weaving, the interlacing of threads [lines of action] alternated between visibility and invisibility, and the sense of hidden action gave force to the sequence as much as the action literally displayed on the screen" (23:424). And, as he will argue with respect to Stan Brakhage's *Mothlight* (1963), the logic of weaving can be applied to the very materiality of the filmstrip itself, as it moves in and out of the viewer's awareness: "The natural elements rush past us, appearing and disappearing, but the strip maintains a continuum of flow, which bears the stuff, like a current carrying flotsam and jetsam" (26:471). It is, he says, like a "game of hide-and-seek."

From early cinema to the avant-garde and back again. Weaving provides a ground-level concept capable of explaining the force of cinematic form in all its complexity, one in which structure is present—even dominant—yet does not have the full and final say. The weaver, after all, creates their own path, their own variations. We can see the way this metaphor moves from the operation of film history to an analysis of individual films. In a discussion of the opening of Child's *Mutiny* (1983), for example, Gunning notes a set of images that will recur throughout the film, arguing that they function as the "threads" that hold it together. "Each of these images represents a thread that will be carried through the film, and dozens more threads are gathered and interwoven as the film progresses." The speed of Child's editing makes the felt presence of the threads all the more vital to the viewer who is trying to keep up. "The interweaving creates unity out of this diversity," Gunning argues, and allows for unexpected intersections to emerge: "Child's montage associates the loving embrace with images of overt aggression and violence, all using the same apparent gesture" (23:435). Unlike montage, it's not just one image plus another, always moving forward. Weaving—a craft, a game, a dance, an activity—is a model in which the hidden energies of threads left unseen are always there to impact how we experience what we do see.

I take the title of this introduction, "The Energies of Cinema," from a line in one of Gunning's essays on the legacy of the nineteenth century, which he describes as an "age of energy." He insists that the energies that gave rise to cinema were inherently multiple, that they could not be contained in a single form or field. The new kind of image that cinema presents is thus one structured by a set of paradoxes: "an image that seems simultaneously alive and immaterial, powerful yet dead (or deadly), present yet absent."[27] And fascination with such paradoxes, he argues, is not a historically defined phenomenon: "It persists in our experience of cinema to this day." If we ignore the paradoxical energies that pulse across cinema's history, energies that offer us unique pleasures and form the ground for wild flights of fantasy, we lose sight of what makes cinema compelling. Indeed, the idea of "energies of cinema" runs across Gunning's entire career; from the first essays describing the force of early cinema to later studies of the avant-garde, readers will find the term cropping up throughout this collection.

From microcosm to macrocosm, from history to theory to criticism—Gunning's thought ranges across methods and debates, drawing in every aspect of the history of cinema, as well as its prehistory. The result is an account of cinema that is both wild and wildly exciting, a unique vision and way of thinking about phenomena both strange and familiar. Across his essays, we encounter films and technologies we know, and are introduced to others as the hidden keys to problems in oft-disparate fields. The leaps can be breathtaking at times, and it can feel like we need to see everything together to understand why each moment works.

Underlying all the intellectual virtuosity is a belief that the work of cinema—the work of any film—is to unleash the energies that emerged at the outset of cinema and never went away. Cinema, Gunning says over and over again, succeeds when it surrenders itself to these energies while simultaneously creating new paths for them to explore. The pleasures of studying cinema with Gunning—encountering him here, through his writings—involve seeing all the directions those paths might take.

A BIT OF HISTORY

The Attractions of the Moving Image—the first collection of writings by Tom Gunning—contains essays that have shaped the field of cinema and media studies, lesser known but equally powerful pieces that have appeared in a range of venues, and several new, previously unpublished works. Taken together, the essays showcase the depth and range of one of the most important contemporary scholars of film and other moving images. Gunning's writings articulate a distinctive and powerful model for thinking about cinema's histories, its present conditions, and its ongoing transformations.

Tom Gunning grew up outside of Columbus, Ohio. Moving to New York in his teenage years, he studied religion as an undergraduate at NYU before moving, in graduate school, into the newly emerging field of film studies, where, in the 1970s, he was part of the first generation of film scholars to attend doctoral programs. At NYU, he worked under some of the pioneers of the field, especially Annette Michelson, Jay Leyda, and P. Adams Sitney, and was deeply involved in New York's then-burgeoning avant-garde scene. Gunning would go on to hold teaching positions at SUNY Purchase, at Northwestern University, and at the University of Chicago, where he taught from 1996 until his retirement in 2018.

The work Gunning produced during these decades is massive in scope and scale. It can seem at times that his career has encompassed all the fundamental shifts in the discipline since it began to coalesce. Among his contemporaries, no other figure has so persistently and carefully tied so many aspects of cinema—from form to theory to genre to ontology to aesthetics—to pre- and early cinematic histories, or been able to treat cinema as simultaneously unique and part of the longue durée of cultural history. No one else has been so attuned to the origins of cinema and to its contemporary manifestations, or so adept at history and theory while supporting it all with an encyclopedic knowledge of cinema and related media. Such a scope poses a problem for any collection.

Gunning is the author of two monographs, both of which are about—among many other topics—the way that films tell stories. The first, *D. W. Griffith and the Origins of American Narrative Film* (1991), emerged out of his legendary dissertation. The book traces the evolution of Griffith's style, practice, and themes during his early years at Biograph, showing how he gradually developed a flexible approach that allowed him not only to tell stories but to add psychological complexity, formal and thematic resonances, and emotional intensification. While Gunning sees in Griffith's early work the articulation of many of the aspects of cinema that would emerge in the classical era, from the use of a "narrator system" to the logic of off-screen space, the book is far from a formalist study, showing how deeply Griffith was immersed in the social and political debates hovering in and around cinema. Gunning's second book, *The Films of Fritz Lang: Allegories of Vision and Modernity* (2000), is the kind of monumental study of a director that is rarely produced. While partly about the way Lang's films are enmeshed with the emergence of industrial and media-focused visions of modernity, focusing in particular on the logic of allegory, the book also traces two key devices that Lang develops and deploys. Gunning argues that these techniques—"visionary scenes" and the "destiny machine"—serve as ways of creating narrative forces that stand outside the actions and intentions of characters yet still catch the characters in their overarching logic. What we get in these monographs are studies in the flexibility of cinematic narrative, examinations of how basic templates of narration emerge and can then be adapted in new ways and for new ends. It is part of the power of Gunning's work that he embeds these studies of narrative within so many other arguments without losing sight of any of the threads.

In addition to these two books, and an ongoing book-length manuscript on the emergence of cinema out of a longer culture of vision and technologies of images, Gunning has edited several collections. *An Invention of the Devil? Religion and Early Cinema* (1992), coedited with Roland Cosandey and André Gaudreault; *Pathé 1900: Fragments d'une filmographie analytique du cinema des premiers temps* (1993), coedited with André Gaudreault and Alain Lacasse; *The Fantasia of Color in Early Cinema* (2015), coedited with Giovanna Fossati, Jonathan Rosen, and Joshua Yumibe; and *The Image in Early Cinema: Form and Material* (2018), coedited with Scott Curtis, Phillipe Gauthier, and Joshua Yumibe. While three comprise scholarly essays, *The Fantasia of Color* has a broader appeal, with a surge of glorious images showing everything color could do in early cinema.[28]

Despite these books, Gunning remains known primarily as an essayist. Part of this owes to sheer volume: he has published well over a hundred essays, and more emerge every year. But it is due also the range of topics. It can seem, starting to work in cinema and media studies, as though Gunning has already written on every topic you're interested in. Race in American cinema after Griffith? There's an essay about that.[29] The use of formal techniques, such as flashbacks or camera movement? There are essays about them.[30] There's a study of method, bringing together history, theory, and criticism.[31] There's a study of city symphonies.[32] What about a classic auteur like Hitchcock? Of course.[33] The history of film theory? Yes, that too.[34] American film genres? There are essays on those, and even an appearance in a documentary on horror.[35] British cinema? Yes, especially for Powell and Pressburger.[36] The relation between dance and film? Indeed.[37] Cinema and painting? Definitely.[38] And topics like digital special effects? Need you ask?[39] This could go on, topic after topic after topic—from eroticism in the cinema to the dynamics of spirit photography. And all without mentioning any of the myriad of essays on early cinema, Griffith, the avant-garde, and film history. What is remarkable is not just the breadth of topics but how many of these essays are vital contributions to their respective fields.

Amid all this variety, how should we make sense of Gunning's career? It's tempting to describe his intellectual trajectory as moving through several distinct stages. There is a focus in the 1980s on film history, and the avant-garde; an engagement in the 1990s with the logic of modernity, and how cinema shapes and is shaped by changes in the world; an orientation in the early 2000s around what he calls "cultural optics";[40] and then, starting around 2010, a new focus on the intertwined issues of movement and the digital image. These would be general trends, not programmatic ambitions, an outline of key shifts in Gunning's work that simultaneously tracks broader changes in the field and responds to the films and other moving image works being made over these decades. Yet reviewing the essays collected here reveals continuities rather than discontinuities, overlaps rather than distinct processes. There is a core, a kernel, that runs across his career. In his 2011 essay "The Play between Still and Moving Images: Nineteenth Century Philosophical Toys and their Discourse," Gunning writes, "Since the beginning of culture, movement has played a role within art works through the physical movement of actors and dancers, puppets and automatons, or shadows and pictorial figures. But with these mechanical devices we actually see moving images produced optically. I maintain this marks a revolutionary moment in the history of the image—one we have not fully appreciated or explored." This is the methodological crux of Gunning's decades-long project: an attempt to reckon with our enduring fascination with the image in motion. *The Attractions of the Moving Image* shows how vital Gunning's evolving insights into the domain of moving images—their origins, their histories, their possibilities—are for the present day.

This volume does not aim to represent the full range of topics on which Gunning has written, or to provide a complete account of his work on specific topics such as early cinema. That would be an impossible task. Instead, it is organized according to the three main categories that Gunning lays out in "The Cinema of Attractions," and which play a structuring role across his career: History, Theory, and the Avant-Garde. While it was tempting to relabel the final category as "criticism," in keeping with the broad division of the field, the importance of the avant-garde—and the post-1960s American avant-garde in particular—to Gunning's understanding of cinema makes the more focused category a better fit. Of course the divisions are porous. The essays in "History" often have an explicit theoretical focus, while those in "Theory" are grounded in historical analysis; the avant-garde runs through many of the essays in those two parts, and those in "Avant-Garde" are suffused with debates in history and theory as well—indeed, they contain, as I'll argue below, some of Gunning's deepest reflections on questions of film theory.

The organization of each part attempts to balance celebrated essays with lesser-known work. "History" includes two of Gunning's three major essays on the cinema of attractions: "The Cinema of Attractions" and "An Aesthetic of Astonishment." (The other, " 'Now You See It, Now You Don't': The Temporality of the Cinema of Attractions," is less central. A contemporaneous essay, "The Whole Town's Gawking: Early Cinema and the Visual Experience of Modernity," focuses less on the logic of attractions and more on an articulation of their cultural context, a project taken up in more detail by other essays in this section.[41]) The other essays in part I take up problems of film form and historiography, ranging from questions of point of view to the place of landscape aesthetics in early cinema, from the cultural history of photography to the role of optical devices in thinking about media. Taken together, these essays trace Gunning's evolving thinking about both the emergence of cinema and the methods used to study it.

Part II, "Theory," shows how Gunning addresses a range of theoretical problems. The essays include studies of cinema in the context of a culture of modernity, notably "The Exterior as *Intérieur*: Benjamin's Optical Detective" and—of course—a major account of Griffith, represented by the brilliant study of *The Lonedale Operator* (1911) in "Systematizing the Electric Message." Mostly, however, the focus is on arguments Gunning has developed in the twenty-first century, largely in response to challenges to the historic assumptions of film theory brought on by the rise of digital technologies. "Moving Away from the Index: Cinema and the Impression of Reality" has been frequently cited, especially in discussions of animation, digital aesthetics and technologies, and the history of film theory. The essay also marks a key turn in Gunning's thought, a moment where the topic of movement becomes explicitly pressing. Here, it is augmented by a series of essays that lead up to and follow from it, focused especially around historical and theoretical investigations into the nature of the cinematic image. Much of Gunning's approach turns on what he perceives as an ontological uncertainty at the heart of images, an instability about their nature and force. To explain the powers and appeals of cinema, both celluloid and digital, he often turns—as in "To Scan a Ghost"—to the history and logic of magic, moving from a history of the phantasmagoria to a rethinking of media by way of ghosts and ghostly apparitions.

Finally, the essays reprinted in "Avant-Garde" are among the hardest to find, and part of the work of *The Attractions of the Moving Image* is to bring them to a wider audience. While the importance of the avant-garde for Gunning is clear in "The Cinema of Attractions," part III showcases his more focused writings on the subject, including seminal essays on individual filmmakers: Ken Jacobs, Ernie Gehr, Mark LaPore, Gustav Deutsch, Abigail Child, David Gatten. But there are also essays trying to articulate more general trends. "Towards a Minor Cinema: Fonoroff, Herwitz, Ahwesh, LaPore, Klahr, and Solomon," published in 1989/1990, takes aim at the idea that the avant-garde had reached a permanent crisis. Written partly in response to an essay by Fred Camper arguing that "major" work by "major" avant-garde filmmakers had ended—a powerful critique that is at once aesthetic, ethical, and institutional—Gunning rejects those terms of evaluation and proposes an alternate system, a new grid or set of coordinates.[42] Published in a journal that it is now out of print, "Towards a Minor Cinema" has circulated informally for years, serving as the inspiration for several film festivals and as the basis of a study of Peggy Ahwesh.[43] There are also three unpublished essays in "Avant-Garde"—including Gunning's only treatment of Kenneth Anger and his only sustained reflection on the films of Stan Brakhage—that will provide new models for thinking about the power and significance of the American avant-garde.

The aims and ambitions of Gunning's essays across all these sections are important, and rarely does he attempt anything less than to describe a fundamental piece of cinematic history or experience. Yet one can also be struck by more minor discussions that swirl alongside the main argument like eddies in a river: unexpected turns or movements of thought that seem to come out of the blue and yet open up a new way of thinking about a familiar topic.

Some of these minor discussions are substantial in their own right. In his essay on Deutsch's *Film ist.* (1998), for example, Gunning takes up the Kuleshov experiment, reading it as a demonstration not simply of the power of editing but also of the project of the found-footage film. "The use of the familiar face of émigré movie star Mozhukin gave Kuleshov's experiment a polemical edge. Editing not only imposed specific meanings on neutral material, but also overcame whatever reactionary bourgeois meanings the prerevolutionary footage originally intended to convey." It's a brilliant argument, which Gunning uses not just to talk about revolutionary politics but also to introduce the two modes of temporality operating through found-footage films—the time the footage was shot and the time of the (new) film—that then open out further. We have, condensed into a brief section, an original account of the powers of film in the context of revolutionary politics alongside an investigation of the ability of found footage to negotiate temporal paradoxes. As he puts it, "Beyond simply recycling images of the past, the editing of found footage triggers a truly new moment, not only a new sense of presence but a prophetic sense of future possibilities." Such provocative reflections—another takes on the role of color in Brakhage's work—are found throughout the essays in this volume.

There are also turns of Gunning's thought that feel more digressive but no less exhilarating or essential. There is a dive into Charcot's use of photography in "In Your Face: Physiognomy, Photography, and the Gnostic Mission of Early Film"; a discussion of Emily Dickinson in "To Scan a Ghost"; a meditation on the genre of the travel film in the essay on Mark LaPore. The list could go on, and any reader of Gunning's work tends to have their own favorites. These sparkling moments of insight often range far beyond the familiar terrain of an academic field, but they are central to what makes these essays such a joy to read, such a continual source of insight and intelligence. The hope is that the reader will find value, delight, and insight in such moments, while still learning from—and taking in—the bigger arguments that guide Gunning's thinking.

THE LIMITS OF MODERNITY

One of the difficulties in assessing Gunning's career is his ambivalent relation to debates within the field. At a first glance, he seems deeply attuned to them, part of the ebb and flow of trends and debates: early film history in the 1980s, the modernity polemics of the 1990s, reflections on digital media in the 2000s. Essays by Gunning have been central to each of these. Yet from a longer perspective, and tracing out the resonances these essays have had across Gunning's own career, his position is less settled. So I want to look at the way Gunning moves in and out of synch with the rest of the discipline, picking up on the force of contemporaneous debates while moving them into distinctly different areas of discussion. A later section picks up his reflections on the nature of the cinematic image; here, I discuss the kinds of historical arguments Gunning makes.

In constructing this volume, I minimized the essays that helped define the "modernity debates" of the 1990s and early 2000s. Many of these essays are already available, having been collected and discussed in well-known volumes, and the arguments also appear in Gunning's monograph on Lang.[44] In these works, Gunning often draws on arguments from Frankfurt school theorists to analyze how forms of viewing were shaped by the new experiences of modern, urban, and industrial life in the first decades of the twentieth century. Gunning not only provides archival evidence to support his position, but makes the case that changes in perceptual habits could be observed in contemporaneous developments in film style. While this line of thought is found here in essays like "An Aesthetics of Astonishment: Early Films and the (In)Credulous Spectator," "In Your Face: Physiognomy, Photography, and the Gnostic Mission of Early Film," and "The Exterior as *Interieur*: Benjamin's Optical Detective," it is not their primary focus.

The modernity debates can now seem like a historical matter themselves. But there was a moment in which cinema's relation to modernity seemed one of the field's most pressing questions. The argument ran roughly like this. Cinema, as a technological medium, emerged amid ongoing transformations of urban space, sites and techniques of work, and modes of transportation—developments that in turn changed social habits and practices, modes of public and mass experience, and forms of entertainment. As Leo Charney and Vanessa Schwartz put it in the introduction to their influential collection *Cinema and the Invention of Modern Life*, "The culture of modernity rendered inevitable something like cinema, since cinema's characteristics evolved from the traits that defined modern life in general. At the same time, cinema formed a crucible for ideas, techniques, and representational strategies already present in other places."[45] This last point was crucial. Cinema was not simply part of modernity; it could, as an artistic form, constitute what Miriam Hansen would describe as a "sensory-reflexive horizon" for the experiences of modernity.[46] Hansen's work was central to this debate. Drawing heavily on writings by Siegfried Kracauer and Walter Benjamin, she argued that our basic perception of the world changed with the rise of urban, industrial modernity, and that older forms of cultural and social practice were inadequate to the new and dynamic world in which people found themselves. Modernity was destructive as well as liberatory, terrifying as well as exciting. Again, cinema had a dual role: "the cinema was not only part and symptom of the crisis and upheaval as which modernity was experienced and perceived; it was also, most importantly, the single most inclusive, cultural horizon in which the traumatic effects of modernity were reflected, rejected, disavowed, transmuted or negotiated."[47] In anonymous, collective spaces, watching the modern world removed from actual experience, cinema could help audiences come to terms with it. This was the utopian potential of cinema, one that depended, for Hansen, not on narrative organization but on its opposite: "sensory experience and sensational affect."[48]

It's not hard to see the affinity with Gunning's delineation of a "cinema of attractions." Attractions, after all, emerge from popular entertainment in the context of modernity and focus less on narrative than on "a generally brief dose of scopic pleasure." Indeed, it is precisely this intersection that

Gunning emphasizes: "If the experience of modernity finds its *locus classicus* in big city streets and their crowds, the unique stimulus offered by this new environment discovers its aesthetic form in attractions. . . . Attractions express the fugitive nature of modern life, with their brief form and lack of narrative development, as well as their aggressivity."[49] As with Hansen and others, the argument is at once historical, focusing on the visual culture out of which attractions emerged, and formal, drawing on affinities and homologies between early cinema and the new modern life. On this latter point, Gunning writes, "Attractions trace out the visual topology of modernity: a visual environment which is fragmented and atomized; a gaze which, rather than resting on a landscape in contemplation, seems to be pushed and pulled in conflicting orientations, hurried and intensified, and therefore less coherent or anchored."[50] This is modernity par excellence, the lack of stability leading to new kinds of experience.

The modernity thesis quickly faced two kinds of challenges. The first, which I won't discuss here, had to do with claims about the mind, and whether changes in the world around us can impact the way we apprehend the world.[51] The second involved questions of historical explanation, and whether the claims made about the emergence of modernity could account for the facts of cinema. This is what I want to dwell on, as it gets to Gunning's uniqueness as a historian. David Bordwell, for example, challenged Gunning's position, arguing that if attractions are an essential part of the new modernity, the fact that attractions are not defining elements of all films made in the first decade of cinema means that modernity's break with the past could not be as strong as proponents of the modernity thesis argue. How else, he asks, can early cinema's heterogeneity of styles and forms be explained?[52] Another criticism looked to the emergence of a narrative cinema with Griffith and the one-reel short. If attractions are meant to resonate with the fugitive temporality of modern life and the affective charge of urban experience, how can we explain the rise of narrative forms that seem counterposed to those tendencies? And what does one do, as Charlie Keil asked, with all the films of the transitional period that either ignore the signs of modern life or treat new technologies—the car, the telephone—as prosaic rather than disruptive?[53]

Such arguments matter for a range of methodological debates: about the role of the exceptional case or statistical sampling; about the place of cognitive studies in the analysis of visual culture; about the relation between individual artworks and the cultural contexts that surround them; even about the meaning of modernism and modernity itself. These were, and remain, important questions. To get at Gunning's place in the debates, however, I want to highlight a curious exchange with Bordwell. Responding to the latter's criticism of his arguments, Gunning remarks that "I never make a causal claim" between early cinema and modernity, "which indeed I would find very dubious in its simplistic sense of how culture and style interact, bereft of mediation."[54] Bordwell dismisses this response, saying that causal claims do exist in "The Whole Town's Gawking," and proceeds to use Gunning's words as an occasion to argue against the terms of the modernity thesis broadly writ.

Yet in focusing on the general position, Bordwell misses Gunning's original point. While it is true that Gunning makes claims of causation with respect to modernity, his argument is about the range of factors involved: the emergence of early cinema is not—it could not be—attributable to a single phenomenon, even a phenomenon as broad and significant as "modernity." It is central to Gunning's understanding of how cinema emerged, and the factors behind its emergence, that we recognize modernity as an important but by no means unique aspect of the context within which moving images emerged and succeeded. As he put it in a later essay, "Cinema has never been one thing. It has always been a point of intersection, a braiding together of diverse strands" (9:234; also see 8:225–26). This view of the essential complexity of historical causation is central to the arguments and paradoxes that run through the heart of Gunning's major essays on history and historiography.

We can see how this dynamic works by looking at a curious aspect of "An Aesthetic of Astonishment," a 1989 essay that was reprinted in the influential collection *Viewing Positions: Ways of Seeing Film*, edited by Linda Williams. "An Aesthetic of Astonishment" recapitulates the central arguments about attractions, returning to the idea of attractions as an "underground current flowing beneath narrative logic and diegetic realism" that pops up across later film history. But the essay also invokes the modernity debates. Gunning provides one of his first sustained treatments of Benjamin and Kracauer, using their work to show how attractions could be understood as "respond[ing] to the specifics of modern and especially urban life." Attractions, he says, embodied "the particularly modern entertainment form of the thrill," and were a way to pierce the shield that individuals threw up around themselves to ward off the sensory assault of the urban metropolis.

All of this seems familiar to the modernity thesis, though buttressed not just by theory but by archival documentation (far more than in "The Cinema of Attractions" itself). But there is another line of thought in the essay, one that feels distinctly separate from, even contradictory to, the modernity argument. As Gunning positions the logic of attractions against the dominant form of nineteenth-century realism (or absorption), highlighting in particular the way early films seemed to "reach outward and confront" the spectator, he suddenly introduces a different context:

> By tapping into a visual curiosity and desire for novelty, attractions draw upon what Augustine, at the beginning of the fifth century, called *curiositas* in his catalogue of "the lust of the eyes." . . . For Augustine, *curiositas* led not only to a fascination with seeing, but a desire for knowledge for its own sake, ending in the perversions of magic and science. . . . Attractions imply the danger of distraction, a cardinal sin in Augustine's contemplative and vigilant model of Christian life.

The paradox is apparent. On the one hand, attractions emerge with and respond to—are a direct symptom of—modern life in all its vicissitudes. On the other, attractions can be understood in relation to fifth-century debates, partaking of a vastly wider history of a (moral) theory of vision.

It's important, I think, not to ignore how striking and strange this move is. It's one thing to argue, as Gunning does in "The Long and the Short of It: Centuries of Projecting Shadows, from Natural Magic to the Avant-Garde," that a particular technical phenomenon—e.g., the images thrown onto a screen in darkness—has a history that can be traced back into older practices. But what he is doing in "An Aesthetic of Astonishment" is looking back from modernity to Augustine, and connecting a seventeen-hundred-year-old account of vision to modern cinema. There is no sense of an intervening history that could bridge the gap, no sense of why Augustine should be the point of reference for attractions. There is simply a straightforward declaration: "While the impulse to *curiositas* may be as old as Augustine, there is no question that the nineteenth century sharpened this form of 'lust of the eyes' and its commercial exploitation." It's a sweeping gesture, a move that positions cinema's emergence within a much wider cultural framework. Indeed, Gunning returns to this point elsewhere, as in his 1997 essay "In Your Face: Physiognomy, Photography, and the Gnostic Mission of Early Film," which traces the way cinema emerged out of a culture of "overdetermined fascination with the close-up and the human face." This culture, he argues, involves discourses and practices that are at once oriented toward a model of scientific knowledge and driven by a fascination with images for their own sake. Going back into the work of Marey and Charcot, Gunning suggests that the attempt to use photography to discover "the laws of motion and the temporal processes of the body and the face"—and in doing so, to divide time into increasingly small increments—"led directly to the technical invention of the cinema." But then he again turns to Augustine: "Thus the first exhibitions of the Cinématographe, the Vitascope, or the Biograph, while certainly part of modern show business, were not as divorced from their scientific progenitors as might at first appear. It is as though the two aspects of Augustine's *curiositas*, the investigation of nature and the fascination in novelties, had been rejoined in a peculiarly modern gnostic impulse."

So why does Augustine reappear, and again with little framing? There is something of an answer, I think, somewhat earlier in the essay, when Gunning remarks on the importance of maintaining the "broader view of the gnostic impulse as preceding modern science and inherent in such metaphor-based systems as physiognomy." If we recognize that Gunning is arguing that this gnostic impulse is part of what makes up cinema, then we can be alert to the ways he places cinema in line with modes of thought that precede "modern science." To understand cinema, Gunning suggests, we need to push beyond the context of modernity and consider the larger historical context in which it emerges—what he calls at one point "an even deeper layer of history."[55] He makes the point over and over. Take his essay on Anne Friedberg's notion of a "virtual window," where he is particularly interested in the way she ties the idea of the "virtual" into medieval systems of thought. Or "To Scan a Ghost," where his approach to understanding contemporary images is by way of older sciences—especially "the premodern worldview . . . after the triumph of a Platonically tinged Christianity." This means turning again to Augustine, and to an account of sight and seeing "before Kepler and the rise of modern optics." These older theoretical models are not there simply as relics; for Gunning, they are central to an understanding of media at its most contemporary.

As with many of the peculiar moves Gunning makes, this argument does not emerge in a vacuum. His immersion in the culture of the 1970s avant-garde shaped his sense that a wider history of culture was always just at the edge of cinema. Take, for example, Hollis Frampton's fascination with older texts, most notably presented in *Zorns Lemma* (1970), which includes Frampton's own translation of Robert Grosseteste's *On Light, or the Ingression of Forms* (ca. 1225). Or there is Brakhage's fascination with Novalis, which would reach its apex in his remarkable *First Hymn to Night—Novalis* (1994), which Gunning analyzes in an essay included in this volume. In criticism, too, Annette Michelson could move seamlessly across the centuries, as in her 1984 essay on Villiers de l'Isle Adam's *Eve of the Future*. Fred Camper's essay "The End of the Avant-Garde," which serves as Gunning's stalking horse in "Towards a Minor Cinema," is likewise suffused with references to artistic and literary cultures, some of which are centuries removed from the emergence of cinema.

For Gunning, the excavation of larger historical lineages aims to show how the appearance of such long-standing impulses comes to center, at each moment in the history of culture, around a fascination with the image. We can see this vividly in his essay on projected shadows, where he traces the history of the idea that "light [can] structure and create its own world" out of nothing more than darkness and an object that will cast a shadow. Gunning focuses on a key technology for such imagery, the phantasmagoria, and the way it created an image that was "a transition between the tangible and the virtual," at once here and not here. For Gunning, the appeal of the phantasmagoria was that it "literally took place on the threshold between science and superstition"—or, put slightly differently, the "entertaining confusion" of faith and reason. It is this same ontological puzzle, a sense of disavowal, that Gunning finds in writings on early cinema, most notably Maxim Gorky's famous account of the Lumière Cinématographe as presenting the "kingdom of shadows." The uncertain ontology of the image that he finds in the responses of contemporary critics to early cinema, echoing earlier technologies of image-making, will be central to his account of the appeal of projected moving images. We can't fully grasp what it is that we're seeing or discern its status, but we also can't look away.

Gunning's point isn't to establish the phantasmagoria as *the* key to early cinema, any more than his argument in "The Whole Town's Gawking" aims to isolate modernity as *the* key to its emergence. Nor is it to find the idea of cinema in earlier media. Gunning certainly does think that modernity plays a causal role in changes of style, and that the phantasmagoria matters to the emergence of cinema, but also that we cannot understand a complex phenomenon like cinema through any single causal chain. Culture and influence, whether in general or in detail, are too complex to be reduced to single explanations or lines of influence. Yet Gunning's thought runs still deeper. We are fascinated by images, he thinks, and by moving images in particular—and were so long before a technical apparatus like the cinema was imagined. Cinema thus emerges not just into a culture of modernity but into something like a primal human fascination, articulated differently depending upon the epoch and the technology. Understanding that history requires that we be willing to open our own minds to the value and importance of images more broadly. If we want to be able to understand the uniqueness of cinema, especially as it emerges in a culture of modernity, we can only do so against this vast canvas. It's an extraordinary gambit, and one that Gunning makes over and over again, in different ways and in different contexts.

A virtuosic example of this kind of argument is found in Gunning's essay on phantom rides, "Landscape and the Fantasy of Moving Pictures." In an earlier essay on these films, he had focused largely on the way they transformed the perceptions of the viewer, the formal technique of the camera mounted on the front of a train producing a unique form of experience.[56] Here, he focuses on their content, especially the presence of the natural world as the setting through which the trains travel, and highlights a broader perceptual innovation. "Perhaps," he remarks, "we should ask in what ways cinema transformed the possibilities of landscape, both as a form of imagery and as a way of experiencing nature." Gunning argues in particular that phantom rides transform a well-established tradition of American landscape painting, a tradition that brings together aesthetic strategies, a critical discourse, and technologies of image-making (from photography to the panorama to the Claude glass). He connects this to the "new relation to the spectator" in cinema, "an embodied physical presence with physiological sensations." For the first time, we move into and through space, a movement that engenders a "breakdown of the Ideal Landscape" and radically alters not only the forms of pictorial illusion but the very logic of point of view. In a sense, Gunning tracks the history of landscape painting to set up the sense of why phantom rides could appear as such an extraordinary innovation, in both aesthetic and sensorial terms.

This complex dynamic may be best emblematized by a moment in "In Your Face." In that essay, Gunning isolates the close-up as a key aspect of early cinema. This appears to be a medium-specific claim, but he then qualifies it by noting that "the study of the face possesses its own history." This in turn allows him to pivot immediately into the "roots in texts from antiquity attributed to Aristotle and Pythagoras." In short, to the Greeks.[57] The open question that his essays raise, and that they attempt in different ways to find answers to, is how deep the history of cinema goes, and what we might discover in those depths.

GUNNING AS THEORIST

Gunning's fit as a theorist is no less idiosyncratic than the position he occupies within a discourse of historical explanation. It is clear that he has theoretical ambitions in mind every time he writes, and he is often engaged with—directly or indirectly—a range of theoretical positions. Yet for all that, there are surprisingly few film theorists who recur as nodal points in his writings. Bazin, who is of paramount importance to Gunning's career, rarely appears, and is the primary focus only in a late essay on the "myth of total cinema." Jean Epstein, another figure whose thought is central to Gunning's work, is largely a background presence. Even Eisenstein, who gives Gunning the term "attractions," doesn't show up much outside that context. I could go on. My point is not that Bazin, Epstein, and Eisenstein—or any of a number of other theorists—do not matter to Gunning; clearly they do, and it is hard to read his reflections, for example, on the nature of the image without these thinkers in mind. I mean, rather, that Gunning is not a theorist in a familiar sort of way. He does not move through a tradition of "theory," accumulating a range of names and positions so as to tell a story *within* theory. Instead, the theories that are present in his writings are used to excavate the deeper principles on which cinema operates—a way of developing concepts that is almost, as Adorno once put it, "guided by the logic of the object."[58]

Montage

One of the primary ambitions of the "new film history" was theoretical, aimed at providing an alternate model of spectatorship to the one that had been predominant during the 1970s. At the start of that decade, Scott Bukatman has observed, "the serious study of film . . . was largely oriented around methods derived from narrative theory."[59] Films, like novels, were seen as immutable texts, the same no matter how many times you showed them. By contrast, what came to be called "apparatus theory" posited the spectator—rather than the text—as the crucial site of meaning. Yet in this theoretical model the position of the spectator was fixed, determined in advance by the arrangement of the projecting apparatus within the space of the theater, then buttressed by the codes contained in the images and sounds of the film. Gunning, along with the new film history, rejected the assumption of fixity carried by both traditions. Indeed, every aspect of Gunning's historical, critical, and theoretical work is predicated on the idea that cinema is open rather than closed, mutable rather than fixed.

In "An Aesthetic of Astonishment," Gunning directs a polemic precisely at that point. He rejects the assumption of the immutability of the text: "Lost sight of now after decades of text-obsessed film analysis, the exhibition situation transforms and structures a film's mode of address to an audience." How a film is shown determines what that film is. But the implications of Gunning's argument also tell against the terms of apparatus theory, which used an image of awestruck early spectators "as a founding myth for the theoreticalization of the enthralled spectator." Instead, he argues, "we must recognize that the experience of these audiences was profoundly different from the classical spectator's absorption into an empathetic narrative." There is not one spectator but many. This is the ground for a new model of theory, one that is inherently open and dynamic.

Yet even as Gunning moves beyond them, the debates of the 1970s never disappear from his work: realism versus modernism; structure versus experience; apparatus versus history; film as language versus film as recording of reality. These are the tensions around which his work is built. We can see this as early as his 1988 essay on point of view, where he argues against the assumption that a point-of-view construction involves the subordination of the spectator's gaze to that of the character. Looking to early film, Gunning argues that we can see that "point of view operates . . . independently of a diegetic character." While Mulvey is certainly on his mind, the main target of the essay is the theory of voyeurism put forward by Christian Metz, in which the spectator's look is bound to that of the camera. "Far from endowing the site of the camera with the reverence Metz describes . . . early film frequently confronts it with an almost titanic energy, invading or threatening it with a carnivalistic overturning of hierarchy." Take the cycle of voyeuristic or "peeping tom" films, in which characters look through keyholes at private scenes. Whereas the classical film spectator "is constructed within a fantasy of a powerful invisible gaze able to insinuate itself into the most private of dramas," the spectator in these early films is directly addressed—often by the characters doing the looking, who "perform a mocking pantomime of what they see and their delight in sharing it)." Not voyeurism, then, but a form of publicness, one that can occasion varying delights.

Gunning's most sustained engagement with film theory of the 1970s, though, comes in his frequent engagement with the writings of Raymond Bellour. Gunning admires Bellour's flexibility in his treatment of structure, as it avoids reductive definitions of segments by focusing on "patterns of alternation, rhyming, repetition, and so forth."[60] The result, he argues, is the effort to "trace an order that regulates the text," in which "the text [is] the product of dynamic tensions that must be worked through and resolved."[61] Yet Gunning still worries over the totalizing or systematizing impulses at work. In his own study of D. W. Griffith's *The Lonedale Operator* (1911), "Systematizing the Electric Message," he provides a sustained reading of and challenge to Bellour's methods. Acknowledging the presence of patterns that clearly structure the film, Gunning proceeds to explore instead the "shots that stand out by *not* being repeated or alternated." What this allows is an understanding of reflexive devices in the film—moments in which the film's network, its modes of connection, become evident—and what stands out from the patterns, in this case the natural world and the dramatic close-up of the wrench at the film's climax. Gunning argues that Griffith uses breaks in the patterns to develop new aspects of cinematic style and to link the film's events to the growing world of interconnected communication and exchange. From this, he develops the model of a "communicative realism" to describe the "systematic aspect of the style of the single-reel era" and its deployment of montage. It's about how one space is connected to another, how aspects of the action can be linked, and how new technologies of communication (from the telegraph to the telephone) become present without having style be entirely about them. Reflexive, yes—but not disruptive. Realism *and* modernism.

Not surprisingly, Gunning's most sustained reflections on the power of montage appear in his discussions of the avant-garde. Of Ken Jacobs, for example, Gunning writes that his "role as filmmaker is not that of a demiurge fashioning a world in his own image. Rather, like a trained analyst, he stays in the background, mutely allowing the secrets to reveal themselves" (17:354–55). Breaking apart the illusions of coherent space and time, "we penetrate the original, observe the rules of its construction and its implicit ideology . . . the release of its hidden meanings and motives" (15:343). Writing about Abigail Child's practice of editing, Gunning places her squarely within the line of thinking inaugurated by Soviet cinema in the 1920s: "Montage," he writes, "remains, I feel, possibly the most powerful voice film has, the tool by which it probes and questions reality." With Gustav Deutsch's found-footage practice, the impetus is "less about simply making new connections than about awakening energies slumbering in old material. This energy comes from chain reactions, splitting the cinematic atom of original meanings." As with Child's montage, Gunning sees in Deutsch's trawling of the history of early cinema not just a process of assigning meaning but of opening up the work to "generate new figures of significance." Meaning is destabilized, and new configurations emerge—not only between images but in the relation of viewer to image, and of any film to film history.

Image

We can see, even in these brief discussions, the way that Gunning frames an argument against an unstated background of film theorists. The approach can sometimes seem knowingly evasive. Gunning compares Child to "the Soviet school" of montage—but of course he knows the differences between Sergei Eisenstein, Dziga Vertov, Lev Kuleshov, and Vsevolod Pudovkin. Is it just a general point? Or are we to infer a reference? It is as if, at times, he is working with the belief that the background against which his arguments are to make sense is simply present in the reader's mind, that the new paths and lines of thoughts he traces will resonate for us as they do for him. This tendency is especially vivid in what becomes Gunning's main preoccupation, which has to do with the nature of the cinema image.[62] It is, arguably, *the* dominant question across film theory. Epstein focused on the ephemeral transformation of the world by means of cinema, what he termed "photogénie"; Eistenstein distinguished between a representation and a conceptual force-field (*obraz*); Bazin emphasized the photographic reproduction or re-creation of the world; Michelson drew out the perils of illusion, buttressed against the material base of the filmstrip. These positions—and many others—lurk behind Gunning's extensive reflections on the topic.

Of course the central interlocutor is Bazin. How could it be otherwise? Bazin's essay "The Ontology of the Photographic Image" remains the touchtone for the argument that there is something in *cinema* that is transformative within the history of images. For Bazin, it was the idea that, because of its photographic base, cinema is a medium that is automatically and necessarily attuned to reality. Gunning, as we'll see, will argue that while realism is central to the cinematic image, photographic reproduction cannot matter—and never did matter—in the way Bazin says it does. There are simply too many obvious limitations to such a theory, from the technological transformations involved in the rise of digital media to the historical exclusion of animation from the precincts of cinema—a rejection emblematized in Cavell's remark that "cartoons are not movies."[63] It is also the case that the historical opposition Bazin draws out of his realist axiom is anathema to Gunning's own taste. How could you accept a theoretical view that rejects the movements Bazin describes as avowing a "faith in the image": Expressionism, Soviet cinema, and the experiments of the 1920s? Gunning, then, wants to do two things: to accept the axiom that there is something transformative in the cinematic image, and that it has to do with realism; and to describe these terms in a way that doesn't invalidate the formal experimentation across wide swaths of the history of cinema.

Gunning's broad project comes into focus with two 2007 essays that are not explicitly linked but which together provide the terms of an alternative path toward such a model of cinematic ontology. The first is better known. "Moving Away from the Index: Cinema and the Impression of Reality" emerges against the backdrop of anxiety engendered by the rise in digital technologies of image production and modification. The anxiety was focused on the status of the photographic image and its relation to the world, which had generally been regarded as indexical: a direct, causal relation between image and the object(s) it is of. The automatic character of this connection, guaranteed by the mechanical nature of the image, was held to be the ground of a realist orientation to the cinema, an orientation at once aesthetic and ethical.[64] Many of the early debates about the implications of new technologies moved around this position.

Gunning's essay attempts to shift the terms of the debate, moving away from the question of photographic reference—while noting that it was always more complex than the common version of indexicality suggested—to argue instead that it is the movement of the image that generates the important impression of reality.[65] This shift has immediate consequences. First, it moves the site of realism from a relation between camera and world to one between image and viewer, from ontology to phenomenology; it is our engagement with the moving image, the "increased sense of involvement with the cinematic image," that is fundamental to the impression of reality. It turns out that a "faith in the image" can itself be a ground for cinema's reality effect. Second, it offers an account of realism not predicated on a set of styles or a kind of look—"nothing restricts movement to a single style"—which enables historically marginalized aspects of cinema, from animation to special effects, to come to the fore. The essay presents an account of cinema that is open rather than closed, based on effect rather than technology, and alive to the complexity of how we respond to images.

While Gunning continues to develop this line of thought, especially in the direction of animation, he also extends his own account of the cinematic image, one that uses the emergence of digital media to rethink broader questions of media history and ontology.[66] For this account, we can turn to his other 2007 essay, "To Scan a Ghost: The Ontology of Mediated Vision." As he puts it there:

> Not the least of my discomforts with the current term *new media* comes from the linear succession it inflicts on our still emerging understanding of media history—as if the prime modernist virtue of renewal followed automatically from technical innovation and commercial novelty. I want in this essay to explode the iron cage of historical succession to which this use of the term *new* unwittingly commits us. (10:248–49)

Deemphasizing the contemporary, Gunning aims to rethink the very category of media, and especially to focus on the "the term *medium* itself, in all its polysemy and historical divagations, its very materiality and its paradoxical aspiration to immateriality."

The answer to this challenge will involve premodern worldviews, in which ghosts and phantasms share the world—as causes that generate effects—with substantial and animate beings. Ghosts present, Gunning thinks, a crisis of vision for a premodern worldview: we see them, and see them as real, yet they are not (in an ordinary sense) there. But a shift happens with modernity and the project of disenchantment: "As the Renaissance phantasms faded from history, their optically manufactured doppelgangers appeared multiplied in a new daily environment of transparency and reflection." Thus we get the phantasmagoria of the French Revolution, with the visages of dead revolutionary leaders suddenly looming before an audience; stage phenomena such as Pepper's Ghost, where lights and mirrors create the appearance of a phantom onstage; and especially spirit photography, where the self-evidence associated with the medium is used to give credence to the appearance of apparitions in the image. Ghosts, and their challenge to perception, become media objects, part of the domain of visual pleasure, the way we enjoy being delighted and having our skepticism overcome.

It is from this terrain "of pure imagery and virtuality" (10:271) that Gunning sees a way to understand the appeal, power, and uncanniness of the digital image. Rather than treat the apparent ungroundedness of the digital image as a problem for photographic media, Gunning argues that a lack of solidity in fact brings such images into the ontological status of ghosts—the realm out of which they first emerged. (Bazin: "No one believes any longer in the ontological identity of model and image."[67]) What images show is not physically there, but we see it as real, something that is especially true with cinema because of the movement of the image. It's a fascinating argument. We get a way of bringing the digital into photographic media, of reckoning with the new by, paradoxically, turning to an even older history.

The implication of this dual move—away from a photographic ontology and toward premodern theories of images—becomes clear in Gunning's response to Anne Friedberg's *The Virtual Window: From Alberti to Microsoft* (2006), an essay written as a memorial tribute after Friedberg's death. Gunning's engagement with the digital image stands out not so much because it treats new technologies as a historical form—a common enough argument—but because it turns on the etymology of the notion of the “virtual.” For both Friedberg and Gunning, what matters in these early accounts is the idea of a “virtue,” namely the capacity for an entity to exert an effect on the world; by contrast, and to their dissatisfaction, the modern usage is largely negative, signifying something that is not quite real (“virtual reality,” for example). Gunning’s appreciation of Friedberg’s project lies precisely in her turn to an older way of thinking about the “virtual” in terms of optics. But Friedberg, Gunning argues, obscures the ontological status of the image, arguing that the difference between a “real” and a “virtual” image has to do with whether an image is formed by “the unmediated use of the eye versus the use of a lens,” whether the image is in the world or in our mind. What Gunning shows, working through texts from early optics alongside theories of natural magic, is that the difference between real and virtual is in fact about different kinds of optical images.

Gunning wants to draw two lessons for more contemporary debates over the status of images. The first has to do with the topics of reality, materiality, and representation, as he will argue that none of those terms—or their negation—can help specify the nature of the image in the digital age. Rather than a consideration of the ontological status of the image, and whether it has “real” existence, Gunning sees the “virtual *image*” as a unique way of defining the force of images regardless of ontological ground. This connects to the second lesson, which he absorbs from Bergson’s writings on the nature of the image. Gunning had once criticized Bergson’s account of motion and movement in cinema, but now he reclaims Bergson for his account of the virtual, and for the way images operate as something at once inside and outside us. Where Friedberg reads Bergson as aligning the virtual with the possible, hence creating an opposition between possible and actual, Gunning posits a more complex relation: “the virtual is not simply the immaterial waiting in the wings to become material, nor is it a refusal of materialization, a purist pursuit of abstraction. The virtual implies the force of invention and creation, never fully given, but moving toward actualization” (14:328). The virtual image is not opposed to the actual but, rather, part of what allows the actual to come into being—along with “an element of the indeterminate in its unfurling” that makes this connection less secure. Again, we have openness, possibility. The virtual image can *do* things; it can have an effect. Whatever its material basis, the point is not to divide images from the world but to think about how they interact.

Across these essays, and in other essays from the time, Gunning thus presents an unfolding position: that cinema’s claim on the world is grounded in movement rather than ontology, and that an uncertain ontology allows us to treat the image at once in terms of likeness and effect.

If "Moving Away from the Index" seems ostensibly about contemporary debates on indexicality, Gunning uses the conceptual space it provides to move into arguments and histories that resonate back across the history of cinema and its voluminous precursors and successors.

Language as Image

There is a curious sense in which Gunning seems to have fallen into a trap that bedevils the history of film theory. On the one side is a theory of montage, and the way images go together; on the other side is a theory of the image, and how it relates to the world and to spectators. How do they go together? Gunning's response is to turn back to the question of film language. In doing so, however, he recasts the nature of language—or, put differently, the theory of language being used to think about cinema—so as to meld the seemingly opposed positions.

We can start to see this happen in a short essay, "The Language of Motion: Moving Images within the Evolution of Human Technology," where Gunning takes up the question of language by aiming to place cinema "within larger patterns of technological development." Rather than the structuralist model adopted by Metz and film theory of the 1970s, Gunning draws here on the research and theories of André Leroi-Gourhan and their use by Bernard Stiegler in his *Technics and Time*. The aim, simply and broadly speaking, is to show how cinema takes its place within larger and longer patterns of the exteriorization of human thought and memory.[68] Cinema is positioned not so much within a history of language as within a history of *writing*, figured as a form of recording, inscription, and preservation. The crucial step here is what Leroi-Gourhan calls "graphism," an initial stage of language that is initially about "expressing rhythms (i.e., gestures) rather than tracing forms (the pictorial transcription of visual evidence)" (13:308). When Gunning says that moving pictures "are already operating like languages," it is not the idea of structure—the relation between paradigmatic or syntagmatic units—that he has in mind. To operate like languages means that these technologies "are already participating in the process of exteriorization," a process central to the fact of technology itself.

It's with the logic of graphism in mind that Gunning revisits a central moment from the history of montage. Directly addressing Eisenstein, he argues that rather than mere linguistic or conceptual meaning, his films "maintain a creative tension with the range of meaning carried by the graphic." These are creative, dynamic films, based in the power of images as well as ideas. Despite Eisenstein's claims for an intellectual cinema, Gunning argues that the significance of the "Gods" sequence in *October* (1928), for example, is not just the form of the logical reduction—as Noël Carroll argued—but the power of the specific images and figures: the lighting, the distortions, the patterns, the control of space.[69] These are Leroi-Gourhan's rhythms and gestures, the presentation of thinking and acting in permanent form. There is nothing like the "unambiguous decoding" of intellectual montage, nor even the more open logic of the ideogram.

Where Gunning most fully develops this theoretical position around language and cinema is in his writings on the avant-garde. In one essay, he focuses on a series of films in which David Gatten treats words as if they were images—filming them in fragmentary close-ups, emphasizing the shapes of letters—while minimizing linguistic meaning. The result is a curious hybrid: a use of words to meditate "on the nature of the image in an era where visual technology surrounds us and pictures proliferate and multiply." Gatten's approach to text, Gunning argues, effectively sidesteps questions of the photographic index, focusing instead on both the logic of technological reproduction—including Leroi-Gourhan's graphism—and the theological legacy of talking about the letter as such. This latter point is a mystical vision that entails "a liberation of letter into spirit as if releasing the creative power of the word and letter from its technological framework and linear clarity" (24:444). The "words as images," and words without images, create an affinity between writing and drawing, a sense in which pictorial forms are not opposed to each other but constituted by the same process. The result is a very different picture of cinematic imagery, "which we could describe as blending trace, writing, and image but circumscribed or limited by none of these."

Gunning also takes up this revised account of language in two other essays on the avant-garde, both of which treat inscription as a form of mediated vision that nonetheless conveys and generates intense experience. In an essay on Kenneth Anger's *Fireworks* (1947), Gunning uses the pairing of queer desire and the avant-garde to open up the idea of "cinema as a vehicle of desire."[70] A meditation at once on the importance of amateur cinema and on the presentation of ecstasy and ecstatic experiences, Gunning's argument moves through the iconography and visual play of Anger's film. But it ends on inscription, with the lover's face scratched out: "The film transforms the body into an impossible amalgam for the final and most significant time. . . . The aura of the sun-face introduces another layer of representation, scratching through the physical and material body of the film emulsion to let the unstained light of the projector through . . . an image of desire so intense it bores through the surface to originating light" (22:418). The permeability of the film surface recurs in Gunning's essay "The Grain of the Scratch: The Precarity of Transparency in Cinema," where he takes up broader theorizations of inscription in the avant-garde. He touches on Anger here, but also on Gatten's *What the Water Said, Nos. 1–3* (1998). And then there is Stan Brakhage, whose use of scratches is initially in the mode of sight and then, gradually, in the form of an expanded conception of vision. As with Anger, the form of ecstatic, personal perception is not opposed to the medium of cinema but constituted by it, "its materiality serving neither as an obstacle nor as a simple neutral channel, but as a matrix for the generation of unexpected effects."

It is in Gunning's full essay on Stan Brakhage, though, that this theoretical orientation gets its fullest articulation. Given Brakhage's importance to Gunning, it is curious that he has not written much on him; perhaps it has to do with the proximity of Brakhage's concerns to the theoretical issues Gunning cares most about. "I am trying," he writes in this hitherto unpublished essay, "to specify the way Brakhage redefined the film medium through his work and created a medium uniquely his own. . . . I would claim that only a few filmmakers have actually redefined their medium in a unique manner. Brakhage is one of these." Gunning moves through the superimpositions in *Mesa Verde* (1989), the drama of nature and techné in *Mothlight* (1963), the role of motion and movement in *Passage Through: A Ritual* (1990), and finally the hand-painted films such as *First Hymn to the Night—Novalis* (1994), the film that constitutes the central preoccupation of the second half of the essay.

Again, Gunning turns to Leroi-Gourhan's account of graphism, but does so here with a knowingly counterintuitive argument. Brakhage, after all, is almost synonymous with the idea of overcoming language: "Imagine a world alive with incomprehensible objects and shimmering with an endless variety of movement and innumerable gradations of color. Imagine a world before 'the beginning was the word.'"[71] Gunning argues that it was actually a *particular* use of language that bothered Brakhage, not language per se. But this becomes clear only with the late painted films, when Brakhage turns to writing by way of painting—and especially the *act* of painting. If graphism, Gunning argues, is about recording the movement of gesture, "late Brakhage reveals that his cinema, and that is to say, his medium, has been about the hand as much as the eye: the hand that marks and moves draws, writes, and gestures."[72] It a medium, a physical presence that can be revealed in multiple ways and which constitutes the affective charge of the films. Even in the scratched surfaces that contain Brakhage's name, the etching into the black leader that marks the authorship of the work, Gunning finds the graphic charge of writing: "one cannot lose a sense of them as meager shaky scratches etched against a broad expanse of blackness." These images pose basic questions about the materiality of the medium: What is darkness? What is light? How is experience shaped? And how does meaning emerge? Brakhage turns to the logic of graphism as a means of posing the full reach of these questions, treating them as simultaneously conceptual, affective, and material.

Much like avant-garde film itself, Gunning's late essays on avant-garde filmmakers allow him to pose arguments about cinema in new ways. He takes up familiar topics, from the logic of montage to the history of the trace in photographic media to the very concept of the medium itself, but now gives them new groundings, new meanings. If the ontology of the image, digital as well as analog, is one of his concerns, so too is the idea of a film language, but with language now grounded less in structuralist and semiotic accounts and more in mysticism, human evolution, and modes of poetic register. In the essay on Brakhage, one of the highest achievements in all of Gunning's critical writings, we find all these arguments and preoccupations coming together. Images are unmoored from considerations of reference but made all the more powerful for it; they are organized into patterns but without the demand of a structuralist logic, following instead the flows of visual and linguistic thought. The result is a theory of language, as Gunning quotes Novalis, that is part of a "*higher linguistic power*," not so much conveying meaning as carrying us, as viewers and readers alike, along with it, "a process of being taken out of our selves somewhere." The precise location of such transport, such transformation, is the art of cinema: we watch to discover, to see where we will be taken, and what we will learn and experience along the way.

ENERGIES FOR THE FUTURE

Gunning concludes his essay on Brakhage on a mystical note, emphasizing what he calls "moving writing." "The energy of these marks," he writes, "denies any connotation of writing as static, past, inert ('for the letter killeth') and opens the way to a writing that is alive and renews itself in every frame. The jittering, so challenging to our eyes, demands 'moving visual thinking' in the most literal sense. The word is animated, brought to life" (26:492). So much of the cinema that Gunning discusses is gone, consigned to history—from the "cinema of attractions," over before the end of the first decade of the twentieth century, to the postwar American avant-garde, which faded away over the course of the twentieth (and early twenty-first) century. His look back, though, is not nostalgic; rather, it seeks to uncover what he calls "tales of cinema's forgotten future" and to bring them into the present.

A vision of the past has always been central to Gunning's work, one in which cinema's history continues to matter to an ongoing sense of its present and future. Part of the appeal of early cinema had to do with what he describes as "the chaotic curiosity shop of early modern life," which includes not just cinematic forms but the "long existing game of fooling the senses and the uncanny pleasures it evoked."[73] Filmmakers and film historians alike can turn to the past to discover energies that haven't yet been fully explored and that can never be fully exhausted. This is the domain of the avant-garde that matters to Gunning. Recall his description of Deutsch creating a montage less as a matter of "making new connections than [of] awakening energies slumbering in old material." Or of Ken Jacobs, who, likewise uncovering new meanings in old footage, "enters an uncanny dimension of the cinema akin to psychoanalysis." "Here, after nearly a century," he writes of Jacobs's *Perfect Film* (1986), "are true *motion pictures* in which motion is never taken for granted but continually encountered in a flux and reflux of perception." We watch ourselves as we watch films, seeing how we see—our trained habits of perception, and also what gets left out of them. Elsewhere, Gunning remarks that Jacobs's "resurrection" of early film "does not lie quietly upon the operating table. It barks with life and stands as a new creation, a deconstructive Frankenstein of a film with new vitality in its borrowed parts." And similarly, there is the work of Ernie Gehr, whose films demonstrate both "an essential mystery at the root of the cinematic process" and "the process of perception as crisis." What we get, Gunning observes, is "a laboratory of perception, where effects of light and shadow, peculiar angles of space, flows of traffic both human and vehicular, and effects of time passing all intersect." Again, the use of footage from early cinema gives this perceptual charge a historical force, making the spectator confront the present moment of the film's projection—and the perceptual transformations that are occurring—at the same time as the pastness of the images shown on screen. Moving back and forth, never settling, a model of uncertain temporality that weaves together history and experience into one.

Tom Gunning's essays cover almost innumerable topics yet present an integrated vision of cinema. They are based in a careful and sustained study of early cinema but always expand beyond these limits: back into the long history of visual culture, from speculations on vision in antiquity to the development of optical technologies across the early modern period; outward across the wide range of nineteenth-century media, the varied entertainments that constitute the cultural horizon amid which cinema emerged; and forward into the continued—and continuing—transformations of the nature of the image. It shouldn't be a surprise that the one essay he devotes solely to the work of André Bazin is not about cinematic ontology but, rather, about the history of cinema and what Bazin calls "the myth of total cinema." Gunning writes, "Tracing the figure of total cinema involves not only a process of historical research but also an engagement with the future, so that the question, what is cinema? never becomes simply, what was cinema? but always asks, what will cinema be?"[74] The essays collected in this volume represent Gunning's attempt to weave together the different elements of the history of the moving image, preserving historical specificity yet insisting on connections between periods and modes that are deep and fundamental. It is with the intent of articulating such connections, not only to new studies of cinema but also to new kinds of films and filmmaking, that Gunning continues to write. His works present a vision of the past and of the present for the future.

*

A note on the text. With several exceptions, the essays in this volume have been previously published. The editing done to them has been slight: names and punctuation standardized, typos and errors corrected, and minor grammatical infelicities resolved. Nowhere has the writing been substantively altered, or the claims revised.

PART I
History

1

The Cinema of Attractions: Early Film, Its Spectator, and the Avant-Garde

Writing in 1922, flushed with the excitement of seeing Abel Gance's *La Roue*, Fernand Léger tried to define something of the radical possibilities of the cinema. The potential of the new art did not lie in "imitating the movements of nature" or in "the mistaken path" of its resemblance to theater. Its unique power was a "matter of *making images seen*."[1] It is precisely this harnessing of visibility, this act of showing and exhibition, which I feel cinema before 1906 displays most intensely. Its inspiration for the avant-garde of the early decades of this century needs to be reexplored.

Writings by the early modernists (Futurists, Dadaists, and Surrealists) on the cinema follow a pattern similar to Léger: enthusiasm for this new medium and its possibilities, and disappointment at the way it has already developed, its enslavement to traditional art forms, particularly theater and literature. This fascination with the *potential* of a medium (and the accompanying fantasy of rescuing the cinema from its enslavement to alien and passé forms) can be understood from a number of viewpoints. I want to use it to illuminate a topic I have also approached before, the strangely heterogeneous relation that film before 1906 (or so) bears to the films that follow, and the way a taking account of this heterogeneity signals a new

This essay first appeared as "The Cinema of Attraction" in *Wide Angle* 8, nos. 3–4 (1986): 63–70, and was subsequently revised and republished in *Early Cinema: Space, Frame, Narrative*, ed. Thomas Elsaesser (London: British Film Institute, 1990), 56–62.

conception of film history and film form. My work in this area has been pursued in collaboration with André Gaudreault.[2]

The history of early cinema, like the history of cinema generally, has been written and theorized under the hegemony of narrative films. Early filmmakers like G. A. Smith, Georges Méliès, and Edwin S. Porter have been studied primarily from the viewpoint of their contribution to film as a storytelling medium, particularly the evolution of narrative editing. Although such approaches are not totally misguided, they are one-sided and potentially distort both the work of these filmmakers and the actual forces shaping cinema before 1906. A few observations will indicate the way that early cinema was not dominated by the narrative impulse that later asserted its sway over the medium. First there is the extremely important role that actuality film plays in early film production. Investigation of the films copyrighted in the US shows that actuality films outnumbered fictional films until 1906.[3] The Lumière tradition of "placing the world within one's reach" through travel films and topicals did not disappear with the exit of the Cinématographe from film production. But even within non-actuality filming—what has sometimes been referred to as the "Méliès tradition"—the role narrative plays is quite different from in traditional narrative film. Méliès himself declared in discussing his working method:

> As for the scenario, the "fable," or "tale," I only consider it at the end. I can state that the scenario constructed in this manner has *no importance*, since I use it merely as a pretext for the "stage effects," the "tricks," or for a nicely arranged tableau.[4]

Whatever differences one might find between Lumière and Méliès, they should not represent the opposition between narrative and nonnarrative filmmaking, at least as it is understood today. Rather, one can unite them in a conception that sees cinema less as a way of telling stories than as a way of presenting a series of views to an audience, fascinating because of their illusory power (whether the realistic illusion of motion offered to the first audiences by Lumière, or the magical illusion concocted by Méliès) and exoticism. In other words, I believe that the relation to the spectator set up by the films of both Lumière and Méliès (and many other filmmakers before 1909) had a common basis, and one that differs from the primary spectator relations set up by narrative film after 1906. I will call this earlier conception of cinema, "the cinema of attractions." I believe that this conception dominates cinema until about 1906–1907. Although different from the fascination in storytelling exploited by the cinema from the time of Griffith, it is not necessarily opposed to it. In fact, the cinema of attractions does not disappear with the dominance of narrative, but rather goes underground, both into certain avant-garde practices and as a component of narrative films, more evident in some genres (e.g., the musical) than in others.

What precisely is the cinema of attractions? First, it is a cinema that bases itself on the quality that Léger celebrated: its ability to *show* something. Contrasted to the voyeuristic aspect of narrative cinema analyzed by Christian Metz, this is an exhibitionist cinema.[5] An aspect of early cinema which I have written about in other articles is emblematic of this different relationship the cinema of attractions constructs with its spectator: the recurring look at the camera by actors. This action, which is later perceived as spoiling the realistic illusion of the cinema, is here undertaken with brio, establishing contact with the audience. From comedians smirking at the camera, to the constant bowing and gesturing of the conjurors in magic films, this is a cinema that displays its visibility, willing to rupture a self-enclosed fictional world for a chance to solicit the attention of the spectator.

Exhibitionism becomes literal in the series of erotic films which play an important role in early film production (the same Pathé catalogue would advertise the Passion Play along with "scènes grivoises d'un caractère piquant," erotic films often including full nudity), also driven underground in later years. As Noël Burch has shown in his film *Correction Please: How We Got into Pictures* (1979), a film like *The Bride Retires* (France, 1902) reveals a fundamental conflict between this exhibitionistic tendency of early film and the creation of a fictional diegesis. A woman undresses for bed while her new husband peers at her from behind a screen. However, it is to the camera and the audience that the bride addresses her erotic striptease, winking at us as she faces us, smiling in erotic display.

As the quote from Méliès points out, the trick film, perhaps the dominant non-actuality film genre before 1906, is itself a series of displays, of magical attractions, rather than a primitive sketch of narrative continuity. Many trick films are, in effect, plotless, a series of transformations strung together with little connection and certainly no characterization. But to approach even the plotted trick films, such as *Voyage dans la lune* (1902), simply as precursors of later narrative structures is to miss the point. The story simply provides a frame upon which to string a demonstration of the magical possibilities of the cinema.

Modes of exhibition in early cinema also reflect this lack of concern with creating a self-sufficient narrative world upon the screen. As Charles Musser has shown, the early showmen exhibitors exerted a great deal of control over the shows they presented, actually reediting the films they had

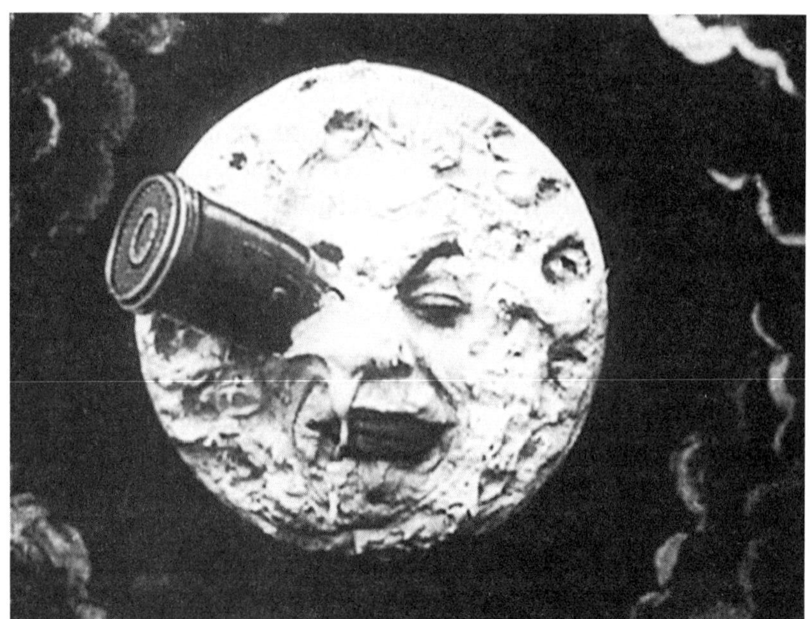

FIGURE 1.1. *A Trip to the Moon* (Georges Méliès, 1902).

purchased and supplying a series of off-screen supplements, such as sound effects and spoken commentary.[6] Perhaps most extreme is the Hale's Tours, the largest chain of theaters exclusively showing films before 1906. Not only did the films consist of nonnarrative sequences taken from moving vehicles (usually trains), but the theater itself was arranged as a train car with a conductor who took tickets and sound effects simulating the click-clack of wheels and hiss of air brakes.[7] Such viewing experiences relate more to the attractions of the fairground than to the traditions of the legitimate theater. The relation between films and the emergence of the great amusement parks, such as Coney Island, at the turn of the century provides rich ground for rethinking the roots of early cinema.

Nor should we ever forget that in the earliest years of exhibition the cinema itself was an attraction. Early audiences went to exhibitions to see machines demonstrated (the newest technological wonder, following in the wake of such widely exhibited machines and marvels as X-rays or, earlier, the phonograph), rather than to view films. It was the Cinématographe, the Biograph, or the Vitascope that was advertised on the variety bills in which they premièred, not *Le Déjeuner de bébé* or *The Black Diamond Express*. Alter the initial novelty period, this display of the possibilities of cinema continues, and not only in magic films. Many of the close-ups in early film differ from later uses of the technique precisely because they do not use enlargement for narrative punctuation but as an attraction in its own right. The close-up cut into Porter's *The Gay Shoe Clerk* (1903) may anticipate later continuity techniques, but its principal motive is again pure exhibitionism, as the lady lifts her skirt hem, exposing her ankle for all to see. Biograph films such as *Photographing a Female Crook* (1904) and *Hooligan in Jail* (1903) consist of a single shot in which the camera is brought close to the main character, until they are in mid-shot. The enlargement is not a device expressive of narrative tension; it is in itself an attraction and the point of the film.[8]

To summarize, the cinema of attractions directly solicits spectator attention, inciting visual curiosity and supplying pleasure through an exciting spectacle—a unique event, whether fictional or documentary, that is of interest in itself. The attraction to be displayed may also be of a cinematic nature, such as the early close-ups just described, or trick films in which a cinematic manipulation (slow motion, reverse motion, substitution, multiple exposure) provides the film's novelty. Fictional situations tend to be restricted to gags, vaudeville numbers, or re-creations of shocking or curious incidents (executions, current events). It is the direct address of the audience, in which an attraction is offered to the spectator by a cinema

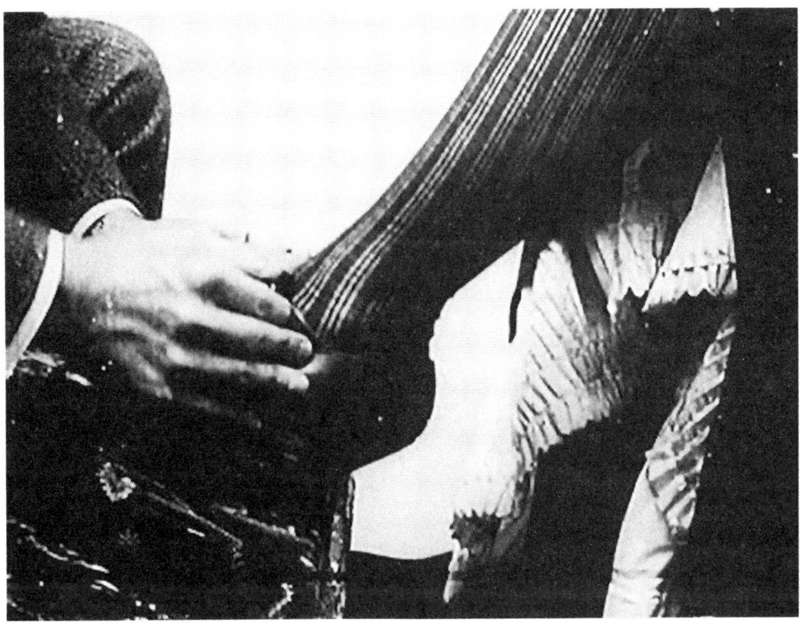

FIGURE 1.2. *The Gay Shoe Clerk* (Edwin S. Porter, 1903).

showman, that defines this approach to filmmaking. Theatrical display dominates over narrative absorption, emphasizing the direct stimulation of shock or surprise at the expense of unfolding a story or creating a diegetic universe. The cinema of attractions expends little energy creating characters with psychological motivations or individual personality. Making use of both fictional and nonfictional attractions, its energy moves outward toward an acknowledged spectator rather than inward toward the character-based situations essential to classical narrative.

The term "attractions" comes, of course, from the young Sergei Mikhailovich Eisenstein and his attempt to find a new model and mode of analysis for the theater. In his search for the "unit of impression" of theatrical art, the foundation of an analysis that would undermine realistic representational theater, Eisenstein hit upon the term "attraction."[9] An attraction aggressively subjected the spectator to "sensual or psychological impact." According to Eisenstein, theater should consist of a montage of such attractions, creating a relation to the spectator entirely different from his absorption in "illusory depictions."[10] I pick up this term partly to underscore the relation to the spectator that this later avant-garde practice shares with early cinema: that of exhibitionist confrontation rather than diegetic absorption. Of course, the "experimentally regulated and mathematically calculated" montage of attractions demanded by Eisenstein differs enormously from these early films (as any conscious and oppositional mode of practice will from a popular one).[11] However, it is important to realize the context from which Eisenstein selected the term. Then, as now, "attraction" was a term of the fairground, and for Eisenstein and his friend Yutkevich it primarily represented their favorite fairground attraction, the roller coaster, or as it was known then in Russia, the American Mountains.[12]

The source is significant. The enthusiasm of the early avant-garde for film was at least partly an enthusiasm for a mass culture that was emerging at the beginning of the century, offering a new sort of stimulus for an audience not acculturated to the traditional arts. It is important to take this enthusiasm for popular art as something more than a simple gesture to *épater les bourgeois*. The enormous development of the entertainment industry since the 1910s and its growing acceptance by middle-class culture (and the accommodation that made this acceptance possible) have made it difficult to understand the liberation popular entertainment offered at the beginning of the century. I believe that it was precisely the exhibitionist quality of turn-of-the-century popular art that made it attractive to the avant-garde—its freedom from the creation of a diegesis, its accent on direct stimulation.

Writing of the variety theater, Marinetti praised not only its aesthetics of astonishment and stimulation but, particularly, its creation of a new spectator who contrasts with the "static," "stupid voyeur" of traditional theater. The spectator at the variety theater feels directly addressed by the spectacle and joins in, singing along, heckling the comedians.[13] Dealing with early cinema within the context of archive and academy, we risk missing its vital relation to vaudeville, its primary place of exhibition until around 1905. Film appeared as one attraction on the vaudeville program, surrounded by a mass of unrelated acts in a nonnarrative and even nearly illogical succession of performances. Even when presented in the nickelodeons that were emerging at the end of this period, these short films always appeared in a variety format, trick films sandwiched in with farces, actualities, "illustrated songs," and, quite frequently, cheap vaudeville acts. It was precisely this nonnarrative variety that placed this form of entertainment under attack by reform groups in the early 1910s. The Russell Sage Survey of popular entertainments found vaudeville "depends upon an artificial rather than a natural human and developing interest, these acts having no necessary and as a rule, no actual connection."[14] In other words, no narrative. A night at the variety theater was like a ride on a streetcar or an active day in a crowded city, according to this middle-class reform group, stimulating an unhealthy nervousness. It was precisely such artificial stimulus that Marinetti and Eisenstein wished to borrow from the popular arts and inject into the theater, organizing popular energy for radical purpose.

What happened to the cinema of attractions? The period from 1907 to about 1913 represents the true *narrativization* of the cinema, culminating in the appearance of feature films, which radically revised the variety format. Film clearly took the legitimate theater as its model, producing famous players in famous plays. The transformation of filmic discourse that D. W. Griffith typifies bound cinematic signifiers to the narration of stories and the creation of a self-enclosed diegetic universe. The look at the camera becomes taboo and the devices of cinema are transformed from playful "tricks"—cinematic attractions (Méliès gesturing at us to watch the lady vanish)—to elements of dramatic expression, entries into the psychology of character and the world of fiction.

However, it would be too easy to see this as a Cain and Abel story, with narrative strangling the nascent possibilities of a young iconoclastic form of entertainment. Just as the variety format in some sense survived in the movie palaces of the 1920s (with newsreel, cartoon, sing-along, orchestra performance, and sometimes vaudeville acts subordinated to, but still coexisting with, the narrative *feature* of the evening), the system of attraction remains an essential part of popular filmmaking.

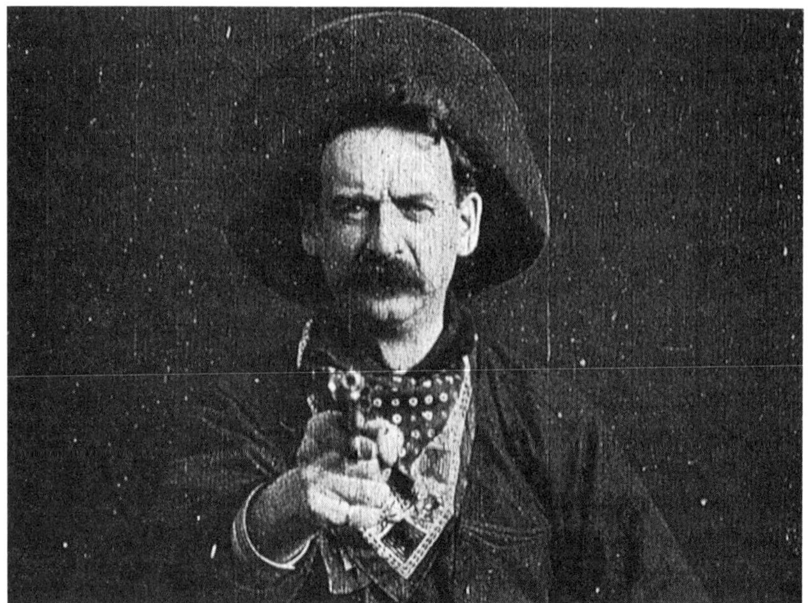

FIGURE 1.3. *The Great Train Robbery* (Edwin S. Porter, 1903).

The chase film shows how, toward the end of this period (basically from 1903 to 1906), a synthesis of attractions and narrative was already under way. The chase had been the original truly narrative genre of the cinema, providing a model for causality and linearity as well as a basic editing continuity. A film like Biograph's *Personal* (1904), the model for the chase film in many ways, shows the creation of a narrative linearity, as the French nobleman runs for his life from the fiancées his personal column ad has unleashed. However, at the same time, as the group of young women pursue their prey toward the camera in each shot, they encounter some slight obstacle (a fence, a steep slope, a stream) that slows them down for the spectator, providing a mini-spectacle pause in the unfolding of narrative. The Edison Company seemed particularly aware of this, since they offered their plagiarized version of this Biograph film (*How a French Nobleman Got a Wife through the New York Herald "Personal" Columns*) in two forms, as a complete film or as separate shots, so that any one image of the ladies chasing the man could be bought without the inciting incident or narrative closure.[15]

As Laura Mulvey has shown in a very different context, the dialectic between spectacle and narrative has fueled much of the classical cinema.[16] Donald Crafton, in his study of slapstick comedy, "Pie and Chase," has shown the way slapstick did a balancing act between the pure spectacle of gag and the development of narrative.[17] Likewise, the traditional spectacle film proved true to its name by highlighting moments of pure visual stimulation along with narrative. The 1924 version of *Ben Hur* was in fact shown at a Boston theater with a timetable announcing the moment of its prime attractions:

8.35	*The Star of Bethlehem*
8.40	*Jerusalem Restored*
8.59	*Fall of the House of Hur*
10.29	*The Last Supper*
10.50	*Reunion*[18]

The Hollywood advertising policy of enumerating the features of a film, each emblazoned with the command "See!" shows this primal power of the attraction running beneath the armature of narrative regulation.

We seem far from the avant-garde premises with which this discussion of early cinema began. But it is important for the radical heterogeneity I find in early cinema not to be conceived as a truly oppositional program, one irreconcilable with the growth of narrative cinema. This view is too sentimental and too ahistorical. A film like *The Great Train Robbery* (1903) does point in both directions, toward a direct assault on the spectator (the spectacularly enlarged outlaw unloading his pistol in our faces), and toward a linear narrative continuity. This is early film's ambiguous heritage. Clearly in some sense recent spectacle cinema has reaffirmed its roots in stimulus and carnival rides, in what might be called the Spielberg-Lucas-Coppola cinema of effects.

But effects are tamed attractions. Marinetti and Eisenstein understood that they were tapping into a source of energy that would need focusing and intensification to fulfill its revolutionary possibilities. Both Eisenstein and Marinetti planned to exaggerate the impact on spectators, Marinetti proposing to literally glue them to their seats (ruined garments paid for after the performance) and Eisenstein setting firecrackers off beneath them. Every change in film history implies a change in its address to the spectator, and each period constructs its spectator in a new way. Now in a period of American avant-garde cinema in which the tradition of contemplative subjectivity has perhaps run its (often glorious) course, it is possible that this earlier carnival of the cinema, and the methods of popular entertainment, still provide an unexhausted resource—a Coney Island of the avant-garde, whose never dominant but always sensed current can be traced from Méliès through Keaton, through *Un Chien Andalou* (1928), and Jack Smith.

2

What I Saw from the Rear Window of the Hôtel des Folies-Dramatiques, or the Story Point-of-View Films Told

> Celui qui regarde par le trou de la senure c'est pas au théâtre; Cocteau a justement démontré dans *Le Sang d'un poète* qu'il était déjà au cinéma.
>
> ANDRÉ BAZIN, "THÉÂTRE ET CINÉMA," 1951

> "I used to think seein' and hearin' was the only regulation aids to ascertainin' facts, but as we get older we get more accomodatin' . . . Biograph or cinematograph was what I was alludin' to."
>
> FROM "MRS BATHUST," BY RUDYARD KIPLING, 1904

Few critical terms are as powerful as "point of view" or as ambiguous (and in criticism ambiguity often *is* power). In cinema the concept of point of view resounds with multiple associations. On the one hand it refers to a very specific figure of filmic discourse, known in English as the POV shot. From this specific denotation the term can be expanded outward until it threatens to take in the whole realm of filmic narration, encompassing not only the POV shot but all devices relating to character subjectivity, and extending, for some theorists, to the "point of view" of narrator or even author.[1] My task in this article will extend somewhat beyond the classical conception of the POV shot, but will not attempt to take in the full range of narrative discourse in early film.

This essay first appeared in *Ce que je vois de mon ciné: La représentation du regard dans le cinéma des premiers temps*, ed. André Gaudreault (Paris: Méridiens Klincksieck, 1988), 33–43.

Perhaps the best way to define the sense of point of view I will pursue is through François Jost's extremely useful concept of ocularization, which he defines as "la relation entre ce que la caméra montre et ce que le héros est censé voir."[2] I will concern myself only with those moments in filmic discourse which refer to an act of seeing as well as to what is seen. I will not deal with those representations of subjectivity (such as dreams, memories, or fantasies) which do not involve visual perceptions, or with those filmic means of indicating subjectivity metaphorically which Edward Branigan terms "character reflection and projection."[3]

However, if point of view in my understanding does not engulf all of filmic narration, it cannot be understood apart from its narrative context. As both Jost and Branigan make clear in their respective studies, cinematic point of view can only be approached within a consideration of narrative context. As Jost says:

> Autrement dit, le problème de la signification sémiologique d'un plan ne peut être traité complètement qu'à condition d'être restitué dans le champ du récit, c'est-à-dire dans un contexte ou l'on suppose quelqu'un qui raconte (un narrateur) et quelqu'un dont on raconte l'histoire (un personnage): sans cette opération, l'analyse de l'image touche très vite le bout d'une impasse.[4]

Although I will modify a bit the conception of this context as narrative in the classical sense (particularly its necessary relation to diegetic characters), I firmly agree that point of view must be placed within the context of a film as *énonciation*.

However, for my purposes another context intervenes as well, one not included in the theoretical and synchronic projects of Jost and Branigan. Branigan makes it clear that his own approach to the issue of point of view is not concerned with historical questions (although he acknowledges the importance of history for a full understanding of the concept).[5] The context of film history forms my ultimate horizon, and the purpose of this essay will be to put in play an interaction between the theoretical and the historical, allowing one to inform (and transform) the other. This means that another context, that of the historical role of point of view, surrounds and redefines the very important narrative context which Jost and Branigan describe. Although this historical context could be established in a number of ways, I will deal with two primary sources: the films themselves and their description in original catalogue publicity.

How does one undertake a historical investigation of an aspect of film like point of view? If we take seriously the principle that different periods of film history are organized in different ways and that a film historian must recognize and respect these differences, then clearly we can not simply catalogue early instances of point-of-view cutting.[6] We must examine how the notion of point of view operates in early cinema and how it relates to the later classical point-of-view shots which convey a character's viewpoint. And if in fact early film shows a different understanding and treatment of point of view, we must not only describe that difference but indicate its relation to later forms, tracing patterns of historical transformation.

Point of view has been approached primarily as a relation between narration and character, and secondarily, between narration and spectator. Although I would not claim such narrative structures are irrelevant to early films, I do believe that they are often secondary to the presentation of spectacle. And following from this, I find that in early film the relation between narration and character is often secondary to the relation between spectacle and spectator. The relevant context for the *énonciation* of early film is not always a *narrative* context, at least as this term is usually understood. I believe that a close examination of point of view in a number of early films will reveal this difference. But a historical treatment of early films also reveals a shift in attitude toward point of view which sketches the tranformation that leads to later forms.

André Gaudreault and myself use the term "the cinema of attractions" to highlight a driving force of early cinema that differs from classical cinema's dedication to storytelling.[7] The cinema of attractions directly solicits spectator attention, inciting visual curiosity and supplying pleasure through an exciting spectacle. This cinema is based in theatrical display rather than narrative absorption, emphasizing the direct stimulation of shock or surprise at the expense of unfolding a story or creating a diegetic universe. The cinema of attractions expends little energy creating characters with psychological motivations or individual personality. Making use of both fictional and nonfictional attractions, the cinema of attractions is directed outward toward an acknowledged spectator rather than inward toward the character-based situations essential to classical narrative.

Serving as an index for character's perception and psychological reactions, the classical point-of-view shot seems quite opposed to the dominant energy of the cinema of attractions. The classical point-of-view shot as defined by Branigan is "a shot in which the camera assumes the position of a subject in order to show us what the subject sees."[8] Branigan further specifies that the effect of point of view most frequently depends upon two shots in a relation of temporal continuity. The first shot establishes a point from which a glance originates which refers to an object. In the second shot (the actual POV shot) the camera is situated at the point established in shot one and reveals or highlights the object of the glance. Point of view in this sense refers to a unit that integrates these elements. However, Branigan makes it clear that it is the integration of the elements which defines the POV unit, which could be "scattered in various ways in any number of shots, a single shot, or fragment of a shot."[9] As Branigan makes clear at several points in his text, point of view depends on narrative context and structure rather than formal features alone.[10]

Branigan's description of the formal elements of the classical POV shot does in fact apply perfectly to most of the early films I am going to discuss. The specificity of point of view in early cinema cannot be revealed simply by a formal description, but demands to be placed in the context of narrative (or nonnarrative) functions. Some discussion of the narrative functions of point-of-view shots within the classical cinema will provide a basis for differentiation.

Although POV units (I use this term rather than POV *shot* to acknowledge Branigan's insight that the POV effect depends on the interrelation among narrative elements rather than shots) undoubtedly serve a number of functions within the classical film, I believe that two are primary. First, presenting a shot as the perception of a character accents the content of the shot, focusing added attention on it. Following the basic economy of classical narrative, such accenting becomes an indication of narrative significance. Further, through manipulation of the limited knowledge of events attainable through a character's viewpoint, the POV unit becomes a way of shaping that significance by holding back or revealing information. In Jost's terminology, although *ocularization* is not identical with *focalization*, what a character sees often indicates what she knows.[11] As Branigan points out, such epistemological boundaries "may be used to conceal and measure our knowledge pertaining to the enigmas of the text."[12] POV structures can play an essential role in the suspenseful development of narrative information, so important to the classical text.[13] Secondly, placing the shot within the perceptual awareness of a specific character highlights that character's subjectivity, so that the POV unit frequently carries information about what the character thinks or feels (often supplied by the reaction shot which follows a POV shot and forms an optional element of the POV unit). As Branigan states, the concept of character provides the coherence of the POV unit, justifying "the unity and meaning of all the elements."[14] These two aspects often combine; for example, the narrative significance of a POV shot may lie precisely in what a character thinks or feels about what she has seen.

A film like Hitchcock's *Rear Window* exemplifies this classical use of the POV unit to build up significant story information (e.g., what is happening in Lars Thorwald's apartment and what it means—suspensefully developed through L. B. Jeffries's limited access) while at the same time revealing reactions of the characters (e.g., Jeff's growing obsession; his desperation as he watches Lisa assaulted by Thorwald). Such narrative functions of POV units appear rather early in film history. Three shots from D. W. Griffith's *The Red Man and the Child* fulfill all the classical functions of the POV unit. In this sequence an Indian is encouraged to look through a surveyor's telescope. Peering through in curiosity he suddenly sees the murder of an old man, the theft of the Indian's hidden gold, and the kidnapping of a young boy. These actions occur within a single(!) POV shot, framed by a circular matte to indicate the Indian's view through the telescope. The third shot returns to the Indian as he reacts to this sight with alarm and rushes off to rescue the boy and retrieve his gold. The POV shot provides Griffith with a dramatic way to present this key event, while portraying the Indian's knowledge of and reaction to it. The POV unit is firmly embedded in the film's narrative architectonics of suspense and character motivation.[15]

How does point of view in a cinema of spectacle differ from point of view in classical character-based cinema? Although I have no doubt that Griffith drew on uses of point of view that preceded him, I also believe that his use of the device, and its later function in classical filmmaking, is quite different from its usual function in early cinema. This difference is rooted in the attitudes of the cinema of attractions, even though POV units in early films often follow Branigan's description of the classical POV shot. In early cinema, the POV unit's relation to narrative structure and character motivation differs from its function in the films of Griffith and Hitchcock. However, I will show that certain early films also channel scopic energies in ways which sketch the later bond between point of view and the act of storytelling.

The films which relate most strongly to the cinema of attractions do not make use of the classical POV unit but play with the concept of point of view in a radically different way. In these films, the concept of POV is both invoked and exploded. Rather than the classical two-shot unit, films by Cecil Hepworth and James Williamson create a sense of POV within a single shot.[16] But most importantly, the point of view established by these films does not correspond to the diegetic point and glance provided by the first shot in Branigan's schema. Rather it is the viewpoint of camera and spectator that these films address, that area outside the film which, Jacques Aumont points out, in painting supplied the original meaning of point of view.[17] Point of view operates in these films independently of a diegetic character. In its outward trajectory, the cinema of attractions addresses a viewpoint from which both the look of the camera and the look of the spectator originates.

Christian Metz refers to this point as the "empty emplacement for the spectator-subject" which allows binding the look of spectator with the look of the camera. For Metz this "primary cinematic identification" with the camera provides the basis for the secondary identification with characters. The classical POV unit operates by identifying a character's position with the camera's, therefore binding the spectator/camera gaze with the look of a diegetic character.[18] But this presumes a narrative context which provides a diegetic character who can assume this position and the act of looking.[19] It is precisely this subordination of the gaze to a diegetic character that the cinema of attractions avoids. Far from endowing the site of the camera with the reverence Metz describes ("an all powerful position which is that of God himself, or more broadly of some ultimate signified"), early film frequently confronts it with an almost titanic energy, invading or threatening it with a carnivalistic overturning of hierarchy.

Two very early, but fascinatingly sophisticated, films carry this acknowledgment of the camera/spectator to the *reductio ad absurdum* of physical assault, Williamson's *The Big Swallow* (1901) and Hepworth's *How It Feels to Be Run Over* (1900). Both films direct movement in a threatening manner right at the camera, using the effect of perspective and enlargement to create a nearly hallucinatory experience. In Williamson's film a man walks toward the camera mouthing an angry tirade (the film's publicity bulletin transcribes it as "I won't, I won't. I'll eat the camera first") and flailing his cane, until first his face and then his lips (become as monumental as an Egyptian collossus) fill the frame.[20] Saturn-like, these giant lips now gape open, filling the frame with darkness. We then see a cameraman and his apparatus topple headfirst into this maw. The lips close and the man withdraws, smacking his lips, apparently satisfied. To convey the experience described by his title, Hepworth assaults the camera/spectator with a motorcar. This brief film shows a car moving down a country road. It swerves to avoid hitting a dogcart and heads toward the camera. At last the front of the car overwhelms the frame, and the film then cuts to black leader on which the message "Oh! Mother *will* be pleased" appears in desperate scratches. The film's original catalogue description is explict about the direct address to the audience, describing the last action as "the car dashes full into the spectator, who sees 'stars' as the picture comes to an end."[21]

Both these films directly invoke the camera/spectator viewpoint. Rather than identifying this viewpoint with a character within the diegesis, the

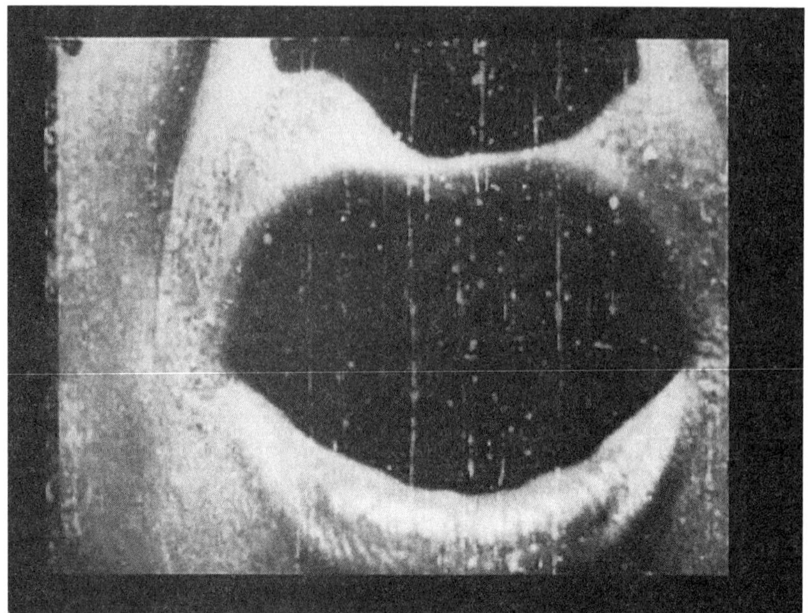

FIGURE 2.1. *The Big Swallow* (James Williamson, 1901).

direct reference to the viewpoint bursts diegetic boundaries with enunciative force. Point of view here directly confronts both camera and audience, eclipsing the image in a darkness which invokes the darkness of the theater itself.[22] These films are extreme examples that show the cinema of attractions operating at maximum difference from the classical point of view. However, *The Big Swallow* shows the precarious nature of this extreme separation from a character-based diegesis. As he is swallowed, the cameraman becomes in effect a character engulfed by the world of the film (how, in this literal *mise en abyme*, is this act of cannibalism and the giant's satisfied grin recorded?). Thriving on disorientation and shock, the cinema of attractions often flirted with its own destruction, pushing toward contradictory forms of representation. However, most films in this mode indulge in less flamboyant forms of display and less dramatic invocations of the camera/spectator viewpoint, such as the actors' glance or gesture to the spectator which typifies performances in early film.

Such delightful plays upon the technique of cinematic point of view do not constitute the only approach found in early film. A pattern closer to the classical point-of-view unit, involving mediation through a diegetic character, *does* appear in early film and creates an intricate problem for historical analysis. One of its earliest examples can be found in British filmmaker G. A. Smith's *As Seen through a Telescope* from 1900. This film (at least in its extant form) consists of a single point-of-view unit. The first shot shows a street corner as an old man in foreground glances about through his telescope. He eventually focuses on a couple who appear in the background walking with a bicycle. As they lean against the bicycle, we cut to a closer view of this action, framed within a circular matte indicating a view through the telescope. Within this closer view we see the lady's foot and lower leg as the man's hands tie her shoe. The shot centers on the lady's ankle, providing an erotic focus, as the lady lifts her skirt a bit revealing her calf, which the man pats. We then cut back to the original wider angle as the old man sits down and retracts his telescope, expressing his pleasure as he gestures toward the camera. The couple walk toward the foreground, and, as they pass the old man, the cyclist knocks him off his seat. This prototype for later point-of-view films adds the secondary cue of the circular telescope matte and concludes with a reaction shot. Both elements will recur in other examples of what I will call the "peeping tom" series. *As Seen through a Telescope* shares with many films in this series an erotic motivation for the act of looking and achieves closure by inflicting a punishment on the voyeur character.

Not limited to a single dose of scopic pleasure, many early point-of-view films string together a series of acts of voyeurism carried out by a single character. This "peeping tom" series reflects a consistent and enduring international pattern, nearly a genre. Smith again sets the prototype for this string of point of view units, with *Grandma's Reading Glass* (1900). The catalogue description for this film can serve as a description as well for the structure of the series:

> Grandma is seen at work at her sewing table, while her little grandson is playfully handling her reading glass, focussing same on various objects, viz., a newspaper, his watch, the canary, grandma's eye, and the kitten, which objects are shown in abnormal size on the screen when projected. The conception is to produce on the screen the various objects as they appeared to Willy while looking through the glass in their enormously enlarged form. The big print on the newspaper, the visible working of the mechanism of the watch, the fluttering of the canary in the cage, the blinking of grandma's eye, and the inquisitive look of the kitten, is most amusing to behold. The novelty of the subject is sure to please every audience.[23]

Other films in this series include the Pathé and Biograph imitations of Smith's film, *La Loupe de Grand-Maman* (1901) and *Grandpa's Reading*

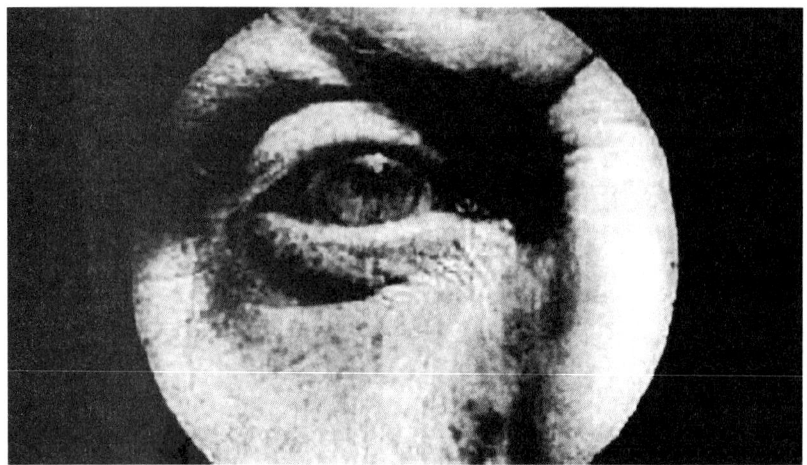

FIGURE 2.2. *Grandma's Reading Glass* (George Albert Smith, 1900).

Glass (1902); *Ce que l'on voit de mon sixième* (Pathé, 1901); *La Fille de bain indiscrète* (Pathé, 1902); *A Search for Evidence* (Biograph, 1903); *The Unclean World* (Hepworth, 1903); *Un coup d'oeil par étage* (Pathé, 1904); *The Inquisitive Boots* (Hepworth, 1905); *Le Déjeuner du savant* (Pathé, 1905); *Les Cartes lumineuses* (Pathé, 1905); and *Peeping Tom* (Pathé, 1901). These films share a common pattern of alternation, cutting from a curious character who uses some sort of looking device (reading glass, microscope, keyhole, telescope, transom window, or in one case, a deck of magically suggestive playing cards) to the scenes which these devices make visible (frequently presented within a matte—circular or keyhole-shaped—to indicate the viewing device). This pattern basically corresponds to the classical POV shot. This formal similarity raises our key issue: do such scenes of voyeurism diverge from the direct display that defines the cinema of attractions?

A number of anticipations of later classical cinema seem evident in these films. First, they involve a closely linked chain of interdependent shots. While the cinema of attractions is best exemplified by the single-shot film (or a film which appears to be a single shot by maintaining a unity of point of view, such as *The Big Swallow*), the "peeping tom" film requires at least two interrelated shots and usually involves a larger number, closely bound by a consistent pattern of alternation. When films of the cinema of attractions do contain more than one shot, these tend to consist of a series of semiautonomous tableaux with distant spatial and noncontinuous temporal relations. The act of looking in the "peeping tom" series entails a very direct temporal and spatial interrelation (as Branigan's schema indicates). Secondly, portraying a specific point of view highlights a character's perception and moves toward the construction of a diegetic world which mediates the spectator's relation to the film through a character's reaction to a dramatic situation.

In spite of these formal similarities and their implications, I believe that the essential function of these POV units in the "peeping tom" series relates more strongly to the cinema of attractions than to later narrative films. The drive toward display in the cinema of attraction which subverts the creation of self-contained diegesis operates at full force in these films. However, a close examination of editing and narrative patterns in some of these films does indicate the means by which this scopic force was absorbed and channeled in later narrative films.

In his penetrating treatment of point of view in early film, Ben Brewster has already pointed out the tenuous narrative function of point of view in such films as *Grandma's Reading Glass*, seeing this structure as "the pleasure point of the film, its attraction."[24] Rather than providing narratively significant information, or indications of character knowledge or psychology, these glimpses deliver bits of scopic pleasure, spectacle rather than narrative. The motivation for these visual investigations is simply curiosity, frequently of a salacious sort.[25] Although closely linked in time and space, the revealed scenes are sharply discontinuous and self-contained, maintaining the autonomy of the single shot films of the cinema of attractions in spite of their place within a point-of-view unit. This is especially clear in the films which involve peeking through keyholes. The scenes glimpsed by voyeurs in these films have no relation to each other, existing in splendid isolation. In fact, in at least one case, Pathé's *Un coup d'oeil par étage*, some of the point-of-view shots were also sold as separate, autonomous films. Such films find their heir in Cocteau's Hôtel des Folies-Dramatiques sequence from *Blood of a Poet*, with its dreamlike discontinuities and sense of wonder, rather than in the highly narrativized *Rear Window*.

Far from excluding the spectator from these viewpoints, the very raison d'etre of the series is his or her participation in these revelations. The frequent matte framing directs and solicits the spectator's gaze as much as it portrays that of the character. Most importantly, in the majority of these films the voyeurs perform a mocking pantomime of what they see and their delight in sharing it with the spectator, directly addressing the camera.[26] While these films involve voyeurism, the spectator they address is still far from the voyeur spectator of classical narrative film, that invisible witness who watches unobserved by any of the inhabitants of the film's world, secure in his isolation in the dark.[27] The classical spectator is constructed within a fantasy of a powerful invisible gaze able to insinuate itself into the most private of dramas. In contrast, the "peeping tom" series forces private dramas into the public space of corridors and the invoked space of the place of exhibition itself. As in the cinema of attractions, its power is projective rather than absorptive, relishing the uncovering of hidden dramas and spectacles.

However, if the "peeping tom" series profoundly relates to, and indeed thematizes, the essential scopic drive of the cinema of attractions, a specific, if tenuous, storyline does develop from the structure of these films. This storyline avoids the involvement with character subjectivity and narrative structure which marks the function of point of view in later narrative cinema. Its story-forming energies are directed differently. With a few exceptions, the "peeping tom" series present the act of looking as a mischievous act, violating social mores. Thus they form a subgenre of the mischief comedies that provide a recurring narrative structure in early story films. The protagonist of this genre occupies a marginal social status, usually a child, a servant, or a country rube (in the "peeping tom" series, servants, with their professional access to domestic spaces, predominate).[28] The narrative action of the film comes from this character merrily (and sometimes violently) puncturing some social structure. The film celebrates this release from social repression either in a single gag (as in *As Seen through a Telescope*) or (as is more frequent in the "peeping tom" series) through a concatenation of such violations. As Noël Burch has pointed out, these gags form a potentially endless series which is brought to a halt only by a violent punishment of the mischief-maker.[29] Repression returns to end the film usually in a scene which, though justified as punishment, also diverges from civilized behavior, and presumably provoked as much laughter as the antics of the mischief-maker. Viewed from this perspective, these films provide a series of visual attractions, bursts of scopic pleasure for the spectator, and end with an action which attacks the protagonist as the bearer of the guilty look. The punishment becomes yet another attraction for the audience, as well as providing closure to the film's unfolding. As in *The Big Swallow*, the spectator can watch the attack on the character voyeur as one more finalizing spectacle.

The ambivalence of early film allows for varying mixes of pure indulgence of scopic attractions and the channeling of visual involvement toward narrative ends. A comparison between two films of the "peeping tom" series shows the contrasting orientations possible toward spectator, character, and narrative function in early point-of-view structures. Both films were made in 1903, although on different continents: Hepworth's *The Unclean World* and Biograph's *A Search for Evidence*. Hepworth's film exemplifies the direct relation to the spectator found in the cinema of attractions. The Biograph film certainly maintains the "peeping tom" genre's fascination with a discontinuous series of visual attractions. However it pushes point of view closer to its later narrative functions.

The Unclean World, like Hepworth's earlier *How it Feels*, demonstrates the sophistication of the cinema of attractions and its potentially radical divergence from the assumptions of later cinema. Incredibly, at this early date, *The Unclean World* parodies the very concept of point of view in film. The film burlesques the situation portrayed in Pathé's *Le Déjeuner du savant*, in which a scientist about to eat a bit of cheese and drink a glass of water first places them under a microscope and finds them riddled with creepy crawly organisms. Since the Pathé film is later than *The Unclean World*, there were undoubtedly earlier prototypes. Most specifically, Hepworth lampoons a series of nonfiction scientific films released by Charles Urban in 1903 under the title *The Unseen World*, which consisted of microphotography of such subjects as *Cheese Mites* and *Typhoid Bacteria*.[30] Williamson's film begins much like the later Pathé comedy with a scientist eating bread with cheese, which he very ungentilely spits out in disgust. He then places the cheese under his microscope.

The next shot is framed within the circular matte that serves as the mark of the POV in many early films. The matte functions as a signifier of mediated vision, an indication of the visual instrument being used—which Hepworth will unmask as an arbitrary convention. Within the matte two cockroach-like creatures crawl, fluttering their wings. Suddenly human hands invade this circular matte from right and left, pick up the bugs, and turn them over. The presumed microscopic creatures are revealed as mechanical toys which the hands proceed to wind up. This comic intervention works on a number of levels. First, it reveals the fiction of the microscopic view—not tiny creatures revealed by wonders of science, but children's toys intended to trick us. The film undoes the trick, revealing the clockwork mechanism which produced the illusion.

Further, this comic revelation destroys the conventional understanding of the circular matte as point of view. First the hands destroy our sense of scale. We have assumed that these creatures inhabit the tiny space of the microscope. Now we see them as full-sized. Therefore our understanding of the circular matte as authorized by the scientist's gaze is totally exploded. And with the collapse of this intradiegetic look, the coherence of the fictional world disappears, and the film is thrust back on the acknowledged

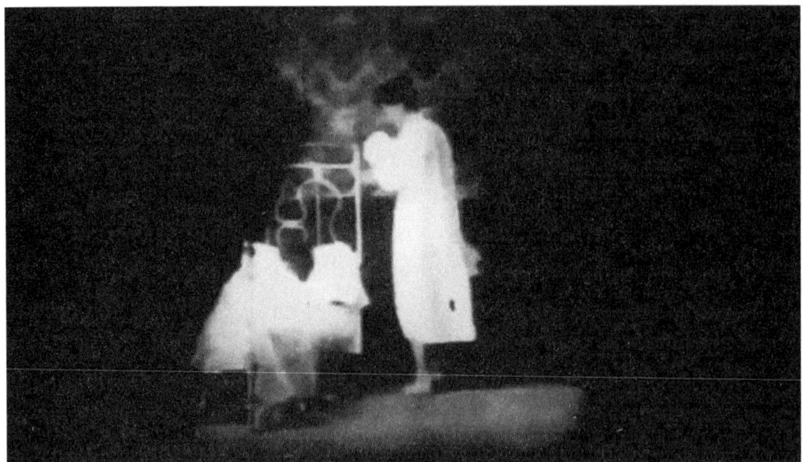

FIGURE 2.3. *A Search for Evidence* (Biograph, 1903).

gaze of the spectator. The hands turn the bugs over in order to demonstrate them to the spectator, revealing the conventions of a character's point of view as a trick, like the mechanical bugs themselves, an illusion which the film delights in undoing.

Its role as comic parody should limit viewing *The Unclean World* as a subversive, self-reflective film. It belongs to the tradition of gags in comic films such as *Sherlock Jr.* (1924), *Hellzapoppin'* (1941), or *The Nutty Professor* (1963), which punch holes in audiences' expectations of a coherent diegesis. With its emphasis on nonnarrative spectacle, film farce preserves a number of the attitudes toward the spectator found in early cinema. However, in 1903, *The Unclean World* does not parody the yet-to-be-established narrative functions of the point-of-view shot but rather the actuality film, whose satisfaction of visual curiosity belongs to the cinema of attractions. The gag structure of the film works by switching suddenly from one sort of visual pleasure to another, from "scientific" curiosity to comically surprising revelation and direct address.

A Search for Evidence leads in the exact opposite direction. In other films of the "peeping tom" series the motivation for the voyeur's gaze remains scopic curiosity explicitly shared by character and spectator. In this Biograph film, peeping through keyholes is given a specific narrative function and character-based motivation, one which the viewer does not share directly. The search is undertaken by "a detective and a discarded wife" with the intention of obtaining the "evidence necessary to secure a divorce." The various private rooms are spied upon until the "guilty pair, the husband and his sweetheart" are discovered, which leads to a confrontation between wife and sweetheart and "an exciting denoument."[31]

While the action of this film and its cinematic treatment correspond very closely to the other films of the series (particularly Pathé's *Peeping Tom*), the narrative functions of point of view contrast sharply with *The Unclean World* and relate more closely to those I attributed to later classical film. The detective and abandoned wife are very different figures from the bathhouse girl, the bootblack, or concierge in the other "peeping tom" films. Rather than mischievous embodiments of the joy of forbidden curiosity, the detective and wife are embedded in an already initiated drama of deceit and transgression. Instead of sharing their delight with the spectator, they are embarked on a mission of discovery and retribution. As elementary as these characters may be, they are nonetheless provided with a more complex set of intentions than the simple scopic pleasure motivating the previous peeping toms, and the scenes glimpsed through the keyholes are scrutinized for narrative significance. Rather than a simple concatenation of attractions, this series of views follows a narrative trajectory; the characters move from one view to the next, not from a seemingly unquenchable visual appetite, but in order to solve the narrative enigma, in search of evidence. This search ends not with its interruption but by achieving its end, the discovery of the guilty couple. In place of the voyeur being punished as a mischeivous prankster, the act of looking becomes the means of determining guilt and preparing punishment.

A Search for Evidence does maintain links to the cinema of attractions through its invocation of scopic drive. The scenes glimpsed through the keyhole remain discontinuous vignettes, both comic and serious (a man with a crying baby; a rube trying to light an electric bulb with a match; an old maid doffing her wig; a doctor at a sickbed), whose interest within the film seems rather divorced from the uncovering of the narrative enigma. However, by framing these scenes within a purposeful and even suspenseful search they become more fully narrativized than in the other films. As if illustrating Laura Mulvey's schema of the movement from spectacle to narrative as paralleling a shift from fetishistic scopophilia to one dominated by sadism, *A Search for Evidence* dramatizes a gaze whose motivation lies precisely in "the ascertaining of guilt."[32] Such a guilt-baring and punishment-bearing scenario enlists point of view in the narrative task of revealing significance and conveying character motivations and reactions.

A Search for Evidence moves historically toward the classical point-of-view shot and a more fully narrativized cinema. In this new narrative economy the significance of point of view lies precisely in its role as transfer between the private and the public. Instead of functioning primarily as visual attractions, these private scenes now become evidence of social transgressions. The detective-voyeur, agent of the law who justifies visual curiosity by tracking down such evidence, plays a key role in this new narrative structure. Walter Benjamin has noted that beyond the usual identification of the detective with the voyeur, one can trace a perhaps deeper connection to the technology of photography. In industrializing capitalism, photography posited a technological solution to the problem of establishing and maintaining the personal identity of malefactors and subversives:

> Photography made it possible for the first time to preserve permanent and unmistakeable traces of the human being. The detective story came into being when this most decisive of all conquests of a person's incognito had been accomplished. Since then the end of efforts to capture a man in his speech and action has not been in sight.[33]

The narrative implications of this evidence-gathering technology found its way into cinema as well, binding point of view to the apparatus itself. In the narrative imagination of the turn of the century, the cinema became another viewing device able to penetrate into private worlds. But unlike the keyhole, microscope, or telescope, this viewing device possesses the possibility of reproduction and can function as evidence of guilt. English film historian Stephen Bottomore has noted that the earliest published stories involving the cinema repeatedly describe situations in which a projected film reveals a person unknowingly caught in a compromising act (from adultery to murder). Bottomore suggests that the almost obsessive nature of this recurring theme reveals the anxiety induced by the introduction of an apparatus with an ability to both penetrate and record private life, an anxiety which began, of course, with still photography.[34]

As Bottomore points out, the scenario moved quickly from literature to cinema (although the cluster of literary works he has located seem more numerous than their cinematic counterparts). Biograph offers a felicitous example in a film which crossbreeds the "peeping tom" series with the motion picture camera's ability as a recorder and public exhibitor of scenes. This film, which faithfully follows the pattern of the mischief cycle, is appropriately titled *The Story the Biograph Told*. This 1903 (a key year in the evolution of early film) film tells the story of a businessman who is surreptitiously photographed by a mischievous office boy while he is romancing his secretary. The resulting film is projected as part of a vaudeville program which the businessman attends with his wife. The wife is outraged, attacks her husband, and the next day follows him to the office, where she demands the secretary be fired.

Although not exactly corresponding to the classical POV unit, point of view operates in this film on two levels. First, at the vaudeville theater, the cut to the film image projected on the screen indicates that the film is being witnessed by the wife and husband (who were shown in their seats in the previous shot). But the film itself is also a mediated point of view of the scene previously witnessed and recorded by the office boy. This is stressed in the film by the fact that the film projected was shot from a different angle and closer than the previous view of this action, matching the position of the office boy as he filmed it.

The film reworks the dynamics of the "peeping tom" series, maintaining its delight in erotic visual display, as well as the mischievous pleasure in making such private scenes public. It also contains a punishment scene in which infractions of propriety are physically redressed. However the reallignment of these energies is significant. It is not the voyeur who is punished but the object of his gaze. The making public of this private scene is likewise pushed further and diegetized. It is not the actual spectator that this private moment is shared with but the diegetic vaudeville audience. As in *A Search for Evidence*, the voyeur presents evidence of an adulterous relation that leads to moral punishment. The film maintains the "peeping tom" series's relation to comedy and the mischief cycle. But the tattletale visual attraction offered in this film does tell a story and, as in *A Search for Evidence*, reveals the process of transformation from a cinema of attractions to one of narrative integration, that is, from a discontinuous series of scopic displays to a vengeful search for guilty parties.

Biograph as well as other companies returned to such themes in a number of later films.[35] Shortly before Griffith's advent as film director at the company, *Bobby's Kodak* replays the same basic situation as a mischievous boy's picture-snapping captures a series of compromising images within the domestic environment. A home exhibition of these embarrassing moments culminates with a snapshot of father philandering (he reacts by destroying the incriminating still camera and punishing Bobby). In *Falsely Accused* (filmed one month earlier), photographic evidence provided Biograph with material for melodrama, as a motion picture camera creates the denouement of a courtroom drama. The film's heroine is falsely accused of the murder of her father, an inventor of a motion picture camera. When it is discovered that the camera recorded the murder, the film is projected in court to clear the young lady's name "by showing the actual murder, of the old man by the villain . . . who is taken into custody for the heinous crime he committed."[36] As Eileen Bowser has pointed out, the court official who spreads the screen for this bit of filmic evidence is played by D. W. Griffith, in what appropriately seems to be his screen debut.[37] In these films, the photographic image solves narrative enigmas through its claim on the truth. In this way, the photographic image assumes the role Branigan assigns to point of view in cinema: "a device internal to the text through which the text attempts to create an *external* reference to a level of narration and so manage (affirm, qualify, restrict, deny) the truth of the text."[38]

In the period from 1900 to 1908, we can locate three basic shifts in the use of point of view. In films that clearly belong to the cinema of attractions (such as the Williamson and Hepworth films), the acknowledged point of view is nondiegetic, a direct address to the spectator. The "peeping tom" series employs a schema formally very close to the classical POV shot, in the service of a more mediated but still acknowledged and shared indulgence of scopic pleasure. Developing almost at the same time, films such as *A Search for Evidence* place point-of-view units in a significant relation to an unfolding narrative. Although one should avoid overstating the linear development of this pattern, it does reveal an essential transformation in the relation to the spectator in early film. The immediate relation of spectator to visual pleasure becomes subordinated to narrative causality through a new channeling of scopic drives, pleasures, and repression. Instead of displaying a discontinuous suite of images, the act of voyeurism takes on the role that Peter Brooks sees as essential to melodrama—the applying of pressure to the surface of things in order to extract moral truth.[39] The scenes glimpsed behind doors become evidence, elements in a narrative and moral argument which uncovers villains and malefactors. In contrast to Williamson and Hepworth's lampooning assault on the apparatus, the camera now stands as an authority, a means of ascertaining the truth, that "moral occult" which Brooks finds at the center of the melodramatic imagination. The camera as detective unmasks villainy or impropriety through an explosion of truth, providing the film with narrative closure in which punishment is more than a comic attraction.

3

An Aesthetic of Astonishment: Early Film and the (In)Credulous Spectator

TERROR IN THE AISLES

> The damming of the stream of real life, the moment when its flow comes to a standstill, makes itself felt as reflux: this reflux is astonishment.
>
> WALTER BENJAMIN, "WHAT IS EPIC THEATRE?" (FIRST VERSION)

In traditional accounts of the cinema's first audiences, one image stands out: the terrified reaction of spectators to Lumière's *Arrival of a Train at the Station*. According to a variety of historians, spectators reared back in their seats, or screamed, or got up and ran from the auditorium (or all three in succession). As with most myths of origin, the source for these accounts remains elusive. It does not figure in any report of the first screening at the Salon Indien of the Grand Café that I have located.[1] And as with such myths, its ideological uses demand probing as much as its veracity. This panicked and hysterical audience has provided the basis for further myths about the nature of film history and the power of the film image.

The first audiences, according to this myth, were naive, encountering this threatening and rampant image with no defenses, with no tradition by which to understand it. The absolute novelty of the moving image therefore

This essay first appeared in *Art and Text*, no. 34 (Spring 1989): 31–45, and was subsequently republished in *Viewing Positions: Ways of Seeing Film*, ed. Linda Williams (New Brunswick, NJ: Rutgers University Press, 1995), 114–33. The original essay was dedicated to Miriam Hansen.

reduced them to a state usually attributed to savages in their primal encounter with the advanced technology of Western colonialists, howling and fleeing in impotent terror before the power of the machine. This audience of the first exhibitions exists outside of the willing suspension of disbelief, the immediacy of their terror short-circuiting even disavowal's detour of "I know very well . . . but all the same." Credulity overwhelms all else, the physical reflex signaling a visual trauma. Thus conceived, the myth of initial terror defines film's power as its unprecedented realism, its ability to convince spectators that the moving image was, in fact, palpable and dangerous, bearing toward them with physical impact. The image had taken life, swallowing, in its relentless force, any consideration of representation—the imaginary perceived as real.

Furthermore, this primal scene at the cinema underpins certain contemporary theorizations of spectatorship. The terrorized spectator of the Grand Café still stalks the imagination of film theorists who envision audiences submitting passively to an all-dominating apparatus, hypnotized and transfixed by its illusionist power. Contemporary film theorists have made careers out of underestimating the basic intelligence and reality-testing abilities of the average film viewer and have no trouble treating previous audiences with similar disdain. The most subtle reading of this initial terror comes from Christian Metz. But Metz's admirable subtlety renders his analysis all the more deficient from a historical point of view. Metz describes this panicked reaction on the part of the Grand Café audience as a displacement of the contemporary viewer's credulity onto a mythical childhood of the medium. Like the childhood when one still believed in Santa Claus, like the dawn of time when myths were still believed literally, belief in this legendary audience, Metz claims, allows us to disavow our own belief in the face of the cinema. *We* don't believe in the screen image in the manner that *they* did. Our credulity is displaced onto an audience from the infancy of cinema.[2]

Metz's penetrating analysis of the mythical role of this first audience does not lead to demythologization. He instead introjects this primal audience, removing it from historical analysis by internalizing it as an aspect of a presumably timeless cinema viewer. No longer a historical spectator in the Grand Café in 1895, the naive spectator "is still seated *beneath* the incredulous one, or in his heart."[3] Thus removed from place and time, this inner credulous viewer supplies the motive power for Metz's understanding of the fetishistic viewer, wavering between the credulous position of believing the image and the repressed, anxiety-causing knowledge of its illusion. The historical panic at the Grand Café would be, according to Metz, simply a projection of an inner deception onto the mythical site of cinema's "once upon a time."

Although I have my doubts whether actual panic took place in the Grand Cafe's Salon Indien, there is no question that a reaction of astonishment and even a type of terror accompanied many early projections. I therefore don't intend to simply deny this founding myth of the cinema's spectator, but rather to approach it historically. We cannot simply swallow whole the image of the naive spectator, whose reaction to the image is one of simple belief and panic; it needs digesting. The impact of the first film projections cannot be explained by a mechanistic model of a naive spectator who, in a temporary psychotic state, confuses the image for its reality. But what context does account for the well-attested fact that the first projections caused shock and astonishment, an excitement pushed to the point of terror, if we exclude childlike credulity? And, equally important, how could this agitating experience be understood as part of the *attraction* of the new invention, rather than a disturbing element that needed to be removed? And what role does an illusion of reality play in this terrified reception?

Only a careful consideration of the historical context of these earliest images can restore an understanding of the uncanny and agitating power they exerted on audiences. This context includes the first modes of exhibition, the tradition of turn-of-the-century visual entertainments, and a basic aesthetic of early cinema I have called the cinema of attractions, which envisioned cinema as a series of visual shocks. Restored to its proper historical context, the projection of the first moving images stands at the climax of a period of intense development in visual entertainments, a tradition in which realism was valued largely for its uncanny effects. We need to recognize this tradition and speculate on its role at the turn of the century.

As I have shown elsewhere, many early spectators recognized the first projection of films as a crowning achievement in the extremely sophisticated developments in the magic theater, as practiced by Georges Méliès at the Théâtre Robert Houdin and his English mentor John Nevil Maskelyne at London's Egyptian Hall.[4] At the turn of the century, this tradition used the latest technology (such as focused electric light and elaborate stage machinery) to produce apparent miracles. The seeming transcendence of the laws of the material universe by the magical theater defines the dialectical nature of its illusions. The craft of late nineteenth-century stage illusions consisted of making visible something which could not exist, of managing the play of appearances in order to confound the expectations of logic and experience. The audience this theater addressed was not primarily gullible country bumpkins, but sophisticated urban pleasure seekers, well aware that they were seeing the most modern techniques in stage craft. Méliès's theater is inconceivable without a widespread decline in belief in the marvelous, providing a fundamental rationalist context. The magic theater labored to make visual that which it was impossible to believe. Its visual power consisted of a trompe l'oeil play of give-and-take, an obsessive desire to test the limits of an intellectual disavowal—I know, but yet I see.

Trompe l'oeil as a genre of aesthetic illusion underscores the problematic role perfect illusion plays within traditional aesthetic reception. As Martin Battersby puts it, trompe l'oeil aims not simply at accuracy of representation but at causing "a feeling of disgust in the mind of the beholder." This disquiet arises from "a conflict of messages": on the one hand, the knowledge that one is seeing a painting, and on the other, a visual experience sufficiently convincing as "to warrant a closer examination and even the involvement of the sense of touch."[5] The realism of the image is at the service of a dramatically unfolding spectator experience, vacillating between belief and incredulity. Although trompe l'oeil shares with *The Arrival of a Train* and the magic theater a pleasurable vacillation between belief and doubt, it also displays important differences from them. The usually small scale of trompe l'oeil paintings and the desire to reach out and touch them contrast sharply with the "grandeur naturale" of the Lumière train film and the viewer's impulse to rear back before it, as well as with the spectator's physical distance from the illusions of the magic theater.[6] But all three forms show that, rather than being a simple reality effect, the illusionistic arts of the nineteenth century cannily exploited their unbelievable nature, keeping a conscious focus on the fact that they were only illusions.

In fact, in the most detailed and articulate account we have of an early Lumière projection, Maxim Gorky (reporting on a showing at the Nizhny-Novgorod Fair in July of 1896) stresses the uncanny effect of the new attraction's mix of realistic and nonrealistic qualities. For Gorky, the Cinématographe presents a world whose vividness and vitality have been drained away: "Before you a life is surging, a life deprived of words and shorn of the living spectrum of colours—the grey, the soundless, the bleak and dismal life." The Cinématographe, Gorky explains, presents not life but its shadow, and he allows no possibility of mistaking this cinematic shade for substance. Describing *The Arrival of a Train*, Gorky senses its impending threat: "It speeds right at you—watch out! It seems as though it will plunge into the darkness in which you sit, turning you into a ripped sack full of lacerated flesh and splintered bone." But, he adds, "this too is but a train of shadows." Belief and terror are larded with an awareness of illusion and even, to Gorky's sophisticated palate, the ennui of

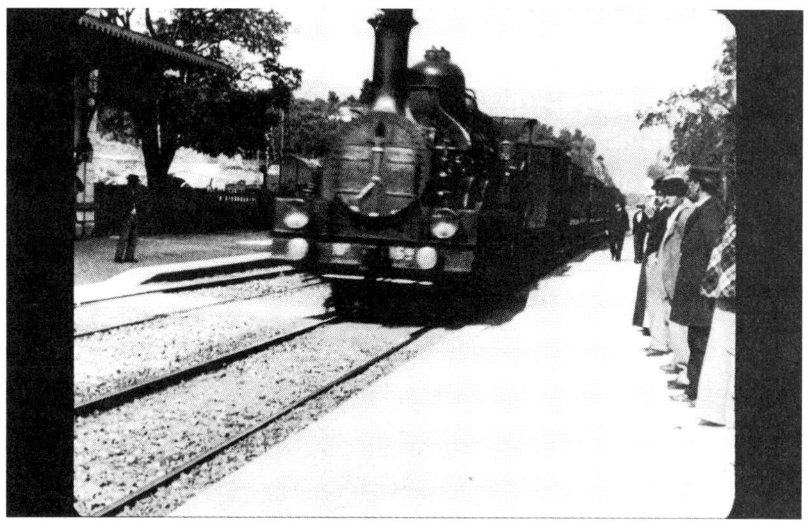

FIGURE 3.1. *The Arrival of a Train at La Ciotat* (Lumière Co., 1896).

the insubstantial, the bleak disappointment of the ungraspable phantom of life.[7]

One might dismiss Gorky's reaction as the sophisticated disdain of a cultured intellectual, deliberately counter to the more common reception of early film images. Gorky's negative assessment of the cinema *was* unusual in a period when new advances in the technology of entertainment were generally hailed with excitement and satisfaction. But his recognition that the film image combined realistic effects with a conscious awareness of artifice may correspond more closely to general audience reaction than the screaming dupes of traditional accounts. While contemporary accounts of audience responses, particularly of unsophisticated viewers, are hard to come by, the very mode of presentation of the Lumière screenings (and of other early filmmakers as well) contains an important element which served to undermine a naive experience of realism. It is too infrequently pointed out that in the earliest Lumière exhibitions the films were initially presented as frozen unmoving images, projections of still photographs. Then, flaunting a mastery of visual showmanship, the projector began cranking and the image moved. Or as Gorky described it, "suddenly a strange flicker passes through the screen and the picture stirs to life."[8]

While such a presentation would seem to forbid any reading of the image as reality—a real, physical train—it strongly heightened the impact of the moment of movement. Rather than mistaking the image for reality, the spectator is astonished by its transformation through the new illusion of projected motion. Far from credulity, it is the incredible nature of the illusion itself that renders the viewer speechless. What is displayed before the audience is less the impending speed of the train than the force of the cinematic apparatus. Or to put it better, the one demonstrates the other. The astonishment derives from a magical metamorphosis rather than a seamless reproduction of reality. The initial impact of this transformation at the Lumière premiere is described by an expert in such effects, Georges Méliès:

> A *still* photograph showing the place Bellecour in Lyon was projected. A little surprised. I just had time to say to my neighbor:
>
> "They got us all stirred up for projections like this? I've been doing them for over ten years."
>
> I had hardly finished speaking when a horse pulling a wagon began to walk towards us, followed by other vehicles and then pedestrians, in short all the animation of the street. Before this spectacle we sat with gaping mouths, struck with amazement, astonished beyond all expression.[9]

This coup de théâtre, the sudden transformation from still image to moving illusion, startled audiences and displayed the novelty and fascination of the Cinématographe. Far from being placed outside a suspension of disbelief, the presentation acts out the contradictory stages of involvement with the image, unfolding, like other nineteenth-century visual entertainments, a vacillation between belief and incredulity. The moving image reverses and complicates the trajectory of experience solicited by a trompe l'oeil still life. The film first presents itself as merely an image, rather than appearing to be the actual butterflies, postcards, or cameos which the initial apperception of a trompe l'oeil canvas seems to reveal. Instead of a gradual disquiet arising from the divergence of what we know and what we see, the shock of the film image comes from a sudden transformation while the hardly novel projected photograph (Gorky also stressed his initial disappointment at this "all too familiar scene") gives way to the astonishing moment of movement.[10] The audience's sense of shock comes less from a naive belief that they are threatened by an actual locomotive than from an unbelievable visual transformation occurring before their eyes, parallel to the greatest wonders of the magic theater.

As in the magic theater, the apparent realism of the image makes it a successful illusion, but one understood as an illusion nonetheless. While such a transformation would be quite capable of causing a physical or verbal reflex in the viewer, one remains aware that the film is merely a projection.

The initial still image demonstrated that irrefutably. But this still projection takes on motion, becomes endowed with animation, and it is this unbelievable moving image that so astounds. The initial projection of a still image, withholding briefly the illusion of motion which is the apparatus's raison d'être, brought an effect of suspense to the first film shows. The audience knew that motion was precisely what the Cinématographe promised (hence Méliès's restlessness). By delaying its appearance, the Lumière exhibitor not only highlights the device but signals his allegiance to an aesthetic of astonishment which goes beyond a scientific interest in the reproduction of motion.

Another account of early projections, this time from the other side of the Atlantic, further demonstrates the theatricality of this device and clearly aligns the terror of early spectators with a conscious delectation of shocks and thrills. The memoirs of Albert E. Smith, one of the founders of the Vitagraph company, describe his early years as a traveling exhibitor with Vitagraph cofounder J. Stuart Blackton. Smith had toured earlier with Blackton, a quick-sketch artist, as an illusionist combining "sleight of hand and invisible mechanical appliances of his own invention."[11] But like a large number of stage illusionists, they had turned to the exhibition of moving pictures as the most technologically advanced form of visual entertainments. Smith contributed a mechanical improvement to the Edison projecting Kinetoscope—a water cell between the film and the light source that absorbed heat and allowed the film to be projected as a still image a bit longer without danger of the celluloid bursting into flames.

The most popular item on Smith and Blackton's exhibition tours was *The Black Diamond Express*, a one-shot film of a locomotive rushing toward the camera. As in most early film shows, a patter spoken by Blackton accompanied the projection, preparing the audience for the film and providing dramatic atmosphere. Smith describes Blackton's role in presenting *The Black Diamond Express* as that of a "terrorist mood setter." As he recalled it, Blackton's lecture (delivered over the frozen image of the locomotive) went like this:

> Ladies and gentlemen you are now gazing upon a photograph of the famous Black Diamond Express. In just a moment, a cataclysmic moment, my friends, a moment without equal in the history of our times, you will see this train take life in a marvellous and most astounding manner. It will rush towards you, belching smoke and fire from its monstrous iron throat.

Although Smith's memory of Blackton's oration decades later may not be entirely reliable, it captures the address of the first film shows and places the audience's terror in a new light. Blackton directly addresses the audience, mediating between it and the film and stressing the actual act of display. Like a fairground barker, he builds an atmosphere of expectation, a pronounced curiosity leavened with anxiety as he stresses the novelty and astonishing properties which the attraction about to be revealed will possess. This sense of expectation, sharpened to an intense focus on a single instant of transformation, heightened the startling impact of the first projections. Far from being a simple reality effect, the impact derives from a moment of crisis, prepared for and delayed, then bursting upon the audience. This suspenseful presentation of an impossible transformation, Smith reports, caused women to scream and men to sit aghast.[12]

THE AESTHETIC OF ATTRACTIONS

> There came a day when a new and urgent need for stimuli was met by the film. In a film, perception in the form of shocks was established as a formal principle.
>
> WALTER BENJAMIN, "SOME MOTIFS IN BAUDELAIRE"

While these early films of oncoming locomotives present the shock of cinema in an exaggerated form, they also express an essential element of early cinema as a whole. I have called the cinema that precedes the dominance of narrative (and this period lasts for nearly a decade, until 1903 or 1904) the cinema of attractions.[13] The aesthetic of attraction addresses the audience directly, sometimes, as in these early train films, exaggerating this confrontation in an experience of assault. Rather than being an involvement with narrative action or empathy with character psychology, the cinema of attractions solicits a highly conscious awareness of the film image engaging the viewer's curiosity. The spectator does not get lost in a fictional world and its drama, but remains aware of the act of looking, the excitement of curiosity and its fulfilment. Through a variety of formal means, the images of the cinema of attractions rush forward to meet their viewers. These devices range from the implied collision of the early railroad films to the performance style of the same period, when actors nodded and gestured at the camera (e.g., Méliès on screen directing attention to the transformations he causes) or when a showman lecturer presented the views to the audience. This cinema addresses and holds the spectator, emphasizing the act of display. In fulfilling this curiosity, it delivers a generally brief dose of scopic pleasure.

And pleasure is the issue here, even if pleasure of a particularly complicated sort. When a Montpellier journalist in 1896 described the Lumière projections as provoking "an excitement bordering on terror," he was praising the new spectacle and explaining its success.[14] If the first spectators screamed, it was to acknowledge the power of the apparatus to sweep away a prior and firmly entrenched sense of reality. This vertiginous experience of the frailty of our knowledge of the world before the power of visual illusion produced that mixture of pleasure and anxiety which the purveyors of popular art had labeled sensations and thrills and on which they founded a new aesthetic of attractions. The onrushing train produced not simply the negative experience of fear but also the particularly modern entertainment form of the thrill, embodied elsewhere in the recently appearing attractions of the amusement parks, such as the roller coaster, which combined sensations of acceleration and falling with a security guaranteed by modern industrial technology. One Coney Island attraction, the Leap Frog Railway, literalized the thrill of *The Arrival of a Train.* Two electric cars containing as many as forty people were set toward each other at great speed on a collision course. Just before impact one car was lifted up on curved rails and skimmed over the top of the other. Lynne Kirby has also noted the popularity of staged collisions between railroad locomotives at the turn of the century, both at county fairs and in such films as Edison's 1904 *The Railroad Smash-Up.*[15]

Confrontation rules the cinema of attractions in both the form of its films and their mode of exhibition. The directness of this act of display allows an emphasis on the thrill itself—the immediate reaction of the viewer. The film lecturer focuses attention on the attraction, sharpening viewer curiosity. The film then performs its act of display and fades away. Unlike psychological narrative, the cinema of attractions does not allow for elaborate development; only a limited amount of delay is really possible. But such a film program consists of a series of attractions, a concatenation of short films all of which offer the viewer a moment of revelation. The succession of thrills is potentially limited only by viewer exhaustion. This concatenation may have some thematic structuring and builds toward a climactic moment, a final *clou* (such as Smith and Blackton's *Black Diamond Express*). The showman rather than the films themselves gives the program an overarching structure, and the key role of exhibitor-showman underscores the act of monstration that founds the cinema of attractions.[16]

A film like Edison's *Electrocuting an Elephant* (1903) shows the temporal logic of this scenography of display. The elephant is led onto an electrified plate and secured. Smoke rises from its feet, and after a moment the elephant falls on its side. The moment of technologically advanced death is neither further explained nor dramatized. Likewise a fictional film produced by the Biograph Company in 1904, *Photographing a Female Crook*, presents a single shot of a woman held between two uniformed policemen, who try to steady her for a mug shot. The camera tracks in on this group, ending by framing the woman in medium close-up. Attempting to sabotage the photographing of her face for identification purposes, the female crook mugs outrageously, contorting her face. The inward movement by the movie camera and the progressive enlargement of the woman's face emphasize the act of display which underlies the film. While both these films show considerable formal differences from *The Arrival of a Train*, all three demonstrate the solicitation of viewer curiosity and its fulfilment by the brief moment of revelation typical of the cinema of attractions. This is a cinema of instants rather than developing situations.

As I have stated elsewhere, the scenography of the cinema of attractions is an exhibitionist one, opposed to the cinema of the unacknowledged voyeur that later narrative cinema ushers in.[17] This display of unique views belongs most obviously to the period before the dominance of editing, when films consisting of a single shot—both actualities and fictions—made up the bulk of film production. However, even with the introduction of editing and more complex narratives, the aesthetic of attraction can still be sensed in periodic doses of nonnarrative spectacle given to audiences (musicals and slapstick comedy provide clear examples). The cinema of attractions persists in later cinema, even if it rarely dominates the form of a feature film as a whole. It provides an underground current flowing beneath narrative logic and diegetic realism, producing those moments of cinematic *dépaysement* beloved by the surrealists.[18]

This aesthetic so contrasts with prevailing turn-of-the-century norms of artistic reception—the ideals of detached contemplation—that it nearly constitutes an anti-aesthetic. The cinema of attractions stands at the antipode to the experience Michael Fried, in his discussion of eighteenth-century painting, calls absorption.[19] For Fried, the painting of Greuze and others created a new relation to the viewer through a self-contained hermetic world which makes no acknowledgment of the beholder's presence. Early cinema totally ignores this construction of the beholder. These early films explicitly acknowledge their spectator, seeming to reach outward and confront. Contemplative absorption is impossible here. The viewer's curiosity is aroused and fulfilled through a marked encounter, a direct stimulus, a succession of shocks.

By tapping into a visual curiosity and desire for novelty, attractions draw upon what Augustine, at the beginning of the fifth century, called *curiositas* in his catalogue of "the lust of the eyes." In contrast to visual *voluptas* (pleasure), *curiositas* avoids the beautiful and goes after its exact opposite "simply because of the lust to find out and to know." *Curiositas* draws the viewer toward unbeautiful sights, such as a mangled corpse, and "because of this disease of curiosity monsters and anything out of the ordinary are put on show in our theatres." For Augustine, *curiositas* led not only to a fascination with seeing, but a desire for knowledge for its own sake, ending in the perversions of magic and science.[20] While beauty, in Augustine's Platonic schema, may form the first rung of an ascent to the ideal, *curiositas* possesses only the power to lead astray. Attractions imply the danger of distraction, a cardinal sin in Augustine's contemplative and vigilant model of Christian life.

The aesthetic of attractions developed in fairly conscious opposition to an orthodox identification of viewing pleasure with the contemplation of beauty. A nineteenth-century satirical engraving shows London's Egyptian Hall (which existed as a home for natural curiosities—freaks and artifacts of natural history—before it became the home of Maskelyne's magic theater) proclaiming itself "the Hall of Ugliness" and advertising the "Ne Plus Ultra of Hideousness."[21] This attraction to the repulsive was frequently rationalized by appealing to that impulse which Augustine found equally dubious, intellectual curiosity. Like the early film exhibitions, freak shows and other displays of curiosities were described as instructive and informing. Similarly, a popular and long-lasting genre of the cinema of attractions consisted of educational actualities, such as Charles Urban's *Unseen World* series (beginning in 1903), which presented magnified images of cheese mites, spiders, and water fleas.[22] As late as 1914, a proponent of the reform movement in cinema objected to the vulgarity of films displaying such "slimy and unbeautiful abominations," which he claimed repulsed spectators with more refined sensibilities.[23] But showmen were well aware that a thrill needed an element of repulsion or a controlled threat of danger. Louis Lumière understood that his films, which directed physical action out at the audience, added a vital energy alongside the scientific curiosity addressed by his reproduction of motion and daily life.

DISTRACTION AND THE AMBIVALENCE OF SHOCK

> The film corresponds to profound changes in the apperceptive apparatus—changes that are experienced on an individual scale by the man in the street in big city traffic, on a historcal scale by every present day individual.
>
> WALTER BENJAMIN, "THE WORK OF ART IN THE AGE OF MECHANICAL REPRODUCTION"

While the impulse to *curiositas* may be as old as Augustine, there is no question that the nineteenth century sharpened this form of "lust of the eyes" and its commercial exploitation. Expanding urbanization with its kalcidoscopic succession of city sights, the growth of consumer society with its new emphasis on stimulating spending through visual display, and the escalating horizons of colonial exploration with new peoples and territories to be categorized and exploited all provoked the desire for images and attractions. It is not surprising that city street scenes, advertising films, and foreign views all formed important genres of early cinema. The enormous popularity of foreign views (already developed and exploited by the stereoscope and magic lantern) expresses an almost unquenchable desire to consume the world through images. The cinema was, as the slogan of one early film company put it, an invention which put the world within your grasp. Early cinema categorized the visible world as a series of discreet attractions, and the catalogues of the first production companies present a nearly encyclopoedic survey of this new hypervisible topology, from landscape panoramas to microphotography, from domestic scenes to the beheading of prisoners and the electrocution of elephants.

If not all the attractions of early cinema express the violence of an onrushing train, some sense of wonder or surprise nonetheless underlies all these films, if only wonder at the illusion of motion. Even a filmed landscape panorama does not lend itself to pure aesthetic contemplation. One is fully aware of the machine which mediates the view, the camera pivoting on its tripod. The most common form of landscape panorama—films shot from the front or back of trains—doubled this effect, invoking not only the motion picture machine but the locomotive which pulls the seated viewer through space. These train films provide an even more technologically mediated example of what Wolfgang Schivelbusch, in his description of the transformation of perception occasioned by the railway journey, calls panoramic perception. In contrast to the traditional traveler's experience of a landscape, the train passenger "no longer belongs to the same space as the perceived objects: the traveler sees the objects, landscapes, etc., *through* the apparatus which moves him through the world."[24] A film taken from the front of a train, an "unseen energy swallowing space" (as one journalist described the experience of such a train panorama), doubled this effect imposed by industrial apparatuses, intensifying the alienation *and* the dynamic sensation of train travel.[25] Such train films might turn the onrushing Black Diamond Express inside out, but still provoked viewer amazement through a technologically mediated experience of space and movement.

Ultimately the encyclopedic ambition of this impulse of early cinema, transforming all of reality into cinematographical views, recalls Gorky's vague discomfort and depression before the Cinématographe. While the cinema of attractions fulfills the curiosity it excites, it is in the nature of curiosity, as the lust of the eye, never to be satisfied completely. Thus the obsessional nature of early film production and the early film show the potentially endless succession of separate attractions. But beyond the unlimited metonymy of curiosity, Gorky's unease derived from the abstraction and alienation of this new pursuit of thrills.

Gorky also found a pervasive ennui in the dreamworld home of attractions, Coney Island (which he visited in 1906), calling it "a slavery to a varied boredom." For Gorky, Coney Island purveyed "an amazement in which there is neither transport nor joy."[26] While the tone of a European intellectual's distaste for the mass pleasures of a capitalist society is unmistakable, Gorky also provides insight into the need for thrills in an industrialized and consumer-oriented society. The peculiar pleasure of screaming before the suddenly animated image of a locomotive indicates less an audience willing to take the image for reality than a spectator whose daily experience has lost the coherence and immediacy traditionally attributed to reality. This loss of experience creates a consumer hungry for thrills.

The cinema of attractions not only exemplifies a particularly modern form of aesthetics but also responds to the specifics of modern and especially urban life, what Benjamin and Kracauer understood as the drying up of experience and its replacement by a culture of distraction. While Benjamin's writing provides the most brilliantly dialectical (and ambivalent) description of the modern transformation of perception and experience,[27] Kracauer's essay "The Cult of Distraction: On Berlin's Picture Palaces" provides a specific focus on the role of cinema and particularly that element foregrounded by the cinema of attractions—exhibition.[28]

Lost sight of now after decades of text-obsessed film analysis, the exhibition situation transforms and structures a film's mode of address to an audience. In early cinema, the act of presentation was stressed by both exhibition context and the direct address of the films themselves. By the 1920s, when Kracauer wrote, the architecture of the picture palace and the variety format of the evening's program played a major role in defining moviegoing as a succession of attractions, what Kracauer describes as the "fragmented sequence of splendid sense impressions."[29] The opulence and design of the Berlin movie theaters served to offset the coherence that classical narrative cinema had brought to film. As Kracauer described it:

> The interior design of the movie theatres served one sole purpose: to rivet the audience's attention to the peripheral so that they will not sink into the abyss. The stimulations of the senses succeed each other with such rapidity that there is no room left for even the slightest contemplation to squeeze in between them.[30]

The spectacular design of the theater itself (accented and temporalized by elaborate manipulations of light) interacted with the growing tendency to embed the film in a larger program, a revue which included music and live performance. The film was in a larger program, a revue which included music and live performance. The film was only one element in an experience that Kracauer describes as a "total artwork of effects" which "assaults every one of the senses using every possible means."[31] For Kracauer, the discontinuity and variety of this form of cinema program (juxtaposing a two-dimensional film with three-dimensional live performances) strongly undermined film's illusionistic power. The projected film "recedes into the flat surface and the deception is exposed."[32] As in the first projections, the very aesthetic of attraction runs counter to an illusionistic absorption, the variety format of the picture palace program continually reminding the spectator of the act of watching by a succession of sensual assaults. As if in defiance of the increased length and the voyeuristic fictional address of the featured films, the effect of a discontinuous suite of attractions still dominates the evening.

But in spite of (or rather motivating) this smorgasbord of sensual thrills, Kracauer discerns an experience of lack not unrelated (even if differently interpreted) to Gorky's malaise. The unifying element of the cult of distraction lies in what Kracauer calls pure externality And this celebration of the external responds to a central lack in the life of its audience, particularly that of the working masses,

> an essentially formal tension which fills their day without making it fulfilling. Such a lack demands to be compensated, but this need can only

> be articulated in terms of the same surface which imposed the lack in the first place. The form of entertainment necessarily corresponds to that of enterprise.[33]

The sudden, intense, and external satisfaction supplied by the succession of attractions was recognized by Kracauer as revealing the fragmentation of modern experience. The taste for thrills and spectacle, the particularly modern form of *curiositas* that defines the aesthetic of attractions, is molded by a modern loss of fulfilling experience. Once again, Schivelbusch's understanding of the changes in modern perception brought about by railway travel provides a theoretical tool. Crossbreeding Freud's metapsychological formulations with the urban sociology of Georg Simmel (and thus following a trajectory traced by Benjamin), Schivelbusch describes a stimulus shield, which inhabitants of the overstimulated environments of the modern world develop in order to ward off its constant assaults.[34] But one could also point out that this stimulus shield dulls the edge of experience, and more intense aesthetic energies are required to penetrate it. As Miriam Hansen points out in her reading of Benjamin, the modern experience of shock corresponds to "the adaptation of human perception of industrial modes of production and transportation, especially the radical restructuration of spatial and temporal relations."[35] Shock becomes not only a mode of modern experience but a strategy of a modern aesthetics of astonishment. Hence the exploitation of new technological thrills that flirt with disaster.

Attractions are a response to an experience of alienation, and for Kracauer (as for Benjamin) cinema's value lay in exposing a fundamental loss of coherence and authenticity. Cinema's deadly temptation lay in trying to attain the aesthetic coherence of traditional art and culture. The radical aspiration of film must lie along the path of consciously heightening its use of discontinuous shocks, or as Kracauer puts it, "must aim radically towards a kind of distraction which exposes disintegration rather than masking it."[36] As Hansen has indicated, Benjamin's analysis of shock has a fundamental ambivalence, molded certainly by the impoverishment of experience in modern life, but also capable of assuming "a strategic significance—as an artificial means of propelling the human body into moments of recognition.[37]

The panic before the image on the screen exceeds a simple physical reflex, similar to those one experiences in a daily encounter with urban traffic or industrial production. In its double nature, its transformation of still image into moving illusion, it expresses an attitude in which astonishment and knowledge perform a vertiginous dance, and pleasure derives from the energy released by the play between the shock caused by this illusion of danger and delight in its pure illusion. The jolt experienced becomes a shock of recognition. Far from fulfilling a dream of total replication of reality—the *apophantis* of the myth of total cinema—the experience of the first projections exposes the hollow center of the cinematic illusion. The thrill of transformation into motion depended on its presentation as a contrived illusion under the control of the projectionist-showman. The movement from still to moving image accented the unbelievable and extraordinary nature of the apparatus itself. But in doing so, it also undid any naive belief in the reality of the image.

Cinema's first audiences can no longer serve as a founding myth for the theoreticalization of the enthralled spectator. History reveals fissures along with continuities, and we must recognize that the experience of these audiences was profoundly different from the classical spectator's absorption into an empathetic narrative. Placed within a historical context and tradition, the first spectators' experience reveals not a childlike belief but an undisguised awareness (and delight in) film's illusionistic capabilities. I have attempted to reverse the traditional understanding of this first onslaught of moving images. Like a demystifying showman, I have frozen the image of crowds scattered before the projection of an onrushing train and read it allegorically rather than mythically. This arrest should astonish us with the realization that these screams of terror and delight were well prepared for by both showmen and audience. The audience's reaction was the antipode to the primitive one: it was an encounter with modernity. From the start, the terror of that image uncovered a lack, and promised only a phantom embrace. The train collided with no one. It was, as Gorky said, a train of shadows, and the threat that it bore was freighted with emptiness.

4

In Your Face: Physiognomy, Photography, and the Gnostic Mission of Early Film

I. THE GNOSTIC IMPULSE

Béla Balázs, writing in the 1920s, declared, "At present a new discovery, a new machine, is at work to turn the attention of men back to a visual culture and give them new faces."[1] This claim exemplifies an almost forgotten utopian tradition of film theory, one that saw cinema not only as a new art form or a new language, but as a new instrument of knowledge. For theorists such as Balázs, the motion picture camera had the ability not only to capture reality but to penetrate it as a new instrument of the visible which had a revelatory mission. We could call this potential for uncovering new visual knowledge the gnostic (from *gnosis*, knowledge) mission of cinema. For Balázs and other utopian theorists, the gnostic potential of the cinema was especially evident in the conjunction of the cinematic device of the close-up and the subject of the human face:

> It is the "microphysiognomics" of the close-up that have given us this subtle play of feature, almost imperceptible yet also so convincing. The invisible face behind the visible has made its appearance.[2]

This essay first appeared in *Modernism/Modernity* 4, no. 1 (1997): 1–29, with the following acknowledgment: "I would like to thank a number of people for formative comments on this paper, in particular Lawrence Rainey, Mikhail Yampolski, Yuri Tsivian, and Jan Holmberg."

One could find parallel quotes from other utopian theorists of the 1920s (as well as parallel ideas in Benjamin's somewhat later essay, "The Work of Art in the Age of Mechanical Reproduction"), such as Dziga Vertov ("a shot of the banker will only be true if we can tear the mask from him, if behind the mask we can see the thief") or Jean Epstein ("I am sure . . . that if a high speed film were made of an accused person during his interrogation, then beyond his words, the truth would appear, unique, evident, written out").[3]

I would like to use this detour into film theory to highlight something about the origins of cinema and this overdetermined fascination with the close-up and the human face. In earlier canonical accounts of film history, the close-up transformed cinema from a mere means of reproduction into a unique art form, a transformation often attributed to D. W. Griffith. Not only is this account discredited on factual grounds (Griffith did not invent the close-up, and in fact it occurs rather infrequently in the films he made for the Biograph Company, which are generally seen as the foundation of his later film style), it also obscures the complex archaeology of the facial close-up in early cinema.[4] A close examination of this archaeology underscores the key role that the gnostic view of cinema played in both the invention and the form of early cinema.

Behind the gnostic impulse that motivates the invention and the practice of early cinema lurk ambiguous relations woven among visuality, technology, knowledge, representation, and entertainment in modern culture. Uncovering the role that capturing the face played in both cinema and its antecedents traces a saraband between seeing and knowing within the new visual terrain opened up by photographic technology, which could not only reproduce human eyesight but exceed it. At the center of this figure lies the expressive human face, whose relation to knowledge and communication forms a central preoccupation of Western culture, serving as a pivot between individuality and typicality, expression and destiny, body and soul. The attempt to bring photography, and especially motion photography, to bear on this most polysemous of human objects reveals a crisis in understanding visual representation beneath a proclaimed confidence.

It is well known that close framings of human faces appear at the origin of cinema. The early Edison Kinetoscope films *Fred Ott's Sneeze* (shot in 1894) and *May Irwin Kiss* (1896) frame figures at the waist in a manner that clearly emphasizes the transformations of their faces as they perform simple biological actions. Even earlier, one of the first cinematic or protocinematic apparatuses was fashioned by George Demenÿ in 1891 precisely to obtain a moving image of the human face (and especially the mouth as it spoke) in order to aid in teaching deaf children to speak.[5]

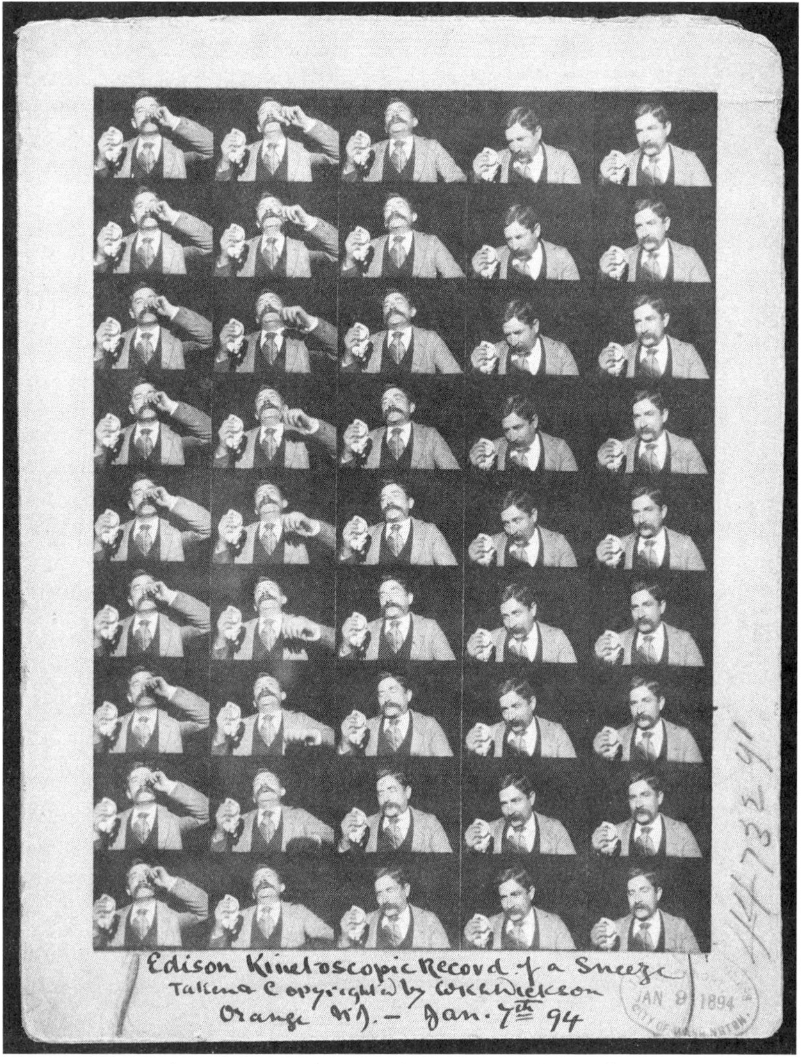

FIGURE 4.1. *Fred Ott's Sneeze* (Thomas Edison, 1894). Library of Congress Prints and Photographs Division, Washington, DC.

The Edison and Demenÿ motion pictures may seem to diverge sharply in purpose and audience (education versus entertainment; a small, specialized audience versus a mass one), but I would claim that they are in fact dialectically interrelated. Early cinema, whether designed as entertainment, pedagogical tool, or instrument of scientific investigation, maintained an important relation to the gnostic impulse, although often operating as parody.

The gradual perfection of still photography stimulated the pursuit of visual phenomena that might otherwise slip below the threshold of conscious observation and opened up new possibilities of visual knowledge. A continual attempt to make photography ever more sensitive to the ephemeral and instantaneous events of physical nature was a major motivation for cinema's invention and perfection. Early cinema owes its gradual technical realization to this gnostic impulse driving the work of Muybridge, Marey, Londe, Demenÿ, and others. Beyond the technical invention of photography, the origin of this impulse lies in a redefinition of the role of visual evidence and new methods for investigating the visual world. The successive ways the human face was categorized, investigated, and visualized in the pursuit of knowledge provides one way of tracing this gnostic impulse through to the cinema.

But the study of the face possesses its own history, as well as its own ambivalent relation to systems and methods of knowledge. Balázs's term "microphysiognomics" invokes (with the added precision of "micro") the somewhat antiquated term "physiognomy," a science of facial classification that had been basically discredited by the twentieth century.[6] In many ways the decline of this pseudo-evidence paralleled the growth in new methods of visual observation, such as photography. Physiognomy has its roots in texts from antiquity attributed to Aristotle and Pythagoras, which trace the relation between physical appearance and character, a practice that ultimately derives from magical forms of interpretation and divination such as chiromancy. It finds its most influential formulation in the work of Giambattista della Porta at the end of the sixteenth century, in which the shape of the elements of the human face were interpreted by a series of analogies to animals, the elements, and the stars within a neoplatonic cosmic system. In this system of resemblances and affinities, the human face took on meaning by way of a series of metaphors which joined man's physical appearance to the powers that rule his soul and destiny via emblematic animals (e.g., facial resemblance to a lion indicates strength and hot temper) as well as the astral and planetary influences of astrology. As an exemplar of magical thinking, physiognomy worked on the basis of visual resemblance, tracing, as Foucault describes it, similitudes as "visual marks of invisible analogies."[7]

At the beginning of the modern age (and under the direct influence of Descartes), physiognomy became reinterpreted as a guide to visual representation in the arts, detouring from a means of knowing man's destiny to a system of aesthetic signification. The work of Charles Le Brun, first painter to Louis XIV, in *Conférence sur l'expression générale et particulière* (1688),

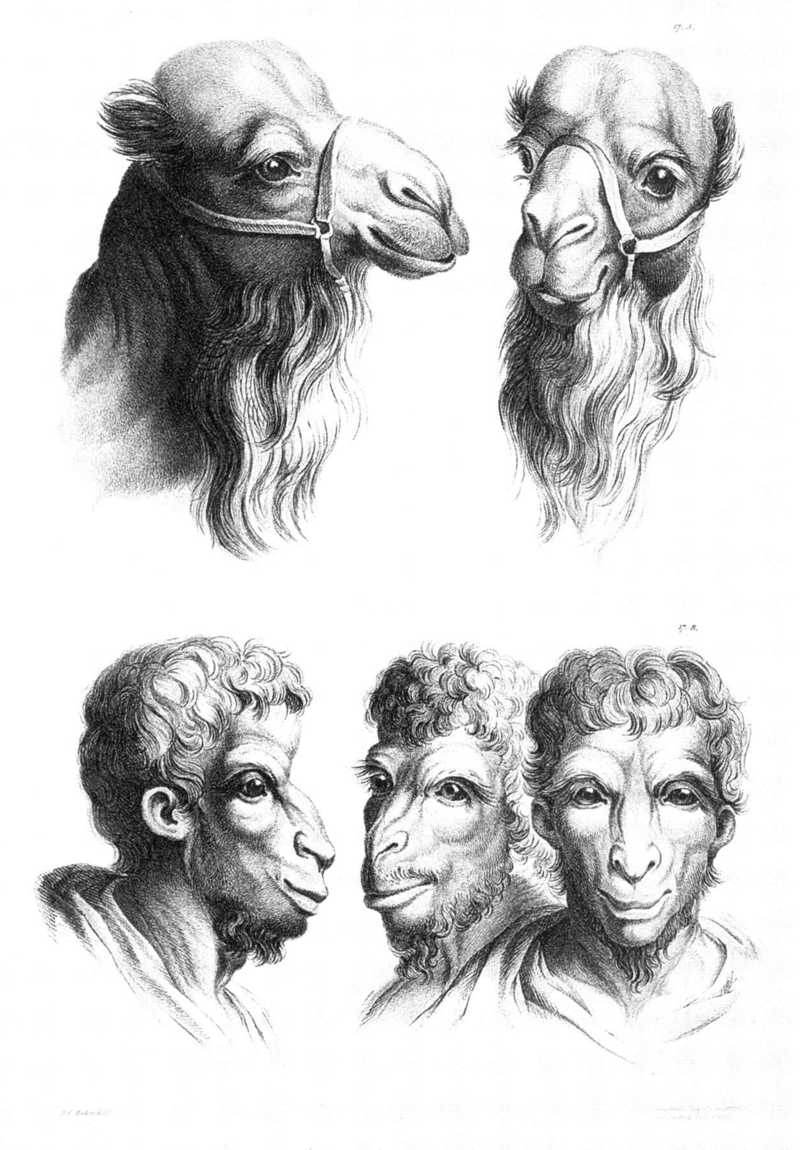

FIGURE 4.2. Charles le Brun, *Conférence sur l'expression générale et particulaire* (1698). Image: Wellcome Collection.

assembled physiognomic principles as a method for the proper way for painters to portray emotion and character through facial expression, dealt both with facial structure, the traditional domain of physiognomy, and the more transient passions, the domain of facial expression rather than type. His discussion of the passions is modeled on Descartes's last work, *The Passions of the Soul* (1649), providing drawings for each of the simple and complex passions as Descartes had outlined them, understanding his task in terms of Cartesian relations between mind and body: "Whatever causes passion in the soul creates also some action in the body. It is necessary to know which are the actions of the body that express those passions and what action is."[8] In doing this, however, he placed himself in unacknowledged opposition to Descartes's own declaration that facial expressions are difficult to discern as signs of the passions and, being easily feigned, are often misleading.[9] Le Brun's discussion of physiognomy, the structure of the face as a sign of character rather than as expression of passion, further developed traditional analogies between human faces and those of animals and the qualities they represented. As Patrizia Magli says, "In his links with ancient traditions, and in his merging them with more innovative trends, Le Brun both fell behind and preceded his own times."[10]

Physiognomy entered into the age of reason and sensibility (and strongly influenced both realist and romantic aesthetics of the nineteenth century) through the famous *Physiognomische Fragmente* of the Swiss theologian Johann Caspar Lavater, first published in 1775.[11] Basically a further systematization of the ancient tradition, Lavater's work no longer approached physiognomy as divination but, developing Le Brun's understanding of body as the expression of the soul, presented the science as a means of deciphering the mysterious inner world through bodily signs.

Existing on the other side of Descartes's split between the mind and body, the Romantics believed Lavater's physiognomy reunited mind and body in an act of symbolic reading, as Novalis's notes on physiognomy reveal: "The religious essence of physiognomy. The divine and infinitely meaningful hieroglyphs of each human body. . . . The way in which these hieroglyphs have their occasional moments of revelation."[12] The Romantics also recognized Lavater's method as revealing the unique qualities of each individual physiognomy, analyzing each face as a combination of individual elements rather than as a master table of analogies. Lavater's physiognomy exerted as much influence on aesthetics as on scientific discourse, and was directly responsible for the increased popularity of the silhouette as a mode of representation. Not only did the silhouette accurately capture the facial profile so important in Lavater's method, its indexical process of production—directly tracing the shadow of its subject—announced the importance of new visual technologies in sciences of observation, directly anticipating photography.[13]

While the tradition of physiognomy is complex, one can see a consistent drift in its conceptions as it moves from traditional systems of occult knowledge to a modern discourse with at least pretenses to being a science. Physiognomy became less of a system by which one reads an individual's fate, inscribed in facial features through cosmic and symbolic analogies, than a means of observation in which the face is mobile and expressive, revealing a person's accumulated history as much as predetermined fate (Lavater emphasized that a person's way of life could affect his physical appearance).[14] Features no longer embodied the coded writing of destiny. They spoke the language of emotion conveyed through expressions, the changeable signifiers of varying moods. The facial traits which reflected character served less as predictions of a person's future than as traces left by their profession or way of life, less occult symbols than the residue of a scientific logic of cause and effect. For instance, the French editor of Lavater, Dr. Moreau de la Sarthe, described the physiognomies of professions as reflections of habitual behavior:

> Skillful and very experienced surgeons have in their physiognomy a particular dominant trait, which comes from a habitual movement of raising the upper lip—which can be attributed the effort they make to resist the impression caused by the sight of suffering and pain which they have before their eyes during major operations.[15]

But however systematized and rationalized, physiognomy still carried a promise of knowledge that verged on the occult. Since our reactions to faces seem immediate and untutored, physiognomy exemplified the Romantic concept of universal hieroglyphic language, more intuitive than analytical, a signifier that, far from being arbitrary, still carried the surplus value of visual similarity. It is no coincidence that one of the few attempts at film theory that preceded Balázs's, that of Vachel Lindsay, declared cinema to be a "hieroglyphic" art.[16]

Physiognomy became a popular social science in nineteenth-century Paris, where it provided a visual means to order the diverse and anonymous masses that surrounded the urban dweller. These typologies of observation greatly affected the novels of Balzac and the caricatures of Daumier and Grandville.[17] It was suggested that choosing a wife or hiring a servant should never be undertaken without the aid of physiognomic analysis. The physiognomic studies of Lavater and his disciples became transformed into the "physiologies" which appeared as a sort of literary fad in the 1840s. Somewhat broadening the physiognomies into a description of specific manners and lifestyles, these physiologies outlined the various "types" of Parisians, through a somewhat ironical "scientific" observation.[18] As Walter Benjamin has indicated, these physiologies attempted to reduce classes and professions to stable and recognizable stereotypes, reassuring to a petty bourgeois worldview:

> The long series of eccentric or simple attractive or severe figures which the physiologies presented to the public in character sketches had one thing in common: they were harmless and of perfect bonhomie. Such a view of one's fellow man was so remote from experience that there were bound to be uncommonly weighty motives for it.[19]

Weighty indeed. The physiologies were a last gasp of a confidence in one's ability to sort people into types that were not only stable but easily recognizable, an attempt that gained urgency as the fluid contours of a modern world made such methods of classification increasingly difficult. Balzac, who authored several physiologies, nonetheless was aware of the new precariousness of sorting people into general types. He bewailed the fact that, whereas previously "the caste system gave each person a physiognomy which was more important than the individual; today the individual gets his physiognomy from himself."[20]

2. THE ILLEGIBLE FACE: PHOTOGRAPHY, INDIVIDUALITY, AND MADNESS

> We owe to M. Londe, the chemist of Salpêtrière, the following anecdote. . . . [Blanche] Wit[man] was in a state of [hypnotic] somnambulism, and [Londe] showed her a photograph of a view of the Pyrenees with donkeys climbing one side, and told her, "Look, this is your portrait; you are absolutely naked." On coming out of the trance the patient saw by chance the photograph and, furious to see herself there represented in a "state of nature," threw herself upon it and destroyed it.[21]

If the future of such social physiognomy as social science was doomed by the dissolving of the visual signs of caste, profession, and type (or their slipping below the threshold of the immediately recognizable), the extremely individualizing processes of photography allowed for a new positivist science of observation of the face and its expressions. The physiologies were accompanied by the growth in the art of caricatures, which were frequently used to illustrate them. But with the advent of photography, the human face became less a realm described in generalities (such as Moreau's description of surgeons) than a zone of intense scrutiny on an individual basis. An anonymous British author writing on physiognomy in 1861 saw the progress of the science as lying precisely in its use of photographs:

> It is equally true that with such portraits and engravings of portraits as we have had, it has been utterly impossible to get beyond the nebulous science of a Lavater. We required the photograph. . . . It must be remembered that to give a general likeness is one of the easiest strokes of art. With a half-a-dozen lines the image is complete, as anyone may see in the million wood-engravings of the day; while at the same time it would be difficult to gather from these rough sketches, where two dots go for eyes and a scratch for a mouth, what is the precise anatomy of any one feature. So while we can accept as in the main truthful the portraits that have come down to us, it is impossible to place perfect reliance on any particular lineament.[22]

In this new method of investigation of the face, rooted in individual faces and their transient momentary expressions, photography served as the optimal tool of investigation. From this new empirical perspective, physiognomy no longer served primarily as a guide to aesthetic representation, but demanded the accuracy of new mechanical modes of image-making.[23]

A seminal figure in this research was G. B. Duchenne de Boulogne. Duchenne was a founder of neurology in France, the teacher and master of Jean-Martin Charcot.[24] Duchenne's pioneering work in the classification of neurological disorders was often based on his innovative use of electricity to stimulate directly muscles and nerves. His use of new technology for medical purposes also extended to photography, as he began in the 1850s to photograph the debilitating results of neurological diseases. He combined electricity and photography in his investigation of the mechanism of human facial expression which was published in 1862. Duchenne wished first of all to accurately map out the muscles of the human face which created the common expressions of emotion. Direct application of electrodes to the faces of human subjects allowed Duchenne to cause involuntary contractions of facial muscles. In this way he literally sculpted expressions or grimaces onto the faces of his subjects. Photography could fix these momentary contractions and allow them to be studied at leisure, to be scrutinized and compared.

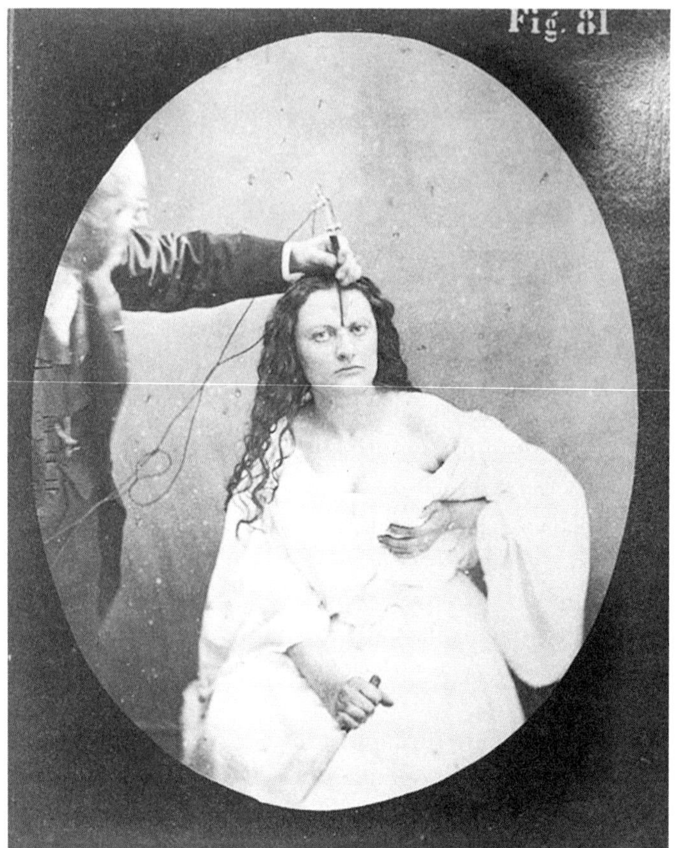

FIGURE 4.3. G. B. Duchenne de Boulogne, *Mécanisme de la physionomie humaine ou analyse électro-physiologique de l'expression des passions* (Paris, 1876).

Duchenne's distance from the earlier physiognomies comes from both his positivist scientific ambitions and his use of modern technology. Instead of a permanent physical imprint of fate or character, he sought to understand the face in motion, describing facial expressions as mobile muscular phenomena. This interest in motion set him apart from Le Brun, who, as Duchenne stated, "represented the diverse aspects of facial expression produced by the emotions but without worrying about their laws of motion," as well as from Lavater, who "entirely omitted the study of facial expression in movement."[25] This interest in the phenomenon of motion and the belief that the physical effects of motion had laws indicate Duchenne's place within a modern line of scientific investigation that would lead directly to the invention of the cinema. What had seemed contingent and below the threshold of knowledge for the earlier physiognomists was precisely suited to the possibilities of new technology. The electrode could affect a facial muscle in isolation while photography could capture a facial contraction that was much too brief to be otherwise recorded. As Duchenne put it:

> Skillful artists have tried in vain to represent the faces of my subjects; for the contractions provoked by the electrical currents are of too short a duration for an exact reproduction of the expressive lines that develop on the face to be drawn or painted. Only photography, as truthful as a mirror, could attain such a desirable perfection.[26]

Since Duchenne's major goal was to identify the muscles and motor nerves in the face and their role in a variety of expressions, he literally tried to reveal the "invisible face behind the visible." Yet for Duchenne, following the Cartesian tradition, facial expression had another interior—the spirit. "The spirit is thus the source of expression. It activates the muscles that portray our emotions on the face with characteristic patterns."[27] But in Duchenne's experiments the spirit as the motive force of facial expressions was replaced by the electrode that caused the face involuntarily to "speak the language of emotions and the sentiments."[28] However artificial such expressions might be when electrically induced for purposes of demonstration and investigation, Duchenne had no doubt that he was investigating a language that was universal and God-given:

> In the face our Creator was not concerned with mechanical necessity. He was able in his wisdom or—please pardon this manner of speaking—in pursuing a divine fantasy, to put any particular muscles into action, one alone or several muscles together, when he wished the characteristic signs of the emotions, even the most fleeting, to be written briefly on man's face. Once this language of facial expression was created, it sufficed for him to give all human beings the instinctive faculty of always expressing their sentiments by contracting the same muscles. This rendered the language universal and immutable.[29]

But if Duchenne represents a modern scientist devoted to empirical observation through the use of modern technology rather than a traditional physiognomist tracing mystical signatures and resemblances, the strong tie between the study of the face and codes of aesthetic representation continued to compel aspects of his work. Duchenne hoped to reformulate Le Brun's work and provide artists with documentary proof of the visual language of the human emotions.[30] He divided the photographic plates that illustrated his thesis into "Scientific" and "Aesthetic" sections. In place of the predominantly male models imaged in the scientific section, the aesthetic section makes use exclusively of a female model, while the close framing of the face frequently gives way to dramatic tableaux in which the female model is posed in costume with props.

Duchenne glosses these images with narrative situations that might explain or specify the emotions he evokes with his electrode. If somewhat less aggressive in their framing and less agonized in their facial contortions, these images seem even more bizarre as the electrode and its manipulator intervene into the stage sets and poses of genre painting. The photographs display disturbing tensions between the conventional sentiments and narrative of the poses and scenarios and a nightmarish scene of a metanarrative of control and technological manipulation which the intervening electrode indicates. Further complicating his simple narratives, Duchenne deconstructs the unified effect of the facial expression by attempting to create distinct expressions within different zones of the face. For instance, he describes his plate 80:

> The young lady photographed in this figure is visiting a poor family; we recognize, from her tender laughter (cover the left side of the face) or from her kind smile (cover the right side of the face) that she is touched by the misery and suffering of this unhappy family, and that this sentiment has inspired an act of charity.[31]

Although Duchenne frequently apologizes for the lack of aesthetic value and physical beauty of the older male model who appears frequently in the scientific section of his work, he never explains why he exclusively uses a female model (whom he describes as neither pretty nor ugly and mentions was nearly blind).[32] Undoubtedly a belief that a female model would be more pleasing to viewers corresponded with his desire in this section "to please those who possess 'a sense of beauty.'"[33] However, more deeply imbedded cultural conceptions of gender clearly operate here, relating the female model not only to the aesthetic but to an atmosphere of drama and mystery created by the use of the fictional settings and narrative scenarios. Although experiments in electrically creating different expressions on each side of the face appear in the scientific section as well, here it becomes a nearly constant practice, as if the conjunction of a woman model and drama led naturally to a succession of facial expressions and moods. For instance, his gloss on plate 77 describes not only diverse expressions but a typology of female desire: "Earthly love at right and celestial love at left.

Ecstasy of human love, by covering the left half of the face; gentle rapture of divine love (ecstasy of St. Teresa), by covering the opposite side."[34]

This division of the sides of the face into separate expressions became for Duchenne a means of expressing the ambivalence of a dramatic scene, as in his extraordinarily revealing discussion of plate 78 which he elaborates with a complete drama:

> In Plate 78 I wanted to show a little comedy, a scene of coquetry, a gentleman surprises a lady while she is dressing. On seeing him, her stance and her look become disapproving (cover the bottom half of her face). Nevertheless, we note her nudity, which instead of covering she seems to reveal with a certain affectation. It is the mannered pose of her hand, which supports a rather overtly revealed bosom. All this betrays her coquetry. The young man was becoming more audacious, but the words "get out" pronounced in a scornful way by the girl, stop him in his enterprise (see only the left side of the lower half of her face). The mocking laughter that accompanies the amorous rejection (see the right side of the lower half of the face) we believe to mean, "Conceited ass." Perhaps she says also, much lower: "The fool, if he had dared . . ."[35]

For Duchenne, the face was an extremely flexible medium on which the spirit writes a translatable message of emotions in a language created by God himself. However, his investigation via an arbitrary stimulation of the diverse muscles of the face could also produce the face as a sort of collage, in which contrasting emotions occupied different zones of the face. Duchenne also found that he could produce nongrammatical expressions, which he termed grimaces, "where it was hard, sometimes nearly impossible, to make any meaningful interpretation."[36] Such grimaces serve only as the noise within his system of facial expression, in which a mask of muscles sculpts the invisible impulses of the spirit. But the very bizarre nature of Duchenne's aesthetic section may betray anxiety at the arbitrary expressions he has induced on the face by substituting electrical impulses for the passions of the soul. Narrative scenography imposes itself as a means of containing (though not dispelling) his own intervention, as if familiar situations and cultural clichés of feminine roles provided a context of ideologically reassuring recognizability necessary to allow the viewer to see these shocking demonstrations of the human face as the play of muscles as part of a visible "natural language." In any case, it would seem that Charcot learned the effectiveness of staging a scenography of female performers under the dominance of a male "operator" from his master.

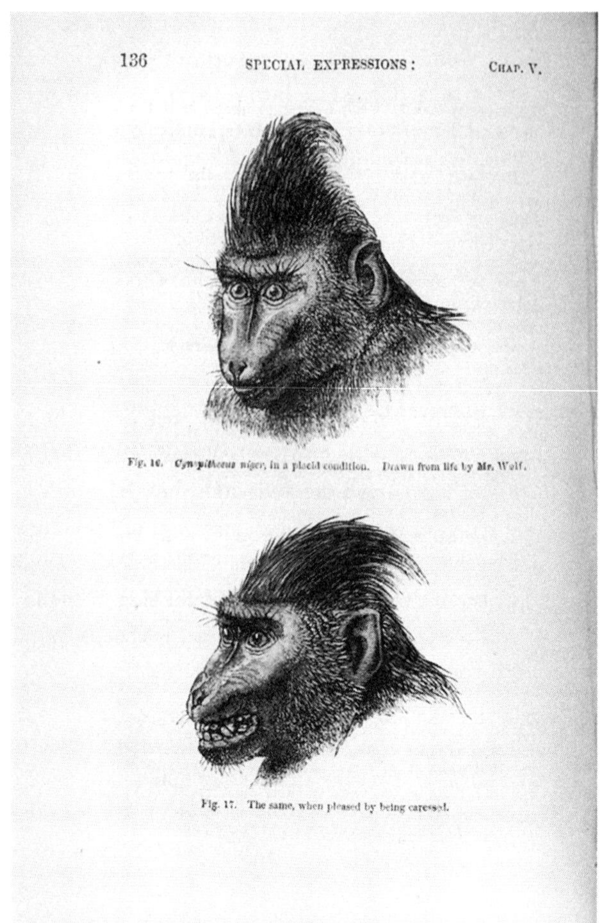
136 SPECIAL EXPRESSIONS: CHAP. V.

Fig. 16. *Cynopithecus niger*, in a placid condition. Drawn from life by Mr. Wolf.

Fig. 17. The same, when pleased by being caressed.

FIGURE 4.4. Illustration by T. W. Wood for Charles Darwin, *The Expression of the Emotions in Man and Animals* (1872).

Charles Darwin drew heavily on Duchenne in his 1872 study *The Expression of the Emotions in Man and Animals*. He particularly praised the use of photography in the investigation of facial expression: "I have found photographs made by instantaneous process the best means, as allowing more deliberation."[37] However, he strongly rejected, as contrary to the principles of his theory of evolution, any claim that expressions were a language designed by the Creator to allow humans to communicate, as Duchenne had believed. Darwin tried to explain the communicative aspects and forms of expressions through recourse to a deeper history than the personal one of habit or profession. Expression provided a link between men and animals. "With mankind some expressions, such as the bristling of the hair under the influence of extreme terror, or the uncovering of the teeth under that of furious rage, can hardly be understood, except on the belief that man once existed in a much lower and animal-like condition."[38]

Darwin was probably unaware of the irony of this return to the most ancient form of physiognomy, the comparison between humans and animals. However, Darwin's method was historical and evolutionary rather than analogical, discovering, like most nineteenth-century systems of thought, the traces of the longue durée of history on the forms of nature, rather than the timeless semantic tables of resemblance that guided Della Porta and even Le Brun's physiognomy. But Darwin also sought the survival of this evolutionary past in the present through a different sort of analogy. If the investigation of expression led directly to the extensive evolutionary past of man, he felt it essential to investigate not only man's animal ancestors but also human subjects whom he believed might be closer to this ancestry due to their distance from civilizing influences, such as infants, the insane, and different races of man.[39] Darwin's investigation sought to strip the face of its civilized mask of convention and reveal a language of expression which derived from the struggle for survival and various forms of adaptation to environmental or physical forces. But to understand the laws of the human face a new importance was accorded to faces that were somehow alien to "normal" human behavior. A science of deviant faces took on a new importance, in contrast to physiognomy's traditional search for the typical and ideal.

Facial photographs held a special place in the treatment of the insane, with Hugh W. Diamond pioneering the use of photographic portraits in both the study and treatment of the insane. The photographs Diamond took at the Surrey County Lunatic Asylum in the 1850s were used not only in his public lectures on mental illness but in the therapy of patients, using "the effect they [the photographs] produced upon the patients themselves" to help the progress of their cure.[40] Diamond's associate Dr. John Conolly discussed these photographs in 1858 in an article entitled "Case Studies from the Physiognomy of the Insane," in which he portrayed these faces as traces of a battle between original character and the physical effects of mental aberration. The idea of a physiognomy of the insane had already been described in 1838 by J. E. D. Esquirol, who made drawings of mental patients in order to trace similarities between them.[41] As Conolly's essay shows, this was a system of description still indebted to the ancient forms of analogy and metaphor, but inflected by a modern concern for individual case history, clearly showing the influence of Lavater.[42] Describing a

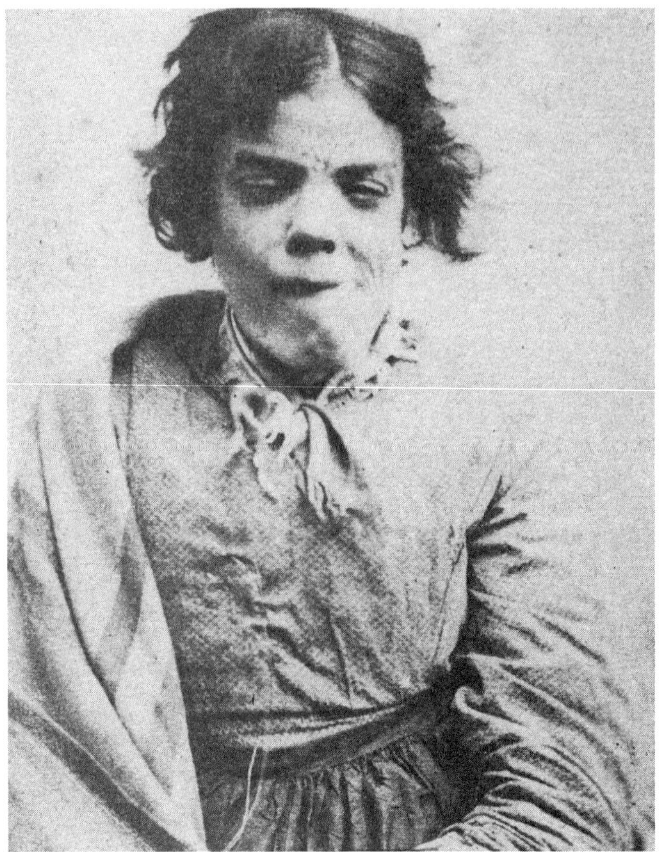

FIGURE 4.5. Hugh W. Diamond, *Photograph of Patient*, ca. 1855. The Royal Photographic Society Collection at the V&A, acquired with the generous assistance of the National Lottery Heritage Fund and Art Fund. © Victoria and Albert Museum, London.

pathetic case of what he termed "suicidal melancholy," he portrayed the face as a battleground of emotional struggles:

> The features are unrefined; but the wide and high head indicates intellectual qualities that cultivation might have improved; so as to control perhaps a now dominating ideality. The copious and disheveled hair, which we feel sure must be black mingled with grey, is parted with no care, but straggles in sympathy with the tortured brain. Those many and curved wrinkles in the brow are not wrinkles of ordinary trouble. The raised and equally curved eyebrows; the large, melancholy, and uplifted eyes, declare that the sense is fixed on some image of fear, which no other eye can detect; and the intensity of the prevalent emotion is forcibly expressed

in all the other parts of the face. The upper eyelids disappear; the lower are strongly depressed; the muscles of the cheeks are drawn down, the lower lip being, as it were, spasmodically acted upon, showing nearly all the front teeth of the lower jaw. The chin has been scratched and scarred by her own fingernails. The very ears seem starting forward. Everything bespeaks terror.[43]

The face photographed becomes a text to be read by the male doctor employing a bewildering variety of interpretive means, ranging from deviation from norms of behavior (the unparted hair), to traces of past behavior (the scarred chin), through a range of analogies (the hair which "straggles in sympathy with the tortured brain") to a general sort of allegorical method which sees the face as "bespeak[ing] terror." These faces stand primarily as deviant faces, horrifying visual evidence of the mental sufferings the subjects have undergone. Diamond underscored these aspects in assembling in one plate four photographs of a woman in different stages of illness and cure, in which the variety of expression seems perhaps less remarkable than the variety of clothing which clearly differentiates the deviant expressions from the controlled face of convention.

Succeeding decades saw a general adoption of photography for medical and scientific purposes (the *Revue photographique des Hopitaux de Paris*, for instance, was established in 1869), and toward the end of the century increasingly short exposure times allowed a relation between photography and the recording of motion for scientific purposes that moved asymptotically toward the invention of cinema.[44] Undoubtedly the most famous and complex use of photography to record facial movement and expression came from Jean-Martin Charcot and the *Iconographie photographique de la Salpêtrière*. In 1878, Charcot, the head physician of the Salpêtrière (a Parisian charity hospital for women), had installed there a Photographic Service complete with a glass-roofed studio and a photographic laboratory.[45] Albert Londe, who was placed in charge of the Photographic Service in 1884, lauded the gnostic possibilities of photography, describing the latest photographic plate as "the true retina of the scientist," a means of seeing that could, in fact, be more sensitive than the human eye.[46] Charcot's greatest fame came from his description and treatment of hysteria. Documenting the behavior of hysterics was especially important since this elusive disease exhibited a scenario of behavior rather than clearly isolatable physical symptoms (leading frequently to the claim that hysterics were simply malingerers who "mimicked" the symptoms of others to gain attention).[47] Charcot claimed to have discovered predictable patterns to this behavior (such as the succession of different physical actions in a consistent order that made up the hysterical fit), giving the disease a character that could be analyzed and diagnosed.

Observation was essential to the diagnosis of hysteria, and photography increases this power of observation as well as providing its faithful record. Charcot had actually compared his method to that of photography, declaring, "In truth I am absolutely nothing but a photographer; I inscribe what I see."[48] In diagnostic use, medical photography mediated between the patient's individual body and the general characteristics of the disease. Determining this general aspect, or *facies*, of a disease called for a specific use of photography. As Londe explained:

> To determine the *facies* belonging to each disease, to each illness, to place it before the eyes of all, this is what photography is capable of. In certain doubtful or uncertain cases, comparing photographs taken in diverse places or at quite different times allows one to be sure of the identity of the illness of diverse patients whom one has not had under one's care at the same time. This has been accomplished with great success by M. Charcot and the *facies* belonging to this or that illness of the central nervous system is now well-known.[49]

Visual demonstration as well as diagnosis played a key role in Charcot's investigation of hysteria. Both were evident at his famous public "Tuesday lessons," in which women patients and their symptoms were paraded before an audience made up of interns, doctors (such as the Viennese physician Sigmund Freud—who later overturn Charcot's theory of hysteria—attending the lectures on a travel grant), and invited members of high society (including such luminaries as Henri Bergson, Emile Durkheim, Guy de Maupassant, and Sarah Bernhardt).[50] In these sessions, Charcot not only displayed the symptoms of his female patients but experimentally influenced their behavior through hypnosis, drugs, or various forms of physical manipulation (including, during photographic sessions, sudden exposure to a magnesium flash, as Ulrich Baer has stressed).[51]

But the *facies* revealed by these means of investigation and observation was the paradoxical typicality of the deviant. Charcot used hypnosis to provoke effects similar to those his teacher Duchenne had induced by electrical current, occasionally invoking contradictory impulses within a patient so that "the subject found herself in some way divided in two."[52] Charcot also on occasion used electrodes to effect his hysterics, but found that such force was unnecessary to provoke facial contractions. Slight pressure from a simple metal rod would produce the same sorts of facial contractions Duchenne had induced by more powerful means.[53] Sudden loud noises, flashes of electrical light, or dramatic gestures on the part of the doctor could produce extraordinary physical results, from cataleptic postures to violent seizures.

The extremely theatrical nature of Charcot's demonstrations and treatments, as well as his use of hypnosis, led to widespread suspicion and criticism of his methods and conclusions. Charcot's critics portrayed him as the histrionic impresario of his mimicking hysterics, inducing symptoms through suggestion and training his subjects (knowingly or unwittingly) to perform for himself and his invited audiences.[54] The collapse of Charcot's view of hysteria led to alternative scenarios, most obviously that of psychoanalysis, and one can see Charcot's highly visualized and dramatic performances as an attempt to give this paradoxical disease a recognizable visual face, an attempt, on the cusp of modernity, to tie once more the act of seeing to the act of knowing.

The role of photography in all of this is perhaps more complex than previous treatments, such as Georges Didi-Huberman's, have indicated, as insightful as they have been. Charcot's patients and their symptoms were paraded before the camera as well as before interns and the public. The resulting photographs were published in the three volumes of the *Iconographie photographique de la Salpêtrière*, in 1876, 1877, and 1879. After a significant hiatus, the photographic series reappeared in a new format in 1888, as *Nouvelle Iconographie de la Salpêtrière*. These photographs include a number of facial close-ups, although framing that includes the posture and contortions of the full body predominates. However, in contrast to Diamond and other earlier photographers of mental illness, there is no attempt to create a physiognomy of madness here. The *facies* of hysteria demands a specific etiology of an elusive disease. The contorted faces of women were fit into a pattern that made hysteria conceivable as a disease and visually recognizable. Londe described the importance of facial close-up photography in capturing the characteristics of the disease:

> Certain modifications of the face which by themselves were not recognized as constituting in isolation a clear indication of a particular illness took on a very great importance when they were found over and over in similar sufferers. Unless one happened by chance to have patients show the same expressions at the same time, they might go unnoticed. However, with close-up photographs of them, one can make comparisons between

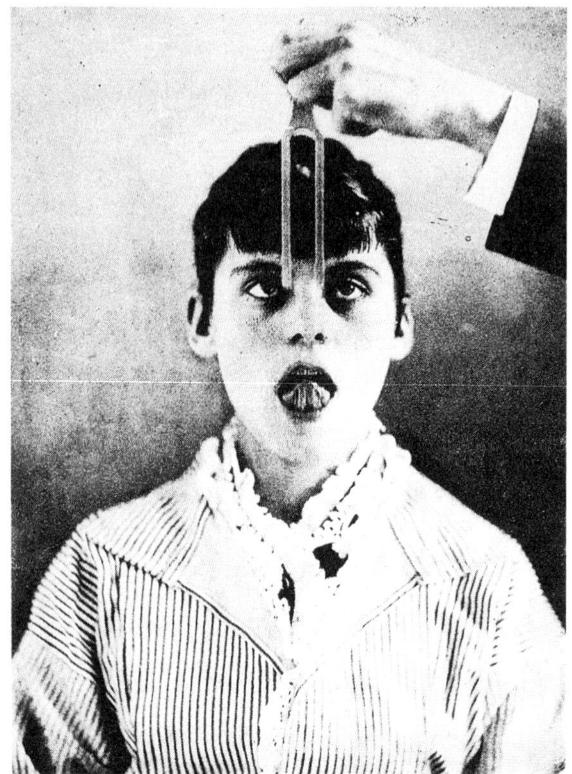

FIGURE 4.6. Paul Richer, "Gonflement du cou chez un hystérique," *Nouvelle Iconographie de la Salpêtrière* 2 (1889), plate 34. Image: Wellcome Collection.

> a number of examples and deduce the typical modifications of different aspects.[55]

Londe here perhaps knowingly recalls Bertillon's system of criminal photography, which allowed photographs of suspects and convicts to be compared in terms of physical characteristics and the identity of malefactors to be established. However, as in the case of Bertillon, we see that the satisfaction of pure visual recognition remains elusive. No one photograph could finger a guilty party or portray the *facies* of the disease. The act of recognition relies on comparison, and knowledge resides not in the single photograph but within vast photographic archives, cross-indexed by systems of classification.[56]

Recent biographers of Albert Londe, Denis Bernard and André Gunthert, have questioned Charcot's personal devotion to photography as a method of medical investigation. They point out that the *Iconographie* was instigated by Désiré Bourneville and that its hiatus coincided with Bourneville's departure from Salpêtrière for Bicetre in 1879.[57] They also claim Bourneville rather than Charcot was the driving force behind photography at Salpêtriere, and that the Photographic Service, as well as the *Iconographie*, fell into stagnation until Londe took charge in 1884.[58] From this perspective, Charcot's self-identification with the photographer may indicate he felt his own gaze was sufficient as the major device of visual investigation. As Bernard and Gunthert indicate, "The gaze (*regard*) and the image are not synonymous." Photographic sessions at Salpêtrière took place without Charcot present, and the "most serious rival of the photographic plate remained the clinician's gaze."[59]

Londe, a devoted advocate of medical photography (whose book on the subject was published in 1893), understood that a photograph, in order to become scientific, had to be placed within a system.[60] Each photograph had to find its place within a series. Besides the comparisons that a physician could make by rummaging through the *Iconographie*, Londe also explored the possibilities of serial photography to indicate the succession of actions typical of hysterical attacks. The need to obtain successive photographs led Londe to photographic inventions that brought him to the cusp of cinema, including a number of multilens cameras capable of taking a series of separate images in rapid succession. His crowning apparatus possessed twelve lenses and was therefore able to take, at brief intervals, twelve images of an ongoing action.[61] Such images inscribed a temporal progression into photography. Still photography in the late nineteenth century had gained a scientific and gnostic role not only through its iconic resemblance and indexical reliability, but through its increasing mastery of increments of time and its ability to freeze an instantaneous event, such as a sudden facial expression or the convulsions of a hysteric's limbs. The ambition of nineteenth-century science to discover not only the characteristic lineaments of the face as interpreted by physiognomy but the laws of motion and the temporal processes of the body and the face led directly to the technical invention of the cinema.

As a leader in bringing photography (and especially scientific and medical photography) to the attention of the public, Londe knew the motion-analysis photographs of Eadweard Muybridge and the chronophotography of Étienne-Jules Marey very well. A pioneer in the development of instantaneous photography, Londe was enthusiastic about the scientific possibilities of new photographic techniques.[62] Not only chronophotography (the taking of series of stills in rapid succession to analyze the phases of a motion) but stereoscopic three-dimensional photography were employed by Londe

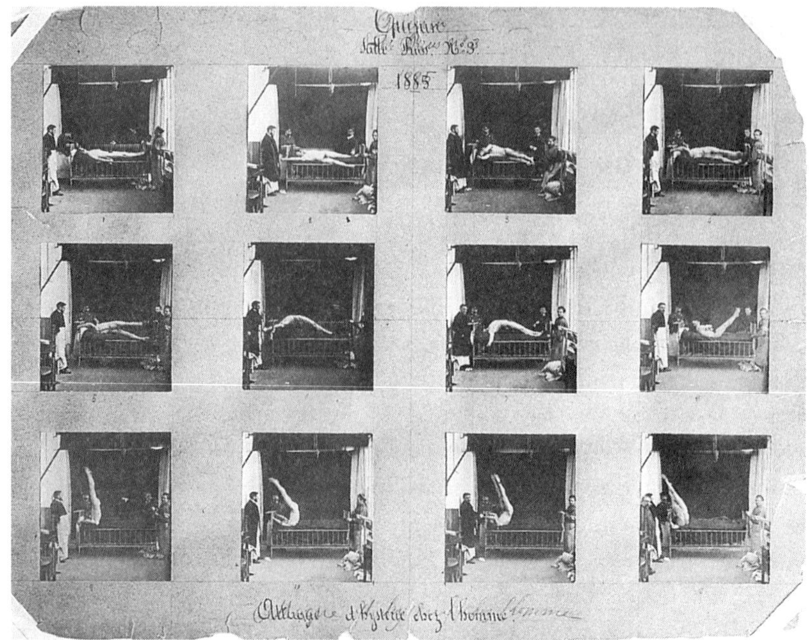

FIGURE 4.7. Albert Londe, *Attaque d'hystérie chez l'homme*, Hôpital de la Salpêtrière, Paris, 1885. Chronophotographic image.

to capture the symptoms of medical patients.[63] In his drive to master the analysis of space and time through photography, Londe seems to have created a counterforce to his subjects' bodies out of control—attempting to master on the level of technology what defied orderly behavior. But, like Marey, he at least initially found the Cinématographe, the device for projecting motion pictures to create an illusion of movement, a mere novelty, bereft of scientific interest.[64] In place of photographic processes which could fix and analyze temporal processes in order to reveal phenomenon otherwise difficult to perceive, motion pictures seemed simply to reproduce the experience of the normal eyewitness.[65]

For Londe, scientific photography mastered its visual subject, moving beyond the simple resemblance and illusion of motion that Lumière's Cinématographe offered. Through still photography's control of time, the hysteric fit was frozen, delivered to the physician's gaze with movement tamed. We find here, at the moment of the invention of cinema, a dilemma which thwarts any simple tracing of a linear progression in film's genealogy. The gnostic impulse pushes toward cinema's control of time and motion, but also expresses suspicions of its illusory potential. At this critical point, the bifurcation between cinema as a device of mass entertainment and its use as a scientific tool becomes evident, as the conflict between Marey and his assistant Demenÿ dramatized. However, one should not assume too quickly an absolute separation. The two impulses continue to infect each other, indicating less a parting of the ways based on principle than a crisis of representation based on the illusory power of technological imagery and a new mimesis of time. Cinema's destiny as a modern technological popular medium derives from this conflict and continues to show its effects for at least its first decade.

How, then, are we to understand Londe's turning his experimental photography on nonscientific subjects, photographing acrobats from the Hippodrome in stereo in 1887 and the tightrope walking act of Mlle. Barenco of the Nouveau Cirque in 1893?[66] Clearly such subjects were ideal for demonstrating the new powers of photography to capture action. The twelve images of La Barenco demonstrate her delicate control of balance in a manner that the naked eye, absorbed in the ongoing moment-to-moment drama of her act, might not catch. But the sequence also anticipates the strong link that early cinema, as a popular art, will forge with vaudeville, circus, and the attractions of popular culture.

If Marey and Muybridge stand as the best known and most influential of cinema's scientific progenitors, the focus of chronophotography on the face owes more to the experiments of Marey's assistant Georges Demenÿ, whose attempt to bring the motion picture into the realm of show business (even before the Lumière brothers) led to the loss of his position as a researcher. Discussing his cinematic work some years later, Demenÿ still presented himself as a savant rather than a showman, claiming that for him, "the cinema was only a means of study momentarily rendering me the same service that a microscope provides for the anatomist."[67] Demenÿ had served as Marey's *preparateur* and trusted assistant from 1881, when he approached the renown physiologist and investigator of the science of movement about the application of Marey's methods to a system of gymnastic training Demenÿ had been perfecting.[68] Demenÿ oversaw the construction and subsequent functioning of Marey's Station Physiologique. In 1891, Marey turned over to him a project brought to the physiologist by the director of the National Deaf Mute Institute to study the physical mechanics of speech. The director hoped that a series of chronophotographs showing the positions of lips and tongue during speech might aid deaf mutes in learning to lip-read and, hopefully, to speak.[69]

For this project, Demenÿ substituted a much closer camera position than had been customary for Marey's chronophotographic studies of the body in motion, framing speaking subjects above midchest. However, since the aim was not only analytical but synthetic—helping deaf mutes to imitate the processes of speech as well as observe them—devising a means of presenting the photographs in such a manner as to reconstitute their motion became a primary issue to an extent it had not been for Marey's earlier motion studies. Attempting to create the illusion of a human face in motion, speaking, brought Demenÿ even closer to the cinema than Londe had ventured. While both Muybridge and Marey had also employed various means of reconstituting motion from their analytical photographs, Demenÿ was certainly a pioneer in the production of motion pictures, even if his technology was heavily indebted to his mentor. He cut and pasted the images captured on the chronophotographic strips around the edge of a circular wheel based on an earlier "philosophical toy" for the production of the illusion of motion, the phenakistiscope.[70] Two initial series of images were produced, both with Demenÿ himself (his eyes closed from the blinding light necessary for the brief exposure) speaking the emblematic phrases "I love you" and "vive la France!" When this device was presented to the public in 1892 (three years before the Cinématographe and a year before the first public demonstration of Edison's Kinetoscope), it generated a fervent interest which overwhelmed the pedagogical purposes for which it was designed.

Demenÿ, long concerned about financial security, hoped that this interest in his moving photographs could be exploited commercially. He patented his apparatus, which he called the "phonoscope," demonstrated it at the 1892 Photographic Exposition, and was approached by carnival operators with offers to exploit it as an entertainment device. For Demenÿ, however, the possibilities of the phonoscope were firmly linked to the image it provided of the human face in motion. He described his new invention as a "living portrait," saying, "The future will replace the static photograph, fixed in its frame, with the animated portrait that will be given life with the turn of a wheel. The expression of physiognomy will be presented as the voice is preserved by the phonograph."[71] The living portrait, Demenÿ believed, would deliver the traditional family portrait from an effect of mummification, allowing it "to live again like a veritable apparition."[72]

Although the device which presented the moving image was of Demenÿ's design (although based on the traditional phenakistiscope), the chronophotographic camera which took the images was Marey's invention, and a growing conflict over the commercial exploitation of the phonoscope led to a bitter rupture between the savant and his protégé. While the issue revolved around what Marey perceived as Demenÿ's appropriation of his work, the prospect of marketing chronophotography as a fairground attraction undoubtedly further annoyed Marey. Marey's deep and abiding suspicion of the fallibility of human vision was even more intense than Londe's, and his lack of interest in the illusion of motion strongly expresses the scientific disdain of motion pictures as betrayals of the possibilities of scientific photography.[73] Demenÿ continued his attempt to make a commercial success of his invention and, adapting it to flexible film, designed both a camera and a projector, setting up his own studio where he filmed living portraits as well as other subjects. After approaching the Lumières about a partnership and getting a cold response, Demenÿ eventually sold the rights to his patents to Louis Gaumont and returned to his first passion, gymnastic and physical training.[74]

We find among the films that Demenÿ shot before the dissolving of his company, catalogued by Laurent Mannoni, one which Mannoni entitles "Demenÿ making a grimace." Mannoni adds this brief speculative description: "An illustration perhaps intended to represent two different human expressions, as Le Brun had done in the seventeenth century in his work *The Expression of the Passions*."[75] Demenÿ's interest in the motion picture of the face clearly embraced not only the "living portrait" but the investigation of expression that extends from Della Porta to the grimaces of the facial expression films to come.

3. THE GRIMACE OF CURIOSITY AND MOTION PICTURES

> Take this kinetoscopic record of a sneeze, a topic intended to excite a smile, and let us rise higher.[76]
>
> BARNET PHILIPS

Given the seeming interruption of the scientific tradition with the triumph of actual motion pictures, can we assert that early cinema still owes something to the gnostic impulse? While the cinematic devices of Edison and the Lumière brothers owe a great deal to the technical path traced by their scientific predecessors, does the illusion of cinema invert and betray their own anti-illusionary impulse, as Marey and Londe suspected? Does the synthesis of motion supply nothing but a parlor trick, limited to a dubious entertainment value, bereft of scientific interest because it relies on a simple visual mimesis rather than the scientific possibilities of analysis and manipulation of time and motion? While the road in the development of cinema does fork here, the interchanges between the gnostic impulse and entertainment continue to assert themselves, something that becomes clearer if we maintain our broader view of the gnostic impulse as preceding modern science and inherent in such metaphor-based systems as physiognomy.

The scientific impulses that gave birth to modern science derive from a more primal curiosity, that *curiositas* which was condemned as a sin against the faith by St. Augustine in the fifth century, a fascination with the unusual which the theologian saw as the root of both a sideshow theatricality and an unseemly concern with the nature of God's universe, in other words, the root of both popular entertainment and scientific investigation:

> Because of this disease of curiosity monsters and anything out of the ordinary are put on display in our theaters. From the same motives men proceed to investigate the workings of nature, which is beyond our ken—things which it does no good to know and which men only want to know for the sake of knowing.[77]

The monumental work of Hans Blumenberg has traced the gradual overturning of this theological stricture and the eventual validation of curiosity as a positive force and power of man in the sixteenth and seventeenth centuries, supplying one of the major transformations in the legitimation of a modern secular world.[78] In the more immediate era of modernity, the nineteenth and twentieth centuries, the exploitation and exercise of such curiosity outside the disciplines of actual science constituted a major impulse of popular entertainment, and operated explicitly in the presentation of motion pictures as a show business novelty. While the pseudo-educational and scientific claims of P. T. Barnum's nineteenth-century museum of curiosities were partly a response to American puritanical suspicion of entertainment, they also tapped a growing popular curiosity about scientific and technological innovations. While claims of scientific value could serve as camouflage for simple forms of popular entertainment, a peculiarly modern exploitation of curiosity may also introduce new regimes of aesthetic appreciation, ones which conflict sharply with traditional modes of contemplation and absorption, revealing parallels with modernist attacks on traditional aesthetics. Therefore, we need to question how thoroughly illusionistic the earliest exhibition of motion pictures were, and in what ways they may have continued the scientific probing of illusionistic coherence, but now for the sake of curiosity rather than coherent knowledge.

Londe and Demenÿ found their photographic experiments intersecting with the world of popular entertainments. And certainly part of the fascination with Charcot's Tuesday lessons came less from their scientific demonstrations than from the complex scenography of attractions—erotic, sadistic, and simply curious—that Charcot evoked from his women patients. In fact, one of Charcot's critics, Leon Daudet, described the sessions as Grand Guignol.[79] But more is at issue here than an unmasking of the motivations behind scientific display. Curiosity indicates an audience that remains skeptical, capable of devising his or her own explanation of the phenomenon before them.

It was precisely this skeptical but curious spectator that Barnum wished to attract to his museum, employing what Neil Harris has called an "operational aesthetic."[80] According to Harris, the operational aesthetic draws viewers who want not only to see a marvel but to understand and speculate on how it works. An impresarial technique tailored to an age of technology and its fascinations, this aesthetic both excites and satisfies curiosity and supplies a very different aesthetic experience from that of traditional art forms. It was precisely such curiosity that drew the first spectators to the premieres of motion picture devices. They came to see a new technology demonstrated, and they received it with discussions of how it was achieved. Thus the first exhibitions of the Cinématographe, the Vitascope, or the Biograph, while certainly part of modern show business, were not as divorced from their scientific progenitors as might at first appear. It is as though the two aspects of Augustine's *curiositas*, the investigation of nature and the fascination in novelties, had been rejoined in a peculiarly modern gnostic impulse.

It should come as no surprise, then, that motion pictures of faces, films consisting entirely of facial close-ups, formed an important genre of early film, dating, as I indicated earlier, from the very first attempts at motion pictures undertaken by Edison and Demenÿ. These first experiments became in cinema's first decade a genre known as "facial expression" films, which display very clearly this early motion picture aesthetic founded on curiosity.[81] In line with the operational aesthetic, such films demonstrated to early audiences cinema's ability to capture complex and detailed motions. Although Fred Ott's sneeze and May Irwin and John Rice's kiss were ordinary, everyday actions, captured on film they became subjects of curiosity. The close framing of these brief films endowed them with a sense of physical proximity that was particularly startling given the actions portrayed, inviting scrutiny and delivering surprise. While the ideology of the close-up in later narrative cinema invited emotional intimacy, the physical closeness of these early images seems rather to be confrontational and comical.

Once these images had emerged from the confines of Edison's Kinetoscope (a peepshow device into which a single viewer peered to see small moving images through a magnifying lens) and were projected on the screen, the new possibility of giganticism added to their unfamiliarity. The huge enlargement of the close-up was advertised as an attraction of facial expression films, as in this announcement from 1902 by the English film company Hepworth for the film *Comic Grimacer*: "A human face shown the full size of the screen is always a comic and interesting sight."[82] If this sort of novelty satisfied the curiosity of popular culture, it could stick in the throats of traditional genteel culture, whose modes of aesthetic representation seemed to be upset by such unsublimated attention to the human face. The editor of the Chicago literary journal *The Chap Book* sputtered in 1896 after seeing *May Irwin Kiss* projected on the screen: "When only life size it was pronounced beastly. But that was nothing to the present sight. Magnified to Gargantuan proportions and repeated three times over it is utterly disgusting."[83] The Rabelaisian reference here may be more significant than the author intended. Early facial close-ups, whether in single-shot facial expression films or as emblematic shots in early multishot films, frequently show the mouth in action, eating, slobbering, kissing, guffawing, and generally partaking of the carnivalesque pleasure of the open orifice in a most unseemly manner. As with Charcot, the camera once again aimed at bodies out of control, but with a very different viewing perspective in mind. Rather than supplying the intimate moments that furnish narrative emphasis or reveal psychology, as is typical of close-ups in later cinema, close-ups in early cinema display monsters and giants, their mouths swallowing and chewing, before viewers who are fascinated (and sometimes repulsed) by the new revelations of such unusual sights. In their very physicality and lack of aesthetic sublimation, such images are closer to the images of scientific facial photography than to the romantic close-ups of shimmering movie stars in later cinema. Thus the simple illusionism that motion pictures seemed to afford could also be experienced as a new mode of perception, as motion reconstituted and defamiliarized by the technology of enlargement. Clearly motion pictures breached new modes of representation.

But if such images seem to subject the human face to an enlargement that relates more to scientific scrutiny than to enraptured absorption, we must not lose sight of the comic nature of these close-ups, quite at odds with the sober discourse of scientific investigation. The popular curiosity that delights in these odd and marvelous expressions and facial behavior parts company with the use of photography as a means of investigation and operates more like a parody of the gnostic impulse. In their delight in the ridiculous and nonsensical, the uncivilized aspects of the body, the contortions rather than the expressions of the face, early facial expression films derive from a long clowning traditions of grimaces which stretches from

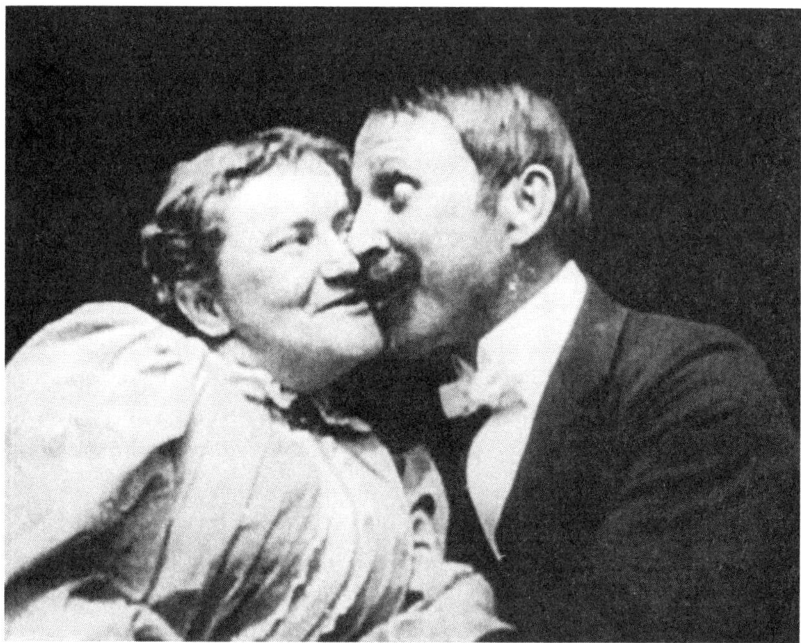

FIGURE 4.8. *May Irwin Kiss* (Thomas Edison, 1896).

medieval jesters through circus traditions to nineteenth-century vaudeville. Seen within this tradition, we can understand the way these early close-ups not only denied access to the psychology of characters but celebrated the very meaninglessness of their swiftly changing grimaces, overturning the gnostic attempt to endow the face with meaning, whether through occult resemblances or photographic scrutiny of its phases.

The grimaces that Duchenne exiled from his system become in these films the major motivation for the facial play. Enlarged enormously, such grimaces became even more grotesque than any performer in the circus or the caf'conc could manage, a true carnival of flesh brought to visual acuity through modern technology. In these films the face cavorts on an open playing field, freed from any relation to narrative or drama or any labor of conventional signification. The performer faces the camera and viewer directly and goes through a succession of expressions dazzling in their range and rapidity.

Of course, the evolution of popular traditions of grimace humor and of scientific investigations in the era of modernity did not take place in hermetically separated realms. Daudet could compare Charcot's demonstration to the Grand Guignol, while at that Parisian theater of horrors, André de Lorde took the *Leçons de Mardi* as the subject for his grim drama *Une leçon à la Salpêtrière*, in which a hysteric patient tosses acid in the face of an intern who has been sadistically torturing her, after her accusations have been dismissed as hysteric symptoms.[84] And as Rae Beth Gordon has shown, the performance styles that were used by such turn of-the-century *caf'conc' grimaciers* as Paulus were compared by fans such as J. K. Huysman to the hysterics of Charcot, who may even have served as models for such performers.[85] In tracing the intersections between scientific investigation and the curiosity of popular culture in the emergence of cinema at the end of the nineteenth century, I want not only to relate these two traditions but to uncover a dialogue between them, centered on the semantically loaded and unceasingly ambiguous representation of the human face. In this encounter, the popular tradition has something to say to the scientific, and vice versa.

Unlike his predecessor Duchenne (who rested secure in his belief in a God-given language of facial expression from which grimaces were excluded), Charcot did investigate facial contortions (and perhaps this is why he strikes us as so modern), seeking behind their chaos for the *facies* of hysteria. Within the amphitheater of his clinic and in the studio of the Photographic Service, his female patients' facial gymnastics were presented to the public. His women patients were doubly victims, subject both to the symptoms of their disease and the control and manipulation of their doctors, who provided, as Didi-Huberman and others have shown, the mise-en-scène of both the Tuesday lessons and the photographs of the *Iconographie*.

But in the early facial expression films, such grimaces explode any framework of interpretation, seeking only the curiosity and laughter of onlookers. Films such as Edison's *Facial Expressions* (1902) or *Goo Goo Eyes* (1903) seem to fulfill Didi-Huberman's fantasy about Charcot's "star" patient Augustine, in which her impulse toward "making a scene" might subvert Charcot's effort to create a mise-en-scène. In her performances, Didi-Huberman declares, Augustine shows "the mastery not of an autocrat, but of an acrobat."[86] Similarly, in Edison's films the female performers contort their faces endlessly in a dazzling display of dexterity and absurdity, invoking amusement, curiosity, occasional revulsion, and ultimately a certain admiration for their novel skill as facial performers.

Clearly, we must resist the impulse to see the images presented by such early films simply as fulfillments of a utopian desire that defies narrative order and scientific symptomology in pursuit of an ethos of pure play and physical transformation, a mode of representation using mimesis to subvert cultural logic. As products of popular culture, these films are deeply complicit in the stereotypes of patriarchal, racist, and economically exploitative ideologies, and the marks of these systems are clearly legible in their imagery. However, they also contain, like the dream world of commodity culture evoked by Walter Benjamin, the seeds of utopian urges.[87] Utopian possibilities are opened by early cinema's nonnarrative configurations of time and its direct confrontation of the viewer with images that seem familiar and yet are also uncanny. If the history of the close-up ultimately extends to the nearly religious absorption in the mystery of the human countenance, the sort that Roland Barthes expresses in his rapture over the face of Garbo, we can see its origins in a very different gnostic impulse, a curiosity about the meanings of the face and an attempt to assert mastery over it through the analysis and classification of its muscle structure, its evolutionary derivation, and its forms of deviance.[88] The desire to know the face in its most transitory and bizarre manifestations was stimulated by the use of photography; but that desire, in turn, also stimulated the development of photography itself, spurring it to increasing technical mastery over time and motion, prodding it toward the actual invention of motion pictures. Paradoxically, once the illusion of motion was technically feasible, emphasis could shift from the dominating eye of the scientist to the skill of the performer as the facial close-up became an arena for grotesque grimaces and goo goo eyes, a delight of facial play.

The face had formerly served as a guarantor of meaning and significance, a mode of communication that exceeded any conventional or cultural system of exchange; but modern science and medicine first dissolved this guarantor into pure physical materiality or a welter of chaotic symptoms. Yet as the techniques of photography attempted to penetrate this apparent chaos and discover new patterns of regularity, the popular art of early cinema again allowed this investigation to dissolve into curiosity and amusement, rehearsing an encounter with representation that the techniques of aesthetic modernism would replay on a different level, borrowing, as Surrealism in particular acknowledged, a great deal from its popular predecessors.

5

Landscape and the Fantasy of Moving Pictures: Early Cinema's Phantom Rides

PLACING THE WORLD IN A FRAME: THE TECHNOLOGIES OF LANDSCAPE

Da nun alles, ales sich bewegte,
Baume, Fluß und Blumen und der Schleier
Und der zarte Fuß der Allerschönsten,
Glaubt ihr wohl, ich sei auf meinen Felsen
Wie ein Felsen still und fest geblieben?

Now everything, but everything was moving,
Trees, the flowers, filmy robe, the river
Delicate feet of the girl in all her beauty—
Do you think I sat so calm and steadfast
Rocklike on my rock a moment longer?

GOETHE, "AMOR AS LANDSCAPE PAINTER" (1787)

Landscape is not a genre of art, but a medium.

W. J. T. MITCHELL, "IMPERIAL LANDSCAPE"

What makes nature into a landscape? What aesthetic and technical processes transform the formal possibilities of natural surroundings into im-

This essay first appeared in *Cinema and Landscape*, ed. Graeme Harper and Jonathan Rayner (Bristol: Intellect, 2010), 31–70, with the following dedication: "For Iris Cahn who started me thinking, Scott McDonald who focused my argument and Claribel Cone, the painter."

ages? Alberti inaugurated the theory of Western painting by defining a picture as something traced within a quadrilateral that served as a window onto the world. Placing a view of nature within a frame, fixing that view within a geometrical frame of reference, defined landscape as an art form. A frame that organizes a composition geometrically, while simultaneously opening a view into a depth—this describes the double aspects of the landscape. As Renzo Dubbini puts it:

> In Western Europe the invention of landscape painting coincided with the elaboration of the *veduta* or "view" as a space contained within a picture, but which opened up the setting to the world beyond. The discovery of an adequate technique for framing and defining depth signalled the invention of landscape as a cultural space, visible in all its aspects.[1]

Landscape painting displayed the mastery of perspective and composition that defined Western easel painting as an aesthetic form. The work of seventeenth-century landscapist Claude Lorrain (as well as the work of Gaspar Poussin) provided an archetype for landscape, balancing compositional frame and recessive depth—containment and distance. Claude created synthetic ideal landscapes, artistic visions that never claimed to be records of actual topographies (as Edgar Poe said in his landscape fantasy "The Domain of Arnheim," "No such paradises are to be found in reality as have glowed on the canvass of Claude").[2]

This "Ideal Landscape" schema provided painters with a structure for centuries. In a Claude landscape, towering trunks of backlit trees crowned by fanlike foliage framed a recessive arrangement of space, theatrical in effect. These powerfully vertical trees served as *coulisse* (a theatrical term for the flats that conceal and naturalize the offstage space of the wings) or *repoussoirs*, darker elements framing the foreground, setting off the landscape's glowing central depth and drawing the viewer's gaze into a distance dissolved in a luminous blur of aerial perspective.[3] Claude created a clearly marked succession of planes, based in an ordered presentation of natural elements. A darkened, largely empty, horizontal foreground came first, often populated by fairly small human figures or *staffage*. Towering trees provided the vertical frame, while streams or lakes led the viewer's gaze into a middle distance where water shimmered with reflected light. An atmospherically diffused vista of mountains defined the distance, outlining a horizon dominated by a luminous sky. Ideal Landscapes wove together these clearly marked stages of recession with a harmonic gradation and variety of light that unified the image.

By the late eighteenth century such visual schemata served not only as a template for landscape painting, but as a new model for viewing and experiencing nature, finding its clearest articulation in England in the concept of the "picturesque." As both a new mode of aesthetic experience and a means of defining what constituted a proper landscape, the picturesque not only served as a guide to creating and viewing painting, it also directed the gaze of tourists and inspired the ground plans of gardeners. In 1734 poet Alexander Pope had declared that "all gardening is landscape-painting," and gardens in the eighteenth century provided optical experiences as much as spaces for wandering or the display of plant life.[4] Even in the seventeenth century, formal French gardens applied perspectival and visual effects taken from theatrical designers, while somewhat later the more "natural" English gardens frequently took Claude's landscapes as their model.[5] British landscape artists even added the "prime ingredient of picturesque view"—crumbling ruins made to order—to satisfy the "love for broken and rough surfaces" so praised by James Gilpin, chief theorist of the picturesque.[6] The picturesque defined gardens as a succession of images, carefully ordered and artificially created by the gardener's construction, employing colors and textures as well as devices of framing and (often forced) perspective.

"The picturesque moment"—the passion for experiencing nature as a picture that reached a climax in the late eighteenth century—also introduced the "Claude glass," a device used by artists, artistic amateurs, and simple tourists to transform the natural world into a source of endless images.[7] Named for the landscapist (who most likely never used one), the Claude glass consisted of a handheld mirror, usually darkly tinted and convex, most often oval but sometimes rectangular. As Hunt puts it, "the use of the mirror . . . concentrated for its owner all picturesque possibilities":[8]

> To the picturesque tourist and amateur artist [the Claude glass] reflected the real world, yet also collected carefully chosen images within the oval or rectangular frame and colored them with its one coordinating tint.[9]

More than earthmoving, fake ruins, or even carefully arranged belvederes and observation towers, the Claude glass exemplified the process of turning nature into landscape through a technology of vision. Arnaud Maillet describes the subtle but essential optical transformations the mirror accomplished: "The sensible reduction of objects reflected in the mirror occurs on two levels: one concerns colors, the other involves the visual field."[10] The tinting of the mirror lowered the level of light, "reducing not only the lights and shadows but also the colors to a tonal unity," casting the scene into an artificial twilight in which the values of disparate colors merged.[11] The convex mirror (like a wide-angle camera lens) creates an artificial sense of distance, reducing the scene, as Maillet puts it, "in order to unify."[12] Gilpin claimed this allowed viewers "to grasp the landscape in a single glance, like a painting."[13] The Claude glass processed nature optically, yielding an epitome of the visual qualities valorized by the picturesque: an image carefully framed and optically lifted out of an undifferentiated visual field—automatically creating a landscape.

While the "picturesque" landscape model encountered challenges in the nineteenth century—from, successively, the Romantic sublime, the less ideal compositional schemata emerging from the Barbizon school of plein air painting, and eventually the Impressionists—the Ideal Landscape remained the model against which innovations in landscape painting were measured. The schema's longevity depended on balancing landscape's essential tension between geometrical framing and illusionistic depth. The Claudean recessive landscape solicits a voyage of both eye and body into the depth of the scene, inviting spectator fantasies of entrance and exploration into this bounded and avowedly artificial space.

How does cinema relate to this landscape tradition? Too often, discussions of landscape in cinema simply assume that films, at least certain films, contain landscapes, positing a simple transfer of visual principles and effects from canvas to cinema screen. I believe we must first ask what the concepts of the landscape and the picturesque offered to cinema as it emerged at the end of the nineteenth century. Perhaps even more vitally, we should ask in what ways cinema transformed the possibilities of landscape, both as a form of imagery and as a way of experiencing nature. In this essay I will attempt to sketch aspects of this question, focusing primarily on nineteenth-century American landscapes and their interaction with technology.

LANDSCAPE AND TECHNOLOGY: THE RAILROAD

> . . . this admirable invention of the railroad . . . is destined to do away with those stale ideas of home and fireside, and substitute something better.
>
> NATHANIEL HAWTHORNE, *The House of the Seven Gables* (1851)

In a footnote buried in perhaps the most serious discussion of the inspiration landscape painting has offered American cinema, *The Garden in the Machine*, historian of American avant-garde cinema Scott McDonald seems to question the relation between landscape and early cinema that he explores in the body of the work. Referring to a pioneering essay by Iris Cahn that related early American films to the "Great Picture" tradition of Frederic Church, McDonald notes:

> The Library of Congress lists dozens of titles that claim as their central focus not only American landscapes but also, in a good many instances, precisely those landscapes made so popular by the Hudson River and Rocky Mountain painters of the mid-nineteenth century: The Catskill Mountains, Niagara Falls, Yosemite Valley, Yellowstone.

But McDonald then demurs:

> However, while titles of many of these early films identify landscapes as their subject, it must be said that many of the films are really about railway travel through landscapes and are more fully focused on the railroad tracks into the landscapes than on the landscapes themselves.[14]

While I might question what it means to "really" make a landscape "the subject" of a film, I take seriously McDonald's sense that these early films of famous tourist landscapes project a different experience of place than the nineteenth-century painting that may have inspired them. While this difference needs to be explored rather than assumed, I believe it opens essential questions about landscape's relation to modern space and technology as exemplified by the cinema.

Seemingly offhandedly, McDonald contrasts "landscapes themselves" with films "fully focused on railroad tracks *into* the landscapes" (my emphasis). A true landscape, it would seem, maintains a certain distance from the viewer, an invisible barrier to actual penetration. Early films, shot by cameras mounted on the fronts of locomotives tracking into famous landscapes, violated the barrier that defines contemplative beauty. As opposed to the carefully framed, distanced, and *static* picture offered by Claudean Ideal Landscape, early landscape films actually moved into the landscape via technology. Not only do the tracks travel into the frame, but the camera that rides upon them as well, transporting the viewer as an ersatz passenger, rather than framing a view for a transfixed and immobilized viewer. In doing so these films make explicit a fantasy of penetration and visual voyage implied in the Claudean model, described by Rachael DeLue: "Nothing obstructs the passage of the eye from zone to zone; indeed, its traversal is made easy by alternating strips of light and dark, Claudean in origin, that ferry it from foreground to depth in an orderly fashion."[15] But to literalize and actually achieve such transit—indeed to industrialize it, as in early train films—involves an extreme transformation in the landscape tradition. This essay will explore this transformation in spectatorship and the transformations in landscape technology that made it possible.

The title of McDonald's book wittily inverts another famous title: Leo Marx's 1964 *The Machine in the Garden: Technology and the Pastoral Ideal in America*. Marx analyzed the encounter of American culture with the machine, typified by the intense experience of the invasion of the American landscape by the locomotive, which he described as a "sense of the machine as a sudden, shocking intruder upon a fantasy of idyllic satisfaction."[16] Henry David Thoreau's description of a locomotive passing by Walden Pond captured the vulnerability of the American wilderness (and the pastoral ideal it represented) to the onslaught of industrialism. McDonald claims American avant-garde film- and video-makers as Thoreau's ideological heirs, creating a reservation of wildness and pastoral contemplation in opposition to the industrial filmmaking of Hollywood. These often avowedly pastoral or ecological motion pictures, McDonald claims, ultimately owe inspiration to the visionary tradition of the American landscape exemplified by Thomas Cole, Frederic Church, and Albert Bierstadt. McDonald and Marx avoid an inert dichotomy between nature and culture in favor of a dialectical narrative of the way landscape depends on technology, even as it is threatened by it. Extending this intricate and often traumatic interaction between nature and technology to early cinema, I would claim landscape must be viewed not simply as a refuge from technology but, in a complex manner, as its product.

The railroad initially carried the freight of this encounter between wilderness and technology. As a mode of transportation, as a business dependent partly on tourism, and as the beneficiary of the greatest federal land grants in US history, the railroad literally opened up the American countryside to appropriation as landscape. The railroad used aestheticized images of American nature (including landscape paintings commissioned by the railroads themselves) as tools of commerce. Thus, rather than posing polar opposites, technology and the industrial expansion of American business simultaneously generate and exploit the idea of natural landscape. Indeed, as Richard Grusin argues in *Culture, Technology and America's National Parks*, even the wilderness reserves of national parks

> need to be understood as technologies for the reproduction of that very nature which is being threatened and destroyed. . . . Neither gardens in the

machine nor machines in the garden, national parks are machines that are made up of gardens, or gardens that function as machines.[17]

Marx's work outlined a uniquely American conception, a faith that a pastoral ideal could be realized, not as a mythical Golden Age nostalgically contemplated, but as a national ideal charting plans for future development. Envisioned by such figures as Thomas Jefferson, a pastoral state could be attained through cooperation with technology, rather than in opposition to it. In this vision, to quote Marx, "the railroad is the chosen vehicle of bringing America into its own as a pastoral utopia."[18] However, the harmony initially imagined by this pastoral vision gave way to a growing sense of ambivalence and danger, embodied in Thoreau's warning, "we do not ride upon the railroad; it rides upon us."[19] But even within this minatory mode, the convergence between landscape as the redeeming force of natural energy (what Thoreau called "wildness") and the force of technology remains. The modern American landscape envisioned a new "technological sublime" that cast its spell even over Thoreau as the harbinger of a new mythology: "When I hear the iron horse make the hills echo with his snort like thunder, shaking the earth with his feet, and breathing fire and smoke from his nostrils . . . it seems as if the earth had got a race now worthy to inhabit it."[20] This dialectic between the seemingly pastoral landscape and modern technology penetrates deeply into the history and concept of American landscape painting. To understand the transformation the railroad brought to this tradition, we need to trace the long-standing fantasy of entering into a landscape painting.

Ideal Landscapes, including American versions, frequently place diminutive *staffage* figures in the foreground in postures of beholding (backs to the viewer, facing into the scene and occasionally gesturing reactions of delight or pointing into the depth) strongly evoking a mood of contemplation and its religious connotations of awe. While these figures posed on the threshold of the composition maintain a certain distance from the view, beholding the wonders of nature, they also inaugurate imagined narratives of entrance into the represented space. Landscape as a form did not wait for the cinema to provide an image of entrance into the landscape, although the new medium certainly transformed both the means and meaning of doing so. The pronounced perspective of the Ideal Landscape and such compositional devices as streams, pathways, or minute travelers traditionally lead the viewer's eye into the distance, generating a fantasy of penetration and exploration.

Denis Diderot, in his description of the Salon of 1763, first verbalized this fantasy of entering into a landscape in response to a painting by Philippe-Jacques de Loutherbourg (whose optical device the Eidophusikon offered an early mechanical form of motion pictures), imagining lingering among grazing herds and then wandering into the distance.[21] As Rachael DeLue points out, "for Diderot the success of specific types of landscape representations could depend on the encouragement of this fiction."[22] With its display of perspective as an invitation to voyage, the landscape seduces the gaze into fantasies of physical entrance.

In American landscape painting these imagined trajectories into the distance increasingly manifested a national sense of destiny in the westward course of the empire.[23] Albert Boime calls the view from a height into the distance characteristic of American landscapes "the magisterial gaze," in which the fantasy of penetration takes on a national imperative of spatial expansion and historical progress,

> taking us rapidly from an elevated geographical zone to another below and from one temporal zone to another, locating progress synchronically in time and space. Within this fantasy of domain and empire gained from looking out and down over broad expanses is the subtext of metaphorical forecast of the future.[24]

The image of the locomotive impinging on a natural landscape that Marx traced through American literature also infiltrated modern American landscape painting. Images produced by artists associated with America's first great school of landscape painting, the Hudson River School, portrayed the ideal pastoral vision of technology that Marx described, with trains and railroads integrated into Claudean views framed by foreground trees, with waterways or pathways snaking toward the distant horizon where luminous skies meet mountains blurred by aerial perspective (see Thomas Cole, *River in the Catskills*, 1843; Thomas Doughty, *A View of Swampscott*, 1847; Jasper Cropsey, *Starrucca Viaduct, Pennsylvania*, 1865; George Inness, *Delaware Water Gap*, 1861). However, as Barbara Novak claims, trains and railways hardly dominate these compositions: "How remote and insignificant are the trains that discreetly populate the American landscape paintings of the mid-century!"[25] Placed in the middle distance, Thoreau's titanic locomotive appears miniaturized and firmly integrated into an ordered and hierarchical schema, its trail of smoke or steam, as Novak points out, blending with the billowing clouds.[26] Marx notes that "these artists were bent on making the new machine blend as inconspicuously as possible into its natural surroundings."[27]

However, these seemingly harmonic Ideal Landscapes also interwove ambivalence into their celebration of America's errand into the wilderness, typified by the complex composition of *The Oxbow*, painted in 1836 by Thomas Cole, dean of American landscape painters. A view from Mount Holyoke in Massachusetts of a point where the Connecticut River takes on an "oxbow" shape, circling in on itself, the composition divides between untamed nature on the craggy mountain on the left and an agricultural landscape, with fields and villages viewed below along the riverbanks on the right. While the nearly allegorical composition seems to reflect the westward trek of civilization, clearing the land and making it fertile, it also reflects Cole's own questioning of the *Course of Empire* (the title of a sequence of five allegorical paintings he was working on at the same time as this landscape, chronicling a pessimistic view of man's—and America's?—progress from savage and pastoral states to decadence and destruction).[28] Angela Miller convincingly reads the curve of the oxbow as forming a question mark, posing Cole's own uncertainty about American expansion into the wilderness (the painting includes a minuscule self-portrait of Cole as contemplative figure, a painter sketching at his easel, firmly placed on the wilderness side of the image).

America's greatest and most complex landscape painter, George Inness, supplied a similar riddling image in his *The Lackawanna Valley* from 1856 or 1857. In contrast to Inness's extraordinary experimental paintings of the decades to come, this landscape basically follows the Claudean formula, including a *repoussoir* tree framing the left of the image, mountains dissolving in aerial perspective in the distance, and a recumbent *staffage* figure in the foreground gazing toward the horizon. However, in the middle distance a medium-sized locomotive steams toward the foreground, leaving behind a marked trail of smoke and steam, with the industrial structure of a railway roundhouse visible beyond. While still not dominating the foreground, this locomotive nonetheless breaches the discretion maintained by trains in most landscapes of the era. Novak draws our attention to the manner that tree stumps mark the foreground edge of the painting and dominate the zone of middle distance that bridges the contemplative figure and the locomotive. While the tree stump served as a recognized symbol of the march of civilization into the wilderness, clearing the land for future planting and building, this field of stumps seems excessive.[29] Not all critics share Novak's critical reading of technology in Inness's painting, and Inness himself indicated his preference for "the civilized landscape" that bore the signs of "every act of man, everything of labor, effort, suffering, want, anxiety, necessity, love," over "the savage and untamed."[30] The fact that the painting was commissioned by the Delaware and Lackawanna Railway indicates its sponsors felt it celebrated their achievements (although that Inness found it years later in a curiosity shop in Mexico and bought it for a few dollars may indicate something else!). I feel that what Novak calls the "shocking" quality of the painting comes from the mismatch between the contemplative Claudean schema and the new dynamics of motion and transformation in the subject. The recumbent figure seems to have wandered in from another painting as he gazes into this new realm of speed and energy.

Inness's commission from the Lackawanna Railway was hardly unique. The railroad industry, which completed a transcontinental network during the greatest period of American landscape painting, forged commercial alliances with landscape painters. Boime claims the "magisterial gaze" he isolates in landscape paintings was "converted into the diagonal of a line of tracks and speeding locomotive."[31] The railroad industry understood that, while their major commerce was freight transportation, tourism could form an important side business. To encourage the traffic in tourists searching for picturesque landscapes, tours for painters were arranged by railroad companies even before the Civil War and became a common practice in the next decades.[32] Landscapes were produced that depended on railroads to carry painters to their sites, and were commissioned by the companies in order to incite a desire to see such views on the part of potential passengers. Railway magnates were major patrons of such painters as Inness, Church, Bierstadt, and, most gloriously, Thomas Moran. Train travel extended the tradition of the picturesque tour, with guidebooks describing the most picturesque locations railroads could reach, and indicating the sights available to the train passenger from her window.[33] Even when railroads or trains were not featured in American landscapes, the railroad stands outside the frame as a major motivation for the vision they created.

But the new technology of the railroad did more than appropriate the older landscape tradition; as in Inness's painting, tensions inherent in the encounter led to visible transformations and the rise of new media. Susan Danly points out:

> Painters tended to include the railroad as a small compositional detail fully integrated into the overall format of their landscape, while photographers more often monumentalized railroad structures and emphasized innovative building techniques rather than the natural world.[34]

Mass-produced chromolithographs aimed at a popular audience often placed the dramatic locomotive at the center of compositions, belching smoke and flame and speeding through the landscape.[35] Was the Ideal Landscape, amazingly stable for centuries, irrevocably challenged by new technological modes of travel, new spaces defined by industrial appropriation, and new media better suited to portraying these transformations? Would this convergence of technology end in the elimination of landscape both as form and as experience? Historian and theorist of the transformations the railway brought to the nineteenth century Wolfgang Schivelbusch claims the experience of train travel transformed perceptions of space and time. The traditional experience of landscape deriving from other forms of travel changed with train travel, as the train's velocity diminished visual perception of the passing countryside, blurring the foreground, eliminating detail, and abolishing the stasis of contemplation.

But rather than simply erasing the view, Schivelbusch claims, "The railroad creates a new landscape."[36] For detail it substituted variety and transformation, the pleasures of speed and rapid succession replacing contemplation. Schivelbusch dubs this new mode of viewing landscapes "panoramic perception." Seated unmoving in her upholstered seat, watching the landscape roll by through the glass window of her compartment, the train observer simultaneously seemed physically immobilized and perceptually mobile. Thus, as Schivelbusch describes it, "Panoramic perception, in contrast to traditional perception, no longer belongs to the same space as the perceived objects: the traveler sees the objects, landscapes, etc., *through* the apparatus which moves him through the world."[37]

But as important as this transformation in landscape perception might be, it may pose less a radical break with the model of the Ideal Landscape than a shift along the gamut of the picturesque. Not only had the Claude glass already set up the essential mediation of an apparatus of viewing mediating between observer and nature, but the charm of picturesque gardens and the reflections captured in the glass derived as much from motion and changing viewpoints as from the contemplation of fixed compositions. In his 1770 essay "On Modern Gardening," Horace Walpole had described the enjoyment of a garden as mobile, claiming, "Every journey is made through a succession of pictures."[38] Gilpin used his Claude glass while traveling in a chaise, savoring not only the singularity of an image but its transformation: "Forms, and colours in brightest array, fleet before us, and if the transient glance of a good composition happen to unite with them, we should give any price to fix and appropriate the scene."[39] The fixed image and its contemplation still provided the privileged mode of landscape viewing, but the pleasures of transience, motion, variety, succession, and, especially, mediation through an apparatus of viewing already played a key role. Throughout the nineteenth century, fascination in the mobile view of a landscape gave rise to new technologies of motion pictures and mobile viewpoints, transforming the picturesque model by radicalizing its implication of motion and penetration.

TECHNOLOGY OF LANDSCAPE: PANORAMA

> To reflect rigorously on the particular pathos that lies hidden in the art of the panoramas. On the particular relation of this art to nature, but also, and above all, to history.
>
> WALTER BENJAMIN, *Passagenwerke*, CONVOLUTE Q

Schivelbusch took the term "panoramic," of course, from a major technological transformation in the nature of landscape in the nineteenth century, one which rivaled photography in innovation and popularity: the panorama. This form of visual entertainment was once so omnipresent and its name so popular (historian Stephan Oettermann calls it "the first visual mass medium"), it became absorbed into common language and is generally used today with little sense (and rarely any direct experience) of its original reference.[40] The nearly total eclipse of the panorama in the twentieth century has led to a lack of acknowledgment of its very great influence over the way landscapes were conceived. A technical device first and foremost, the panorama was patented in 1787 by Robert Barker in its original form: a painted canvas of such unaccustomed scale and shape, housed in such a manner as to create the effect of an image without limits—*tableau sans bornes*.[41] The panorama brought the landscape image to a crisis, destroying its defining aspect—the frame. As historian of panoramas Bernard Comment comments, "Abolishing the frame was the only way of transcending the limits of traditional representation."[42] Displayed in a specially designed building whose unique construction constituted the core of Barker's invention, the panorama depended as much on architecture as on painting for its effect. As in garden landscaping, the panorama functioned as an environmental, rather than simply a representational, form, creating a new space as much as it represented one. (As Comment puts it, "The aim of the panorama was to produce—using all available means—the illusion of another space.")[43] From the moment of entrance, the design of the panorama space determined the spectator's experience as much as (or more than) the composition of the canvas, truly becoming an apparatus of vision. Comment summarizes the control of the viewing process through control of point of view and lighting:

> To gain access to a panorama canvas, the spectator had to walk along a darkened corridor so as to forget the reality of the world outside and so that the effect of being plunged into the total illusion of the representation would have more impact. Viewers were confined to an observation platform and could not approach the canvas. A canopy concealed the overhead lighting that entered from behind a glass panel.[44]

The viewer was completely surrounded by the circular painting, while architectural design concealed the upper and lower limits of the image, giving the illusion of a boundless view. The construction of the building carefully controlled the lighting, filtering the daylight that shone on the painting and leaving viewers in relative shadow. As in the 1831 panorama of the Battle of Navarino, in which the audience stood on a realistic mock-up of the deck of a naval man of war, the viewing area and the space situated between it and the canvas frequently became the site of three-dimensional props (and even figures) that merged into the two-dimensional images of the canvas.

As Oettermann points out, the panorama liberated landscape vision from the constraint of the frame, delivering a complete view of the encompassing horizon. However, the observer was completely subject to the exhibition schema, a 360-degree space that confined the observer in "a complete prison for the eye."[45] A German aesthetician, J. A. Eberhardt, described this sensation as "this ghastly dream from which I have to wrench myself against my will."[46] But the drive toward this panoramic viewpoint remained a product of the picturesque impulse. Oettermann relates the panorama to a late eighteenth-century passion for viewing the horizon evident in the observation towers constructed in picturesque gardens and landscapes, as well as the popularity of balloon ascents as a means of viewing landscapes. The picturesque certainly sought to confine a view within a frame, but it passionately desired to extend that frame into new, unexplored spaces and into greater and more expansive dimensions, "surrounding and seizing the whole," as Oettermann puts it.[47] More than any previous form, the panorama realized Diderot's fantasy of the viewer's entrance into a fictive world, but it also transformed it.

Instead of the single perspective of Claude's theatrical space with its enframed central view into the depth, the panorama embraced the viewer, or more properly, the viewers, offering what Oettermann describes as a "democratic perspective" as "the infinite number of points of view are matched—theoretically—by an infinite number of viewing points from which observers can look at the picture without distortion."[48] Rather than a single observer regarding the scene in isolated contemplation, the panorama attracted an "audience," a commercial mass made up of varied classes, who wandered from viewing point to viewing point to obtain the full effect of the image. The German explorer and scientist Alexander von Humboldt, whose epic account of his global travels, *Cosmos*, greatly influenced American landscape painters, praised the totalizing effect of the panorama, which surrounded "the spectator, inclosed [*sic*] as it were, within a magic circle, and wholly removed from all the disturbing influences of reality."[49] Viewers attested to the realistic effect of the panorama on a number of levels. Panoramas featuring the sea, for instance, caused seasickness in a number of viewers, reportedly even Queen Charlotte of England.[50] Some decades later, a large Newfoundland dog supposedly tried to leap into the sea in a panorama of Malta.[51]

These stories indicate two aspects of panorama spectatorship that challenge the tradition of landscape contemplation. First, they were the responses of an audience rather than a single viewer withdrawn into himself. The panorama audience was not only multiple but varied, made up not only of connoisseurs but of gawkers from the middle and even the working class.[52] Further, whether attributed to queens or dogs, physical sensations and reactions rather than intellectual contemplation emanated from the panorama. Although the panorama might seem an absolute fulfilment of the fantasies of being absorbed into a representation, for many observers it crossed the line that separated art from popular spectacle and modern technology.

Jacques-Louis David told his students to attend Prevost's panorama "to study nature." David's purported comment carries a double edge; if he praised the panorama's verisimilitude, he did not claim it to be the best place to study art. A triumph of perceptual realism, to the neoclassical ideal, the panorama was too real.[53] Britain's great landscape painter John Constable declared, after visiting Daguerre's diorama, "It is without the pale of art, because its object is deception. Art pleases by reminding, not deceiving."[54] The panorama's verisimilitude, art critics repeated throughout the nineteenth century, aimed at fooling the eye, not the true blending of realism and idealism that art should aspire to. A critic praising the effect of a German panorama in 1880 still had to add parenthetically, "The fundamental aim of the whole—to create the greatest possible illusion and confound appearances with reality—is not artistic."[55]

The panorama had many predecessors and successors, from Loutherbourg's Eidophusikon to Daguerre's diorama, all of which offered what I have called elsewhere the supplement of realism, the addition to traditional representations of something felt to be "missing" for the achievement of total verisimilitude, whether the scale and circular format of the panorama, lighting effects of the diorama, or the movement given to the Eidophusikon.[56] These technologies exemplify a new anxiety about the limits of representation that was repressed as beyond the pale of aesthetics by academic discourse, but exerted a fascination over the broader public. In the United States the influence of the panorama was pervasive, but the greatest enthusiasm was reserved for a native variation, the moving panorama. The vast lengths of these panoramas were measured in miles. (Banville's panorama of the Mississippi was advertised as three miles in length, while Smith's rival panorama was claimed to measure four miles.) Mounted on twin sets of rollers and like a gargantuan version of a Chinese scroll painting, the moving panorama unrolled bit by bit before theatrical audiences, accompanied by music and a spoken lecture commenting on the views.[57] Eschewing the effect of total immersion via the 360-degree format, the moving panorama instead emphasized an ever-expanding image, presenting a succession of views for a seated audience, an experience whose duration simulated the impression of a condensed journey by train or railway.

This literalization of the temporal and spatial expanse of the imaginary journey, endowed with epic portions far beyond the Claudean horizon promised by the Ideal Landscape, strikes many critics as a peculiarly American response to the landscape tradition (Oettermann dubs it "an art form for American tastes").[58] As Angela Miller claims, "The vehicle of the grand plot embedded within American landscape was the road, or its fluid counterpart, the river, connecting the incidents of the landscape in a unified whole."[59] From the pioneering treks of Western expansion to the counter-journeys of Huck and Jim down the Mississippi, or Ahab and crew across the ocean, the sense of movement and journey offered a central image of the protean American identity.

Perhaps pressured by the popularity of moving and static panoramas as a new stage in the portrayal of landscape, American landscape painters seemed to respond (or in some cases anticipate) the new forms within their work. Most obviously Fredric Church's display of his massive canvas *The Heart of the Andes* as an elaborately stage-managed quasi-theatrical event, complete with paid admission, recalled the viewer address of the panorama. Iris Cahn describes the exhibition of this and similar "Great Pictures":

> Viewers would pay admission, enter a *darkened* room and sit on benches to stare at one single enormous, *illuminated* canvas. The frame surrounding the painting was often dark wood (unlike the prevailing gilt of the day) and so blended into walls draped with light absorbing fabrics. Gaslight and skylight controlled by draperies created illusion that light was emanating from the canvas itself, that one was looking, perhaps, onto a real scene. Opera glasses were used, allowing the observer to enlarge and reframe the parts of the larger canvas. Pamphlets were distributed, their words functioning much like slide lecture narrations, or as film intertitles would later. The words traced a visual path for the eye through the various planes of the painting, explaining exotic locations, unfamiliar plants, animals and geographic formations.[60]

The Great Pictures of the American landscape painters of the mid-nineteenth century aspired to the domains of high art. But in their pursuit of a more expansive form of the picturesque, the romantic sublime, and a unique sense of American terrain, like the panorama, they pushed against the limits of the Ideal Landscape, creating new attitudes toward framing and spectatorship. Perhaps ironically (or perhaps inevitably) these experiments converged with the commercial technological modes of emerging mass media.

Gilpin had theorized that the titanic scale of the American landscape might exceed the possibilities of the picturesque. The lakes of Switzerland or Italy could serve as material for picturesque landscapes, but, Gilpin claimed, "the *larger* lakes, like those of America, are disproportioned to their accompaniments: the water occupies too large a space, and throws the scenery too much into the distance."[61] Thomas Moran's sublime Turneresque portrayal of the Great Lakes, Longfellow's "shining Big-Sea-Water," in his series of paintings based on *Hiawatha*, demonstrate the inspiration such scale could provide in expanding, if not exploding, the concept of the picturesque. Thomas Cole, in his famous essays on American scenery, admitted there were those who claimed that the American landscape was "rude without picturesqueness, and monotonous without sublimity."[62] Cole's own attempts to blend the Ideal Landscape with the sublime show the dynamics of American landscape, tensions that he manages to hold in equilibrium, while the next generation found it necessary to seek new solutions. Cole's tendency to create series of paintings in which action unfolded through a succession of canvases also seems related to the panorama tradition. Scott McDonald has beautifully detailed the protocinematic flow of action and meaning in Cole's 1840 series *The Voyage of Life*, moving from one canvas to the next, the river providing a constant pathway for the voyage, even as the apparent "screen direction of the boat reverses from 'shot' to 'shot.'"[63] Likewise, the five canvases of his *Course of Empire* fix the same basic geographical spot (the distant mountain with its precarious balanced boulder providing a point of reference for each view, shifting a bit but never radically switching viewpoint). Such stable spatial reference underscores the temporal transformations of each scene, as the course of empire runs through its historical cycle. This practice particularly recalls Daguerre's diorama, in which a change in lighting radically transformed a scene of a single location—from day to night, from spring to winter.

Using a variety of means—scale, a use of seriality, or theatrical modes of presentation—American landscape painters in the nineteenth century absorbed the challenges to framing and spectatorship exemplified by the various forms of panorama entertainments. We see in these landscapes the mastery of framing contending with an energy striving to burst them asunder in pursuit of a new relation to the spectator. The location of the spectator, increasingly addressed as an embodied physical presence with physiological sensations, became a contested site.

HOW CAN A LANDSCAPE EXPERIENCE BE FRAMED?

> I long for the return of the dioramas, whose brutal and enormous magic has the power to impose on me a useful illusion. I would rather go to the theater and feast my eyes on the scenery, in which I find my dearest dreams treated with consummate skill and tragic conclusions. These things, because they are false, are infinitely closer to the truth, whereas the majority of our landscape painters are liars, precisely because they fail to lie.
>
> CHARLES BAUDELAIRE, "SALON OF 1859"

In the nineteenth century, American landscape painting confronted a series of challenges: new subject matter—such as the titanic proportions of the expanses of American nature; technological transformations—such as the railroad; and new models of spectatorship—such as those offered by the panorama. While the picturesque tried to maintain the balance of framing and recession exemplified by the Ideal Landscape, these new challenges pushed the landscape increasingly toward a companion concept: the sublime, the romantic experience of the infinite, of experience itself pushed beyond limits, which appeared both as the intensification of the picturesque and its explosion. However, the older models of the sublime, supplied by Salvatore Rosa and his landscapes of wild trees and stormy mountains populated by banditti, hardly seemed adequate for a new technological age, which could be satisfied only with a new technological sublime. The sublime supplied less a model for new compositions than an impulse to explore new technical options, pursuing new effects for the viewer. The increased canvas size introduced by Moran, Church, and Bierstadt did more than simply contain the scale of the American landscape; massive paintings sought to convey the overwhelmingly sublime effect of the American landscape on the observer, especially as the Rockies replaced the White Mountains and the Colorado superseded the Hudson.

In this respect the tradition of the Great Painting took up the challenge of the panorama, aspiring to its power over a spectator. New concepts of spectatorship were emerging—yet these concepts do not so much reverse the traditional stance of the viewer as force artists and viewers to confront contradictions inherent in the sublime form of landscape. Andrew Wilton, speaking of J. M. W. Turner's massive and sublime landscapes (which exerted a decisive influence on the American landscape), claimed, "Landscape was no longer to be contemplated from afar, but participated in an immediate experience."[64] In fact, the nineteenth-century landscape spectator seems torn between several positions: the traditional distanced contemplation called for by the Ideal Landscape; Diderot's fantasy of lingering penetration and transversal; the domineering and surveying magisterial gaze of exploration and appropriation; the intense sensual subjection to the overwhelming sublime experience of nature (in Turner, Friedrich, or Church); the technological illusion of being engulfed by the image of the panorama; and the fascinated, but distanced, mobile gaze of the panoramic train traveler.

The affinity between the Great Paintings and the panorama did not pass unnoticed, or uncensored, since the panoramas themselves were considered outside the bounds of art. The subtlest American critic of the era, James Jackson Jarvies, satirically invoked the country bumpkin who, seeing Bierstadt's Great Painting *The Rocky Mountain* (1863), "mistook [the painting] for a panorama, and after waiting a while asked when the thing was going to move." The rube, Jarvies claimed, "was a more sagacious critic than he knew himself to be."[65] Jarvies himself criticized the painting: "All this quality of painting is more or less panoramic from being so material in its artistic features as always to keep the spectator at a distance. He can never forget his point of view, and that he is looking at a painting."[66] We find here a contradictory welter of metaphors, like Baudelaire's oxymoron of truthful illusions, that reveal the contested nature of landscape spectatorship at the middle of the nineteenth century. Did the Ideal Landscape or did the panorama keep the spectator at a distance? Was this distance a good or a bad thing, a product of artistic contemplation or the inevitable disillusioned reaction to a spectacle aimed at deception? In what sense could a spectator "forget his point of view"? Did panoramic perception bring one into the landscape, fulfilling a longstanding fantasy, or did it further separate viewer and spectacle by affirming the power of the apparatus through which things were viewed?

This series of nearly irresolvable contradictions points, I believe, to an anxiety about the nature of direct experience in the modern era, a desire for modes of representation intended to reproduce not simply a landscape, but the full sensual experience of being there, often employing sensual supplements (late panoramas added simulations of breezes, smells, and kinesthetic experiences such as the pitching of a boat).[67] But the pursuit of direct experience need not take such a literal path in its final manifestation. In preparing for perhaps the greatest nineteenth-century painting of the new technology of the locomotive, Turner's *Rain, Steam, Speed* (1843), the artist reportedly stuck his head out a train window during a torrential downpour for some nine minutes, then sat soaked in streaming water, contemplating his experience with closed eyes for another quarter of an hour.[68] A similar story is told about Turner being lashed to a ship's mast during a storm.[69] Whether the artist directly experienced seasickness beforehand or the observer felt nauseous as a result, the forms of aesthetic experience were reaching for a new identification with bodily sensation.

But we encounter again the paradox of the panoramic. Did the new technology, such as train travel, bring one closer to a more intense, more sublime experience of "rain, steam, and speed," or did it remove one from the world it traveled through? Recall that Schivelbusch defined panoramic perception not in terms of being environmentally engulfed by a represented space to the point of physical reaction—enclosed in Humboldt's "magic circle," forgetful of all else—but, rather, in terms of separation, as the viewer "no longer belongs to the same space as the perceived objects: the traveler sees the objects, landscapes, etc., *through* the apparatus . . . ," and he cites numerous nineteenth-century descriptions of train travel to support this view.[70] As if confirming Schivelbusch's definition, American poet Bayard Taylor described a trip on the Eire Railroad as

> a rapidly unrolling panorama. . . . We sped along . . . in a warm and richly furnished chamber, lounging on soft seats, half arm-chair and half couch. Apparently as disconnected from the landscape as a loose leaf blown over it by the winds.[71]

One technology, an apparatus of representation, the panorama, strove to represent an experience so intensely it could trigger nausea. Another technology, a mode of transportation, the train journey, became an apparatus of vision that transformed real landscapes into virtual ones, and travelers into spectators. Traveling becomes a frictionless form of transportation typified by the fictional global traveler of record-breaking speed Phileas Fogg, whom Jules Verne describes as "not travelling, but only describing a circumference . . . he was a solid body traversing an orbit around the terrestrial globe, according to the laws of rational mechanics."[72] No wonder Turner felt compelled to stick his head out the window!

Focusing once again on the frame may help us gain a handle on this contradiction. The panorama appeared almost simultaneously with another new medium whose history ultimately lasted longer: photography. Photography also posed a challenge to the tradition of the Ideal Landscape. The American landscapes from Cole and Durand through Church and Bierstadt, while drawing on sketches from nature, understood their relation to nature to be synthetic, aestheticizing, and idealizing, composing landscapes that never claimed to correspond precisely to the views that originally inspired them. Photography, by contrast, according to aestheticians seemed unlikely to become a true art form precisely because it was condemned to an accurate portrayal of the scene it depicted, the handmaiden rather than the master of nature. As Peter Galassi puts it, "The camera's inability to compose rendered the old standards nearly obsolete from the outset."[73]

However, Galassi's pioneering essay on the relation between photography and the composition of "views" explored the complexity of the relation between technology and aesthetics. The breakdown of the Ideal Landscape in certain forms of landscape views and sketches can by no means be attributed simply to the invention of photography. Galassi claims the invention of photography (or at least its aesthetic use) should instead be understood in relation to changes in artistic composition that occurred before it. Almost from its origins, the picturesque carried an impulse toward the casual and aleatory that seems to contradict its investment in carefully framed pictures. While the picturesque favored the rearrangement of nature into more balanced composition, the very tools it used in venturing into nature, the camera obscura and the Claude glass, directly anticipate the fragmentary, "taken directly from nature" aspect of both photography and the new models of landscape composition.

It is useful to return to the Claude glass. This capturing of reflections also raises the complex question of what it means to "frame." The German

Romantic painter Carl Gustav Carus criticized the Claude glass from the point of view of composition in a letter to Caspar David Friedrich:

> Look at a natural landscape in a mirror! You will see it reproduced with all its charms, all its colours and shapes; but if you capture this reflection and compare it to the effect a finished work of art representing a landscape has on you, what do you notice?—It is obvious that the work of art falls short of the truth; for whatever it is that makes the beautiful natural shapes so charming, the colours so luminous, it is never entirely achieved in the painting. You experience at the same time the feeling that the authentic work of art constitutes a whole, a little world (microcosm) in itself; a reflection in retrospect will always appear to be a fragment, a part of infinite nature, detached from its organic links and circumscribed within its limits from nature.[74]

The Ideal Landscape pursued through its balanced composition the creation of a fragment that seemed self-contained. But the very genre of the landscape, with its invitation to voyage, introduced the leaven that would undermine this illusion of self-containment. The landscape implied a voyage inside its frame, soliciting other viewpoints, like the succession of images the Claude glass gave to the tourist, which Gilpin claimed he would give any price to fix and appropriate. In spite of Carus's objection, in the nineteenth century both Realism and Romanticism (to invoke two massive concepts) encouraged a taste for the fragmentary rooted less in ideal models than in the selection of a point of view. From Friedrich to Degas (or from Church to Inness), painting explored what Galassi calls "the formative role of the vantage point," implicit already in perspective, but increasingly wandering away from the architectonic composition that theatricalized the space viewed.[75]

Various technological responses to this tension loomed, including the chemical fixing of camera obscura images that Daguerre, Niépce, and Fox Talbot sought and achieved before the middle of the nineteenth century—photography. But the photograph seemed condemned to the fragmentary, if not the random. The panorama offered another response, combining photography's detailed accuracy and adherence to nature with a form that aspired less to a microcosm than to imaging Humboldt's totalizing Cosmos.[76] While the contrast between photography and the panorama might seem as absolute as that between fragment and whole, in their common purpose of conveying accurate topographical information, each overthrows the Ideal Landscape, abolishing synthetic ideal composition in favor of an image of a place determined by the apparatus of view. As Comment put it, "The panorama therefore had no composition other than that implied by the chosen vanishing point."[77] Fundamentally, both media exploit the "formative role of the vantage point." Photographs soon served panorama artists as guides in the preparation of their massive canvases, and photographic panoramas appeared, including Eadweard Muybridge's two versions of a photographic panorama of San Francisco.[78]

The panorama seems to embody the imperial ambitions inherent in the "magisterial gaze," a role recognized in its use as a tool of nationalist propaganda from Napoleon's plan to establish a series of rotundas displaying military victories of the Revolution and Empire through to twentieth-century panoramas of the defense of Stalingrad, the (still existing?) Battle of Al-Qadissiyah (installed by Saddam Hussein outside of Baghdad), or the Battle of Tetshou in North Korea, or celebrating colonial ambitions, as in the massive 1913 Belgian panorama of the Congo.[79] Evoking on the one hand visual and physical mastery, the panorama also provoked a feeling of being physically overwhelmed, of vertigo, rather than mastery, as Comment describes it, "an exquisite switching from feelings of dominance to those of dissolution, of loss."[80] One might claim the ideological effect of identification with a masterful gaze is dependent upon an experience of disorientation, but I would agree with Comment that this simplifies the dialectical nature of the experience, ignoring the panorama's essential relation to the sublime tradition of Turner, Friedrich, and Church, "to destabilize their viewers, to make them lose their bearings, to destructure the background so that they could be sucked into the vertigo of the image, to be as it were immersed in the forces of nature and painting."[81]

The panorama underwent a commercial climax around 1900 with a dramatic proliferation and new technological sophistication evident in the variety of panoramas offered at the 1900 Universal Exposition at Paris.[82] Then, as a mass medium, it died a lingering death. The history of the emergence of cinema, while acknowledging cinema's debt to several centuries of visual entertainments, unfortunately often adopts a Darwinian arc of ascent in which the cinema fulfills, as it abolishes, a series of predecessors, including the panorama. Approached more broadly, the proliferation of mechanically produced images readily available through a complex modern visual culture ended the commercial possibility of an artisanal product like the panorama, however industrialized its production had attempted to become. But modern landscape painting was undoubtedly shaped by this rival in more ways than imitation of scale and mode of presentation by the Great Paintings. Barbara Novak subtly shows that the American luminists, while absolutely avoiding the theatricality and monumentality of the Great Picture, worked out their own appropriation of the lessons of the panorama. While in their landscapes, John Frederick Kensett and Martin Johnson Heade made no attempt to rival the panorama's scale, they also abandoned the classic proportions of the Ideal Landscape, producing horizontally extensive canvases:

> Significantly the luminist artists duplicated the horizontal extensions of the panorama in their picture's proportions. I say significantly because I am suggesting that they had a profound understanding of the structural means whereby the popular panorama could be transformed back into high art.[83]

Likewise, Comment reminds us that Monet's conception of *The Waterlilies* originally envisioned display within a circular, panorama-type structure which would maximize the experience Monet described as "a whole without end, of a wave without horizon and without shore."[84] Even if it disappeared as a medium, the panorama pioneered a new relation to the frame and the viewer whose influence on modern art and new media endured.

AN UNSEEN ENERGY

> As we become accustomed to the gloom, we see an EYE, far ahead; a half-closed eye, growing larger and larger as we approach. It glistens on the converging rails; it grows larger; it grows brighter. We see a delicate picture outlined in that tiny space; a picture of a station, a tower, bright trees, shining meadows; and suddenly we're right in the midst of it all.
>
> EDISON, 1900 CATALOGUE DESCRIPTION OF *Running through Gallitzen Tunnel, Penna., R.R*

The relation between landscape and cinema must be understood in relation to a long history of transformations in framing, the view framed, and the role of the spectator. Approaching landscape and *early* cinema also demands attention to transformations in film history. I have argued that, in contrast to later cinema, for at least the first decade of film history, narrative played a secondary role.[85] Rather than primarily telling stories, early films displayed things, placing a variety of attractions on display for curious audiences. These attractions included vaudeville acts, magical camera tricks (disappearances and transformations), brief gags, and views of various sights, both man-made (famous buildings, World's Fairs, city streets) and natural (rivers, waterfalls, mountains, canyons—the sort of things panoramas initially featured). This cinema of attraction, with its emphasis on the "view," showed a greater affinity with the genre of landscape painting than we find in later films. Films presenting landscape views formed a major genre of early cinema, gradually transforming into the travelogues of the classical cinema program, lasting until the end of the studio system.[86] Filmed views of natural landscapes recall more directly the still photographic views printed on postcards, projected as magic lantern slides, and pasted in tourist albums, yet these fairly recent practices had absorbed lessons in composition and a canon of worthwhile sights from landscape painting—even as the photograph introduced new models of framing.

Travel films composed a major genre of early cinema, fitting in seamlessly with such popular traditions as lantern slide travel lectures and illustrated guidebooks. All of these forms presented to audiences views of sights and sites that either they were thinking of visiting, enjoyed recalling—or knew they would never be able to afford to see and therefore particularly valued through this ersatz form of tourism.[87] Like landscape painting and landscape photography (such as the work of William Henry Jackson and Eadweard Muybridge), early films were often sponsored by railroads in the hope these cinematic views would spawn the curiosity of tourists when they were shown. At the turn of the century, American railroads sponsored filmmaking tours along their routes, just as they had sponsored (and continued to sponsor) tours for painters and photographers. Edison made films with the cooperation of the Lehigh Valley Railroad and the Southern Pacific Railroad. The Mutoscope and Biograph Company made a series of films in cooperation with the New York Central, the Union Pacific, the Canadian Pacific, and the Sante-Fe Railways. Travel had become an industry in which the technologies of transportation and image-making were mutually beneficial.

The affinity between the railroad and the cinema as emblems of modernity has been widely commented on.[88] Film capturing the dynamic speed of the locomotive, especially when filmed from an angle so that the train moves rapidly toward the camera, formed a major genre of the novelty phase of film exhibition in the 1890s. Starting with Lumière's famous *Arrival of a Train at La Ciotat*, shown at the premiere projection of the Lumière Cinématographe in Paris in 1895, the image of a locomotive apparently charging out from the screen became a defining image of the new medium internationally. Edison filmed the world's fastest locomotive, the Lehigh Valley's Black Diamond Express, while its rival film company, Biograph, filmed the New York Central's rival contender for fastest locomotive, the

Empire Express.[89] More than simply a choice of dynamic subject matter, filming locomotives in this manner implied new attitudes toward the frame and the spectator.

These forward-charging trains gave birth at some later point to an enduring myth, a sort of cinematic primal scene, in which audiences, mistaking the moving images for reality and the train's motion for a violent assault upon them, ran out of the theater. No one has ever documented an instance of such behavior among the first cinema audiences.[90] But if not literally true, such stories raise important issues for the newly forming film spectatorship. The legend confuses sensory experience and intellectual belief. If we keep these separate, we can better describe the spectator address of panoramas and cinema, in which conventions of representation took second place to the delivering of sensual experiences.

When the *New York Telegraph* covered the premiere projection of Biograph films in 1896 New York City, it reported that two women in the audience "screamed and fainted" during the projection of the Biograph film of the Empire Express (a claim later modified to read "screamed and *nearly* fainted");[91] this reaction recalls Queen Charlotte's seasickness at the panorama, or the report of an anonymous woman's attack of the hysterics at Langlois's panorama of the Naval Battle of Navarino.[92] Even if these reports are reliable, they tell us little about spectator belief in the reality of the illusion, but rather indicate that sensual stimulation can trigger psychophysical reactions. Probably no one ever ran from such a screening in fear of a train wreck, yet spectators undoubtedly screamed, made sudden reflex motions, or had other physical reactions to the movement on the screen (as they continue to do during highly kinetic scenes in movies, especially when shown in such exhibition situations as three-dimensional movies or the semipanoramic Cinerama).

Like the panorama, moving pictures also redefined the interaction of frame and spectator. The poster Albert Truchet designed for the 1896 Lumière Cinématographe exhibitions shows fashionably dressed ladies watching an arrival of a train on the screen in front of them.[93] But as Klaus-Jurgen Sembach points out, the train track emerges irrationally from the left corner of the screen frame extending into the space of the audience. The anomaly reflects more than a stylistic flourish. A British commentator writing under the name O. Winter described the effect of the Lumière film: "And a train, running (so to say) out of the cloth, floats upon our vision."[94] The fantasy of the train's emergence from the screen was omnipresent and powerful in the novelty era, attested to by numerous journalists, including Maxim Gorky, who in 1896 sadistically imagined the Lumière train's "plunge into the darkness in which you sit, turning you into a ripped sack full of lacerated flesh and splintered bone and crushing into dust and into broken fragments this hall"— fantasy he then deflated by adding, "but this too is but a train of shadows."[95]

Cinema simultaneously maintains the frame (the screen rectangle fixed and visible in the front of the auditorium) and ruptures it. The quadrilateral on which the film is projected does not vary, but, as the Truchet poster illustrates and as the fantasies of emergence testify, movement extends beyond the frame, "out of the cloth"—or seems to. The creation of off-screen space fascinated and confused early film spectators. Yuri Tsivian describes the effect of what he calls the "disappearing figure," as moving figures came to the edge of the frame—and then seemingly disappeared.[96] Reviewers of the premiere of Biograph films, which included a film of presidential candidate William McKinley, noticed with confusion that when McKinley "came to the edge of the curtain he vanished."[97] The moving panorama had mimed landscapes slipping past a viewer seated in a train or boat and disappearing from view, anticipating the lateral displacement of movement through a film frame. But the arrival of the train, or similar films featuring motion aimed at the camera (such as the delightful 1900 film by Cecil Hepworth, *How It Feels to Be Run Over*), opened up a new space beyond the frame, not simply on either side. This novel movement toward the camera—that is, *toward the spectator*—prompted cries of alarm and fantasies of collision. The panorama, moving or fixed, maintained a constant and safe distance between spectator and the spectacle.[98] Movement toward the camera seemed to undermine that traditional separation, collapsing the contemplative distance in the anticipation of collision and heightening the physical sensations evoked in the panorama to an intense shock. Did the cinema therefore abolish the sense of separation between observer and scene that Schivelbusch calls "panoramic perception," attested to by so many nineteenth-century train travelers? Or did it simply redefine its effects?

The symbiosis between the panorama and the cinema that occurred at the turn of the century, strongly transformed the effects of the older medium, rather than simply absorbing it. The cinematic "pan"—short for "panoramic shot"—a pivoting camera movement as the camera turns on a stationary tripod, marks one of the terms of this merging of the forms. This camera movement was introduced quite early. Barry Salt claims Robert Paul designed the first pivoting camera in order to cover Queen Victoria's Diamond Jubilee in 1897, and the manufacture of camera heads that could pan smoothly and steadily institutionalized the shot's place in the cinema's vocabulary to the present day.[99] Although also used to follow the action of an event (a parade or a sporting event), its earliest uses tended to acknowledge the pan's derivation from the panorama. Early film companies offered "panoramas" or "panoramic views" of sites, natural and man-made. Not all early films that included the term "panorama" in their titles used such "panning" motion, and likewise not all films that used a pan mentioned it in their title, but a large number did, often modifying the term to "circular panorama" to indicate a sweeping view (occasionally, but not always, a full 360 degrees). Edison made circular panoramas of the Niagara Falls (one of the many examples Cahn noted of early cinema picking up locations familiar from American landscape painting)[100] as well as of 360-degree views of the 1900 Paris Universal Exposition.

But the term "panorama" or "panoramic view" also described another sort of landscape film, undoubtedly the most popular and most dynamic visually. These panoramas did not simply show locomotives moving toward the camera, but instead mounted a camera on a train, capturing a mobile view of a landscape. Edison first shot such a film in June of 1896, *View from Gorge Railroad*, which the *Boston Herald* described as "a panoramic picture obtained from the rear end of a swiftly-moving train on the Niagara Gorge railway."[101] The term "panoramic" first designated an Edison train film in 1897, with *Panoramic Scene, Susquehanna River*. Titles like Biograph's *Panorama from Incline Railway* (1902; shot from Mt. Beacon, New York) or Edison's *Panoramic View, Kicking Horse Canyon* (1901) all refer to films shot from the front of moving trains. These films deliver an experience of movement more extensive and dynamic than the pivoting pans. Whereas the arc of vision in a pan presents a sweeping circular view of a scene from a fixed center, these films, made with the camera mounted on the front of a train, actually travel through space, like the train itself moving through the landscape. Thus the films realize the centuries-old fantasy of penetration that had remained literally impossible in landscape painting. Besides "panoramic views," catalogues and exhibitors called such films "phantom rides," a term richly evoking the uncanny effect of ghostly movement that I feel was central to their popularity.

Many historians see these films simply as simulacra of train travel or other sorts of tourist journeys (some were filmed from other forms of transportation, such as boats, trolley cars, or automobiles). As such, they seem to provide the ultimate form of Schivelbusch's panoramic perception, with the distance between traveler and unfolding landscape now become the ontological difference between live audience and filmed image on the

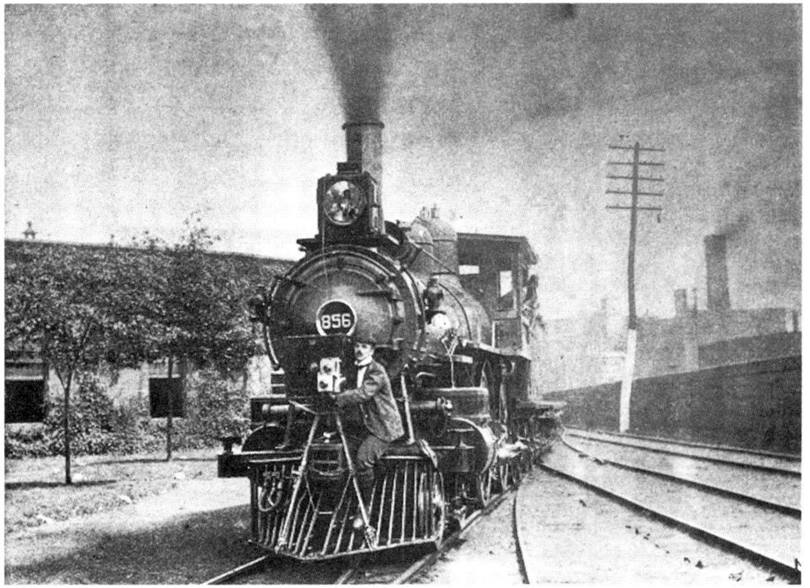

FIGURE 5.1. Billy Bitzer filming a phantom ride (1896).

screen. Certainly the essence of this genre resides in what Charles Musser has called the "viewer as passenger" convention.[102] But most of these films show a strong deviation from the tourist experience, firmly embodied in point of view. As the Edison catalogue stressed in its description of the 1903 film *Phantom Ride on the Canadian Pacific*, "The view taken from the front of the train running at high speed is one even tourists riding over the line are not privileged to enjoy."[103] The viewpoint of the train traveler primarily remained lateral, looking through the train window as it moved past the landscape. The moving panoramas mimed this lateral motion, with the most elaborate versions, such as the panorama of the Trans-Siberian Express at the 1900 Paris Universal Exposition, providing mock-ups of compartment windows for spectators to gaze through (and, in this case, an elaborate system of multiple rolls of canvas to simulate the apparently different rates of speed that objects at various distances move past the viewer: more rapidly for the foreground fields, more slowly for the distant vista of mountains).[104] But the cinematic phantom rides dived straight into the landscape and presented this plunging point of view directly to the viewer.

Some contemporary descriptions of such films recall Diderot's imaginary itinerary into an Ideal Landscape, as in the Edison catalogue description of *Panorama of Susquehanna River Taken from the Black Diamond Express*:

> There is hardly a lovelier spot along the whole Lehigh Valley railroad than this stretch of road. We are on a gently curving bit of track, mountains on both sides. We glide beneath a slender bridge, pass a crossing and a wayside station and run out on a steep embankment. Suddenly the road dips into the hills, then out again, round a point, and the valley of the Susquehanna bursts out upon our view. Far away in the blue distance the river glistens like a silver thread. There are bridges and houses and barns and steeples. There are checkerboard farms, and broad patches of virgin forest. All calm and serene in the glory of God's sunshine.[105]

Thus films of "panoramic views" seemed to fulfill desires inherent in the Ideal Landscape, exploring a new literal portrayal of motion into the landscape.

However, other films (or perhaps other marketing strategies) promoted spectator experiences that contrasted sharply with contemplative visual voyages. The Edison Company in 1902 advertised the film *Panoramic View of Lower Kicking Horse Canyon* for its physical thrills and the appearance of danger: "Of all panoramic mountain pictures this is the most thrilling, as the audience imagines while they are being carried along with the picture the train will be toppled over thousands of feet into the valley below." Of a companion film of the same canyon, the catalogue claimed: "The train seems to be running into the mountains of rock as each curve is reached and rounded, making the scene exciting from start to finish." The key attraction of Edison's *Panoramic View of Mt Tamalpias, Cal.* according to its publicity, lay in "the sensation of momentarily expecting to be hurled into space."[106]

These films fully exploit the dynamics of their unique frontal point of view, driving a wedge between the "phantom ride" and the distanced panoramic perception of the train tourist. The view from the front of the train created a more thrilling perspective, allowing the suspenseful anticipation of collisions and derailments described in the Edison catalogue for their Lower Kicking Horse Canyon panoramas. Far from a contemplative mode, this viewpoint summoned up the possibility of shock and intense sensual involvement that had migrated from the painted panorama and intensified as it found its home in the new electrical fairground with thrill rides such as the Leap Frog Railway, which threatened passengers with a direct collision between train cars—only to have one car "leap over" the other at the last moment. Such fairground attractions strove to create a sense of physical danger while passengers were actually nestled in a device guaranteed to keep physical collision and injury in abeyance.[107]

If the panorama films shot from the front of the train seem to abolish the traditional reception of landscapes by accelerating the fantasy of travel into a landscape with a vengeance, one might note that the early excursions mounted by railway companies for artists also frequently featured rides on the front of the locomotive.[108] Whatever inspiration such rides provided artists, they do not seem to have literally inspired the viewpoint of any canvas. Like Turner sticking his head out from the train compartment window, such experiences might deepen an artist's experience of a landscape but were unlikely to inspire a choice of compositional viewpoint. But in the early films taken from a camera mounted on the front of the train, the effect of this viewpoint often becomes nearly overwhelming, to my mind the richest and most dialectical experience offered by early cinema in its exploration of movement and point of view. Such phantom rides substitute sensation for contemplation, overcoming effects of distance in a rush of visual motion.

The longevity of phantom-ride filmmaking testifies to the inherent power of its effect. I have found examples as early as 1896, and many exist as late as 1907, when the cinema of attractions had become increasingly seduced by the tasks of narrative. Indeed, there are similar tracking shots from the front of locomotives integrated into later narrative films that deal with the railway (and viewers of European television will recognize the final survival of the form in long-lasting videos of train rides broadcast on certain channels in the wee hours of the morning, apparently for the pleasure of trainspotters, insomniacs, and a few sleepless devotees of the power of visual kinesis). Intuiting the energy slumbering within the form, a number of panoramic train films have also been reworked by avant-garde filmmakers, most gloriously by Ernie Gehr and Ken Jacobs.

From 1905 to about 1907, toward the end of the era of the cinema of attractions, this genre was renewed by George C. Hale, who returned it to its roots in the panorama and brought it closer to the new electric amusement parks. Hale adopted the exhibition strategy of many panoramas by fashioning a viewing area that imitated an aspect of the panorama, such as the Trans-Siberian Express panorama. In Hale's Tours and Scenes of the World, the audience was seated in a mock-up of a train car, complete with sound effects (the clickety-clack of wheels running over the rails, the hiss of the air brakes), as they watched the films projected in the front of the car, narrated by lecturers dressed as train conductors. These theaters were briefly very popular, and films taken from the front of trains are often referred to as Hale's Tours films, somewhat anachronistically, since the genre had been in existence for nearly a decade before Hale introduced his specialized theaters.[109]

The increased mimesis of train travel that these theaters offered reaffirm their role as ersatz tourism, like the panoramas themselves, a new technological version of what Comment refers to as "a dream that had been prevalent since the beginning of the nineteenth century, to travel without having to move."[110] But the intensity of this experience, as I have argued, exceeded a simple reproduction of travel and transformed the experience of landscape. Only a thick description of this experience, both phenomenological and historical, reveals its radical transformation of the landscape tradition. With their front-on viewpoint, the phantom rides provide a unique realization of the fantasy of penetrating a landscape, of chasing the horizon into the depth of an ever-unfolding image. The displacement from the lateral view provided by the train (and the moving panoramas) to a head-on plunge into the center of the image fundamentally transforms the distance Schivelbusch described as inherent in panoramic perception.

In previous essays I have quoted an anonymous journalist's account of his experience of one of Biograph's earliest phantom rides.[111] I find it such a rich description of the experience of a film traveling down the train tracks I feel compelled to return to it once again in this new context:

> The way in which the unseen energy swallows up space and flings itself into the distances is as mysterious and impressive as an allegory. A sensation is produced akin to that which Poe in his "Fall of the House of Usher" relates was communicated to him by his doomed companion when he sketched the shaft in the heart of the earth, with an unearthly radiance thrilling through it. One holds his breath instinctively as he is swept along in the rush of the phantom cars. His attention is held almost with the vise of a fate.[112]

The terms of comparison that journalist offers probe deeply into the novelty of this experience of spectatorship. The locomotive, which never appears on the screen but is present only in its motive force, literally embodies an unseen energy that compels the camera, the film, and the viewer down the track. Since it remains off-screen and invisible, the locomotive takes on a basic characteristic of a phantom, a presence evident in its effects, while remaining unseen. Although we *know* the camera was perched on the front of a train, the film delivers a fantasy of total visual dominance. It is *our eyes*, liberated from any visible body, that fly down the track, "swallowing up space," like the film spectators described by Christian Metz decades later as "taking everything in with their eyes, nothing with their bodies."[113]

The head-on confrontation between the viewer's vantage point and the direction of movement into space evoke the possibility of shock and collision, in contrast to the lateral view of the traditional train rider that created the sense of separation essential to panoramic perception. Nonetheless, a fundamental fissure between viewer and spectacle remains, dependent less on visual viewpoint, yet physically more absolute. As much as the expectation, even the sensation, of collision may be evoked by such film, no collision is ever possible. As with the fantasy of the emergence of the train from the screen, we remain in a realm of shadow, not substance. No physical shock is possible, no meeting between our bodies and the space on-screen can occur, however much we may seem to penetrate into it.

This ultimately ontological separation between viewer and screen therefore posits a new form of the distance characteristic of panoramic perception, the return of the unreality of the image repressed by the apparent sensual immediacy delivered by the cinematic experience of motion. As film viewers, we seem to be there, to actually fulfill the desire for entrance into an illusionary landscape. Space streams right at us—yet, it only invites our eyes to enter, our bodies remain seated, on the other side of the screen. We experience our exile from this represented space, like a phantom hovering over our seeming participation. In an uncanny way, as film viewers, we experience that transcendent experience that Emerson described in his essay "Nature" and that has become an emblem not only for American Transcendentalism but for the experience of the nineteenth-century American landscape: "Standing on the bare ground—my head bathed by the blithe air, and uplifted into infinite space—all mean egotism vanishes. I become a transparent eye-ball; I am nothing; I see all . . ."[114] In a more concrete (but not less extraordinary) manner, in these films the spectator vanishes physically, leaving only the energy of travel, the sensation of movement through the landscape. Yet this all-seeing eye is also a physiological eye, one alert to the possibility of collision and ready to flinch at the sensation of danger, even as it is protected by its very medium from physical contact. In spite of its fulfilment of the centuries-old fantasy of penetration, it remains what Benjamin describes as a modern "protective eye," alert to potential dangers rather than "daydreaming surrender to distance and faraway things." As Benjamin speculates, the magic of distance may be broken.[115]

The convergence of tracks in the distance, the ultimate image of perspective in our culture—parallel lines merging at the vanishing point of infinity—sets up the dynamic balance of the visible and the invisible in these films. The energy forcing us down the tracks remains unseen. The space we travel through, once we have moved past it, slides around the frame, and vanishes as well, forming an invisible wake of remembered space trailing behind us. As we move toward the ever-receding horizon, new bits of landscape seem to come into existence at the limits of our vision; hills, bridges, train stations, towns, cliffs, and forests burst into sight. An ever-renewed landscape emerges from the distance that remains, continuously bisected by the tracks in front of us, which hold steady not only our trajectory but, as the journalist cannily observes, our *attention*, as in a vise of fate. Our track cannot deviate, nor can we look in any other direction than straight ahead, any more than we can retain a sight of the passing landscape that we only catch a glimpse of. All space is in constant motion; all is continuously both approaching us and slipping away from us. Diderot's fantasy of a voyage into a landscape becomes a nightmare of infinite regress, impelled by a fatelike irresistible resistible force.

Noël Burch, in his influential and pioneering work on early cinema, figured the spectator in the phantom rides as an anticipation of the classical spectator of later cinema around whom all space is organized—the coherent subject of ideology sutured into a continuous narrative of illusory domination.[116] This interpretation fits, just as the panoramic viewpoint corresponds to the magisterial gaze of manifest destiny. However, as Comment claimed for the panorama, another experience seems dominant, one prompted by physical sensations of vertigo, perhaps even more powerful than the relation the panorama had to dissolution and loss. The vanishing point, the fixed convergence of classical perspective, its point of coherence, becomes in the phantom ride a point of constant transformation and instability. From it, new vistas emerge like ants swarming up from an unseen anthill. Instead of the point where things vanish, the far distance becomes the point of entrance into visibility. Our point of view, as stand-in for the camera, becomes the point at which everything converges and then disappears, reversing the traditional schema of perspective. The reversal reworks perspective's inherent sense of visual dominance into an experience of an abject subjection to the course of movement and the logic of the track. As shaped by the camera lens, instead of offering a broad and inviting foreground, a stable viewing point on which traditional landscape *staffage* figures can loll at ease to gaze into the distance, the foreground of a phantom ride represents the narrowest point of the image, as well as the point of greatest velocity, the anticipated site of collision. To watch a phantom-ride film, I find, provokes not only a crisis within the spectator's relation to space and landscape, but a heightened awareness of perception and consciousness itself, its temporal protensions and retentions, its constant reach into the distance, balanced by its sense of passing by and leaving behind.

If the phantom ride is "a mysterious and impressive allegory," one might describe it as an allegory of spatial perception itself.[117] Yet this one-tracked mind flies obsessively in a nightmare inversion of the contemplative gaze Diderot imagined, picking its leisurely way through the varied zones of the Ideal Landscape.

In one of his papers on technique, Freud advised patients beginning analysis to imagine "you were a traveller next to a window of the railway carriage and describing to someone inside the carriage the changing views which you see outside."[118] Access to the unconscious unfolds like a sightseeing trip. But the phantom ride's direct stare down the track seems to invoke more closely the hypnotic state that Freud increasingly rejected as a means of reaching unconscious experience. In the opening of his film *Zentropa*, Lars von Trier has the voice of Max von Sydow address the audience as a hypnotist, inducting them into a trance that will be the film, entered into by following the camera movement down these train tracks. The tracks appear gleaming within darkness, passing through no visible landscape, other than the abstract pathway they lay down. We could see this prologue as cinema's ultimate anti-landscape, the nightmare armature on which fantasies of domination and of being dominated are carried.

GHOST DANCES

> After I had looked at five or six of them, they gradually began to separate themselves from their surroundings, and I was no longer able to see them as moons. They became holes in the canvas, apertures of whiteness looking onto another world. Blakelock's eye perhaps. A blank circle suspended in space, gazing down at things that were no longer there.
>
> PAUL AUSTER, *Moon Palace*

In describing the uncanny effect of the Biograph train film, the journalist compared it to the painting produced by Roderick Usher in Poe's "The Fall of the House of Usher." Poe's description could stand, I believe, as the exemplar of an anti-landscape:

> A small picture presented the interior of an immensely long and rectangular vault or tunnel, with low walls, smooth, white, and without interruption or device. Certain accessory points of the design served well to convey the idea that this excavation lay at an exceeding depth below the surface of the earth. No outlet was observed in any portion of its vast extent, and

> no torch, or other artificial source of light was discernible; yet a flood of intense rays rolled throughout, and bathed the whole in a ghastly and inappropriate splendor.[119]

While the American landscape tradition more immediately brings to mind as a literary correlative a figure like James Fenimore Cooper, whose description of the Adirondacks inspired a major painting by Thomas Cole, I would claim no major American author thought as deeply or wrote as profoundly about the composition of landscape as Poe. Two of his most obscure late works, "The Domain of Arnheim" (1847) and "Landor's Cottage" (1849), consist entirely of descriptions of the composition of landscapes and discussions of the art of landscape architecture. His sketch "The Island of the Fay" performs an imaginary exploration of an Ideal Landscape based on an engraving, while his article "Morning on the Wissahiccon" provides a gentle satire on the passion for picturesque landscapes.

But we properly associate Poe more with interior spaces (as Charles Olson said, Poe's response to the American landscape was to dig in).[120] Poe, we might claim, turned American space inside out (in his amazing fantasy of landscape gardens, "The Domain of Arnheim," Poe imagines a garden whose configuration could only be appreciated and understood by a perspective beyond the human and terrestrial).[121] The interior portrayed in Usher's picture empties out our consciousness of space and place. Usher's painting has sometimes been described (anachronistically) as an exercise in abstract art. More accurately, it performs an act of ascesis, a landscape sunk beneath the surface, composed exclusively of formal aspects of framing and depth, illuminated by a light whose deathly quality and lack of source invert Claude's golden varied sunlight and shade. Walter Benjamin called Poe's story "The Man of the Crowd" "the x-ray" of a detective story.[122] I believe we could call Usher's picture the x-ray of a landscape.

Is it too far a flight of speculation, spurred by a journalist's comparison, but also by the uncanny experience generated by most of the scores of phantom rides I have seen from film archives around the world, to identify early cinema's seemingly realistic genre of mobile landscapes with Poe's picture that strips landscape of all spatial and temporal moorings? I feel it is greatly significant that phantom-ride films appear around the time that artists such as Monet, Cézanne, and Seurat crafted a new era in painting partly by rethinking the form of the landscape. But rather than rehearse a well-known European-based narrative, I want to return to the American tradition and consider two final heirs of the Hudson River School and its gradual reworking and dismantling of the Claudean Ideal Landscape: George Inness and Ralph Blakelock.

Both painters could be described as heirs of the original school of American landscape painting, the Hudson River School of Cole, Durand, Cropsey, Gifford, and others, which had revivified the Claudean Ideal Landscape by giving it an American urgency. Working primarily in the latter half of the nineteenth century, both Inness and Blakelock were aware of later developments in European landscape painting, of first the Barbizon school and then the Impressionists.[123] While each acknowledged an influence from these movements, they also maintained their distance from them, especially in regard to painting from nature. With only a few exceptions, neither attempted to paint existing landscapes, remaining faithful to the ideal of the Claudean landscape as a synthesis of various elements, recalled and reassembled.[124] Blakelock's landscape seemed to recycle a nocturnal shadow of the Claudean Ideal Landscape, the golden sunlight given over to a pale moonlight that seems more like a dark melancholic sun than a nocturnal view. I am certainly not claiming that these artists, perhaps the least photographic of American landscape painters, produced "cinematic images." But I feel they both bring the American landscape tradition to a culmination, in ways that recall (but never actually resemble visually) the uncanny aspect of the phantom rides, especially seen through the filter of Usher's anti-landscape.

Rachael DeLue reminds us that the original reception of Inness's landscapes found them violent and shocking, even describing them as seeming to rush toward the viewer from off the wall.[125] Partly because Inness still makes reference to the schemata of the Ideal Landscape, less ignoring its constraints than contradicting them, his late paintings seem to me to recall the phantom ride's reversal of spectator position from the Ideal Landscape through its extreme fulfilment of its fantasy of penetration. Using painterly means rather than contradictory psychophysical sensations of motion, Inness too transforms our sense of horizon and foreground, disorienting our relation to the imaginary scene. As DeLue describes it, some of his paintings seem to stack multiple horizons on top of each other.[126] Likewise Inness frequently transfers the blurring, which as atmospheric perspective gave the Ideal Landscape an effect of distance, to the foreground.[127] Rather than a stable foreground providing an inviting entranceway and place for contemplation to the viewer, DeLue sees Inness's foregrounds as "expanding and recalcitrant" and describes his later landscapes as "sliding."[128] These reversals, DeLue argues powerfully, "compromise any fantasy of entrance and traversal."[129] DeLue demonstrates that in his engagement with and undermining of the conventions of the Ideal Landscape, "Inness's landscapes are ever in process, are ever engaged in working out a proper way to conceive of the relation between self and world, eye and truth."[130] Inness's work challenges viewers to renegotiate their sense of space and image, a process keenly aware of its own stages of development, as DeLue puts it, "creating an effect of gradual unfolding and continual flux."[131] As such, they both recall the irresistible motion of the phantom ride and offer a response, reclaiming a form of contemplation proper to a world in dissolution.

The dissolution one senses in Ralph Blakelock's *Moonlights*, the series of almost obsessively similar nocturnal landscapes he produced in the 1880s through the 1890s, seems to chronicle a more personal struggle with the coherence of the landscape, whether one relates it directly to the artist's growing madness or more generally to a sense of a crisis of subjectivity attempting to define a stance in the face of not only incoherent space but disillusioning history.[132] The usually minuscule Native American figures that populate many of Blakelock's landscapes recall a long tradition of Indian *staffage* figures contemplating the landscape, providing a recognizable allegory not only of wilderness, but of a vanishing past. These Native American figures cast a wistful gaze at the landscape, inevitably evoking their ultimate displacement from their homeland as one of the consequences of the magisterial gaze. These images sentimentalize the Indians even as compositional schemes naturalize their vanishing, like the brilliantly colored foliage of a Hudson Valley autumn. Blakelock, while clearly drawing as much on romantic clichés as on his own direct experience of Native American life in his youthful trips to the West, rarely sentimentalizes his figures, yet the sense of their transience extends to every aspect of the canvas.[133] It is not simply the Indians that are being displaced here: a whole world appears to be fading, growing darker and paler in moonlight.

Compared to Inness's constant experimentation with spatial effects—his demand on the viewer to find new ways of orienting oneself to his montage of compositional schemes—Blakelock seems fixated on an inflexible version of the Ideal Landscape, almost schematic in form. Particularly in the *Moonlight* canvases, Blakelock's skein of spiky-leaved trees punctured by irregular patches of moonlight seem highly theatrical in effect, recalling the two-dimensional coulisses of the baroque theater that inspired Claude. These arboreal frames, protective in their embracing gesture and yet carrying a sinister overtone in their prickly form, sharpened by the impasto of Blakelock's paint, seem to frame a fairyland set, both enchanted and haunted. Fantasies here derive less from imagined voyages into a depth that appears too blurred to ever be physically navigable, than from the almost hallucinatory varied textures and colors that Blakelock built up through his fanatically worked-over surface, applying layer upon layer of paint, then scraping, polishing, and gouging with palette knife and pumice stone and even subjecting the canvas to running water.[134] The effect not only is deeply tactile, creating a modernist push-pull between surface and depth, but sparkles with points of color and a variety of textures, evoking the experience of sight at low light, levels in which the physiology of the eye competes with the forms of the world, creating a swim and play of colors, phosphemes, and optical eccentricities. In complete contrast to the sunlit vision of the Impressionists, Blakelock evokes a uniquely beautiful night-vision, uncanny in its familiarity, surprising in its continually renewing variations.

One of Blakelock's last canvases before his decades-long institutionalization for dementia praecox bears the title *Ghost Dance*, or alternatively *The Vision of Life*. Blakelock's trees framing a moonlit distance provide a theatrical backdrop to the image. The foreground, made up of a field of variegated colors and textures, provides a stage for a cluster of midground figures primarily on the right of the canvas. A fairly uniform yellowish brown defines these figures, whose outlines are impossibly blurred and vague, but human forms and postures are recognizable, even if individual features remain effaced. The composition recalls to some extent Blakelock's *Pipe Dance*, and this resemblance (along with the title) encourages the viewer to see these hardly identifiable figures as Native Americans performing a dance. Scrutiny of the figures can yield only Rorschach-like projections, but to my eye they are not exclusively Native Americans, as some forms recall figures in evening wear, creating an allegorical *danse macabre* rather than an ethnographic image.

Nonetheless, I strongly believe that Blakelock intended the canvas to recall his Native American landscapes. Although it has been questioned whether Blakelock intended the title *Ghost Dance*, it opens the painting to a rich series of associations.[135] The image seems to show ghosts, whether of Native Americans or of humanity in general, vanishing as they dance. In the mid-1890s, when the canvas was painted, the term would evoke the Ghost Dance of the Plains tribes, the millenarian movement headed by the prophet Wovoka, which predicted a return of the original Native American way of life, the replenishing of the buffalo herds, the vanishing of the White Men, and the return of the dead, who would arrive carried on a huge train. The dance that Wovoka taught the tribes took the form of a solemn circling motion lasting sometimes for days, designed to invoke visions and generate the energy needed to bring the dead to life. The movement represented the

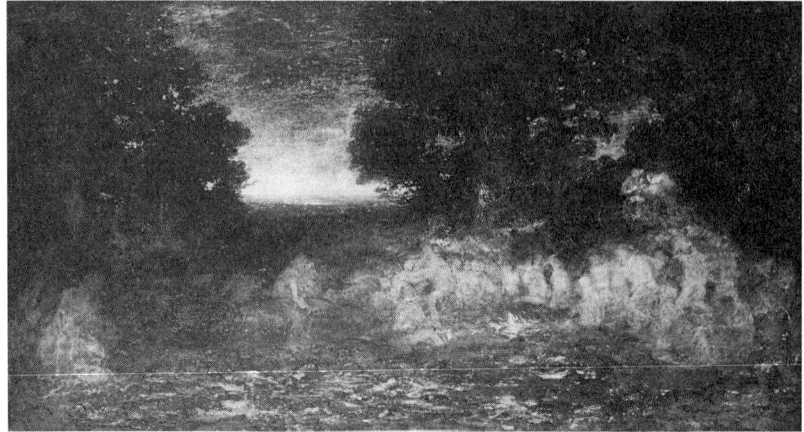

FIGURE 5.2. Ralph Albert Blakelock, *Ghost Dance (The Vision of Life)*, ca. 1895–1897. Oil on canvas. The Art Institute of Chicago.

last gasp of Native American resistance to White Manifest Destiny. The federal government responded brutally to the basically peaceful movement and in 1890 massacred over 150 Lakota men, women, and children at Wounded Knee.[136]

Both Inness and Blakelock (who certainly knew each other, occasionally painting in the same studio buildings in New York City and living in the same area of northern New Jersey) were members of congregations devoted to the teachings of the eighteenth-century Swedish visionary Emanuel Swedenborg, who exerted a profound influence on nineteenth-century American culture.[137] Both were also involved with the Spiritualist movement, that pervasive nineteenth-century attempt to found a new religion on communication with the dead (which may have influenced Wovoka as well). Inness was the more articulate, both visually and verbally; as DeLue shows, quoting him, his experimental approach to landscapes derives from a desire to push vision beyond itself, "endeavouring to give men sensuous apprehension of . . . that which is unseen—of that which the Spirit of God working in it reveals." Inness added in another instance: "But God is always hidden, and beauty depends on the unseen, the visible upon the invisible."[138]

As one of the culminating inventions of the later nineteenth century, the cinema emerges from a crisis in the conception of the visible and the invisible, a crisis provoked by progressive pressure placed on the technologies of sight, what film theorist Jean-Louis Comolli called a "frenzy of the visible," which took many forms, both physical and metaphysical.[139] Early cinema's most powerful landscape form, the phantom ride, grew out of a centuries-long process by which nature was turned into pictures, culminating in the concept of the picturesque. In America the encounter with a vast and virginal natural terrain provoked an ambivalent confluence of aesthetic appreciation with a technologically accelerated penetration of nature. American landscape painting charted a growing crisis inherent in a pastoral ideal achieved by technological means. New technologies in the representation of landscape, from the panorama to the motion pictures, endeavored to increase the sensation of immersion into a represented space, pursuing an almost obsessive goal of total spectator involvement. But the dialectic such systems set up between immersion and insulation created new paradoxes of spectatorship. As the phantom ride seemingly achieves a complete grasp and penetration of a landscape, this new technological sublime simultaneously encounters a sense of loss, of dissolution, a phantomization of the experience of self and world. Thus the dawn of cinema, rather than simply perfecting a new technology for the portrayal of landscapes, also inaugurates a new representation of loss in which the pas de deux of spectator and landscape becomes a ghostly dance of presence and absence, sensation and distance.

6

The Play between Still and Moving Images: Nineteenth-Century "Philosophical Toys" and Their Discourse

Cinema is an art of the moving image, yet materially it could be said simply to be made up from a series of still images. This apparent paradox between still and moving images has been noted by nearly all accounts of cinema, but resolving this exchange between stillness and motion, or rather the transformation of one into the other, still eludes both empirical scientific explanation and, I feel, reflects deeply rooted ideological prejudices. The moving image, I claim, constitutes a sort of a scandal, which has been consistently resolved by being described as an illusion, something in other words that does not "really" exist. I want to explore the complexities of the introduction of the moving image in the nineteenth century and the limitations that come from seeing it simply as an illusion.

PERSISTENCE OF VISION: VISION AND ITS FALLACIES

Jonathan Crary has claimed that nineteenth-century visual devices focused on the question of the body and the senses, emphasizing, defining, and measuring the processes of the body and the senses and thereby disciplining them. Thus the nineteenth century approached vision in a new mode: "Vision, rather than a privileged form of knowing, becomes itself an object of

This essay first appeared in *Between Stillness and Motion: Film, Photography, Algorithms*, ed. Eivind Røssaak (Amsterdam: Amsterdam University Press, 2011), 27–44.

knowledge, of observation. From the beginning of the nineteenth century a science of vision will tend to mean increasingly an interrogation of the physiological make-up of the human subject, rather than the mechanics of light and optical transmission."[1] Optical illusions do not simply obscure the truth about the world, but rather offer new information about the process of perceiving and the perceiver's body.[2]

Focusing on human perception redefined the complex problem of seeing things that are "not there." Discovering the nature of visual illusion revealed the essential processes of vision, just as knowledge of disease reveals the processes of health. The most common form of seeing something which was "not there" may be the afterimage, which at the turn of the nineteenth century became the subject of intense investigation. Close attention to this subjective phenomenon exemplified the new attitude toward perception that Crary describes. The way afterimages were described and the role they played within the optical devices known as philosophical toys, which produced moving images, vividly reveals the assumptions generated and the tensions raised by the moving image in this new intellectual and technological context.

Contemporary perceptual psychologist R. L. Gregory defines afterimages (of which there are both positive and negative types) as "the continuing firing of the optic nerve after the stimulation."[3] In other words, after an object has been removed from the field of vision an image of it lingers, due, in Gregory's explanation, to a physical process within the retina, especially if the object were bright or the gaze fixated. By means of an afterimage we paradoxically see an object even in its absence. This phenomenon had been observed for centuries, including discussions by Aristotle, Ptolemy, Ibn al Haytham, and Leonardo da Vinci.[4] The afterimage forms the most dramatic example of what are often called "subjective visual phenomenon," i.e., seeing images that result from a bodily response rather than from a "sampling" of the world. Studying and demonstrating this phenomenon led to the first proliferation of optical philosophical toys. As Crary puts it, "Beginning in the mid-1820s, the experimental study of afterimages led to the invention of a number of related optical devices and techniques."[5] These devices announced the invention of modern motion pictures and popularized the concept of the persistence of vision as the means of creating an illusion of apparent motion.

"The persistence of vision" exemplifies the nineteenth century's understanding of visual illusions as primarily a physiological phenomenon, which can be demonstrated, triggered, and even measured through mechanical and optical devices. Few concepts have been evoked so often in relation to visual devices and especially moving images, and yet so disputed, as this one. As an explanation of the phenomenon of apparent motion it has now basically been discarded, but it still must be dealt with as a revealing historical and cultural legacy (and one that displays its own phantom persistence, as perceptual psychologists like Joseph and Barbra Anderson have lamented).[6] As Mary Ann Doane has put it, "The theory of persistence of vision may be 'wrong,' but the question remains—why was it so firmly ensconced and what function did it serve in the 19th century?"[7] The attitude toward vision maintained by the persistence of vision thesis reveals the interface nineteenth-century scientists thought they had discovered (and in many senses, had *manufactured*) between human perception and the machine. The attraction of the theory for the nineteenth century, I believe, lies largely in its essentially mechanical view of the human sensorium (and its persistence in some accounts of cinema to this date indicates how much a mechanical view of perception and cognition still underlies the assumptions most people maintain about vision). Persistence of vision and the optical devices I discuss here form a circular logic in which the devices are the cause of visual illusions as well as demonstrating their explanation. Besides spawning images of motion, these devices forged a new dependent relation between the still and the moving image, as each enacted the trick of a transition from a static image to a moving image. However, we might claim the real trick lies in making the moving images appear as nothing more than a peculiarly tricky modification of the still image, an epiphenomenon founded in the inert and reliable still image. That the theory of persistence of vision has been debunked therefore takes on more significance than simply a passing moment in the explanatory fashions of science. Persistent afterimages offered a theory of perception which parsed movement into static phases and still images, an attempt thereby not only to discipline the moving image, but to dissolve its movement into its opposite.

So what is this theory in which movement is paradoxically explained through persistence? The theory is founded on the fact that motion picture devices (whether the first nineteenth-century devices such as the phenakistiscope or zoetrope or the later motion picture films) all employ a continuous series of still drawings or photographs depicting separate phases of an action on some sort of material support. A device moves these still images through some sort of viewer at a sufficient speed to create what is often called "apparent motion." A dancer dances, a horse gallops, a man walks. How does this happen? In 1912 one of the earliest books published on the nature of cinema, Frederic Talbot's *Moving Pictures: How They Are Made and Worked*, provides an especially vivid description:

> Suppose, for instance, that a series of pictures depicting a man walking along the street, are being shown on the screen. In the first picture the man is shown with his left foot in the air. This remains in sight for 1/32 of a second, and then disappears suddenly. Though the picture has vanished from the eye, the brain still persists in seeing the left foot slightly raised. One thirty second part of a second later the next picture shows the man with his left foot on the ground. The shops, houses, and other stationary objects in the second image occupy the positions shown in the first picture, and consequently the dying impression of these objects is revived, while the brain receives the impression that the man has changed the position of his foot in relation to the stationary objects, and the left foot which was raised melts into the left foot upon the ground. The eye imagines that it sees the left foot descend.[8]

The first book written about film by an experimental psychologist, *The Photoplay: A Psychological Study*, was published in 1916 by Hugo Munsterberg and offered a summary—as well as an early rejection—of the persistence of vision theory in psychological terms:

> Every picture of a particular position left in the eye an afterimage until the next picture with the slightly changed position of the jumping animal or the marching men was in sight, and the afterimage of this again lasted until the third came. The afterimages were responsible for the fact that no interruption was noticeable, while the movement itself resulted simply from the passing of one position into another. What else is the perception of movement but the seeing of a long series of different positions? If instead of looking through the Zoetrope we watch a real trotting horse on a real street, we see its whole body in ever-new progressing positions and its legs in all phases of motion; and this continuous series is our perception of the movement itself.[9]

Munsterberg wryly comments on the theory: "This seems very simple. Yet it was slowly discovered that the explanation is far too simple . . ."

Munsterberg put the crux of the critique (which has basically stood to today, although many film scholars seem unaware of it) succinctly as, "The perception of movement is an independent experience which cannot be reduced to a simple seeing of a series of different positions."[10] Munsterberg claims that a "higher mental act" is superadded to the physiological process, which he admits does not fully explain the phenomenon.[11] While contemporary theories of perception do not deny the phenomenon of an afterimage and the apparent motion that the older theory sought to explain, they agree that simply retaining a series of afterimages in different positions cannot automatically yield a moving image (the effect would more likely be that of multiple superimpositions). Contemporary theories have broken motion into multiple interrelating factors, whose complexities still allow some degree of controversy and uncertainty, even if the inadequacy of the old theory cannot be disputed. As the Andersons show, the phenomenon of persistence of vision as the explanation of the continuous moving image can be broken into two issues:

> Why is the image continuous, and why does it move? In other words, why do the separate frames appear continuous rather than as the intermittent flashes of light which we know them to be? And why do the figures on the screen appear to move about in smooth motion when we know they are in fact still pictures?[12]

Not long after the emergence of cinema, perceptual psychology already supplied alternative explanations to the persistence of vision thesis, as Munsterberg was aware. In 1912 Max Wertheimer took up the issue of apparent motion and his critique of the persistence of vision theory inaugurated the beginning of Gestalt psychology by questioning the mechanistic assumptions of previous perceptual psychology. Wertheimer attributed apparent motion to three factors, summarized by the Andersons as (1) beta movement (the object at A seen as moving across the intervening space to position B), (2) partial movement (each object seen moving a short distance), and (3) phi movement (objectless or pure motion).[13] Writing more recently, R. L. Gregory's recent classic account of visual perception, *Eye and Brain*, simplifies the situation and states that the continuous action as seen in a motion picture film "relies upon two rather distinct visual facts. The first is *persistence of vision*, and the second the so-called *phi phenomenon*."[14] Most perceptual psychologists today agree that multiple factors contribute to apparent motion.

PLAYING WITH VISION: THE THAUMATROPE

Picking up and playing with a nineteenth-century optical device allows anyone to reexperience the transformation of a still image into . . . something else. Beyond demonstrating the phenomenon of the afterimage or apparent movement, the fascination these images draw from us endures. A true

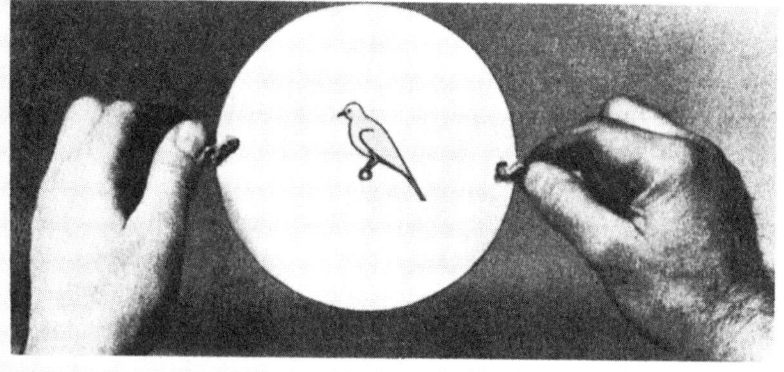

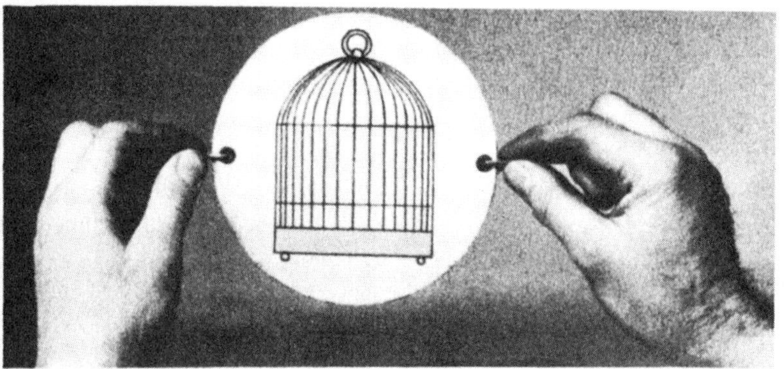

FIGURE 6.1. The thaumatrope. Image: Bridgeman Images.

phenomenology of that experience may be sharpened through attention to successive theories of vision, but it also exceeds the context of the history of science. The moving image breaks out of its intended context when its playfulness triumphs over its philosophy.

The thaumatrope, one of the earliest optical philosophical toys, has a somewhat indirect relation to apparent motion but demonstrates the flicker fusion aspect of persistence of vision quite dramatically, through its ability to fuse a continuous image from two rapidly alternated separate images. As Crary says of the thaumatrope, "Similar phenomenon had been observed in earlier centuries merely by spinning a coin and seeing both sides at the same time, but this was the first time the phenomenon was given a scientific explanation *and* a device was produced to be sold as a popular entertainment. The simplicity of this 'philosophical toy' made unequivocally clear both the fabricated and the hallucinatory nature of its image and the rupture between perception and its object."[15]

The purveyor and promoter of the thaumatrope, John Ayrton Paris, was a distinguished medical doctor and scientific author who had used his philosophical toy to demonstrate the principle of persistence of vision to the Royal Society in 1824. But he aggressively promoted the device's role as an educational toy and wrote a rather long novelistic account of how toys and games could teach young people the nature of the universe and their own perceptions. This 1827 book (so popular it went through several editions and revisions) embeds these devices into a very revealing discourse of popular nineteenth-century science. Its title says it all: *Philosophy in Sport Made Science in Earnest: An Attempt to Illustrate the First Principles of Natural Philosophy by the Aid of Popular Toys and Sports*. The chapter he devotes to the thaumatrope opens with a clear argument for the educational use of illusions: questioning human senses and demonstrating their unreliability. According to Paris, the trick of the thaumatrope lies not just in the hand, but lurks concealed in the eye itself, whose nature is revealed by the device. Paris's narrator, Mr. Seymour, declares to his young charge, "I will now show you that the eye also has its source of fallacy." His adult interlocutor, the local vicar, exclaims, "If you proceed in this manner, you will make us into Cartesians." Paris provides a useful footnote to explain the term:

> The Cartesians maintained that the senses were the great sources of deception; that everything with which they present us ought to be suspected as false, or at least dubious, until our reason has confirmed the report.[16]

Mr. Seymour translates the toy's name to mean "*Wonderturner*, or a toy which performs wonders by turning round." The thaumatrope's wonder is "founded upon the well-known optical principle, that an impression made on the retina of the eye lasts for a short interval after the object that produced it has been withdrawn."[17] The twirling of the card causes the images on each side to appear before the eye as if present at the same instant, which Seymour describes as "a very striking and magical effect."

As with most philosophical toys, the lessons of the thaumatrope depended on the manipulator not only being in control of the device, but also being able to examine its elements both in motion and in stillness. Anyone could see that each side of the disk presented only a part of the composite image which spinning produced. Thus the illusion could be both produced and deconstructed by the child who operated the device. The classic thaumatrope composite images (e.g., a bird + a cage; a vase + flowers; a horse + a rider; a bald man or woman + a wig) did not present a moving image at all but, rather, a sort of superimposition, merging two separate pictures into a new unity.

The thaumatrope displays the fascination produced by an optically produced image. Paris claims the composite image derives from a "fallacy" of the eye. Most discussions of persistence of vision claim it results from a "defect" or "weakness" of the eye. Herein presumably lies at least one basis for the production of motion being described as a trick or deception (Talbot says "the camera is a more perfect trickster than the most accomplished prestidigitator"[18]). The spinning disk is faster than the eye. The illusion presumably derives from the lingering, persistent afterimage, by which we see something after it has, in fact, vanished from our visual field, or, in the case of the thaumatrope's composite image, we see an image which does not strictly correspond to anything in reality (there is no "bird in a cage," only a bird on one side of a card and a cage on the other). This image is the product, Paris seems to claim, of a collusion between the device and our eye, or, alternatively the tricky device has taken advantage of the weakness of our eye (C. W. Ceram in fact refers to the "laggard sense of sight" in describing Plateau's experiments with afterimages, and Talbot intones about motion pictures, "The illusion is wholly due to one glaring deficiency of the human eye, of which the utmost advantage has been taken") in order to make us believe we see something that does not, in fact, exist.[19]

I have always found such descriptions of this ability to blend two images into a single one as an imperfection of the eye curious and extremely Cartesian, in the sense of driving a wedge between what we know and what we see—and decidedly valuing what we *know* over what we *see*. Following Paris's cue, we might view the thaumatrope as a machine for producing young Cartesians, as much as illusions. But to understand this new form of image, I think we must let the movement speak rather than concentrate exclusively on the explanation. When I twirl a thaumatrope, although I do see a composite image, I do not mistake it for the equivalent of the images imprinted on either side of the disk. The image has an unfamiliar quality. It is less material than the printed images and, as Paris stresses, less opaque; I can in effect see through it. I am inclined to think of it as visual rather than tactile, something I can see but not touch. And yet I am very aware of its production (and my manual role in producing it). Mary Ann Doane, one of the few film scholars who attempts to describe the image produced by optical devices, captures its odd nature, which she indicates aligned it with the possibility of deception and trickery: "The image of movement itself was nowhere but in the perception of the viewer—immaterial, abstract, and thus open to practices of manipulation and deception. The toys could not work without this fundamental dependence upon an evanescent, intangible image."[20] Most likely this is best described as a "virtual image," an image whose existence consists in its appearance and effects rather than its materiality, and which, in relation to optics, the *OED* defines as an "image resulting from the effect of reflection or refraction upon rays of light" (thus David Brewster used the term in 1831 to describe the effect of an image appearing behind the mirror caused by a convex mirror). As a trick, this virtual image surprises me, not only because I know it isn't "really there" but because I participate in its appearance. As simple as the device is, the thaumatrope cannot function without someone serving as simultaneous viewer and manipulator. The image appears as the result of this interaction. As Doane states about early optical devices, "The tangibility of the apparatus and the materiality of the images operated as a form of resistance to this abstraction, assuring the viewer that the image of movement could be produced at will, through the labor of the body, and could, indeed, be owned as a commodity."[21] The viewer of the thaumatrope was both the astonished spectator and the producer of the image. Mannoni reproduces a thaumatrope with a painter before a blank canvas on one side and a small portrait of a lady on the other. Twirling the disk, the resulting composite image places the lady on the canvas, as if stressing the device's role in creating, not just a composite, but a composite *image*.[22]

But if we are aware of the act of twirling the thaumatrope as a form of production, we are also aware that it produces only an ephemeral image that vanishes as soon as the turning stops. While the implication of Paris's Cartesian discourse is that the thaumatrope should make us aware of the feeble and deceptive aspect of our senses, I wonder if the imagery of the disks, their often irreverent sense of humor and fantasy, encourages such sober disillusionment. I want to stress the ludic and aesthetic dimension of the toy, the delight that comes from playing with oneself and one's perception. Why, in fact, shouldn't this ability to see the superimposed image be viewed as a faculty, an ability, rather than a defect? I experience the production of this virtual image as extending my conception of vision rather than experiencing some sort of failure to maintain the distinction between the two images. After all, this is a toy, a device to give pleasure, not cause frustration. We certainly feel as we twist the thread of the thaumatrope and watch the image it produces that we are escaping the ordinary, that we are seeing in a different manner; we glimpse a virtual world. Although the superimposed image may not necessarily produce an image *of* motion, it is an image *in motion* and therein lies its uniqueness. What it does not resemble is the fixed and static image that constitutes the norm of pictorial expression (a norm, I believe, we could claim that the art of picture-making also constantly challenges and reconceives). To claim that the thaumatrope-produced image does not exist, or exists simply as an illusion, reveals a prejudice toward perception as a static process, veracity as something viewable only from a fixed and stable perspective, vision understood as a still picture. I am claiming that the moving image fascinates partly because of its constant impulse to exceed what is already known and already grasped, in favor of mobile possibilities.

WHEELS OF LIFE: FLICKERING MOVING IMAGES

The optical devices that succeeded the thaumatrope produced not just superimposed virtual images, but images that moved, using revolving wheels or drums with slots or indentations through which the viewer peered. The aperture provided by the viewing slot not only turns what would otherwise be a continuous blur into a stable visible image, but also inscribes the viewer into the apparatus, setting a place and means for observation and controlling it with precision. The breakdown of a continuous movement into a series of flashes or flickers—basically the creation of shutter effect—would be essential for the production of motion in nearly all cinematic devices to come. As Austrian scientist Simon Stampfer explained its function in his stroboscopic disk in 1833, "the light falling on the change of the images is interrupted, and the eye receives only a momentary visual impression of each separate image when it is in the proper position."[23] The production of motion was founded upon a breakdown of vision into flashes, flickers of instantaneous vision produced by a rapidly revolving shutter. The complexity of effects triggered by this simple device is worth extensive contemplation. Stampfer indicates the role of the aperture and shutter in aligning image and viewer and exposing the still images to a brief view in such a way that the transition between images is occluded. Like a mechanical conjuror, the shutter hid the moment of change (when one image replaced another) from view.

Paris's book for young scientists explains the apparent movement produced by these devices in terms of a theory of motion which claims that perceived motion is less something *seen* than something *deduced*: "Now it is evident, that before the eye can ascertain a body to be in motion, it must observe it in two successive portions of time, in order to compare its change of place." He supports this statement with a quote from Lord Brougham (Lord Chancellor and member of the Royal Society), "Our knowledge of motion is a deduction of reasoning, not a perception of sense; it is derived from the comparison of two position; the idea of a change of place is the result of that comparison attained by a short process of reasoning."[24] This claim seems somewhat different from the more physiologically based persistence of vision theory, but it reveals a central prejudice about the actual perception of motion: that motion must be the product of a mental (or physical) processing of still images. This persistence of the still image as the true substance of the moving image is the specter that haunts the nineteenth-century understanding of the moving image.

While the explanations of vision offered by Lord Brougham resolve motion back into still images, the toys more commonly ran the other way, as is seen in the phenakistiscope, invented by Belgian scientist Joseph Plateau (and basically identical in principle and manufacture to the stroboscope invented and presented about the same time by Simon Stampfer).[25] Curiously, Plateau first produced a device whose turning wheel and aperture-and-shutter mechanism produced a still image rather than a moving one. In the anorthoscope (described by Mannoni) a distorted anamorphic drawing rotated and viewed through a revolving slotted disk produced a "perfectly steady and recognizable image."[26] Although produced for sale in 1836, the anorthoscope was a commercial failure, while Plateau's next revolving wheel toy set off what Mannoni has called a "Phenakistiscope craze."[27] It could be claimed that this latter device provided the first unambiguous example of an optical moving image. The name of the device, derived from the Greek *phenax*—cheater or deceiver—marked the view it offered as deceptive. Here is Plateau's physical description of the device:

> The apparatus . . . essentially consists of a cardboard disc pierced along its circumference with a certain number of small openings and carrying painted figures on one of its sides. When the disc is rotated about its center facing a mirror, and looking with one eye opposite the opening . . . the figures are animated and execute movements.[28]

The viewer holds the device by a handle in one hand while peering through the slots and sets the wheel turning, usually spinning it with a single finger of her other hand. The slots punctuate the vision of images on the moving disk as Stampfer described, converting the passing figures into a flickering series of individual images (or rather, producing a single moving image) rather than a continuous blur.

Apparently the idea of a moving figure came to Plateau only after his experiments with the "illusion" of a still image produced by the anorthoscope.

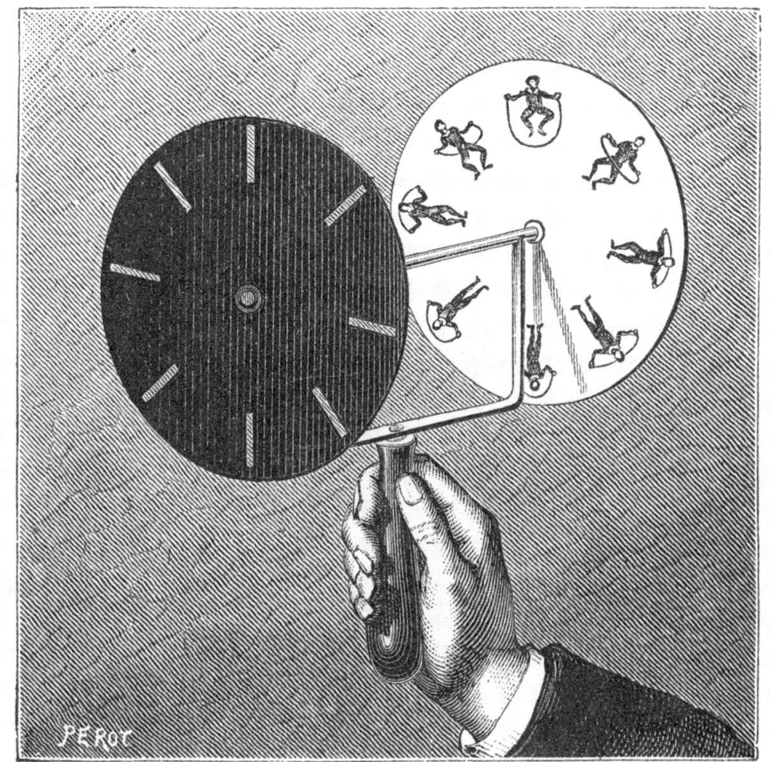

Fig. 99. — Phénakisticope de Plateau. (Page 125.)

FIGURE 6.2. The phenakistiscope, 1885. Image: Chronicle/Alamy Stock Photo.

He had also demonstrated the apparent stillness of a rapidly revolving device with a repeated identically drawn figure. As the wheel revolved with some sixteen figures of a standing man drawn on its periphery, the figure appeared within the viewing slots as a single static image. Mannoni theorizes that the example of the thaumatrope may then have inspired Plateau to the next crucial move. Now the figures drawn on the periphery portrayed a single figure engaged in the successive stages of a simple repetitive motion: a dance, sawing wood, opening one's mouth in a grimace, juggling balls, or, perhaps most mesmerizingly, a series of abstract geometrical gyrations and transformations. As William B. Carpenter, vice president of the Royal Society, pointed out in 1868, the phenakistiscope substituted "for the repetition of similar impressions . . . a series of gradationally varied impressions, produced by drawings of the same figure in different positions."[29] Although the succession of poses yields a single progressive action, the revolving wheel makes it a potentially endless cycle, with no clear conclusion, other than that caused by the operator/viewer's boredom or manual fatigue. The movement portrayed is posed between brevity and endlessness, an instant of action or an eternity of Sisyphean repetition, the first appearance of the cinematic loop that evades the linearity of action through its circular technology. The most famous of Plateau's phenakistiscope disks shows a male dancer performing a pirouette.[30] The dancer performs a 360-degree turn.

Like most of his contemporaries, Plateau believed the device demonstrated the natural outcome of optical afterimages, for the first time explicitly subsumed under persistence of vision:

> If several objects that differ sequentially in terms of form are represented one after another to the eye in very brief intervals and sufficiently close together, the impression they produce on the retina will blend together without confusion and one will believe that a single object is gradually changing form and position.[31]

One could see the pirouetting dancer as the origin of the optical moving image (in other words, as a continuous moving image produced by an optical device). Like the thaumatrope, the phenakistiscope or Stampfer's stroboscope create a virtual image, an optical phenomenon that is not identical to any of the images that make it up. Rather than an image with a single material base, it is a perceptual image produced by motion, and thus virtual. In this sense it could be called a "trick," produced as it is by a device that must be operated. But the same process of revolving disk and slotted shuttered viewing could produce an equally "tricked" *still* image, as in Plateau's anorthoscope (or the more famous Faraday wheel). Motion is necessary for the trick, but the trick does not have to yield a moving image.

But the effect of the motion produced remains powerful, and Paris describes "the great astonishment they felt, at observing the figures in constant motion, and exhibiting the most grotesque attitudes." In spite of these uncanny and grotesque effects, Paris (or his narrator) uses the device to explain our normal perception of motion:

> Each figure is seen through the aperture and as it passes and is succeeded in rapid succession by another and another, differing from the former in attitude, the eye is cheated into the belief of its being the same object successively changing the position of its body. Consider what takes place in an image on the retina when we actually witness a man in motion; for instance, a man jumping over a gate, in the first moment he appears

> on the ground, in the next his legs are a few inches above it, in the third they are nearly on a level with the rail, in the fourth he is above it, and then in the successive moments he is seen descending as he had previously risen. A precisely similar effect is produced on the retina, by the successive substitution of figures in corresponding attitudes as through the orifices of the revolving disc; each figure remaining on the retina long enough to allow its successor to take its place without an interval that would destroy the illusion.[32]

The true sleight of hand employed here is that the devices that produce motion from a series of still images are now being used to explain—not the process of the toy itself—but normal human perception. If the toy creates an illusion of motion, one wonders if the precisely similar process of the toy and what happens "when we actually witness" motion indicates that all perception of motion should also be considered an illusion, and if not, why not? Like Lord Brougham's description of movement as a process of reasoning and comparing, Paris's explanation of actually witnessing movement starts from the assumption that in perception the still image is primary, that movement consists of a mental deduction based on comparing static positions. What we see happening in Brougham's explanation and Paris's lesson drawn from the phenakistiscope—and this is one reason the discourse about the invention of cinema involves more than simply a technical history—is human perception being modeled on a mechanical explanation of a mechanical device (rather than exploring the new device in terms of human perception).

The phenakistiscope generated a number of offspring, all of which similarly animated drawn successive figures in loops of repetitive motion when viewed through revolving devices. The most popular was the zoetrope, in which, as Carpenter described it, "We look through slits in the side of a vertical revolving drum at the interior of the opposite side of the drum . . . and when one of the long strips covered with figures is placed in the lower part of the drum, and is viewed through the slits in its near side, the effect is exactly the same as that produced by looking through the slits near the margin of the disks of the Phenakistiscope."[33]

THE MOVING IMAGE: MORE THAN AN ILLUSION

It is worth pausing at this threshold in the nature of imagery that the phenakistiscope and its successors crossed. Since the beginning of culture, movement has played a role within art works through the physical movement of actors and dancers, puppets and automatons, or shadows and pictorial figures. But with these mechanical devices we actually see moving images produced optically. I maintain this marks a revolutionary moment in the history of the image—one we have not fully appreciated or explored. To describe the perception achieved by these devices without recourse to the mechanical description of how they operate remains a challenge, precisely because their effect overturns our dominant concept of representation as a picture. We are more comfortable describing how the devices work than how they affect us as viewers.

Let me be clear. These devices do not represent motion; they produce it. They do not give us a picture of motion (such as a comic strip panel of Ignatz Mouse's brick sailing through the air with lines indicating its trajectory); they *make pictures move.* For perceptual reasons, which we still understand only in part, we actually see movement, provided the apparatus is properly made and operated. Earlier devices represent, or allude to, movement through multiple pictures. Magic lantern slides, protean or transforming pictures (pictures showing different images depending on a change in light), and even thaumatropes could represent different phases of an action, although in a limited number (usually two). A trick lantern slide showing a dancer in two successive poses could be manipulated rapidly and smoothly and give an impression of motion through this alternation. But a viewer is always aware of the individual static phases and the gap between them. The phenakistiscope generated a new sort of image, an image that moved.

The reader might observe that my task in describing this threshold might be easier if I simply described what the phenakistiscope produces as an "illusion" of motion. But this is a thorny term and I don't want to descend into philosophical conundrums. From one viewpoint I would agree we are dealing with something like an illusion, in that the successive drawings of Plateau's dancer never move—*except in a phenakistiscope.* But I am not willing to say that when the wheel is spun and I look through the aperture I do not see a figure of a dancer moving. My position is obviously phenomenological; that is, I maintain that perceptions need not be dissolved into their physiological process (I am not against doing this—if we are studying physiology rather than moving images). But my task here is to describe our perception as we experience it. The riddle of the perception of the moving image lies in the fact that no one can explain it purely physiologically, and the psychological explanations are still debated. In other words, we have a true challenge to explanation here. Yet the phenomenological description, while still difficult, is, I think, possible. We see motion, and yet it is somehow truly different from a physical dancer or puppet. We see a moving image, two-dimensional in appearance. As an image, it has something of the virtuality of the composite picture in the thaumatrope, provided that, as I believe we do, we sense the flicker fusion occurring.

A moving image delights us with its novelty, because most images do not move, but also for its familiarity, since it recalls for us the way we perceive the world, *which is primarily moving*. Recent investigators of perception claim the greatest distortion in our understanding of visual perception comes from assuming it is founded on static images, pictures to which somehow movement is superadded. As the ecological and phenomenologically minded perceptual psychologists (such as J. J. Gibson and Alva Noë) have demonstrated, movement provides the norm for visual perception because our eyes are moving, our bodies are moving, and the world around us moves as well, in concert and independently of us. The static retina image is a myth created in the perceptual laboratory. I believe our investigation of the discourse surrounding the early moving image devices shows that the mechanistic worldview of the nineteenth century was determined to see human perception in terms of machines. Thus the education offered by philosophical toys included not only the disciplining of the body that Crary finds embedded in these devices, but a worldview in which the viewer identified his (and others'!) perception with the operation of a machine. This is an education with social and political consequences. Sometimes the greatest trick lies in claiming something is only a trick and that one can unmask it easily.

However, I would maintain that reexamining the experience of the moving image, even in these devices, need not be limited to this lesson. While I resist describing the moving image as an illusion, I think one might still see it as a trick, a trope, a turn, a transformation that surprises, partly because we do indeed see it, not simply mistake it. The moving image is an illusion only if we assume our eyes are defective. If we think of seeing as a multifaceted way of exploring the world (and indeed of delighting in it), then a trick need no more be an illusion than is a difficult gymnastic or acrobatic turn or a feat of juggling. While the educational logic of *Philosophy in Sport Made Science in Earnest* labors to transform astonishment and delight into earnest discipline, it also exceeds its purpose. The dancer pirouettes endlessly, and if its visual fascination may serve the end of seduction into taking one's place willingly within the apparatus (or before the screen, or at the keyboard), this need not be the only pleasure produced (nor need pleasure only lead to complicity).

This apparatus, while it subjects our vision and behavior to a specific regimen necessary for the transformation into a moving image to take place, also remains very much in our hands and within our sight. The productive gestures are highly visible rather than concealed; we operate the phenakistiscope and zoetrope with the flick of our hands or fingers. We see the whole apparatus and its parts and can observe the still images before we set them into action. These philosophical toys display what Crary calls "the undisguised nature of their operational structure," their evident "mechanical production" based in "the functional interaction of body and machine."[34] They lack the concealing of the operational mechanism that Theodor Adorno would identify with the phantasmagoria, and which become part of the regimen of the classical cinema.[35] Mary Ann Doane states it explicitly: "The optical toy is anti-phantasmagoric in this respect—it does not hide the work of its operation but instead flaunts it."[36]

The moving image entered the nineteenth century in peculiar circumstances. First, it displayed a dialectical relation between still and moving images. But the educational discourse surrounding philosophical toys remained fixed upon the primacy of the still image, and describing the "illusion of motion" as the product of the rapid presentation of still images before a "defective" eye. This reduction of motion to an illusion served philosophical ends. William Carpenter in his 1867 history of "the Zoetrope and its Antecedents" claimed that the study of these devices allowed young people to cultivate a "scientific habit of thought" founded on a comparison "between the *apparent* and the *real*."[37] Even more radically, it was claimed such devices taught young people that the process of seeing motion somehow depended on atomistic still images, and then "cheating" the eye into seeing things that were not actually there. In this scenario, maintained by many to this day, the eye is deficient and weak, while the machine is powerful.

As Doane has emphasized (and Crary indicated), optical devices present the machine as a toy, unthreatening and inviting. Part of its attraction lies in the manipulation of the apparatus itself, which one holds in one's hand, as much as in the evanescent image it produces, which Doane characterizes as their tactility, manipulability, and materiality. These optical toys, as she elegantly puts it, mark a moment when the viewer "seemed to hold movement in his or her hands."[38] Yet, even acknowledging the nostalgia that such a simple control of the device evokes, the production of the moving virtual image remains a crucial threshold in the modern transformation of the image I am tracing. As Doane describes it, "A hesitation in the transition from still to moving image underscores the wondrous nature of its effect, its alliance with the toy that takes on life."[39] While the trick of motion undoubtedly partakes of the uncanny effect of the animating of the inanimate, the stuff of childhood fables and myth for millennia, it takes on new meanings in the modern era. No longer restricted to the myths of archaic culture or the fairytales of the nursery, we now dwell within an environment enlivened by moving images, even though the new dimensions implicit in this modern revolution in image has now been rendered banal by its omnipresence. It is our duty as theorists to rediscover and pay attention to it.

My survey of several nineteenth-century devices for the production of moving images has tried to break away from simply drawing up a linear series of devices that "led" to the movies. While not denying that narrative, in this chapter I tried to show the deeply dialectical relation between still and moving images which these devices reveal, especially when approached phenomenologically, rather than simply technically. Most centrally, I am arguing that the absolute novelty of the moving image—so delightfully evident in all these devices—posed a source of anxiety (or at least confusion) for its early explicators, who used their explanation to reduce the moving image to an "illusion" founded in the "reality" of still images and the fallacy of human perception. A strong prejudice against recognizing the mobile nature of visual perception is revealed by this discourse, a prejudice that the cinema and media studies must still labor to overturn.

The best introductory textbook on cinema, David Bordwell and Kristin Thompson's *Film Art: An Introduction*, still promotes this view, claiming in its opening pages, "Moving-image media such as film and video couldn't exist if human vision were perfect."[40] One wonders how to imagine this "perfect" vision in which all motion would presumably cease and dissolve into a succession of still images. Although Bordwell and Thompson simply invoke this perfect vision as a rhetorical heuristic, it reflects the distrust, and indeed pedagogical discredit, of the senses that much of film studies has adopted from the nineteenth century. Although Bordwell particularly offered a trenchant criticism of the description of film spectatorship known as apparatus theory, which saw cinema and especially the "illusion of motion" as part of the ideological swindle of the basic cinematic apparatus, that suspicion of the moving image seems to persist.

My investigation of the moving image offers another take on the theory (and history) of the apparatus. Although being vigilant about the nature and method of ideological deception remains a duty of the theory of media, assuming an Enlightenment critique of perception seems to me a distraction rather than a foundation for a political praxis. I share Jonathan Crary's attempt to provide apparatus theory with historical, technological, and phenomenological specificity. However, if the optical devices serve as a mode of disciplining subjects and workers and citizens, I find the realm of the moving image provides equal opportunities of criticism and analysis. And I do not believe that delight necessarily cancels those possibilities out. The proliferation of devices of the moving image demands a critical history of their uses and experiences. But if a utopian celebration of new media can blunt the edge of criticism (and produce an amnesia about what we have learned from previous practices of visual images), puritan suspicions of the senses and their playfulness seems to be an equally deadly route to take. There may yet be uses for philosophical toys.

PART II
Theory

7

The Exterior as *Intérieur*: Benjamin's Optical Detective

Here is a riddle for you *unheimlicher* bird.
What is so strange it feels like home?

SUSAN MITCHELL, "BIRD, A MEMOIR," IN *Erotikon: Poems*

Benjamin's arcades need to be grasped as a topographical fantasy, something like those phantom objects André Breton glimpsed in dreams that caused him to haunt the flea markets and arcades of Paris to find their equivalents—the "Cinderella Ashtray" or the "Nosferatu Necktie"—objects that, like a dream, combined seemingly irreconcilable aspects.[1] The arcade, Benjamin frequently reminds us, is an exterior space conceived as an *intérieur*. A one-line entry in *The Arcades Project* summons up topographical contradictions like a Mobius strip: "Arcades are houses or passages having no outside—like the dream."[2] By their very nature of enclosing an alley-way, or, rather, forcing a passage through a block of buildings, the arcades present a contradictory and ambiguous space that allows an interpenetration—not only of spaces, but of ways of inhabiting and using space. "More than anywhere else, the street reveals itself in the arcade as

This essay first appeared in *boundary 2* 30, no. 1 (2003): 105–30, with the following acknowledgment: "This essay has benefited greatly from a conversation at its origin with Thomas Elsaesser in a London restaurant and, just before its final revision, a long phone conversation with Miriam Hansen. I was also aided by comments at the conference 'Benjamin Now: Critical Encounters with *The Arcades Project*' at Brown University and the comments of Philip Rosen. None of the above, however, should be assumed to be in agreement with my argument."

the furnished and familiar interior of the masses" (*AP*, d°,1). Thus the arcade embodies the fundamental dreamlike experience of the flaneur as the city "opens up to him as a landscape, even as it closes around him as a room" (*AP*, e°,1).

The exterior as interior becomes a crucial emblem for Benjamin's analysis of the nineteenth century, because this ambiguous spatial interpenetration responds to an essential division on which the experience of the bourgeois society is founded, the creation of the interior as a radical separation from the exterior, as a home in which the bourgeois can dwell and dream undisturbed by the noise, activity, and threats of the street, the space of the masses and of production, a private individual divorced from the community. A cocoon of consumption, the *intérieur* becomes "not just the universe of the private individual; it is also his étui" (*AP*, 20). Encased within an upholstered environment, the inhabitant of the *intérieur* is cushioned, like the railway passenger for whose comfort Wolfgang Schivelbusch claims the modern shock-absorbing techniques of upholstered furniture were first designed.[3] But what collision is being warded off by such protection? This new interior betrays signs of the previous violence of demarcation by which the *intérieur* and its privileges were claimed—as Benjamin observes, "pieces of furniture retain the character of fortifications" (*AP*, I1a,8). The "unconscious retention of a posture of struggle and defense" (*AP*, I2,3) that Benjamin quotes Adolf Behne as finding in the bourgeois furniture arrangement belies any taking for granted the success of this exclusion. In spite of attempts to fashion an impermeable cloistered space, a summons from without, Benjamin claims, such as an insistently ringing doorbell, cannot be exorcised simply by being ignored (*AP*, I1a,4).

Through a defensive posture, the *intérieur* constitutes itself as a space cut off from the world, but this process of private appropriation relies not only on separation and insulation but also on disguise and illusion, as the optics of interior space take on the complexity of the phantasmagoria. As Benjamin says, "The space disguises itself" (*AP*, I2,6). Ultimately the interior cannot withstand the exterior; it can only transform the nature of its looming invasion optically. While the aural summons of the ringing doorbell may not be successfully ignored, the inhabitant of the interior can still optically dominate the exterior through a "window mirror," a device Theodor Adorno describes as "a characteristic furnishing of the spacious nineteenth- century apartment." A carefully positioned mirror, also known as "a spy," it reflects who, or what, waits outside. As an optical device of the *intérieur*, the window mirror, in Adorno's words, allows the exterior to enter the room "only [as] the semblance of things."[4] This control of semblance defines the *intérieur* as much as does the defensively conceived furniture. Through semblance, Benjamin claims, the interior can pretend to be a space of universal representation: "In the interior [the private individual] brings together remote locales and memories of the past. His living room is a box in the theater of the world" (*AP*, p. 19). Thus the nineteenth-century parlor became not only the protective shell one fashions for oneself (*AP*, I4,5) but also the locus of optical devices and philosophical toys of all sorts—the stereoscope, the kaleidoscope, the magic lantern—that seem to open the viewer's gaze onto a different world, but only under the dominion of the image and semblance.

But optical transformation of the interior could cause, rather than assuage, anxiety, figuring a return of the repressed. Benjamin returns frequently to the opening pages of Proust's *Swann's Way*, invoking the relation the process of dreaming and awakening bears to the *intérieur*, as Marcel, on awakening, would try to reconstruct both the structure of his own body and the shape and arrangement of the furniture in his bedroom.[5] A few pages on, in a passage Benjamin does not refer to directly but that introduces the theme of the optical uncertainty of the *intérieur*, Proust describes the attempt by family members to ease Marcel's fear of slipping into sleep with an optical device, the parlor magic lantern:

> It substituted for the opaqueness of my walls an impalpable iridescence, supernatural phenomenon of many colors, in which legends were depicted as on a shifting and transitory window. But my sorrows were only increased thereby, because this mere change of lighting was enough to destroy the familiar impression I had of my room, thanks to which, save for the torture of going to bed, it had become quite endurable. Now I no longer recognized it, and felt uneasy in it, as in a room in some hotel or chalet, in a place where I had just arrived by train for the first time. . . .
>
> I cannot express the discomfort I felt at this intrusion of mystery and beauty into a room which I had succeeded in filling with my own personality until I thought no more of it than of myself. The anaesthetic effect of habit being destroyed, I would begin to think—and to feel—such melancholy things.[6]

The encasing forms of the bourgeois interior, its protective shell, are literally shaped by habit (AP, I4,5). The plush material that swaddles the bourgeois not only cushions its inhabitants but, of all materials, most retains the imprint of their habits. The furnishings of the *intérieur* become molded (as Marcel fantasizes as he awakes) to the very shape of his body and bear the imprint of his deeds. As Benjamin puts it in his essay "Experience and Poverty," in the bourgeois room of the 1880s, "there is no spot on which the owner has not left his mark. . . . [A]nd conversely, the *intérieur* forces the inhabitant to adopt the greatest number of habits—habits that do more justice to the interior he is living in than to himself."[7] Benjamin contrasts this with the new environments of glass and metal being built by Le Corbusier, Adolf Loos, and the Bauhaus, and imagined by Paul Scheerbart—the glass houses that so fascinated both Benjamin and Sergei Eisenstein, "rooms in which it is hard to leave traces."[8]

Imprinted in the velour and plush of the *intérieur*, Benjamin locates "the origin of the detective story, which inquires into these traces and follows these tracks" (*AP*, p. 20). One might find this claim somewhat surprising, given Benjamin's frequent claim that the detective is the heir of the flaneur, taking over the persona of the former's street-wandering idleness as a cover for his sharp-eyed surveillance, whether in the street or in the new department stores that, like the arcade, move the human circulation of the street into the confines of a building.[9] Benjamin's analysis of Poe's "The Man of the Crowd" sketches out this transformation from flaneur to detective when the narrator leaves his position at the plate-glass window from which he surveyed the passing urban crowd in order to surreptitiously follow one of its members whose appearance has aroused his suspicion.[10]

In spite of occasional nocturnal rambles, Poe's most famous detective, C. Auguste Dupin, confined within his shuttered daytime apartment, remains very much a man of the *intérieur*, for his most famous cases, the murder in the Rue Morgue and the purloined letter, depend on his careful consideration of the arrangement of furniture and objects in interiors. However, our consideration of Benjamin's topography should have revealed to us that the opposition between street and *intérieur* does not form a simple dichotomy; the significance of the arcade lies partly in its simultaneous embodiment of both aspects of this apparent contradiction. A dialectical development of this spatial contradiction must unfold through its optics: both the close-up scrutiny of the detective and a disorienting process of reflection.

THE ANGLE OF VIEW: THE OPTICS OF DETECTIVE WORK

> Interpenetration as principle in film, in new architecture, in colportage.
>
> WALTER BENJAMIN, *Arcades Project*, O°,10

Benjamin quotes H. Pene's 1859 reaction to police solving a London murder through examination of a piece of clothing: "So many things in an overcoat!—when circumstances and men make it speak" (*AP*, I5a,2).

The methods of Emile Gaboriau's Monsieur LeCoq and Sir Arthur Conan Doyle's Sherlock Holmes are figured here. The traces left in personal belongings, which detectives examine, take the form of incriminating clues. Impressions of the human personality and its deeds become absorbed without one's awareness by the nearly animate objects of the *intérieur* and eventually betray the owner or user. But Carlo Ginzburg has already beautifully examined this aspect of the scrutiny of the trace as the origin of detective fiction, and I see no need to rehearse it further here.[11] Rather, I want to follow Benjamin's lead and locate the dynamics of the detective story not only in the scrutiny of clues but in the optical exchange between interior and exterior. The optics of the detective has primarily been investigated in terms of Foucauldian panoptics of surveillance, an essential aspect I grant, but one that Benjamin's analysis of optics complicates. Commenting on *Panoptikum* as a popular name for wax museums at the turn of the century, Benjamin glosses it in a typically dialectical manner that goes beyond Jeremy Bentham and Michel Foucault: "Panopticon: not only does one see everything, but one sees it in all ways" (*AP*, Q2,8). The nineteenth-century detective not only observes and investigates but also—at least potentially—investigates his or her point of view.

Benjamin's optics relates to a tradition deriving from Marx's rhetorical use of optical devices such as the camera obscura and the phantasmagoria to describe the illusory nature of relations and appearance under capitalism and its ideologies, a tradition developed, as well, by Benjamin's friends Adorno (whose Marxian definition of the phantasmagoria Benjamin quotes as "a consumer item in which there is no longer anything that is supposed to remind us of how it came into being" [*AP*, X13a]) and Bertolt Brecht (especially in the last scene of *Galileo*, in which superstition and religion are reduced to optical phenomena when the shadow cast on a wall that appears to a child as a witch at her cauldron is shown to be simply an old woman cooking when he is hoisted up to look into the interior through a window).[12] Likewise, Adorno's account of the window mirror sees the exterior as penetrating into the *intérieur* only by passing through an optical transformation into semblance, that is, illusion. But Benjamin also dialectically develops this tradition by understanding optical devices (including the cinema) not simply as deceiving or creating illusion but as articulating the dialectic of interior/exterior, the relation between the private dreaming self and the public space of production and history. In his analysis of popular literature (colportage, such as detective stories), Benjamin reveals the access that optical devices and entertainment may provide to unconscious adumbrations of revolutionary perception.

In two different entries in *The Arcades Project*, Benjamin speaks quite gnomically of the truth exemplified by what he calls "the house without windows." Thus, in one of his first sketches:

> The true has no windows. Nowhere does the true look out to the universe. And the interest in the panoramas is in seeing the true city. "The city in a bottle"—the city indoors. What is found within the *windowless* house is the true. One such windowless house is the theater; hence the eternal pleasure it affords. Hence, also, the pleasure taken in those windowless rotundas, the panoramas. In the theater, after the beginning of the performance, the doors remain closed. Those passing through arcades are, in a certain sense, the inhabitants of a panorama. The windows of this house open out onto them. They can be seen out these windows but cannot themselves look in. (*AP*, F°,24)

This note is nearly reproduced in Convolute Q, slightly edited and rearranged, with the rather difficult last sentences perhaps clarified as, "The windows that look down on it [the arcade] are like loges from which one can gaze into its interior, but one cannot see out these windows to anything outside" (*AP*, Q2a,7). I would be the first to confess I find these statements more intriguing than obvious. I am speculating that the "true" invoked here is not ironic (possibly a dangerous assumption). But I believe it allows us to keep the dialectic of optics in play, liberating it from a simple opposition of truth/illusion. It seems certain that Benjamin here refers to a statement by Leibniz in the "Monadology": "Monads have no windows, through which anything could come in or go out."[13] Yet the relation between the self-enclosed monad and the permeable arcades remains rather obscure to me. What seems to be at issue, however, is a truth that depends not on looking out at the world, on simple accuracy of representation, but rather on a system of representation coming through the interconnection of all created things, which makes a monad, in Leibniz's words: "a perpetual living mirror of the universe."[14] The nature of the "true," of "the living mirror" within the windowless room, will be one of "the MacGuffins" of the optical detective story I am about to spin.[15]

An entry in *One Way Street*, entitled "Manorially Furnished Ten-Room Apartment," presents the detective story as a critique of the *intérieur*:

> The furniture style of the second half of the nineteenth century has received its only adequate description, and analysis, in a certain type of detective novel at the dynamic center of which stands the horror of apartments. The arrangement of the furniture is at the same time the site plan

> of deadly traps, and the suite of rooms prescribes the path of the fleeing victims. . . . This character of the bourgeois apartment, tremulously awaiting the nameless murderer like a lascivious old lady her gallant, has been penetrated by a number of authors who, as writers of "detective stories"—and perhaps also because in their works part of the bourgeois pandemonium is exhibited—have been denied the reputation they deserve. The quality in question has been captured in isolated writings by Conan Doyle and in a major work by A. K. Green. And with *The Phantom of the Opera*, one of the great novels about the nineteenth century, Gaston Leroux has brought the genre to its apotheosis.[16]

In addition to the familiar citing of Poe and Conan Doyle, Benjamin speaks here of two writers of detective fiction, neither of whom is as well known today as they deserve to be: Anna Katharine Green and Gaston Leroux. Leroux has regained some attention in the last decades due to the Broadway adaptation of his most famous work. Green remains out of print and largely ignored, except for a few feminist literary critics and historians of the genre who recognize that this American woman writer was a bestselling author of detective novels decades before Conan Doyle.[17] Green is undoubtedly the most important figure in nineteenth-century detective fiction between Poe and Gaboriau.[18]

In contrast to the hard-boiled film noir detective who roams the mean streets of the city, the detectives created by Green and Leroux remain primarily inhabitants of the interior. *The Phantom of the Opera* revolves around one of the greatest architectural fantasias in modern literature, adapting the gothic castle with its crypts and secret passageways to a modern structure in an urban location, the Paris Opera, designed by Charles Garnier. As a temple of illusion and display, "the stage on which imperial Paris could gaze at itself with satisfaction" (*AP*, L2a,5), as Benjamin quotes one historian as saying, the Opera included not only the famous area of visual display—the grand stairway and theater—but layer upon layer of subterranean levels in which props, sets, and even horse stables were housed, depths that allowed the illusions created on the surface to operate. The construction of the Opera took over a decade (1861–1875), beginning under the Empire and finishing in the Republic, including the period of the Prussian siege and the Commune. In its depth, at least according to Leroux, the structure retained signs of this repressed recent history, as well as of the primal geology of Paris, incarnating another of that city's subterranean realms, like the sewers explored by Hugo and Nadar, which fascinated Benjamin as well. The lowest level of the Opera sinks into a lake, the center of which the phantom Erik has made his unrestricted domain. But it is through its many passageways, including the one formerly used by the communards, known as the "Communist way," that Erik exerts his influence throughout the Opera, as the seemingly invisible "spirit of music." In the center of Erik's subterranean dwelling lies another architectural fantasy in which the structural meets the optical, a hexagonal torture room composed of mirrors, in which illusions are conjured and multiplied to infinity and in which Erik's victims are driven mad by a succession of illusory scenes combined with oppressive heat and thirst.

Leroux's inspiration for these fiendish optics was avowedly the Salle du Illusions, a central attraction of the 1900 Universal Exposition in Paris, which the narrator claims Erik had originally invented in Persia to entertain a sultan.[19] As an actual commercial attraction, its illusion was provided with a guaranteed exit, rather than subjecting customers to the nightmare of being lost in infinity, which drives Leroux's characters mad. This attraction was later transported to the Parisian wax museum, the Musée Grevin in the Passage Joffroy (where it remains to this day), and rebaptized as the Cabinet des Mirages. Benjamin recognized it as an essential *topos* in his discussion of the arcades:

> Here were united, one final time, iron-supporting beams and giant glass panes intersecting at countless angles. Various coverings make it possible to transform these beams into Greek columns one moment, Egyptian pilasters the next, then into street lamps; and according as they come into view the spectator is surrounded with unending forests of Greco-Roman temple columns, with suites, as it were, of innumerable railway stations, market halls, or arcades, one succeeding another. (*AP*, R1,8)

The bell whose sound announced each change recalled for Benjamin the Kaiserpanorama of his childhood, in which a similar bell would sound as, "before our eyes, that were full of the pain of departure, an image would slowly disengage from the stereoscope, allowing the next one to appear" (*AP*, R1,8).

The optics of this attraction, another windowless house, literally revolves around a key figure in Benjamin's optics of the arcade: the mirror, which forms the subject of Convolute R. For Benjamin, unlike most Romantics and psychoanalysts, mirrors do not primarily serve as the means of self-reflection and reproduction but provide another instance of the optically created dialectic of interior and exterior: "The way mirrors bring the open expanse, the streets, into the cafe—this too, belongs to the

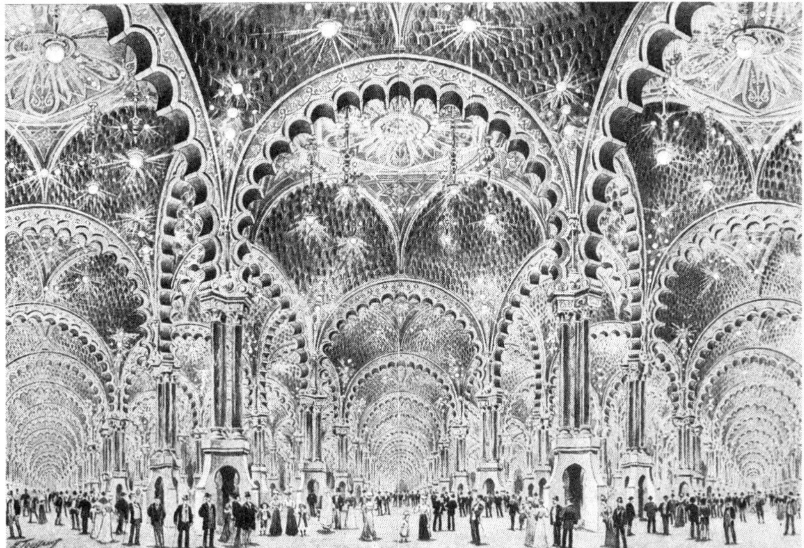

FIGURE 7.1. Palais des mirages Musée Grévin, originally in 1900 Paris Universal Exhibition. Photo © akg-images.

interweaving of spaces, to the spectacle by which the flaneur is ineluctably drawn. . . . Where doors and walls are made of mirrors, there is no telling outside from in, with all the equivocal illumination. Paris is the city of mirrors" (*AP*, R1,1; R1,3). Benjamin was well aware of both the attraction and the danger of these illusory spaces, so vividly envisioned in the torture chamber in the climax of Leroux's work. "Let two mirrors reflect each other; then Satan plays his favorite trick and opens here in his way (as his partner does in lovers' gazes) the perspective on infinity" (*AP*, R1,6). The satanic multiplication of perspectives risks losing all track of its original dialectic and seems to open space to endless elusive attempts at mastery (as it does in Erik's torture chamber, and—Benjamin indicates—in the broad perspective of Haussmann's panoptical construction of Paris). For the truth contained in these windowless houses lies in their hollow core. Benjamin's evocative analysis recalls both the Cabinet des Mirages and Erik's sinister tortures: "For although this mirror world may have many aspects, indeed infinitely many, it remains ambiguous, double edged. It blinks: it is always this one—and never nothing—out of which another immediately arises. The space that transforms itself does so in the bosom of nothingness" (*AP*, R2a,3). It is this pivot on nothingness that the Cabinet des Mirages reveals, the optical process of reproduction in which nothing is produced—except our sense of nothingness.[20]

But if Leroux's Erik expresses his villainy through his mastery of illusions, conjuring an infinite landscape within a small chamber, can this trick also be worked within the bourgeois parlor? Erik's glass-covered room would seem to recall the unyielding spaces of modernity rather than the plush- and velvet-furnished domain of the *intérieur*. Leroux himself underlines the contrast by having Raoul de Chagny, the novel's romantic hero, regain consciousness within the bourgeois *intérieur* Erik has created as his own dwelling within his subterranean realm. As with Proust, Raoul's awakening is one of disorientation and gradual recognition guided by the typical outlay of middle-class furniture:

> After the deceptions and illusion of the torture chamber, the precision of the middle-class details in that quiet little room seemed invented for the express purpose of once more puzzling the mind of the mortal rash enough to stray into that abode of living nightmare. The wooden bedstead, the beeswaxed mahogany chairs, the chest of drawers, the brasses, the little square antimacassars carefully placed on the backs of the chairs, the clock on the mantelpiece and the harmless looking ebony caskets at either end . . . and lastly the what-not filled with shells, with red pin cushions, with mother of pearl boats and an enormous ostrich egg . . . the whole discreetly lighted by a shaded lamp standing on a small round table: this collection of ugly, peaceful, reasonable furniture, *at the bottom of the Opera cellars*, bewildered the imagination more than all the late fantastic happenings.[21]

Raoul here discovers a secret convergence between the overstuffed bourgeois interior and the seemingly deserted optical illusions of the mirrored torture chamber. In this intersection of seeming opposites, Leroux inscribes and also deconstructs the horror of the *intérieur* Benjamin claims as his true subject, the product of a detour into the optically absurd.

While Poe may have pointed the way, Green, as Catherine Ross Nickerson's recent treatment of early detective fiction by American women shows, supplied a gendered sense of the domestic and its discontents that allowed the detective story to attain to the novelistic. For Dupin and his legacy of sleuths, a crime leaves its imprint in an object, a thing whose handling and use have converted it into a hieroglyphic of crime, a bearer of signs to be deciphered and read. The optical domain of detective fiction may originate in the masterful detective's gaze, but it has other visual regimes that often deflect the direct gaze into a mediated course of reading and reflecting.

As a genre, the nineteenth-century detective story seems often to aspire to a form of hieroglyphic writing, straddling both arbitrary and pictorial modes of signification, through its visual presentation of the text to the reader, such as its frequent use of diagrams and visual facsimiles. Readers of Sherlock Holmes might not know the illustrations that accompanied the original publications of the Holmes stories in the *Strand* magazine, which are not considered an essential part of the text, but they must recall the various diagrams and maps that appear embedded in the narrative as well as the printed text. These include messages that are literally hieroglyphic, such as the cavorting cryptogram that capers through "The Adventure of the Dancing Men," or the torn or damaged written messages whose fragmentary nature is reproduced, forbidding any reading of it as a nonmaterial sign but rather demanding it be examined as a very material signifier, whose matching with a signified has been blocked.[22] Semiotically, this disjunction and later reunion might define the genre, for Holmes's solutions relieve material objects of their embarrassing obtuseness as they are cannily read by the knowing detective.

Although no responsible historian takes claims of invention too seriously, Green is often credited as the originator of these typographical devices. Her first novel, *The Leavenworth Case* (1878), provided diagrams of both the scene of the crime and of a later location, as well as the reproduction of a fragmentary letter whose lacunae the detective must fill in and read correctly.[23] Apparently in the original edition of this novel, these letter fragments were not illustrations but actual irregular pieces of paper bound into the book.[24] Similar diagrams appear in the novels of Leroux's most famous detective, Rouletabille, *The Mystery of the Yellow Room*, one of the most famous locked-door mysteries, and *The Perfume of the Lady in Black*, perhaps the most satisfying Oedipal mystery of the early twentieth century.[25] Such diagrams function differently from the maps in which turn-of-the-century authors try to locate fictional events, in either a naturalist (as in Thomas Hardy's maps of Wessex) or fantastic genre (as in L. Frank Baum's maps of Oz and its surrounding territories). In contrast, these diagrams map out domestic spaces—of interiors—that have become as threatening as a jungle. They indicate the possibility (or impossibility) of passage, the routes of escape, and even the trajectory of a gunshot. As Benjamin puts it, Leroux and Green transform the bourgeois interior into pandemonium, and these diagrams lay out its threats and dangers.

But while these diagrams are clearly visual and seem to illustrate the systemic and panoptic view of a detective, sailing above the scene and witnessing it from a cartographer's point of view, do they express the complex dialectical optics, the transforming pivot between exterior and *interieur*, that I have

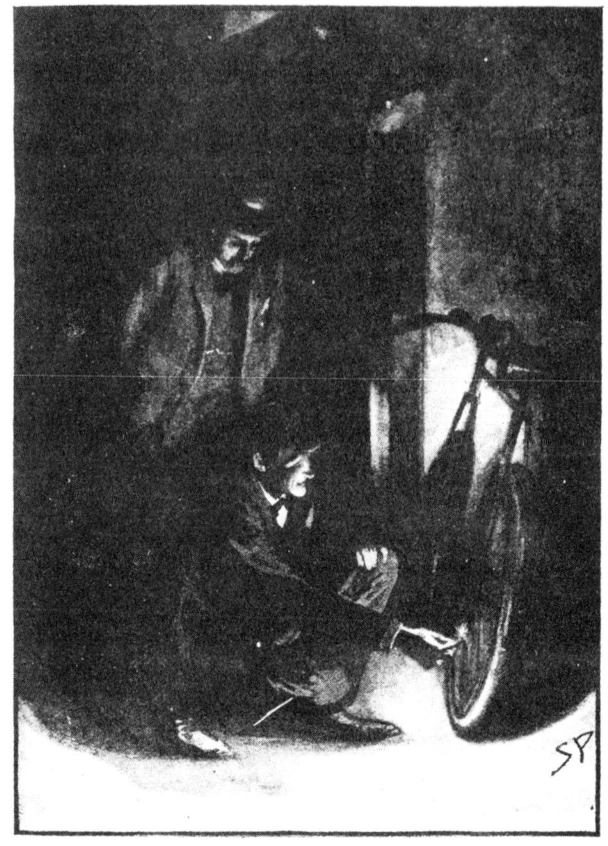

"I HEARD HIM CHUCKLE AS THE LIGHT FELL UPON A PATCHED DUNLOP TYRE."

FIGURE 7.2. From Arthur Conan Doyle's "The Adventure of the Priory School."

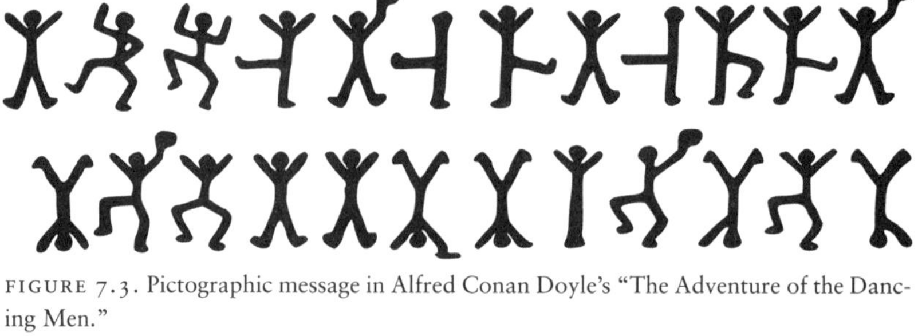

FIGURE 7.3. Pictographic message in Alfred Conan Doyle's "The Adventure of the Dancing Men."

claimed Benjamin found in the detective story? Beyond these topographical diagrams that are so common in nineteenth- and early twentieth-century detective stories that they could be considered as much *topoi* of the genre as the locked room or the dinner party, there also occur—not as frequently, but therefore with more startling force—scenes in which complex optical situations reveal the entrance of the criminal into the midst of apparent bourgeois order. The optical acuity and ambiguity captured in the primal scene from Green's novel *The Woman in the Alcove* (1906) is worth detailing.

The novel's protagonist, an eventual amateur detective seeking to clear her fiance's name, is the plain and slightly shy Rita van Arsdale. At a large dinner party, while seating herself at the table, she experiences a strange episode:

> I had not moved nor had I shifted my gaze from the scene before me—the ordinary scene of a gay and well-filled supper-room, yet I found myself looking, as if through a mist I had not even seen develop, at something as strange, unusual and remote as any phantasm, yet distinct enough in its outlines for me to get a decided impression of a square of light surrounding the figure of a man in a peculiar pose not easily described. It all passed in an instant, and I sat staring at the window opposite me with the feeling of one who has just seen a vision.[26]

Immediately after this experience, which seems to waver between the supernatural and the pathological, the dinner party is interrupted by the announcement that a woman, Mrs. Fairbrother, who was wearing a large and famous diamond, has been found murdered in an alcove off the dining room, her diamond missing. Rita's fiance, Anson Durand, is suspected of committing the murder, for he was last seen with the victim. Even more damning, the diamond is actually discovered on Rita's person in a pair of gloves Anson had handed to her.

During interrogation by a police detective, everything seems to incriminate her lover and perhaps even herself. Realizing she has no "witness" to her probity, Rita suddenly recalls her vision:

> Instantly (and who can account for such phenomena?) there floated into view before my retina a reproduction of the picture I had seen, or imagined myself to have seen, in the supper room; and at that time it had opened before me an unknown vista quite removed from the surrounding scene, so it did now, and I beheld again in faint outlines, and yet with an effect of complete distinctness, a square of light through which appeared

> an open passage partly shut off from view by a half lifted curtain and the tall figure of a man holding back this curtain and gazing, or seeming to gaze, at his own breast, on which he had already laid one quivering finger.[27]

In this second manifestation, the vision is fully psychologized as a memory, its sudden floating into visibility clearly an act of recall. But curiously, this "reproduction" of the vision is more distinct, or described more fully. Details both of its background (an open passage half concealed by curtains) and of the man's curious gesture and stance (gazing at his breast, which he touches with his finger) are now recounted.

With this increased clarity come further realizations: "Feeling anew the vague sensation of shock and expectation which seemed its natural accompaniment, I became conscious of a sudden conviction that the picture which had opened before me in the supper-room was the result of a reflection in a glass or mirror of something then going on in a place not otherwise within the reach of my vision; a reflection, the importance of which I suddenly realized when I recalled at what a critical moment it had occurred."[28] Convinced that she had seen the murderer of Mrs. Fairbrother, Rita persuades the police to let her return to the dining room. Resuming her seat at the table, Rita discovers that a large window facing her across the table could be swung on a pivot. The police manipulate this window until Rita declares, "For the second time I was to receive the impression of a place now indelibly imprinted on my consciousness."[29] However, the vision she saw was not a simple reflection, but rather a reflection of a reflection, the window bouncing to Rita's retina an image it caught from a mirror, reflecting in turn the very alcove in which the murder took place. The novel includes a diagram of the house on the eve of the dinner party and the murder. But this is more than a plan produced from the abstracted viewpoint of cartography; it also traces with a broken line the ricocheting glance by which Rita catches sight of the murderer. What we see here is not simply the panoptic gaze of the detective but the contingent flash of insight.

If less elaborate and less revolutionary in implication than this glimpse offered by the female protagonist of a female author, a similar relayed view occurs in Leroux's *The Perfume of the Woman in Black*. The major female character (revealed at the end to be the long-lost mother of the detective Rouletabille), Mme. Mathilde Darzac, lives in fear that her ex-husband, the notorious murderer and intriguer Larsan, still lives, despite reports of his death. Boarding a train with her new husband, she lets out a scream. Her husband explains: "In the compartment a small door leading into the dressing room was half open, so that anyone entering the compartment got an oblique view of it. A mirror was fixed to the small door. Now in that mirror Mathilde had seen Larsan's face!" Rushing onto the platform, Mons. Darzac also glimpses the sinister ex-husband lurking. However, he and Rouletabille decide that for the sake of Mathilde's sanity they must convince her that she saw only an optical illusion, based on a "curious reflection."[30] Mathilde stays up all night in the compartment with the light on, veiling the mirror with her handkerchief to avoid seeing Larsan's face again, as if unconsciously following the Jewish rituals of mourning, in which mirrors are veiled after a death in order to avoid seeing apparitions.

While I don't want to overstress the contrasting approaches these two works have to their scenes of mediated vision, I do want to emphasize their common theme of uncanny vision, of the sudden appearance of another scene within this one. Mathilde's vision almost involuntarily recalls Freud's account of his uncanny experience riding in a train compartment, when a jolt "swung back the door of the adjoining washing-cabinet, and an elderly gentleman in a dressing-gown and a traveling cap came in. . . . Jumping up with the intention of putting him right, I at once realized to my dismay that the intruder was nothing but my own reflection in the looking glass on the open door. I can still recollect that I thoroughly disliked his appearance."[31] Freud interprets his dislike as a vestigial trace of the uncanny fear of mirror reflections, but we might describe his reaction in more Benjaminian spatial terms.

The railway compartment, with its attempt to provide all the comforts of home while traveling, in effect constitutes (as Schivelbusch shows) another of the contradictory spatial figures of modernity, an unmoored *intérieur*, rolling through space at great speed. Everything in the design of the railway compartment strives to make the traveler forget that he is not at home. The mirror image functions, then, less as an uncanny double than as what Freud names it, an "intruder," a messenger from the outside disrupting the illusion of homey security. This reminder of the true state of affairs—the compartment's insecure mastery of privacy, its actually mobile and insecure place within a public and technological system—is conveyed optically. The truly uncanny moment comes—as anyone who has had a similar experience can testify, despite Freud's silence—from the lack of self-recognition. The dreamer of the *intérieur* has so defensively identified with his precarious privacy that even his own image appears as an alien intruder.

The fascination that Freud's essay "The 'Uncanny'" exerts owes less to his psychoanalytical explanation of the experience offered than to his complex description of the effect itself. Performing an essential and canny transformation of Freud's method, Benjamin explains such experiences in terms of the conflict between individual and collective psychologies that capitalism engenders. The unconscious that operates in Benjamin's arcades, while certainly not unrelated to Freud's analysis of dreams and parapraxis, opens itself up to the invasion of social history. This invasion operates via the optical unconscious that Benjamin describes in "The Work of Art" essay, a perceptual mechanism that takes in more than it can consciously account for.[32] This unconscious, therefore, cannot be reduced to a dream from which one must be awakened—just as its complex optics generates something more than an illusion that must be dispelled. These optical experiences of a sudden invasion of the interior by the exterior, and vice versa, undermine maintaining any absolute separation between the realms. As critical moments, they act like the monads that Benjamin frequently evokes as the basis of his method. But these fragments do not simply contain the whole but expand and redefine it. They are explosive monads, moments that shatter the apparently secure dichotomies on which a system of social control and illusory satisfactions are founded. This may be why Benjamin refers to his method in *The Arcades Project* as comparable "to the splitting of the atom," liberating the energies of history from the narcotic of the "once upon a time" (*AP*, N3,4).

Like the visual attractions of popular culture, the phantasmagoria, the panorama, the kaleidoscope, or the halls of mirrors, the detective story activates the complex dialectical optics of modernity, an optics based not only on the visual mastery of surveillance but also on the uncanny experience of transformed vision, glimpsing a presence where it is not, a space where it does not belong, and triggering a frisson of possible recognition, "the flash of wakened consciousness" (*AP*, K1,2). The optical trick that may occasion this flash involves turning the methods of psychoanalysis inside out, so that we see Freud less as a psychologized Sherlock Holmes rifling through the archives of personal memory for clues to a primal crime than as a ruthless surveyor of the modern barriers between self and society. Benjamin urges us to transfer Freud's methods "from the individual to the collective" (*AP*, K1,5). This reversal becomes a method itself, because, as he adds immediately:

> Of course much of what is external to the former [the individual] is internal to the latter [the collective]: architecture, fashion—yes even the weather—are, in the interior of the collective, what the sensoria of organs, the feeling of sickness or health, are inside the individual. And so long as they preserve this unconscious, amorphous dream configuration, they are

> as much natural processes as digestion, breathing, and the like. They stand in the cycle of the eternally selfsame, until the collective seizes upon them in politics and history emerges. (*AP*, K1,5)

The uncanny déjà vu that overcomes the flaneur in the arcade foreshadows this method, because it leads "into a past that can be all the more profound because it is not his own, not private . . . it is not a past coming from his own youth, from a recent youth, but a childhood lived before then that speaks to him" (*AP*, e°,1). Thus, the dream, the uncanny intoxication, is not the logical contradiction of awakening but its basis. As in Rita van Arsdale's flash of vision, reexperienced as recognition, the images granted by unconscious optics must "be secured on the level of the historical, and collectively. There is a not-yet-conscious knowledge of what has been: its advancement has the structure of awakening" (*AP*, K1,2). But far from dispelling the dream, this process of awakening relies on remembering it: "The new dialectical method of doing history presents itself as the art of experiencing the present as waking world, a world to which the dream we name the past refers in truth. To pass through and carry out *what has been* in remembering the dream!" (*AP*, K1,3).

This method coincides with what Benjamin describes as the "dialectical optic," which Surrealism foresees in its nesting of the mysterious within the everyday, rediscovering the dialectic of *heimlich* and *unheimlich* through turning inside out the dream, revealing its collective interior, concealed within an individualist psychology: "For histrionic or fanatical stress on the mysterious side of the mysterious takes us no further; we penetrate the mystery only to the degree that we recognize it in the everyday world, by virtue of a dialectical optic that perceives the everyday as impenetrable, the impenetrable as everyday."[33] The surrealists offered Benjamin the glimpse of a method in which the mystery and its solution were not antithetical but mutually engendered each other. The flash of dialectical optics reveals both the solution of the mystery and the truth of the dream. One learns something from the flash of recognition, but one also discovers through it a mode of knowledge that exceeds logical categories of verification. One could say that the optics of the detective reveals the canny aspect of the uncanny, not simply that which can be logically verified but, following up the associations of *canny* in English, a sort of knack, a knowledge, that comes from practice and tradition, the ground on which subjective insight opens onto a collective culture.[34]

The uncanny, properly understood, evokes the seduction of the strange, the revelation through déjà vu that our deepest memories do not belong to us alone. As a figure of colportage, the detective enacts within a popular medium a new dramaturgy based precisely on the topologies of bourgeois space that Benjamin analyzes in his discussion of both detective fiction and the arcades: the interpenetration of public and private, interior and exterior, which exposes the antinomies of bourgeois subjectivity and experience. The truth the detective seeks is inadequately figured as disciplinary surveillance (Foucault), as the influence of scientific empirical investigation on popular culture (Régis Messac), or even as an emblem of the divine justice unreachable in modern times (Siegfried Kracauer).[35] Rather, the detective exploits and develops the new dialectical optical experience of modernity, employing a vision simultaneously uncanny and canny, piercing to the foundations of nothingness on which bourgeois culture rests in the period of late capitalism. The detective announces the method that Benjamin's *Arcades Project* exemplifies. "Nevertheless, truth is not—as Marxism would have it—a merely contingent function of knowing, but is bound to a nucleus of time lying hidden within the knower and the known alike. This is so true that the eternal, in any case, is far more the ruffle on a dress than some idea" (*AP*, N3,2). The detective's methodical scrutiny of objects and ability to respond to unconscious optical experience adumbrates a method that will turn that ruffle inside out, finding within its immemorial folds both the space within a space and the time within time.[36]

8

Systematizing the Electric Message: Narrative Form, Gender, and Modernity in *The Lonedale Operator*

> Open the story by bringing two strongly contrasted places and strongly contrasted sets of people, into the connexion necessary for the story, by means of an electric message. Describe, the message—*be* the message—flashing along through space—over the earth and under the sea.
>
> CHARLES DICKENS, *Book of Memoranda Begun in January 1855*

> "How can you tell a story jumping about like that? The people won't know what it's about."
> "Well," said Mr. Griffith, "doesn't Dickens write that way?"
>
> LINDA ARVIDSON, *When the Movies Were Young*

The Lonedale Operator (1911) may be D. W. Griffith's most frequently viewed and best-known film from the "transitional" era. Indeed, the film's star, Blanche Sweet, whose winsome charm and plucky moxie dominate the film, told me in later years that she finally refused to appear with it anymore because she had gotten so weary of its constant screenings. The film became available readily by the 1960s in 16mm prints. VHS versions now are easy to rent or purchase, and most recently a DVD version appeared as part of

This essay first appeared in *American Cinema's Transitional Era: Audiences, Institutions, Practices*, ed. Charlie Keil and Shelley Stamp (Berkeley: University of California Press, 2004), 15–50, with a dedication—"For Sophia Moxie"—and the following acknowledgment: "This essay was probably conceived decades ago during conversations with Lynne Kirby, whom I miss; was gestated through arguments with Charlie Keil, my friend; and brought to term through discussions with Jennifer M. Bean, whom I am glad I met, finally. I want to thank Charlie Keil and Shelley Stamp for their patience."

the Treasures from American Film Archives set, presenting a Museum of Modern Art restoration of the film that gives us a tinted version, an aspect long missing from most modern prints and essential not only to the aesthetics but even the narrative logic of this film.

THE SYSTEM OF THE SINGLE-REEL FILM

As Kristin Thompson has pointed out, *The Lonedale Operator* provides a perfect example of Griffith's Biograph style, or at least of his race-to-the-rescue melodramas, and of his use of parallel editing with the effect Griffith termed "sustained suspense."[1] Could the film stand, as well, as representative of the "transitional" era, defined by Charlie Keil as existing between 1907 and 1913,[2] that point between what has become known as "early cinema" and the later classical mode supposedly instituted around 1917?[3] Here the thicket of problems becomes tangled, involving not only the issue of typicality but also the term *transitional* itself. Although I have used the term, increasingly I feel it begs many questions, not the least of which is the implication that American cinema accommodated only one transitional period. Further, the term seems to indicate that this period's significance lies less in itself than in the eras it comes from and leads to. Serving as a bridge between an earlier cinema that was somehow different and a later classical cinema in which difference was repressed in favor of a fairly static and consistent pattern of both stylistic norms and production modes, the transitional era would serve mainly as a way station, a pit stop on the course of history.

Questioning the monolithic nature of Hollywood cinema between 1917 and 1960 lies beyond the scope of this essay. I would theorize provisionally that every period of American cinema could be seen as a "transitional" one, but acknowledging this fact does not invalidate the investigation of this key period of early film history. Seeing this period as more than "preclassical" may help us discover its unique qualities, revealing more than a period of apprenticeship in which the regimens of classical narrative structure were rehearsed and tested with an aim toward perfection. If anything typifies the period between 1907 and 1913, it would seem to be the rapid rate at which film style changed during the period so that the films from 1907 seem radically different from those released in 1913. This period may distinguish itself from others primarily through its protean nature. It might be better named a period of transformation than a period of transition.

In my own work on Griffith I have defined this period as one of "narrative integration" in which the various devices of the cinema were worked over with an eye to creating narratives that were not only easily comprehensible but also fully engaging. To make stories move quickly and clearly, Griffith (and other directors during the transitional period) clarified temporal and spatial relations between shots, working out the logic of such editing figures as parallel editing, reverse-angle cuts, and "sight links" or point-of-view shots. But these devices were not introduced simply to render stories more comprehensible (after all, *The Great Train Robbery*, from 1903, conveyed the basic action of its story without any of these devices) but more complex and involving as well. Character motivation and psychology, moral judgments, and devices of suspense were all introduced through editing and other means in order to transform film stories from distanced chronicles of action-dominated events to emotionally meaningful and exciting narratives, often carrying a moral message.

Charlie Keil's important new work, *Early American Cinema in Transition*, and my book on Griffith's early Biograph films both see 1913 as the end point of this era, largely because after this year the dominance of the single reel begins to give way in favor of the multiple-reel feature film.[4] Longer films led to new conceptions of narrative form, as filmmakers more frequently looked to the theater or the novel as models. The one-reel film understood itself in relation to the short plays presented in vaudeville and, especially, the short story.[5] Important as these models were, however, the sort of narrative condensation found in the films of the transitional period created new conventions, a sort of narrative shorthand unique to motion pictures. This condensed format rendered narrative strategies especially visible.

Thus, the "transitional" period feeds off a dialectical energy, as opposing forces rub against each other. On the one hand, the brevity necessitated by the limited length of the one-reel film, which was the industry standard during the transitional period, posed an inflexible format. This set length ran up against the expanding ambitions of the film industry, calling for more complex story lines and characterizations.[6] Instead of simply leading to an artistic standoff, however, this conflict inspired filmmakers such as Griffith to generate complex and very noticeable narrative conventions and formal systems. Combined with other constraints (such as limited budgets, extremely short shooting schedules, reliance on stock acting troupes and compressed multipurpose film studios, and release schedules that demanded a set number of films be completed each week), this tension between ambition and limitation led not only to an almost factorylike mode of production but also shaped stylistic aspects of the films, promoting highly systematic and schematic approaches. This system revolved around the standardization of the single reel as the basic industry product, the basis on which the industry was organized.[7] Thus, I would propose calling this period the "single-reel era" to avoid the assumptions implied by calling it "transitional." The best films of the single-reel era, such as *The Lonedale Operator*, demonstrate the way art can thrive in the midst of constraints and triumph creatively over formulas, even as it employs them.

SYSTEMS OF NARRATION: REPETITION AND ALTERNATION

> I must create a system or be enslaved by another man's.
>
> WILLIAM BLAKE, *Jerusalem, the Emanation of the Giant Albion*

I have described Griffith's style as a "narrator-system."[8] By this term I wished to express that Griffith approached the process of narration systematically, working on the various levels of cinematic expression in order to create the narrative effects of suspense, characterization, and moral lessons. Such narrative devices were appearing in the films of other American production companies in this era as well. The conflict between narrative ambition and the one-reel format yielded differing outcomes. These conflicting demands could end in a fatal collision, exemplified, as Ben Singer has pointed out, in an episode from the Thanhouscr 1914–1915 serial *Zudora*, in which narrative coherence and characterization remain, as he puts it, "baffling."[9] But films by other production companies did employ systematic devices of repetition, alternation, and rhyming that guaranteed not only narrative clarity but also an aesthetic sense of coherence and unity. For instance, Ben Brewster has shown that Vitagraph one-reel films were often structured around a single object whose exchange unites the film, providing not only an economic narrative flow but a device that literally pulls the film together.[10] This interaction among constraints, clarity, and stylistic ambition could even, as in the case of *The Lonedale Operator*, produce a film in which formal systems interpenetrate narration to such a degree that the film not only achieves narrative clarity and the emotional involvement of the audience but also attracts the viewer's attention to the film's systematic approach.

What does the term *system* contribute to this discussion of early film narration? In many ways I use it as a synonym for *structure* and indicate by it the way the individual elements of the film are arranged into clear patterns. I prefer *system* to *structure* because *structure* often carries a connotation of something static and rigid, whereas *system* seems to denote a process, the way something is done, rather than simply how it ends up. *System* is also the term used during the strongest period of film semiotics, in the analyses of Raymond Bellour (as in "The System of the Fragment") and Christian Metz's *Language and Cinema*, in which Metz examines not only the cinematic language system generally (that is, the codes of cinema) but also the unique system of a single cinematic text.[11] Indeed, in Bellour's magisterial analysis of *The Lonedale Operator*, "To Alternate/To Narrate," Bellour seeks to demonstrate "the systematicity at the heart of American high classicism."[12]

In Griffith's Biograph films, action is channeled and funneled by devices of alternation and repetition in such a way as to make them orderly and clear. My analysis in many ways supplements Bellour's but seeks to explore *The Lonedale Operator* less as an exemplar of a larger system (such as the classicism Bellour seeks to highlight), or even as preparatory to a later system (the "Classical Hollywood Cinema" that the transitional era supposedly anticipates), and more as fashioning a unique system. I do, however, reach beyond the singular here to speculate on a somewhat smaller system than the classical: the unique qualities of the period of single-reel production.

Let me begin by relating the systematic nature of a film's editing to the organization of its actual filming, relating narrative form to the exigencies of production. After 1908 the single-reel film became the standard and basically unvarying commodity sold to exchanges and exhibitors by film production companies. The single-reel forms a unit in a grand scheme that embraces and controls the entire film market. The Motion Picture Patents Company was founded in 1909 not only to protect the patents of its members but to regulate the motion picture industry, uniting production, distribution, and exhibition of films in a predictable flow of product. Every production company had a determined number of single-reel films it was required to place on the market on fixed release dates. Film exchanges, the distribution agents of the era, placed a set number of "standing orders" with the companies, guaranteeing they would take a constant amount of the company's reels every week. Exhibitors had slightly more freedom in deciding how many films they would rent from the exchanges, but almost every film theater presented a program that included more than one film, and most of them changed their bills daily. A constant flow of films had to be guaranteed for these voracious exhibition outlets, and the production of any single film could not slow down the process. Each film had to be carefully planned and, in effect, standardized, in terms of days devoted to its shooting, the locations in which it was shot, and even the camera setups used in order. Predetermined systems of filming had to be in place to guarantee the smooth operation of systems of exchanges and exhibition.

At the same time, however, filmmakers during this period gradually increased the number of shots used in a single reel. Before 1907 films rarely consisted of more than a dozen shots. According to Charlie Keil's sampling of American film up to 1911, the average number of shots per reel had doubled.[13] From 1908 to 1913, Biograph led the way in hyperediting, and *The Lonedale Operator* set a formidable standard. Griffith squeezed ninety-eight shots into its seventeen-minute length, as well as six intertitles, one main title, and two written inserts! Since this is the largest number of shots found in any of Griffith's films to this date (the film was released on 23 March 1911), and Griffith was the leader in hyperediting, it is unlikely any film released before *The Lonedale Operator* contained more shots. Yet Griffith and his cameraman, Billy Bitzer, shot this film in only four days! Only a systematic plan of shooting could mediate between the industry's demand for quickly made films and Griffith's desire to make his film more exciting through hyperediting.

Preplanning shooting through carefully constructed shooting scripts introduced a new economy of shooting and editing during the single-reel era, allowing cameramen to shoot films out of order. This meant every scenario had to be broken down into shots and the camera setups for those shots predetermined. In this way many shots could be taken from one camera setup and the process of shooting streamlined. *The Lonedale Operator* consists of ninety-eight shots but uses only twenty-three camera setups.[14] On average a single setup yielded four shots. Some setups were used for only one shot (nine, mostly shots of the train rushing down the track during the climactic race to the rescue), whereas others (such as the doorway to the station and the telegraph operator's office) were used for a dozen shots or more.

This system of camera setups yielding multiple shots also meant that a series of repetitions would appear across the film because of these recurring locations. Besides the obvious benefit of efficiency on the production level, on the level of narrative form, such repetitions would anchor spatial relations in the minds of viewers. By always seeing the doorway to the

Lonedale station from the same camera setup, the viewer quickly learns to recognize it. In addition to the recurrence of individual setups, Griffith employs repeated trajectories of spatially linked shots. Early in the film we follow the heroine from the exterior doorway through the interior ticket office and into the office of the telegraph operator. The trajectory of movement lays out the space of the station, setting up not only the primary location of the film but also the basic action (will the tramps penetrate from the exterior door to the operator's inner office?). Griffith repeats this three-shot trajectory through the office space four times over the film, fixing it in the viewer's memory.

Repetition structures *The Lonedale Operator* on both the level of single shots and multishot segments. But other forms of repetition stand out in the film through patterns of alternation. Parallel editing plays a key role in single-reel films and especially in the Biograph films. Parallel editing first appeared at the beginning of the single-reel era, primarily in films produced by the French film company Pathé Frères. In its simplest form, parallel editing alternates between shots of two threads of action in different locations in order to indicate that they are interrelated, usually that they are simultaneous. The best example of this simple form of parallel editing in *The Lonedale Operator* occurs during the sequence in which the heroine, having seen the tramps skulking around the station, telegraphs for help. Eleven shots alternate between a closely framed shot of the heroine telegraphing and a medium shot of another telegraph office as a male operator first dozes, then responds to the message, transcribes it, then rushes out. The telegraph connection underscores the effect of simultaneity (supplying narrative clarity), and the parsing of the action and the movement back and forth also creates suspense, provoking questions: Will the male operator wake up? Will he get the message? How will he react? Will he act in time?

Lonedale's major sequence of parallel editing adds a further complication. In the dramatic race to the rescue, which brings the film to its climax, Griffith introduces a three-pronged editing pattern. Instead of simply alternating between two threads of action, the film rotates among three different actions: the locomotive rushing to save the heroine, the tramps breaking through the various doorways of the station, and the heroine in her inner office.[15]

This three-pronged rotation allows *Lonedale* to maximize all the effects of suspense the simpler form of alternation creates but also avoids the predictability an extended sequence of simple back-and-forth cutting entails. Although each shot returns to one of the three elements (thieves, rescuers on locomotive, heroine), Griffith also introduces variations. First, the thieves themselves are mobile, progressing into and through the station.

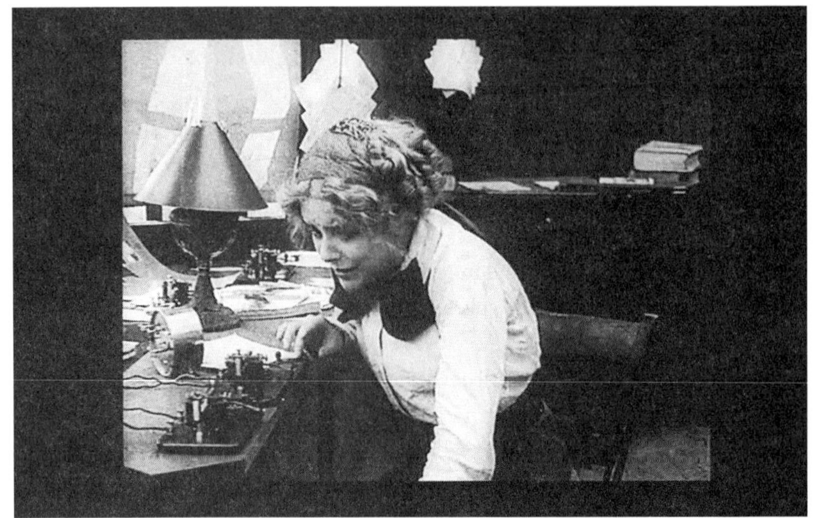

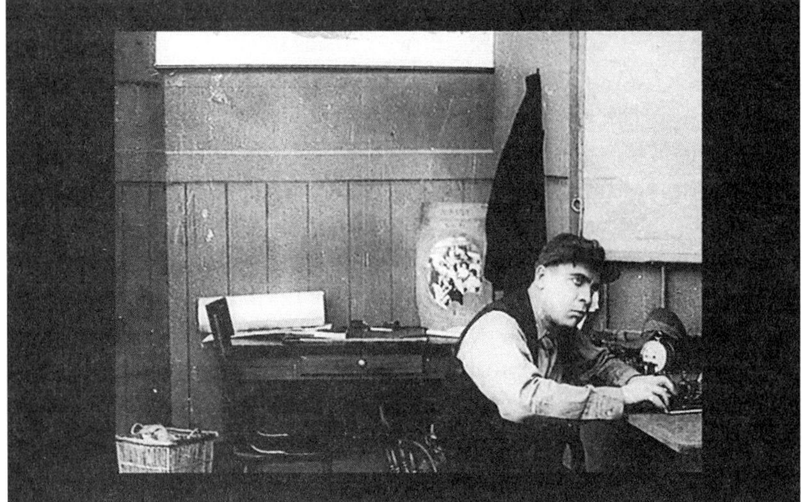

FIGURE 8.1. D. W. Griffith, *The Lonedale Operator* (1911).

Second, the series of shots devoted to the rescuers alternates among three views: a medium shot of the engineer from inside the engine cab (dynamically framed to reveal the landscape slipping by the window), a shot from outside the train showing the tracks as the engine barrels toward the camera, and a less frequent wider shot of the engine cab from the tender.[16] Thus, in moving among thieves, rescuers, and heroine, the editing pattern, rather than simply stuttering, endows its repetition with variations, highlighting a complex system of alterations within set parameters.

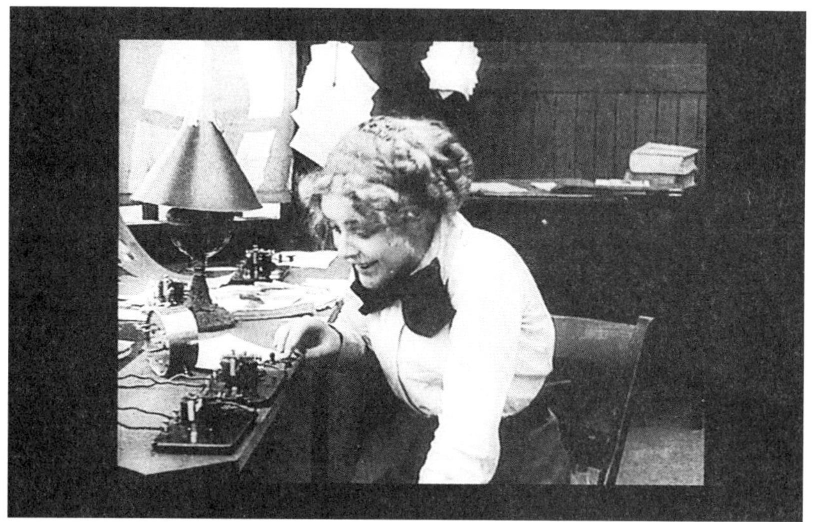

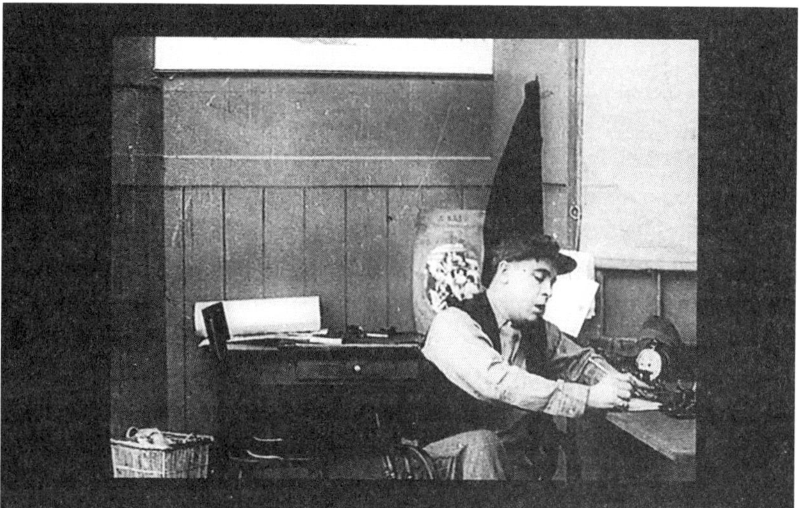

FIGURE 8.1. (*continued*)

The restoration of the film's original tinting pattern reveals another system of repetition and variation. A review of *The Lonedale Operator* in the *New York Dramatic Mirror* commented on the blue tint of the latter part of the film as "really looking like night." The reviewer added, "Tinted scenes in a Biograph is enough of a novelty to call for special praise anyway."[17] Tinted scenes appear in a number of 1911 Biograph films, usually the conventional blue for night, but sometimes with symbolic overtones, such as the golden tint used in *The Broken Cross*. More unusual is the red cast given to the shots within the engine cab in *The Lonedale Operator*. The realistic motivation for the tint comes from the glow of the overstoked boiler of the steam engine. As with most "red for fire" tints in early silent film, however, the monochrome carries as much abstraction as realism.

The rotation among the tints provides another formal system. As in the intercutting of action elements, the shots again rotate three possibilities: red (the engine cab), blue (darkness, including the train tracks, the exterior of the station, and the telegraph office once the heroine turns off the lamp), and no tint at all (used as the equivalent of sunlight or lamplight and restricted to interiors in this section of the film). The tints do not change with every cut, since several dark shots might appear in succession. But they do change frequently and underscore the pace of the editing; after the heroine recovers from her faint, nearly every shot changes tint. Given the relative brevity of these shots (most less than five seconds, none more than fifteen seconds), one almost has the impression of an abstract color flicker film rhythmically moving between red, blue, and black and white. Although for the most part, the change in tinting comes on a cut, in two instances the tinting changes during a shot (when the lamp is turned off and when it is turned on again), indicating tinting's relative independence from editing as a system of variation.

Kristin Thompson has also discovered other symmetrical patterns, less immediately apparent. Describing the race-to-the-rescue sequence as an alternation between shots of the train and shots of the station, she points out that the sequence returns to the station six times. Fascinatingly, the number of shots in each of these returns sets up a symmetrical order. The first return consists of a single shot (the thieves at the exterior door); the second return consists of four shots, the next return of two, the following return of two shots again; the penultimate return swells again to four shots, and the final return (before the engine arrives, that is) consists of a single shot of the heroine holding the tramps at bay with the wrench. As Thompson concludes, "Whether Griffith deliberately made his shots of the station balance symmetrically in this fashion or simply intuited the optimum rhythm for the presentation of the action cannot be known. Either way the rescue scene in *The Lonedale Operator* demonstrates Griffith's mastery of this technique."[18]

All these patterns serve the narrative—either through clarifying spatial and temporal relations between shots or by creating suspense and increasing audience involvement. Thompson points out that the number of shots in each of the station sequences fits the action being portrayed. In addition, the sensual rhythm of the editing, the brevity of shots combined with intense action (the speeding locomotive, thieves breaking through doorways), and the rotation of the tints create a visual experience of sharp alternations triggering a heightened sensual, physical excitement. The system of strong formal devices—repetition, symmetry, alternation, and variation on several levels—supports the film's obvious commercial purpose of telling a story in a clear and exciting manner.

I would claim that this impression of a strong formal system subtending the narrative operates as a key feature of the single-reel era, albeit one developed most fully by Griffith at Biograph. The brevity of the one-reel films dictated a limited number of elements, allowing spectators to notice repetitions that might be missed in a longer film. Devices of symmetry, alternation, or repetition were encouraged by the need to maximize the number of shots obtained from a single camera setup. Production efficiency and economy led to formal economy, a systematic use of elements that could take on artistic or poetic overtones. The coherence of the single-reel form (its use of symmetries and resolved asymmetries, as Raymond Bellour would put it) certainly gives these films a "classical" appearance, if by this we mean a formal unity and coherence. This foregrounded formal system contrasts sharply, however, with the classicism attributed to the Hollywood film, which requires not only narrative coherence but also formal transparency, as narration as a self-conscious or noticeable aspect of the film tends to "fade out," in deference to the apparently unmediated unfolding of the story.[19] Although I believe the transparency of later Hollywood cinema has been asserted more than it has been analyzed, a unique aspect of the single-reel era may lie in the foregrounding of editing, tinting, and other means of narration by an emphasis on their formal as well as expressive qualities.

SYSTEMS: BEYOND ALTERNATION AND REPETITION

> Time—the time appropriate to the production of exchangeable goods, to their transport, delivery and sale, to payment and the placing of capital—now served to measure space. But it was space which regulated time, because the movement of merchandise, of money and nascent capital, presupposed places of production, boats and carts for transport, ports, storehouses, banks and money brokers.
>
> HENRI LEFEBVRE, *The Production of Space*

The Lonedale Operator not only is systematic in telling its story but also foregrounds its formal system through repetition, alternation, and rotation. But the film's system also includes shots that stand out by *not* being repeated or alternated. Figures of alternation or rotation are obviously systematic because they organize individual shots into larger patterns. But in a film like *The Lonedale Operator*, where so many shots can be absorbed into figures of alternation or rotation and in which most shots are filmed from camera setups that are repeated multiple times, one might neglect the special role played by shots whose camera position appears only once and is never repeated. Searching out such a unique camera setup to be used in only one shot indicates a special role for the shot that overrides the economy gained by shooting multiple shots from a single camera setup. It is likely, therefore, that each of these shots plays a key role in both the film's narrative and its formal system. In addition, thematic elements, systems of oppositions and tensions that link the film to historical issues of the era of its production and reception, such as class and gender, are welded to the film's narrative by these unique shots. Analyzing these images and patterns will allow us to move beyond the film as a closed formal system, to relate the film to the systems of society and history in which it was formed, as well as to us as viewers living in the wake of that history.

The largest group of unique shots in *The Lonedale Operator* doesn't seem to carry special significance, however: the long shots of the train barreling toward the camera as it passes through various landscapes. But these shots do not really operate as independent shots. Although photographed from a series of unique camera setups, the shots are similar in their depiction of action and in their composition, and this similarity clearly inscribes them as part of a series rather than as independent pivotal shots.[20] The remaining four shots that are taken from unique camera setups, however, do mark out highly significant points within both the narrative and the referential systems of the film. The earliest unique shot provides the simplest, and perhaps the most elegant, example. The heroine and her engineer boyfriend enter a bucolic location dominated by the backlit foliage of a willow tree that frames the image. In the background we see a hilly country path with rustic buildings in the distance. The couple approach from the background right until they are embraced by the foliage. Framed at the hip, they act out a flirtatious scene: the heroine shakes her head "no" to some plea from her beau; he pouts at this rejection, but she reassures him, and they hold hands. When he tries to kiss her, she playfully twists his ear. Then, pulling out his railway watch, she reminds him of his schedule. They exit happily toward the camera on the left.

For this love scene Griffith and cameraman Billy Bitzer selected a unique location with a diffused natural light that enfolds the tender scene and expresses a romantic mood. Ensconced in a natural landscape, it is the only shot in the film in which the world of technology is truly absent (with the exception of the engineer's watch, produced at the shot's end and motivating the characters' exit from this romantic locale). The composition fuses actors and landscape into an expressive unity. In this little oasis of nature, the lovers enact their romance, as this lyrical setting contrasts with the modern environment (represented by the railway and the telegraph office). Unique setups next appear in a pair of consecutive shots that introduce the central object of the film: the mine payroll. In the first, the payroll is gathered from a cashier; in the next shot, it is loaded on the train that will transport it to Lonedale. These two shots in some distant station remain isolated from the rest of the film. None of the characters we encounter here (the delivery boy who picks up and loads the payroll, the official who gives it to him, the typist in the office) appear again. Only the object, the money-laden payroll bag, will make the journey from this central station to the center of the story—distant Lonedale. Money, however, is the object that is no object, merely the medium of exchange.[21] Early in the system of telegraphy, the possibility of "wiring" money could eliminate its actual transport, opening up the information age.[22] *The Lonedale Operator* does not penetrate that far into the systems of modernity, however; its "MacGuffin" remains tangible.[23]

Why include these shots at all? The narrative introduction of the film's MacGuffin, or, to use the contemporary term mischievously reintroduced into scholarly discourse by Ben Singer, the "weenie," the object of desire that motivates the film's action, could be conveyed by the telegraph message the heroine receives in the following shot or, even more simply, by its delivery at Lonedale.[24] Such repetition may anticipate the redundancy of later classical Hollywood cinema that repeats key information (it even follows the "rule of three," since we learn about the payroll shipment three ways: seeing it loaded, seeing the telegraph message that announces its arrival, and finally seeing it being taken from the train by the heroine).[25] But these shots of the shipping station also anchor Lonedale within a larger railway system.

These two shots stand out by being loaded with detail and a strong use of background action. The office in which the payroll is picked up teems with incidental details and explanatory inscriptions. Two complementary desks (one closer to the foreground on the right with an elderly man facing right, the other a bit further back on the left, with a woman typist facing left, busily at work) split the cramped and shallow space. On the back wall above the head of the typist a large clock marks time with a continually swaying pendulum, and on the right edge of the frame a calendar decorates

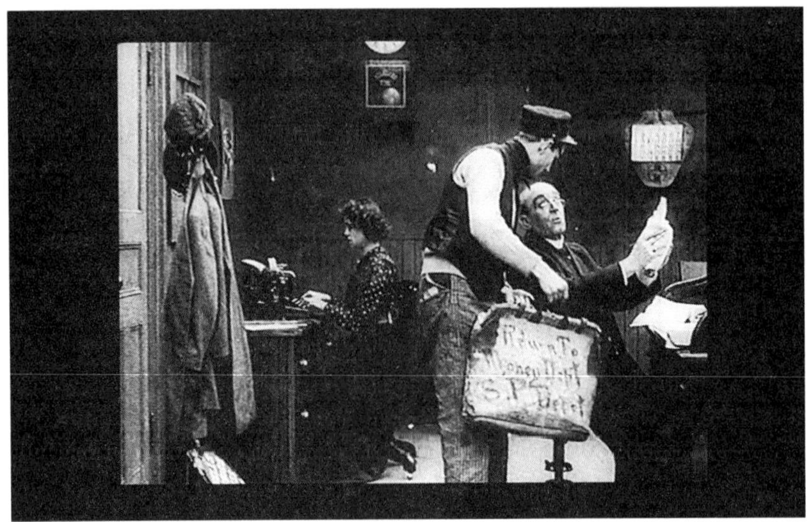

FIGURE 8.2. D. W. Griffith, *The Lonedale Operator* (1911).

a partition. At each desk a man gives or takes orders from the cashier and the typist. Both of these incidental characters exit when the delivery boy enters. After a moment, a door on the left opens and a delivery boy enters, bearing with him a panoply of written signs: the opened door reveals the word *Office*; the delivery boy carries a placard reading "Wells Fargo Express," which he puts down after he enters; the canvas bag he carries is emblazoned with "Return to Money Dept. S. F. Depot." Even the back of his ledger, which he gives to the elderly man to sign, briefly shows the words "W. F. C. Express." The whole environment tells us we are in the realm of business, of words and messages, of records and carefully measured time.

Griffith was strongly influenced by naturalistic stagecraft, the ideal represented by David Belasco of recreating a world in miniature onstage, complete in all its details.[26] More than anything else in *The Lonedale Operator*, this office embodies that naturalistic ideal. But the constriction of space here, the cramming in of so much information and detail, gives the composition an excessive quality. The symmetry of the shot also strikes one: two desks facing opposite directions in two separate planes of action, the complementary men standing before each desk. While foreground position and extended interaction with the delivery boy marks the exchange of the payroll as the key action, we can hardly help our eye's wandering over to the woman's energetic typing, the rapid movement of her fingers matching the swaying of the clock pendulum above her. Griffith encourages our divided attention (without subverting the hierarchy of action that contributes to narrative clarity) by choreographing contrasting actions across the screen. As the delivery boy and the elderly man bend over the desk, signing and countersigning the ledger, the typist pauses, leans forward, and erases a word from her text.

The office presents a realm of money but also of words, order, and routines. The delivery boy gathers the money, but mutual signing of a record closes the deal, while in the background another written record is prepared and corrected. The clock and the calendar watch over these orderly and symmetrical actions, marking time and schedules. Although we are more likely to recall the charging locomotive and the heroine fervently clicking her telegraph key, such actions depend on this realm of business, words, and order. The systematic order of *The Lonedale Operator* extends beyond its narration and becomes part of its diegetic world, the modern environment of similarly systematic networks in which time and space are connected through technology, just as Griffith connects them via new patterns of editing. In effect, by bringing this systematic narration to a story about modern systems of transportation and communication, Griffith bares the device, accenting the modern nature of his style. Griffith edits his film as if inspired by the telegraph, constructs his dramaturgy as if mirroring the railway networks of interconnecting speed and urgency.

The railway and the telegraph were essential technologies in creating a new topography of space and time in the modern world.[27] This new topography overturned previous conceptions of space and time through new thresholds of speed. The railway not only transported people and goods from one place to another in drastically shortened periods, but it absorbed the points along its route—individual stations such as Lonedale or the depot shown in these shots—into a single network. The telegraph sprouted along railway routes as means of letting stations communicate (as both other stations in this film communicate with the Lonedale operator). This network not only interrelated spaces but transformed time as well, as schedules were devised to regulate the speed and direction of trains (thus the innovation of the pocket watch, known originally as the railway watch, such as the one the heroine pulls out, keeping her engineer lover on schedule).[28] Standardized "railway time" maintained along a railway network preceded (and prepared the way for) Standard Time, overcoming the tyranny of individual town clocks, each with its own, often quite different, time.[29]

Led by Lynne Kirby, film historians have noted the congruence between the mastery of space and time by new technologies and the establishment of flexible but systematic spatial and temporal relations in cinema during the era of the single-reel film. Even Charlie Keil, although critical of making "correlations between formal change and large scale social observations,"[30] claims that "the moving picture stood as the culmination of a series of inventions that emphasized the capacities of technology to collapse conventional boundaries of time and space . . . that stretched from the telegraph and the telephone . . . through to the locomotive and automobile."[31] Thus, *The Lonedale Operator* not only displays the most advanced devices of film narration—its systematic use of editing, tinting, and composition—it also ties them directly to a story that foregrounds the systematic nature of the modern world.

The systematic nature of modernity in *The Lonedale Operator* does not appear only in the parallel edited sequences of telegraphic communication or the race of the speeding locomotive to "get there in time" that forms the film's climax. The overloaded accumulation of significant objects (typewriter, money bags, clock, calendar, ledger), actions (transfer, transcription, correction, signing, conferring), and written messages found in this shot, as well as the formal and symmetrical arrangement of all this, portrays the modern systems that subtend the action of the film. The publicity bulletin that the Biograph company issued for this film emphasized Lonedale's ("the most isolated spot in the Western country") direct relation to "the city office," describing the run the engineer makes as stretching "between Lonedale and civilization." Within the network of the railway and telegraph, even a remote rural station participates in the topography of modernity (a point that should be brought home to those who assume modernity could only be experienced in crowded city streets).

The second unique shot, portraying the bustling central station, uses depth of composition to contrast it with isolated Lonedale. A wide shot shows a train pulling in, moving past another train idling on a sidetrack (as opposed to Lonedale's single track). In contrast to the nearly deserted platform at Lonedale, the train yard here teems with activity. Griffith utilizes three separate planes: conductors help passengers on and off the train in the background, while a large crate is unloaded from a freight car onto a cart in midground, and in the narratively privileged foreground the delivery boy entrusts the payroll to an attendant on the train, getting him to sign for it in the ledger. The attendant writes a message on another form, which the delivery boy places in his hat as the train pulls out.

The intertitle that follows informs us, "The Operator Is Notified of the Money Shipment." The following shot shows the heroine tapping the telegraph key and transcribing the message she has just received. The cut joining these shots indicates the form that the delivery boy put in his hat contained the telegraph message the heroine received. Thus these three shots trace not only the process of sending off the payroll but also its paper trail, the information sent to precede and announce it. *The Lonedale Operator* traces a spatial and temporal drama in which, not only does the engineer race to rescue his sweetheart, but telegraph messages always outstrip locomotives, as the communication of information jockeys with the transport of objects and people. Like an "electric message," Griffith's editing moves as swiftly as thought itself, tracing a parallel not only between film and telegraphy but between the telegraph operator and the film narrator. Even outside a pattern of parallel editing or repetition, Griffith reveals the film's basis in the modern network of transportation and communication; from the center to far-flung reaches, all locations and events are connected by technology as well as by narration.

THE CLOSE-UP: DRAMAS OF VISIBILITY AND INVISIBILITY

> My primary task is to make you see.
>
> D. W. GRIFFITH (PARAPHRASING JOSEPH CONRAD)

Our fourth and final shot from a nonrepeated camera setup unquestionably plays a pivotal, indeed resolving, role in the film, performing the film's essential revelation, and provides one of the strongest uses of close-ups in American cinema to this point. The penultimate shot of the film, this shot presents a close-up of the nickel-plated wrench with which the heroine holds off the tramps. From several points of view, this shot pushes the envelope of the style of the single-reel era, but it also stays within the systematic foregrounding of techniques that marks the era, rather than the routinization and naturalization of techniques that seem to typify the classical period that follows. As a close-up it uses a form of editing less common in this period and different from the parallel editing that dominates the film: editing within a single space, or intrascene editing.

Parallel editing serves as Griffith's primary narrative device during his Biograph years. Griffith most frequently cuts from one space to a different space. In addition, he frequently uses patterns of alternation between spaces that are contiguous, often from one side of a door to the other, as in the cuts between the heroine in the telegraph office and the tramps forcing the door in the ticket office. Whether the shots are distant or proximate, all but three cuts (out of ninety-seven!) in *The Lonedale Operator* cut from one space

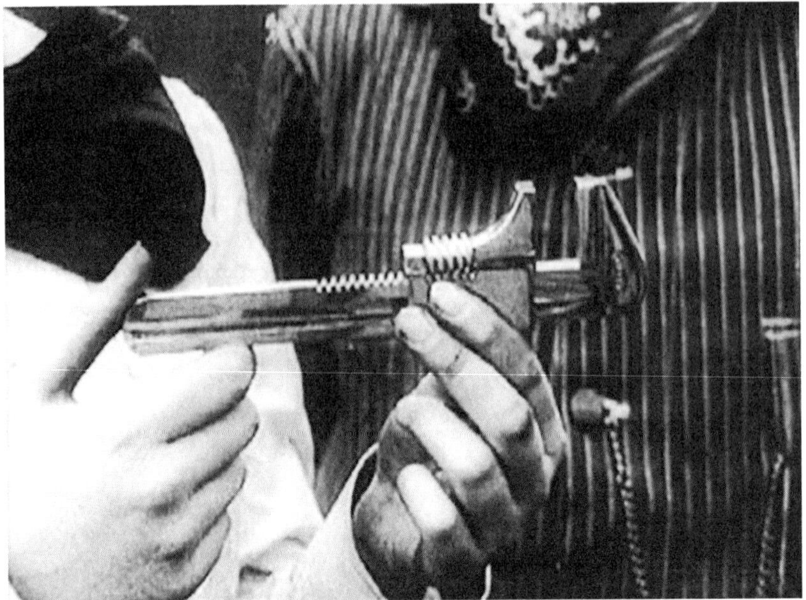

FIGURE 8.3. D. W. Griffith, *The Lonedale Operator* (1911).

to an entirely different one.[32] In these three cuts the spaces overlap, and we move from one view of a single space to another view of the same space, with the camera setup either closer or farther back and with a change of angle. The first example of these overlapping shots switches from a medium close-up of the heroine as she first receives the message about the payroll to a subsequent shot filmed from a more distant position, showing the telegraph office in long shot. This "cut-back" from medium close-up to long shot is motivated by the heroine's rising to get out a large canvas bag.[33] The second overlapping cut repeats and reverses these camera positions. After the heroine glimpses the tramps outside, a long shot first shows her huddled against the door. Then, as she sits down at the telegraph to send her message, we cut to the medium-close framing. This "cut-in" plays a dramatic role. Although the switch to a closer view may be motivated by the need to enlarge a small object (the telegraph key), the cut-in also intensifies the action, supplying an exclamation point and building suspense. Further, the closer position focuses our concern for the heroine, anticipating a practice in classical cinema, in which closer shots often express alignment or sympathy with a character.

During the single-reel era, cutting within a single space, overlapping or intrascene cutting, remained relatively underdeveloped compared with patterns of alternation across distant or proximate spaces. The emergence of intrascene cutting as the dominant form of editing marks the end of the single-reel era. Increased emphasis on character psychology, which the facial close-up supplies by highlighting expressions and reactions, motivates this change. This increased focus on characters naturalizes filmic narration—anthropomorphizes it—by directing viewer attention toward human emotions rather than formal systems. The new mode of facial close-ups also anchored cutting more closely to interaction between characters, giving rise to shot/countershot editing as the means of expressing a conversation or/and exchange of glances between characters. In contrast to the more character-based cutting of the later period, during the single-reel era, space took priority over character. Although in this era of narrative integration the focus became increasingly tied to character, spatial environment plays a more fundamental narrative role than emotional reactions conveyed by facial close-ups.

If we divide the narrative use of close-ups between those focused on objects (intended to reveal or emphasize a detail) and those focused on a face (intended usually to indicate a psychological reaction) in the single-reel era, objects appear much more frequently, especially before 1911. The close shots of the heroine at the telegraph desk in *The Lonedale Operator* move toward increased audience investment in characters. But the lack of such a facial close-up at its climax marks this film as belonging to an earlier paradigm. The close-up of the wrench that does supply the climax of the film pivots on visibility and on the film's displaying its own devices rather than focusing on character psychology. It fulfills the most frequent role of the closer view in single-reel films: the enlargement of a small object. Serving as a revelation and the denouement of the film, the wrench necessarily appears in a unique shot, showing something not seen before.

Nonetheless, Griffith uses this object-revealing close-up in an uncommon manner, tailored to supply the film's second climax. In most films of the single-reel era, such close-ups appear at the moment the object is introduced, as in the close-up of the syringe injecting a chocolate with poison in Griffith's *The Drive for Life* (1909). In *The Lonedale Operator*, the wrench had been introduced earlier, but our attention was not directed to it. Early in the film, framed in long shot, the heroine picks the wrench up after her father has gone home and she has refused his offer of a revolver. Although she handles the wrench for an extended time (she even waves it in her hand as she bids farewell to her engineer sweetheart), the shot's wide angle renders the object very small, almost unrecognizable. It remains part of an incidental action, sandwiched between two major events (her father's and her sweetheart's departures), although it clearly has been "placed" for its later dramatic use. The wrench reappears later in the film, again in long shot, as the tramps batter the door to the telegraph office. Moving away from the door, desperate, the heroine looks around and sees it on the table. She grasps it excitedly and then almost immediately turns off the lamp. Since the climax of the film takes place at night, extinguishing the lamp plunges the telegraph office into darkness, rendered dramatically through the blue tint that immediately suffuses the image, obscuring our vision. Griffith fashions the film's climax around issues of invisibility/visibility through the convergence of filmic devices (close-up and tinting).

The climactic close-up of the wrench, therefore, stands out in a number of ways. First, its delayed revelation creates a narrative strategy not common in the single-reel film: withholding key information from the audience.[34] The heroine's second discovery of the wrench, although strongly marked by Sweet's performance, still does not receive a close-up. A sharp-eyed viewer, remembering the earlier scene where the wrench was placed on the desk, might recognize and correctly identify the object.[35] But by filming the action in long shot and compromising our view almost immediately through tinting, Griffith intentionally obscures recognition of the wrench. Like a good mystery writer, he has not prevented any possibility of identification. Hence he cannot be accused of breaking faith with the viewer; all the pieces are there if we watch the film carefully. But they are not emphasized.[36] Earlier in the single-reel era (and, as Singer has shown, even later), filmmakers do not always make narratively important elements visually salient, leading to unintentional obscurities in the narrative. In this penultimate close-up, however, Griffith flaunts his ability to display a privileged object clearly and unambiguously. In contrast, his refusal of a close-up earlier intentionally keeps visual certainty from the audience.

In the film's play with visibility the close-up of the wrench reverses the obscurity of the blue-tinted long shot. The unarmed heroine protects the payroll through subterfuge and cleverness, staging a scenario of visual trickery. Keeping her back to the window (from which, the publicity bulletin emphasizes, the moonlight glints off the metal in her hand), she deftly uses the cover of darkness and an ambiguous object to realize her performance of threatening the tramps with a pistol.[37] On their arrival, her engineer sweetheart and his fireman produce a real pistol and turn the lamp back on, flooding the room with light. The heroine steps forward and dramatically flourishes the "pistol" in her outstretched arm. The succeeding shot, our climactic close-up, similarly displays its object, the light gleaming from the highly polished nickel-plated wrench. As Bellour puts it, "The unseen or badly seen object appears in its true colors."[38] This triumph of visual clarity celebrates both the heroine's and Griffith's expert manipulation of concealment and revelation.

A review in *Moving Picture World* praises Griffith's use of the locomotive's rush to the rescue but notes that "such scenes had been enacted before"; the added plot twist of the pistol constituted the film's "novelty," its distinctive feature.[39] This final nonrepeated shot not only demonstrates the systematic nature of *The Lonedale Operator* but flaunts its devices, not only the close-up but the suspenseful withholding, then revealing, of an object. The close-up, the actors' performance, and the narrative structure all chorus, "Look at this!" in this final revelation. Griffith's climax exemplifies that "prominence of . . . deployment" of particular devices that Charlie Keil finds typical of the transitional period and that he attributes to the experimental process of introducing new devices. Keil interprets this style as primarily anticipating, through trial and error, a classical style in which such devices, far from being flaunted, would become automatic and conventional.[40] The teleology of this interpretation defines it, assuming filmmakers were always striving toward the classical ideal of stylistic transparency, sometimes with success, sometimes in failure. But Griffith's delight in this moment does not resemble a stab in the dark groping toward a device he would naturalize and render transparent if only he knew how. Other assumptions operate here: this narrative style flaunts not simply a single device as a novelty but its whole system. Rather than absorbing this happy ending into the beaming face of the heroine, as might happen in a later era, Griffith favors an object and, in so doing, demonstrates how the trick was done.

GENDER IN THE SPACE OF MODERNITY

> They [women telegraph operators] are more or less public, and this is a disadvantage. Instead of meeting employers only (like a typist) the telegraph operator is thrown directly with the public.
>
> HELEN CHURCHILL CANDEE, *How Women May Earn a Living*

Earlier filmmakers frequently shot close-ups against dark or neutral backgrounds, abstracting the enlarged view from the diegetic world of the film. But Griffith clearly strives to place the wrench within the space of the action. Behind the wrench, instead of a neutral background, we see the heroine's white blouse and part of her decorative bow and the engineer's striped uniform, part of his bandanna, and even the watch chain that hangs from his button. These costumes are meticulously matched with the ones the characters have worn throughout and immediately identify the couple, even without showing their faces. This background detail serves other purposes than diegetic realism. As Raymond Bellour interprets it: "It unites the couple, as if over and above the action that re-forms it, by isolating fragments of their body which suddenly seem made, despite the contrast in clothes . . . of a continuous material."[41] The close-up of the wrench does seem to bolt together the romantic couple of the film.

Bellour tends to privilege alternation in his analysis of this film, founding the systematicity he seeks in "the reduction of a fundamental form of cinematographic discourse—alternation."[42] Noting figures of repetition and symmetry/asymmetry, Bellour pays careful attention to the opposition between shots, tracing their patterns of alternation in terms of time and space as I have. However, a larger semantic figure of alternation regulates the film, especially its resolution: gender. The initial four shots of the film alternate between the heroine and her sweetheart (a pattern Bellour describes as "He/She/He/She"). The couple are joined in the fourth shot and fifth shot (the unique nonrepeated camera setup at the willow tree I analyzed earlier), stroll together in the next shot, then separate, shaking hands at the station's exterior doorway. The departure of the engineer sets up an alternation between them, as Griffith cuts from the train leaving Lonedale station to the heroine waving from her telegraph office.

Bellour sees the alternation that subtends the race to the rescue not only as a suspenseful temporal/spatial articulation but as a gendered figure. The conclusion of the film not only rescues the heroine from danger but also rejoins the romantic couple parted near the film's beginning. Bellour summarizes the gender and narrative logic of the film: "the diegetic couple scarcely formed ([shots] 4–7), apparently only separates in order to meet again, to strengthen its image by the test of a dramatized separation whose internal form is alternation."[43] *The Lonedale Operator* conforms to one aspect of classicism Bellour finds in the American cinema: the creation of a romantic couple (whose symmetry of union is interrupted by the asymmetry of separation, followed by the resolution of reunion and triumph over obstacles) provides both story logic and narrative form in American cinema. Later American films work out patterns of alternation, not only on the shot level but also on the level of sequences or even diegetic actions.[44] Lynne Kirby, in her commentary on Bellour's analysis and its particular relevance to early railway films, refers to this type of resolution as "coupling."[45]

To lose sight of the key role Bellour ascribes to gender would gravely impoverish our understanding of this film. Gender, as Bellour demonstrates, creates essential terms for the film's use of alternation. Although I claim alternation (and rotation) represent only one aspect (albeit a key one) of the film's system, analysis of my other axis, the significance of unique non-repeated camera positions, also reveals the central role of gender and the romantic couple. The initial and final unique camera positions are given to the couple: the first position presents their tryst beneath the willow tree, and their reunion serves as background for the revelation and display of the wrench in the penultimate close-up. Gender roles, their definition and redefinition, their establishment and their subversion, play an essential role in the era of the single-reel film, both in terms of narrative structure and—the issue, I maintain, cannot be ignored in early cinema—the accommodation and acting out of modernity's beginning. A great benefit to the study of early cinema has come from paying attention to the role of gender in the first two decades of cinema history.[46]

However, the analysis of gender in relation to early film narration as offered by Bellour and some analysts following him has sometimes been limited by approaching these films through the lens of later classical cinema, focusing on the pernicious seeds of an insidious patriarchy. I would not deny these seeds are there, but I would encourage attention to differences, as well, and the way these films (or at least some of them) rehearsed new modern forms of gender, engaging with the polyvalent figure of the New Woman. This approach was initiated by Ben Singer's seminal essay on the Serial Queen, work expanded in his recent book *Melodrama and Modernity*, as well as Lynne Kirby's *Parallel Tracks*.[47] An emerging group of scholars has expanded this issue into a new paradigm, as in Jennifer Bean's essay on female action stars or Vicki Callahan's work on Musidora.[48] That this work has often centered on the serial or series films seems to me significant, since these forms mediated between the multireel feature and the single-reel film, in many ways maintaining the earlier form through episodes consisting of one or two reels.

Any intelligent undergraduate can probably produce an immediate Freudian reading of *The Lonedale Operator* that would seem to address feminist issues. Our heroine takes over her father's place in command of technology; however, she does not take on true phallic authority, as imaged in her refusal of the revolver he offers her. When she and her trust are threatened by males outside society, she enacts a series of traditionally feminine defenses: she hides her treasure (the conflation of robbery and rape recurs in Griffith's melodramas) in a chest; she locks the door, taking refuge in the most interior room; and, with the aid of the telegraph, she calls for help. Her call is heard by a male telegrapher who passes it on to her engineer lover, who races to rescue her (the conflation of rescue and coupling is also constant in Griffith), as control of the truly mobile apparatus, the locomotive, remains in the hands of the male hero. Her cry for help accomplished, the heroine dutifully performs Victorian femininity and faints. However, when the tramps continue their invasion of her space, clever girl that she is, in effect she performs masculinity and pretends to have a revolver in her hand. But order is restored, first, when the male lover arrives in the nick of time, bringing a real phallus—or real revolver. Final resolution is achieved and gender roles restored as the heroine's implement is proved not to be a revolver but a *faux de mieux*. This joke of her brief inversion of gender roles restores traditional authority, as she embraces her lover and presses her face shyly into his chest.[49]

I would not deny that this interpretation explicates the dynamics of the film in a coherent manner, but it also leaves energies unaccounted for. What appears as a critical ideological reading reproduces, rather than explores, the strictures of patriarchy. The possibility that the film might be telling another story seems foreclosed. In place of such an interpretation, I am not pleading for a "resistant reading." Rather, I believe that a historical reading of *The Lonedale Operator*, one that places it not only within a logic of the development of narrative and filmic systems but also into larger cultural systems, helps us determine what is at stake here. A consideration of the way the women in this film (and there are more than one) find their place within the film's stylistic narrative and cultural system produces not necessarily a positive or redemptive reading but, hopefully, a more complex one.

Historicizing the role of the telegraph operator within labor history complicates the view of gender and technology offered in the reading above. Like the locomotive engineer, the telegraph "operator"[50] possessed specialized technological skills and training, was difficult to replace on short notice, and therefore could be a powerful labor force difficult to control.[51] Although the failed Great Strike against Western Union broke the telegraph union in 1883 and operators' wages began to fall, telegraphy remained an attractive alternative to factory labor, and telegraph schools turned out graduates eager to join the profession. Even though women operators were loyal supporters of the Great Strike, there is no question Western Union systematically hired women as telegraph operators as a means to drive down wages.[52] Women promised not only lower wages, employers believed, but, as Katherine Stubbs puts it, a putative docility, a perceived willingness to be servants of the technology and the company. The "feminization" of telegraphy (like the parallel feminization of clerical work) was not fully accomplished until the twentieth century and was at points strongly resisted by the previously dominating male operators.[53] Although largely a fait accompli by 1911, what Stubbs calls the "crisis of feminization" constitutes an important background for *The Lonedale Operator*.

The male resistance to female operators, although primarily based in economic issues—competition for the same jobs and fear women would work for lower wages—largely took the form of sexist claims about women's technological incompetence. Executive officer of the telegraph union, Eugene T. O'Connor, even testified before the Senate in 1883 that the "nervous system of women would not allow" them to handle the most demanding assignments.[54] Women operators denied these claims, however, asserting that females in the job possessed superior skills.[55] The bulk of stories written during the close of the nineteenth century portraying female operators, primarily written by male operators, argued that women operators could or would cause disasters. The small amount of telegraphic fiction published by women operators, in contrast, celebrates, or at least explores with levity and enthusiasm, the possibilities the new technology opened to women, including new gender roles. As Stubbs summarizes her study of this material: "In the space of the circuit, then, the female operator experiences a different relation with her self; she earns the right to speak. Rendered invisible, temporarily freed from her body, she is also freed from conventional rules of female behavior, and seems no longer subject to the traditional forms of discipline, prejudice, and violence that exploit corporeal difference."[56] Stubbs wisely cautions against reading utopian achievement into this experience (temporary liberation primarily attests to permanent systems of containment). Nonetheless, at the beginning of the century, however exploited and controlled it may ultimately have been, the position of operator offered women a glimpse of a new world of work and technological mastery.

Observed against this background, the gender drama of *The Lonedale Operator* shifts a bit. Far from demonstrating female incapacity to deal with technology, the parallel-edited sequence of telegraphy demonstrates the heroine's competence, albeit with a major qualification: the heroine's faint, precisely the sort of overwhelmed emotional reaction male operators claimed women were subject to and that rendered them incompetent in the performance of their duty.[57] But the place of the heroine's loss of consciousness within the narrative logic of the film reveals the inherently contradictory nature of this film ideologically. Rather than letting it interfere with her duty, the heroine seems to willfully fight off her syncope until not only has she sent her message, but she has been assured it has been received. Thus the sequence seems to superimpose (almost in the form of a dream condensation, in which contradictions cohabit within an image rather than being resolved) different views of female operators, as competent but also as liable to be overwhelmed by dangerous situations. The sequence, as Bellour indicates, involves a curious symmetry along gender lines as it alternates between male and female operators.[58] The opening suspense of this sequence derives from the unconsciousness of the *male* operator sleeping on the job (ordinary incompetence or lack of professionalism as a result of boredom), which delays communicating the message. In contrast, the heroine's fainting plays no key narrative role, delays no action. The fainting resembles a residual appendage, a souvenir of a traditional heroine, passive and incapable of protecting herself, grafted briefly onto a resourceful New Woman. This badly spliced-on character trait undoubtedly expresses the film's anxiety about fully acknowledging the heroine's autonomy and cues us not to deny the conservative aspects of the film's resolution but also not to ignore its struggle against older forms.

The climax displays a similar doubling, with two solutions to the thieves' threat provided: the traditional rescue by the male hero but also the New Woman's solution, achieved through pluck and cleverness. It is the latter that *Moving Picture World* found to be the film's real claim on audience interest. Rather than exclusively delivering a balanced resolution (and who would deny Bellour's demonstration of this?), the film could also be seen as duplicating solutions, offering less a convergent alternation than a systematic exploration of competing options, even ones that seem contradictory. Obviously, the imaginary resolution of contradictions, as opposed to their rational sorting out, is one definition of the operation of ideology. But contradictory terms unreconciled also indicate condensation, expressing not only the repression but also the signification of desire and the unconscious. The narrative doubling in *The Lonedale Operator* does not simply exemplify a rush toward classical order but rather juggles contradictory attitudes toward gender roles—projecting fantasies that are both reactionary and progressive.

The nature of the female telegrapher's work, the particular technology with which she is engaged, also forms part of *The Lonedale Operator*'s system. Historians of early cinema, including Eileen Bowser, Jan Olsson, Yuri Tsivian, and myself, claim that early narrative cinema mastered cutting freely through space and time and rendered it comprehensible to audiences partly through portraying telephone calls, the alternation between the communicating parties expressing the essence of modern communication technology: instantaneity over long distances.[59] The use of the telegraph in *The Lonedale Operator* recalls the portrayal of telephone calls through parallel editing in other single-reel films. In a recent essay, however, Paul Young has questioned equating the two technologies, pointing out key differences that are vital for understanding *The Lonedale Operator*.[60]

The telephone primarily puts domestic and private spaces in communication, supplying as well the intimacy of the voice. The telegraph shows a much more public face, as a place of publicly conducted business, carrying news and information for large public entities such as the railway, businesses, and newspapers, as well as individuals, and translating all messages into the professional Morse code.[61] According to Stubbs, one resistance to women serving as operators was the claim that the job was "too public."[62] Although both the telephone and the telegraph overcome spatial distance through instantaneous electronic communication, the spaces each medium opened up and put into communication differ.

This contrast can be explored by comparing *The Lonedale Operator* with the Griffith Biograph film that rivals it as exemplary of Griffith's narrative and editing style, *The Lonely Villa*, from 1909. *Lonedale* has frequently been approached as an elaboration of the parallel-edited suspenseful race-to-the-rescue plot of the earlier film. As Shelley Stamp has shown in her careful reading of *The Lonely Villa*, the earlier film exemplifies a melodramatic situation of the threatened female/family (a mother and her three daughters) and the invasion of domestic space by alien male intruders. The female family retreats before the male intruders into ever deeper and (as Stamp points out) ever more confining interior spaces, moving from room to room and barricading doors, whereas exterior space seems restricted to male characters—the thieves, and the husband racing to the rescue.[63] The vulnerable domestic space is not effectively protected by technology, which balances its successes in this film (such as communicating the danger that faces his family to the husband) with its failures and breakdowns (the cutting of the phone wire, the automobile's engine problems, the unloaded pistol).[64] In *The Lonedale Operator*, on the other hand, technology functions smoothly (the only glitch being the sleeping male operator), and the spaces invaded are public offices. Although the scenario of spatial retreat seems identical in the two films, the female operator's active defiance of the thieves with her ersatz pistol sharply contrasts with the action of the earlier film.[65] The wife is directed to a revolver left by her husband, but when she realizes it is unloaded she abandons it, quite a different action from the operator's redefinition of a seemingly irrelevant tool.

The character traits of ingenuity, clear thinking, improvisation, and the ability to create a convincing scenario of defiance that the Lonedale operator displays match her profession and the technology over which she maintains control. The wife in *The Lonely Villa* can make use of the telephone and call for help, but she does not master technology in any manner. Whereas the Lonedale operator persists and gets her message through in spite of the initial glitch in communication, the wife can do nothing when the telephone line is cut, except retreat more deeply into her domestic space. The telephone link directly connects the wife with her husband, whereas the Lonedale operator's connection plugs her into a whole system of messages and transportation, as the male operator she contacts not only conveys the message to her lover but supplies him with a revolver and clears the tracks for his race to the rescue "with right of way over all trains," as an intertitle informs us. Rather than a simple alternation between the domestic space of the threatened house and the space of the husband attempting to get home offered by *The Lonely Villa*, the spatial world of *The Lonedale Operator* operates as a nexus of points, embodying the modern interconnection of spaces that the telegraph enabled. The bourgeois ideology of domesticity seeks to exclude the outside world, providing a private haven ruled over by traditional gender roles (*The Lonely Villa* dramatizes the breakdown of this ideology). The Lonedale operator introduces a modern New Woman heroine whose action in protecting herself and her professional trust lies partly in her ability to plug into that nexus of spaces and information and to master its technology, codes, and discourses.

If the unique shots of the trysting couple beneath the willow and the close-up of the wrench that connects them after the threat of narrative disruption has been resolved embody the classical order of the couple as described by Bellour, the shots of the central station marshal the forces of modernity—especially the shot of the office that dispatches the payroll. This space has also been penetrated by working women, the typist in the left midground of the office reminding us of the feminization of clerical work that occurred around the same time as the feminization of telegraphy. The "pretty typewriter" (the term referred originally to the operator of the machine rather than the machine itself) replaced male secretaries in the late nineteenth century, following the change from handwriting to technological inscription. As the term *typewriter* seems to predict, these women appeared to merge with, rather than dominate, their technology.[66]

This subordinated presence of the typist pictures other futures for the working woman that might curtail the fantasies inspired by the "girl operator." Both are employed to manage new apparatuses of language, technologies that resolve messages into mechanical units.[67] But to what extent does their mastery of technology allow them to function as masters of discourse? If the woman operator opens a portal of liberation, placing working women in public space with skills that provide them with employment while making them a nexus of the flow and transfer of information through new modern space, nonetheless the question of agency persists. The heroine in *The Lonedale Operator* enacts a fantasy that balances threat with agency, mastery with dependence, but primarily displays female competence and imagination. But does she find her dark twin, and possibly her future (or even unglamorous present), in this typist blocked into a subordinate position, staring only at her apparatus with the clock pendulum pressing down upon her? What agency does she possess? Irony rears its head as we recognize this bit actress as Jeanie Macpherson, a regular member of the Biograph stock troupe who (in spite of her beauty and strong sense of presence) never was able to become a featured player in Griffith's company but was to become one of the major Hollywood scenarists during the feature period, working especially for Cecil B. DeMille. Friedrich Kittler claims the introduction of the typewriter transformed the idea of authorship, undoing the traditional author's hand and authority.[68] The cinema, too, has made the question of authorship problematic (who was the author of *King of Kings*? Cecil B. DeMille or Jeanie Macpherson? Is it authored at all?). Within the networks, systems, and circuits of modernity, the issue of agency becomes redefined, as does gender.

INSIDE OR OUTSIDE THE CAGE? GENDER, AUTHORSHIP, AGENCY, AND TECHNOLOGY

> Most of the elements swam straight away, lost themselves in the bottomless common, and by so doing really kept the page clear. On the clearness, therefore, what she did retain stood sharply out; she nipped and caught it, turned it over and interwove it.
>
> HENRY JAMES, *In the Cage*

In search of relations connecting the systematic nature of narration in the single-reel film, the systems of modernity, and the role of gender, is it permissible to make a telegraphic leap from popular culture to high culture, from cinema to literature? Rubbing D. W. Griffith's *The Lonedale Operator* against Henry James's 1898 novella *In the Cage* may produce sparks of illumination. As has frequently been pointed out, James was one of the first major authors to compose texts by dictating to a typewriter, moving enthusiastically into the circuits of modernity after 1897.[69] Yet few texts seem more different than this action-packed single-reel film produced for nickelodeon audiences and James's elegant and ambiguous, extremely interiorized novella published by the progressive Chicago house of Herbert S. Stone (whose literary magazine *The Chapbook* two years earlier had denounced motion pictures as the acme of vulgarity).[70] Operating from very different assumptions about the fantasies of a working girl and providing distinct conclusions, both works address the limits and possibilities of female agency within modern technological employment.

The operator at Lonedale and the telegraphist at Crocker's who serves as heroine for James's tale contrast as sharply as their respective stations at the global wire. Only sending messages electronically links isolated Lonedale and the corner of Crocker's London grocery given over to a telegraph office. Although placed in the midst of a metropolis and its ebb and flow of activity, James's heroine experiences rigid separation between the class of people that send telegrams and her confinement within the cage of her occupation. Yet like her American counterpart's, her corner of the world abuts onto greater systems: "There were times when all the wires of the country seemed to start from the little hole-and-corner from which she plied for a livelihood."[71] A gentlewoman of declined fortunes, she has taken an occupation open to respectable young women. Gifted with imagination, insight, and a powerful memory, she also embodies the anxiety many held about the telegraph as the conveyer of information, that a conscious human being read the message before sending it. Such knowledge threatened the "violation of all secrecy," a writer in the British magazine the *Quarterly Review* quailed: "The clerks . . . are sworn to secrecy, but we often write things that it would be intolerable to see strangers read before our eyes."[72]

Rather than simply serving as the mechanical transfer of messages she is given to transmit, James's heroine reads, remembers, and speculates on them. In this era writers of telegrams, both personal and commercial, devised unique codes that served either to shorten the message via conventional abbreviations or to conceal meanings from prying eyes.[73] James's telegraphist cracks the code of a pair of her upper-class customers and discovers their romantic affair. But rather than use this knowledge as the basis for blackmail, as the *Quarterly Review* writer feared, she elaborates the fragmentary aspect of the texts available to her to construct a novelistic entertainment for herself. As Richard Menke, following James's own lead in his preface, demonstrates, the telegraphist operates like a novelist, following the clue of her impressions, weaving her threads into a romance.[74] Becoming a participant observer of this affair, she actually performs a significant service to the couple by remembering the encoded text of one of their messages. Exactly what this accomplishes for the couple James leaves ambiguous (as though we, the readers, remained outside the code), but the death of the woman's husband and the couple's marriage follow, as well as the telegraphist's disillusionment with her romance, whose sordid nature becomes clear to her.

Where do these very different telegraphic texts converge? Clearly on the figure of the female operator and the degree of her agency. Employed to fit within a system, to understand a technology and master its coded discourse, the female telegraphist maintains an ambiguous relation to the medium within which she operates. Transmitter and reader of private messages, James's character indulges in fantasies of authorship until she is reminded of her truly marginal role. Her American cousin moves within the realm of telegraphic melodrama rather than novelistic realism, the arena of action cinema rather than the domain of interiority and consciousness probed by James. Operating from her remote station, her office briefly becomes the convergent center of the whole system in a drama in which she plays the central role. Her agency pivots on her skill as an operator, her ability to perform clever substitutions, and her pluck in the face of danger. Griffith's heroine enacts a romance, whereas James's romantic telegraphist descends into realist disillusionment.[75] But both dramas imagine a fantasy that could be described with the terms Menke uses to discuss James's heroine: "She represents telegraphy not just as a mode of communication but also as a social practice, a medium of discourse come to life, an information exchange no longer transparent."[76] But can this medium remain lively and visible and not fade back into the automatic and transparent? In James's novella, after her telegraphic memory has somehow saved the adulterous couple, the heroine watches the hero of her imagined romance leave her behind in her cage "without another look."[77] Provided with the final bits of the true story, and deeply reflective about her own role in this sordid business, James's heroine walks off in a deep London fog, coming after several "sightless turns" to the edge of the Paddington canal, while she contemplates her life, "perhaps still sightlessly looking down on to it."[78] Resignedly, she decides to marry her grocer fiance and leave the telegraph cage.

The Lonedale operator, in contrast, ends her romance in a blaze of visual display, flourishing her wrench and her triumph so theatrically (and so cinematically!) that her villainous thieves seemed cowed into being polite schoolboys, doffing their hats (marking that she is still a lady, deserving of good manners). Much more than James's fog-shrouded, sightless consciousness, she is telegraphy made visible, her triumph within the public arena and before an audience. But we can see a split trajectory looming. As Lynne Kirby has claimed, one path pulls our filmic heroines into ever more active scenarios and public action. One year later, when Griffith remakes

The Lonedale Operator as *The Girl and Her Trust*, Grace the heroic telegraphist will actually follow the safe she guards out onto the railway tracks when the thieves attempt a getaway, severing the relation of women to interior space still lingering in *The Lonedale Operator* and preparing the way for Helen Holmes and the railway and girl telegraphist serial queens of the later teens.[79] But another path recalls the forlorn typist in the central station office, remaining in the background, taking dictation from her male superiors, apparently more in thrall to her apparatus than master of it.

In his essay on the telegraph and early cinema, Paul Young finds another way the telegraph system works as a figure for early cinema, related to, but not restricted to, their common ability to coordinate space and time. Young draws on a neglected claim by America's first film theorist, poet Vachel Lindsay. Lindsay spoke of the narrative structure of film in the mid-1910s not simply as the switching about within space and time but as presenting "a conversation between two places."[80] Working Lindsay's metaphor, Young recognizes a link between cinematic narration and the telegraph, describing editing in terms of a transfer of messages rather than a transparent switch in spatial viewpoints. Developing this idea of a cinematic conversation, Lindsay commented, "And as to jumping over geographical spaces, the photoplay dialogue that technically replaces the old stage interchange of words is a conversation between places, not individuals."[81] Young terms this style, which he sees as functioning during most of the 1910s, as "communicative realism," a narrative style that counts on the spectator's actively reading and decoding the film—entering into a conversation with it—as opposed to the transparency of later classical conventions. Young describes this style as well understood to be a code, a lattice work for "conversations" between producers and viewers "that had to be self-consciously invented, taught, and learned before it could become naturalized."[82]

"Communicative realism" could describe the blatantly systematic aspect of the style of the single-reel era, in which systematic alternations, rotations, repetitions, and even unique shots not only aided narrative comprehension but also made narration a palpable relation between audience and film. Rather than an automatic, naturalized, or transparent style of self-effacing narration, this style drew attention to its processes. Griffith's *The Lonedale Operator* may serve as an extreme example. Not every single-reel film displayed a systematic relation between shots to the same degree. But the conditions of production of the single-reel era made such systematic construction a feasible option and, indeed, encouraged it. Lindsay's presentation of his theory of cinematic conversation in 1917 extends this style into the feature era, and many early feature films seem to maintain aspects of the single-reel style. Indeed, one should resist erecting an absolute barrier between different periods. Analysis of style after the single-reel period demands a less unified approach, one that takes notice of the styles used by different genres. My description of the single-reel era style as visibly systematic narration should not immediately assume the transparency and naturalization of all film narration across the board after 1917. As Jennifer Bean has claimed, genres such as the serial action film, slapstick, and mystery thrillers play their own games, balancing narration and spectacular effects. Bean's revisionist work on these orphan genres also asks that we reexamine the way gender is negotiated in American cinema of the silent era.[83]

Cinema, as a major form of mass entertainment employing technological representation and narrative, always engaged the experience of modernity. Critics of what they term the "modernity thesis" may shake their heads at such a broad pronouncement, claiming that if all eras of cinema engage modernity, then that relation becomes a commonplace that offers us nothing to investigate.[84] But as the exploration of early cinema demonstrates (and research into the 1910s and 1920s also shows), engagement with modernity differs in each period. If the cinema of attractions dealt with the shocks of modernity, the cinema of the period of narrative integration and the single-reel film seem rather to subordinate those shocks to larger systems, generating thrilling narratives in which shocks and spectacles interpenetrate a logic of story development, sometimes propelling it, sometimes derailing it (as in many early slapstick films).[85]

If the cinema of attractions resembles a series of shocks, we might compare a single-reel film like *The Lonedale Operator* to an internal combustion engine, in which the systematic triggering of contained explosions is harnessed to produce a forward drive. The development of narration during the single-reel period responds in a complex manner to many factors: economic organization, modes of production, changing audiences, new contexts of viewing, and the experiences of modern life that audience members brought into the theaters. To try to describe the development of film style in terms of a linear conception of singular cause and effect is simply foolish. To claim the style(s) of early film were "caused" by the demands of modern life surrounding them is to speak in a naive fashion. But one should not ignore the way these films and their formal operations portrayed and made use of the modern systems that surrounded them. Nor can one deny that these films were consumed and enjoyed by audience members who were living through the new demands made by the transformations of modern life. To do so would sever cinema from its life world, reducing it to a series of formal plays. As I hope I have shown, the formal systems of early cinema in the single-reel era provided more than occasions for academic exercises. They were the means by which new systems of space and time were processed, were made the basis for both insight and fantasy, and provided schemata through which changing gender roles could be rehearsed. Through these films audiences could recognize, laugh at, confront, and even enjoy images of the world they lived in and its challenges and novelties.

9

Moving Away from the Index: Cinema and the Impression of Reality

INDEXICAL REALISM AND FILM THEORY

While cinema has often been described as the most realistic of the arts, cinematic realism has been understood in a variety of ways: from an aspect of a sinister ideological process of psychological regression to infantile states of primal delusion, to providing a basis for evidentiary status for films as historical and even legal documents. Cinematic realism has been praised as a cornerstone of film aesthetics, denounced as a major ploy in ideological indoctrination, and envied as a standard for new media. I believe the time has come to return to this issue without some of the polemics that have previously marked it but with a careful and historically informed discussion of cinema's uses and definitions of the impression of reality. In film theory over the last decades, realist claims for cinema have often depended on cinema's status as an index, one of the triad of signs in the semiotics of Charles Sanders Peirce. Film's indexical nature has almost always (and usually exclusively) been derived from its photographic aspects. In this essay I want to explore alternative approaches that might ultimately provide new ways of thinking about the realistic aspects of cinema.

This essay first appeared in *differences: A Journal of Feminist Cultural Studies* 18, no. 1 (2007): 29–52.

Peirce defined the index as a sign that functions through an actual existential connection to its referent "by being really and in its individual existence connected with the individual object."[1] Thus, frequently cited examples of indices are the footprint, the bullet hole, the sundial, the weathervane, and photographs—all signs based on direct physical connection between the sign and its referent—the action of the foot, the impact of the bullet, the movement of the sun, the direction of the wind, or the light bouncing from an object.[2] A number of these examples (such as the weathervane and the sundial) perform their references simultaneously to the action of their referents. This fact reveals that the identification of the photographic index with the pastness of the trace (made by several theorists) is not a characteristic of all indices (and one could point out that it only holds true for a fixed photograph, not the image that appears within a camera obscura).

For Peirce the index functions as part of a complex system of interlocking concepts that comprise not only a philosophy of signs but a theory of the mind and its relation to the world. Peirce's triad of signs (icon, index, and symbol), rather than being absolutely opposed to each other, are conceived to interact in the process of signification, with all three operating in varying degrees in specific signs. However (with the exception of Gilles Deleuze, for whom Peirce's system, rather than the index, is primary), within theories of cinema, photography, and new media, the index has been largely abstracted from this system, given a rather simple definition as the existential trace or impression left by an object, and used to describe (and solve) a number of problems dealing with the way what we might call the light-based image media refer to the world. In fact, Peirce's discussion of the index includes a large range of signs and indications, including "anything which focuses attention" and the general hailing and deixic functions of language and gesture.[3] Peirce therefore by no means restricts the index to the impression or trace. I do not claim to have a command of the range of Peirce's complex semiotics, but it is perhaps important to point out that the use of the index in film theory has tended to rely on a small range of the possible meanings of the term.

I have no doubt that Peirce's concept has relevance for film and that (although more complex than generally described) the index also provides a useful way of thinking through some of these problems; indeed, even the restricted sense of the index as a trace has supplied insights into the nature of film and photography. However, I also think that what we might call a diminished concept of the index may have reached the limits of its usefulness in the theory of photography, film, and new media.[4] The nonsense that has been generated specifically about the indexicality of digital media (which, due to its digital nature, has been claimed to be nonindexical—as if the indexical and the analog were somehow identical) reveals something of the poverty of this approach. But I also feel the index may not be the best way, and certainly should not be the only way, to approach the issue of cinematic realism. Confronting questions of realism anew means that contemporary media theory must still wrestle with its fundamental nature and possibilities. I must confess that this essay attempts less to lay a logical foundation for these discussions than to launch a polemic calling for such a serious undertaking and to reconnoiter a few of its possibilities.

It is worth reviewing here the history of the theoretical discourse by which a relation was forged between cinematic realism and the index. Without undertaking a thorough historiographic review of the concept of the index in film and media theory, the first influential introduction of the concept of the index into film theory came in Peter Wollen's groundbreaking comparison of Peirce to the film theory of André Bazin.[5] But to understand this identification, a review of certain aspects of Bazin's theory of film is needed. Bazin introduced in his essays and critical practice an argument for the realism of cinema that was, as he termed it in his most quoted theoretical essay, "ontological." The complexity and indeed the dialectical nature of Bazin's critical description of a realist style have become increasingly recognized.[6] For Bazin, realism formed the aesthetic basis for the cinema, and most of his discussion of cinematic realism dealt with visual, aural, and narrative style. Although Bazin never argued the exact relation between his theories of ontology and of style systematically (and indeed, one could claim that Bazin's discussion of realism across his many essays contains both contradictions and a possible pattern of evolution and change in his work taken as a whole—not to mention multiple interpretations), at least in the traditional reception of Bazin's theory, cinematic realism depended on the medium's photographic nature.

A number of frequently quoted statements containing the essence of Bazin's claim for the ontology of the photographic image and presumably for motion picture photography warrant consideration. Bazin's account of the realism of photography rests less on a correspondence theory (that the photograph resembles the world, a relation Peirce would describe as iconic), than on what he describes as "a transference of reality from the thing to its reproduction," referring to the photograph as "a decal or approximate tracing."[7] Bazin extends these comments, saying:

> The photographic image is the object itself, the object freed from temporal contingencies. No matter how fuzzy, distorted, or discolored, no matter how lacking in documentary value the image may be, it proceeds, by virtue of its genesis, from the ontology of the model; it is the model.[8]

He adds, shortly after this:

> The photograph as such and the object in itself share a common being, after the fashion of a fingerprint. Wherefore, photography actually contributes something to the order of natural creation instead of providing a substitute for it.[9]

To cite one more famous description from another essay, Bazin also describes the photograph as "the taking of a veritable luminous impression in light—to a mold. As such it carries with it more than a mere resemblance, namely a kind of identity."[10]

Bazin's descriptions are both evocative and elusive, and Wollen was, I think, the first to draw a relation between Bazin's ideas and Peirce's concept of the index. In his pioneering essay "The Semiology of the Cinema," Wollen said of Bazin:

> His conclusions are remarkably close to those of Peirce. Time and again Bazin speaks of photography in terms of a mould, a death-mask, a Veronica, the Holy Shroud of Turin, a relic, an imprint. . . . Thus Bazin repeatedly stresses the existential bond between sign and object, which, for Peirce, was the determining characteristic of the indexical sign.[11]

The traditional reception of Bazin's film theory takes his account of the ontology of the photographic image as the foundation of his arguments about the relation between film and the world. Wollen's identification of Bazin's photographic ontology with Peirce's index has been widely accepted (although critics have rarely noted Wollen's important caveat: "But whereas Peirce made his observation in order to found a logic, Bazin wished to found an aesthetic").[12]

I must state that I think one can make a coherent argument for reading Bazin's ontology in terms of the Peircean index, as Wollen did. However, I have also claimed elsewhere that this reading of Bazin in terms of Pierce does some disservice to the full complexity of Bazin's aesthetic theory of realism.[13] Likewise, Daniel Morgan makes a convincing and fully argued case (different from mine) that Bazin's theory of cinematic realism should not be approached through the theory of the index at all.[14] I would still maintain, however, that parallels between aspects of Bazin's theory of cinematic realism and the index do exist, even if they cannot explain the totality of his theory of cinematic realism (or, as Morgan would argue, its most important aspects).

I do not intend to rehearse here either my own or others' arguments about why the index might not supply a complete understanding of Bazin's theory of cinematic realism, but some summary remarks are in order. The chief limitation to the indexical approach to Bazin comes from the difference between a semiotics that approaches the photograph (and therefore film) as a sign and a theory like Bazin's that deals instead with the way a film creates an aesthetic world. When Bazin claims that "photography actually contributes something to the order of natural creation instead of providing a substitute for it," he denies the photograph the chief characteristic of a sign, that of supplying a substitute for a referent. While it would be foolish to claim that a photograph cannot be a sign of something (it frequently does perform this function), I would claim that signification does not form the basis of Bazin's understanding of the ontology of the photographic image and that his theory of cinematic realism depends on a more complex (and less logical) process of spectator involvement. Bazin describes the realism of the photograph as an "irrational power to bear away our faith."[15] This "magical" understanding of photographic ontology is clearly very different from a logic of signs. In Peirce's semiotics, the indexical relation falls entirely into the rational realm.

BEYOND THE INDEX: CINEMATIC REALISM AND MEDIUM PROMISCUITY

The indexical argument no longer supplies the only way to approach Bazin's theory. Rather than assuming that the invocation of Peirce's concept of the index solves the question of film's relation to reality, I think we must now raise again the question that Bazin asked so passionately and subtly (even if he never answered definitively): What is cinema? What are cinema's effects, and what range of aspects relates to its oft-cited (and just as variously defined) realistic nature? Given the historically specific nature of Bazin's arguments for cinematic realism as an aesthetic value (responding as he did to technical innovations such as deep-focus cinematography and to new visual and narrative styles such as Italian Neorealism), it makes sense for a contemporary theory of cinematic realism to push beyond those aspects of cinematic realism highlighted by Bazin. Specifically, we need to ask in a contemporary technical and stylistic context: what are the bounds that cinema forges with the world it portrays? Are these limited to film's relation to photography? Is the photographic process the only aspect of cinema that can be thought of as indexical, especially if we think about the term more broadly than as just a trace or impression? If the claim that digital processing by its nature eliminates the indexical seems rather simplistic, one must nonetheless admit that computer-generated images (CGI) do not correspond directly to Bazin's description of the "luminous mold" that the still photograph supposedly depends on. But can these CGI images still be thought of as in some way indexical? In what way has the impression of reality been attenuated by new technology, and in what ways is it actually still functioning (or even intensified)? But setting aside the somewhat complex case of computer-generated special effects, is it not somewhat strange that photographic theories of the cinema have had such a hold on film theory that much of film theory must immediately add the caveat that they do not apply to animated film? Given that as a technical innovation cinema was first understood as "animated pictures" and that computer-generated animation techniques are now omnipresent in most feature films, shouldn't this lacuna disturb us? Rather than being absorbed in the larger categories of cultural studies or cognitive theory, shouldn't the classical issues of film theory be reopened? I will not attempt to answer all these questions in this essay, but I think they are relevant to the issues I will raise.

Within the academy, the study of film theory has often been bifurcated between "classical film theory" and "contemporary film theory." Insofar as this division refers to something more than an arbitrary sense of the past and present, "classical" film theories have been usefully defined as theories that seek to isolate and define the "essence" of cinema, while "contemporary" theories rely on discourses of semiotics and psychoanalysis to describe the relation between film and spectator.[16] While the classical approach has been widely critiqued as essentialist, it seems to me that a pragmatic investigation of the characteristics of film as developed and commented on through time hardly needs to involve a proscriptive quest for the one pure cinema. Therefore, if I call for new descriptions of the nature(s) of the film medium, I am not at all calling for a return to classical film theory (and even less to a neoclassicism!). But I do think the time has come to take stock of the historical and transforming nature of cinema as a medium and of its dependence and differentiation from other media.

Considering historically the definitions of film as a medium helps us avoid the dilemma of either proscriptively (and timelessly) defining film's essence or the alternative of avoiding any investigation into the diverse nature of media for fear of being accused of promoting an idealist project. As a new technology at the end of the nineteenth century, cinema did not immediately appear with a defined essence as a medium, but rather, displayed an amazing promiscuity (if not polymorphic perversity) in both its models and uses. Cinema emerged within a welter of new inventions for the recording or conveying of aspects of human life previously felt to be ephemeral, inaudible, or invisible: the telephone, the phonograph, and the X-ray are only a few examples. Before these devices found widespread acceptance as practical instruments, they existed as theatrical attractions, demonstrated on stage before paying audiences. Indeed, the X-ray, which appeared almost simultaneously with the projection of films on the screen, seemed at one point to be displacing moving pictures as a popular attraction, and a number of showmen exchanged their motion picture projectors for the new apparatus that showed audiences the insides of their bodies (and unknowingly gave themselves and their collaborators dangerous doses of radiation). It is in this competitive context of novel devices that Antoine Lumière, the father of Louis and Auguste Lumière, who managed the theatrical exhibition of his sons' invention, warned a patron desirous of purchasing a Cinématographe that it was an "invention without a future."[17]

Rather than myths of essential origins, historical research uncovers a genealogy of cinema, a process of emergence and competition yielding the complex formation of an identity. But cinema has always (and not only at its origin) taken place within a competitive media environment, in which the survival of the fittest was in contention and the outcome not always clear. As a historian, I frequently feel that one of my roles must be to combat the pervasive amnesia that a culture based in novelty encourages, even within the academy. History always responds to the present, and changes in our present environment allow us to recognize aspects of our history that have been previously obscured or even repressed. At the present moment, cinema finds itself immersed in another voraciously competitive media environment. Is cinema about to disappear into the maw of undefined and undifferentiated image media, dissolved into a pervasive visual culture? To be useful in such an investigation where theory and history intertwine, the discussion of cinematic realism cannot be allowed to ossify into a dogmatic assertion about the photographic nature of cinema or an assumption about the indexical nature of all photography.

My history lesson resists either celebration or paranoia at the prospect of a new media environment, seeing in our current situation not only a return to aspects of cinema's origins but a dynamic process that has persisted in varying degrees throughout the extent of film's history—an interaction with other competing media, with mutual borrowings, absorptions, and transformation among them. Cinema has never been one thing. It has always been a point of intersection, a braiding together of diverse strands: aspects of the telephone and the phonograph circulated around the cinema for almost three decades before being absorbed by sound cinema around 1928, while simultaneously spawning a new sister medium, radio; a variety of approaches to color, ranging from tinting to stencil coloring, existed in cinema as either common or minority practices until color photography became pervasive in the 1970s; the film frame has changed its proportions since 1950 and is now available in small, medium, and supersized rectangles (television, cinemascope, IMAX, for example); cinema's symbiotic relation to television, video, and other digital practices has been ongoing for nearly half a century without any of these interactions and transformations—in spite of numerous predictions—yet spelling the end of the movies. Thus anyone who sees the demise of the cinema as inevitable must be aware they are speaking only of one form of cinema (or more likely several successive forms whose differences they choose to overlook).

Film history provides a challenge to rethinking film theory, arguing for the importance of using the recent visibility of film's multiple media environment as a moment for reflection and perhaps redefinition. In contemporary film theory, a priori proscriptions as well as a posteriori definitions that privilege only certain aspects of film have given way to approaches (like semiotics, psychoanalysis, or cognitivism) that seem to ignore or minimize differences between media in favor of broader cultural or biological conditions. My view of cinema as a braid made of various aspects rather than a unified essence with firm boundaries would seem to offer a further argument against the essentialist approach of classical film theory.

But we also increasingly need to offer thick descriptions of how media work, that is, phenomenological approaches that avoid defining media logically before examining the experience of their power. And while I maintain that various media work in concert and in contest rather than isolation, I also maintain that the formal properties of a specific medium convey vital aesthetic values and do not function as neutral channels for functional equivalents. An attempt to isolate a single essence of cinema remains not only an elusive task but possibly a reactionary project, yet most earlier attempts by theorists to define the essence of cinema can also be seen as attempts to elucidate the specific possibilities of cinema within a media environment that threaten to obscure or dismiss the particular powers that film holds. In other words, while the naming of a specific aspect of cinema as its essence must always risk being partial, it once had the polemical value of drawing attention to those aspects, allowing theorists to describe their power. This was true of the emphasis given to editing by the Soviet theorists in the 1920s, who established not only that film could function as a mode of mechanical reproduction but that it could create a poetics and a rhetoric that resembled a language. Partly as a corrective to this earlier claim that editing formed the essence of film as a creative form, the emphasis on film's relation to photography, found after World War II in the work of Bazin, Siegfried Kracauer, and Stanley Cavell, also performed this sort of vital function of attracting attention to a neglected aspect of cinema. In the current environment, probing the power of cinema, its affinities with and differentiations from other media, must again take a place on our agenda.

WHAT REALLY MOVES ME . . .

Photography's relation to cinema comprises one of the central concepts in classical film theory's attempt to characterize the nature of cinema, and it remains a rich area for investigation. However, to offer alternative paradigms, I want to return to the generation of film theorists of the 1920s, primarily the work of filmmaker theorists such as Sergei Eisenstein, Jean Epstein, and Germaine Dulac, who wrote before the dominance of photography that marks the work of Bazin and Kracauer (and arguably Walter Benjamin).[18] Although photography played a key role in film theories of the 1920s as well, (especially in the concept of *Photogénie*—the claim that film produced a unique image of the world more revelatory than other forms of imagery—championed by Epstein, Dulac, and Louis Delluc), I want to focus on the centrality of cinematic motion in the discussions of cinema's nature that marked this foundational period of classical film theory. Dulac declared in 1925, "Le cinéma est l'art du mouvement et de la lumière" (Cinema is the art of movement and light). In her writings and her innovative abstract films, she envisioned a pure cinema uncontaminated by the other arts (although aspiring to the condition of music), which she described as "a visual symphony, a rhythm of arranged movements in which the shifting of a line or of a volume in a changing cadence creates emotion without any crystallization of ideas."[19] The concerns that preoccupied both the French Impressionist filmmakers and the Soviet montage theorists of the 1920s—cinematic rhythm as a product of editing, camera movement, and composition; the physical and emotional reactions of film spectators as shaped by visual rhythms; even the visual portrayal of mental states and emotions—were all linked to cinema's ability both to record and create motion.[20]

The role of motion in motion pictures initially appears to be something of a tautology. Rather than simply recycling this seemingly obvious assumption—that the movies move—theories of cinematic motion can help us reformulate a number of theoretical and aesthetic issues, including film spectatorship, film style, and the confluence of a variety of new media. Further, a renewed focus on cinematic motion directly addresses what I feel is one of the great scandals of film theory, which I previously mentioned as an aporia resulting from the dominance of a photographic understanding of cinema: the marginalization of animation.[21] Again and again, film theorists have made broad proclamations about the nature of cinema, and then quickly added, "excluding, of course, animation." Perhaps the boldest of new media theorists, Lev Manovich, has recently inverted this cinematic prejudice, claiming that the arrival of new digital media reveals cinema as simply an event within the history of animation.[22] While I appreciate the polemic value of this proclamation, I would point out (as Manovich's archaeology of the cinema also indicates) that far from being a product of new media, animation has always been part of cinema and that only the overemphasis given to the photographic basis of cinema in recent decades can explain the neglect this historical and technological fact has encountered.

Stressing, as Manovich does, the nonreferential nature of animation implies that only photography can be referential—a major error that comes from a diminished view of the index. But if cinema should be approached as a form of animation, then cinematic motion rather than photographic imagery becomes primary. Spectatorship of cinematic motion raises new issues, such as the physical reactions that accompany the watching of motion. Considering this sensation of kinesthesia avoids the exclusive visual and ideological emphasis of most theories of spectatorship and acknowledges instead that film spectators are embodied beings rather than simply eyes and minds somehow suspended before the screen. The physiological basis of kinesthesia exceeds (or supplements) recent attempts to reintroduce emotional affect into spectator studies. We do not just see motion, and we are not simply affected emotionally by its role within a plot; we feel it in our guts or throughout our bodies.

Theories of cinema's difference from the other arts that appeared in the 1920s derived from the excitement that filmmakers of the teens and twenties experienced in their newfound ability to affect viewers physiologically as well as emotionally through such motion-based sequences as chase scenes involving galloping horses or racing locomotives, rapid camera movement, or accelerated rhythmic editing. While kinesthetic effects still play a vital role in contemporary action cinema, nowadays these devices of motion rarely generate theoretical speculation or close analysis. Nonetheless, critical attention to cinematic motion need not be limited to action films, however rich this mainstay of film practice may be. Motion, as Eisenstein's analysis of the methods of montage makes clear, can shape and trigger the process of both emotional involvement and intellectual engagement.[23] Analysis of motion in cinema should address a complete gamut of cinema, from the popular action film to the avant-garde work of filmmakers such as Stan Brakhage, Maya Deren, or Abigail Child.

In many ways these avant-garde filmmakers took up the legacy of Dulac's pure cinema and explored the possibilities of filmic motion outside of narrative development. Although Deren in particular stressed the importance of the photographic basis of film in her theoretical writings, she made the analysis and transformation of motion essential to all her films, especially her later films inspired by dance and ritualized bodily movement such as *Ritual in Transferred Time* (1946), *Choreography for the Camera* (1945), *Meditation on Violence* (1948), and *The Very Eye of Night* (1958).[24] Brakhage's use of handheld camera movement and complex editing patterns, as well as frenetic kinetic patterns created by painting directly on celluloid, produced patterns of motion that evoked a crisis of perception and lyrical absorption in the processes of vision.[25] Filmmaker Abigail Child's recent volume of writings on film and poetry is actually titled *This Is Called Moving*, testifying to her commitment to cinema as a means of deconstructing the dominant cultural forms of media through an intensification of cinematic perception that relies in part on new patterns of motion, often created through editing.[26] As cinematic experience, motion can play an intense role both in sensations of intense diegetic absorption, fostering involvement with dramatic, suspenseful plots à la Hitchcock, and in kinetic abstraction, thrusting viewers into unfamiliar explorations of flexible coordinates of space and time.

Theoretical exploration of cinematic motion need not contradict, but can actually supplement, photographic theories of cinema such as those of Kracauer and Bazin. Kracauer in particular deals extensively with cinema's affinities with motion (discussing especially the cinematic possibilities of the chase, dancing, and the transformation from stillness to motion) as a part of cinema's mission to capture and redeem physical reality.[27] Even if movement never receives a detailed discussion as a theoretical issue within Bazin's work, he clearly sees camera movement as an essential tool within a realist style, as in his analysis of the extended track and pan in Jean Renoir's *The Crime of M. Lange*,[28] or his description of the shot in Friedrich Murnau's *Tabu* in which "the entrance of a ship from left screen gives an immediate sense of destiny at work, so that Murnau has no need to cheat in any way on the uncompromising realism of a film whose settings are completely natural.[29]

METZ AND CINEMATIC MOVEMENT

While Bazin and Kracauer saw motion as contributing to (or at least not contradicting) the inherent realism of the film medium, another film theorist went farther and made movement the cornerstone of cinema's impression of reality. I want to turn now to a neglected essay by a theorist usually associated with postclassical film theory, Christian Metz. "On the Impression of Reality in the Cinema," a short essay that directly superimposes the issues of motion and cinematic realism, opens the first volume of Metz's writings and is among his presemiotic essays that the section heading characterizes as "phenomenological" (and that most theorists have zoomed past, treating them as juvenilia).

Metz attempts in this essay to account for the "impression of reality" that the movies offer ("Films release a mechanism of affective and perceptual participation in the spectator . . . films have the appeal of a presence and of a proximity").[30] While later apparatus theorists (including Metz himself in later writings) would see realism as a dangerous ideological illusion (while Bazin, on the contrary, would deepen cinematic realism into the possibility of grasping the mysteries of Being), in this early essay Metz simply attempts to give this psychological effect a phenomenological basis. Metz begins by contrasting media, claiming that this degree of spectator participation and investment does not occur in still photography. Following Roland Barthes, Metz claims that still photography is condemned to a perceptual past tense ("This has been there"), while the movie spectator becomes absorbed by "a sense of 'There it is.'"[31]

Metz locates the realistic effect of cinematic motion in its "participatory" effect. *Participation* seems to be a magic word in theories of realism that seek to overcome the dead ends encountered by correspondence theories of cinema. For Bazin, participation describes the relation between the photographic image and its object. Likewise, his description of the spectator's active role in the cinematic style that makes use of depth-of-field composition ("it is from [the spectator's] attention and his will that the meaning of the image in part derives") indicates an active participation by the viewer.[32] For Metz, similarly, participation in the cinematic image is both "affective and perceptual," engendering "a very direct hold on perception," "an appeal of a presence and proximity."[33]

Metz points out that "participation, however, must be engendered." What subtends this sense of immediacy and presence in the cinema? "An answer immediately suggests itself: It is movement . . . that produces the strong impression of reality." While Metz admits other factors in film's effect on spectators, he ascribes a particular affect to the perception of motion, "a general law of psychology that movement is always perceived as real—unlike many other visual structures, such as volume, which is often very readily perceived as unreal."[34] In terms that seem to recall Bazin's claim that a photograph "is the object," Metz adds:

> The strict distinction between object and copy, however, dissolves on the threshold of motion. Because movement is never material but is always visual, to reproduce its appearance is to duplicate its reality. In truth, one cannot even "reproduce" a movement; one can only re-produce it in a second production belonging to the same order of reality, for the spectator as the first. . . . In the cinema the impression of reality is also the reality of the impression, the real presence of motion.[35]

Metz gives here a very compressed account of a complex issue, and his assumptions would take some time to isolate and explicate (such as exactly what the "reality of an impression" might be and the begging of the question through the assertion that cinema delivers "the real presence of motion"). But the relation he draws between motion and the impression of reality provides us with a radical course of thought. We experience motion on the screen in a different way than we look at still images, and this difference explains our participation in the film image, a sense of perceptual richness or immediate involvement in the image. Spectator participation in the moving image depends, Metz claims, on perceiving motion and the perceptual, cognitive, and physiological effects this triggers. The nature of cinematic motion, its continuous progress, its unfolding nature, would seem to demand the participation of a perceiver.

Although Metz does not refer directly to Henri Bergson's famous discussion of motion, I believe Bergson developed the most detailed description of the need to participate in motion in order to grasp it. Bergson claims, "In order to advance with the moving reality, you must replace yourself within it."[36] For Bergson, discontinuous signs, such as language or ideas, cannot grasp the continuous flow of movement but must conceive of it as a series of successive static instants, or positions. Only motion, one can assume, is able to convey motion. Therefore, to perceive motion, rather than represent it statically in a manner that destroys its essence, one must participate in the motion itself. Of course, analysis provides a means of conceptual understanding, and Bergson actually refers to our tendency to conceive of motion through a series of static images—a distortion he claims our habits of mind and language demand of us—as "cinematographic." Great confusion (which I feel Deleuze increases rather than dispels) comes if we do not realize that the analytical aspect of the cinematograph that Bergson took as his model for this tendency to conceive of motion in terms of static instants derives from the filmstrip in which motion is analyzed into a succession of frames, not the projected image on the screen in which synthetic motion is recreated.

Cinema, the projected moving image, demands that we participate in the movement we perceive. Analysis of perceiving motion can only offer some insights into the way the moving image exceeds our contemplation of a static image. Motion always has a projective aspect, a progressive movement in a direction, and therefore invokes possibility and a future. Of course, we can project these states into a static image, but with an actually moving image we are swept along with the motion itself. Rather than imagining previous or anterior states, we could say that through a moving image, the progress of motion is projected onto us. Undergirded by the kinesthetic effects of cinematic motion, I believe "participation" properly describes the increased sense of involvement with the cinematic image, a sense of presence that could be described as an impression of reality.

Metz claims that the motion we see in a film is real, not a representation, a claim I take to be close to Bergson's discussion of the way movement cannot be derived simply from a static presentation of successive points. According to Metz, what we see when we see a moving image on the screen should not be described as a "picture" of motion, but instead as an experience of seeing something truly moving. In terms of a visual experience of motion, therefore, no difference exists between watching a film of a ball rolling down a hill, say, and seeing an actual ball rolling down a hill. One might object to this identification of motion and its visual sensation by pointing out that our sensation of motion (kinesthesia) does not depend entirely on vision but on a range of bodily sensations. But I believe Metz could respond to this in two ways. First, the most extreme sort of kinesthesia primarily refers to the sensation of ourselves moving bodily, traversing space, not simply watching a moving object. Insofar as we do experience kinesthesia when we observe a moving object other than ourselves, the same sensations seem to occur when we watch a moving object in a film. Thus, perceiving motion in the cinema, while triggered by visual perception, need not be restricted to visual effects. Clearly, cinema cannot move us, as viewers, physically (we don't, for instance, leave our seats or get transported to another place, even if we have a sensation of ourselves moving as we watch films in which the camera moves through space). However, while acknowledging that Metz can only claim that cinema possesses visual motion, not literal movement through space—a change of place—the fact remains that even visual motion, such as camera movement, doesn't only affect us visually but does produce the physiological effect of kinesthesia.

Metz questions whether there could be a "portrayal of motion" that did not actually involve motion, a representation parallel, say, to the use of perspective drawing to render volumes. In a way, it is not hard to conceive of such a portrayal. A diagram conveying the trajectory of a moving object, such as a graph of the parabola described by a baseball hit by David Ortiz, could be said to portray motion. The speed lines used by comic book artists to indicate a running figure also portray the idea of motion visually but in static form. Indeed, the chronophotographs of Étienne-Jules Marey, with their composite and successive figures tracing the path of human movement, or the blurred image of simple actions like turning a head found in the photo-dynamist photographs of Futurist Anton Giulio Bragaglia, all portray motion without actually moving. But that is the point, precisely. These diagrammatic portrayals of motion strike us very differently from actual motion pictures. Such portrayals of motion recall Bergson's descriptions of attempts to generate a sense of motion from tracing a pattern of static points or positions, which miss the continuous sweep of motion. In contrast to these diagrams of the successive phases of motion or indications of its pathways, we could say, perhaps now with even more clarity, that cinema shows us motion, not its portrayal.

Ultimately, I think there is little question that phenomenologically we see movement on the screen, not a "portrayal" of movement. But what does it mean to say the movement is "real"? As I understand Metz's claim, it does not at all commit us to the nonsensical position that we take the cinema image for reality, that we are involved in a hallucination or "illusion" of reality that could cause us to contemplate walking into the screen, or interacting physically with the fictional events we see portrayed. In the cinema, we are dealing with realism, not "reality." As Metz makes clear, "on the one hand, there is the impression of reality; on the other, the perception of reality."[37] Theater, for instance, makes use of real materials, actual people and things, to create a fictional world. Cinema works with images that possess an impression of reality, not its materiality. This distinction is crucial.

THE REALISTIC MOTION OF FANTASY

Metz's description of cinematic motion supplies at least part of (and probably a central part of) an alternative theory of the realistic effect of the cinema (one I find much more compelling and flexible than the ideological explanation of psychological regression offered by Jean-Louis Baudry and, in a sense, the later Metz of *The Imaginary Signifier*).[38] But we should keep in mind that this is a theory of the impression of reality (based, as Metz says, on the reality of the impression), rather than an argument for a realist aesthetic such as that offered by Bazin or Kracauer. Part of the flexibility of Metz's theory of the reality of cinematic motion lies in its adaptability to a range of cinematic styles. As Metz indicates, the "feeling of credibility" film offers "operates on us in films of the unusual and of the marvelous, as well as in those that are 'realistic.'"[39] But his description also shows that movement can be an important factor in describing a realist style (one need only think of the role of camera movement in Welles and Rossellini, undertheorized by Bazin, or in Renoir, which Bazin describes beautifully). But the fantastic possibilities of motion, or rather its role in rendering the fantastic believable, and I would say visceral, shows the mercurial role motion can play in film spectatorship and film style.

It is this mercurial, protean, indeed mobile nature of cinematic motion that endows it with power as a concept for film theory and analysis. Not only does the concept of cinematic movement unite photographic-based films and traditional animated films (not to mention the hybrid synthesis of photographic and animation techniques that computer-generated images represent), movement displays a flexibility that avoids the proscriptive nature of much of classical film theory.[40] While the formal aspects of cinematic movement (and the range of ways it can be used, or even the number of aspects of cinematic motion possible) make it an important tool for aesthetic analysis (and even useful in a polemical argument like Dulac's or Bazin's for a particular style of film), nothing restricts movement to a single style.

The impression of reality that cinematic movement carries can underwrite a realist film style (think of the use of handheld camera movement in the films of the Dogma 95 movement), a highly artificial fantasy dependent on special effects (the importance of kinesis in the Star Wars films), or an abstract visual symphony (animator Oskar Fischinger). Metz describes the role of the impression of reality enabled by cinematic motion as "to inject the reality of motion into the unreality of the image and thus to render the world of imagination more real than it had ever been."[41] Like Mercury, winged messenger of the gods, cinematic motion crosses the boundaries between heaven and earth, between the embodied senses and flights of fancy, not simply playing the whole gamut of film style but contaminating one with the other, endowing the fantastic with the realistic impression of visual motion.

The extraordinary writings Sergei Eisenstein produced in the 1930s on the animated films of Walt Disney accent this double valence of movement, tending not only toward realism but also, as the animated film and new digital processes demonstrate, toward fantasy. Movement in the cinema not only generates the visual sense of realism that Metz describes; bodily sensations of movement can engage spectator fantasy through perceptual and physical participation. Thus, movement created by animation, freed from photographic reference, can endow otherwise "impossible" motion and transformations with the immediacy of perception that Metz claims movement entails. In some ways this returns us to Dulac's concept of a pure cinema based entirely on the motion of forms (and the forms of motion). In his writings on Disney, Eisenstein focuses on the possibility of the animated line to invoke precisely this aspect of motion, which he calls "plasmaticness" and defines as "a rejection of once-and-forever allotted form, freedom from ossification, the ability to dynamically assume any form."[42] Rather than simply endowing familiar forms with the solidity and credibility that Metz describes, movement can extend beyond familiarity to fantasy and imagination, creating the impossible bodies that throng the works of animation, from the early cartoons of Emile Cohl to the digital manipulation of Gollum in *The Lord of the Rings*.[43] While flaunting the rules of physical resemblance, such animation need not remain totally divorced from any reference to our lived world. As I once heard philosopher Arthur Danto explain, the cartoon body can reveal primal phenomenological relations we have to our physical existence, our sense of grasping, stretching, exulting.[44] For Eisenstein, this plasmatic quality invokes

> a lost changeability, fluidity, suddenness of formations—that's the "subtext" brought to the viewer who lacks all this by these seemingly strange traits which permeate folktales, cartoons, the spineless circus performer and the seemingly groundless scattering of extremities in Disney's drawings.[45]

Motion therefore need not be realistic to have a "realistic" effect, that is, to invite the empathic participation, both imaginative and physiological, of viewers. Eisenstein's discussion of motion as a force that does not simply propel forms but actually creates them not only refers back to the theories of Bergson but makes clear the multiple nature of the participation that motion invokes, from the perceptual identity described by Metz to the realm of anticipation, speculation, and imagination of the possibly transforming aspects of line described by Eisenstein. Unlike the literalness of pointing to an actual individual that a narrow adherence to the diminished indexical theory of film and photography forces on us, as Metz emphasizes, the cinematic impression of reality affects the diegesis, the fictional world created by the film, and thus escapes the straitjacket of exclusive correspondence or reference to any preexisting reality. Metz's concept of cinematic movement's "novel power to convince . . . was all to the advantage of the imagination."[46]

The realist claim offered for cinema's indexical quality, based in still photography, actually operates in a diametrically different direction than the role Metz outlines for cinematic movement in the medium's impression of reality. An indexical argument, as it has been developed, based in the photographic trace, points the image back into the past, to a preexisting object or event whose traces could only testify to its having already been. Metz's concept of the impression of reality moves in the opposite direction, toward a sensation of the present and of presence. The indexical argument can be invoked most clearly (and usefully) for films used as historical evidence. It remains unclear, however, how the index functions within a fiction film, where we are dealing with a diegesis, a fictional world, rather than a reference to a reality. Laura Mulvey, in her extremely important discussion of indexicality in film, has pointed out how it relates to the phenomenon of the Star, clearly an existing person beyond the fictional character he or she plays and therefore a reference outside the film's diegesis.[47] The effect of an index in guaranteeing the actual existence of its reference depends on the one who makes this connection invoking a technical knowledge of photography, understanding the effect of light on the sensitive film. Metz's cinematic impression of reality depends on "forgetting" (that is, on distracting the viewer's attention away from—not literally repressing the knowledge of) the technical process of filming in favor of an experience of the fictional world as present. As he claims, "The movie spectator is absorbed, not by a 'has been there' but by a sense of 'There it is.'"[48]

Even if the indexical claim for cinema is granted, I am not sure it really supplies the basis for a realist aesthetic. Although Bazin invokes something that sounds like an index in his description of the ontology of the photographic image, maintaining the exact congruence of his claims with a strictly indexical claim seems fraught with difficulty. Rather than an argument about signs, Bazin's ontology of the photographic and filmic image seems to assert a nearly magical sense of the presence delivered by the photographic image. In any case, at best, the index would only function as one aspect of Bazin's realist aesthetic.[49] Once again, I am not claiming no use exists for the index in theories of film and photography, but simply that it has been entrusted with tasks it cannot fulfill and that reading it back into classical realist theories of the cinema probably obscures as much as it explains.

But I would also have to admit that "motion," even when specified as "cinematic motion," probably includes multiple aspects, not just one perceptible factor. The extreme spectator involvement that movement can generate needs further study, both in terms of perceptual and cognitive processes (which I think call for both experimental and phenomenological analysis) and in relation to broader aesthetic styles. Metz's description is based on the classical fiction film: what role does motion play in nonclassical films? (I have, of course, argued for its vital role in avant-garde film.) I am offering only a prolegomena to a larger investigation; my comments here aspire to be provocative rather than definitive. Motion, I am arguing, needs to be taken more seriously in our exploration of the nature of film and our account of how film style functions. At the same time, giving new importance to movement (or restoring it) builds a strong bridge between cinema and the new media that some view as cinema's successors. Like the animated line Germaine Dulac described, whose movement directly creates an emotion, motion involves both transformation and continuity (film history involves both the transformation of its central medium and a recognition of an ever-shifting continuity, a trajectory, to this transformation). As an art of motion, cinema has affinities to other media: dance, action painting, instantaneous photography, kinetic sculpture. But it also possesses its own trajectory, one in which I suspect the new media of motion arts will also find a place, or at least an affinity.

10

To Scan a Ghost: The Ontology of Mediated Vision

1. RENDERING THE INVISIBLE WORLD VISIBLE

> Though in many of its aspects this visible world seems formed in love, the invisible spheres were formed in fright.
>
> HERMAN MELVILLE, *Moby Dick* (1851)

Friedrich W. Murnau's 1922 "Symphony of Horror" *Nosferatu* cuts directly from a swarm of plague-bearing rats (one of which has just bitten a sailor on the foot) emerging from the hold of a ship in which the vampire lies in his coffin filled with earth, to Prof. Bulwer, "a Paracelsian," in a lecture room laboratory initiating his students into the night-side of Nature. Murnau intercuts Bulwer's lecture with shots a film historian (and likely a contemporary viewer) would recognize as taken from (or closely patterned on) the scientific films of the era, including a close-up of a Venus flytrap closing around its prey and a spider crawling along its web toward a trapped insect. Murnau uses complex and highly symbolic intercutting

This essay first appeared in *Grey Room*, no. 26 (Winter 2007): 94–127, with the following acknowledgment: "This essay is based on a paper delivered to the conference 'Dark Rooms: Photography and Invisibility' arranged by Anne McCauley at Princeton University, October 2005. I want to thank the participants of the conference for their comments, and especially Karen Beckman for encouraging me to submit the paper to this journal and for her careful reading and advice on revision. For reasons that should be obvious to him, I offer the essay to my friend Stefan Andriopoulos. And, as always, for Aelia Laelia."

in this scene and throughout the film, less to arouse Griffithian suspense than to create a series of magically interlocking events carried by sinister correspondences and analogies.[1] Thus, although the cut to the spider web confirms Bulwer's demonstration to his students of the pervasive cruelty of nature, its vampirelike system of feeding on other species, this spider web does not cling to some untidy corner of Bulwer's lecture room. Rather, through editing's ability to juxtapose different spaces, this web hangs in the asylum cell of the vampire's minion, Knock, whom we have just seen devour insects, proclaiming, "Blood is life!" Just as Bulwer compares the carnivorous plant to the vampire, Murnau's editing compares the madman and the scientist, each the center of a dark system of deadly metaphors and hysterical imitations. Murnau cuts back from the asylum cell to Bulwer and his students bent over a water tank, as the scientist isolates another vampire of the natural world. A "polyp with tentacles" appears not merely enlarged by a close-up but obviously filmed through microcinematography, a frequent technique of scientific films since the invention of cinema.[2] As the microscopic monster's tentacles grasp another cellular creature and seem to devour it, this glimpse into an invisible world made possible by the conjunction of two emblematic modern optical devices (the microscope and the movie camera) still compels our wonder. In an intertitle Bulwer describes the creature: "transparent, almost ethereal . . . but a phantom almost." (Indeed one can see, in this silent film, the actor's lips form the word *phantom*, evoking another phantom presence in silent cinema, the voice—eluded to, visualized, even translated into intertitles—but never heard directly.[3])

Murnau's intercutting gives Bulwer's analogies and metaphors a natural, if not a supernatural, demonstration. Cinema visualizes nature's sinister powers through the intercutting of predators across the various locales of the story (dockside, madman's cell, scientific lecture hall). The sequence also demonstrates the uncanny powers of the cinema. By supplying literal and disturbing images of nature's vampiric appetite through close-ups taken from (or closely imitating) scientific films, Murnau not only roots his horror tale in the seemingly objective world but aligns the medium of cinema with other optical devices of observation and display, such as the microscope. If we take this conjunction of the scientific and the supernatural merely as a motif of the horror genre, we miss Murnau's reference to German Romantic *Naturphilosophie*. Bulwer represents more than a horror-film mad scientist, exceeding even the Victorian-era biologist Van Helsing from Bram Stoker's *Dracula*, who provided the source for the film's scientist character in this free adaptation.[4] Murnau and his scriptwriter (the shadowy Henrik Galeen) backdated Stoker's tale from the end to the early nineteenth century, transforming Van Helsing into a Romantic scientist modeled on figures such as J.W. Ritter, Lorenz Oken, and Alexander von Humboldt.

These pioneers of Romantic life sciences took as their principle the unity of nature and the existence of archetypal forms (like Goethe's *Urpflanze*) throughout nature, uniting the vegetable and animal world (and even the organic and inorganic) in similar dynamic processes of growth, transformation, and decay. As Ritter put it, "Where then is the difference between the parts of an animal, of a plant, of a metal, and of a stone—Are they not all members of the *cosmic-animal*, of *Nature*?"[5] Describing plants as composing "the language of nature," Ritter, like most Romantic scientists influenced by the *Naturphilosophie* of Schelling, conceived of Nature not as inert material but as an organic entity shot through and enlivened by a system of correspondences and metaphors.[6] By the end of the nineteenth century, however, the logic of such correspondences had been excluded from serious consideration by a positivist and empiricist current in science that had critiqued and replaced the Romantics. But in 1922 Murnau used editing to visualize such metaphors, reviving, through modern technology, an untimely system of thought. For Murnau the medium of cinema appears to demonstrate a system that science no longer endorsed.

In *Nosferatu*, Murnau provided world cinema with one of the first masterpieces that systematically reflected on the artistic possibilities of the new medium of cinema. Far be it from me to underestimate the achievement of cinema during its previous two and a half decades (the works of Lumière, Méliès, Bauer, Griffith, and many others). Whereas Griffith aspired (rather disingenuously) to an appearance of transparency in his emulation of historical epic narrative in *The Birth of a Nation* and *Intolerance*,[7] Murnau synthesized the pictorial heritage of the cinema of the 1910s (Tourneur, Bauer, Hofer)[8] with Griffithian strategies of crosscutting, transforming both traditions in the process. *Nosferatu* explored the play between the visible and the invisible, reflections and shadow, on- and off-screen space that cinema made possible, forging a technological image of the uncanny. One senses throughout *Nosferatu* this excitement of innovation, of redefining a medium by testing and transforming its relation to its own history and to other media (the strong use Murnau makes of painting, literary texts, scientific discourse, and even musical rhythms). As such, the film offers lessons not only in the nature of cinema as a visual medium but also in the question of what a "new medium" can create by reflecting upon itself and its differences from and similarities to other media.

Not the least of my discomforts with the current term *new media* comes from the linear succession it inflicts on our still emerging understanding of media history—as if the prime modernist virtue of renewal followed automatically from technical innovation and commercial novelty. I want in this essay to explode the iron cage of historical succession to which this use of the term *new* unwittingly commits us. In its place, I want to celebrate the impact of untimely discovery (which often involves a recycling of the supposed "outmoded") that frequently motivates artistic renewal. But if the term new in "new media" seems to be easily critiqued, what about the term *media*? Too often the accent is placed exclusively on the first term with the assumption that the second goes without saying, a transparent channel of transmission, a technological conduit for communication. If the novelty of media is to be granted a purchase in aesthetic analysis, its historical lineage needs explication. What is it that mediates between the seen and the seer? What pathways do vision and the other senses take—rather than being the mere vehicles of transmitting messages and meaning? As I want to explore and question in this essay the trope of vision and transparency, I also want to focus on the term *medium* itself, in all its polysemy and historical divagations, its very materiality and its paradoxical aspiration to immateriality.

This essay reflects on the occasionally untimely and potentially uncanny nature of modern media, visual and auditory, through a consideration of a premodern conceptualization of visual perception and the imagination in Western thought, guided by philosopher Giorgio Agamben's discussion of the "phantasm" and, more literally, by the untimely figure of the ghost or phantom, especially in visual form.[9] A "phantasm" denotes an image that wavers between the material and immaterial and was used by premodern philosophy and science to explain the workings of both sight and consciousness, especially the imagination (*phantasia*). Although a discredited and untimely concept in both philosophy and science, the phantasm provides a tool for thinking through modern—including "new"—media. I believe that in the new media environment based in the proliferation of virtual images, the concept of the phantasm gains a new valency as an element of the cultural imaginary. The ghost has emerged as a powerful metaphor in recent literary studies, cultural history, and even political theory. An examination of their history of representation, including the newly emerging visual devices can sharpen and renew these metaphors.

The polyp vampire projected by Murnau's microscopic cinema embodies a mediated, phantasmatic imagery whose visual appearance wavers ambiguously between the visible and the invisible. Bulwer's emphasis on the transparency of the predator polyp floating on the screen so highly magnified, its body almost as translucent as the water that bears it, offers not only a literal image of a phantasmatic body (visible, yet seen through); it also recalls for us the transparent nature of film itself, its status as a filter of light, a caster of shadows, a weaver of phantoms. "Transparent, almost a phantom." The act of seeing encounters a bizarre entity whose quasi-ethereal nature marks the limit (or contradiction) of visibility. By displaying the most primitive form of cellular life through the most modern of media, Murnau employs an untimely anachronism, suggesting the anticipation of cinema in this early nineteenth-century lecture hall. Bulwer and his students are not shown peering into microscopes to see this creature. Instead, the image looms before us, oddly abstracted from any specified means of seeing it, a product of cinema not wholly absorbed back into the film's diegesis, a self-reflective moment that seems to float, in more ways than one, upon the movie screen. Bulwer's demonstration not only makes the drama of microscopic vampirism visible but also makes the medium of its presentation (whether thought of as microscope or cinema) seem to disappear, as the medium becomes transparent in the wake of its message. This elegant demonstration not only visualizes a gaze of scientific mastery but explores an uncanny dialectic of the visible and the invisible introduced by technologically mediated images.

Bulwer's lesson, despite using scientific footage, occurs in a fictional film, but the attempt to establish an occult invisible world of phantoms through the modern devices of photography has historical foundation. The recent exhibition of spirit photography (originating in La Maison Européenne de la Photographie in Paris, then brought to the Metropolitan Museum of Art in New York City in September 2005), focused unprecedented attention on nineteenth-century photographic images that were offered as evidence of the existence of spirits or ghosts.[10] While many reviewers treated the exhibition as a joke, it confronted alert viewers with more than a risible encounter with discredited beliefs or even an eccentric episode in photographic history. If these images continue to fascinate us, this may come less from what they indicate about a belief in ghosts than from what they reveal of our beliefs about photographs. Rather than focusing on the claims made for such photographs as proof of the existence of a spirit world, I want to explore their formal, visual nature—what supposed photographs of ghosts or spirits *look like*—and their phenomenological aspect—how these images *affect us* as viewers. The convergence between phantoms and photography may prove more than fortuitous. In discussing these spirit photographs, the term *phantasmatic* denotes images that oscillate between visibility and invisibility, presence and absence, materiality and immateriality, often using transparency or some other manipulation of visual appearance to express this paradoxical ontological status. Beyond the literal sense of survival after death, ghosts, as phantasms revealing hidden assumptions about the nature of the visual image, still haunt our modern media landscape.

Ghosts or spirits appear in spirit photographs primarily as phantoms—bodies rendered optically strange, semitransparent or out of focus, dissolving into shrouds of gauze or simply incongruously "floating" in the space of the photograph. This iconography of phantoms not only draws on a widespread tradition in portraying the ghostly but mimes a visual experience that exceeds or contradicts normal conditions of sight and recognition. Most spirit photographs portray spirits alongside "normal" figures in familiar spaces (posed subjects in a studio or room), but the two sorts of bodies appear oddly superimposed upon each other or illogically juxtaposed. This collision of separate orientations betrays the technical means by which the photographs were produced (superimposing two or more images photographed at separate times) and therefore undermines their claim to be evidence of a spirit world. Nonetheless, their incongruous juxtaposition yields an eerie image of the encounter of two ontologically separate worlds. Like the free-floating polyp of Bulwer's demonstration, spirit photographs portray a fissured space, one that allows visitors from another dimension to peek through, hovering within (or beyond) the space occupied by the "normal" figures.

Even if we did not take these unconventional images as rendering actual spirits, a clash of different representations of bodies confronts us (at least on a formal level), the one familiarly solid and positioned, the other somehow filtered by the process of transmission into a virtual body, weightless or permeable—a phantom. Spirit photography juxtaposes physical presence with its contrary, a phantomlike transformation of the human body that does not remove it from our vision but does render it somehow unreal. Instead of simply being present, the phantom occupies the ontologically ambiguous status of "haunting"—enduring and troubling in its uncanny claim on our awareness and sense of presence yet also unfamiliar and difficult to integrate into everyday space and time. Such phantasms, with their haunting blend of presence/absence, not only formed the subject of spirit photography but cast a continued, if occluded, influence over our experience of mediated visual images and photographs in a contemporary culture increasingly dedicated to the virtual.

More than a decade ago, I wrote a pioneering essay on spirit photography, whose research is now far surpassed by more recent work such as the essays included in the catalogue for the Metropolitan Museum exhibition.[11] But the theoretical issues I raised in that earlier essay (and several related essays dealing with the emergence of modern media recording of both sound and images in the nineteenth century) remain crucial.[12] The modern media environment, the proliferation of virtual images and sounds that ever-increasingly surround us, recalls earlier models of the relation between consciousness and the cosmos that drew on magical or supernatural analogies.[13] I am far from proposing here a project of reenchantment of technology. Rather I want to probe the unique cultural nature of modern media, which confront us with representations that are fundamentally different from conventional realist theories of mimesis based simply in resemblance. However, rather than offering yet another review of the ontology of the photographic image as proposed by André Bazin, Roland Barthes, and others, I want to explore the ontology and phenomenology of modern media of reproduction (the debates surrounding photography can be extended to both moving image and sound recording) through the metaphor of the ghostly and the phantasm. The ontological argument claims that photography not only portrays things but participates in, shares, or appropriates the very ontology of the things it portrays. In what way does the medium disappear in photography, abdicating in favor of the object portrayed? How does the photographic medium mediate? Spirit photography opens one way of raising this question, with its ghostly conception of the medium as message.

2. GHOSTLY VISION/GHOSTLY IMAGES: MEDIUMS AND MEDIA

> There would be as great an inconvenience in seeing spirits always with us, as in seeing the air that surrounds us, or the myriads of microscopic animals that flutter around us and on us.
>
> ALLAN KARDEC, *The Book on Mediums* (1878)

Described in an intertitle as a "Paracelsian," Bulwer not only recalls the early nineteenth-century Romantic scientist but also represents the heritage of "natural magic," an ancestor of experimental science, whose major authors, from Giambattista della Porta and Athanasius Kircher through to David Brewster, dealt with the wonders of nature more than its regularities and explored especially its visual illusions.[14] Scientific and occult beliefs, as well as a fascination with devices of wonder, mixed promiscuously in sixteenth- and seventeenth-century natural magic, creating a tangle that later scientists and philosophers tried hard to sort out. The optical effect of lenses, including microscopes and telescopes, even as they revealed new worlds of the infinitesimal or the seemingly infinitely distant, often got caught in this thicket.[15] Controversies and skepticism initially met images mediated by new optical devices, partly because the effects of mirrors and lenses were primarily associated with the catoptric illusions managed by conjurers and charlatans.[16] Natural magic remained associated with the world of illusions and entertainments, the display of curiosities and extraordinary devices, staging spectacular demonstrations of electricity, magnetism, and optical phenomenon, but often yoked to scientifically dubious explanatory systems.[17] Although accounts of the evolution of scientific thought and experiment privilege the dominant current of Enlightenment mechanistic investigation and explanation, the heritage of natural magic follows scientific thought and practice for centuries like a shadow. The Romantic scientists of the early nineteenth century wished to reform scientific thought by returning it to its roots in the correspondences and metaphors that made up the magical system of Paracelsus, the Renaissance occultist scientist and doctor, but they also endeavored to enrich this esoteric tradition through scientific observation, including employing new visual devices, as well as integrating new conceptions of electricity, magnetism, and the nature of life.[18]

Nineteenth-century American Spiritualism, a loose-knit ideology based on communication with spirits of the dead, primarily through "mediums" who conveyed messages while in a trance, in many ways continued this Romantic tradition.[19] Spiritualists embraced recent scientific devices, such as telegraphy and photography, both as tools for conveying or demonstrating their ideas and as central metaphors for their communication with the spirit world. In an ideology in which "mediumship" played the central role, a fascination with "new" media abounded, allowing a convergence of modern media of communication with occult systems.[20] As Jeffrey Sconce observes in his study *Haunted Media*, discussing the simultaneous development in the mid-nineteenth century of technological messages sent by telegraphy and supernatural messages conveyed by trance mediums, "the historical proximity and intertwined legacies of these founding 'mediums,' one material and the other spiritual, is hardly a coincidence."[21] Romantic *Naturphilosophie* and, in a more popular form, Spiritualism each sought the dialectical reenchantment of science as well as the scientific foundation of supposed supernatural phenomenon. This quest to rediscover ancient knowledge and revelations implicit in new scientific discoveries encapsulates the untimeliness peculiar to the modern occult—torn between archaic and progressive energies. Bulwer's brief microscopic film, besides scientifically demonstrating the pervasive influence of the vampire throughout nature, also shows what the night side of nature looks like—displaying a devouring phantom, ethereal yet material, visible yet transparent. This convergence of modern media and the spirit world revolves, at least in its visual manifestation, around a phantasmatic body—visible yet insubstantial, an image, separated from its physical basis or somehow strangely rarefied, become transparent—a phantom, almost.

What does a ghost look like? A ghost puts the nature of the human senses, vision especially, in crisis. A ghost, a spirit, or a phantom is something that is sensed without being seen. But this does not necessarily mean that ghosts are more easily heard, smelled, or felt (the sense of taste and ghosts seem to have rarely been paired, although orality plays a recurrent role in Spiritualism, as in the extrusion of ectoplasm from the mouths—and other orifices—of mediums). Ghostly presences may be betrayed by each of these senses, but the confluence of the senses that we think of as making up an ordinary reliable perception of reality seems somehow disaggregated in the case of ghosts. In fact, when encountering a ghost, the senses may contradict themselves rather than cohere. One of the earliest testimonies of an encounter with a ghost, given by Emperor Charles IV in the fourteenth century, describes the night the emperor and a companion endured in his castle in Prague during which they repeatedly heard the sound of a man walking and saw a chalice thrown across the room, but no specter ever became visible.[22] Likewise, ghosts frequently appear substantial but allow other bodies and objects to pass through them without resistance. The senses do not converge on ghosts: they can be heard without being seen, smelled without being touched, seen without registering a tactile presence, and so on. Further, the presence of a ghost is often sensed without generating a normal sensual experience. The ghost is there but is not really heard, smelled, felt, or seen.

The essential aspect of a ghost, its terrifying presence, comes from this uncertainty, this problematic relation to the senses and therefore to our sense of the world. One can, of course, discuss this uncertainty in terms of the ontology of the phantom itself, its mode of existence ambiguously perched between the living and the dead, the material and the incorporeal, rather than its mode of being perceived. From St. Augustine at the beginning of the Middle Ages, through the Protestant Reformation, to the polemics of orthodox Christians against the Spiritualists in the nineteenth century, the nature and even the possibility of ghosts have been hotly debated by theologians.[23] The uncertainty sowed by a ghost, then, would be metaphysical rather than phenomenological. But my focus precisely targets the phenomenological, how ghosts present themselves to the living, their mode of apprehension if not perception. The mode of appearing becomes crucial with ghosts and spirits because they are generally understood, by both believers and skeptics, to be apparitions rather than ordinary material objects. What does it mean for a ghost to be an appearance, to be an image? In the late nineteenth century, when people looked at spirit photographs, beyond the essential question of individual recognition—how did they know it was the late Uncle Harry?—lay a more basic question: How did they know it was a ghost? What does a ghost look like?

According to the admirable study by Jean-Claude Schmitt, the earliest attempts to give a visual representation of ghosts, illustrations included in medieval manuscripts, usually miniatures worked into the text itself, portrayed ghosts no differently than living people. Thus even ghosts in tales describing them as invisible were portrayed with conventional bodies (as in the illustration included in manuscripts of Charles IV's account of the Prague ghost). Sometimes their ghostly nature was indicated by macabre details: the wearing of a shroud, evidence of bodily decay, or outright portrayal as a cadaver. Toward the end of the thirteenth century, ghosts first appear portrayed as phantoms. Schmitt describes an example from a Spanish manuscript: "He is lacking all color and material density; the description of his face and his clothing is reduced to a drawing that is uniformly diaphanous and scarcely visible."[24] As Schmitt puts it, this image "announces from afar those that, since the nineteenth century, have been imposed on us to the exclusion of all others."[25]

My interest in this question goes beyond the iconography of the ghostly; it circles back on the ghost as paradoxical figure of vision, the shadowy ontological status of the ghost as a virtual image, a visual experience that somehow differs from common perception and whose means of representation seek to convey that ontological waver. To fully explore this, I want to probe traditional understandings of visual perception and the role images play in the process as mediation between objects and human perception, a tradition gradually attenuated in the modern era of optics yet strangely reemerged in the phenomena of photography and Spiritualism. In theories of human vision, the ghostly and the phantasmatic play a complex role, as sight has often been conceived as quasi-spiritual, somehow ethereal, as if the process of vision itself were almost phantomlike.

3. THE GHOSTLY MEDIUM OF VISION: THE PHANTASM

> These visible things come inside the eye—I do not say the things themselves, but their forms—through the diaphanous medium, not in reality but intentionally, almost as if through transparent glass.
>
> DANTE ALIGHIERI, *Convivio* III.9

Before Kepler and the rise of modern optics explained vision as a relation between light and lenses—that is, media that carried and shaped light, whether a lens precisely ground, a glass of water, or the human eye—the medium by which sight occurred was understood as consisting of images, *phantasmata*, that in effect worked as relays between objects seen and human vision. According to Aristotle, both perception and thinking rely on *phantasia* (usually translated as "images" or "imagination"), "for when the mind is actively aware of anything it is necessarily aware of it along with an image: for images are like sensuous contents except in that they contain no matter," adding, "the name *phantasia* (imagination) has been developed from *phaos* (light) because it is not possible to see without light."[26] In its sensual yet immaterial nature, *phantasia* works through the virtual image, *phantasm*. The Stoics and Epicureans, while holding that these images possessed a more physical nature than Aristotle claimed (by which means they were able to impress their form on the soul in perception and thought) and disagreeing among themselves about their exact processes, still maintained the existence of such an imagistic intermediary.[27]

The premodern worldview, especially after the triumph of a Platonically tinged Christianity, constructed hierarchies and chains of being in which reality relied on a communication across gradations of distance from the divine. Across such distances, intermediaries played essential roles. Thus St. Augustine described vision as threefold, corresponding to the triple nature of human being: intellectual vision (reason), physical vision (body), and spiritual vision (the soul). Human beings saw the physical world through corporeal vision, *sensus*, and recognized abstract ideas through intellectual vision, *mens*, which in its contemplation of God went beyond any image. But between these extremes, spiritual vision constituted a hybrid process, the realm of imagination; it experienced the images of things but separate from their bodily being. Imagination included memory as well as fantasy and the realm of dreams. But all three realms of sight depended on intermediaries, whether the abstract ideas used by the intellectual vision or the images that carried the imagination.[28] As Jean-Claude Schmitt summarizes this tradition in the Middle Ages, even physical sight involved the "concrete, physical interaction of the eye and the object through an external medium: *species* circulated and penetrated into the eye."[29]

This conception of sight pictured the eye's ability to form an image less as an optical process, as currently understood, than as a more material process as the human perceptive faculty became imprinted by an intermediary, the *phantasm* or *species* that already bore the nature of an image. While Greek authorities, followed by their Arabic translators and commentators, supplied numerous variations and modifications on this scheme, the extreme description provided by the Epicurean and atomist philosopher Lucretius remained both influential and typical.[30] Vision, Lucretius claimed, was carried by images (*simulacra*), which he described quite materially as *films*, "a sort of outer skin perpetually peeled off the surface of objects and flying about this way and that through the air."[31] He explained their effect on human vision as one of direct contact: "While the individual films that strike upon the eye are invisible, the objects from which they emanate are perceived."[32] As David Lindberg summarizes this tradition, "Films or *simulacra* . . . communicate the shape and colour of the object to the soul of the observer; encountering the *simulacrum* of an object is, as far as the soul is concerned, equivalent to encountering the object itself."[33] Roger Bacon's thirteenth-century synthesis of theories of vision, aligned with an Aristotelian understanding of vision as involving a transformation of the medium of air (rather than the atomists' assumption of actual material, albeit rarefied "films" that separated from visible objects), nonetheless depended upon intermediaries that ferried the image from object to observer moving through the medium of the air, explaining, "and this power is called 'likeness,' 'image' and 'species.'"[34]

To a modern eye, this explanation of the phenomenon of vision seems not only unduly complex and redundant but oddly ghostly. Lucretius's description of a universe in which "objects in general must correspondingly send off a great many images in a great many ways from every surface and in all directions simultaneously" evokes a world thick with ghosts, a hall of reflecting mirrors (or perhaps a contemporary airport lounge stocked with successive monitors all broadcasting CNN).[35] Among the terms that Bacon listed as synonyms for his *species—lumen*, *idolum*, *phantasma*, *simulacrum*, *forma*, *similtudo*, *umbra*—are terms used then and now for ghosts.[36] Indeed, before the nineteenth century the world of imagination and images, *phantasia* and *phantasmata*, constituted the medium not only of vision but of psychology generally, as images were the means by which objects penetrated consciousness, dreams occurred, artists created works, lovers became obsessed, magical influences were conveyed, memories were preserved—and ghosts appeared. The Renaissance system of magical influence depended, as Iaon Couliano showed, on the manipulation and control of phantasms, powerful intermediaries that human action could direct, intensify, and control.[37] Giorgio Agamben describes this system of *phantasma* as "a kind of subtle body of the soul that, situated at the extreme point of the sensitive soul, receives the images of objects, forms the phantasms of dreams, and, in determinate circumstances, can separate itself from the body and establish supernatural contacts and visions."[38] Of course, different philosophical schools elaborated distinctions among these processes and debated various theories of their nature, but until relatively recently phantasms or similar intermediaries constituted a realm of images that determined contact between human beings and the world. Within such a worldview, filled with mobile insubstantial images, an atmosphere of virtuality, the experience of seeing ghosts seems almost natural, rather than supernatural.

Kepler's explication of vision as the interaction between light, the eye, and the retinal image can be considered to be as revolutionary as the almost simultaneous displacement of the earth-centered theory of the universe that he and Copernicus theorized.[39] Compared to Kepler's schema of vision, the unnecessary duplication created by the model of free-floating images posed a barrier to a true scientific understanding of perception.[40] This new optical understanding of the process of vision rendered the category of phantasms unnecessary for the understanding of vision and therefore made the medium that joined the mental and the physical (and by which ghosts were also experienced) no longer a necessary part of the explanation of ordinary experience. In the premodern system, insubstantial ghosts had shared the ontology of the phantasms that conveyed emotion, dreams, and artistic imagination. But in the modern era, in which vision directly communicated with the world through the optical operation of the eye, ghosts' lack of clearly defined sensual properties placed them beyond the categories of scientific observation or consideration.

4. THE APPARATUS OF VISION: OPTICAL ILLUSIONS AND OPTICAL DEVICES

> Is it hard for you to accept such a mechanical and artificial system for the reproduction of life? It might help if you bear in mind that what changes the sleight-of-hand artist's movements into magic is our inability to see!
>
> ADOLFO BIOY CASARES, *The Invention of Morel* (1940)

After the Enlightenment, the question of what a ghost looked like bifurcated into issues of psychology (in which the concept of *phantasia* survived, albeit through a transformation of the understanding of psychic processes) and of optics. In contrast to traditional speculation on what ghosts might look like and how they were able to appear to the living, or theological arguments for or against the existence of spirits of the dead, optics or psychology primarily provided the means of explaining ghosts away, reducing them to mental delusions or visual illusions. Psychological explanation remains our major hermeneutic of the ghostly. As Terry Castle has put it, discussing the phantoms that haunt the Gothic novels of Anne Radcliffe,

"Ghost and spectres retain their ambiguous grip on the imagination; they simply migrate into the space of the mind."[41] The optical explanation of ghosts primarily took the form of debunking ghosts as deliberately manufactured illusions, often by revealing the purely scientific means by which optical illusions that resemble ghosts or phantoms could be created. In this context, ghosts no longer had any body, material, subtle, or phantasmatic. They consisted simply of virtual images produced by optical devices. A new modern history of phantoms as optical phenomenon, images scientifically explainable and therefore natural, yet uncanny in their sensual effects, emerges once phantasms no longer explain the process of perception. Exiled from the realm of physical effects, phantasms (to paraphrase Castle) migrate to a new realm, that of the virtual image, whose uncanny sensual and psychological effects linger like the residue of a lost explanatory system, haunting new optical media such as the magic lantern, camera obscura, and, eventually, photography.

Much of this debunking discourse emerged as a Protestant critique of Catholicism and "popery mystifications."[42] Theologically, the Protestant denial of the existence of purgatory abolished a major argument for the existence of ghosts as visits from the souls of the dead (a possibility that had sometimes been controversial within Catholicism as well). If purgatory existed, souls there might visit the living to complain about their suffering and beseech the offering of alms or the saying of masses to ease their torments. But if purgatory did not exist, or ghosts did not visit the living, how could one explain ongoing testimonies of such apparitions?[43] Keith Thomas cites seventeenth-century Protestant polemicists who claimed that Jesuits had faked apparitions in order to convert impressionable women to the Roman faith.[44]

Skepticism about the existence of ghosts was not new, but the new science of optics could explain away the ghost as a visual illusion created intentionally by means of an optical apparatus. This tradition began in the sixteenth century, partly cued by the Reformation. Scot's *Discoverie of Witches* (1584) skeptically approached the issue of witchcraft, primarily attributing it to the magical illusion of juggling, sleight of hand, and fooling the eye and attempting to explain in this way the invocation of the ghost of Saul by the witch of Endor, as described in the Old Testament (a source of controversy throughout church history as one of the few places where spirits of the dead are mentioned in the Bible).[45] Charles Musser has pointed out that the key work on optical devices of illusion (and natural magic) from the seventeenth century, the Jesuit Athanasius Kircher's *Ars magna lucis et umbra*, recommended a similar strategy of demystification, not only describing the scientific basis for optical devices such as catoptric lamps and mirrors (adding, in its second edition, the magic lantern) but urging that such devices be fully explained when displayed to the public.[46]

Creating optical phantoms became a form of entertainment in the eighteenth century and supplied a convention of the Gothic novel.[47] Schiller's novella "The Ghost-Seer" (1784), described by the author as a contribution to the "history of deceit and artifice so often imposed upon mankind," revealed an apparent appearance of a ghost in its plot as the result of a concealed optical device, a magic lantern combined with mechanical effects of light and dark.[48] As if acting out Schiller's scenario, the phantasmagoria exhibitions staged in France in the late eighteenth century by Paul de Philipstahl and Étienne-Gaspard Robertson incorporated the demystification process into their elaborate magic lantern spectacles, which claimed to present "phantasms of the dead or absent" to a paying public.[49] Thus when Philipstahl (using the name Philip Philidor) presented his phantasmagoria in Paris in 1793, he introduced his spectacle with this demystifying preamble:

> I will not show you ghosts, because there are no such things; but I will produce before you enactments and images, which are imagined to be ghosts, in the dreams of the imagination or in the falsehoods of charlatans. I am neither priest nor magician. I do not wish to deceive you; but I will astonish you.[50]

When Robertson presented an even more elaborate version of this ghost show in Paris a few years later, he actually proclaimed his optical spectacle to be "a science which deals with all the physical methods which have been misused in all ages and by all peoples to create belief in the resurrection and apparition of the dead."[51] In the context of revolutionary Paris, these optical demonstrations attacked religion as dependent on contrived illusions and claimed to reveal the optical means of deception that had been used by priests for centuries. Reproducing by optical devices the Old Testament account of the witch of Endor's evocation of the ghost of Saul, Robertson attempted to demonstrate the long history of such deceptions and proclaimed his entertainment a sterling contribution to the revolutionary energy of the era.[52]

Likewise, Sir David Brewster's *Letters on Natural Magic* (1832) defined his subject as the exposing of the means by which tyrants of all ages had enslaved mankind through superstitious belief in their supernatural power, claiming that priests of ancient eras

> must have been familiar with the property of lenses and mirrors to form erect and inverted images of objects. . . . There is reason to believe that they employed them to effect the apparitions of their gods; and in some of the descriptions of the optical displays which hallowed their ancient temples, we recognize all the transformations of the modern phantasmagoria.[53]

Brewster's retrospective reading of supernatural beliefs or events as the product of optical conjuring reveals how firmly scientific explanation based in optics had replaced visual theories that blurred the line between object and phantasm in explaining supernatural effects. Premodern practices and beliefs were now reinterpreted from an optical point of view, with a typically modern hermeneutic of suspicion. Brewster devotes some time to discussing the physiology of the eye and claims that mental images, or phantasms, can in some circumstances overwhelm normal sight and cause hallucinations. His explanation extends Kepler's model of the physiology of the eye with a claim that even in these psychological cases the retinal image is involved: "The 'mind's eye' is actually the body's eye, and . . . the retina is the common tablet on which both classes of impressions are painted."[54]

However, such a radical shift in models of explanation also produced untimely palimpsests in which older models remain legible beneath the inscription of new concepts, especially on the level of popular explanation or artistic metaphor, as if supernatural explanations still haunted the optically obtained virtual image. As ancient accounts of seeing ghosts were anachronistically redefined in terms of modern optical devices, advances in technology were often reinterpreted in an untimely fashion in terms of older, scientifically discredited systems. Some initial receptions of photography exemplify this untimely persistence of older beliefs. In a well-known memoir, the great nineteenth-century photographer Nadar described a theory of the daguerreotype offered by novelist Honoré de Balzac to explain why he avoided being photographed:

> All physical bodies are made up entirely of layers of ghost-like images, an infinite number of leaf-like skins laid one on top of the other. Since Balzac believed man was incapable of making something material from an apparition, from something impalpable—that is creating something from nothing—he concluded that every time someone had his photograph taken, one of the spectral layers was removed from the body, and transferred to the photograph. Repeated exposures entailed the unavoidable loss of subsequent ghostly layers, that is, the very essence of life.[55]

In an era when a classical education still formed part of French culture, one wonders if Nadar failed to recognize Lucretius's theory of detached visual films emanating from objects as the source of Balzac's explanation (or perhaps assumed it was so evident he need not bother to mention it?). This description, which Nadar described as Balzac's resistance to the "purely scientific explanation of the Daguerreotype," added a macabre aspect to the phantasm.[56] The photograph becomes not only the harbinger but a possible cause of death and decay, with an emphasis on the "ghostly" quality of the detaching films. Nadar's account of Balzac's theory was based on several personal discussions, but he added that the author had developed it "in a little alcove somewhere in the immense edifice of work."[57] Balzac's discussion of this theory in *The Human Comedy* consists of a rather short passage in the novel *Cousin Pons*, in which the narrator seems to be celebrating the novelty of the invention of Daguerre rather than resurrecting an aspect of ancient philosophy:

> If anyone had come and told Napoleon that a man or a building is incessantly and continuously represented by a picture in the atmosphere, that all existing objects project into it a kind of *spectre* which can be captured and perceived, he would have consigned him to Charenton as a lunatic . . . and yet that is what Daguerre's discovery proved.[58]

However the untimeliness of this modern conception still plays a role in Balzac's conception of photography because this description occurs within a claim for the possibility of divination, albeit based on new discoveries within the occult sciences.

5. PHANTASMS OF AMUSEMENT AND THE MODERN EVERYDAY ENVIRONMENT

> Every fixture and every movement conjures up shadow plays on the wall—immaterial silhouettes that hover through the air and become mixed with the mirror-images from the glass room itself. The raising of this impalpable glassy ghost, which transforms itself like a kaleidoscope or light reflex, signifies that the new dwelling is not the last solution.
>
> SIEGFRIED KRACAUER, "DAS NEUE BAUEN" (1927)

For Balzac, the new optical device of photography, a direct application of Kepler's theory of the retinal image to a mechanical device, supplied proof of the existence of the visual phantasms that Kepler's optics had rendered redundant. This untimely revival of an ancient tradition is similar to Bulwer using microcinematography and biology to demonstrate the existence of vampires. In both these instances the appearance of the photographic image is so powerful, so unusual (in Balzac's case, partly because of the novelty of photography at the time he was writing), that it takes on an uncanny aspect even if fully scientific explanations are available. Uncanny aspects of the photographic image seem to outrun its more ordinary explanations because a photograph renders visible in objective form the immaterial phantasms that the optical revolution had exorcised. The virtual image becomes the modern phantom. Terry Castle has even described photography as "the ultimate ghost-producing technology of the nineteenth century," the true heir of the phantasmagoria.[59] Indicating that Balzac's uncanny sense of the photographic process still has resonance, Castle even claims that modern culture has

> felt impelled to find mechanical techniques for remaking the world itself in spectral form. Photography was the first great breakthrough—a way of possessing material objects in a strangely decorporealized yet also supernaturally vivid form. But still more bizarre forms of spectral representation have appeared in the twentieth century—the moving pictures of cinematography and television, and recently, the eerie, three-dimensional phantasmata of holography and virtual reality.[60]

The fascination kindled by a decorporealized virtual body partly explains the uncanny experience we often have of spirit photographs, even when we know precisely the photographic means used to create them. As I described them earlier, the ghostly "extras" that appear in these images as either semitransparent superimpositions or oddly placed opaque interventions visualize a collision between the free-floating phantasm of Lucretius and a world of flesh-and-blood creatures. The disproportionate montage of these visually distinct realms makes a spirit photograph visually compelling—spooky, in fact. Ultimately, what emerges in these images may be less ocular evidence of another world (whether microscopic or ghostly) than the way photography itself, as a medium, becomes foregrounded. In these images, we no longer see *through* the photograph but become aware of the uncanny nature of the process of capturing an image. Our gaze is caught, suspended, stuck within the transparent film itself.

But perhaps the most extraordinary historical fact about spirit photographs lies in the fact that such images existed for years before any Spiritualist seemed to have claimed them.[61] Numerous amateur photographers had inadvertently produced them before, as when in 1856 Sir David Brewster, historian of science and magic, inventor of such optical devices as the kaleidoscope and one version of the stereoscope, described the effect of "ghostly" photographs. Brewster had observed (in this era which required long-lasting photographic exposures) that if someone moved out of the frame too soon, she either did not appear on the final plate at all (like the passersby erased from Daguerre's famous 1839 photo of the Boulevard Temple) or, if she lingered a bit longer (but not long enough to be fully registered), left a semitransparent image of herself. These accidentally spoiled photographs amused Brewster, who pointed out that they could be composed intentionally to produce "ghost photographs."[62] In his earlier work on natural magic, Brewster had thoroughly explored the creation of optical illusions intended to create supernatural effects. The purpose of such manufactured photographic ghosts, he stressed, must be restricted to amusement and entertainment. For at least a decade such images were produced, domestically and commercially, before William Mumler famously proclaimed his photographs as images of actual ghosts or spirits. Although we don't know if such claims were made outside of the public sphere before Mumler, his images and *his claims* of their supernatural provenance caused such a stir that one has to assume that a shift in definition had taken place.[63] The supernatural explanation of such photographs ran contrary to readily available technical accounts (described in texts by Brewster and others) and the apparently fairly widespread practice of manufacturing similar superimpositions without any supernatural claim. Yet the photographic production of transparent superimposed bodies still offered an ocular experience of the image of ghosts or spirits (which were taken by some viewers as proof of their existence).

Around the same time as Mumler's claims, a theatrical device for the production of phantoms appeared whose visual acuity surpassed even the phantasmagoria and whose imagery and process closely resembles spirit photography: the famous Pepper's Ghost illusion, invented by Henry Dircks and perfected and presented at London's Royal Polytechnic Institute in 1862 by John Henry Pepper.[64] Designed as stage machinery for the creation of transparent phantoms, the illusion used a pane of glass that emerged from slots in front of the stage and could be lowered as needed. The glass was angled so that it caught a reflection of a highly illuminated figure (usually an actor) posed in an area unseen by the audience. The glass also remained invisible to the audience, and only the reflection appeared, a transparent figure superimposed over the stage scene that was visible through glass. Thus, while the actors seen on stage would remain fully opaque and three-dimensional, the reflections on the glass would seem virtual and transparent, as one could see scenery and actors through the glass in the foregound. Further, actors on the stage seemed to pass through the reflections. Used primarily to stage simple ghost stories of apparitions and hauntings, the Pepper's Ghost illusion achieved an enormous success and became part of the stage machinery of the late Victorian spectacular theater. The device offered the optical experience of living, moving figures that nonetheless remained virtual and insubstantial within the space in which they seemed to appear. Alien visitors, the reflections appeared as detached images floating on air. A product of the science of optics (angles of reflection, the transparency of glass), the device superimposed flesh-and-blood bodies with phantoms in an uncanny and undeniably sensual experience.

Pepper's Ghost illusion partly owed its success to the novelty of the large pane of glass without imperfections so necessary to the illusion. During the late nineteenth century, the manufacture of large panes of glass became commercially and technically possible and enormously increased the visual attraction of the emerging commercial display culture, as reflective surfaces moved from being luxury items found only in palaces to mass-produced commodities adorning city streets. Instead of being restricted to multiplying the image of the king and his courtiers, store windows and mirrors greeted passersby on busy streets, endowing them with optical doubles, mixing passing crowds with their visual phantoms. Optical devices designed entirely as entertainment, such as the stereoscope and kaleidoscope that Brewster produced, joined scientific optical devices that had emerged in the seventeenth century and spawned a new realm of visual amusements ranging from the theater to the parlor to the nursery.[65] As the Renaissance phantasms faded from history, their optically manufactured doppelgangers appeared multiplied in a new daily environment of transparency and reflection.

Further, as glass windows became part of modern transportation systems, transparent and reflecting surfaces began to move, as one looked through (or looked at) windows on trains and trolleys. Yuri Tsivian has given me a rich description from the turn of the century of this new urban visual environment that mingled real and virtual images, visions transmitted or reflected by glass, written in 1899 by a Dr. M. V. Pogorelsky for a Russian occult journal named *Rebus*. "The quality of multiple reflections that the modern city provides us with has turned it into the natural medium of haunting," Pogorelsky claimed, as he described a trolley trip through St. Petersburg:

> In the window opposite you see the real street; it also reflects the side of the street behind the observer's back. Reflections of the front and rear windows of the car fall on it as well; apart from that, the *double* reflection of the real part of the street under observation is imprinted on it. The

> fact that the car itself is in movement makes the whole picture especially complex. In clear air and bright sunlight both real objects and their mirages look particularly lifelike, and what you get as a result is a magic picture, extremely complex and mingled. . . . Passing carriages are not one-directional anymore; they move in a chaos overtaking themselves or passing *through* each other. Some carriages and passersby look as if they were rushing forward, but at the same time you are aware that, in fact, each step they make takes them backward. If your attention wanders for a second you also lose the criterion that separates real objects from their equally lifelike apparitions.[66]

Pogorelsky's visual experience of the new mobile modern city with its clash of reflective surfaces navigates through a perceptual space that would also inspire Cubist and Futurist painters about a decade later, painters often (as in the case of Severini, Kupka, or Duchamp) inspired by occult sources as well. For Pogorelsky, this novel visual environment produced a haunted space, the reflections capturing images he understood as ghostly.

In the modern environment the virtual visual image interpenetrates the everyday world of corporeality and solidity. For the Spiritualist, the spirit world intersects with the material world; perceiving it is simply a matter of the sensitivity of the medium. While a worldview based in scientific explanation may leave no room for the supernatural, modern spiritual movements, such as Spiritualism and Theosophy, strove to find resonance between their beliefs and the discoveries and devices of science, in effect reenchanting the disenchanted world but also fashioning a new synthesis between the occult and the technological.[67] The invisible world of modern science revealed by X-rays and radioscopes—beyond the immediate evidence of the senses, shot through with the vibration of invisible particles, interpenetrated by invisible rays or energy—provided the mystically inclined with a new vocabulary of occult forces drawn primarily from scientific metaphors rather than the scientific method.[68]

The convergence of the scientific dematerialization of the perceptual world with the possibility of its hypervisualization via optical devices could convert the whole of the cosmos and its history into a series of virtual images. Camille Flammarion, who popularized both recent scientific developments and Spiritualist beliefs to the French public in the nineteenth century (including a strong endorsement of spirit photography), composed such a vision of the cosmos and history in his science fiction fantasy *Lumen*. Flammarion's extraterrestrial narrator declares that all events "became incorporated into a ray of light; thus it will transmit itself eternally into the infinite."[69] Cosmic history appears as a succession of disembodied visual images projected into outer space and visible to an ideally placed observer aided by optical devices:

> All the events accomplished upon the earth's surface, since its creations are visible in space at distances proportional to their remoteness in the past. The whole history of the globe and the life of every one of its inhabitants, could thus be seen at a glance by an eye capable of embracing that space.[70]

All of time can be conceived as a motion-picture beam projected into the infinite, envisioned by Flammarion decades before Edison's invention. Such purely optical images allow the possibility of witnessing all of past history as it streams through space.

The instruments of science gave birth to specters as scientific photography completed a circuit through avant-garde art and occult concepts. The chronophotographic images Étienne-Jules Marey produced in the 1880s for the straightforwardly materialist purpose of the detailed observation of the physical human body in motion registered transparent specters as the bodies moved through the frame that Kupka (and perhaps Duchamp) reinterpreted in terms of the occult multiple bodies described by Theosophy.[71] The most complete synthesis of occult lore, combined with a highly creative interpretation of Hindu and Buddhist conceptions, in the late nineteenth century Theosophy devised a theory of bodies and perception that outdid the premodern system of correspondences and phantasms in complexity.[72] Human beings, according to Theosophy, have, even during life, a multiplicity of bodies—the physical, the astral, the mental, and the causal—all of which correspond to various types of extrasensory perception. A true clairvoyant can see each of these bodies and their variety of forms and colors, which indicate a person's stage of spiritual evolution. These bodies take the form of egglike auras surrounding the person, rippling with continually changing energies and flowing patterns of color.[73] For the Theosophist, the visual appearance of these occult bodies indicates a person's physical health, their dominant emotions, and their level of spiritual evolution.

Refusing to limit the total reality of the human body to the manifest physicality of the body examined by modern science, the occult devised a variety of visual forms to express a bodily existence that transcends ordinary sensual evidence. But the visual imagery of science in the twentieth century, while still determinately indexical and empirical, deviates sharply from the classical medical gaze of anatomy and has become increasingly abstract and technologically mediated, producing images often unrecognizable to the layperson, with appearances seemingly as fanciful in their deviation from ordinary vision as the most bizarre occultist imagery. As we move more and more into a world in which data takes on visual form, these forms seem to become less and less familiar. Modern scientific imaging, supplemented not only by complex lenses but by other forms of data collection often associated with the other senses (ultrasound, night vision's sensitivity to heat, the tactile bouncing of radar off objects) has produced new images of the body that reflect this constant transformation and defamiliarization. Looking at the rather naive superimpositions of transparent bodies in spirit photographs, we respond less to the images of the dearly departed than to the first impulse toward a new image of the body, captured by new technologies of vision and seemingly liberated from the constraints of mortal physiology. In comparison to the phantasms of modern medical imaging, they now seem quaintly pictorial.

6. LOOKING AT DEATH IS DYING: THE VIRTUAL IMAGE AND THE APORIA OF VISION

> Alas, how is't with you,
> That you do bend your eye on vacancy,
> And with th'incorporal air do hold discourse?
>
> SHAKESPEARE, *Hamlet*, ACT III, SCENE IV

We do not *believe* in ghosts, we are *haunted* by them. We do not see ghosts. Rather, our senses of vision and perception are brought to a crisis by them. As revenants of things past, ghosts make vivid to us the pairing of memory and forgetting. The ghostly returns even after being shown the door, even after death, just as metaphors of the phantasmatic endure after scientific explanations seemingly triumph. As Jean-Claude Schmitt shows us, to forget the dead we must first remember them: traditionally, hauntings are the result of an inability to forget, due to an incomplete process of memorialization.[74] As harbingers of the future, ghosts show what we are to become in minatory mode: as they are now, so we shall be . . .

The ghostly fascinates us as a complex of two fundamental fantasies. First, it envisions a phantasmatic body, fundamentally different from ordinary bodily experience, whose appearance seems to make us doubt or rethink the nature of our senses, our grasp on reality. Corporeality, the sign of the real and material, becomes tricked out in the guise of the incorporeal. The fascination this paradox exerts reveals our discomfort with the original dichotomy of body and soul, material and spiritual. Second, the ghostly represents a fundamental untimeliness, a return of the past not in the form of memory or history but as a contradictory experience of presence, contained, as Derrida has shown us, in the term *haunting*.[75]

Technological bodies made of light, seizing and exceeding all the possibilities of physical movement, or an ability to overcome linear time, to navigate through, anticipate, or recycle past and future moments—such ghostly gifts also provide the substance of popular media fantasies. Yet if these modern media phantasms enact basic fantasies of release from limitations, they also carry, even if repressed, a warning of mortality and limitations, of the inevitable horizon of death. Roland Barthes has analyzed the deeply resonant association of still photography with death.[76] While Barthes's discomfort with the moving image prevented him from extending this discussion to the cinema, all virtual images and recorded sound also invoke the ghostly ontology of phantasms rather than a simple triumph over death. As Garrett Stewart has brilliantly demonstrated, the still image haunts the cinema and emerges most frequently as a harbinger of death and the ghostly.[77] If the virtual escapes death, it is simply because, as a phantom, it also escapes life. It delights us because it shows us that which remains impossible for embodied human existence. It chills us because it crosses a barrier we cannot.

This essay takes its title from one of the most enigmatic poems by one of our most enigmatic poets, Emily Dickinson. I am not a Dickinson scholar, simply a devoted reader, but in closing, I feel compelled to grapple with her text. Even more than most Dickinson poems, this one defies quick reading. Nearly every line ends with a dash, creating not so much a pattern of pauses as a sequence of gasps, as if each sentence suspends itself in a sharp intake of breath, or perhaps a final choke. The poem seems to exist in fragments that refuse to cohere, replicating the frenzied yet halting viewing that a ghost might cause:

'Tis so appalling—it exhilarates—
So over Horror, it half Captivates—
The Soul stares after it, secure—
A Sepulchre, fears frost, no more

A subsequent stanza probes even more uncertain expression and syntax:

To scan a Ghost, is faint—
But grappling, conquers it—
How easy, Torment, now—
Suspense kept sawing so—

What does Dickinson mean by "to scan a ghost"? Whereas I chose it as my title partly due to its untimely pun on the most contemporary means of reproducing images, the computer scanner, what did Dickinson mean by scanning a ghost? "To scan" has two basic meanings, which curiously combine in the modern use of a computer scanner: to analyze a poem in terms of metrics, line by line, and, according to the *Oxford English Dictionary* (*OED*), "to look at searchingly, examine with the eyes." Dickinson primarily intends the second meaning (i.e., it is difficult to examine a ghost closely), but as a poet writing a verse that, in fact, scans quite unconventionally, she also intends at least an echo of the first meaning. To follow the patterns of stresses, the number of feet, would seem to characterize grappling with something, calculating its rhythm and weighing its meter, even more than a searching gaze. The unbalanced, unfinished syntax of these lines invokes the sawing of suspense, both the process of cutting in two and the up-and-down balancing of a seesaw.

The last stanzas increase this rhythm of suspended conclusions and unfinished statements left lingering in ambiguities and syntactical interruptions:

> The Truth, is Bald, and Cold—
> But that will hold—
> If any are not sure—
> We show them—prayer—
> But we, who know,
> Stop hoping, now—
>
> Looking at Death, is Dying—
> Just let go the Breath—
> And not the pillow at your Cheek
> So Slumbereth—
>
> Others, Can wrestle—
> Yours, is done—
> And so of Woe, bleak dreaded—come,
> It sets the Fright at liberty—
> And Terror's free—
> Gay, Ghastly, Holiday!

Depth of analysis is not needed to see this poem as driven by its ambivalence toward the sight of a ghost as the harbinger of death; it succinctly sums up what I have wanted to say in this essay about the challenge seeing a ghost offers to perception in its line "Looking at Death, is Dying—." Sight itself proceeds by phantoms, at least in reflection. While vision remains our prime image of presence, reflecting on sight also evokes the possibility of illusion, the delusion of bending the eye on vacancy. Dickenson's third and fourth stanzas maintain a struggle. Wrestling with hope and prayer contends with gestures of release, a stopping of hope, a letting go of breath, a slumbering. With this release, the last stanza offers the proclamation that carries more finality than clarity—"Yours is done"—and an invocation to "bleak dreaded" Woe to "come." This invocation releases things—fright at liberty, terror free—but the final uncertainty resides in the linguistic ambiguity of such release. What does it mean to set free Fright and Terror? That is, once freed, do they depart from us, leaving us alone? Or are they simply set unconfined, allowed to roam the earth? Almost humorous in its oxymoron, the final line seems to imagine the grim celebration found in traditional representations of the Dance of Death: "Gay, Ghastly, Holiday!"

To scan a ghost is faint. Like the medieval Spanish illustration of a phantom that Schmitt discusses, the image fades; it no longer seems to hold our gaze, which, instead, passes through it, transparently. But seeing through a phantom does not mean overlooking a ghost. Instead, the transparency of vision terrifies the viewer. However, to liberate a ghost may also indicate a process of exorcism, "laying a ghost," as the traditional phrase puts it. Schmitt speculates that the faint appearance of the Spanish illustration may indicate a ghost that has been dead for some time; its connection with the physical cadaver has disappeared as the fleshly body has decayed.[78] In this view, ghosts would fade continuously. As Freud makes clear in his great essay "Mourning and Melancholy," surviving the dead depends on our ability to slowly and purposefully forget them, to let them leave our world. But this work of mourning involves as well a task of remembrance, the conscious process that differentiates mourning from the disease of melancholia. Perhaps the ultimate power of spirit photographs lies in acting out our attempt to hold onto the dead, an attempt to retain them by capturing their image, balanced, however, with an uncanny visual image that, unlike, say, a snapshot of a loved one when still alive, expresses their alien nature, their bodies transformed even if recognizable, departed from our world. They appear to us, but they also elude us. They do not let us grasp them. Rather they may allow us to release them into the realm of pure imagery and virtuality—of mourning and untimeliness.

But surrounded by the plethora of virtual images that throng our modern media, do we simply witness that aspect of Spiritualism that most disturbed the symbolist (and occultist) J. K. Huysmans, its vulgar democratization of the supernatural, opening the sacred realm to the floodgates of the crowds of the dead?[79] Should we simply marvel with Eliot (and Dante) at the throngs of dead, unaware "death had undone so many"? The virtual often seems to offer less a mode of mourning and release than a Sisyphean process of endless proliferation and compulsive repetition and return, the mechanical reproduction of the image gone wild, with each person (to quote André Breton's marveling description of the climax of a silent American serial) "followed by himself, and by himself, and by himself, and by himself."[80] Understanding the virtual world that surrounds us as the legacy of long traditions of mediating images, of phantasms, allows us, however, to probe this confluence of presence and absence that both the phantasm and the virtual represent.

Freud understood the disease of melancholy as a regression, from a world in which the loved one has died, into an obsession with the introjected image of the lost loved one into the unconscious in order to preserve it from death and deny its loss "through the medium of a hallucinatory wishful psychosis."[81] As Agamben demonstrates in *Stanzas*, Freud's description of melancholia reproduces a long tradition of understanding this disease as springing from an obsession with the phantasm of the unattainable loved one. The dominant Western tradition of thought, especially after Christianity, eyes the phantasm with suspicion as the medium not only of imagination but also of lovesickness, madness, and magic.[82] But within some traditions of Western poetry and some schools of mystical contemplation, the phantasm exists as more than a path to melancholia understood pathologically. Agamben defines the peril of melancholia as taking the phantasm as an illusion of presence. Poetically understood, the phantasm mediates between presence and absence, possession and loss, reality and sign, opening up a realm not only of mourning and symbolic action but also of play and artistry: "the phantasm generates desire, desire is translated into words, and the word defines a space wherein the appropriation of what could otherwise not be appropriated or enjoyed is possible."[83]

Since the writing of her poem and her own death, the word Dickinson chose, *scan*, has continued to transform. This goes beyond naming a recent form of proliferation and reproduction of images via a computer scanner. More curious (and perhaps revealing), "to scan," which in the nineteenth century primarily meant "to examine closely," has taken on the meaning of its near opposite, defined in *Merriam-Webster's Collegiate Dictionary* as "to glance from point to point often hastily, casually, or in search of a particular item." In common parlance, "scan" seems now more frequently to indicate a rapid glance over a text (as several generations of students have "scanned" their reading assignments) than to indicate careful scrutiny. The earliest reference the *OED* gives for this newer meaning—to which it gives a slightly more strenuous sense than is found in the *Merriam-Webster's* definition, or in student practice: "To search (literature, a text, a list, etc.) quickly or systematically for particular information or features"—comes from 1926 and seems to have emerged around the same time as the technical meaning of the term: "To cause (an area, object, or image) to be systematically traversed by a beam or detector; to convert (an image) into a linear sequence of signals in this way for purposes of transmission or processing" (whose first *OED* citation comes from 1928, in an early description of experimental television).

Dickinson could not have intended either meaning, but in the survival of her poem to the present day, in terms of a historical hermeneutics, it has become infected with these new meanings and holds its own in relation to them. We return to one of my key themes, the untimely nature not simply of phantoms but of our cultural interaction with media. If the more recent meaning of *scan* as a cursory glance seems beyond Dickinson's intention, nonetheless it seems to probe directly at the paradox of vision that seeing a ghost occasions, which she describes as "faint" (evoking both visual vagueness and the syncope with which heroines since Anne Radcliffe traditionally greeted phantoms). Scanning a ghost is difficult because in some sense we cannot scrutinize them. They remain virtual, rather than embodied, images. As such, phantoms make us reflect on the aporia of sight, the way the visible strives after the invisible, agonistically.

Photography represents the desire to capture an image of the real, that bald and cold Truth that Dickenson invokes—a faith that a scientifically designed visual apparatus can deliver us from our subjectivity. But, as Dickinson says of Truth—oh so ambiguously—"that will hold—" Hold what? Hold the Truth? Hold us? Hold on? Put us on hold? To return to one of the enigmas contained in Dickinson's poem, what is it that we show those that "are not sure"? Will whatever it is that we show make them "stop hoping?" Believers in spirit photographs saw these images less as photographs conveying what spirits "looked like" than as media of communication with the other world, a token of recognition, a *symbolum* passed between realms of existence.[84] The faith they held in these odd photographs lay in their ability to speak to them, enigmatically to deliver oracles about the nature of death and loss. What a photograph gives us remains an image, peculiarly modern, uniquely technological, and strangely inhuman. Therein lies its fascination: a photograph seems to imprint directly the phantasm of reality. But phantasms also serve as the vehicle of our dreams or desires, our phantasies, and even our delusions. Likewise, the most powerful works of new media seem to evoke precisely the limits of our current environment of hypervisuality to make us again both soothed and frightened by the darkness.

It is up to us to keep these different roles seesawing in play, in a Gay, Ghastly Holiday.

11

The Long and the Short of It: Centuries of Projecting Shadows, from Natural Magic to the Avant-Garde

AN OPTICAL EXHIBITION: ILLUSIONS, SPECTERS, AND DEMYSTIFICATION

First, imagine darkness.[1] Although it does not come first, its effect remains primary and overwhelming. That projection mostly takes place in a dark environment, or at least in shadow, radically distinguishes it from most Western traditions of theater. Until the end of the nineteenth century, both the stage and the auditorium were brightly lit, since the audience formed as much a part of the spectacle as the performance itself (the plebeian "Gods" in the balcony giving signs of approval or contempt; the aristocrats in their boxes wanting to be seen as much as they wanted to see). Only at the end of the century did the darkened theater appear, first in Wagner's Bayreuth (with audience sinking into a dreamlike obscurity), then in Antoine's Theatre Libre (a dark auditorium increasing the naturalism of the "fourth wall"), and later in the cinema. In all of these cases, having the audience sit in blackness caused something of a scandal.

Imagine, then, this unaccustomed gloom, its velvety eclipse of space, its obscuring of orientation. As Maurice Merleau-Ponty said of night, "It is pure depth without foreground or background, without surface and without any distance separating it from me. All space for the reflecting mind is

This essay first appeared in *The Art of Projection*, ed. Christopher Eamon, Mieke Bal, Beatriz Colomina, and Stan Douglas (Ostfildern: Hatje Canz Verlag, 2009), 23–35.

sustained by thinking which relates its parts to each other, but in this case, the thinking starts from nowhere."[2] What happens in the dark? How does light structure and create its own world? Projection indicates a throwing forward, in this case of light, but also of shadow, with a collision occurring between light, shadow, and a surface or screen. There is a space in front of a screen that seems to be canceled out by darkness, the "throw" of the beam of projection. If darkness cancels out this space, the screen or projection surface opens up another space, a space of illusion perhaps, or representation, or simply of the play of light. As Maya Deren described the walls of her apartment when she first projected her film *Meshes of the Afternoon*: "The walls of this room are solid except right there. That leads to something. . . . I've got to get it open because through there I can go through to someplace instead of leaving here by the same way that I came in."

I want to trace this play of projection back to its most elaborate spectacle—the phantasmagoria as presented by Étienne-Gaspard Robertson in Paris at the end of the eighteenth century—and use it to think about the nature of shadow and illusion, but most of all about its dual role of canceling out and conjuring up space. To engage space in this way, as a transition between the tangible and the virtual, means most obviously to engage the most basic aspects of human perception and cognition, the *données* of space but also of movement, and to play there with our most fundamental categories of world formation and orientation, of belief and confusion, of certainty and play. The screen is only the final destination of Robertson's spectacle, a point reached after a complex trajectory.

One approached the entrance to Robertson's phantasmagoria picking one's way past the crumbling walls of a convent and walking between the gravestones of deceased nuns. After one had moved through the court of Capuchins in the evening twilight and entered the former cloister, one walked down a long corridor, which Robertson, trained as a painter as well as a scientist (and originally ordained as a priest), had decorated with dark and fantastic paintings. At the end of the corridor, one arrived at the first exhibition space, the Salon de Physique, which was set aside for scientific experiments and devices. Here Robertson demonstrated the newly discovered power of electricity or, as he called it, "galvanism," causing luminous sparks to leap up before the onlookers' eyes. This room's attractions included optical and aural devices—a variety of distorting mirrors, peepshows that revealed miniature tableaux of familiar landscapes, a ventriloquist who could throw his voice into every corner of the room, and, in later years, the mystery of the "invisible woman," an apparently disembodied voice that answered the visitors' questions.

Galvanism was not presented simply as a physical force, but as a power

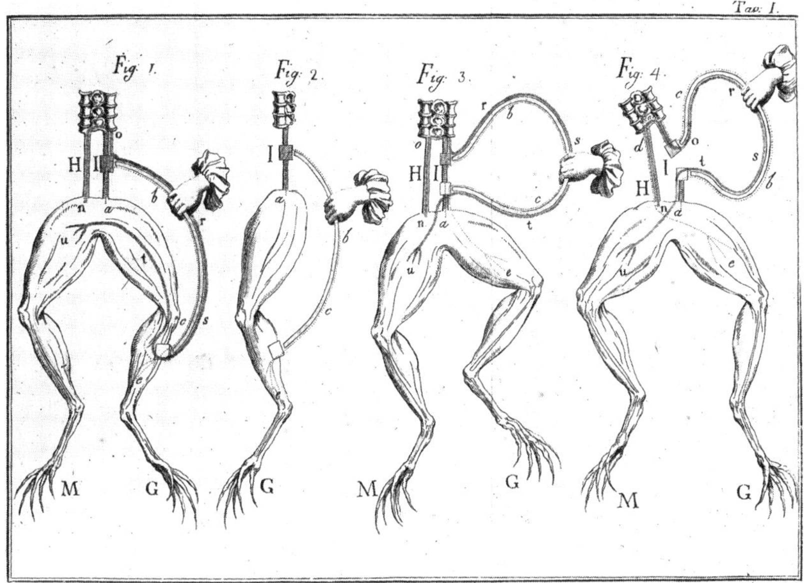

FIGURE 11.1. Galvanism experiment on dead frog. Luigi Galvani, *Memorie sulla elettricità animale* (Bologna, 1797). Image: Wellcome Collection.

that ruled a strange new world with visible effects: Robertson advertised it as "a new fluid . . . that temporarily gives movement to dead bodies."[3] One of Robertson's demonstrations recreated Galvani's application of electrical shock to the leg of a dead frog, which then twitched uncontrollably. Such demonstrations presented science as a succession of wonders and surprises, while the various optical and acoustical devices scattered throughout the room were designed to confuse and transform the senses, demonstrating the way human beings could be made uncertain whether what they were seeing and hearing was actually what it seemed to be. Thus the phantasmagoria literally took place on the threshold between science and superstition, between the Enlightenment and the Terror. Robertson's gathering of phantoms took place behind a huge archaic door covered with mysterious hieroglyphics (those ancient Egyptian symbols whose mysterious meaning had not yet been deciphered) that connected the Salon de Physique to the main auditorium of the phantasmagoria. The scientific demonstration taking place in this anteroom was meant to convince viewers that at the end of the eighteenth century, humankind was about to enter a brave new world and embark on a new path of scientific progress.

An aural cue, the unearthly tones of the glass harmonica, signaled the opening of this passage from the rationalistic, if uncanny, Salon de Physique to the reality of the main hall of the phantasmagoria. Nearly

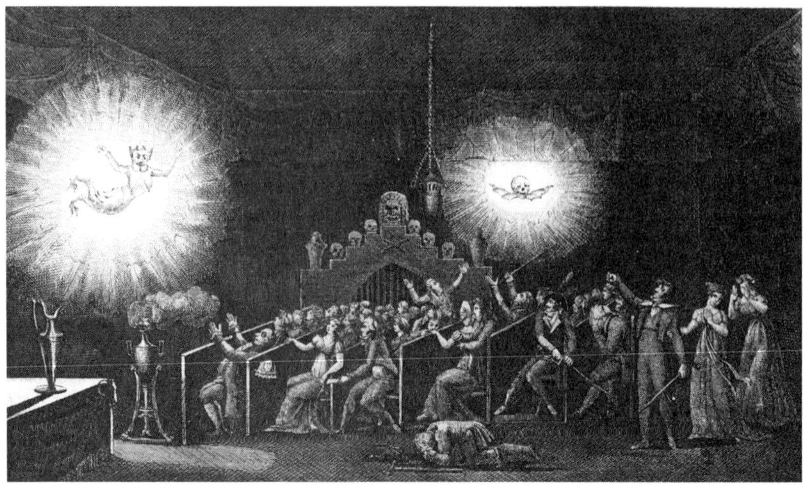

FIGURE 11.2. Étienne-Gaspard Robertson's Phantasmagoria.

forgotten today, the eerie sound of this newly invented musical instrument fascinated composers and audiences alike in the late eighteenth and early nineteenth centuries. A succession of glasses with different tonalities rubbed by fingers dipped in water, the glass harmonica produced music that to many seemed ethereal, possibly angelic. However, music historians commonly attribute the instrument's gradual loss of popularity to claims that its tones adversely effected the nerves, causing mental deterioration and other severe health problems.[4] The most important association for Robertson most likely lay in the use Franz Anton Mesmer made of the "celestial harmony" of the glass harmonica in his cures through animal magnetism.[5] On the other hand, Benjamin Franklin, the master of elecritcity and exemplar of new scientific discoveries, had invented, or at least perfected, this new instrument, whose novelty therefore recalled the new wonders of sciences as well as echoing the unearthly correspondences of Mesmer's occult system.

As the audience found their seats in the large hall, obscurity and then silence descended. A single hanging lamp initially dimly lit the room, draped in dark curtains, its funereal pall broken only by bleached skulls and ancient masks hanging on the walls. Conversations begun in the adjoining room ceased, as the audience observed what one commentator described as a "religious silence."[6] When this one dim light source was extinguished, plunging the audience into darkness, the silence was penetrated by sound effects imitating rainfall and thunder, tolling church bells, and the return of the glass harmonica. The senses already stimulated and led astray by the illusions in the Salon de Physique, the imagination stoked by the abandoned convent and its associations, were now confronted with a blank canvas, the blackness thickly seeded with expectations and suspense.

The phantasmagoria differed from traditional magic lantern shows primarily in that it concealed the apparatus from the audience's view. The magic lantern, the mechanism itself, had played a visible role. But in the phantasmagoria, the device (Robertson called his lantern a "phantascope") was not only shrouded by darkness, but those operating it redefined the whole spectacle by placing the lantern behind the screen, instead of in front of it, so that viewers saw the projected images but not their source. Furthermore, the screens themselves were concealed, first by curtains that covered them when the room was illuminated, then by the darkness of the room, and finally by the lampblack that surrounded the figures on the glass slides, thus eliminating any visible background which could have anchored them in space.

The phantasmagoria (like the movie projection system that ultimately derived from it) created its illusions primarily by concealing its means of projection. Thus it modernized the long tradition of magic shows, which

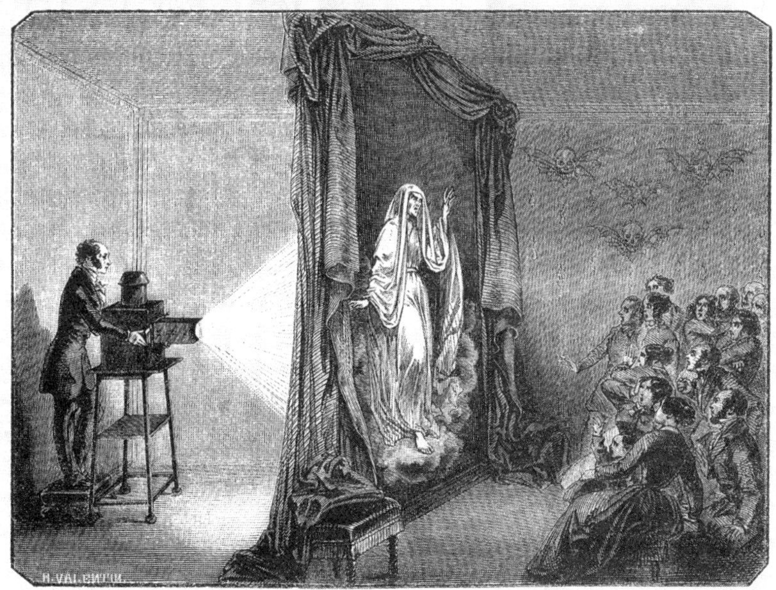

FIGURE 11.3. Phantasmagoria back projection. Image: Chronicle/Alamy Stock Photo.

created the impression of miraculous events by hiding the real processes from view, through the implementation of new optical effects. As an illusion, it worked directly on the people sitting in the audience, limiting their viewpoint, manipulating their perception either by withholding sensual information or by overstimulating the senses (the combination of limited sight due to the gloomy atmosphere while the ears were assaulted with eerie or unfamiliar sounds).

The "phantoms" of the phantasmagoria consisted of lantern projections cast on screens, but they operated in such a way that the audience was unaware of either screen or lantern. Rather than appearing directly on the screen, the images seemed to suddenly loom out of the darkness. This "looming effect" was greatly enhanced by the second major innovation in this new form of lantern entertainment—the illusion of motion.[7] The phantascope could be wheeled smoothly toward or away from the screen along polished brass rails. Combined with controls that simplified adjusting the focus, this movement caused the projected image on the screen to either increase or decrease in size. Since this shifting back and forth and adjusting could be carried out both rapidly and invisibly, and since the spectators were enveloped in darkness without any visible spatial reference, the rapidly magnifying image appeared to be charging out at the audience or, if the lantern was rolled backward, withdrawing. This unusual effect truly shook up the spectators, reportedly causing women to faint and men to rise, striking out with their canes against the apparently threatening phantom.

Robertson varied both the themes and the format of his program. Certain slides emphasized the effects of movement into the audience. The Bleeding Nun (a character from Mathew Lewis's Gothic novel *The Monk*, which exemplified the horrific aspect of the old religion) was portrayed by means of two slides that the projector could seamlessly alternate: one a front view for her "approach" to the audience, the second a back view for her "retreat." Other slides showed images of those who had recently died, including not only protagonists of the Revolution, such as Danton, Marat, and Robespierre, but also the inventor of the glass harmonica, Benjamin Franklin, and—occasionally and controversially—Louis XVI (thanks to trick slides, the latter two figures metamorphosed into skeletons before the viewers' eyes). Other images acted out brief scenarios, as in the images of the poet Edward Young attempting to bury his daughter at midnight, taken from *Night-Thoughts*. Some of the revenants appeared as images projected onto smoke being emitted by a burning brazier, an effect that had been introduced a few years prior to that by German lanternists. The wavering appearance of these phantoms, which seemed to "freely originate upon

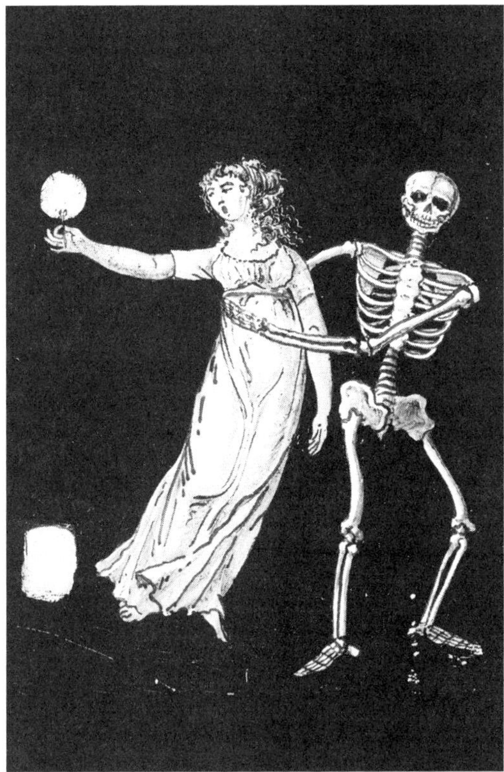

FIGURE 11.4. Phantasmagoria slide figure surrounded by black. *La Mort, représentée par un squelette, entraînant une jeune fille*, 1800–1850. Magic lantern slide © Musée des arts et métiers-Cnam, Paris; photo J.-C. Wetzel.

the air" (as the phantasmagoria showman in London, Paul de Philipstahl, using the name Philip Philidor, advertised), dematerialized the nature of these illusions, further disorienting audiences.[8] Where did they take place? Such immaterial visions seemed to fulfill Shakespeare's description of spirits "melted into air, into thin air / Like the baseless fabric of this vision."[9]

I have claimed the phantasmagoria worked in the space between the Enlightenment and superstition, seemingly summoning the phantoms of "the dead or absent" into the auditorium while displaying the triumphs of the new sciences in the anteroom to its spectacle. Purveyors of phantasmagoria shows not only acknowledged this tension between enlightened science and ancient superstition; they used it to attract the public to their shows. Thus Philip Polidor, who first introduced the phantasmagoria in Paris in 1793 (during the height of the Terror), started his spectacle off with this demystifying preamble:

> I will not show you ghosts, because there are no such things; but I will produce before you enactments and images, which are imagined to be ghosts, in the dreams of the imagination or in the falsehoods of charlatans. I am neither priest nor magician. I do not wish to deceive you; but I will astonish you.[10]

Thus the spectator of the phantasmagoria displayed a divided consciousness that was singularly modern. A sophisticated Parisian described the effect it had on him as follows:

> It is certain the illusion is complete. The total darkness of the place, the choice of images, the astonishing magic of their truly terrifying growth, the conjuring which accompanies them, everything combines to strike your imagination and to seize exclusively all your observational senses. Reason has told you well that these things are mere phantoms, catoptric tricks devised with artistry, carried out with skill, presented with intelligence, your weakened brain can only believe what it is made to see, and we believe ourselves to be transported into another world and another century.[11]

The effect, then, involves overcoming what "reason has told you," which is only possible in an age of reason. The phantasmagoria did not manufacture belief or faith, but rather generated entertaining confusion.

GHOSTS OF IDEOLOGY, APPARATUSES OF THE SENSES

The radical possibilities of the phantasmagoria might be summarized by describing it as an art of total illusion that also contained its own critique. This startling experience in the darkened room denied its own reality even as it was being presented, simultaneously overwhelming and calling the senses into question. One could think about avant-garde art of the ensuing century and a half as moving between these two poles—a direct and overwhelming appeal to the senses on the one hand, and the critique of illusion on the other. The critique seems to carry on the Enlightenment project, while the sensual approach often questions the powers of the rational mind and circumvents rather than demonstrates its powers.

The image of the phantasmagoria remains very much a part of critical tradition. In his posthumously published collection *Pensieri*, the great Italian poet and philosopher of modern skepticism and pessimism, Giacomo

Leopardi, recounted an event he said took place in Florence in 1831. A terrified crowd had gathered in front of a ground-floor window crying, "The phantom, the phantom!" A shadow cast on the wall, visible from the street, resembled a woman flailing her arms in a mysterious fashion. A friend of Leopardi offered to look into the room if a policeman would boost him up to a higher vantage point. From there he saw that the phantom was nothing but a woman's smock that had been draped over a chair, its arms stirred by the wind while a distaff behind the chair projected a shadow resembling a head. Leopardi commented ironically that "in the nineteenth century, in the very heart of Florence, which is the most learned city in Italy and whose inhabitants are particularly discerning and sophisticated, people still see ghosts that they believe to be spirits—ghosts that are distaffs."[12] The modernity of Leopardi's story comes not simply from the uncovering of suspicion still lurking within a supposedly sophisticated metropolis, but from the explanation of the ghosts as a visual phenomenon.

Thus almost a century after Leopardi's Florentine phantom, Bertolt Brecht restaged the event in one version of his great drama about science at war with authoritarian doctrine and superstition, *The Life of Galileo*. In the final scene, after his surrender to the Church, Galileo's disciple Andrea smuggles a book across the border in which the scientist has recorded his continued research. As Andrea steals past the customs inspectors, a group of urchins claim that a witch lives in a nearby house, pointing to a shadow cast on a window that resembles a witch stirring her cauldron. The witch, one child claims, rides a broomstick and casts spells on the coachman's horses. When Andrea casts doubt on this, the boy asks if he is denying that Marina is a witch.

ANDREA: No, I can't say she isn't a witch. I haven't looked into it. A man can't know about a thing he hasn't looked into, can he?

BOY: No,—But THAT! [*He points to the shadow*] She is stirring hell broth.

ANDREA: Let's see. Do you want to take a look? I can lift you up.

BOY: You lift me to the window mister! [*He takes a slingshot out of his pocket*] I can really bash her from there.

ANDREA: Hadn't we better make sure she is a witch before we shoot? I'll hold that.

[*The Boy . . . follows him reluctantly to the window. Andrea lifts the boy up so that he can look in.*]

ANDREA: What do you see?

BOY: [*Slowly*] Just an old girl cooking porridge.

ANDREA: Oh! Nothing to it then. Now look at her shadow, Paolo.

[*The Boy looks over his shoulder and back and compares reality and the shadow.*]

BOY: The big thing is a soup ladle.

ANDREA: Ah, a ladle! You see, I would have taken it for a broomstick, but I haven't looked into the matter as you have.[13]

Ironically, even after acknowledging that the old woman was stirring porridge, the boy still affirms she is a witch. Ironically, this production was staged in Hollywood shortly before the House Un-American Activities Committee witch hunt and Hollywood blacklist that drove Brecht (and film director Joseph Losey, who directed this theatrical production of *Galileo*) from the United States. This little shadow play (not included in other versions of the play) brings together the themes of projected shadows, superstition, and perspective essential to a critique of the phantasmagoria.

If Brecht was familiar with Leopardi's text, he filtered it through Karl Marx's frequent use of visual metaphors to describe the process of false consciousness under capitalism. The most famous of these was Marx's use of the image of the camera obscura in *The German Ideology*. The basis of the modern photographic camera, the camera obscura works on the principle that within a dark chamber (as small as a box or as large as room), if a small aperture is made in one wall or partition, allowing the rays of the sun to enter, an image of the outside world will appear on the opposite wall or surface, albeit upside down. Exploited by both scientists and artists such as Leonardo da Vinci, the camera obscura served both as a tool aiding artists to sketch from life and a form of visual entertainment. In his sixteenth-century book *Natural Magic*, Giambattista della Porta described elaborate pantomimes and dramas that could be staged outside an auditorium and then projected "live" onto the wall (in effect, an early anticipation of television) by means of a camera obscura.[14] Cameras obscura eventually employed lenses, both to make the image clearer and brighter and to project it right side up.

For Marx, this optical device with its upturned image provided a metaphor for distorted experience and ideology under capitalism, in particular the reversal in which ideas rather than material and social circumstances apparently determine the nature of things: "If in all ideology men and their circumstances appear upside down as in a camera obscura, this phenomenon arises just as much from their physical life processes as the inverted objects on the retina do from their physical life processes."[15] The camera obscura metaphor not only imaged the reversal of values and cause and effect apparent in capitalist ideology, but indicated that this distortion, like an optical effect, was fully explainable and operated according to set laws—just as Robertson and Philidor had indicated that their illusions were products of science and technology, not supernatural forces.

The phantasmagoria also appears in the famous passage in volume 1 of Karl Marx's *Capital: A Critique of Political Economy* with respect to the commodity fetish. In the process of becoming a commodity, an object for sale, a product of human labor (Marx's example is a table) ceases to exist either as simply the result of human labor or as an object with a specific purpose. Instead, when it enters the market, it acquires a different value, which Marx refers to as "exchange value." In place of a primary relation between human beings, the exchange value—in effect, the price tag on the object—asserts a relation between commodities. Marx describes this value as "phantasmagoric." As with the camera obscura, he is describing a false perception in which the actual forces operate in hiding or appear as something they are not. "There is a definite social relation between men, that assumes in their eyes the fantastic form of a relation between things."[16] In German, the phrase translated here as "fantastic form" is *dies phantasmagorische Form.*

By focusing on the technology of the device and not simply its fantastic effect, Marx emphasizes ideology's central task: to transfer agency from the effective causes (in the phantasmagoria, the operator and the magic lantern behind the screen; in the case of the commodity fetish, the social labor of human beings, which creates the commodity) to the actual inert effects (images on the glass that appear to be alive; commodities which seem to take on power). The phantasmagoria's confusion of point of view and orientation, created by its hidden lantern and screen and an environment of enveloping darkness, may provide the most important aspect of Marx's reference. The phantasmagoria not only conceals the human agent and the technical process involved but directly affects human perception. Within this critical tradition, the phantasmagoria not only manifests as a visual phenomenon but has powerful spectatorial impact. The consumer under capitalism preeminently becomes part of an audience at a spectacle—a spectator.

As I move my phantascope from illuminating the shadows of ideology to shedding light on the creation of works of art, let me focus this transformation through one of Walter Benjamin's richest insights: that in the nineteenth century, the work of art took on the form of a commodity (and hence potentially, a phantasmagoria). Paradoxically, the lyric poetry of Baudelaire, Benjamin claimed, derived precisely from "the devaluation of the human environment by the commodity economy."[17] But a dialectical opposition also asserts itself in Baudelaire's and the Symbolist's inherent resistance to this commodification through a redefinition of the artwork as a sensual experience rather than a material object.

From the demystifying point of view, the phantasmagoria asserted the ultimate truth of the rational and the fallibility of the senses. But from the point of view of showmanship, audience pleasure, and aesthetics (particularly if we take the term from its Greek root *aisthetikos*, "of or pertaining to things perceptible by the senses"), the novelty of the phantasmagoria lay in its manipulation of the senses—not to foster credulity, but simply to produce startling effects. Rather than seeing the phantasmagoria exclusively as either an ideological machine sustaining illusions or a process of demystification, it might be worth pursuing it as a new model for the manipulation of the senses. For a group of poets, critics, painters, and dramatists, the phantasmagoria signified not simply an illusion, but a new paradigm for works of art.

Thus Arthur Rimbaud, who described himself in *Season in Hell* as a "master of phantasmagorias," also announced a new art based in "a long, gigantic, and rational *derangement of all the senses*."[18] To accomplish this, Rimbaud announced he was inventing a new, universal language "accessible someday to all the senses."[19] Baudelaire had already articulated the experience of synaesthesia as the ideal of Symbolist art: artworks that not only addressed all the senses, but blended and transformed each sense into the others. Baudelaire in part conceived of this new model when he listened to Wagner's music for the first time. This aural experience filled him with a sense of space and light, "an immense horizon and a wide diffusion of light; an immensity with no décor but itself."[20] A few decades later, a Symbolist journal which inscribed the source of its inspiration in its title, *La Revue wagnerienne*, championed Wagner's *Gesamtkunstwerk* as initiating a new approach to art that recognized its basis in sensation. Although it embraced the experience of transcendence the Symbolists found in Wagner, Teodor Wyzewa's manifesto for the journal rooted transcendence in sensual experience: "In the beginning, our soul experiences sensations. . . . These consist of the diverse colors, resistances, smells or sonorities. . . . At a later stage, our sensations become linked. . . . The sensations become thought; the soul thinks after having felt."[21]

Situating the artist's power in his or her ability to manipulate sensations through form, texture, and color, tone and rhythm, or movement in order to create a direct route to emotions and thoughts, this new conception opened the way to an art no longer conceived as the imitation of either appearances or ideal models.

As Symbolist drama came into its own with the production of the plays of Maurice Maeterlinck, the atmosphere of evocation moved toward a deliberate invocation of unreality. Maeterlinck even argued for the elimination of living actors from the stage: "Will the human being be replaced by a shadow? A reflection? A projection of symbolic forms, or a being who would appear to live without being alive? . . . It also seems that any being apparently alive but deprived of life elicits extraordinary powers . . ."[22] A review of a Parisian Maeterlinck production complained, in fact, that the actors seemed like "a succession of images projected by a magic lantern."[23]

Adorno might have perhaps dismissed such attempts to found a new art on the uncertainty of the senses as part of the cultural deception he critiqued in one of their main inspirations, Richard Wagner, and which he termed "phantasmagoria." But we might wonder if another alternative is not laid out here: a deeply sensual art, certainly evocative of dreams and illusions, but which does not attempt to found a new religion or uphold an old mythology. Simultaneously popular in its address and yet often abstract in its forms, it plays with its audience, causing sensations that resolve themselves into both fear and laughter. Unlike canonical high modernist art, this art is not overly concerned with objecthood or even the materiality of the artwork. Rather, it manufactures machines and devices for shaping light and darkness, constantly aware that its true material consists less in its projections than in the sensual experience of the viewer. It seems to me to be a model that continues to have an uncanny hold on life.

EPILOGUE: CONTEMPORARY PHANTOMS, FUTURE PROJECTIONS

Today, with another fin de siècle under our belts, can the complex history and implications of the phantasmagoria still haunt us? In an era of media saturation, suffused with hyper- and virtual reality, can this antiquarian medium (necro-techno, to coin a phrase) inspire anything other than vague nostalgia? Without serving as an apologist for my profession as a media historian, I actually believe the answer is yes. A new generation of artists is exploring the possibilities of image projection from film, video, or computer sources outside the usual contexts of experimental film and video, thus dealing less with the established formal paradigms of frame and screen and audience, and playing with ambiguities of space, motion, and ontology.

In many ways, this recent work operates in opposition to the media saturation of Hollywood, television, and the internet, seeking to fashion a critical space for its practice strongly influenced by the Marxist or critical tradition. This ambition to use the medium in itself as a critical tool could be seen as continuing Robertson's and Philidor's dialectical and demystifying showmanship. Contemporary artist Judith Barry claims her work tries "to make technology in its many guises visibly part of a larger *ideological* context."[24] Barry's variety of projection surfaces (including public buildings) not only makes technology visible, but redefines public spaces and familiar shapes, as images challenge spectators to reorient themselves in positions other than the traditional audience-screen configurations. Curiously, the uncanny aspect of the phantasmagoria persists in some of these recent works as well, such as in Zoe Beloff's invocations of spiritualist photography and séances. Unlike the Spiritualists of the late nineteenth century, Beloff does not present her images as evidence of a supernatural presence, but rather as a simulacrum of an untenable belief whose spectacular fascination nonetheless remains unquestionable. In this respect, her work is reminiscent of the late nineteenth-century performances by magicians such as Maskelyne and Méliès, who recreated Spiritualist séances but introduced them, as Robertson and Philidor did with the phantasmagoria, with the announcement that all miraculous manifestations were achieved without spirit aid, offering them to audiences as avowed tricks and a lot of fun.[25]

Ultimately, I believe that as diverse as it is in its effects, technology, and aims, this new work marks a fundamental change of emphasis within the modernist paradigm, one closer perhaps to Rimbaud and the Symbolist model of works of art as the overwhelming of the senses than to the canons and concepts of modernist art established after World War II. While high modernist theories of self-referentiality led to self-contained and eminently marketable luxury commodities and signs of distinction, one wonders if the immateriality of this technology-driven new art continues aspirations of alternative cultures or simply supplies the new succession in the phantasmagoria of novelty.

12

Chaplin and the Body of Modernity

James Agee opened his novel *A Death in the Family*, the chronicle of young Rufus's loss of his father, set in 1915 and published shortly after Agee's untimely death in 1955, with this exchange:

> At supper that night, as many times before, his father said, "Well, 'spose we go to the picture show."
>
> "Oh, Jay!" his mother said. "That horrid little man!"
>
> "What's wrong with him?" his father asked, not because he didn't know what she would say, but so she would say it.
>
> "He's so *nasty*!" she said, as she always did. "So *vulgar*! With his nasty little cane; hooking up skirts and things, and that nasty little walk!"[1]

This opening elegantly not only brings us into a family situation, a child positioned somewhat precariously in the middle of a conversation between his parents, but also defamiliarizes a figure so recognizable he need not be named. Seen through the distortion of nostalgia (as opposed to Agee's sharply etched, ungilded memories), we are unlikely initially to recognize Charlie Chaplin in the horrid, nasty, vulgar little man. But indeed that was how Chaplin was received initially by guardians of culture, suspicious of

This essay first appeared in *Early Popular Visual Culture* 8, no. 3 (2010): 237–45, with the following acknowledgment: "A version of this article was given as a keynote presentation at the BFI Charles Chaplin Conference in London in 2005 and can be found on the Charlie Chaplin pages of the BFI website." Reprinted by permission of Taylor & Francis Ltd., http://www.tandfonline.com.

vulgar slapstick, with its too-fast action, its love of speed and violence, and its hatred of authority and propriety. Chaplin's behavior flaunted social inhibitions, provoking censure or laughter depending on your point of view. But, as Rufus's mother indicates, it wasn't simply what Chaplin did that made him nasty but his physical being—not just hooking up skirts, but "that nasty little walk!"

Agee, of course, was a novelist and a poet, and the author of a seminal modernist work combining photography and prose, an ethnography of Southern tenant farmers during the Depression, *Let Us Now Praise Famous Men* (1941), anticipating by generations current anthropological work in thick description and personal participant observation and whose style rivals Herman Melville. As you probably know, he was also a scriptwriter (*The African Queen* [1951], *The Night of the Hunter* [1955]), and a film critic, author of "Comedy's Golden Age," perhaps the seminal account of silent film comedy, and in the 1950s one of the few to raise his voice publicly against the shameful treatment of Charles Chaplin by American right-wing organizations and their government sympathizers. By the 1950s, some of the original disgust at Chaplin had resurfaced, albeit with an apparently new focus—not that he had ever been fully embraced by official culture (recall the 1927 Surrealist manifesto in defense of Chaplin in the face of his pending prosecution for alleged sexual crimes, entitled "Hands Off Love").[2] I invoke Agee here, as I could many other modernist artists who appreciated Chaplin, not only for the clarity of his insight, but to stress our need to recover Chaplin, not as an enshrined genius, but in his original energy, as a controversial modern artist whose art not only delighted and entertained, but also helped transform the world he was born into. Chaplin's work offered something new; he laughed the world into a new physical realm, exploring the ambiguities—indeed the comedy—of the body of modernity.

Chaplin's cinematic body defies verbal description—and that's the point. His body transforms before our eyes; it even occasionally sprouts wings and flies. However, as the crumpled body of Chaplin's Icarus-like fallen angel in *The Kid* shows us, he never loses his physical nature: his grace defies, but cannot deny, gravity. In the face of propriety, he asserts the body's less than genteel functions. But besides enacting the clown's traditional role of affirming the body's appetites against social convention, Chaplin's physical nature also exceeds his human identity and transforms itself into the mechanical, the animal, and even the vegetable. His body seems at points to disaggregate itself, with limbs operating independently of each other, or to merge with other bodies and create new creatures. Chaplin slides up and down the great chain of being, achieving a plastic ontology in which inanimate objects become bodily appendages, and the body itself suddenly seems inert.

THE NATURAL MAN: BODILY FUNCTIONS, OR WHAT WAS WRONG WITH THAT WALK?

Despite his mother's objections, Rufus and his parents do attend the picture show and watch an unnamed (and seemingly synthetic) Chaplin short supporting a William S. Hart western. The walk was there: "everyone laughed the minute they saw him squattily walking with his toes out and his knees wide apart, as if he were chafed."[3] Seen through Rufus's five-year-old eyes, Chaplin's walk has a direct physical significance, chafed thighs, an association less likely to be recalled by an adult. These childhood associations continue as Rufus watches the film and they become increasingly—well, nasty. Chaplin has stolen some eggs and hidden them in the seat of his pants. Later, when Charlie gets shoved onto the sidewalk, "he sat down straight-legged, hard enough to hurt," and of course the eggs smashed in his pants. Chaplin's miming and facial expression intensely convey the sensation to Rufus, as well as an embarrassing memory:

> The way his face looked, with the lip wrinkled off the teeth and the sickly little smile, it made you feel just the way those broken eggs must feel against your seat, as queer and awful as that time in the white pekay suit when it ran down out of your pants-leg and showed all over your stockings and you had to walk home that way with people looking; and Rufus's father nearly tore his head off laughing and so did everyone else, and Rufus was sorry for Charlie, having been so recently in a similar predicament, but the contagion of laughter was too much for him, and he laughed too.[4]

Agee's description of Rufus's experience watching Chaplin highlights the first point I would want to make about Chaplin's bodily humor: its connection to the body's biological functions, especially those whose control (and indeed concealment, if not denial) form the first line of defense in adult social behavior. Chaplin not only recalls the child who has not yet been thoroughly housebroken, but the "natural man," whose urges and bodily needs outweigh the demands of society and his own attempts at dignity.

Clowns traditionally represent the demands of the body against the strictures of civilization. Mikhail Bakhtin's analysis of the place of laughter in the culture of carnival, especially the demands of what he called the body's "lower strata," has been nicely applied to Chaplin by William Paul in his essay "The Annals of Anality."[5] In the topsy-turvy logic of carnival, authority is inverted and the lower organs of both excretion and generation overturn the logic of the head. The carnivalesque body, according to Bakhtin, is a body in process, growing, giving birth, eating, excreting.[6] This body possesses orifices, is permeable, taking things into itself and pushing things out; as such, it remains open to the world and merges with other bodies, both biologically and socially. This body, which Chaplin shares with the long tradition of carnival clowns, contrasts sharply with what Julia Kristeva, one of Bakhtin's critical heirs, calls "the clean and proper body"—the body of bourgeois individualism, cosmetically enclosed and complete unto itself, never openly emitting noises, smells, or embarrassment.[7] Chaplin's bodily humor was the "nasty" Chaplin, rather than the sentimental Chaplin, that cliché that so many critics use to avoid dealing with Chaplin's actual complexity.

A sequence from one of Chaplin's Mutual films from 1916, *The Pawnshop*, exemplifies the triumph of bodily functions over sentimentality in Chaplin's comedy. Working in a pawnshop, Chaplin listens to the sad tale delivered by an old man who comes to pawn his wedding ring. The elderly gentlemen uses broad theatrical gestures as he pantomimes his deep sorrow in being forced by dire circumstances to part with the ring. Chaplin at first reacts cynically to the old man's tale, but gradually he begins to give in to the dramatized emotions. This does not, however, prevent Chaplin from continuing to eat a cracker (appetites come first). As Chaplin becomes emotionally and physically affected by the tale of woe, he begins to blubber. Moved finally to sobs, Chaplin literally expresses his grief by spitting his mouthful of cracker crumbs across the room. In *A Dog's Life* (1918), the copious tears shed during Edna Purviance's "sad song" likewise undercut the invoked sentimentality by becoming so excessively physical that they take on a urinary force as the spray of tears drenches the weepers and their neighbors. Chaplin avoids outright scatological jokes of the sort that appeared in the less regulated early comedies at Pathé (such as *Erreur de Port* [1905]), but the uncontrolled, explosive body nonetheless makes it itself both seen and heard. Lest we attribute such vulgarity only to the early Chaplin, recall his use of bodily sounds in *Modern Times*. Although Chaplin avoids having speech come out of people's mouths, he doesn't hesitate to let the stomach speak, creating extended gurglings and bubblings of digestion.

In our cultural tendency to equate the body (and children) with the primitive, this attention to the body's functions may seem to move in the opposite direction from the modern. And certainly, the celebration of the carnivalesque body has a long history. But relating Chaplin, as has often been done, to the Dionysian release of the ancient satyr play should not be done so quickly. Art historian Aby Warburg compared the caprices of the satyr play to a Kachina dance among the Pueblo Indians that he witnessed in 1896. Directly following the solemn dance of the priests and chorus, three men appeared dressed as women and performed "a thoroughly vulgar and disrespectful parody of the chorus movements." But Warburg adds immediately, "And no one laughed," explaining, "The vulgar parody was regarded not as a comic mockery, but, rather, as a kind of peripheral contribution by the revelers in the effort to ensure a fruitful corn year."[8] Although Chaplin's parody may derive from this lineage of fertility rituals, it also breaks with this tradition, remaining secular—and hilarious. Chaplin's natural "body in process" provokes laughter because of his violation of social taboo, breaching the codes of repression that had been imposed with the growth of middle-class propriety in bourgeois culture. Thus even this "natural" body, this return to the clowns of carnival, has a modernist dimension, one closely related to the modern preoccupation with portraying the physical body in its grotesque, rather than idealized or eroticized, forms, an impulse evident in key modern works by Degas, Schiele, and Picasso, among others.

THE MODERN MACHINE BODY OF COMPONENT PARTS AND NERVOUS ENERGY

Fernand Léger performed perhaps the most memorable tribute of a modernist artist to Chaplin in his avant-garde film *Ballet Mécanique* (1924), introducing his film with a title—"Charlot presents *Ballet Mécanique*"—as a puppet of Chaplin emerges on the screen, an image that fractures Chaplin's body in a typically cubist manner. The puppet returns at the film's end, manipulated in such a way that his limbs seem to be in the process of falling apart.

While Chaplin's bodily vulgarity places him in a long tradition (a tradition that plays a lesser role with such other American silent comedians as Buster Keaton and Harold Lloyd), many viewers, especially the intelligentsia and avant-garde artists, celebrated Chaplin's peculiarly modern body,

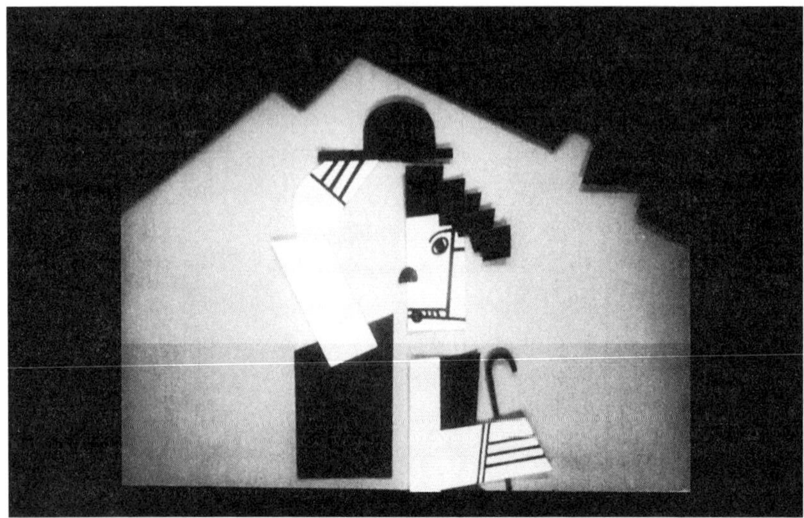

FIGURE 12.1. Chaplin puppet in Fernand Léger and Dudley Murphy, *Ballet méchanique* (1923–1924).

with its series of grotesque motions (that walk again) that recalled for them both the staccato rhythms of a machine and the uncontrollable physical spasms of nervous energy and physiological reflexes.

Like Léger's puppet, Chaplin's body could seem at points to behave like a machinic assembly rather than an organic whole. For modernist artists and critics like Bertolt Brecht, Siegfried Kracauer, Walter Benjamin, and Jean Epstein, as well as Léger, Chaplin offered perhaps the first mechanical ballet: a synthesis in which the hard-edged rhythms of the machine had become part of the human sensorium. The term was intended as an oxymoron, the replacement of the grace of *Les Sylphides* with the clamor and jerkiness of the flywheels, interlocking gears, and pistons, captured in both Georges Antheil's musical composition and the imagery and montage of Léger's film. Chaplin was the first performer, many believed (although in honesty, I would have to nominate French comedian Jean Durand as a precursor in this regard), who transferred the mechanical rhythm inherent in the cinema machine, both camera and projector, into a performance style for film.

The image most of us have of Chaplin as a machine-man comes from his late masterpiece *Modern Times* (1936): the sequences of Chaplin on the assembly line and afterward, involuntarily repeating the abrupt, jerky gesture of tightening a bolt he has been limited to; Chaplin caught in the innards of a vast machine he was trying to repair; and, most unforgettably, Chaplin forced by a machine to eat lunch with the same mechanical rhythms by which the production process has been programmed, culminating in Charlie being forced to consume a bolt. These scenes so vividly stage the interaction of the human body and the machine that I need not cite them in detail. However, made in the depth of the Depression, *Modern Times* stresses the dark side of the equation. Rather than exclusively the sign of oppression, Chaplin's machinelike gestures—their repetition, their strange rhythms, their odd combination of stiff limbs and sudden agility—violated a certain understanding of the human body and thereby seemed to some viewers in the 1910s and 1920s to open up new realms of acrobatic expression and even physical liberation.

Although never without some penumbra of misgiving, in the early twentieth century the machine supplied the model for the new technological body that promised to be the final step in achieving a modern utopia. The regulation of the body in the industrial production process introduced by Frederick Taylor and his disciples initially seemed to offer exciting modes of physical behavior for actors (Vsevolod Meyerhold's biomechanics) and even dancers (the choreography of Valentine de Saint-Point). This new machine-body, attuned to the rhythms of work, efficiency, and speed, would sweep away centuries of stultifying bodily propriety, the studied achievement in ballet of a grace that had absolutely no relevance to the everyday life of modern people. Rather than simply summoning up images of the body subject to the demands of production, the idea of taking performance rhythms from the modern realm of work, the factory, or everyday encounters of the urban crowd—shoving onto subways, crossing busy streets—inspired modernist artists, and Chaplin seemed to supply one of the first examples available on film to avant-gardists around the world.

It is, conceivably, a fruitful misunderstanding. In many ways, both Keaton and Lloyd seem more in tune with the machine age, as exemplified by the central role played in their films by controlling, imposing, modern machines. Keaton and Lloyd master locomotives, motorcycles, tin lizzies, street cars, steamboats, and even ocean liners. Chaplin's encounters with the mechanisms of daily life tend to be more small-scale: he interacts, usually disastrously, with escalators, revolving doors, elevators, roller skates, fold-away beds, and, not infrequently, movie cameras. But these items precisely allow Chaplin to react to their mechanic possibilities with balletic improvisations that teeter between triumph and disaster.

A fundamental difference, whose implications are worth pursuing, seems to appear here between Chaplin and Keaton and Lloyd. Although all initially encounter their share of failures, ultimately, at least in the features,

Lloyd and Keaton gain control of their mechanical complexes and use them to resolve their films, to solve their problems—if not exactly pragmatically, at least spectacularly. Chaplin's plots are rarely resolved in this manner. Instead, Chaplin's balletic, acrobatic-mechanical physical prowess seems to remain divorced from achieving anything (not that he doesn't try . . .). Thus Chaplin's modern body remains unchanneled, oddly purposeless, filled with a nervous energy that discharges itself without effect (or rather, often with countereffect).

Another Mutual film from 1916, *One AM*, reproducing Chaplin's music-hall act, captures Chaplin's body as a crazy machine whose main production seems to be failure, sketching the farthest distance between two points. Although Chaplin's apartment set hardly reproduces a modern industrial environment (in the way, say, that Keaton's *The Electric House* [1922] does), Chaplin's actions turn it into a modern machine of frustration ruled over by a constantly swinging pendulum.

Chaplin's relation to the machine, then, frequently short-circuits its apparent purposes. After all, Chaplin was a Tramp; or, as Keaton described him, "a bum," in contrast to his own honest workingman or Lloyd's social-climbing go-getter. Tramps (among them, the antagonist of one of Lloyd's first features, *Grandma's Boy*) roamed around the edges of society, avoiding the modern regimes of work and social responsibility. In the modern era, these vagabonds were considered by social scientists and doctors to be victims of a form of hysteria. The modern body that Chaplin manifested may well be closer to the pathological body that Rae Beth Gordon describes in her provocatively titled essay "From Charcot to Charlot" than to the Taylorized being that the Russian Constructivists (especially) saw in him.[9] This pathological diagnosis corresponds almost precisely to the way at least one modernist saw him: Jean Epstein spoke of Chaplin's "photogenic neurasthenia" and described his mechanical gestures as "the reflex actions of a nervous tired person."[10] Epstein seems to predict Chaplin's hysterical satyr ballet from *Modern Times* in which Chaplin makes clear that the modern body is subject to nervous breakdown when the efficiency demanded of it fails.

When Chaplin does explicitly imitate the machine, he resembles less the industrial and mechanical devices that, in *Modern Times*, attempt first to force-feed him and then to swallow him whole, than the mechanical toys and automata of earlier centuries, machines designed primarily to delight rather than to produce goods. Thus Chaplin's most perfect imitation of a mechanical body comes in *The Circus* (1928) as, appropriately, a carnival automaton outside a fun house. Chaplin imitates perfectly the stiff motions of this machine, its jerk of inertia between jolts of movement, its sense of endless repetition, and, perhaps most hilariously, the grotesque expression the machine makes when it tries to imitate human laughter. This Chaplin-machine becomes uncannily effective, allowing the Tramp to hide in plain sight and clobber his opponent, the pickpocket, with impunity, even under the gaze of the law. As his ruse begins to crumble, we watch with amazement as the inert machine-Chaplin gives way to the fleeing Tramp. Chaplin's art does not consist simply in a new physical language that speaks to modern experience, or in a power to imitate and redefine the rhythms of that new life, but in an astonishing ability to transform, to metamorphose from one physical identity into another.

DISSOLVING VIEWS: THE DEVOLUTION OF THE MODERN BODY

Even before Darwin, the "natural man" was often represented as a monkey, his affinity with the human not as the origin of the species, but in his playful imitative nature. If Chaplin's relation to the machine ultimately reads as a satirical parody expressing an essential antipathy to mechanical control, he shows a very different affinity with animals. Chaplin's grotesque body language as frequently references the animal as the machine, his reflexes often more like Pavlov's dogs than automatic gears meshing. Agee, through Rufus, describes Chaplin's final reaction to the smashed eggs after removing them from his pants:

> [He] shrugged his shoulders and turned his back and scraped backward with his big shoes at the broken shells and the slimy bag, just like a dog, and looked back at the mess (everyone laughed at that) and started to walk away, bending his cane deep with every shuffle, and squatting deeper, with his knees wider apart, than ever before, constantly picking at the seat of his pants with his left hand, and shaking one foot, then the other, and once gouging deep into his seat and then pausing and shaking his whole body, like a wet dog, and then walking on.[11]

Chaplin's body language, his lack of propriety, related directly to animal behavior. His winged angels in *The Kid* flex their feathered wings with animal awkwardness rather than spiritual grace, and shed their feathers like dogs in August, looking more like composite beings than messengers of the Lord. In this realm of composite beings, even a dog can sprout wings, while Charlie, a recent arrival getting used to his new wings, finds they

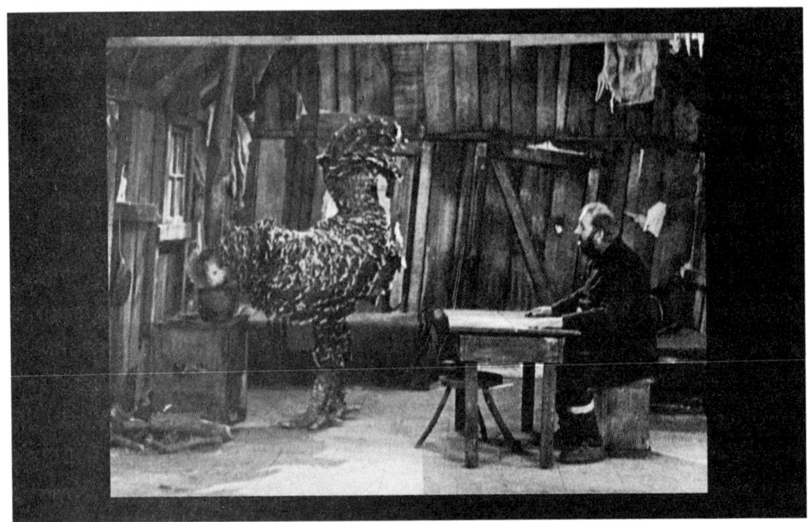

FIGURE 12.2. Charlie Chaplin, *The Gold Rush* (1925).

itch. When he scratches them, his leg jerks reflexively, as a dog's does when it scratches itself. It is the way Chaplin so thoroughly merges with this animal behavior, retaining always his identity as Charlie even as he convincingly joins another species, that marks the modernity of this aspect of Chaplin's body, the effect of a montage between human and animal rather than a simple metamorphosis. Thus even when thoroughly concealed by a man-sized chicken suit, and giving a totally convincing pantomime of a chicken's walk and drinking habits, the chicken that Big Jim McKay hallucinates in *The Gold Rush* (1925) remains unmistakable Charlie—Charlie *as* a chicken. The image of Chaplin drawn by Marc Chagall that Yuri Tsivian introduced me to insightfully shows Chaplin with chicken feet and wings behind him, capturing the composite superimposed montage effect that Chaplin's animal nature allowed him to project and its uncanny modernist style of representation.

Chaplin's most thorough exploration of his affinity with animals comes in *A Dog's Life* (1918). The film expresses the Tramp's affinity with the stray dog, their common struggle for survival and shelter against larger and more powerful beings, often expressed through the similarity of their physical behavior. But, most unforgettably, in one scene they merge into a single composite body. Chaplin enters a cabaret that does not allow dogs by concealing the pup in the voluminous seat of his pants, making the dog, in effect, a new part of his costume. Chaplin's pants, as we have seen, form the true seat of the natural man and are capable of receiving extensive borrowings from the outside world. Just as Chaplin's original character-defining costume consists of a montage of disparate items that somehow form a new, albeit grotesque, being, the addition of a dog to his pants seat generates a new composite character. Through a hole in the seat of his pants, Charlie sprouts a doggie tail, wagging in delirious reflex. The range of associations that this emergence from Chaplin's pants provokes would be as obvious to Rufus (and the rest of the audience) as to the most sophisticated Freudian critic in pursuit of displacements. While the embarrassment of having something extrude from one's pants may be a universal experience (or at least a universal fear), ultimately the doggie tail becomes part of Chaplin, his link to his animal nature, and the clear sign of his new composite body. The rhythm of the wag becomes auditory, as Charlie bends to tie his shoe near a large drum and the tail beats a constant tattoo, whose source baffles the drummer, until Charlie reveals the dog and lifts him lovingly from his pants. (In *The Gold Rush*, the Tramp again finds himself joined to a dog at the pants, as an attempt to save his dignity and keep his pants from falling down, becoming instead a disastrous choreography of man being led on a leash by dog.)

A body in process, in transformation, an incomplete body able to merge with other bodies—or other things—and create new bodies, grotesques that are part human, part something else, exceeding our categories of knowledge and extending our experience. And yet—and this is the clue to Chaplin's popularity (although a clue cannot explain the mystery itself)—this new body, for all its composite weirdness, strikes us as immediately recognizable rather than entirely alien: an insight into our own bodily experience, whether remembered from childhood or glimpsed in dreams. And this unexpected recognition makes us laugh, partly because we see the transformation happening before our eyes. Chaplin's fluid interspecies identity goes beyond not only the human, but even the animate. In *Shoulder Arms* (1918), Chaplin undertakes a spying mission behind enemy lines, disguised as a tree. The conceit and the costume in itself make us laugh; but, again, it is Chaplin's pantomime that makes this vegetable-human composite body so hilarious. Once again, even as he transforms into a tree, the tree remains identifiable as Charlie, his extensive arm/branch becoming the arboreal doppelganger of his cane (as his cane, from film to film, increasingly seems a prosthetic extension of his arms). Indeed, Chaplin can become a tree without costumes, as Jennifer Bean reminded me, in the exquisite pantomime he performs for Claire Bloom in *Limelight* (1952) of the Japanese tree that grows crooked.

Chaplin's pantomime, gestures, facial expressions, the entirety of his body

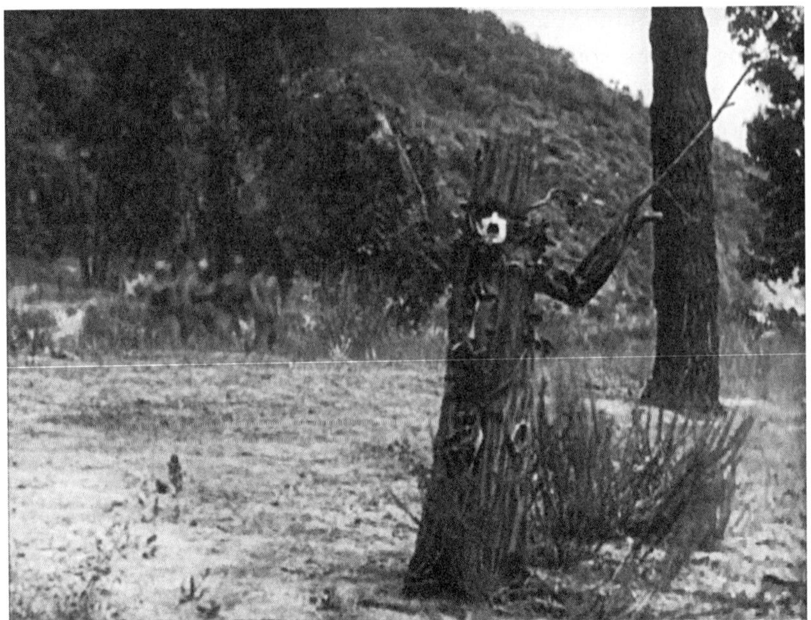

FIGURE 12.3. Charlie Chaplin, *Shoulder Arms* (1918).

art, delivers to us a renewed sense of corporeal experience. His performance remains profoundly rooted in our bodily experience, undermining years of socialization and bodily control, gaining an atavistic intensity by reversing the upward arc of man's evolution and reminding us of our affinities with animals and even plants. But ultimately I want to stress again the fact that Chaplin performs these metamorphoses before our eyes. As in Chaplin's mismatched tramp costume, we recognize the separate elements, but the absurdly appropriate effect of their union overwhelms us. As Sergei Eisenstein recognized, in spite of his limited use of editing, Chaplin's performance, costume, and character embodied the logic of montage. We could translate this insight to say that Chaplin, through his body language, taught the principal syntax of modernity to the world at large.

Grasping this montage principle allows us, I think, to return anew (though it is Chaplin's art that always renews our experience of his films, not any analysis) to one of the signature scenes of Chaplin's art: the dance of the Oceana Rolls in *The Gold Rush*, which the Tramp performs in place of making the speech demanded of him. Again, the disparate elements are evident: Chaplin's face, some forks, two rolls, and—between the highly illuminated face and the rolls—an expanse of relative darkness. But through the interaction of head position, facial expression, the strutting of the forks, and the posing of the rolls, a composite body emerges before us. The silverware and dinner rolls cavort with humor and acrobatic precision, with a physical style that is immediately identified as Charlie's. We see this seemingly giant head fuse with the implements and bread through the vital motion Chaplin enacts with the rhythm of a comic dance. In the film, this all takes place, of course, in a dream; a dream that ends with a unanimous expression of love and delight for the little man who can so enthrall us with the image of a body conjured out of nothingness.

13

The Language of Motion: Moving Images within the Evolution of Human Technology

Cinema first appeared as a particular technology at the end of the nineteenth century, but what it was designed to do was not immediately clear. The work, both historical and theoretical, of my friend and colleague André Gaudreault indicates that its purposes were originally less well defined than its mechanics. As Gaudreault has shown, cinema as a cultural form emerged gradually from a number of differently defined uses and separate "cultural series": from Marey's need for a means of recording scientifically the movement of bodies, human, animal, and inanimate; from the Lumières' company's desire to extend the market and methods of amateur photography; from Edison's attempt to "do for the eye what the phonograph does for the ear," following one successful invention with another.[1] Such examples could be multiplied. Clearly defined goals play less of a role in technological development than we tend to think. Paul Spehr's massive monograph on William Kennedy Laurie Dickson's work on the Edison kinetograph and other motion picture devices reveals how the project of inventing commercial motion pictures grew out of the conception and construction of the Edison laboratory, which opened in 1888, just before Dickson's research in cinema began. As Spehr describes it:

> It was to be the largest, most complete research laboratory in the world . . . The focal point of the main building was a two-story library which was

This essay, previously unpublished, is based on a talk delivered in 2011.

> to have reference books on every conceivable subject, scientific journals, published patents and other documentation that would support the work of his experimenters. There were to be two machine shops. A general shop with the most up to date equipment and a specialized shop for precision work. A large supply room was to be stocked with every imaginable type of material so that an experimenter could find what he needed on site and not have to wait. The advance publicity claimed that the lab would be capable of making anything from a lady's watch to a locomotive and that the stock room would have everything from screws, nut and bolts to walrus hide, swan's down and porcupine quills. There would be a carpentry shop, a blacksmith and glass blowers. On the third floor there was a large room for meetings that became a music room and occasional recording studio. There was a room for photography on the second floor.[2]

Dickson's duties in the photo room, Spehr shows, moved from documenting experiments and supplying photos of Edison at work to the media to the project of inventing the kinetograph, which eventually expanded to the Black Maria motion picture studio constructed on the grounds of the laboratory.

Less than following a specific plan and defined purpose, the Edison research lab explored various possibilities in materials and methods, often unsure of, or radically revising, their ultimate goal. The lab was not designed to realize a specific project, but to generate projects. The materials, apparatuses, and skills it assembled functioned as a sort of technological lexicon, a standing reserve of materials and processes that exemplified the technological world and its possibilities. We sense here a technological drive, less the expression of a singular human will than impelled by principles of mechanics and vagaries of application, an almost more Darwinian natural selection than preconceived intelligent design. As Bernard Stiegler has claimed, approaching technology as simply a means to an end distorts its nature.[3] The technical object itself (and even more, an ensemble such as the Edison laboratory) possesses, as Stiegler puts it, a genetic logic of its own that is not simply attributable to human intention.

The technical object, Stiegler shows us, must be understood as more than an inert utensil, a means to a predetermined end.[4] Following Heidegger, *techne* should be conceived as a process of growth and unfolding.[5] This is not to claim that the technological processes that resulted in cinema were random or irrational but, rather, that their outcomes are not necessarily inscribed in their original intentions. The shapes of development emerge only afterwards, in retrospect. However, if I am partly arguing against a narrow teleology in understanding technology, I am also interested in exploring cinema's place within larger patterns of technological development, asserting less an analogy between technological development and evolution than an actual homology and merging of the two. In this I am following the lead of Stiegler, and others inspired by the work of paleontologist André Leroi-Gourhan, who see the history of technology as an extension of the processes of human evolution. Rather than being in opposition, the human and the technological define each other. Indeed, Leroi-Gourhan would claim we become human through our technology.[6]

As historians of cinema, I believe we need to deal with both technology and aesthetics. I understand this to mean dealing both with machines, their construction and development, and with the way human beings use them, the pleasures they take in them and the purposes they inscribe in them. Although aspects of these two issues can be approached separately, I believe a full understanding of either implies the other. Approaching technology as an extension of human evolution undoes a facile separation of technology into means and ends, material and spirit, tools and meanings, and reveals the close interdependence of *techne* and *aesthesis*. Leroi-Gourhan's work plots a continuity from physiological evolution to the production of tools, as human adaptation moves from physical transformation into cultural production. As he states, "The hand, already formed in the monkey, stops changing . . . from the moment it begins to hold a tool."[7] The production of tools involves a process of exteriorization, a projection of the human into nature, with all the danger of alienation and delight of discovery that entails. Stiegler describes this transformation of the world through our use of objects as "the pursuit of life by means other than life."[8] Exteriorization, Stiegler says, "must not be understood as a rupture with nature but rather as a new organization of life—life organizing the inorganic and organizing itself therein by that very fact."[9]

If I find this approach to technology especially relevant for understanding cinema, I am not referring to Stiegler's recent critique of the role commercial cinema plays in contemporary society, which I believe leads us in another direction that I could not endorse.[10] Rather, the continuity between evolution and technology provides for me a new way to think through the history and origins of cinema, as well as its relation to new media, by defining the active role technology plays within these processes, past, present, and future. Technology as a force of development, rather than a narrow "technical" issue for investigation, appears especially clearly, I would claim, at the point of cinema's origin. Thus I return to the early cinema (which French theory continues largely to bypass in favor of their love/hate affair with classical Hollywood cinema and its successors). In its technical hardware and its function as an apparatus (which includes human operators and observers, filmmakers and film spectators), the cinema forms a particularly modern node in the process of exteriorization that defines technology as an evolutionary force. From its beginnings, cinema aspired, as the names of its first machines indicate—Cinématographe, Kinetograph, Vitascope, Vitagraph, Biograph, Bioscope—to the technical enfolding of life and movement itself.

Almost as persistently as terms for life and movement, the first forms of cinema inscribe their relations to writing and language, the suffix "-graph" appearing if anything more often than "-scope." For Leroi-Gourhan, the acquisition of language and then of writing represents an essential phase of human evolution's extension into technological exteriorization. Understanding language as an aspect of technology allows us to reopen the comparison between cinema and language that emerged with its first inventions and then guided the origins of film theory and film stylistics. One might claim that film theory has oscillated between the dominance of the *graph*, the significant mark, and of the *scope*, something to look at. Approaching cinema as a technology demands that we think of it in terms of these two models, writing and seeing, simultaneously, preserving the productive tension between them. Cinema is both an image *and* a form of writing, and is neither of these in isolation. As a technology it brings them together through a radical act of exteriorizing the human processes of perception and language in a form of technological memory.

The reference to writing inscribed in the names of early cinema devices seems, initially, quite simplistic and hardly refers to the systematic nature that defines language. The "graph" simply parallels the "graph" of "photograph" and "phonograph" and indicates less a reference to language than to a simple act of inscription and recording. The cinematic machine records motion, or life. The terms may carry an echo of the "graphic method" of Marey's chronophotography, but although cinema's debt to the photography of Marey and Muybridge was often cited by Edison and other pioneers, Marey's scientific interest in graphing the abstracted patterns of motion was rarely mentioned in these acknowledgments. In subsequent decades, seeing cinema as a pictorial mechanical recording medium seemed to pose an obstacle to its claim to be an artistic and expressive form, as early film theory fought to establish film's status as an art.

Describing cinema as a language constituted a strategic move in this effort. If cinema could claim to be a language, the new medium would gain the capacity to carry a message and to be expressive, in spite of its initial lack of sound and therefore speech, its essential "muteness." The essence of language (and its difference, per Leroi-Gourhan, from the limited signals of distress or desire given by animals) lay in the abstraction of words from a specific and concrete situation (such as the mating call of a bird) and its combination of signs into a syntax. Thus in the 1920s and later, an emerging semiotics of cinema traced the transformation of film stylistics from single-shot films of events to arrangements of shots structured through editing. The creation of meanings abstracted from concrete reference depended on their position within an edited pattern (Sergei Eisenstein's montage trope, for example).[11] As an art form, film in the 1920s aspired to the condition of language.

Thus a film theory emerged in the 1920s, primarily in the writings of the Soviet montage theorists and the Russian Formalists, based in a more or less rigorous comparison of film editing to the abstraction and syntactical arrangement of language. This privileging of montage often led to a denigration of the recording capacity of the cinema, the "graph" aspect of the original invention. The photographic shot was valued less than the cut, the camera less, as Eisenstein might put it, than the scissors. Consequently, the first decade of cinema was exiled, as it is in Gilles Deleuze's *Cinema* books, to a sort of "pre-cinema," bereft, apparently, of both the time- and the movement-image, which result only from the appearance of montage.[12] In this view, privileging editing, the simple act of filming was not seen as enough to make cinema.

While I would never deny the importance of the articulation between shots in either the history or the theory of cinema (indeed, I devoted my first book to its origins), I would also claim that declaring editing to be the defining aspect of either the history or the essence of cinema remains a limited perspective. While a structural comparison to language undoubtedly appears most clearly when dealing with the cinematic syntagm and the differential unit of the shot, the most careful of film semioticians, such as Christian Metz and Yuri Lotman, were well aware of the comparison's limits.[13] The reef on which the semiotics of cinema foundered lay, of course, in the uneasy fit between the cinematic shot and the linguistic unit. First, nothing in film corresponds to the double articulation of language (in which meaningful units can be broken down into elements that are nonsemantic and purely differential—e.g., phonemes).[14] Further, even a single shot could not be seen as the equivalent to a word or, to use the linguistic term, a morpheme.[15] A shot, even a close-up, contains so much contextual information—in Leroi-Gourhan's sense, is too concrete—to function as an abstract element of the lexicon. As Metz indicated, a shot always carries more than a simple signified: a shot of a gun is never just the sign for {gun} but rather displays a specific gun (partly due, it would seem, to its individualizing photographic and indexical nature).[16] Lotman in some sense cut a Gordian knot by maintaining that cinema uses two sorts of signs: the linguistic and the pictorial or iconic (the latter often ignored in linguistically oriented semiotics).[17] The clarity of these semiotic or semiological analyses came partly from their modesty, their acknowledgment that the systematic aspect of language applies to cinema only in limited contexts (these included for Metz the closed set of spatiotemporal segmentation of narrative, which he analyzed systematically in his "Grande Syntagmatique").[18] This admirable acknowledgment of the limits of the relevance of linguistics to film also seemed to close a period of renewed enthusiasm for the language/film analogy, as ideological, psychoanalytical, and perhaps even historical research took center stage with ambitious agendas, more attractive to many students than the narrow space left to cinema's linguistic parallels.

Once again, I am not denying the value of this classic era of film semiotics, which all too often tends to be overlooked, nor the interest of the extensions offered by the slightly later, semiotically inspired approaches to cinematic enunciation and narrative analysis. But I am recommending another model of the relation between cinema and language, which follows less closely the analysis of the language system and derives instead from a relation among language, technology, and human evolution. This new understanding of cinema's relation to language illuminates aspects of early and even pre-cinema, as well as new media, through its emphasis on cinema considered as technology rather than simply as texts to be analyzed.

Leroi-Gourhan provides a clue that may lead us through this labyrinth and reminds us of the suffix so prominent in the naming of the technology of cinema: *-graph*. Language constitutes an essential moment in human evolution, embodied in the coordination Leroi-Gourhan traces between speech and gesture, mouth and hand. Language reaches another level with the introduction of writing, or more broadly what he calls "graphism":

> While it can at a pinch be claimed that tools are not unknown to some animal species and that language merely represents the step after the vocal signals of the animal world, nothing comparable to the writing and reading of symbols existed before the dawn of *Homo Sapiens*.[19]

With this concept of graphism, Leroi-Gourhan marks out a space in which the opposition Lotman asserted between picture and language is not absolute. He claims, based on archaeological evidence, that "graphism did not begin with naïve representation of reality but with abstraction."[20] Tied to the essential motor evolution of the hand, as in relation to the tool and technology, Leroi-Gourhan sees graphism as initially expressing rhythms (i.e., gestures) rather than tracing forms (the pictorial transcription of visual experience). The interaction of the rhythm of oral speech and the gestural rhythms of inscription determined the original scene of writing and reading. As he puts it, "In both signs and words abstraction reflects a gradual adaptation of the motor system of expression to more and more subtly differentiated promptings of the brain."[21]

Investigating Paleolithic cave paintings, Leroi-Gourhan finds a consistency not simply in stylistics of depiction but in the arrangement of figures, a syntactical pattern in the succession of animals depicted that leads him to underscore their relation to writing and language: "They [the cave paintings] are really 'mythograms,' closer to ideograms than to pictograms and closer to pictograms than to descriptive art."[22] He sums up his claim: "Figurative art is inseparable from language and proceeds from the pairing of phonation with graphic expression. Therefore the object of phonation and graphic expression obviously was the same from the outset. A part—perhaps the most important part—of figurative art is accounted for by what, for want of a better word, I propose to call 'picto-ideography.'"[23]

If moving from Leroi-Gourhan's analysis of cave paintings and their inscriptions to cinema seems a bit of a stretch, I nonetheless suggest we make it. Leroi-Gourhan's own understanding of the homology between the acquisition of language, and especially "graphism," and the longue durée of the evolution of human technology invites us to extend his insights to the present era of rapid transformation. He proposes not a simple theory of origins but an understanding of a still-evolving history. Graphism unites picture and language through the concept of the word, not in its systematic lexical sense but as a symbol, through which "humans could now express themselves beyond the immediate present."[24] Graphic symbols maintain a relation between the pictorial and the linguistic, a relation that became more distant and distinct as language and writing developed: "Two languages, both springing from the same source, came into existence at the two poles of the operating field—the language of hearing, which is linked with the development of the sound-coordinating areas, and the language of sight, which in turn is connected with the development of the gesture co-coordinating areas, the gestures being translated into graphic symbols."[25] The tension between the gestural/graphic mode of language and language as a phonetic system (the linguistic model referenced by most film semiotics) remains a productive process through history, according to

Leroi-Gourhan: "The invention of writing, through the device of linearity, completely subordinated graphic to phonetic express, but even today the relationship between language and graphic expression is one of coordination rather than subordination. An image possesses a dimensional freedom which writing must always lack."[26]

To summarize this schema: Coming from a common origin, written language develops in two modes: the graphic, or as Leroi-Gourhan refers to it, the mythographic ideogram, and the linear phoneticized writing that developed with the tasks of bookkeeping and genealogy. The increasingly linear and speech-dependent aspect of written language serves as an efficient tool for the conveying of information, as "writing is viewed as an economical method of transcribing narrow but precise concepts—an object achieved most efficiently by linear alignment. The language of science and technology meets such a definition, and alphabets meet its requirements."[27] But Leroi-Gourhan doubts the wisdom of seeing this as an entirely positive progression as the graphic quality of the ideographic writing becomes eliminated. While instrumental writing renders tasks of organization and communication more effective and economical, eliminating the mythographic aspect of writing risks eliminating too a vital aspect of human culture:

> Language was placed on the same level as technics; and the technical efficacy of language today is proportional to the extent to which it has rid itself of the halo of associated images characteristic of archaic forms of writing. . . . Such unification of the process of expression entails the subordination of graphism to spoken language. . . . However, it also entails an impoverishment of the means of nonrational expression.[28]

Thus Leroi-Gourhan's dynamic and evolutionary approach to language and writing not only ties it to technology but provides us with a complex model of language practice that extends beyond a structural logic based in spoken language. His concept of graphism relates language to the body through the gesture, and demonstrates the connection of the graphic process not only to the phonetic transcription of speech but to the visual symbol, the mythogram that exceeds the model of the spoken word, without necessarily being condemned to the concreteness of the picture as understood by Metz.

One could read the comparisons the Soviet montage filmmakers—Lev Kuleshov, Sergei Eisenstein, Vsevelod Pudovkin, and, to a certain extent, Dziga Vertov and the Russian Formalists—made between language and cinema as attempts to subject the mythograms of cinema to a linearization and specification of the sort found in phonetic language. Thus the syntax of montage in Kuleshov's Mojukine experiment entailed narrowing the indefinite halo of associations possible in Mojukine's expression down to a specific significance through its juxtaposition with an image bearing a definite emotional meaning: grief, hunger, desire.[29] Eisenstein's montage tropes strove for a similar legibility, pursuing an intellectual or emotional abstraction from its specific context. Yet even if the polemic launched by Constructivist montage theory stressed this systematic aspect of the dialectic, watching the films convinces us that they maintain a creative tension with the range of meaning carried by the graphic rather than simply repressing it.

Further, the fascination montage filmmakers showed in conveying physiological rhythms and emotional tones and overtones sometimes strove to submerge significance in an intense somatic experience. This aspect of film stylistics demonstrates how useful Leroi-Gourhan's theory can be in constructing an embodied understanding of the effects of technology. The gestural nature of the act of writing—and even reading—an ideogram cannot be limited to an unambiguous decoding of a definitive significance. It is worth recalling in this context Eisenstein's own invocation of the Japanese and Chinese use of ideograms as his ideal for cinematic language and model for montage models. Chinese writing, with its strong graphic and even figurative dimension, exemplifies for Leroi-Gourhan as well the multidimensionality of ideogramatic writing. Eisenstein's later work, both films and theoretical writings, pursued an immersion in the mythographic. Even a cursory glance at shots from *Que Viva Mexico* and the stills surviving from *Bezhin Meadow* reveals an interest in the mythic dynamics of composition that goes beyond the syllogisms he claimed in his silent films. His essays following the 1935 "Film Form: New Problems" define an attempt to explore the mythic roots of cinematic expression.[30] Eisenstein's later work could profitably be read in relation to Leroi-Gourhan (and I think the somewhat tangled issue of "inner-speech" that Eisenstein adapted from the Russian Formalists might also be clarified if compared to Leroi-Gourhan's idea about the rhythmic and gestural aspects of language and writing).[31]

Thus Leroi-Gourhan's theory of the interrelation of language and writing with the physical and technological evolution of human being sheds light on traditional theories of the interrelation of language and cinema, showing both their limitations and areas of possible agreement that could be developed. But my initial claim was more radical. Cinema, as well as the welter of moving picture technology that has appeared in the last half century, offers more than simply a technical means of recording and preserving the visual (and aural) aspects of events. This is not to deny that visual and aural moving image media can accomplish this task, but rather to stress that in accomplishing it, they make a major transformation of our human world. Even without a formal analysis of the complexities that may be communicated through the language of these media, moving picture technologies are already operating like languages; they are already participating in the process of exteriorization that defines technology for Stiegler and evolution for Leroi-Gourhan.

For both these thinkers, photography, cinema, television, and computer systems are recent phases in the human exteriorization most specifically of memory, the same impulse that was behind the development of writing, both phonetic and graphic. "Audiovisual techniques," Leroi-Gourhan reflects, "really seem to represent a new stage of human development."[32] Although they greet this ongoing development with excitement, both are also concerned about the tendency of the technical reproduction of vision, sound, and movement to render the receiver passive, thus limiting the processes of the imagination and of creative intervention. While these concerns seem crucial, they also recall the concerns of critical theory with which our field is very familiar. What seems more novel to me (although possibly just as ambivalent in its implications) is the critique of the process of automatization in which the operation of technology is no longer related to the directly human controlled hand tool or handheld device but to the self-propelling machine. As Leroi-Gourhan puts it:

> Tools detached themselves from the human hand, eventually to bring forth the machine: In this latest stage speech and sight are undergoing the same process, thanks to the development of technics. Language, which had separated itself from the human through art and writing, is consummating the final divorce by entrusting the intimate functions of phonation and sight to wax, film, and magnetic tape.[33]

The implied question is, is this a loss or a gain? In either case it seems to constitute the world we now live in.

The very act of filming, denigrated within the period of film theory Metz has called "Montage roi," represents a fundamental transformation that not only can be compared to the human attainment of language or writing, but seems to involve handing over these processes to surrogates, the machines.[34] This gives us a new way to understand the first filmmakers' impulse to film the world around them: to gather images of a moving reality in a form that could be played again. Early cinema allowed technology to see the world automatically, in a manner that also allowed the world—including aspects never before seen or noticed—to be "spoken" back to viewers. Cinema embarked on a project (unarticulated in most instances, but implicit) of supplying a form of automatic memory. Filmmakers gathered views of events, places, and people that could be replayed, that people could see again and again if desired. While I doubt many of these films were made with a longue durée of preservation in mind, this drive toward repetition itself seems to me a significant part of their technological drive, as the recall of human memory now becomes embedded in the program of a machine.

In an essay I wrote on the travel film, I lingered over a phrase common in one form or another to both early travel lectures (such as those of Burton Holmes) and a number of early film companies: "The world within your reach."[35] Today the trope can only strike us as ambivalent, expressing the literalization of Heidegger's "Age of the World Picture," in which all of nature must be consumed as a picture, as an enframed, graspable form of mastery in which vision claims dominion.[36] But the interchangeability it posits between hand and eye also strikes me. What the observer will grasp as he attends film or lectures is not even a material picture but, rather, an automated sight, an image projected either through the magic lantern or through cinema, a view of a distant locale brought back by the viewer's emissary via the apparatus/camera. In my essay I compared this virtual voyage to that of the veterans in Godard's 1963 film *Les Carabiniers*, returning home from their adventure with the loot of the world—in the form of hundreds of postcards. Suffused as we are by these technological visions of the world, do we nonetheless remain empty-handed?

I have begun to wonder if these critiques (which embody Paul Ricoeur's hermeneutic of suspicion), while in many ways dead-on in their analysis, really catch what is novel in our accumulation of virtual images, what transformation they work in our grasping of a new world.[37] Viewing an assembly of such images from the early part of the century (historical distance yields a sharper perspective)—such as the collection of Lumière autochromes, color still photographs, and short films unedited or assembled, from Albert Kahn's astonishing Archive of the Planet, assembled between 1911 and 1930—we experience a certain melancholy, a sense of lost time and fading glances.[38] But I at least also feel enriched, even when the images make me squirm with their imperialist capturing of views of a vanishing exotic world. I see in this archive less a synoptic vision of the world, seized by the imperial gaze of the new technologies Kahn's cameramen employed, than a series of fragments of the exteriorized, automatized memory of our planet, dollops of embalmed time, condemned to endless repetition (and seeming to sigh, like Petronius's Cumaean Sibyl in the epigram to Eliot's *The Wasteland*, their desire to fade away).

Bernard Stiegler works through Heidegger's contrast of the inauthenticity of clock time, with its mechanical measurement of successive empty nows, to the authentic time of Dasein as a being-toward-death. Heidegger founds authentic human temporality (as opposed to the fallen time of calculation represented by the clock) in Dasein's anticipation in the future of its undoubted, yet indeterminate, mortality. But Stiegler reminds us that this openness toward the future can only be founded on a sense of a past, as Dasein's sense of anticipation is founded on its historicity, which Stiegler finds "fixed" in technics, founded in the *-gram* of writing, which fixes the past in an entirely different way than the tick of the clock marking the abstract now.[39] The past for Stiegler is always transmitted, either inauthentically, in a way that blocks our access to it, or authentically—but how is this accomplished? In this brief essay, I will not attempt to summarize the implications of Stiegler's response, but his essential answer depends on our access to a temporality that relies on "the memory supports that organize the successive epochs of humanity; that is, technics."[40] The way to our past, which is to say the way to our historical temporality, lies through its technological forms.

Is this, then, within our grasp? Does technology deliver our temporality to us, as the early filmmakers claimed they could bring the world within our grasp? Or do our hands remain empty? And is that the only way we can actually receive, with hands open and unfilled?

14

Moving through Friedberg's Properly Adjusted Virtual Window

> Do you know, sometimes on still, quiet evenings like this, I almost get a creepy feeling that they will walk in through that window.
>
> SAKI, "THE OPEN WINDOW"[1]

In an era of dramatic changes in media technology and new theories of visual media, Anne Friedberg's two books, *Window Shopping: Cinema and the Postmodern* (1993) and *The Virtual Window: From Alberti to Microsoft* (2006), provide historical perspective and theoretical depth.[2] As graduate students in the 1970s, Anne Friedberg and I both studied under Annette Michelson at the Department of Cinema Studies at NYU and learned from our mentor to place cinema within broad contexts of cultural practice, both aesthetic and theoretical. Anne was my friend, and although we had less contact after her migration to the West Coast, I felt a kinship between our projects as scholars. I primarily explored the history of cinema as a practice, while she sought to lay foundations for a field of visual studies. Our projects converged, especially my current attempt to plot the long history of the moving and projected image (both before, and now seemingly after, the era of celluloid). I learned a great deal from Friedberg's books, even if I believe they represent an unfinished project whose interruption Anne's untimely death, alas, has rendered more than temporary.

Friedberg named her books with wit and care. *Window* opens new perspectives in both, operating as metaphor and cultural object, framing her theme of visual culture and its display. But another term bridges them: *virtual*, appearing in the title of the newer book and in the earlier book's central concept, "the mobilized virtual gaze." *The Virtual Window* particularly focuses on this term and probes its history within a broader visual practice "from Alberti to Microsoft." Not the least of the book's virtues lies in the range of issues it covers: from Albertian theories of perspective to glass architecture, from the camera obscura to computer desktop design. More than an open window, the book strikes me as a postmodern cabinet of curiosities, housing a range of topics assembled to see how they rub against each other. Its logic is not taxonomic, nor, as Friedberg stresses, a linear narrative of development, but rather "accretive and refractive."[3] But the virtual occupies a central place. In this chapter I examine and, to a degree, criticize Friedberg's treatment of the term, especially in her introduction.

DEFINING TERMS: VIRTUAL

> We must consider that it will be a great help unto us, for the making and finding out of strange things, to know what that is from whence the *Virtues* of any thing do proceed.
>
> GIAMBATTISTA DELLA PORTA, *Natural Magick*[4]

In contemporary use, *virtual* primarily evokes recent media revolutions: the virtual memory of the computer, virtual reality, virtual communities established by the internet. But new turns of language invariably trail streams of history behind them. This history illuminates, and perhaps betrays, assumptions implicit in the term. Friedberg expresses her frustration with current uses of the term *virtual* and proposes to explore its definition historically: "By returning to the term's definition and etymology, I hope to reclaim its considerable utility for making distinctions about the ontological status—and the materiality versus the immateriality—of an object. I find it necessary to challenge accounts that assume that 'virtual' refers only to electronically mediated or digitally produced images and experiences, and to decouple the term from its unquestioned equation with 'virtual reality.'"[5] I agree strongly with Friedberg's assessment that contemporary understandings display a certain amnesia and consequent impoverishment. However, I find the history of this word even more complicated than she suggests.

Recent uses of *virtual* provide a useful starting point. Computer terminology introduced a new technological specificity to the term following its earlier technical uses in optics, mechanics, and physics. The *Oxford English Dictionary* definition of *virtual* under the subcategory of computing includes this meaning: "Not physically existing as such but made by software to appear to do so from the point of view of the program or the user." In 1997 the *OED* added the following entry:

> **virtual reality** *n.* a notional image or environment generated by computer software, with which a user can interact realistically, as by using a helmet containing a screen, gloves fitted with sensors, etc.

In contrast to these more recent technical meanings, Friedberg quotes a broader definition from *Webster's Third International Dictionary Unabridged*: "Of, relating to, or possessing a power of acting without the agency of matter; being functionally or effectively but not formally of its kind."[6] This corresponds to definitions offered by most contemporary dictionaries. Broadly understood, *virtual* corresponds in meaning to the phrase "in effect." (*Cambridge Dictionaries Online* gives its synonym as "almost": "almost a particular thing or quality.") Thus the definition given by the *Merriam-Webster's Collegiate Dictionary*, "being such in essence or effect though not formally recognized or admitted <a *virtual* dictator>." The fourth definition listed by the *OED* is: "That is so in essence or effect, although not formally or actually; admitting of being called by the name so far as the effect or result is concerned." *Virtual* therefore indicates possessing a power or quality, but based on its effect rather than nominally. So-and-so may not be the official dictator of such-and-such a nation, but he functions as dictator, in effect. Virtual means "in effect," but not necessarily in name ("not formally"). The term derives from the Latin *virtus*, virtue or power, the inherent quality and efficacy of persons or things.[7] As Rob Shields puts it succinctly in his treatment of the virtual as a "Key Idea": "Virtue was the power to produce results, to have an effect."[8] Thus originally a virtue exerts an effect, natural or supernatural, on the world of things and people. For example, in the sixteenth century certain precious stones were believed to cure diseases or protect against injury; this constituted their virtue. The knowledge of such virtues inherent (or concealed, as a "secret of nature") in objects constituted one category of "Natural Magic." Giambattista della Porta's 1558 work on this subject devotes several chapters to the hidden virtues of plants, stones, and animals.

However, in the modern era, *virtual* usually indicates a diminished, incomplete ("almost") power, although traditionally it signified a power that could be actualized, if not officially recognized (a *virtual* head of the country or a *virtual* disaster). In a modern, more positivistic culture, the realized fact appears of greater value than does potency. (As Shields says, "No matter how big the effects of the virtual are, they seem somehow to lack a proper ontology."[9]) Although computers and new media add technological specifications, their use of the term derives from the earlier meaning. Virtual memory is not the actual memory contained in the hard drive, but it can function like memory. Likewise, virtual reality is not reality, but it possesses effects of reality (visual acuity and movement, responsiveness to an agent's actions). The virtual has power to act like something that it is not formally recognized as actually being. Note the potential tension between a sense of something not fully actualized or recognized ("almost"), which presents the virtual negatively, and its more positive meaning of power, potency. In this powerful sense, the virtual could even exceed the material limitations of the fully actualized.

Friedberg emphasizes the virtual as visual, and the negative aspect (the virtual's privative nature, lacking something) plays a determinative role. The definition she quotes specifies this as a lack of materiality: "possessing a power of acting without the agency of matter." She declares, "The virtual is a substitute—'acting without the agency of matter'—an immaterial proxy for the material."[10] Friedberg's dictionary labeled this part of the definition obsolete.[11] I believe this obsolete meaning refers to the virtual understood as occult powers, which could have magical effects rather than physical cause and effect. Thus the virtual acts without agency of matter, because its effects are understood as spiritual, relying on occult sympathies derived from cosmic immaterial forces (as when Della Porta states, "And you shall put your *Loadstone* under the table, and stir it there, the *Virtue* of it will pass from this body like a spirit penetrating the solid table").[12]

Friedberg gives this archaic doctrine a modern reinterpretation. She identifies the spiritual immateriality of the virtual with the formal immateriality of the semiotic sign: "The virtual is a substitute—acting without the agency of matter—an immaterial proxy for the material. The term becomes a key marker of a secondary order in the relationship between the real and its copy, the original and its reproduction, the image and its likeness."[13] Friedberg equates the virtual with the sign, representation, or image. In contemporary terms, this seems to make sense. In contrast to the actual and the realized, the virtual appears as a "disembodied" representation, a nonphysical entity, as in the *OED*'s definition of virtual in relation to computing: "Not physically existing as such but made by software to appear to do so from the point of view of the program or the user"—or as Friedberg's text puts it: "Computer terminology invokes 'virtual' to refer to a digital object or experience without physical existence."[14] (However, I would add, virtual memory *acts* as memory; it does not *represent* it.) Virtual reality seems to provide a representation of reality, stripped of its physical material existence, an illusionary copy or image of the physical world.[15] The term can be used as a synonym for the new hyperreal forms of representation, divorced from physical reality. But does this constitute the power of the virtual?

REFLECTIONS AND CONFUSIONS: WHAT IS THE VIRTUAL IMAGE?

> The Optical writers say it is an image, when the object itself is indeed perceived along with its colors and the parts of its figure, but in a position not its own, and occasionally endowed with quantities not its own.
>
> JOHANNES KEPLER, *Paralipomena to Witelo*[16]

Friedberg criticizes contemporary identifications of the virtual with the digital as reductive. The virtual, she stresses, cannot be simply identified with a few processes, such as the dematerialization of bodies into information (as in Katherine Hayles's account), or the abolishment of the frame in predigital immersive forms, such as the panorama described by Oliver Grau.[17] She broadens the historical context of the relation between the virtual and the image by considering the revolutionary optics of Johannes Kepler in the seventeenth century. Kepler redefined theories of vision through his description of the retinal image. The eye functions, he claimed, like a camera obscura. Light enters the eye, becomes focused by its lens and humors, and then projects an image onto the retina.[18] To explain this system and the image it formed, Kepler introduced a contrast between what he termed *pictura* and *imago*.[19] The concept of the virtual image originates from this contrast, as Friedberg stresses. However, her account confuses the terms.

The retinal image is in Kepler's terms a *pictura*: a projected image actually caught on a surface, in this case the retina. The *imago*, in contrast, refers to the perceived visual image, seen by an observer. Kepler does not locate the *imago* as an optical image formed in the eye, but rather describes it as perceived in the mind (or the imagination). The *imago* depends on the *pictura* on the retina, but Kepler avoids speculating on how the mind actually converts the retinal image into sight: "I leave it to the natural philosophers to discuss the way in which this image or picture is put together by the spiritual principles of vision."[20] In contrast to the immaterial *imago*, the optically produced *pictura* possesses physical dimensions; in terms used by later optics, the *pictura* is a "real image." As historian of science Alan Shapiro makes clear:

> A *pictura* is a replica of an object that is projected on to a paper or screen. It has a real existence independent of any eye that observes it. In contrast, an *imago* is only a "rational entity" that is perceived by the eye and exists only in the imagination. As truly revolutionary as Kepler's theory of vision was, the concept of *pictura* likewise demanded a revolution in geometrical optics and the theory of optical imagery—even if a lesser one—for projected images had no place in the medieval optical tradition.[21]

Kepler reconceived sight by introducing the projected image, a novel phenomenon in the sixteenth century made possible by the relatively recent invention of such devices as the magic lantern and especially the camera obscura, which Kepler had experimented with and used for astronomical observations; it also provided his model for the eye.[22] I believe Friedberg is right to see Kepler's analysis of the projected image as an essential moment in the technical history of the virtual. However, terminological confusion sets in when she identifies *pictura* with the later optical term *virtual image*. It is a technical term in optics, introduced after Kepler in 1675 by French optical theorist Claude Deschales to correspond to Kepler's term *imago*, and first introduced in English by Sir David Brewster in his 1831 treatise on optics.[23] This virtual image does *not* correspond to Kepler's *pictura* (which refers to projected images, including the retinal image), but rather—quite the opposite—to his *imago* (cf. Shapiro's statement: "Kepler bequeathed two concepts of image, *imago* and *pictura*, which to us are simply a virtual and a real image").[24] Brewster's definition (and contemporary optics) sharply distinguished the "virtual image" from a "real image." To quote a current optical definition:

> A *virtual image* is an image in which the outgoing *rays* from a point on the object always diverge. It will appear to converge in or behind the optical device (i.e., a mirror). A simple example is a flat mirror where the image of oneself is perceived at twice the distance from oneself to the mirror. That is, if one is half a meter in front of the mirror, one's image will appear to be at a distance of 1 meter away (or half a meter inside or behind the mirror). Because the rays never really converge, one cannot project a virtual image.

> By contrast, a real image is an image in which the outgoing rays from a point on the object pass through a single point. It is easiest to observe real images when projected on an opaque screen.[25]

I confess that I had to draw on high school science lectures to grasp this distinction.[26] The reflection in a flat (plane) mirror gives the most common experience of a virtual image. The reflection we see of our face does not appear "on" the surface of the mirror (or in front of it where the reflecting rays in fact are located), but rather at a depth "within" the mirror, at a distance from us. No light actually emanates from that apparent distance, which would actually be behind the mirror. This image in this position occurs only in our perception. These visual deviations from reality (along with the more apparent left/right reversal of the mirror image) mark the plane mirror image as *virtual.*

The term *real image*, which corresponds to Kepler's *pictura*, may seem a contradiction in terms: How can an image be *real*? What is real here, though, is the *image itself*, the light that forms it comes into focus in the *actual* place where the image appears, rather than simply in our perception. Optically speaking, the picture is formed by converging rays of light. Thus, in the camera obscura, rays of light enter the dark interior through a small aperture, and the rays will project an inverted image (reversed top to bottom, as well as left to right) on a surface placed at the point of convergence. The virtual image, in contrast, is not inverted top to bottom (only left to right), and holding a sheet of paper in front of a mirror will not capture a projected image.

This may seem like more than we need to know. Friedberg, however, seems to indicate that the main difference between the two sorts of images is the unmediated use of the eye versus the use of a lens, whereas in fact, lenses and mirrors of differing qualities can produce *both* sorts of images, real and virtual (a flat mirror or a diverging lens produces a virtual image, while a convex lens or a parabolic mirror can create a real image). Friedberg states:

> A real image is formed by the convergence of rays of light and is visible to the eye, but will also appear on a surface that is placed in a plane with the image. A "virtual image"—perceived in the brain—is visible to the eye but will not appear on a surface placed in its plane. Hence a "virtual image" in Brewster's optics is not recuperable to representation.[27]

The first two statements are correct, but the last remains obscure. Kepler's *imago* needed an eye to be seen, while the *pictura* could be projected onto any screen that intervened at the proper point. While the eye must be positioned to see the virtual image, this does not mean it is imaginary in the sense of fanciful or inaccessible. Since virtual images include mirror reflections, why are they not recuperable to representation? Friedberg increases the confusion when she states that "the virtual image was first described as a purely retinal image."[28] (This is wrong; Kepler precisely claimed the retinal image was a *pictura*, a projected image, not an *imago*. Friedberg actually states this correctly in the previous paragraph.) Friedberg's presentation of the virtual image remains confusing and even contradictory (undoubtedly I have sufficiently confused readers that they will be sympathetic to this!). Friedberg recognized a "semantic slippage" and claims that two meanings for *virtual image* emerged: a mental image (Kepler's *imago*, the product of the imagination) and "an image produced by some optical mediation."[29] But for Kepler and later optics, *virtual* and *real* differentiate not between a mental image and an optical one, but between two types of optical images.

But does this misunderstanding of terms really matter? Given that *virtual image* has a very specific meaning within the science of optics, the misidentification should at least be pointed out—partly because it *is* common. As Friedberg mentions, Jean-Louis Baudry, in his famous essay "Ideological Effects of the Basic Cinematographic Apparatus," also identifies the "virtual image" with the image created by a camera, which of course, optically speaking, would be a real image focused on the film's surface. This mistake seems rampant in film studies, and while not insignificant, I do find it understandable, as I discuss here.

The real question is: How does our understanding of the virtual image affect the broader concept of the virtual and its relation to materiality, representation, and the actual? Although she confused terms, I think Friedberg's turn to optics had a strong motive. Initially she describes the virtual as immaterial, but then she claims that "the virtual image that is formed in representation signifies a subtle shift in its materiality," adding, "A virtual image begins to have its own liminal materiality, even if it is of a different ontological order."[30] She reiterates this, reinforcing, but not exactly clarifying, its paradoxical nature: "Virtual images have a materiality and a reality but of a different kind, a second-order materiality, liminally immaterial." Modifying her earlier association of the virtual with the image and its likeness, she claims, "The terms 'original' and 'copy' will not apply here, because the virtuality of the image does not imply direct mimesis, but a transfer—more like metaphor—from one plane of meaning and appearance to another."[31] Although I find these claims difficult to follow, I think Friedberg is wrestling with radical implications of the virtual, perhaps inextricable from the history of human technology and the creation of a world of human culture. The virtual, especially since the optical revolutions of the early modern era, radically calls into question any simple opposition between the material and the immaterial and redefines the process of representation.

Friedberg's confusion of virtual and real images reflects, I believe, an intuition that *both* these forms of images relate to the virtual (even if only one is properly called a "virtual image"). What Friedberg calls their "liminal immateriality" or "second-order materiality" might best be understood through their optical production. Both forms of image originate in light rays radiating from an object. These rays are mediated and transformed by some device through refraction and/or reflection. Optical devices, whether mirrors, cameras obscura, or lenses, manipulate light according to physical laws. All images produced by these devices can be considered virtual, I claim.

Since it constitutes the opposite of the "virtual image," can the "real" or projected image be described as virtual—or is this a contradiction in terms? Returning to Kepler's term *pictura* may dispel some confusion. The reality of the *pictura* lies in its appearance as a picture projected on a surface, the product of a device or mechanism. As Svetlana Alpers puts it, approaching this image as real rather than an instance of human perception—a picture, rather than a sight—Kepler "had to separate as his object of study the mechanism of the eye—what the eye considered as an optic system does with rays—from the person who sees, from the observer of the world and from the question how we see." Thus he was able to "separate the physical problem of the formation of retinal images (the world seen) from the psychological problems of perception and sensation."[32] With the *pictura*, Kepler focused attention on the mechanics of image formation and the picture that results. The *pictura* is the picture that light paints on the retina focused by the optics of the eye or on a surface within the camera obscura, even without an observer present. Kepler does not assert the reality of the *pictura* as a true representation of the world. Quite the contrary; it is real qua *picture*, projecting its measurable presence at a particular point in the refraction of light rays. He leaves the step from optics to perception to the natural philosophers.

Therefore, I claim that both virtual and real images belong to a virtual visuality, resulting from the manipulation of light. The rise of optical devices in the sixteenth and seventeenth centuries certainly aided Kepler's shift in emphasis from perception to the mechanics of vision. The virtual image involves the play of light through an optical device (the plane mirror or converging lens). Besides serving as a model for human sight, the camera obscura functioned as an optical transformation of tangible objects into two-dimensional moving images. I think Friedberg's inclusion of *imago* and *pictura* within the virtual reflects their common production through optical devices. Even if the terms became confused, her union of them under the aegis of the virtual makes sense. The concept of transformation through an optical device provides, I hope, a tangible basis for considering them as virtual. Thus the "transfer" Friedberg claims the virtual enacts can be specified (not simply taken as a metaphor). First, a material object is transformed into an image through an optical process. Second, this transformation also entails a transfer out of its ordinary position—whether into the illusory space of a reflection or into the projected space of a real image.

I asked previously what was real about the "real image." Perhaps now we need to ask: What is "virtual" in the "virtual image"? The virtual image may resemble the object it reflects, but it shifts its spatial location, both to the point behind the mirror and through the left/right reversal. This helps us understand the virtual not simply as a disembodied abstraction, but as being disembedded from its original place. The "immateriality" of the virtual derives in a fundamental way from this transfer.

VIRTUAL AND ACTUAL

> Mirrors: still no one knowing has told
> What your essential nature is.
> You, entirely filled, as with holes
> Of sieves, you, time's interstices.
>
> RAINER MARIA RILKE, *Sonnets to Orpheus*[33]

The core of Friedberg's book is its rich exploration of the window as metaphor and cultural object. I asked in the previous section whether "the virtual image," especially as understood in specific optical terms, could supply a similar metaphorical valency. Can its unique optical nature help us to think through the implications of the virtual and not simply solve high school physics problems? Henri Bergson uses the virtual image as a metaphor in his presentation of the interrelation of matter and mind. In a passage from *Matter and Memory* frequently quoted (by Friedberg, among others)[34], he explains how perception arises in a universe he claims consists of images.[35] Bergson's view of the relation between consciousness and the material world as the interrelation of different sorts of images remains his most difficult concept, and I tend to agree with Keith Ansell Pearson (who does an exemplary job of explaining it) that it is not always clear.[36] But in spite of my difficulty with metaphysical explanations, Bergson more than any other philosopher declared the centrality of the virtual. He also provided an ambiguous but influential discussion of the cinema (which I discuss at the end of this chapter). Friedberg includes a section on Bergson and the virtual in *The Virtual Window*, although it remains somewhat separate from her own discussion.[37] Aided by commentators including Gilles Deleuze, I offer my summary of Bergson's view of the virtual, which differs a bit from Friedberg's.

The world does not exist as representations in our minds (Bergson identifies such a claim as idealism). Nor does matter exist entirely independent of our consciousness (a position Bergson sees as "realism"). Rather, Bergson claims, "Matter, in our view, is an aggregate of 'images.' And by 'image' we mean a certain existence which is more than that which the idealist calls a *representation*, but less than that which the realist calls a *thing*—an existence placed halfway between the 'thing' and the 'representation.'"[38] There is no "inner" world of ideas, nor an "outer" world of things, but rather something in between. Matter and perception constitute two systems of images. As matter, images interrelate among themselves according to fixed laws and without any particular center (Ansell Pearson compares this to an ever-turning kaleidoscope).[39] In contrast, in the system of images belonging to perception, a center arises, which is my body, and images seem to refer to this center. Perception can be described as the way the aggregate of images (the universe of matter) relates to my body. Perception does not abstract my body from the shifting world of matter, but rather orients it within this aggregate. My body thus forms the center of a system of images, choosing the actions it takes in response to the movements other images exert on it.

Representation need play no role here. The body's function is to receive stimulation (movements) and to respond (with its own movements). These responses are initially almost automatic, direct sensory-motor reactions to the movements that impinge on my body, reflexive and unreflective. Yet conscious perception develops out of these responses. The movements of the images that belong to the material world obey fixed laws; they are *determined*. But in the system of images in which my body acts as the center, the response to these motions becomes *indeterminate*, freely chosen. Perception comes from this "center of indetermination." Conscious perception chooses how to respond to the movements that impinge on it. "In other words, the brain appears to us to be an instrument of analysis in regard to the movement received and an instrument of selection in regard to the movement executed."[40] Thus the process of conscious perception arises from my *action* in response to the material universe, rather than from an interiorized process of mental representation.

Conscious perception arises from a response to movement that is neither automatic nor determined. Its nature comes from its uncertainty, its freedom, and the resulting suspense, which precedes its selection of what action to take and how to take it. In his later essay "The Possible and the Real," Bergson states, "Time is this very hesitation, or it is nothing."[41] Bergson describes this process of suspension as a mastery of time, which lays the foundation of the virtual, the realm of choice and freedom. Instead of a single reaction determined by the lawful movement of material images, the living center confronts a range of virtual actions and chooses among them. As Ansell Pearson puts it, "Bergson will define consciousness as the measure of virtual action."[42] Bergson describes this process as a transformation of matter into virtual images. In the system of images that make up the material universe, each image interacts with every other image in strictly determined, yet uncentered, movement. Perception isolates a part from this shifting whole, suppressing, as Bergson tells us, "all those parts of objects in which their [the living centers'] functions find no interest."[43] This process of isolation subtracts from the aggregate of images, but also performs a transformation into the virtual: "so that the remainder, instead of being encased in its surroundings as a *thing*, should detach itself from them as a picture."[44]

Thus the image that is my body, as a center that takes interest in certain images, differentiates itself from the total aggregate of images whose regular and stable motion constitute the material universe. The virtual image provides the central metaphor for this process of perception. The images that make up the aggregate of the material world influence each other endlessly, as if they were light carried on a constant play of shimmering, refracted and reflected from image to image, indifferently. But when the image system of the body arises as a center, this process no longer remains indifferent or mechanical. As the germ of conscious perception, the living center acts spontaneously rather than mechanically, selecting and taking an interest in the movements exerted on it. The total mechanism of the aggregate becomes subject to a process of isolation and selection, which interrupts the circuit of light passing through the whole. Instead of the total aggregate pursuing its endless course, certain images become virtual images. These form the basis of perception, no longer projected throughout the system, but reflected as a virtual image toward a living center. Thus they form a conscious perception. Bergson portrays the birth of perception as the creation of the virtual out of matter:

> When a ray of light passes from one medium to another, it usually traverses it with a change of direction. But the respective densities of the two media may be such that, for a given angle of incidence, refraction is no longer possible. Then we have total reflection. The luminous point gives rise to a *virtual* image which symbolizes, so to speak, the fact that the luminous rays cannot pursue their way. Perception is just a phenomenon of the same kind.[45]

The metaphor of the virtual image reveals perception as the interdependence of the material world as an aggregate of images with the living center of the body. The relation between them is one of virtualization, understood as a process of transformation and isolation of images. Rather than a brain serving as a container of interior representations, consciousness acts as a zone of selection and interest that isolates images from the total aggregate and thereby perceives them through this process. "Our representation of things would thus arise from the fact that they are thrown back and reflected by our freedom."[46] The living center prises an image from the system of total indifference and constant circulation and receives it as a picture, a reflection, a virtual image—a perception. The act of perception occurs, Bergson claims, through a process best understood by analogy to optics and the virtual image:

> That which is given is the totality of the images of the material world, with totality of their internal relations. But, if we suppose centers of real, that is to say of spontaneous, activity, the rays which reach it, and which interest that activity, instead of passing through those centers, will appear to be reflected and thus to indicate the outlines of the objects which emit them. There is nothing positive here, nothing added to the image, nothing new. The objects merely abandon something of their real action in order to manifest their virtual influence of the living being upon them. Perception therefore resembles those phenomena of reflexion that result from an impeded refraction; it is like an effect of mirage.[47]

Perception occurs when the image of the material world becomes virtual, exists as an image, by being reflected. The mirage effect is not simply a process of illusion, but rather a displacement, a sort of liberation from the mechanism of the material world. This actualization of a perception is made possible by the process of virtualization, lifting the image out of the totality of the material universe into a realm of time understood as indeterminacy, choice based in freedom. It becomes, as Bergson states in his later essay, "a vehicle of creation and choice."[48] Here lies the significance of the virtual for Bergson.

VIRTUAL: "NOT THERE"

> Yes, the only place on earth where all places are—seen from every angle, each standing clear, without any confusion or blending.
>
> JORGE LUIS BORGES, "THE ALEPH"[49]

Optical images offered Bergson new models for thinking through the relation between the mind and the material universe. Understanding images as real and the virtual as a process of isolation and displacement shows the complex relation between the virtual and the real, which is more than a simple logical opposition. Recent philosophical discussions of the virtual, influenced by Deleuze's treatment of Bergson, stress the complex nature of this term and hesitate to describe it as the opposite of the real or actual—or as immaterial. Perhaps most crucially, the virtual is not a static quality but a dynamic process. As Pierre Levy puts it, "Virtualization is one of the principal vectors in the creation of reality."[50] The essence of the virtual lies not in its lack of materiality, Levy claims, but in its "detachment from the here and now" and (like the optical virtual image) its aspect of "not being there, of being deterritorialized."[51]

Deleuze uses a relation of four terms, rather than a simple opposition, to describe the virtual. The virtual, first, must be distinguished from the actual, but this central differentiation should not be equated with the opposition between the possible and the real.[52] The derivation of virtual from *virtue*, a latent power, clarifies this distinction. The virtual lies not simply in the possibility of becoming real, but in the power to make something new happen. For Deleuze the *possible* remains predictable, a realization of something already contained and determined.[53] Bergson explains that, far from preceding the real, the possible appears retroactively. The already realized seems to our ordinary intellect to have always been possible. The concept of the possible buttresses our desire for predictability and stability. The real casts back into the past an image of itself as possible, which Bergson describes as "the mirage of the present in the past."[54] The virtual, in contrast, invokes power and creativity, the capacity to create something unforeseen. Its difference from the actual is therefore not simply negative, a lack of existence, but the positive power to exist.[55] Friedberg presents Deleuze's reading of Bergson's *virtual* this way: "For Bergson the 'virtual' serves as an ontological distinction between the possible and the actual; aligned with the possible, the virtual was posed over and against the actual and the real."[56] Reflecting her understanding of the virtual as primarily immaterial, Friedberg reduces this fourfold relation to a twofold opposition.

The opposition between the virtual and the possible is as crucial to understanding the virtual as its difference from the real and the actual. The real and the possible imply each other.[57] The passage from one to the other, the process of realization, is based in resemblance and limitation; according to Deleuze, the "real is the image of the possible," while the principle of limitation determines which possibilities become real (not all do).[58] Likewise, the process of actualization defines the virtual rather than opposes it. Levy describes this dynamic relation: "Unlike the possible, which is static and already constituted, the virtual is a kind of problematic complex, the knot of tendencies or forces that accompanies a situation, event, object, or entity, and which evokes a process of resolution: actualization."[59] More than logical opposition, the virtual implies the interpenetration of these terms. Actual, virtual, possible, and real all revolve in a continual process that allows both opposition and transformation. Thus the virtual is not simply the immaterial waiting in the wings to become material, nor is it a refusal of materialization, a purist pursuit of abstraction. The virtual implies the force of invention and creation, never fully given, but moving toward actualization. Thus Levy can claim nearly the opposite of Friedberg's statement about the relation between the virtual and the actual without denying their defining differences: "The virtual is by no means the opposite of the real. On the contrary, it is a fecund and powerful mode of being that expands the process of creation, opens up the future, injects a core of meaning beneath the platitude of immediate physical presence."[60] Rob Shields puts this quite succinctly: "The virtual calls into question our preconception about the actual, demanding that we broaden our understanding of reality."[61]

Bergson returns to an invocation of the virtual image of the mirror to contrast the virtual with the conception of the possible as preceding the real:

> One might as well claim that the man in flesh and blood comes from the materialization of his image seen in the mirror, because in that real man is everything found in this virtual image, with, in addition, the solidity which makes it possible to touch it. But the truth is that more is needed

> here to obtain the virtual than is necessary for the real, more for the image of the man than for the man himself, for the image of the man will not be portrayed if the man is not first produced, and in addition one has to have the mirror.[62]

The mirror is essential, not simply as an intermediary between real man and virtual image, but as a means of transforming one into the other, a process both spatial and temporal. Thus the intimate relation between the virtual and actual recalls less a logical paradox than a mutual implication bound up with duration. The virtual becomes creation through its experience of the indetermination of time. As Bergson asks, "Would not the existence of time prove that there is indetermination in things? Would not time be that indetermination itself?"[63]

Bergson viewed the cinema with suspicion, a view many, including Deleuze, Friedberg, and myself, have found puzzling.[64] Bergson even used the phrase "the cinematographical illusion" for the prejudice of understanding time as a series of discrete instants, a view he found limited in contrast to the grasp of duration and the unique flow of movement that intuition allows. It seems surprising that this philosopher who argued the value of the virtual, duration, and movement would condemn cinema, the producer of virtual, moving, and temporal images. His apparent blindness to cinema has been explained by his relative unfamiliarity with the new medium or its undeveloped nature at the time he wrote *Creative Evolution* (1907). I have always stressed that Bergson used the cinematograph as an analogy to a mode of intellect he criticized, rather than condemning the medium itself. However, I have come to the reluctant conclusion that his opposition to the cinematograph cannot be easily dissipated. His understanding of the *possible* clarifies his negative view of cinema. The filmstrip bearing the succession of still images into which the motion picture camera analyzes motion certainly receives the brunt of his critique. This string of frozen snapshots exemplifies the spatialization of time that he claims distorts our ordinary understanding, dividing movement into an accumulation of immobilities, parsing time into mathematical sections.

But does the projected film, the actual moving image, also reflect these attitudes? Bergson seems to condemn projector as much as camera, the tool of synthesis as much as the means of analysis, when he claims, "The movement does indeed exist here; it is the movement of the apparatus."[65] As a repetitive and predictable machine, the cinema apparatus can only manufacture false movement, rather than "the continuous creation of unforeseeable novelty."[66] Cinema, like the possible, can only reproduce the real, creating nothing new. Thus in his 1920 essay "The Possible and the Real," Bergson describes the universe of the possible, "whose successive states are in theory calculable in advance, like the images placed side by side along the cinematographic film, prior to its unrolling."[67] Cinema reproduces the calculable and the determined and can only counterfeit the processes of virtual creation through duration.

Or does it? Bergson than adds, "Why, then, the unrolling? Why does reality unfurl? Why is it not spread out? What good is time?" It is perilous to turn these comments on the nature of the possible into a theory of cinema, but Bergson's references to film seem to cut both ways. A film can present a static succession of fixed pictures, states of being and sections of movements that cancel out the intuitive experience of duration and creation. It can only show what it has already recorded. But is there an element of the indeterminate in its unfurling, a virtual dimension to its capture of the possible?

CLOSING, STILL OPEN A CRACK

> But the important thing for me is that, as I used to sit there and watch the film when it was projected for friends in those early days, that one short sequence always rang a bell or buzzed a buzzer in my head. It was like a crack letting the light of another world gleam through. I kept saying to myself, "The walls of this room are solid except right there. That leads to something. There's a door there leading to something. I've got to get it open because through there I can go through to someplace instead of leaving here by the same way that I came in."
>
> MAYA DEREN[68]

From her first book, Friedberg linked the virtual and movement. In *The Virtual Window* she frames the move from the fixed-perspective image of Alberti's window to the multiple windows of new media within a long history of the virtual. Within this trajectory, I have analyzed a smaller arc between Kepler's description of the optical image resulting from lenses and mirrors to current conceptions of virtual media. I have tried to relate the virtual to a continuing optical revolution, in which devices interrelate bodies and images, redefining representation and the duality of material and immaterial. Guided by the radical role the virtual plays in the thought of Henri Bergson and his followers, I hope to bring the optical aspect of Friedberg's larger project into focus.

I claim the virtual moving image as an ongoing series of technological devices (from nineteenth-century optical toys, to the cinema, to video and digital media); I think Friedberg's virtual window opens itself to such a view. While I caution against simply aligning the virtual with the immaterial or tying it too closely to the process of representation, I think the virtual optical images Friedberg invokes mark a revolution we might call *virtual media*. This does not simply involve a process of reproduction (although Walter Benjamin's analysis of technical reproduction provides a founding text in defining the virtuality of modern media), but rather a process of discovery and transport (quoting Levy again, "by undoing the here and now, it opens the way to new spaces, other velocities").[69]

If we focus more broadly, as Friedberg invites us to do, on virtual media rather than a virtual image, our attention shifts from image to the apparatuses or, better, the technical processes, of virtualization. Nor need we limit the virtual to the visual. Virtual written texts (email, computer programs, experimental interactive novels) define the modern environment marked by their mobility and ease of transfer. The telephone with its "virtual auditory space," as Rob Shields indicates, "implies that the 'virtual' life has been coming for a long time"—not to mention the view of language itself as the source of the virtual.[70] Within the hermeneutic of suspicion (which dominated film studies in the 1970s and 1980s), it was assumed that virtual effects induced a collective state of deception. More recent utopian euphoria over the disembedding effect of new media can be just as simplistic and myopic. Complex political analysis of modes of power and discussions of what constitutes liberation remain necessary to deal with the virtual, not simply utopian or dystopian projections based on theory. We also need an analysis of the relation of virtual media to the long history of technology. Levy's brief and Bernard Stiegler's extended considerations of tools as a virtualization of the world open new pathways to think through the way media involve a constant reinvention (including endangering) of the human.[71]

The virtual window, Friedberg teaches us, opens onto something new, familiar perhaps, but only in the way that the uncanny strikes us as strangely familiar. To reopen one of Friedberg's rich discussions from another perspective, the French window, or *porte-fenetre*, demonstrates that more than light and air can move through a window. As my quote from Deren indicates, not only can a moving projected image become a window to another world, it can also become a door, a portal through which we can pass into something new.

At the very moving memorial service for Anne Friedberg held at the Billy Wilder Theater in the Hammer Museum in the fall of 2009, I sat with hundreds of friends, colleagues, and former and current students, enthralled by a succession of photographs projected on the screen. Most showed Anne with her familiar elegant and even glamorous sense of fashion and sophistication, accompanied by friends and family members. One image, however, struck me through the woman's resemblance to Anne, a sort of hippyish, mischievous young woman (a sister I had never met, I wondered?). Then, on repeated viewings (the photographs were cycled through several times as people took their seats), I realized the image was Anne herself, from the time when I first met her at NYU, showing a very different persona and appearance that I had almost forgotten—and I recalled the unspoken crush I had on her from afar in those early years. Like a Proustian involuntary memory, it overwhelmed me. Déjà vu in reverse, something recovered at the moment of its ultimate loss.

PART III
Avant-Garde

15

Doctor Jacobs's Dream Work: Ken Jacobs's *The Doctor's Dream*

> There is often a passage in even the most thoroughly interpreted dream which has to be left obscure; this is because we become aware during the work of interpretation that at that point there is a tangle of dream-thoughts which cannot be unraveled and which moreover adds nothing to our knowledge of the content of the dream. This is the dream's navel, the spot where it reaches down into the unknown.
>
> SIGMUND FREUD, *The Interpretation of Dreams*

I

Ken Jacobs, working through his film students at Binghamton, has sliced into the body of a film so little known, and of such slight intrinsic interest, that it could be considered discarded. The process brings to mind the image of a surgeon directing his anatomy students in the dissection of a corpse. The original film (a two-reeler of the sort distributed by companies specializing in short subjects, such as Castle Films) was titled *The Doctor*. The result of Jacobs's autopsy is called *The Doctor's Dream*. In an interview with Lindley Hanlon, Jacobs described his method for creating the film:

This essay first appeared, as "Doctor Jacobs' Dream Work," in *Millennium Film Journal*, nos. 10–11 (Fall 1981–Winter 1982): 210–18.

> The new film starts with the shot which was numerically the middle shot in the old film. It then proceeds to the shot that came before that middle shot, then skips over to the other side and shows the shot that followed the middle shot and then keeps skipping back and forth to the outer shots. Finally at the very end of the movie, as you see it now, you see the once beginning shot of the film followed by the original end shot of the film. It's mechanically rigid, except for a couple of mistakes they [his students] made, which I left in because the mistakes balanced each other out.[1]

What Jacobs has done, then, is to pierce an old narrative film through its center. One set of shots moves from this midpoint to the end of the film. Interpolated between each shot of this forward running narrative is another set of shots which moves backward to the beginning of the film. To watch *The Doctor's Dream* is to witness a narrative unfolding forward and backward in turns, reversing direction with each shot.

Lest my metaphor of autopsy be taken too literally, let me stress that this restructured film does not lie quietly upon the operating table. It barks with life and stands as a new creation, a deconstructive Frankenstein of a film with new vitality in its borrowed parts. It is in the maze of meanings this resurrected and transformed film brings with it, that I intend to wander.

II

A farm woman stands on the porch of a country house, her face contorted with unexplained anxiety. She reaches for a horn hanging on the wall and places it to her lips. We then see a buckboard enter a farmyard driven by a father and son. Two blasts from the horn sound and they look off. Jacobs's film begins with this call and response between two images. At this point some narrative coherence operates; even the farm woman's unexplained anxiety could be related to the narrative device of beginning *in medias res*, a strategy in fact avoided by the pedestrian original film, but not inconceivable. However, as Jacobs's film proceeds, the narrative fabric stretches and begins to tear. The third shot, instead of continuing the contact between anxious mother and responsive father and the relative spatial coherence of porch and farmyard, jump-cuts to a shot within the farmhouse as the mother reads a thermometer taken from her sick daughter. She looks alarmed and touches the girl's forehead. In a way, this image supplies a narrative grounding for the look of alarm in the first shot. But the reversal of cause and effect, the violence done our sense of narrative by the reversal of temporality (without any marking of the image as a flashback) subverts ordinary narrative expectation. As the film progresses, this experience grows more intense. The shot-to-shot relations become more distant in terms of space, time, and narrative logic.

In structure, the film somewhat unexpectedly recalls Ernie Gehr's *Serene Velocity*, although the films deal with extremely different material. Gehr's film also begins with a midpoint, the middle focal length of a zoom lens. The film then alternates between different focal lengths as it records the static image of an institutional hall. One set of shots (or four-frame bursts) steadily increases the focal length, while the interpolated images steadily decrease it. We have then an image that stutters between moving down the hall toward a door marked EXIT, and withdrawing ever further back from it, as the differences between focal lengths increase. In the opening moments of *Serene Velocity*, when the differences between focal lengths are small, the images are easy to relate to one another. One tends to see a simple shuddering of a single image. But as the differences in focal lengths become more extreme, it is harder to see the alternations as aspects of the same image. However, in Gehr's film, the single site of filming and the temporal continuity offered by the dawn light slowly emerging through the glass doorway, create the sense of a complex meditation on a unified subject. Jacobs's restructuring of a narrative film is hardly contemplative. It involves a complex relation with audience expectations, producing a film that seems shattered and fragmented, playful and analytical at the same time.

If one catches on to the film's recipe (and I certainly did not on first viewing) one could decide to watch it unfold backward and forward in quick turns, adjusting oneself to the film's skip-a-beat rhythm. This way of engaging with the film relates to the implicit games involving memory and expectation in such participatory films as Frampton's *Zorns Lemma* or *Nostalgia*. Michael Kirby, in an article in *The Drama Review*, understands the film in this way:

> In *The Doctor's Dream* Jacobs exploits, puts pressure upon, and brings to conscious awareness the traditional mechanisms of expectancy structure. Let us ignore, for the moment, the interspersed shots of the backward-moving half of the narrative. Intercut black leader would function to some extent the same way. The forward moving narrative is delayed, slowed; the time before expectancies are confirmed or denied is increased. Facts must be retained longer. The mind must carry and retain information and expectancies in an unusual, non-habitual, way. What was automatic and unconscious in the traditional arrangement of shots may now be forced

> into consciousness in an attempt to make sense out of the new, more difficult arrangement.[2]

Certainly this is an important part of the structure of the film and one relation a viewer may have with it. It is always somewhere in my mind when I watch the film. And I think that the process of making unconscious processes conscious is central to the film in a number of ways, as I will show later. But perhaps it is because I am less systematic (it is an effort for me to get the alphabet straight when I watch *Zorns Lemma*), that it seems to me this is a secondary aspect of the film, one which underlies and allows a more surprising process.

Kirby's momentary ignoring of the interpolated shots, his metaphorical censoring of them with imaginary black leader, masks the very strong experience that comes from the juxtaposition of shots out of their (originally intended) narrative order. The effect of these juxtapositions is not simply formulaic; it becomes creative. This unintentional contact of two images generates new meanings. At the same time that one senses the film's original narrative proceeding and recoiling in staggered rhythm, a new narrative develops, a sort of subversion of the meaning still observable in this palimpsest of the original film. This new subversive narrative is not evenly coherent. Jacobs has not intervened in his formula of rearrangement to coax meaning out of the editing. It remains aleatory, episodic, appearing more strongly at some moments than at others. Yet its phantom visitations are extremely strong, and sensed, I find, by audiences long before they discover the formula underlying the film (laughter tends to accompany each epiphany of this spontaneously generated text).

One specific juxtaposition can exemplify this elusive narrative. It appears in the sequence of the film that intercuts the concerned vigil over Carol Ann, as the climax of her illness approaches, with the Doctor's earlier visit to the farmhouse when he reads Carol Ann fairy tales and tells the legend of the rainbow. The basic alternation in mood between the two scenes produces some startling effects and subtexts. In one shot, the Doctor and Carol Ann stand close together as they look off at the rainbow, the actress playing Carol Ann rolling her eyes and sighing deeply as the Doctor describes the pot of gold at rainbow's end. The following shot (coming originally from the sickbed vigil) shows Carol Ann's father in close-up, his face anxious and drawn as he glances off screen. An eyeline glance seems to present itself over the edit, a reaction-shot pattern. The father's anxiety over his sick child is displaced onto this close and apparently innocent scene of doctor and child. Playfully we see a not-so-innocent subtext in the relation of old man and young girl and read the father's reaction as suspicion or even anger. Certain elements in the original scene (the precocious sensuality of the moppet's acting) emerge to support this reading. We do not simply suspend our habit of reading a film from shot to shot. Nor is our habit of reading simply made conscious to us by it being made more difficult. Shot-to-shot juxtapositions create this countertext which ironically undermines the original narrative. In fact, this subversive narrative of sexual attraction runs throughout Jacobs's film. A number of expressions, gestures, statements, separated from their original context, take on eroticized meanings.

The fact that two juxtaposed images (particularly if they include a facial close-up) will yield a meaning is, of course, one of the bases of narrative logic in film—the famous "Kuleshov effect." However, Lev Kuleshov shot his legendary Mozhukin experiment in order to show how a filmmaker could impose meaning on material through editing. He proceeded from the amorphous nature of the single shot to the clarity of meaning given in an edited sequence. Jacobs's formulaic manipulations of found footage uses the same principle in a different way. Intended meanings are undermined and a whole range of ambiguous overtones is opened up. Only a few of the juxtapositions carry definite meanings. Many of them allow a viewer to find a variety of associations.

Once we realize we are watching a new film with new meanings unfold, not simply tracing an old one backward and forward, a number of structures operate. As in any narrative film, meaning in *The Doctor's Dream* comes not only from shot-to-shot juxtapositions but from chains of images dispersed across the film. The repeated images of the Doctor in his lab (usually in reversed temporal order) punctuate the earlier part of the film with an insistence that being absorbed in the continuity of the original narrative would have masked. Because of the interspersed images of the Doctor treating patients, riding in his buggy, and so on, it seems that he repeatedly returns to his lab. An image of Sisyphean labor is created by the editing pattern. In the last shot in the lab, the Doctor's wife appears in curlers and asks him when he is going to bed.[3] He stretches and replies, "In about four days." This hyperbole has been literalized by the images.

Kirby's thesis that the film makes the viewer conscious of the narrative role of expectancy and memory could be expanded to larger narrative structures. Although "rigidly mechanical," the formula for rearranging the original film also relates to certain rules of classical narrative construction. The exact middle of the film holds the film's climax, the discovery and reaction to Carol Ann's high fever, and Jacobs's film begins at this point. It ends with both the opening and closing of the film's narrative. The symmetry of beginning and ending in the original film becomes very apparent in the last minutes of *The Doctor's Dream*, particularly when the film alternates between shots of the Doctor's first visit to Carol Ann and his final visit. At one point a shot of the Doctor descending from his buggy during his final visit is juxtaposed with an image of Carol Ann on the porch looking up and rising to greet the Doctor on his first visit. The aleatory coherence (an accidental match cut which undermines the viewer's resolve to keep the two strands of the story separate) is further cemented by the gap on a projector between image projection and sound reading, which actually allows the Doctor's voice crying, "Hello Carol Ann," from the first shot, to be heard over the image of Carol Ann running to meet him in the following shot. The symmetrical order aimed at in the original film is also revealed by the two shots (one from the credit sequence and one bearing the words "The End" across it) of the genre painting of the Country Doctor that close the film. Separated by a shot of the Doctor's buggy departing, they are the first and last shots of the original film: the static image from which the action of the film derives and the static image into which it is absorbed. (The genre painting is also reproduced as a tableau vivant within the narrative during the vigil over Carol Ann.) Jacobs's rearrangement both demonstrates and subverts this symmetry. Instead of producing the naturalized feeling of resolution of a well-told story, it startles and surprises, and seems to offer a confluence of the two streams of the narrative at the point they are furthest apart.

Many other examples from the film could be similarly analyzed. What we are faced with is not simply a film that offers a formula a viewer can sense and participate in. We have a film that creates (liberates?) through its formula a series of new meanings from an old and hackneyed film.

III

The preceding formal analysis is only the beginning of an understanding of this film. A number of issues underlie the interrelation between Jacobs's film/original film/and viewer. One point of entry into this is to take the film's title seriously, the conversion from *The Doctor* to *The Doctor's Dream*. The title raises one of the oldest themes of avant-garde filmmaking—the relation between film form and dreams—in a radically new way.

Jacobs's use of found footage provides a starting point. Jacobs has often described his viewing of Joseph Cornell's *Rose Hobart* as one of the definitive experiences in his formation as filmmaker. Jacobs had worked as Cornell's assistant[4] and borrowed the film:

> *Rose Hobart* was a revelation. It was a shit film that just burst in front of you, the whole thing . . . it was such an eruption of energy and it was another re-enforcement, this idea I had for making this shit film, a film that would be broken apart . . .

Jacobs's recalling of his original viewing announces the concerns of *The Doctor's Dream*:

> Any way, we both [Jacobs and Jack Smith] became very interested in shit and the energy that was allowed when you come to the junctures of shit. You could find the seams where the shit would break open, you know, and it was really kind of an atomic fission. You know, this mindless banal crap could break open and give off fantastic aesthetic energy.[5]

In *Rose Hobart*, Cornell isolated images from a Hollywood film, eliminated the original sync soundtrack and projected it at 16 frames per second (rather than the 24 frames at which it was shot) through blue glass, to the accompaniment of a record of commercial Brazilian music. As P. Adams Sitney has shown, the effect is like that of a Cornell collage, a transformation of commercial kitsch into a series of oneiric encounters, veiled with a sense of mystery and delicacy.

Cornell's transformation of found footage in *Rose Hobart* can be related not only to his own work in collage, boxes, and other films, but to the early surrealist interest in commercial cinema. Breton has described his cinema voyages with Jacques Vache that preceded the birth of Surrealism:

> I agreed wholeheartedly with Jacques Vache in appreciating nothing so much as dropping into the cinema when whatever was playing was playing, at any point in the show, and leaving at the first hint of boredom—of surfeit—to rush off to another cinema where we behaved in the same way and so on (obviously this practice would be too much of a luxury today). I have never known anything more magnetising: it goes without saying that more often than not we left our seats without even knowing the title of the film which was of no importance to us anyway.[6]

This disjunctive filmgoing was the basis for a type of creative viewing/transformation of commercial film that would become a surrealist principle.

What was valued was the isolated gesture, movement, glance of the star, or ambiguous object, lifted from the syntagmatic context of its narrative and endowed with an unlimited paradigmatic horizon of meaning and mystery. Cornell's film appears at the intersection of this surrealist transformation of commercial film and the related use of found material in collage.

Found material, material not shot by Jacobs, has played a major role in Jacobs's work. It links together such disparate films as *Blonde Cobra*, *Star Spangled to Death*, *Urban Peasants*, and *Tom, Tom, the Piper's Son*, as well as the projection performances Jacobs has presented dealing with material ranging from World War II newsreels to early erotic films. But the use of this material has varied in each case. And if *The Doctor's Dream* originates in Jacobs's first reaction to *Rose Hobart*, the differences between the two films are fascinating.

Rose Hobart uses only fragments of its parent film, *East of Borneo*, and none of its sound. Only hints of the film's original narrative are obtainable. A few important shots do not even come from *East of Borneo* (the slow-motion water splash, for instance). There is no system behind the selection or editing of the material (several sequences of six or more shots are preserved intact from the original film.) Cornell used material from the original film on an entirely personal basis. The shots seen through veils, doorways, and mirrors recall the theme of mediation so important to Cornell's boxes, as does the projecting of the film through a midnight-blue piece of glass. This is a film made up of "evanescent fragments unexpectedly encountered," beauty released from the prison of silver light that contained the original film.[7] The effect is a total eclipse of the original film, with Cornell's dream image of Rose Hobart appearing in the lunar shadow of the original film. From a film that was originally silly and trite, moments of an unfixed beauty have emerged.

Jacobs's approach to *The Doctor* was quite different. He used every frame of the original film and all of its sound. Although the rearrangement transforms the film, its original narrative is glimpsable through the restructuring. Even without discerning the forward/backward logic of the editing, the basic story line is graspable, the character relations understandable; on repeated viewings it can become totally clear. Cornell's film overrides the logic of the narrative, abolishes it. Jacobs recircuits this logic and reveals something about it (and at the same time subverts it). Cornell presents us with timeless and placeless images as Rose Hobart wanders, enchanted, through a world of oneiric beauty and terror. The imperialist and racist ideology of the original film has been eliminated. In *The Doctor's Dream*, ideological statements become foregrounded precisely because the narrative ceases to absorb them in its natural continuity. They stand exposed like rocks on a beach from which the sea has ebbed. (The father telling his son as he cries, "There now, men don't let go like this," or the Doctor's speech about the road to the pot of gold at the end of the rainbow are just two of many rich examples.)

Jacobs's relation to the original film, then, is one that takes up the burden of its original narrative order and cultural meanings. To watch *The Doctor's Dream* is not simply to see a clever, formally precise rearrangement of an old film. We penetrate the original, observe the rules of its construction and its implicit ideology. Furthermore, as Jacobs describes it, we see the release of its hidden meanings and motives. Let's return to the sexual coloring given the relation between the Doctor and Carol Ann. In the interview with Hanlon, Jacobs stresses that this subtext is not accidental:

> Sequential progression along conventional lines has the magic effect of disguising the real matter at hand from the observer. At the same time, it's what the observer is really drawn to. It's veiled, which allows the observer to have a powerful response to it and at the same time not feel guilty toward the taboo strictures of the society.

Flo Jacobs, the filmmaker's wife, expanded this by saying, "What he is saying is that it is all there, he only exposed it."[8]

The Doctor's Dream reveals meanings that were present but repressed in *The Doctor*. This interrelation between the two films reveals one of the resonances of the title. To call this series of images a dream does not simply refer to its seeming incoherence, its reversals of temporal logic, or the surrealist quality of some of its juxtapositions. In its systematic play with these devices, it departs from the dream cinema of the early avant-garde. But it is precisely this system (which revises and transforms a preexisting text) that relates it to aspects of dreams that are dealt with less frequently by oneiric cinema: viz., the dream work in which repressed material takes the form of a dream, and in which the interpretation that unravels this dream obtains the thoughts beneath it.

In understanding the film in relation to the dream work, one finds a parallel between the relation between Jacobs's film and his source film and the events of the "dream day" (the day preceding the dream) that are found embedded in the dream. The Freudian concept of displacement is key here; the events of the first film are found in the second, but "displaced" by

Jacobs's editing scheme. The repressed themes which attach themselves to these displacements (as in the rainbow scene discussed before) show that the relation between the Freudian concept of displacement and Jacobs's reediting is more than a verbal pun. For Freud, the events of the dream day take an important part in a dream only through their association with repressed material, by a displacement of the dreamer's concern with the repressed subject onto the seemingly neutral events of the day before.

If Jacobs's systematic reediting of the film offers an analogy to dream work, one can also relate it to the technique of dream interpretation. Since Jacobs's reworking exposes the repressed content of the original, the relation between the two films becomes that of manifest to latent content. The story of *The Doctor* masked the erotic relation between the Doctor and Carol Ann behind the drama of illness and cure. In this view, the rearrangement of material in *The Doctor's Dream* merely follows up the displacements of the earlier film and its secondary revision into a tidy two-reel narrative. Jacobs's film functions as the psychoanalysis of *The Doctor*, and Dr. Jacobs becomes both surgeon and psychoanalyst. The analysis became possible because Jacobs's rearrangement interrupts the continuity of the original narrative, much as Freud found his patients came up with associations to their dreams only after he "put the dream before [them] cut up into pieces," revealing it as a conglomerate of psychic material only disguised as a whole.[9]

Clearly the symbiosis of Jacobs's film with its original source bears only an analogy to either the dream work or psychoanalysis. The film is both more and less than either of these activities. Jacobs has by no means illustrated Freudian concepts in his film (the genesis of the film would make that impossible). But the application of an arbitrary system to an already structured narrative yields complex results. The process by which Jacobs's radical restructuring of the film becomes a radical reinterpretation makes both dream work and dream interpretation relevant. In the long history of the interrelation of films and dreams, *The Doctor's Dream* occupies a new place—the intersection of the freedom of surrealist play and the exigencies of dream work. That Jacobs chose a film heavy with the inheritance of Hollywood narrative codes and ideology opens a whole field of issues in the making and unmaking of narratives.

Across the stuttering rhythm of this altered text, one traces a new story. Replacing the pietistic morality of a tale of virtue rewarded, a new drama of Dr. Beast and his patient Beauty appears, of a courting ritual of gift-giving moving from beast to necklace; of rivalry between the Doctor's wife and Carol Ann, and between Carol Ann's father and the Doctor himself. This new drama appears by flickers, then disappears. To fix it precisely is impossible, for it exists only in the play between images.

In the final moments of the film, we see a shot of the Doctor in a bed shrouded in darkness, an image that came near the beginning of the original film. Because of the delay between soundtrack and image, we hear the word "Goodbye" from the preceding shot. Then an off-screen knock sounds. The Doctor jerks awake, crying "I'm coming, I'm coming!" From what dream, we might wonder, was the Doctor awakened?

16

The Critique of Seeing with One's Own Eyes: Ernie Gehr's *Untitled (1977)*

At a program at the Collective for Living Cinema over a year ago, Ernie Gehr speculated on whether he would continue to make films. His sparse comments explaining this speculation were seized upon by an audience anxious to understand and empathize. But Gehr himself was unwilling to define precisely what the causes of such a stance might be, and each audience member was left to decide for himself what Gehr's statement entailed. However, Gehr made it clear that this was not a crisis in personal creativity; that, rather, it reflected a relation to the world in its present state and the situation of avant-garde filmmaking.

I do not bring this up because I feel I have a unique insight into what Gehr was feeling at that moment. As far as I know Gehr *has* continued to make films. But I feel that the sense of crisis that he voiced is one felt by many filmmakers in the avant-garde at this moment, and one that is rarely indicated in the writings of this journal. More specifically, I feel that the apparently cool detachment of Gehr's film style relates fundamentally to an exploration of crisis—the crisis of a filmmaker in relation to his means, and in relation to the world. For me, Gehr's cinema has explored the process of perception as crisis—and, in this sense, his films deal with the relation of eye, mind, and image from a *critical* perspective. I have always experienced the title of *Serene Velocity* ironically. In its explorations of the fissures in

This essay first appeared, as "The Critique of Seeing with One's Own Eyes: Ernie Gehr's *Untitled (1976)*," in *Millennium Film Journal*, no. 12 (Fall 1982–Winter 1983): 134–36.

the persistence of vision and the mind's ability to create space from a filmic image, *Serene Velocity* leads me toward a crisis in seeing and understanding that leaves me astonished, rather than serene.

A film some years old (but only screened recently), *Untitled (1977)* operates with a similar crisis in recognition. (It is worth noting that Gehr's titles are often in flux and this may be only a temporary title for the film. Librarians might take note that the film discussed in *Millennium* no. 3 by J. Hoberman under the title *Geography* has now been known for several years as *Eureka*.) The form of the film follows certain strategies of minimalist filmmaking of the 1960s and 1970s: a single camera roll exposed from a static camera position. Gehr does not use these limitations to produce a simple contemplative image, however. The exploration of human perception in relation to the cinematic apparatus in this film produces an image in flux, in fact, an image of flux in dialectical relation to precise limitations.

Like *Serene Velocity* and *Eureka*, *Untitled (1977)* explores the camera's relation to space through a meditation on penetration. As in the two previous films this penetration is rendered problematic. It is produced as an issue, as opposed to the simple phallic appropriation of the third dimension found, for instance, in Busby Berkeley's camera tracking through the gothic-arched legs of a line of chorus girls. In *Untitled (1977)*, the means of passing through space is exclusively optical. Gehr changes the focal plane of his camera so that the eye moves from foreground to background as successive layers come into sharpness. There is no zoom or camera movement here, but the eye delves progressively deeper into the image as new planes of distance come into focus.

The subject of Gehr's film is a snowstorm. The film is short, lasting about four and a half minutes when projected (as Gehr in the Warhol tradition requests) at 16 frames per second, and is, of course, silent. Gehr has told me that at one point *Untitled (1977)* was to be part of a longer film, but such plans are now abandoned. Again like the early Warhol films, *Untitled (1977)* begins with the flare end of the camera roll, emulsionless leader over which the image spreads after a few seconds. What we see at first is not immediately definable. After some orientation, one recognizes the diagonally slanting white streaks which move across the frame as the paths of snow. At first, however, the image recalled for me Gehr's *Field*, and I wondered if the streaking movement was caused by camera movement across a static subject as in that earlier film. The shallow focus of the image creates this ambiguity, because the background is diffused and vague. But one begins to recognize a static mottled colored mass in the distance across which a semitransparent medium appears to be moving.

I first supposed that this as yet unascertainable background was a stream bed filmed from a high angle and the semitransparent motion was the rush of water. As the camera slowly- refocused, nudging the zone of recognizability deeper into space, I realized this blurred and transparent motion was merely successive layers of falling snow. And the mottled surface which formed the limit of my vision came into focus as an enormous brick wall, filmed straight on and filling the extent of the frame.

The emergence of this wall, its slow materialization from ambiguous forms, produces a pleasure of final recognition, but also a sort of visual start. Our optical penetration of space has run into an ultimate barrier. Both *Eureka* and *Serene Velocity* end with similar limits. However, the light of morning breaking beyond the door in *Velocity* and the old man's windblown beard in *Eureka* offer a sort of counterpoint to the sense of containment. In *Untitled (1977)* the halt is unmitigated. We see in this final image how illusionary our penetration of space has been. The extent of the image is clear now, but we are no closer to it than before. The opening ambiguous image gave a sense of infinite space. The wall now stands before us at a finite distance, but clearly out of reach beyond us. We have run up against a wall, but not physically. It looms beyond us, closing down the horizon of our visual world, without a glimpse of sky above or ground below.

In many ways it seems to me that Gehr's films comment in a witty, ironic, and precise way on the ambitions of the avant-garde filmmakers of the 1920s, particularly the Soviets. His recent film *Shift*, which combines permutations of images of traffic with the sounds of motors, breaking glass, and screaming brakes, seems to literalize Sergei Eisenstein's metaphor of editing as collision. In *Untitled (1977)* (as in many of his other films), Gehr seems to relate to Dziga Vertov's paradigmatic opposition of human eye to camera eye—much of what a man can't see a camera can. However, if Vertov's project was part of a revolutionary optimism that saw the camera as the completion and improvement of human perception, Gehr's attitude seems more modest and more critical. It is the limitation of perception that Gehr explores through the possibilities of the camera, an art of vision founded on a crisis in seeing.

The wall stands beyond us in focus. We sense the opposition between this static monumental man-made structure and the random dance of snowflakes before it. The snow closest to the camera is now out of focus and the layers of swirling particles form a pattern that recalls film grain. Then the image is swallowed by end flare, emulsion washed away in a sort of yellow light.

17

"Films That Tell Time": The Paradoxes of the Cinema of Ken Jacobs

I love to go to the movies; the only thing that bothers me is the image on the screen.

THEODOR W. ADORNO

I. KEN JACOBS AND THE INVENTING OF THE CINEMA

When asked in 1899 to comment on the invention of moving pictures (which his experiments had made possible), the physiologist and inventor of chronophotography, Étienne-Jules Marey, declared, "What [motion pictures] show, the eye can see directly. They add nothing to the power of vision and remove none of its illusions. But the true essence of the scientific method is to supplement the weakness of our senses and correct our errors." As we begin the celebration of cinema's centenary, I believe it is time to take stock of this fin de siècle invention and ask Marey's implied question: has the cinema strengthened our vision and given us the means to overcome illusion? Or has it rather, as he seemed to fear, weakened our

This essay first appeared in the exhibition catalogue *Films That Tell Time: A Ken Jacobs Retrospective*, ed. David Schwartz (New York: American Museum of the Moving Image, 1989): 3–11, with the following acknowledgment: "Many of the ideas in this essay grew from four-way conversations between Kenneth and Florence Jacobs, David Schwartz, and myself. However, I alone deserve any blame for their development which may not represent Jacobs' view of his films. The title for this retrospective, 'Films That Tell Time,' which I have borrowed for the title of my article, comes from Jacobs."

sense and understanding of sight and multiplied the possibilities of visual deception?

While the films of Ken Jacobs may not completely answer this question, they certainly lead us onto the proper paths for its investigation. For the past three decades, Jacobs has probed the nature of the cinema in a way few filmmakers have aspired to. And it is precisely the total body of Jacobs's work (rather than any specific film) that reveals the systematic and profound nature of his investigation. This retrospective allows us to discover the center of an oeuvre that is more fugitive than most, yet essential to a rethinking of the nature of film as it enters its second century.

I wouldn't load such freight on the back of Jacobs's work if I weren't sure it could take it, in spite of its unprepossessing appearance. Looked at over an expanse of time, Jacobs's work might seem disjointed. In a concentrated dose its unities emerge and its ambitions and successes are clarified. But these ambitions are couched within ironies and their most probing questions come as a still small voice rather than a whirlwind. The fragmentary and seemingly modest dimensions of this oeuvre are its riddle and secret challenge. Jacobs has never claimed the position of priest of cinema but rather describes himself as a sort of secondhand dealer in film's curiosity shop, his work bits and pieces showing the wear of time. But as in a nineteenth-century romantic tale, it is in this rag-and-bone shop that the greatest mysteries of film can be obtained, discoveries unavailable in the great halls of bombast and pretension.

On first seeing a number of Jacobs films, one might flip through the program notes to make sure these are the works of one filmmaker. The diversity can be a bit dizzying. To the extent that genres exist in avant-garde film, Jacobs seems to cover them all: picaresque comedies (*Blonde Cobra*, *Little Stabs at Happiness*); diary film/home movie (*Nissan Ariana Window*, *Urban Peasants*); structural experiments in a single fixed take (*Soft Rain*) or rephotography (*Tom, Tom, the Piper's Son*); metaphysical dramas with allegorical tableaux (*The Sky Socialist*); experiments in documentary (*Orchard Street*, *Perfect Film*). But if this succession of phrases describes something of the range of Jacobs's work, they also immediately obscure the films. None of these films can be so easily categorized, and seeing them as parts of a whole makes one aware of subterranean passages linking them.

Jacobs's films pursue the slippery surfaces of experience rather than the deceptive clarity of ideas. None of his films illustrate or grow out of theories, and there is no substitute for the hard-won pleasures of sitting through them and puzzling them out while watching. He has specifically warned me of the dangers of trying to explain his (or anyone's) films, and the reader is hereby cautioned that this essay will be useful only if she has already threaded her own way through the Jacobs labyrinth. To delve into a Jacobs film requires getting one's hands dirty. What I hope to do in this essay is less to take an overview than to trace a series of paths along the corridors, well aware of the finger smudges on the wall and the sticky footprints on the floor. But from my perspective, more is at stake here than simply understanding Jacobs's films. The nature of cinema itself is the issue, a question that Jacobs explores with paradoxes rather than doctrines.

II. THE PARADOX OF THE PERFECT FILM: THE DISCOVERED IMAGE

> All the arts are founded on the presence of Man; only photography delights us with his absence.
>
> ANDRÉ BAZIN, "THE ONTOLOGY OF THE PHOTOGRAPHIC IMAGE"

The first and most apparent paradox of Jacobs's work is the fact that most of his films are made from material shot by other people with other purposes than his own. The sources are varied: footage from abandoned film projects by Jacobs's friend, filmmaker Bob Fleischner (*Blonde Cobra*); a 1905 chase film by the American Mutoscope and Biograph Company, shot by famous cameraman Billy Bitzer (*Tom Tom the Piper's Son*); a short film, probably shot for television, about the sacrifices of a country doctor (*The Doctor's Dream*); home movies from the 1940s shot by a relative of Jacobs's wife, Florence (*Urban Peasants*); outtakes of news footage surrounding the assassination of Malcolm X (*Perfect Film*); and, in the Nervous System performances, a documentary on the colonial history of the Philippines (*The Philippines Adventure*), combat footage from World War II (*Camera Thrills of the War*), antique hardcore stag movies (*XCXHXEXRXRXIXEXSX*), and records of daredevil stunts (*The Whole Shebang*). These films consist almost entirely of found footage; bits of political documentaries, cartoons, and educational films also play important roles in *Lisa and Joey in Connecticut, January 1965* and *Star Spangled to Death*, not to mention the many instances of "found sound" (old 78's, ethnographic recordings, how-to records, vintage jazz) that make up Jacobs's soundtracks.

In most of these films Jacobs works over the original footage, utterly transforming the material into a film of his own, either by reediting it according to his own schema (*The Doctor's Dream*), rephotographing it off

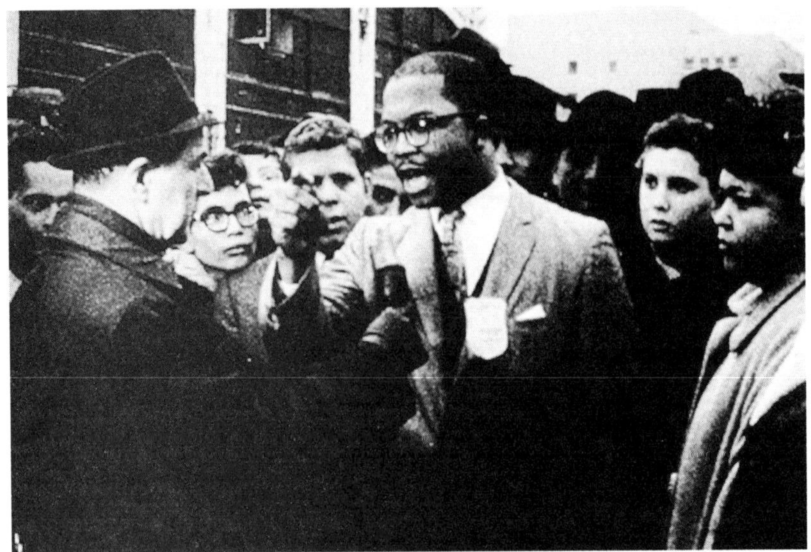

FIGURE 17.1. Ken Jacobs, *Perfect Film* (1986).

the screen (*Tom, Tom, the Piper's Son*), or transforming it through a multiple projection system (as in the Nervous System performances). But in *Perfect Film*, one of Jacobs's most recent works, the transformation has been reduced to a minimum. *Perfect Film* starkly reveals Jacobs's paradoxical view of filmmaking as a process that doesn't necessarily require a filmmaker's conscious intentions to be meaningful.

Perfect Film is literally a found film. Jacobs, foraging through a secondhand shop on Canal Street, found the footage (as well as the film which he reedited into *The Doctor's Dream*) in a bin of used film reels. The metal reels were on sale for a couple of bucks, with the films clinging precariously to them thrown in for free. Jacobs gave the footage a name and made a print, boosting the volume of one section. Otherwise the film remains as he found it. The paradox lies in the fact that, nonetheless, *Perfect Film* stands as an essential Jacobs film, and one that gains its fullest dimension when seen in the context of all his work. *Perfect Film*—a film that Jacobs neither shot, edited, nor "directed," but only found.

Is Jacobs simply playing a dadaist game, signing his name to a discarded readymade? Rather than an action of brash egotism, commandeering the work of someone else, Jacobs's issuing of *Perfect Film* under his name displays a deep humility before the cinematic image and a devotion to its inherent fascination. In this investigation of the cinematic image, Jacobs's lack of manipulation of the original footage is as important as a scientist's disciplined objectivity during an experiment. The film consists of what would generally be considered outtakes, unedited footage from news coverage of the assassination of Malcolm X. We see and hear multiple interviews of an eyewitness to the shooting; interviews with bystanders in Harlem; a statement by a New York City police official; silent footage of the Audobon Ballroom, where the murder took place, and its environs; close-ups of bullet holes in the floor; and briefly an image of Malcolm himself discussing recent threats to his life.

The event which motivates the film galvanizes our attention. But accustomed as we are to broadcast coverage, it is the unmanipulated quality of this unedited footage that begins to intrigue us, provided we are willing to let its powers of distraction overcome our impatience to get the story. The gathering of information brings us no closer to the horror of the actual event. In its multiple retellings we witness an act of murder become a story, then a news item, a bit which will be tailored to the format demands of television journalism. Even the sincere involvement of the eyewitness seems to be overwhelmed by the banality of the interview process. One's attention becomes diverted to odd bits of behavior (the eyewitness's jaw muscles seem to convulse; the bizarre and irrelevant behavior of bystanders, jumping to be included within the camera frame, attracted not by the event but by the camera). The film becomes an anthropological document, giving us the opportunity to observe human behavior in itself, not simply as a vehicle for information or ready-made formulas of human interest.

Since this is raw footage, the awkward moments which would be weeded out before broadcast remain. These rough spots possess the greatest powers of revelation. The police official's demand that the filming be done his way reveals his insecurity and authoritarian stance, rather than his strength and control. Likewise the inarticulateness and clumsy responses of some of the Black bystanders eloquently express the emotional dynamics of the moment. Besides these bits of flotsam and jetsam of reality, the starts and stutters of film itself are retained. The film includes sections of blank leader, occasionally with wild tracks of sound. Shaky silent pick-up shots of street signs and the exterior of the ballroom give a fragmented but strangely expressive feel of the place itself, the scene of the crime.

At one point the cameraman filmed a sign proclaiming that no cameras are allowed in the ballroom. This image, which simultaneously portrays the stricture against its own existence and the transgression of the rule, seems an emblem for the contradictory energy of the film. We see the periphery of an event of historic significance, strongly feeling that we are outside of it, insulated from its reality. If this footage had been edited for television it would have been given a sense of smoothness and narrative coherence, the manufactured intensity of "eyewitness news." But *Perfect Film* reveals such coherence as an artificial process, a trivializing of the event, aimed at producing a piece of easily digestible information. This homogenized product would eliminate all the rough edges, the awkward clumsiness of events that speak so eloquently in the unedited version. It is through the uncontrolled moments, the glitches and inarticulate statements, that life appears in *Perfect Film*. These rough spots also reveal the seams in the constructed veneer of reality that most often covers our screens. Jacobs shows us how to begin to take that apparent coherence apart. By picking at the scabs, he both releases vitality and uncovers rot.

I am not sure that every viewer placed before *Perfect Film* would understand it in this way. And this is why its identity as a Jacobs film plays a key role. It is as though all of Jacobs's previous films teach us to see *Perfect Film*, training us to watch the moving image while remaining alert to the contingent and marginal, to subtexts popping out from behind the apparent subject matter. Jacobs not only found the film itself, he allows us to find many things within it. He abdicates the position of all-powerful creator, maker, fashioner of images, to assume that of witness, observer, investigator, and ultimately, analyst. His contribution to the film lies in the fact that if we have seen his other films we have learned to watch movies with a vision akin to both X-ray and microscope, uncovering what is concealed and paying attention to what is generally ignored.

Perfect Film is, according to Jacobs, perfectly revealing. And all Jacobs has to do is present it to us, having previously made us realize the need to recenter our viewing of images, to be alert for the action in the margins, to watch for the seams in the construction. In this way Jacobs reveals the perfection of film itself, its unique contribution to the arts—the ability to capture the unconscious by penetrating the disguises of the conscious. *Perfect Film* reveals things that the people on camera never intended to reveal. At the same time it also reveals things that the original cameramen (whoever they were) did not intend. In fact, the whole issue of intention becomes irrelevant. In uncovering meanings that were never intended to be revealed, Jacobs enters an uncanny dimension of the cinema akin to psychoanalysis. *Perfect Film* is cinema before secondary revision, before a rational sense has been imposed on the chaos of the image. Jacobs's role as filmmaker is not that of a demiurge fashioning a world in his own image.

Rather, like a trained analyst, he stays in the background, mutely allowing the secrets to reveal themselves.

III. THE PARADOX OF THE NERVOUS SYSTEM: SPACE, TIME, AND IMAGE

> Our taverns and our metropolitan streets, our offices and furnished rooms, our railroad stations and our factories appeared to have us locked up hopelessly. Then came the film, and burst this prison-world asunder by the dynamite of the tenth of a second, so that now, in the midst of its far-flung ruins and debris, we calmly and adventurously go travelling.
>
> WALTER BENJAMIN, "THE WORK OF ART IN THE AGE OF MECHANICAL REPRODUCTION"

> Mayakovsky's going to play a solo
> On a flute made of his backbone.
>
> VLADIMIR MAYAKOVSKY, "THE BACKBONE FLUTE"

Writing fifty years ago, Walter Benjamin declared that cinema shared with psychoanalysis an ability to probe into realms of reality of which we were not previously conscious. The true power of cinema, one rarely tapped by the mainstream commercial cinema, lies in its exploration of an optical-unconscious. *Perfect Film* does this so effortlessly, partly because the intensity of the historical event raises it to an unusual transparency. Jacobs's role as analyst is rarely so simple. More often he uses the basic tools of his filmmaking to fracture the overwhelming familiarity of the moving image, blocking our most ingrained visual habits so that something else could take place.

Freud discovered he could help his patients make sense of their dreams only when he re-presented the seemingly familiar but opaque dream to them cut up in pieces, isolating its elements from their apparent coherence. Jacobs also usually begins by breaking up some basic element of film continuity. In *The Doctor's Dream* he detours the onrush of narrative by systematically reworking the order to the film's shots. Instead of the original film's linear progress to resolution, Jacobs begins with the middle of the film and then alternates shots, one group moving toward the beginning of the film, the other toward the end. This does more than simply undermine the film's narrative flow. In true psychoanalytic fashion, it unleashes currents of energy present, but disguised, in the film's original story: the sexual attraction between the country doctor and his moppet patient.

But Jacobs's most systematic and challenging transformation of our relation to the film image comes in the series of performances he calls the Nervous System. In the past decade, this ever-expanding group of works has absorbed most of Jacobs's filmmaking energy. These works are as vital and challenging as anything done in the history of avant-garde film. Their relative neglect comes partly from the exigencies of their presentation (they are literally performances—Jacobs must be present and operate the apparatus; therefore, unlike most films, they have no existence as canned goods), and partly from the intense offensive they mount against our viewing habits.

Jacobs's apparatus here is not the film camera but the projector. The projection apparatus Jacobs has devised is complex and is basically his own invention. Simply stated, it consists of two analytical projectors which can show the film frame by frame, or freeze it immobile on the screen. Each projector shows an identical print. Jacobs then controls the film's advance (or retreat) frame by frame, the two images getting slightly (usually no more than one frame) out of synch. A specially devised adjustable shutter in front of the projectors controls the relation between the images, at points keeping them separate, at other points overlapping them in a variety of durations. The shutter also creates a range of flicker effects and can even shape the projector light. Additional effects come from a platform which allows the projector to move slightly side to side, up and down, back and forth, and even to tilt a bit. Operating the projectors himself at each performance, Jacobs plays on his apparatus like a musician. We watch the film unfold in retarded time, and process the slightly different images. By breaking the automatic whirr of 24 frames a second, Jacobs returns cinema to its prehistory in Marey and Muybridge's analysis of motion. But besides breaking down the illusion of motion, Jacobs also uncovers how dependent our sense of space in film is on this constant mechanical speed.

The slightly different film frames, diverted from an illusion of motion by the analytical projectors, begin to produce spatial illusions. It has long been known that film could produce an illusion of three dimensions by projecting two images whose deviation matches that of human binocular vision. The use commercial cinema made of this is the gimmick of 3-D movies with lions leaping from the screen. In mainstream movies, 3-D has remained a fad that has never found a permanent place, but whose occasional resurfacing indicates some primal fascination on the part of film viewers. The projection arrangement of the Nervous System paradoxically produces an effect similar to 3-D movies, the deviation produced by motion between two film frames substituting for binocular parallax (Jacobs uses polarized lenses for some of his performances, and in others relies

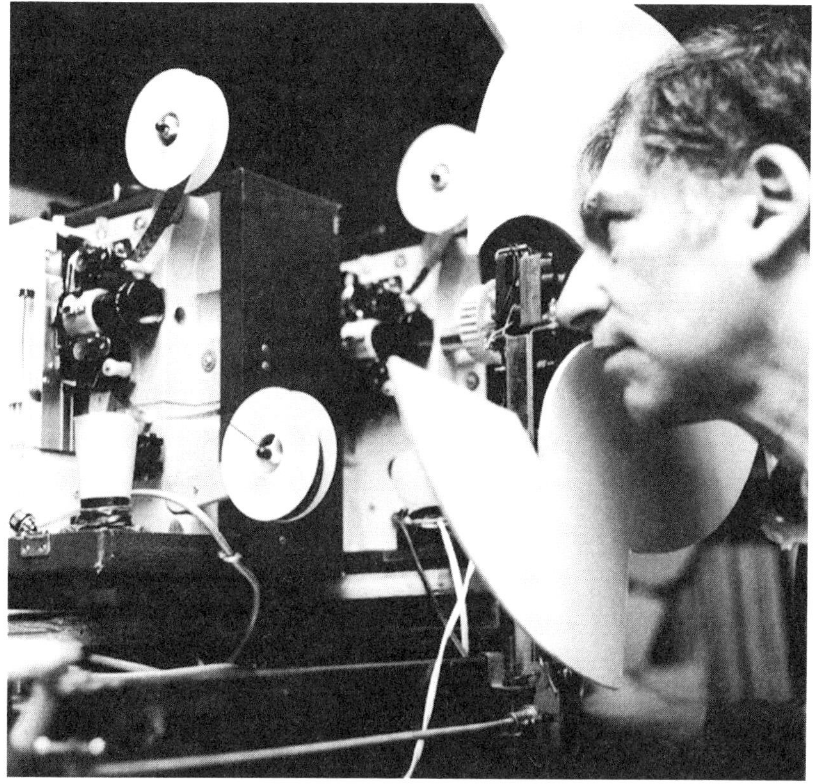

FIGURE 17.2. Ken Jacobs and projector apparatus for the Nervous System. Courtesy of Ken Jacobs.

simply on the mind's power to process the images by itself). Jacobs is the only major filmmaker to consistently mine the untapped potential of 3-D illusion on the screen.

But if the Nervous System undermines the common 24 frames per second seamless illusion of motion on which almost all cinema depends, it never becomes a series of static images. The possibility of motion haunts these trembling images, and Jacobs uncovers a range of illusions of motion in the interstices of film frames. Not only is the moment of transition in human gestures or the sweep of nature agonizingly prolonged and probed, the miracle of transformation from still to motion takes place before our eyes. The Nervous System overcomes Zeno's paradox as motion is built up out of infinitely small increments. Further, manipulations of shutter and projector position often create truly paradoxical experiences of motion as the screen itself seems to rotate slightly or its surface becomes convulsed by a sudden ripple. These images flow and ebb before us, inviting us into their depths or looming out from the screen to meet us. The trajectory of motion pauses, reverses itself, breaks down and reconstitutes itself. Here, after nearly a century, are true *motion pictures* in which motion is never taken for granted but continually encountered in a flux and reflux of perception.

Jacobs's 3-D movies rarely aim at a lifelike illusion (although a few films, such as *Globe*, do invoke it in an ironic fashion). The Nervous System performances don't even use films originally shot in 3-D. Instead Jacobs creates a strange vacillating illusion of three dimensions through his projection process. Rather than being subjected to an illusion, we watch the perceptual process itself evolve. A strange trembling image takes shape before us, seeming always on the verge of breaking into motion or transforming into a steady three-dimensional illusion. But it hesitates, shivering before us, and seems to break down into the basic units of time and motion, space and objects.

The Nervous System plays on our nervous system. Jacobs not only operates his analytical projectors, he also hooks into our most primal processes of perception. Our basic ability to perceive figure and ground, movement out of stillness, to synthesize space and time are played with, as though we were hot-wired to the screen. Space, motion, time, and imagery dance before us, eternally breaking apart and coming together. The Nervous System makes great demands on its audience. It focuses our awareness on processes that are usually unconscious, on our own mental contribution to the images on the screen, synthesizing frames into motion and patterns of light and shadow into space. Never has the position of the film spectator been so perilous, the sutures holding the subject/viewer to the screen so radically unstitched.

Jacobs opens a window onto perception and calls into question the coherence of our position as viewers and masters of vision. The effect is both exhilarating and frightening. In becoming aware of our role in making the moving image we also realize the power the apparatus has over us. I have never watched a Nervous System performance without the vertiginous sensation that I was teetering out of control on the brink of some primal threshold. One begins to synthesize spaces that make no sense (the moments in all the films when foreground and background seem to change places), and to envision images that aren't truly there (the monstrous faces that seem to materialize in the flames of the "wall of death" stunt that opens *The Whole Shebang*).

This process of breaking down the film image into its basic elements (which Jacobs first explored in *Tom Tom the Piper's Son* through frame-by-frame projection and rephotography, combined with magnification of the image down to its grain) coheres with the central concerns of modernist painting. Jacobs began as a painter in the era of abstract expressionism, and both cubism and the ideas of his teacher Hans Hofmann exert a strong influence on the push/pull of space in the Nervous System works. But as important as modernist painting is as an inspiration (and, for those confused by Jacobs's films, as a sort of guide to the perceptual play he invites), the cinematic apparatus remains central. Jacobs never simply undermines the filmic illusion in order to reach a sort of neutral material. He is always making movies, dealing with the intricacies of illusion even as he unmasks them.

Likewise, although these performances uncover essential structures beneath film viewing, they are never merely abstract. Specific images anchor our experience, whether it is the marching American colonial troops in *The Philippines Adventure* or the spurt of orgasm in *XCXHXEXRXRXIXEXSX*. At the same time as he probes the illusion of the moving image, Jacobs uses his apparatus to investigate this record of human behavior. These films never rest on the level of phenomenal play but become profoundly historical works, aware not only of the celluloid surface of the original films, but of their place in history and culture as well. As with *Perfect Film*, the events these films record are reclaimed by Jacobs's method, liberated from structures that were often meant to obscure them. In *The Philippines Adventure*, for instance, the official handshakes between American presidents and representatives of the Filipino people are revealed by the Nervous System as predatory gestures, their essential aggression unmasked by the fracturing of motion.

IV. THE ULTIMATE PARADOX: TELLING TIME

> Time is a river that sweeps me along, but I am the river; it is a tiger which destroys me, but I am the tiger; it is a fire which consumes me, but I am the fire.
>
> JORGE LUIS BORGES, "A NEW REFUTATION OF TIME"

> The only thing that begins by reflecting itself is history. And this fold, this furrow, is the Jew.
>
> JACQUES DERRIDA, "EDMOND JABÈS AND THE QUESTION OF THE BOOK"

While Jacobs derives inspiration from the push/pull of modernist painting, the dimensions of movement continuously propel him into the realm of movies and into a confrontation with the most essential yet slippery property of film—time. While the linear trajectory of narrative seems to exhaust the range of times available to commercial cinema, Jacobs offers a full temporal menu. The Nervous System performances, in their hesitation and prolonged stutter between frames, frequently evoke a time stuck in the groove, a nightmare of endless repetition. As if freeing themselves from some metaphysical mud, the figures in a Nervous System piece often seem caught in the cycles of the same motion. But in the midst of this repetition, one begins to sense the moment of change as the returning flow of time becomes palpable. We skate on the intervals between moments, experiencing time's weight and its release as never before.

Equally important, Jacobs occasionally celebrates an empty, "sitting-around" time, captured so eloquently in his *Little Stabs at Happiness*, made up of 100 foot rolls as they came out of the camera. Jacobs once evoked in conversation the image of a cave family sitting around on a rainy Stone Age day peering out into the drizzle, as the type of essential human time history so often loses track of. While commercial movies seem designed to evoke anxious expectations of an oncoming ending, Jacobs hopes to tune his viewers into the richness of the times that lie between. A moment which promises neither climax nor delay, but which possesses its own weight and presence, provides a utopian image of happiness in a number of Jacobs films.

But time in Jacobs's films also involves a complex transaction between the immediate present moment of watching and the distanced past of the film image itself. Nearly every Jacobs film displays its pastness, whether by the actual marks of wear on the print (scratches and dirt particles on the original material play complex and paradoxical roles in the three-dimensional illusions of the Nervous System films) or the sense of history they capture. As the Nervous System pieces and *Tom Tom the Piper's Son* demonstrate, time can be taken apart, our whole perception of it altered, but it cannot be ignored. Jacobs lacks the romantic's thirst for eternity, and his films constitute a recurring critique of the attempt to deny time. Rather than a liberation, denying the many dimensions of time (or restricting it to only one) becomes an act of oppression.

What Marey (a scientist seeking timeless principles and hoping to wrest a system from the apparent randomness of motion) could foresee about moving pictures was their eventual role as the memory of the twentieth century. The relation between cinema and memory stands at the center of Jacobs's films and asserts its final paradox. Jacobs is well aware that cinema can be the enemy of memory as much as its embodiment. This paradox is ancient. Plato in the *Phaedrus* repeated the legend that when

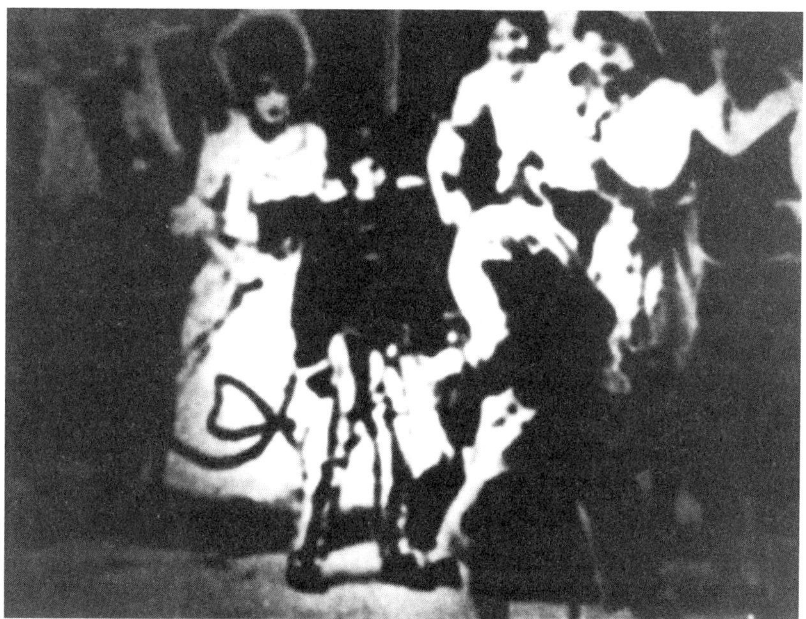

FIGURE 17.3. Ken Jacobs, *Tom, Tom, the Piper's Son* (1969).

Thoth introduced writing as a boon to memory, he was rebuked by the king of Egypt, who recognized that, in fact, writing would bring forgetfulness, since men would now rely on the written reminder and neglect the living memory within them. In the twentieth century the deluge of photographic images has deadened our ability to see, and the constant imaging of the past threatens our experience of memory at the root. Things are filmed and recorded in order to be forgotten.

But where danger is, there grows salvation also. Jacobs realizes that these images of the past need not serve only as inert matter, or as totalizing versions of the past. Unlike the written text, film images may be interrogated, not only to reveal their falsity, but to unearth their hidden truth as well. Jacobs crawls inside the images he finds, and reveals that the camera really did catch it all—provided we know where and how to look. Psychoanalysis, too, involves an art of memory, the excavation of those things not only forgotten but repressed from consciousness. In both Freud and Jacobs, the process of recovery never regains the full embodied presence that commercial cinema seems to deliver, but a fragmented story and a consciousness of loss. With this acknowledgment of loss, the past becomes part of our conscious history, and the wounds of time are acknowledged, if not healed. The past exists only in remnants.

Jacobs once characterized his role as filmmaker as a dealer in remnants. He jokingly (seriously) described it as part of his ethnic heritage, becoming a retailer of other people's discards, recycling the garbage of the culture. Jacobs's wit here cuts in several directions. Referring most obviously to his use of found footage, this invocation of his Jewish identity resonates with multiple meanings. Forced into the peripheries of society, Jews have always found unexpected uses for those things the culture did not value. From the Orchard Street merchant in fabric remnants, to the turn-of-the-century Jewish immigrants who invested in the disreputable movie business, to Sigmund Freud's valuing of the discards of conscious life (dreams and slips of the tongue), the Jew has survived by converting the marginal into the essential.

But for Jacobs, remnants primarily speak of time. Remnants are the remains, what is left over, what has survived in a marginal state. Remnants are the traces of time past, of events passed on, the crumbs from the feast. But like the trickster in Jewish legend who makes soup from a stone, Jacobs understands the feast that can be made on what others discard. It is a feast to which he invites us all, freely. And so let us sit and eat. But be sure you have good teeth.

18

Towards a Minor Cinema: Fonoroff, Herwitz, Ahwesh, LaPore, Klahr, and Solomon

> There is nothing that is major or revolutionary except the minor. To hate all languages of masters.
>
> GILLES DELEUZE AND FÉLIX GUATTARI, *Kafka:Towards a Minor Literature*

Something is happening around here, as if avant-garde filmmaking has suddenly gained a new influx of energy and reached a sort of critical mass, a thaw of previously congealed energies. The controversy around the recent avant-garde-film-conference-as-post-mortem in Toronto served the truly vital purpose of a sudden stock-taking which led to a new consciousness of both how vital the new avant-garde is, and also how new it is. Overviews are not yet possible. Rather than an aerial perspective, I offer a glimpse grabbed in transit, a partial view tied to the specificity of a moment, subject to change and revision, and limited to a particular perspective in space and time. There is a great deal of new work that I have not seen (most importantly, everyone tells me, the work of Leslie Thornton), and some I have not seen enough. (I am deeply indebted to Lewis Klahr for cuing me into this new atmosphere and for tracking down works I should see.) Nor do I claim that the filmmakers I am going to discuss represent the only currently vital approach. Nor do they form a school with a unified aesthetic. They cut across genres and differ in techniques. However, there are a number of

This essay first appeared in *Motion Picture* 3, nos. 1–2 (Winter 1989–1990): 2–5.

attitudes that unite them, not the least of which is their freshness, their distance from the dominant films of the last two decades. Most importantly, I count these films among the strongest works I have seen in many years, tapping new sources in the constant discovery of cinema that constitutes avant-garde filmmaking. Although I will be concentrating on a small number of films due to space, I want to indicate my enthusiasm for the filmmakers I will treat more generally. I hope in the future to discuss in more detail such important films as Peggy Ahwesh's *Martina's Playhouse*, Nina Fonoroff's *A Knowledge We Can Not Lose*, and Peter Herwitz's *Musique de Ténèbres*.

But what do I mean by a minor cinema? Am I simply proposing a group of relatively talented filmmakers? Have I bought Fred Camper's thesis that avant-garde filmmaking has plunged into a downward spiral and decided to name a number of *petite maîtres*? On the contrary. I intend to answer Camper's thoughtful essay in the terms it lays down—by proposing a number of films and filmmakers that rate serious consideration—and, at the same time, to challenge his ground rules. But, a *minor* cinema? Am I aligning myself with Tony Conrad's and others' objection to Camper's view of decline by doing away with the criteria of masterworks? Not really. While I am uncomfortable with the mastery implied in masterworks, I am by no means jettisoning evaluation. I am extremely excited by these filmmakers and believe in the beauty, profundity, and complexity of their works. I borrow my term "minor cinema" from Deleuze and Guattari's study of Kafka, for them an exemplar of minor literature. Minor literature remains exiled from a major literature (e.g., Kafka, a Jew writing in German in Prague), and forswears aspiration to mastery. Minor literature remains aware of, and celebrates, its marginal identity, fashioning from it a revolutionary consciousness. I believe that these filmmakers profoundly understand their place in film history and in the economic realities of film distribution and exhibition. These films assert no vision of conquest, make no claims to hegemony. A minor cinema reshapes our image of the avant-garde, moving away from its image of shock troop battalions. The challenge mounted by a minor cinema calls into question the terms in which the future of the avant-garde has been theorized in recent decades.

THE END OF THE "INTERNATIONAL STYLE" IN AVANT GARDE FILM

Let's start with what's being left behind. The forms of avant-garde filmmaking which seemed still dominant, even if only by inertia, in 1987 (when

Paul Arthur wrote his important overview of the movement since 1966), Structural Film and New Narratives, could not contrast more sharply with the films I am highlighting here. Contemplating the residual energies of Structural Film in the late 1980s, it comes as no surprise that a number of people, critics and filmmakers, pronounced the avant-garde dead. Seeming an extremely imitable form, Structural Film proved the most fugitive of models, as the true complexities of the masterpieces of Michael Snow, Ernie Gehr, Hollis Frampton, and Ken Jacobs eluded their epigones. By the mid-1980s, Structural Film had become something like an International Style, its minimalist lines seemingly adaptable to any content. In contrast to the profoundly exploratory films (frequently much less systematic than their descriptions indicate) of Snow, George Landow, Frampton, Larry Gottheim, Gehr, or Jacobs, later minimalist filmmaking became a style, a "look."

In fact, the filial relation Arthur traced between Structural Film and the New Narrative resulted from the fact that this new look eventually found itself searching for a content. New Narratives laid impersonal minimalist strategies over a largely verbal engagement with Serious Ideas (with footnotes to sources frequently provided at the end of the film or in program notes). While some challenging work came out of this juxtaposition (Yvonne Rainer), even it seemed to be contemplating its own dead end. In recent years the evident exhaustion of the form moved from an intermittently compelling film like Benning's *Landscape Suicide* (which heats up Structural landscapes with tabloid murder accounts) to an occasionally infuriating film like Errol Morris's *The Thin Blue Line* (which uses minimalist techniques underscored by Philip Glass to cool down a *60 Minutes* exposé into an art film). For someone like myself, who decades ago embraced the American avant-garde as a truly subversive alternative to the culturally acceptable pretensions of art house cinema à la *L'Avventura*, it was a shock to find it suddenly aspiring to the respectability of intellectual subject matter treated in coolly dispassionate imagery.

A CINEMA OF RESTRICTION BUT NOT MINIMALISM

Much alternative filmmaking and theory of the past decade declared its intention to break down the ghetto of avant-garde film. The recent films that I find exciting proudly wear the badge of the ghetto. This is a dangerous statement, of course, and I can already predict its misuses. I adamantly am *not* saying that these are films that know their place and keep within it.

But I am saying that these are films that recognize their marginal identity and consciously maintain a position outside the major cinematic languages (including, *pace* Paul Arthur, television), even when—especially when—they make reference to them. The ghetto is not an ivory tower, and it finds an antiseptic, hermetic isolation impossible. The tremors of history are felt with redoubled intensity within the ghetto (as Deleuze and Guattari say, in a minor literature everything becomes political, especially that which seems most personal). Minor cinema recognizes—cannot ignore—the existence of another cinema. Its attitude is both creatively parasitic (e.g., the use of found footage) and insistently oppositional (none of these filmmakers dream of a commercial breakthrough film—breakthrough to what?). But these filmmakers also manifest no desire to supplant dominant cinema. The millennium in which everyone goes to see *The Art of Vision* on Saturday night has been indefinitely postponed. In the meantime (and this is a cinema of *mean times* as much as it is of the ghetto) these filmmakers practice and perfect their own language of images, a language which, while new, also develops the richest traditions of avant-garde cinema.

A minor culture (that is, a culture with a marginal existence within a dominant culture) redefines the cast-offs of the masters, from the Caribbean musician fashioning steel drums from oil containers, to the Black DJ manhandling turntables, to the generations of immigrant junk dealers and bricoleurs that have populated Canal Street. Embracing Super-8 filming long after video dislodged it from the bosom of the family and the kit bags of documentarians, many of these new filmmakers proclaim their resistance to the onslaught of technical progress. Certainly economies dictate here, but stern necessity has bred an affection for the limits of their medium rather than frustration. In the films of Nina Fonoroff, Lewis Klahr, Peggy Ahwesh, Peter Herwitz, and Mark LaPore, the almost tactile surface of Super-8 film creates an experience at odds with the monumentality of much of the previous avant-garde. This encounter with the limits of the medium differs markedly from Brakhage's use of visible splices or film flares as metaphors of vision, or the Structuralist celebration of film's material self-reflexivity. But an exploitation of film's new identity as an endangered species need not be restricted to a use of Super-8. Phil Solomon's work in 16mm, in spite of the complexity and perfection of its optical printing, seems to put his found images through a wringer, torturing and diverting the light which composes them into a demonstration of the fragility of moving images, their fundamentally transient nature. Painting or scratching the film surface in the work of Ahwesh and Herwitz, while pioneered by Brakhage, seems less to supply metaphors for closed eye vision, or an anti-illusionist demonstration of the film surface, than to physically puncture the skin of the film, exposing its tactile and frangible nature.

A RETURN TO MONTAGE AND THE "NARRATIVE" OF IMAGES

A return to Brakhage seems evident in many of these filmmakers, although it is a return with a difference (there is nothing "minor" about Brakhage's work, with the possible exception of the 8mm Songs, which ultimately teetered back into monumentality with *My Mountain* and *Twenty-Third Psalm Branch*). While there are undoubtedly intermediary influences here (such as Saul Levine and Dan Barnett, neglected figures who served as mentors for several of these filmmakers), many of these films return to montage, showing a concern for a flow and rhythm of imagery and a language of juxtaposition that recall the founding generation of American avant-garde filmmakers. Nearly all these filmmakers pitch a great deal of energy into the creation of complex rhythms of motion and highly structured syntagms of images. Fonoroff's *A Knowledge We Can Not Lose*, Herwitz's *Mysterious Barricades*, LaPore's *Medina*, and Solomon's *The Secret Garden* all create a synthesis of movement and tempo that remained taboo in either Structural Film or New Narratives. (Again, works by Gottheim, Gehr, and Snow and the Nervous System performances of Ken Jacobs explore these elements in ways the later minimalists avoided, while the non-Structuralist work of Abigail Child and Warren Sonbert—and others—certainly kept it alive through the 1980s.)

Another lesson from Brakhage can be sensed in the highly meaningful flow of images in these films. Whereas New Narratives restricted the narrative function to dialogue and performances, and tended to oppose it to visual stylistics (following a rather humorless interpretation of the witty structure of *Wavelength*), these films often seem to follow a narrative so densely interwoven with the visualization of each image that it defies complete comprehension. Such films as Klahr's *Morning Films*, Solomon's *The Secret Garden*, and LaPore's *The Sleepers* seem to carry submerged narratives, like those which impel many of Brakhage's longer films. Plots stir just beneath the threshold of perceptibility. The sea swells of these subliminal stories align images into meaningful but often indecipherable configurations. The films invite the reader/detective to pursue the thread of narrative, but no closure is promised, no final answer lies behind the veil. While Bette Gordon managed to create in *Variety* a film noir without any sense of mystery, Klahr's *In the Month of Crickets* fashions a noir world in which one searches for clues to the story itself.

But if Brakhage offered lessons in rhythm, montage, and the devious language of imagery, these films open onto a different landscape. The skeleton key to so much of Brakhage, the sense of the filmmaker behind the camera, does not open many of these films. They are certainly personal films, but for the most part they probe the hieroglyphics of imagery rather then the depths of the self. Fonoroff and Herwitz relate to an autobiographical lyrical tradition, but the driving impulse of their films probes a world they haven't made, rather than creating one out of the Romantic Ego. Fonoroff's attempt to understand her father's life and death in *A Knowledge We Can Not Lose* constantly encounters a check, as the film meditates on the paradoxical union of meaninglessness and significance in the images she has gathered. The film questions the possibility of emotional expression through film while it attempts it. Likewise, Herwitz's films (which most closely resemble the romantic lyricism of Brakhage) constantly acknowledge the ways his imagery falls short of ecstasy, as images of possible liberation (the flight of birds, the gestures of lovers) are curtailed by cutting and rendered conditional. The image, rather than the Self, dominates in minor cinema. This nearly epistemological impulse moves Ahwesh and LaPore toward documentary, but a documentary filmmaking in which the language of images never becomes subjugated to the objectivity of fact. Ahwesh's manipulation of the celluloid surface constantly filters the reality she records, a reality which itself is composed of role-playing, performance, and attempts at seduction of the filmmaker and audience.

THREE FILMS

LaPore's Sudan Trilogy: Medina, Work and Play, The Sleepers

Mark LaPore's trilogy dealing with his experience in the Sudan balances extremely assertive camera movement and juxtaposition of images, in *Medina*, with fixed camera position and unedited camera rolls, in *Work and Play*. Yet both apparent minimalism and hyperactivity display a humility before the world they encounter. Neither the unsteady movement that scans the folds of a garment in *Medina* nor the fixed camera position that frames girls gathering firewood in *Work and Play* function as self-conscious formal gestures. They are varying methods of engaging the rhythms and forms of an endangered culture. The shifting camera movements in *Medina* pursue a shallow tactile space of the hand rather than a deep perspective of the eye, as their lateral motions caress surface patterns and textures. LaPore never tries to process this world, exerting the pressure of close-up and cutting to make it yield information in the mode of traditional ethnographic documentaries. Even the apparent self-effacement of the unedited, fixed shots of *Work and Play* (which followed certain principles of ethnographic information gathering) strike one as an aesthetic strategy in which (as in the films of Peter Hutton) the modesty of the technique allows a deeper participation in the enframed action.

The culminating film of the trilogy, *The Sleepers* (in my opinion one of the most powerful films of the last decade), while verging on the confessional, never loses sight of a world whose structures it must try to penetrate. The discourse quoted in the film, although profoundly insightful about the situation of precapitalist third world cultures in a period of global totalization of technology, are never simply illustrated by the images, which range from North Africa to New York's Chinatown. (What a contrast with Trinh Minh-ha's *Naked Spaces: Living Is Round*, in which images of African culture are made accessible by poetically intoned passages of "wisdom"). In this film LaPore speaks to the profound deterritorialization of the twentieth century in a way only a minor cinema could, neither documentary nor lyrical, neither diaristic nor didactic, but employing elements of all these discourses in order to weave a language of ambiguity and sensual specificity.

Klahr's Lost Camel Intentions

The cut-out animations of Lewis Klahr, with their technical poverty (this is animation that proudly displays its lack of professionalism—Klahr doesn't even use an animation stand—and recycling of cast-off images), could serve as an emblem of minor cinema. Although definitely owing a debt to the work of Harry Smith, Klahr's paper world avoids Smith's abstraction and metaphysical resonance. Rather than ascending to heaven, Klahr's cutouts endure the perils of adolescent adventure tales (plane crashes in the desert, murders of passion and lengthy jail terms, sexual blackmail plots). However, Klahr rarely opts merely for the quick return of condescending irony or camp. His total lack of illusionism, combined with shifting patterns of identity and barely graspable narrative events, create a nightmarish sensation of being trapped in a fictional world one can never comprehend or fully believe in, but whose consequences seem dire. Klahr's submerged narratives breed both paranoia and a zany euphoria, as a series of cultural icons and an unstoppable narrative drive compel viewer involvement. In *Lost Camel*

Intentions, the first film of his cycle *Tales of the Forgotten Future*, his skeleton protagonist journeys from a desert plane wreck to what appears to be a United States car dealership. Klahr's black-and-white landscapes and the persistence of his main character through physical metamorphosis and geographic displacement offer a tabletop odyssey of immigration and acculturation.

Beyond this archetypal ancestral legend, *Lost Camel Intentions* draws on adolescent masculine guilt and embarrassment. As soon as the skeleton gains flesh and escapes the desert, he gets a boner, ridiculously prominent as he walks the streets of an art deco city. But you can take the nomad out of the desert more easily than you can root him in a newfound home. Metamorphosized into cutout snapshots of Klahr's grandfather, the protagonist dwells in a new world primarily composed of road maps. This world fills with automobiles, which provide him with emblems of masculine potency, a site for erotic encounters, and, most importantly, the means of a quick getaway. Deflecting found images from their original univocality, Klahr maps out a fantasized past as well as a forgotten future, fraying the linearity of narrative into a network of metaphors, visual puns, and submerged primal scenes.

Solomon's The Secret Garden

Klahr and Phil Solomon share a fascination with childhood and adolescent fantasy and tap into dreams' multivalent imagery and shifting structure. Compared to the arid, ascetic black and white of *Lost Camel*, *The Secret Garden* is a sensual festival of color and tropical lushness. Yet Solomon's garden holds more terrors than Klahr's desert. Solomon threatens not only the biblical expulsion (images of Dorothy from *The Wizard of Oz* picking forbidden fruit and of the downward tumble of Jack and Jill are the most recognizable iconography in the film) but the more terrifying possibility of confinement and burial within the claustrophobic imaginary of childhood. Solomon evokes, as few filmmakers have, childhood fantasy's incommunicable guilt, rage, and sense of abandonment.

Solomon's debt to Brakhage seems evident in his ecstatic delight in color and in the pure stuff of vision which emerges when imagery escapes the confines of recognition. But Solomon replaces the immediacy of Brakhage's first-person lyricism with the mediation of storytelling. A sequence near the beginning of the film (and returned to recurringly) shows a bedridden boy being spoken to by an adult and, at points, another child. Subtitles from this footage intone the ritual "Once upon a time" of a bedtime story whose verbal fragments invoke both a mysterious past and a promised future. The film initially interweaves this dominantly monochromatic scene of storytelling with startling color footage that seems to envision the secret garden the subtitled story mentions.

As the film moves toward its ending, the framing story becomes contaminated by the intensity and violence of the colorful fairytale it served to contain, as melodramatic action unfolds under veils of optical manipulation. The interrelation of tale and telling implied by the film's structure, as well as its extraordinary transmutation of found footage, gives *The Secret Garden* a turbulent narrative thrust, as if Solomon were both fascinated and repelled by the fable of innocence and betrayal he spins. The final image of the film, a glance out toward the audience by the boy (the original auditor of the tale of the secret garden), pierces the screen with a violated vulnerability and a silent accusation. It also serves as an emblem for the belated quality of minor cinema, its struggle with the promises and deceptions of the dominant narrative cinema.

The dominant cinema of the past decades, both in Hollywood and the avant-garde, has been the cinema of the Concept. The minor cinema, whose advent I am celebrating, as Deleuze and Guattari say of minor literature, "begins by expressing itself and doesn't conceptualize until afterward." These six filmmakers form no school, nor do they propose a method. They share, however, a concern for the expressivity of images and a moment in history. As well as a freshness, richness, and, I believe, promise for the future.

19

Perspective and Retrospective: The Films of Ernie Gehr

A cause for celebration: three new films by Ernie Gehr that mark an especially fruitful period of Gehr's life, and a retrospective which allows us to put these new works in perspective. Only a handful of filmmakers working today have established an oeuvre as consistent in quality and unswerving in purpose, or as sure of enduring as key works in film history. New works by Gehr transform our sense of earlier works, as each film sets up a play of reflection among the earlier ones, illuminating previous areas of obscurity and revealing new aspects of what we thought we knew. For as different as Gehr's films are from each other (and these new films show an astonishing variation in method and imagery), they converge on a common project and exploration. Few filmmakers have been as persistent in pursuing an essential mystery at the root of the cinematic process, a mystery involving the way the internal life of film itself interacts with the internal life of the viewer.

This essay first appeared in *Films of Ernie Gehr* (San Francisco Cinémathèque, March 1993), with the following acknowledgments: "I want to thank Ernie Gehr for his patience in answering my questions with such insight; the San Francisco Cinematheque for commissioning this catalogue essay and Steve Anker for reading it with care; Ann Harris at the Department of Cinema Studies at NYU, M. M. Serra of the Film-Makers' Cooperative, Millennium, Janie Geyser, Lewis Klahr, and Mark LaPore all for helping me see films." It also included the following dedication: "I would like to dedicate this essay to Myrel and Daniel Gehr."

I. THE SECRET LIFE OF MACHINES

Infinite surprises within a finite frame

ROBERT BRESSON

Gehr has placed a confrontation with this mystery at the beginning of his work as a filmmaker. After making some early 8mm films in a manner that he felt he could not continue with, Gehr decided to stop. In an interview in the early 1970s, Gehr recounted, "The thing that did it, that actually stopped me, was suddenly facing the camera on the tripod, standing there, and really being puzzled by what *it* had to do with what I was trying to do." This essential check led to the central intuition of Gehr's early work, which continues to animate his work today although in a transformed manner: that cinema itself, the whole apparatus, lives a secret life of its own. Gehr undertook an exploration of the very intricacies of that alien object which confronted him as a filmmaker and which he could no longer see simply as a tool for the expression of something else, whether story, idea, or emotion. Each of his films explored aspects of this secret life of the machine and the way its elements act upon each other: the pliant transparent celluloid; the light-sensitive and therefore unstable emulsion; the camera with its device to move the film past the lens at different speeds of intermittent motion; the lens with its ability to gather and shape incoming light; and the projector with its speeds and lens designed to reanimate the previously imprinted stains of light, enlarging, blocking, and pulling at the beam of illumination.

Ironically, many viewers and critics saw this work as minimalist, when in fact Gehr was uncovering through the interlocking aspects of cinema intensely dramatic and elaborate processes. Take *History* (1970). If one simply read a description of this film, it could seem the ultimate minimalist work or even a neo-dada joke. Gehr made this film without a lens in the camera, so that the exposed film registered no representational image at all, simply the dance of emulsion as it was eaten up by light and digested by processing. Although this might sound like the driest conception of conceptual art, when projected on the screen, the drama of this process astonishes. Certainly this nearly infinite and constantly renewing dance of threads of darkness and points of light evokes cosmic imagery, as if one were witnessing the birth of stars and night, or the primal chaos before the demiurge separated darkness from light. But this is more than a mystical

Rorschach test. One soon realizes that the process one is watching makes no metaphorical claim, but rather it *demonstrates*. We are actually seeing, not the cosmos but, as Gehr described it, "Film in its primordial state in which patterns of light and darkness—planes—are still undivided." We need not reach here for an image beyond history or language; we see directly the pulsing of film's secret life, a rhythm that invisibly underlies the processing of every film ever made. Gehr is no more minimalist than an X-ray is, and this film is no joke.

History establishes one of the central rules of Gehr's work: that an almost ascetic paring down of means can yield a nearly infinite return in perceptual riches. In any number of Gehr's films we find this pattern: a simplicity of form or approach will lead to a discovery of variation and complexity that was unsuspected. And this takes many forms. For instance, an almost anecdotal example from one of the new films, *Side/Walk/Shuttle*. After viewing this succession of high-angle moving cityscapes twice, I was sure from the absolute lack of repetition of landscape compositions that Gehr had shot the film in a variety of locations. However, after watching it several more times and painstakingly noting landmarks within the frame, I discovered what Gehr confirmed to me, that all the shots were taken at the same site, with a constant exploration of new vantage points within it continually renewing each composition with a sense of discovery.

This understanding of cinema as the locus of an endlessly renewed process of discovery profoundly links Gehr's work to early cinema. Like the first cameramen, Gehr focuses on the novelty of cinema, its ability to present a world previously unseen by us, and he maintains early film's fascination with motion in relation to the edges of the frame. His treatment of a turn-of-the-century actuality film in *Eureka* shows his affinity with the early cameraman's treatment of the dynamics of motion, as well as Gehr's own method of digesting and transforming it. The original film that supplied the material belonged to an early genre known as "panorama films," in which the camera captured views of a natural landscape or cityscape while mounted on some means of transportation: steamship, gondola, railway locomotive, or, as in this trip down San Francisco's Market Street, a trolley. The genre combined two dominant attractions of early films, the ability to transport the viewer to a different part of the world and a vivid experience of the defining innovation of the new invention, its ability to reproduce motion. Gehr's film optically prints the original footage, repeating frames (as well as eliminating some material), creating a sort of stuttered, nearly static, rhythm and extending the film's length while attenuating its pace.

Again a seemingly simple transformation actually multiplies awareness. First, slowing down the motion by reprinting individual frames interrupts the seemingly seamless illusion of motion that cinema introduced. But, paradoxically, rather than destroying the experience of motion, Gehr refocuses our attention on it, as we witness the continual birth of motion out of the succession of still frames. Thus by inverting and nearly destroying the illusion of motion (that is, making us aware of individual frames rather than losing them in the blur of motion), Gehr allows us to reexperience its miraculous dimension, its perceptual surprise. *Eureka* returns us to the position of those first audiences of Lumière's invention who exclaimed with delight as the projected image lurched into motion.

In addition, Gehr's slow pace directs our attention to each change within the frame, allowing us to scan each new bit of information. Noël Burch and Ken Jacobs have commented on the uncentered nature of early cinema, in which any part of the frame became a potential site of information and excitement. This was nowhere more true than in early street-scene films where filmmakers pointed the camera and all of urban life rushed into the shot. Again Gehr's transformation allows us to experience this film as an early audience might have, not simply as a trolley car trajectory with an endpoint in view (although I will return to this aspect of the film), but as an almost encyclopedic survey of visual attractions: the means of urban transportation, the gait and carriage of city folk, written signs and bits of advertising, and the procession of architecture. The camera's frame seems to suck in eyecatching material like a magnet, and then to disperse it beyond its four corners.

Gehr's filmmaking, then, was not inspired by a pursuit of minimal form or a desire for modernist self-reflexivity. Rather, he discovered in the extreme complexity of this late nineteenth-century device, the Cinématographe, a cunningly made little world with its own laws and possibilities whose exploration had only begun. The camera and projector provided means to constantly manipulate and control its raw material of motion, light and time, creating, instead of a representation, a process of transformation and balance directly visible on the screen. This secret life of the machine was visible within the dance of particles of emulsion, as well as in a decades-old recording of the street life of old San Francisco, or an aerial animation of modern San Francisco's skyline. However, as full of surprise and energy as this secret life is, Gehr accesses it through acts of *ascesis*, refusing the immediate possibilities of representation the motion picture camera delivers. The discoveries Gehr offers are purchased by acts of constriction, a focusing of attention through techniques of discipline, concentration, and silence. Infinity is only reached by a thorough mining of the finite.

II. FINDING A PLACE

> Stillness and stimulation around which consciousness oscillates as well as film . . .
>
> ERNIE GEHR, 1971

There is nothing mechanical—that is, predictable and inert—about Gehr's exploration of the machine. In that founding confrontation between Gehr and this mechanism on a tripod, the question Gehr posed himself was what the camera had to do with the filmmaker's own intentions. The secret life that Gehr discovered profoundly involved the relation between the machine's processes and the processes of human consciousness. Once again, *History* provides a vivid example. Rather than a conceptual demonstration of self-reflexivity, this brew of film particles provides an experience, as the life of chemical interactions sparks the life of the mind. As you watch *History*, nothing concrete appears for you to grab onto, except the ceaseless change of light on the screen. But you inhabit that mottled space, or try to, the mind trying to keep up with its unpredictable patterns. As Gehr said in an interview, "But the changes that are taking place on the screen are not—or are they?—the same as the ones going on in the mind." Again the image on the screen is not a metaphor for mental processes, or a representation, but rather a stimulus to thought, one which parallels and diverges from the patterns of mental life. This roiling energy of light and time without configuration both resists and engages a series of mental processes as we watch it. It recalls the description a Buddhist text, the *Hekiganroku*, gives of the consciousness of a newborn baby, "like a ball thrown in the rapids, do you know where it is carried?"

One always tries to find one's place in Gehr's films, and this process plays a key role in watching and understanding them. Even though the landscapes of Gehr's films vary enormously, finding one's footing within them remains a constant challenge and pleasure. In the films of the early 1970s, the floor often seems to give way beneath one's feet, as Gehr creates a radically nonperspectival space "in which a finite orientation seems impossible." However, even within his most nonrepresentational films, such as *History* and *Field*, Gehr refuses to let our vision rest within a flat space. Not only does the swirl of grain in *History* invoke an infinite space, but the right of the frame (where light leaked through to the film stock) creates an edge of clear light, and gives an almost humorous impression of three-dimensional molding to the bubbling mass of emulsion magma. Part of the interaction between the life of the mind and the processes of film in *History* lies in what Gehr describes as "the struggle for space form."

Likewise, although the unbelievably rapid and consistent camera movement in *Field* reduces the image to bands of contrasting gray in which no place can ever be recognized, one never loses the sense of motion transforming space. The screen never becomes a comfortable pattern of striation, like a malfunctioning TV set. Although one can not always determine even the direction of the movement (which changes without signal and can seem radically different depending on where you focus attention—a tilt of the head, for instance, can totally change your sense of spatial flow), the presence of a world streaked with speed never disappears. Cinema's intricate possibilities of representation and transformation encounter perception's inner need to see in three dimensions, our own struggle for space-form and need to place ourselves in relation to what we see. But by blocking the automatic nature of such perceptual processes, Gehr focuses us on them in a dynamic and sensuous manner.

Although Gehr returned gloriously to nonperspectival space in *Mirage* (in which the diagonal black-and-white streaks of *Field* give way to lateral bands of unbelievable color), most of his later films seem rather to invoke perspective in an intense but often playful manner. *Serene Velocity* takes the most perverse orientation imaginable toward perspectival space by shooting down a recessive hallway from a centered position so that the converging orthogonals etch a central X into the frame. The central vanishing point, the doors at corridor's end, have been considerately marked with an exit sign. But if the viewer's gaze is strongly solicited, if not channeled, down this path of exit, the structure of the film (alternating every four frames—or fourth of a second—between different focal settings) constantly yanks the viewer into and out of this depth. As the difference between sequential lens settings increases, the viewer is hard pressed to maintain a coherent sense of depth or even hold onto the constancy of objects on the screen. The exit sign ceases swelling and deflating in a comic puffing rhythm, but emerges threateningly in the most telephoto setting and then retreats to near nothingness. Although *Serene Velocity* asserts a nearly mechanical rhythm lacking in Gehr's other work, the predictability of its structure once again leads to unpredictable results, moving from a familiar inhabitable space that seems to pulse gently, to a nightmare of disorientation as we experience both thrust and resistance to this tunnel-like space of classical depth.

Untitled (1977) also explores the contradictions of the apparent penetration of space that perspective seems to offer through the dynamic of the film lens. But here, rather than the aggressive and rather contradictory effects of the zoom lens, Gehr deals with a gradually changing plane of focus. We begin with a nearly undefinable image—a sense of motion and color, that's about all. Slowly the focus sharpens and we recognize a swirl of snow with an undefined color mass beyond. As the focus continues to change, the zone of recognizability stretches further into the background, until the soft color mass solidifies into a firm brick wall. We have crept across the space of the frame as focus allowed us to define objects until we meet this sudden barrier in the distance. Its final recognizability allows us to construct this deep space, but also immediately confines and closes it down.

Eureka, as well, journeys into deep space, as the converging orthogonals of Market Street and the towering Ferry Building at the terminus supply (as in *Serene Velocity*) a prominently marked vanishing point. But the energy of the film pulls against simple targeted penetration. While the trolley car–borne camera proceeds unswervingly toward its goal, life pours in and out of the edges of the frame, vanishing and intruding. The reprinting of the film allows this lateral unstructured motion to nearly overwhelm the trolley's relentless but stuttered progress into the depth. Further, the printing briefly stills each frame so that the sense of its surface comes forward. Scratches and other marks of wear become as salient as the photographed happenings themselves, as much a sign of history as the outmoded styles of dress and transportation. Gehr undercuts the original film's implacable penetration of space by placing it in tension with these surface phenomena. And just as the freeze-and-release pattern of the reprinting of the film seems to alternately congeal and open up the space of the frame, this stop-and-start rhythm transforms our experience of time. One no longer reexperiences a past moment come to life, but rather the time elapsed between us and the film's original shooting becomes palpable. Temporal progression converges here into a sense of the past, as time becomes history.

While I have primarily dealt with the place we seek for while watching Gehr's films in spatial terms, temporal positioning plays an equally determinate role, allowing the motion in space I have described and the complex sense of progression. *Still*, one of Gehr's most subtle and evasive films, literally superimposes time and space to create ghostly encounters. *Still* consists of eight shots, all but the last of which are double exposures. Although the framing of the shots varies slightly, all present basically the same vantage point, looking across a lower Manhattan street to a luncheonette and furniture store on the other side, observing the traffic and flow of pedestrians both near the camera and across the street. Because the framing of the double exposure is identical (with the exception of one shot where a slight tilting of the camera moves the two images out of alignment), this quotidian street scene becomes criss-crossed with both opaque and transparent traffic and people. The transparent entities move convincingly on the solid surfaces, receding from the camera in perfect perspective, negotiating street and sidewalk with precision. Rather than behaving like dreamlike phantoms, these transparent beings fit perfectly into this everyday scene.

And they are part of it. Their visual permeability results from the camera's play with time, in which the second image registered makes a less vivid and substantial mark on the film. Like the scratches on the original footage used in *Eureka*, this crisscross of people and specters is the trace of time—of two times laid over each other. It invokes a phantasy of the street scene as itself a photographic surface, able to retain the trace of all the day's traffic, a synchronic image of accumulated life and passage. Seeing two times simultaneously within the same space splits our consciousness between different trajectories and expectations.

This collapse of separate times into one image creates another push/pull with the experience of depth. The superimpositions seem to lie *on top* (superimposed) of the image, yet they move into depth, creating what Gehr describes as a "teasing play with planes." But the play with space and position here involves more than tension between layers. The variations in light and shadow on the two levels cause the double exposures to pop in and out of depth. A shadow on the first level can give the superimposition a sudden burst of solidity. Gehr calls our attention to the multiplicity of depth cues that operate in a film in addition to perspective recession. The cue of overlap creates much of the amusement of the film, as the vehicles on one level plow through the phantoms on another, or cars fulfill a New Yorker's dream by parking on top or within each other. Gehr was particularly fascinated by the way the depth cues provided by color (with warm colors coming forward) interact with the logic of space as the red doors across the street seem at points to not only project through the passing phantoms, but even to be in front of more solid passersby.

We can not assume an assigned place before a Gehr film, ultimate positioning eludes us. But we never feel abandoned or ignored by these films. Instead, they directly solicit us to entertain a number of often contradictory positions, to try them out and switch between them. In this way Gehr explores the interaction between those processes of space, motion, and time inscribed in the cinematic machine and our own perceptual and mental processes. Gehr's game with forms of space explores possible contradictions and tensions and invites us to experience zones of place that remain for most of us *terra incognita*.

III. THE CITY

> . . . why the city, where people make the most ruthless demands on one another, where appointments and telephone calls, sessions and visits, flirtations and the struggle for existence grant the individual not a single moment of contemplation, indemnifies itself in memory, and why the veil it has woven out of our lives shows the images of people less than those of the sites of our encounters with others or ourselves.
>
> WALTER BENJAMIN

Still's city street, where an illusionary depth mingles and merges substantial figures with spectral twins, recalls a short article sent to me by my friend Yuri Tsvian, a Latvian film scholar of uncommon perception, which was published at the turn of the twentieth century in *Rebus*, a Russian journal of the occult. The article, written by Dr. M. V. Pogorelski in 1899, has been on my mind for some time. Dr. Pogorelski announces that (to quote Tsvian) "the quantity of multiple reflections that the modern city provides us with has turned it into the natural medium of haunting." Pogorelski illustrated his thesis by a description of a ride through St. Petersburg on a modern horse-drawn trolley with glass windows, a description whose imagery seems to marry *Still*, *Eureka* and *Shift*. I quote from Tsvian's translation:

> In the window opposite you see the real street; it also reflects the side of the street behind the observer's back. Reflections of the front and rear windows of the car fall on it as well; apart from that, the *double* reflection of the real part of the street under observation is imprinted on it. The fact that the car itself is in movement makes the whole picture especially complex. In clear air and bright sunlight both real objects and their mirages look particularly lifelike, and what you get as a result is a magic picture, extremely complex and mingled. . . . Passing carriages are not one-directional anymore; they move in a chaos overtaking themselves or passing *through* each other. Some carriages and passersby look as if they were rushing forward, but at the same time you are aware that, in fact, each step they make takes them backward. If your attention wanders for a second you also lose the criterion that separates real objects from their equally lifelike apparitions.

Gehr's filmmaking remains resolutely rooted in a tangible world and its laws, and is not given to spiritualist musings. However, his exploration of the unnoticed workings of those laws and their effect upon perception, his minute attention to the way light reflects and transforms space—and to the way motion shapes and recreates our visual field—all this leads to images that recall Pogorelski's. The spiritualist's writing shares with Gehr's work a discovery of, and vivid response to, a range of visual phenomenon available in the modern urban environment.

I believe Annette Michelson was the first to point out the key role the urban environment plays in Gehr's films. If this important insight had not occurred before, it is partly because the city Gehr discovers differs sharply from the bustle of crowds and metropolitan distractions found in most city films. One could almost describe Gehr's urban films as meditations, particularly if one acknowledges both the focused attention and occasional desperation of purpose that underlie meditation. The city in Gehr's cinema functions partly as a laboratory of perception, where effects of light and shadow, peculiar angles of space, flows of traffic both human and vehicular, and effects of time passing all intersect. It also forms another complex system whose secret life Gehr explores, the apex of the triangle of mutual influence whose other points are the cinema apparatus and human perception.

For Gehr, the city is also the ultimate place in which one tries to find oneself and often loses oneself as well. If there is a common image in most of Gehr's city films, it is directional signs. These are the indicators which regulate the circulation of traffic: the lines which mark lanes in the street in *Still* and *Shift*; the sharply turning arrows painted on the street that guide turns in *Side/Walk/Shuttle*; the pedestrian and traffic signs posted in *Signal—Germany on the Air*. Few filmmakers have so strongly imaged the city as a circulatory system, a channeling of flows. If the modern city is based on a perspectival logic of commercial centers and receding boulevards, Gehr reveals the twists to this logic, its turns off the main drags, the complexity of its intersections, and the multiple centers that a meditative urban vision can uncover.

If every viewer must find her place in a Gehr film, his city films frequently deal with trying to negotiate the circulatory system of the city. This is most profoundly true in *Signal—Germany on the Air*, where Gehr juxtaposes a series of views of a complex traffic intersection in Berlin. The overlapping vantage points of successive shots tease us with the possibility of mapping out the total space and finally orienting ourselves. At the same time the array of directional signs and the tangle of urban objects which solicit our attention increasingly convey the bewilderment of anyone who pauses to contemplate this intersection rather than simply being channeled by it. His other films sometimes view the constant city traffic with bemusement. The speed of car traffic blurs into superimposition not only in *Still*, but in an even more focused manner in *Shift*, where opaque and spectral cars move forward and reverse, while an often asynchronous soundtrack not only causes amusement but evokes the way traffic in the city is a presence often heard but unseen.

The city piles up layers of history as well as the flow of traffic, as *Still* and *Eureka* show. But whether the city itself retains a memory of its past seems both an ironic and impassioned question in Gehr's city films, The jolting rhythm of *Eureka* almost stereographically superimposes the hurried purposes of these frenzied city folk, all trying urgently to get somewhere, and our awareness of them as frozen in a past, condemned to constantly reenact this effort of transit. *Signal—Germany on the Air* raises the specter of history most centrally, as certain urban signs remind us implacably of the role Berlin played as the circulatory center of an industrial and military war against the human race. Are the traces of the past still here, are they tangible, or have they vanished? The question asked playfully by the title and form of *Still* ("Still?") here becomes anguished. One recalls in the midst of this traffic how important an efficient system of circulation was to the Nazi final solution: the elaborate use of the railway to transport Jews to the death centers, the use even of mobile gas chambers mounted on trucks. If this present-day traffic intersection carries the freight of so much past horror, then how can we escape it? And if it doesn't—if the traces are truly dispersed and lost—then how can anything be saved?

Could we say that history is also a matter of perspective, of finding a place from which to sight it? How can I explain my experience while preparing this essay of watching *Still* for the first time in years? In a dark screening room I discovered (along with its spatial mysteries) its ability to recall the feel of a late spring day and the look of lower Manhattan in the early 1970s—an experience so vivid I could feel the sun on my skin and sense the smells of the city when warmth returns to it. Part of what gives Gehr's city films their intensity (and their meditative character) is their profound immersion in a particular gaze that is alert to the spectacle of the city in its most unspectacular moments. Gehr's city films create a sense of the place from which they are filmed, a place defining some spatial distance, a place arranged for vision. *Shift* often includes the barely noticeable grid of a window screen before its images. And the telephoto lens in *Untitled, Part I* (1981) provides an extraordinary sense of both observation and distance in perhaps Gehr's most subtle and moving city film. Whereas Gehr frequently records the more impersonal aspects of the city, here he focuses on the gestures and circulation of human figures. The magnification of the lens allows him to register intimate details of the texture of skin or the uncertain tread of an elderly foot, while remaining somewhat outside the scene. In documenting the streetside acts of exchange and encounter in a neighborhood dominated by recent emigrants (largely Jews from Russia), Gehr captures a history of circulation and exile written in the bodies of the city's inhabitants.

IV. THREE NEW FILMS

Side/Walk/Shuttle stands as the most spectacular of the new films and certainly is a crowning film in Gehr's urban visions. However, its monumental quality also highlights the more intimate visions of *This Side of Paradise* and the new version of *Rear Window*. The variety of these three films reveals the way Gehr's filmmaking eludes classification or simple definition. Because each film occupies such a separate place, they continue to shed new light on the scope of Gehr's work.

The early cameraman who shot the footage found in *Eureka* was responding to an urban technology of transport (the trolley) and trying to provide a view of a tourist attraction. He captured a street filled with constant interaction, with near collisions as humans and animals negotiated the space between vehicles. Nearly a century later, *Side/Walk/Shuttle* rides a different technology and reveals a different city, although both films were shot in San Francisco. Gehr shot the new film from a glass elevator on the exterior of a big hotel which lifts tourists past a postcard vista of the city to an expensive restaurant. Although repeated viewings of the film make this mode of conveyance obvious (the side of the building and passing window ledges visible in some shots, and the arched niche within which the elevator ascends and descends, function as a leitmotif throughout the film), it is not so clear on first viewing.

Finding one's place in this film becomes especially tricky since that place is in constant motion, and even more because the angle of view never repeats itself. Gehr did not approach this short ride as either a touristic sight or a fast trip to an overpriced meal, but as a place of intensive labor. He rode the lift continuously and made notes on the shots and framings he needed, knowing he would have to work quickly when the time came to shoot. The actual shooting had to be done in the midst of tourists hungry for food and viewpoints, and the positions Gehr had to assume to obtain his framings must have raised eyebrows. Gehr had to do this work of intensive concentration as an interloper, and security guards soon recognized that he was neither a hotel guest nor addicted to the restaurant menu and escorted him out a number of times, causing him to curtail shooting for several months. It makes sense that Gehr's act of filmmaking would be seen as a threat to private property. He chose here a vantage point that was not only mobile but served as a transition between spaces rather than a place of contemplation, reminding one that the dominant locations in Gehr's city films are streets and sidewalks, sites of passage. Beyond his fascination with circulation, it would seem that Gehr seeks out intermediary places that provide fast getaways (even *Serene Velocity* takes place in a hallway).

Although two of the twenty-some shots that make up this film include vistas of the San Francisco skyline or a tourist attraction like Coit Tower, most of the images present the city in unfamiliar framings, the elevator movement endowing these buildings with an unmoored perspective. One rarely feels that Gehr's camera is restricted to the utilitarian lift-and-deposit cycle of an elevator, as canted angles and upside-down framings seem to launch the camera off from solid ground and chart a wayward flight over these man-made structures. But this aerial liberation is a temporary illusion, as the recurrent return or departure from the confining niche of the elevator reminds us.

What we see of the city bears all the marks of the hard-edged geometry of circulation that Gehr has chronicled before, if rarely from so aerial a perspective. We see below (although few films destroy our sense of above and below so completely) pedestrians on the sidewalk, the patterns of traffic (the cars whose bright colors occasionally pop forward, buses bearing numbers on their roofs, and even a cable car) and the painted arrows that swerve traffic from lane to lane. But it is primarily the elevation of buildings that these short trips aloft or rapid descents transform. On the simplest level, the vertical path of the camera charts the shifting perspectives of these quadrilateral structures: orthogonals stretch and switch orientation; roofs and walls exchange dominance in the frame; relative screen sizes shrink, expand, and shrink again; and buildings recede to reveal vistas previously hidden. The frame is so full of transformations that at points one forgets what the actual objects behind these moving aspects really look like. Like an object lesson in the vagaries of perspective, *Side/Walk/Shuttle* stages a constant conflict between what we know (or think we know) about what we see, and what we actually see before us on the screen.

While a moving viewpoint from such a height would inevitably provide visual pleasures (especially if one weren't intent on grasping a familiar tourist vista), Gehr's camera frames its trajectory to maximize defamiliarizing effects. The camera takes up so many positions within its constricted space that one suspects Gehr of being a contortionist. As in *Serene Velocity*, illusion pops up in the most rational of spaces. Buildings seem less to move past than to sprout and expand, like miraculous stop-motion mushrooms. Frequently the pitch of a rooftop appears pointed toward the camera, as if traveling laterally through this space, an interstellar vehicle of massive size floating over a city of the future. The constant vertical motion of the camera combines with such framing to overcome our sense of gravity and weight, as architecture floats serenely past us.

This essential disorientation provides the strongest experience of flying I have had in the cinema, recalling the effortless untrammeled flight of dreams where one overcomes the laws of this world. But Gehr always brings back to us the fictional nature of this freedom, the way it is manufactured by the camera, returning us to the constricted view through the niche archway, and providing instants of visual rest with the flare ends of shots. This does not make the magic any less powerful. The framing recurringly turns orientation on its head and when Gehr literally turns the image upside down so that the tops of buildings grow down into the frame from above, nudging their way into a blue sky, one experiences a freedom of the sky that recalls the enthusiasm for flying shown by the avant-garde in the 1920s—Blaise Cendrars or El Lissitzky. In one shot, Gehr so manages his camera that a brown building remains nearly stationary in the frame and the change of perspective and distance appears as a strange metamorphosis the building undergoes, flexing and extending its sharp-edged boundaries. At points Gehr has flipped the film to get a particular framing which also causes the motion to be reversed, as the traffic in the street flows backward. One realizes the depth of one's disorientation, the way one experiences this film as a world with its own laws, by noticing that the reverse-motion framings don't always seem radically different from the others.

Gehr pointed out that the elevator viewpoint of this film was situated near the point from which Eadweard Muybridge had shot a panorama of San Francisco more than a century before. The panoramic photograph exemplified a nineteenth-century desire to encompass the full extent of the visual world. Muybridge's later motion studies (which paved the way for the motion picture apparatus) extended this visual curiosity to the phenomenon of motion and minute increments of time. Gehr seems to literally take a ride on this ever extensive modern desire to see more and to frame what one sees in a coherent comprehensible image. However, his apparatus yields a more fragmented image, less useful for mapping and surveillance than the various panopticons of the modern age.

Gehr nonetheless deals with the modern desire to encompass expansive space and its claim to power over what it sees. As *Signal—Germany on the Air* used urban spaces to invoke the Nazi system, the aerial perspective of *Side/Walk/Shuttle* also evokes the imperial ambition of space shuttle diplomacy, particularly when the skyscrapers appear like huge motherships hovering over an urban domain, their water towers and air vents gleaming in the sun like the mechanisms of space travel. The synchronous roar on the soundtrack of wind over a microphone sounds for a moment like the revving of mighty engines, further defining Gehr's visual transformation through a complex use of sound. This new film shares with *Signal—Germany on the Air* an intricately devised soundtrack which enlarges the spatial throw of its images.

The title of *Signal—Germany on the Air* encourages hearing the soundtrack as a broadcast, and much of it was recorded from a radio. In *Side/Walk/Shuttle* the spatial throw of the sound partly comes from its initial contradiction of the vertical extension of the imagery. What we hear most frequently is street-level sound, mainly footsteps, the noise of traffic, trolleys, or subway trains, accompanied by sidewalk conversations. The recurring click or shuffle of footsteps' reassuring gravity and traction contrast with the ascension of the seemingly weightless camera. These sounds are nearby and familiar, and the voices we overhear have a down-to- earth quality. However, we soon sense that the sounds extend further than the street below us. The first sounds we hear are muffled conversations that could in fact come from the elevator (although nothing in our visual field relates to them). Then after a period of silence, we hear the bustle of a deli or restaurant, with orders being given and dishes clanking. One doesn't have to be a New York chauvinist to recognize that this particular assembly of noise and energy could come from no other city. Other sounds signal a foreign origin, such as the English accents of street vendors hawking shirts.

Gehr's sound in this film emanated from a number of distant locations in not only New York and London, but Venice and Geneva. While I cannot claim to recognize the unique click of a heel on the stones of Venice or the difference between a Swiss trolley bell and one from San Francisco, I think that one recognizes the sound in this film as extending beyond its vista, setting up a series of links that take one not only to distant places but to purely mental spaces. The sound of birds and a distant airplane which accompany some views of the sky and San Francisco Bay were recorded, I believe, in a backyard in Geneva, but more importantly they help transform these buildings into gentle inhabitants of the air.

The forces of circulation that cities create (and that create cities) extend beyond the city limits, transporting people as well as commodities. Finding a place, a process so central to Gehr's filmmaking, becomes literal in films like *Signal—Germany on the Air* (which deals with Gehr's experience finding his way as a foreigner in Berlin) or *Untitled, Part I* (which observes new immigrants washed up on the shore of Brighton Beach). *This Side of Paradise* deals with another circulation of people and their goods across the borders and directional circuits of a big city. Gehr was in West Berlin in 1989 to record some sound for a film, and stumbled upon an improvised flea market where Poles, weekend visitors from the Eastern Bloc, were trying to sell random objects they had brought with them for Western currency, which they could exchange on the black market at home for substantial profit.

Ironically, almost immediately after Gehr happened upon this rather pathetic attempt at economic circulation, Germany was reunited and the Berlin Wall came down. This small clump of people squatting at the edge of a huge mud puddle and, as Gehr put it, "selling their misery," was the product of that wall, of the construction of borders between ideologies and economic systems that (as abstract as they may sound) have tangible and visual results. The history of Gehr's family as refugees and immigrants during the period of World War II has undoubtedly sharpened his awareness of the precariousness of finding a place in a world given to violent upheavals and reworkings of borders. The ironic sense that such walls can exclude or transform a place into separated sides gives a bitterness to Gehr's title. For these economic refugees on holiday, the West is a sort of artificial paradise, and they hope to exchange their ragtag assortments of commodities for a portable piece of that financial paradise that they can take back to the other side.

In contrast to the careful preparation that preceded the filming of *Side/Walk/Shuttle*, *This Side of Paradise* was shot (and the sound recorded) as a spontaneous reaction to Gehr's discovery of this site, and most of the footage was used (much of it edited in camera). Gehr's shooting shows an immediacy (sometimes he didn't even look through the camera), and he moves through this crowd with a proximity none of his other films have ever shown. The sound emanates naturally from the site, mainly conversation in a sort of Polish-German, none of it synchronous, although the careful pairing of sound and image occasionally has a startling effect (as when a strange metallic clang accompanies a spreading ripple in the mud puddle).

The watery nature of the site particularly fascinates. It gives the market an edge which makes its purchase on the space particularly tenuous. As Gehr phrased it to me, it seems the people are "oozing out of the water." As such they appear as strangely liminal beings, flotsam and jetsam of the world's currents, like the litter of cans and cigarette butts which float in the puddles around them. Gehr was amazed at the indifference with which they stood in the water or even placed their goods for sale in it. In Gehr's frames the water becomes the surface of another world, a watery twin that mimes and even mocks the world above it. In several shots Gehr frames these puddle-borne reflections in such a way that we can't tell at first if we are looking at the world or its reflection. As in *Side/Walk/Shuttle*, our spatial orientations of up and down are often inverted, as the reflection appears right side up (sometimes this seems due to holding the camera upside down, while at other points reverse motion indicates the image has been flipped). In some shots people appear perched on top of their liquid doubles, a man's heels in the water cloning another pair of legs and torso below him.

The surprising solidity and vivid color of this inverted world takes on an intangible ephemerality when a ripple (like the one caused by the wheel of a baby pram) dissolves its image into flux. And yet these reflected images are possibly no more ephemeral than the world above, or the touching and absurdly abject collection of cast-off items offered for sale: a miniature Christmas tree, bits of clothing, a lampshade, rolls of ribbon, scarves, clocks, toys. The inversion of a world in which we see birds flying through the sky in a puddle below makes us uneasy, like the opening shots of Eisenstein's *Strike*, which also show inverted reflections in a factory yard mud puddle. These denizens of a divided world whose barriers were about to fall recall a Chinese myth Borges recounts in *The Book of Imaginary Beings*. At one time, the myth claims, the world of reflections and the world of people interpenetrated each other and both sorts of beings could walk through mirrors. But one night the mirror people invaded the human world. After a bloody battle, the Emperor prevailed and reflections were imprisoned behind their glass surfaces and condemned to ape the actions of their human counterparts. However, a day will come when a revolt begins, as little by little our reflections will cease imitating our actions and will eventually cross their barriers. Just before this invasion the clatter of weapons will be heard from the depths of our mirrors.

Shown some years ago in a silent version, *Rear Window* now reemerges with sound (and apparently some slight changes to the images). It would be hard to imagine a film more different from *Side/Walk/Shuttle* in scale and effect, although many of the same issues of finding oneself within a visual urban world are present here, only in a different key. Few of Gehr's films are as beautiful as this, or as delicate. With its telephoto lens it explores a sort of seeing that is more voyeuristic than most of Gehr's urban films, although the distant magnification of its lens recalls the gentle penetration of the world in *Untitled, Part I* and its view through a window-side fire escape has some relation to *Shifts* window views. But unlike the views of street traffic or sidewalks given in other films, this rear-window vantage point turns toward the other side of city life, where folks hang their laundry out to dry.

Gehr focuses his camera on the most quotidian of sights and reveals a drama of light and space as breathtaking as the cityscapes in *Side/Walk/Shuttle*. Light functions as subject rather than medium (although no Gehr film has ever used light simply as illumination), as the objects we recognize hanging from the line arise out of a flux of light. While the scrutiny of textures of light makes this the Gehr film closest to Brakhage, the comparison makes clear its difference from Brakhage's vision. These luminous images are not the occasion for a free association in editing of an encyclopedic ambition. Rather, even in a film as free as this one, in which the boundaries of individual shots are difficult to determine, Gehr methodically exhausts possibilities by concentrating on the material before him from a basically unswerving vantage point. A bar on the fire escape from which Gehr shot the film remains visible in most shots (although often nearly transparent due to the focal plane of the telephoto lens), and firmly anchors us in a restricted viewpoint from which we observe a constantly shifting world.

But light is more than observed here. Gehr literally molds the world we see with his hands before the lens. His fingers frequently operate as masking devices, obscuring all or part of the scene, recalling the movies we made with our eyes as kids on a sunny day when we watched things through the cracks in our fingers, or shook our hands rapidly close to our eyes to render the solid world insubstantial. The nature of the telephoto lens obscures Gehr's fingers so that the device that shapes our sight is never very clear. But as much as Gehr's hands frame what we see through them, they also literally shape and change the light itself. Gehr used "indoor" film for these outside shots and occasionally left off the orange filter commonly used to balance the cold blueness of outdoor light. Throughout the film Gehr's hands act to warm the light, the light coming through flesh and blood and bringing a tint no manufactured filter could match.

This handheld light relates *Rear Window* to what I consider Gehr's other most delicately beautiful film, *Mirage*, whose streaks of color I always assumed were produced (like the striations in *Field*) by speed of camera movement. However, the camera in *Mirage* remained still and the distortion was caused by replacing the lens with a plastic tube. While the colors of this film came from actual objects (including the blue of the sky), and the distortion into unrecognizable bands from the tube itself, the transformations came primarily from the play of Gehr's hand cupping the plastic tube, again shaping light before it passed through the apparatus to the film.

Gehr's films frequently recall paintings. His investigations of color and space certainly share concerns with visual artists of nonmoving pictures, and *Mirage* has often made me think of the stripe paintings of Kenneth Noland. Such formal comparisons (like the comparison frequently made between *Serene Velocity* and the geometric paintings of Frank Stella) tend to be superficial because Gehr is exploring a process that forms an integral part of the film medium—the image formed by light and motion, not paint on canvas. However, *Rear Window* seems to me profoundly related to the paintings of Morris Louis, although it does not in any sense resemble a Louis painting, but rather delivers a similar experience of veils of light. As in a Louis canvas, a flow of illumination seems to merge with and hover above a supporting fabric, as the flutter of the wind in Gehr's images shake colors and tones of light from sheets glimpsed through a fleshly framing.

Gehr says he always conceived of *Rear Window* as a sound film and spent much time gathering sounds he thought might work with it (including a special trip to Berlin thinking something he heard there might fit the film), but no sound he collected ever satisfied him. The soundtrack now married to the film may be less elaborate than previous plans, but it would be hard to imagine anything more fitting. Midway through the film, after accompanying our exploration of the light and its vicissitudes with silence for several minutes, wind over a microphone supplies a sound as harsh as a thunderstorm, as the laundry on the line is tossed by the breeze until it blows almost transversely across the screen. This storm of light produces an almost sexual frenzy as the hand-warmed light takes on an increasingly fleshly tone. As our vision calms, we see one of the clearest frames in the film, with a towel and a red-tipped sock hanging limply on the line. Over black leader the sound continues briefly.

Like the end of *Signal—Germany on the Air*, where Gehr pairs the sound of a real thunderclap with clear leader to artificially create a flash of lightning, this storm comes from a nonliteral combining of sound and image, an audiovisual mix which both references a real event and avoids simply recreating it (the sound of the ocean barely audible in *Rear Window* beneath the wind guarantees that we don't take the sound as simply emanating from the image). As vivid as the "storm" appears, it is the product of craft and imagination. No such storm actually took place; Gehr simply combined shots filled with motion with this urgent sound. Once again Gehr plots the intersection between the processes of his medium and the play between perception and the world. In this view across a Brooklyn backyard we find a place where the cinema opens onto a world of light and motion, uncovered among the daily wash.

I have not tried to give an overview of Gehr's films, an aerial perspective which his method would frustrate achieving—so much variety of approach, with each film relating in so many different ways to so many others. Rather, I have tried to trace a few routes through the body of his work, which these new films in particular illuminated for me. There are many others.

20

Bodies Rest and Motion: The Films of Mark LaPore

Mark LaPore died on September 11, 2005. I learned of his death from a mutual friend, filmmaker Lewis Klahr. LaPore was fifty-three years old, and while he leaves behind an important body of work, including a number of films I (and many others) value as key films within the American avant-garde cinema, one can't help but feel that he had many productive years ahead of him. But, as with nearly all filmmakers working in an experimental mode, the danger looms that the films he *did* make will never reach as large an audience as they deserve. In an era in which more and more commercial directors have abandoned both craft and vision in favor of calculation and the exploitation of easily fulfilled appetites, filmmakers who make cinema entirely out of a devotion to the medium have little hope of making a living directly from their films, or even of having their works seen, savored, and preserved. There is nothing we can do about the films Mark LaPore did not get a chance to make, but we owe it to him—and to ourselves—to pay attention to the beautiful, demanding, and disturbing ones he leaves us.

When I learned LaPore had died, I realized that I had seen the films he made over the last decade only in a fragmentary manner. I have now seen

This essay first appeared, with no subtitle, in *Film Comment* (November/December 2006): 52–56, with the following acknowledgment: "[Tom Gunning] would like to express his deep appreciation to Mark McElhatten for making LaPore's films available to him."

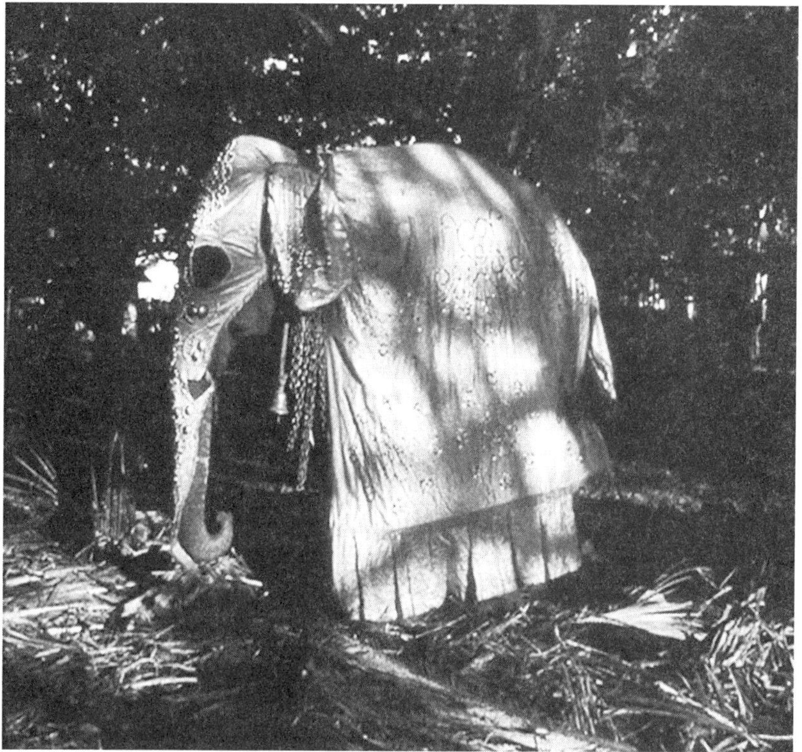

FIGURE 20.1. Mark LaPore, *The Sleepers* (1989).

four films he completed in the last ten years, a powerful cinematic legacy that I will try to describe in this brief essay.

More than a decade ago, LaPore's films took a central place in an article I wrote that argued that avant-garde cinema in America was far from moribund. Those earlier works had many of the qualities found in LaPore's more recent output: compositions that spring from the real world—from landscape, animal life, the human body and face—and an awareness of the physical environment that stands apart in an avant-garde tradition obsessed with subjectivity. His small-gauge films shot in the Sudan were partly inspired by a close friend's project in social geography. While these works are hardly pedagogic, they gained from that context a precision of observation and an extraordinary feel for how things fit together to form a world: men and animals, objects and dwellings. LaPore's most complex film from this period, *The Sleepers* (1989), mixes sounds and images from the Sudan, Europe, and New York City to create a stunningly incoherent geography that evokes the consciousness of the traveler—memories, dreams, associations—as much as the physiognomy of any place.

A peripatetic artist whose films trace his wanderings, LaPore was a traveler who became immersed in the everyday, as opposed to a sight-seeking tourist. He resembles a global flaneur taking his time, staring and contemplating rather than glancing—reflective rather than acquisitive. LaPore fixed himself in front of the world he filmed and dwelt upon what he saw, and in doing so created a unique sense of time and place. His work reminds us that, from its invention, cinema immediately took on two tasks: capturing the human body in motion (Marey, Muybridge, Edison) and bringing images of the far-flung world to the view of everyone (Lumière, Pathé). Even before the twentieth century began, filmmaking had made it to almost every country, recording sights and customs, creating, in a sense, a cinematic universe. But this invasion of the world at large by the image technology of the industrial West also forms an essential part of the colonialist project: to process the world's peoples and cultures as raw material. Martin Heidegger described this impulse to convert everything into images in "The Age of the World Picture." It is an essential component of the full-scale conversion of our environment into material whose significance lies entirely in its utility and profitability.

LaPore grappled with the relation his films bore to this tradition of appropriation. His most beautiful film, *A Depression in the Bay of Bengal* (1996), very knowingly includes footage from *Curious Scenes in India*, an early Edison travelogue whose views are striking both for their occasional beauty and their dependence on colonial labor. Even when dealing with material similar to his own (and at points the footage is intercut directly), Edison's rigidly composed and generally distant shots contrast with LaPore's contemplative and patient gaze. But by intercutting these images, LaPore also indicates his own sense of a certain distance from the world he filmed, and confesses something close to guilt.

LaPore frequently shoots people in a close frame, often standing against a wall and directly facing the camera, in long takes that resemble cinematic staring contests. Although these faces possess beauty and dignity, they are never performing for the viewer. As cinematic portraits they retain something of the scientific observation of the ethnographer. Yet LaPore does not allow the viewer to become an invisible, detached witness. These faces meet our gaze; because they seem so unpicturesque, so lacking in seductive charm, they preserve an individual mystery that confronts us—just as the camera confronts them. At points we almost feel like averting our eyes. Is it possible, LaPore asks, to make a cinema out of views of the world driven by love and unflinching awareness rather than exploitation? The Edison travelogue footage LaPore uses prominently displays the name of its distributor: Conquest Pictures. Are filmmakers inevitably the shock troops of the centuries-old and ongoing march of global capital and exploitation in the form of picturesque images culled from the world for our delectation?

This question forms the crux of LaPore's group of four films shot mainly in South Asia: *A Depression in the Bay of Bengal*, *The Five Bad Elements* (1997), *The Glass System* (2000), and *Kolkata* (2005). In these films, despair and rage constantly contend with a sense of awe at the visual beauty and the courage necessary in a world of labor and survival. Disturbingly, in the arc of LaPore's filmmaking the balance shifts progressively toward darker intuitions. *A Depression in the Bay of Bengal* opens with one of the most sublime images I have ever seen (I would place it beside the image of any master). A rocky landscape extends to a vista of mountains and sky. From the distance a tiny figure rises and approaches, bearing a huge bundle of some sort of fiber. The figure reaches the foreground and tosses down the bundle, revealing a procession of similar people in the distance, one by one coming forward and depositing their burdens, which form a growing heap. Aside from the films of Joris Ivens, I have never seen the process of labor so stunningly conveyed, its repetitive rhythms, its communal nature, but even more its relation to space and landscape. These toiling figures join earth to sky, distance to proximity, evoking Hölderlin's extraordinary line, "Poetically Man dwells upon this earth." But LaPore never monumentalizes this labor. It remains everyday, matter of fact—burdensome. The image, like so many of LaPore's images of work in this film, fluctuates between admiring physical skill and portraying drudgery. Other filmmakers articulate the tension between grace and oppression through contrast (opposing image and sound or image and image). LaPore avoids this sort of juxtaposition. His sounds and images simultaneously contain both promise and terror.

The Five Bad Elements takes its title from a Maoist term used during the Cultural Revolution for class enemies: landlords, rich peasants, counterrevolutionaries, criminals, and reactionaries. The phrase also evokes deep-rooted sinister forces (the Chinese enumerate five essential elements: wood, fire, metal, water, and earth), bad influences circulating at the core of things. LaPore's soundtrack recounts fragments of disturbing histories: a discussion of the court intrigues of Empress Yang Kwei Fei, a description of the colonialization of New England, and a nihilistic letter home from a Korean War–era sailor. These are all heard over images of bodies whose motionlessness seems more moribund than peaceful (a long take of the face of a dead man poses an unsettling variant to LaPore's other prolonged

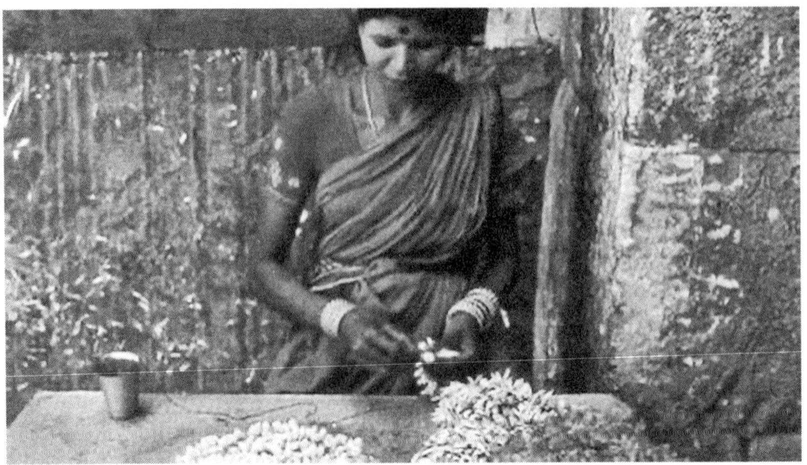

FIGURE 20.2. Mark LaPore, *A Depression in the Bay of Bengal* (1996).

close-ups). A shot of a tethered ceremonial elephant that also appears in *A Depression in the Bay of Bengal* exemplifies the contrast between the elemental rot that spreads throughout *Elements* and the tension between the exquisite and the oppressive in the earlier film. In *Depression*, the elephant appears in color, and its gold-embroidered caparison shines with a sense of celebration. This is undercut by the animal's agitation at being chained to the spot. In *Elements*, similar footage appears in black-and-white, and its monotonality echoes the troubling Edison travelogue shot included in *Depression* of an elephant pathetically pulling at its chained leg. Festive music on the soundtrack makes the elephant's manic swaying resemble dancing—but the effect is ironic rather than uplifting. A penumbra of stories and associations personal to LaPore haunts this film, increasing rather than relieving our distress at the world it brings to us.

I have only been able to watch *The Glass System* on DVD, so I cannot compare the color of the images, but it shares some of *Depression*'s wonder at the skill of manual labor in a world in which the bifurcation between interior and exterior space doesn't correspond to Western ideas of public and private. Although the images derive primarily from the streets of South Asia, the film deviously slips in shots from New York City that seem congruent with the exotic ones: a street vendor in front of Saks Fifth Avenue echoes the Asian sidewalk workers; a glass frame encasing a poster for a Chinese film reflects New York skyscrapers off its surface. The dexterity the small children demonstrate as they perform acts of balance or contortion, or rapidly fold printed pages for pamphlets, evokes LaPore's evident respect for physical processes, but they also show young bodies disciplined into repetitive or risky actions in order to make a living. Basic phrases plucked from language primers compete with street sounds on the soundtrack, but the questions they ask remain not only unanswered but unacknowledged. The final phrase, heard over an image of a shallow pan filled with wriggling fish, reiterates a question posed earlier: "Is that animal still alive?" The query seems to match the shot by chance; in retrospect it raises a question relevant throughout the film. What does survival mean? How is it accomplished in most of the world? As viewers, how do we raise—let alone answer—this question?

The soundtrack of the last film of this quartet, *Kolkata*—dominated by a persistent, repetitive, and severely distorted voice broadcast over a loudspeaker, whose urgency announces either imminent danger or the desire to sell something—comes as close to the aural equivalent of overwhelming depression as I can imagine. The film's black-and-white images, primarily of Calcutta streets, replace LaPore's usually patient contemplation of individual views with a frenetic sense of accumulation. The opening shots create a surreal and hallucinatory quality unusual for LaPore: store

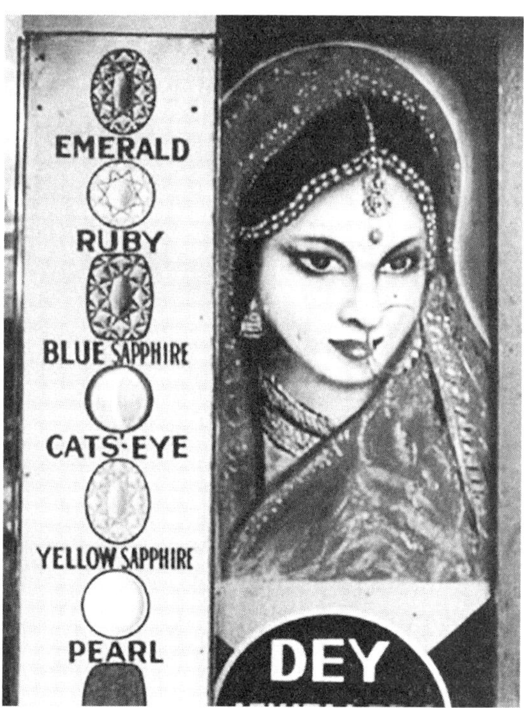

FIGURE 20.3. Mark LaPore, *The Glass System* (2000).

mannequins, racks of baby dolls, children sleeping in doorways, swaying garlands of shiny metallic packages of medicine or candy. Late in the film, extended tracking shots negotiate alleyways and streets lined by market stalls, propelling the action with a relentless drive. The traveling camera moves at a constant speed past people who either react to or ignore it, glimpsing endless piles of goods and materials, and children and adults passing their time or working. The camera claustrophobically maintains a fixed distance that is punctuated by sudden openings into alleys or cross streets. As steady as the pace of this movement may be, it also seems lost, advancing because it no longer has a goal, passing by everything it sees as if making its way through a labyrinth—or the inner circles of Dante's *Inferno*.

LaPore's films achieve a vision that straddles and brings together the modes of experimental film, ethnographic documentary, diarist travel films, lyrical autobiography, and political polemic. They should be seen by anyone who cares about the cinema and who cares about the way this image machine can display the world we have made and, especially, the aspects we prefer to ignore or forget. Their courage matches their beauty and their growing despair. If you teach cinema or if you program film, I urge you to show them. Rest in peace, Mark.

21

From Fossils of Time to a Cinematic Genesis: Gustav Deutsch's *Film ist.*

"Found footage"—the recycling of previously shot film, reworked by later filmmakers—defined a founding moment in both film theory and filmmaking. As is well known, Lev Kuleshov and his students in the revolutionary USSR intercut the same shot of the actor Mozhukin (with a rather neutral expression) with a variety of other shots (usually described as a bowl of soup, a dead baby, and a scantily clad woman) in order to produce widely differing affects (respectively: hunger, sorrow, and lust). Referenced by theorists and filmmakers from Hitchcock to Deleuze, the Mozhukin experiment has particularly fascinated theoretically inclined filmmakers such as Jean-Luc Godard, Vsevelod Pudovkin, and Hollis Frampton—appropriately so, since it was designed to instruct film students in the logic of their craft. For Kuleshov the experiment demonstrated the power of editing to create meaning through juxtaposition, demonstrating that cinematic shots must be read synthetically. Each shot in isolation remains neutral in its meaning; it can only be read through contextualization. The shot of Mozhukin gained its meaning from the cut that juxtaposed it to another shot. A single shot in itself means nothing—or potentially can mean anything. According to Kuleshov, a film's meaning therefore comes not from the act of filming but from the act of splicing.

This essay first appeared in *Gustav Deutsch*, ed. Wilbirg Brainin-Donnenberg and Michael Loebenstein, FilmmuseumSynemaPublikationen, vol. 11 (Vienna, 2009), ISBN/ISSN 978-3-901644-30-6.

I want to shift the lesson of this demonstration from its intended QED about the power of montage, and focus instead on the material underlying its transformation: the preexisting shot of Mozhukin. Kuleshov's demonstration did not necessarily demand using found footage (although according to some accounts, the scarcity of raw stock in postrevolutionary USSR compelled him to scavenge among the leavings from prerevolutionary Russian cinema). However, the choice had strong effects. The use of the familiar face of émigré movie star Mozhukin gave Kuleshov's experiment a polemical edge. Editing not only imposed specific meanings on neutral material, but also overcame whatever reactionary bourgeois meanings the prerevolutionary footage originally intended to convey. One could claim that Kuleshov's iconoclastic (deconstructive?) hermeneutics also asserted a power over time, overcoming a fossilized meaning with the explosive dynamics of a new cut. While Kuleshov may not have specifically seen this renewal of old material as demonstrating montage's revolutionary potential, the other major advocate and theorist of the praxis of montage in early revolutionary USSR, Estir Shub, certainly did. In her compilation film *The Fall of the Romanov Dynasty*, Shub's montage redefined -prerevolutionary footage of the czar's family and the Russian empire, as did the reediting of foreign films to change their ideological message that she undertook with her pupil Sergei Eisenstein in the early 1920s.

While the term "found footage" highlights the role of chance, the lucky *trouvaillee* celebrated in surrealist aesthetics, to my mind the use of cinematic found footage primarily transformed the temporality of the cinematic image. As Alain Robbe-Grillet once theorized, cinema seems restricted to the present tense: we see actions unfolding before us. However, cinema, at least in its photographic aspects, also partakes of the past tense of the photographic image, the trace of the past, the message that Roland Barthes claimed all photography proclaims: "This has been." The cinematic image therefore operates in two different temporalities simultaneously. On the one hand, the moving image's present tense shows actions in the course of unfolding; while on the other hand, as a photographic trace, film consists of records of past events. The context, genre, and stylistics of individual films privilege one aspect over the other (even to the extent of nearly repressing, although never totally eradicating, signs of one or the other). The fictional film usually foregrounds the present tense of unfolding action with effects of anticipation, suspense, and immediate involvement, while the documentary film tends to foreground the past tense aspect of recording an event which has already occurred.

Avant-garde or experimental cinema frequently plays on the tension between these modes of cinematic time. As William Wees has shown, in the past few decades especially, found footage has played a major role in avant-garde cinema in both North America and Europe, almost constituting a genre in itself. More than the chancelike nature of a lucky find, found footage in cinema tends to emphasize the pastness of the image: This image existed before this film, usually in a different context. Experimental filmmakers, of course, subject found footage to a range of technical manipulations and adopt a variety of tones—from the pop-art satirical collage of iconic mass-cultural images of the late Bruce Conner to the utterly transformed, nearly unidentifiable, oneiric working-over of found images in the *Twilight Psalm* series of Phil Solomon (especially such films as *Walking Distance* and *Night of the Meek*). I do not want to reduce the complexity of this cinema of appropriation to a limited number of themes, since found footage refers to material rather than final result and results can be wide-ranging. But the use of found footage, from the experiment of Kuleshov on, brings the paradoxical nature of cinematic temporality, its intertwining of effects of past and present, to a boil. The films of Gustav Deutsch have worked over a range of preexisting footage, from home movies, to educational and scientific films, to pornographic films, to fiction films from both early and classical cinema. Each film he has made has its own individuality, and even within his series *Film ist.* the variations are striking. But within these variations a meditation on cinematic time recurs.

Experimental cinema explores fault lines, slides down slippery slopes, evades definition by definition. Rather than exemplifying theoretical issues of cinematic temporality, the films of Deutsch, like other found-footage films, play with diverse possibilities. Therefore, a critic like myself needs to avoid freezing this dynamic into a theoretical statement. But in this brief essay I want to explore the implications of Deutsch's found-footage film for both temporality and the mechanics of meaning in cinema. To shift a bit from my initial focus on temporality to the more traditional semantic approach to Kuleshov's experiment, the use of footage implies a radical decontextualization and redefinition. Whatever the meaning or intention originally tied to this footage, that tie has been loosened. Kuleshov's method was to supply a new context, to supply a new meaning. While the avant-garde seized upon this dynamic redefinition of meaning, from at least Bruce Conner's early works, the redefinition often celebrated ambiguity and equivocation. Kuleshov demonstrated his control of meaning, while Conner (and others) liberated the image into a wide range of associations—political, sexual, and anarchic. Kuleshov displayed the semantic power of editing; found-footage films in the late twentieth and early twenty-first centuries rerouted this power, multiplying rather than defining it.

In segments 1–6 of *Film ist.*, Deutsch radically separates images from the films he draws on from their original context. Since many of the films in this first part of the series are from educational or scientific films, this original exhibition context defined their original meaning. These films generally served as part of a course of instruction on such things as animal behavior, physiology, or the nature of the larynx. In some avant-garde found-footage films (such as the extraordinary work of Abigail Child or Leslie Thornton), scientific footage wavers between metaphor and sensational attraction as a whole new context is created. In the *Film ist.* 1–6 series, one strongly senses the original purpose of pedagogy in nature of the footage. A tone of instruction dominates: from the subject matter focused on, to composition and lighting, to the devices used in the shooting process (slow motion or stop motion, X-ray photography), as well as the presence in the footage of scientific instruments of measurement. Yet Deutsch has stripped these films of the explanations of physiology or psychology that originally accompanied them. Without these reassuring explanations, much of the footage seems strange, dreamlike, horrifying or amusing, grotesque. Instead of being processed for the information they hold, these images confront us in all their oddness. Deutsch seems to substitute his own pedagogic project for the original one. The series's titles direct our attention to an aspect that the original filmmakers may have considered transparent: the film medium itself. Liberated from the function of simply recording scientific data, these films display the nature of cinema as a moving image, cinema's affinity with the motions of physical bodies and scientific instruments, its control of time and vision. And the dual sense of temporality returns. The sense of surprise and discovery we experience as these images pirouette before us carries a strong present tense, as the movement unfolds before us. Yet our perception of the images as data, their role in recording scientific demonstrations that have already occurred, accents the past tense. Both of these aspects appear defamiliarized; we are as fascinated (and sometimes repelled) by the motion of bodies as by the scientific regimen to which the image is subjected.

But the scientific context of much of this imagery evokes another temporal regime. Scientific demonstration strives to present an abstraction of time in which the unique moment disappears in favor of the unchanging laws of nature. However, in episodes 1–6 of *Film ist.* the images never rest simply in this abstract time. Time seeps into the images. The clothes people wear, the

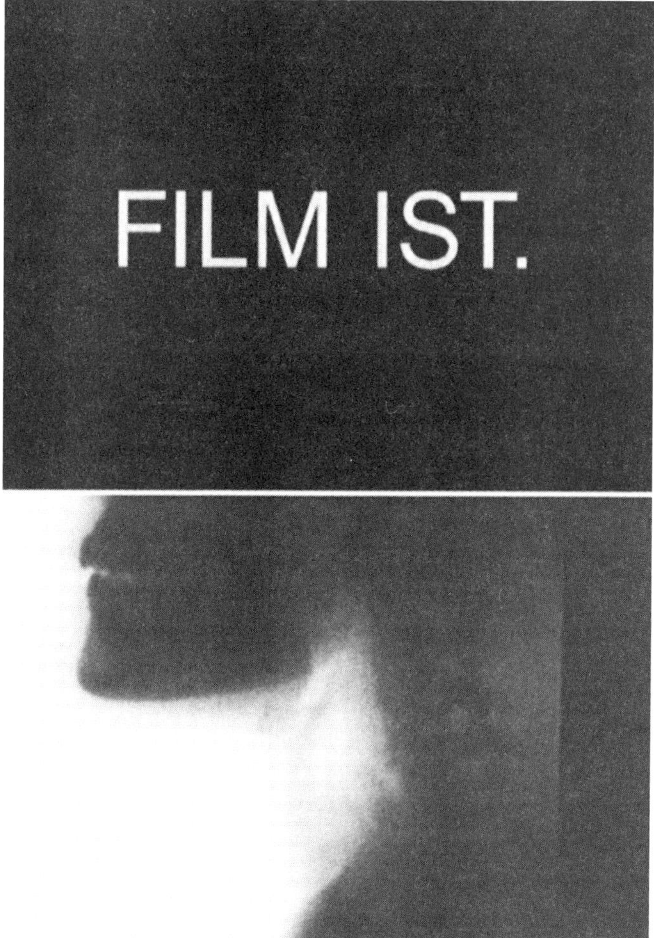

FIGURE 21.1. Gustav Deutsch, *Film ist. (1–6)* (1998).

color of the film stock, the nature of décor—all these background details tend to anchor these images in a specific time that otherwise the films strive to evade. The contingency of the scientific demonstration, its rootedness in certain styles of behavior and attitude as much as clothing or hairstyle swims before us. And yet the fundamental laws of motion and physiology do not simply disappear into this matrix of period reference. These contrasting elements of abstracted scientific laws and contingent filmic details twine about each other, defining a pas de deux that seems to underlie much of *Film ist.* as a whole: an interaction between fundamental laws, urges, and forces, and their material manifestations and individual identities. Rather than simply recycling old scientific films, Deutsch demonstrates the double nature of cinema: its eye for general pattern and recurrence along with its affinity for the particular and unique.

Episodes 1–6 not only explore the scientific aspect of cinema, but Deutsch's own pedagogic project of laying out the fundamentals of cinema. The second group of *Film ist.*, episodes 7–12, focuses on the historical dimension of cinema. The double aspect of history explored in this section can be expressed linguistically in French and German, but unfortunately is less immediate in English. German *Geschichte*, like French *histoire*, translates as both history and story. Episodes 7–12 of *Film ist.* take up the cinematic aspect of this interrelation of narrative and history, evoking the telling of stories and the carrying on of tradition. Episodes 1–6, like all of *Film ist.*, rely heavily on editing, sometimes preserving the sequence of original footage and sometimes creating new juxtapositions. In episodes 1–6, the succession of shots convey a sense of rhythm and process, rather than the devices of suspense, mystery, or comic gags that dominate the second series. The material used in episodes 7–12 comes from a different sort of archive than the primarily educational films that appear in the earlier series. Drawn primarily from the first decades of cinema history, these images, while including the actuality footage so essential to early filmmaking, present films from a very different exhibition context than the first series. These films were primarily intended for theatrical audiences and address the pleasures of sight, the seductions of eye and fantasy, more than the discipline of education. Rather than forming part of a pedagogic demonstration, these images invited spectators to enter their cinematic worlds, whether as travelogues or fictional adventures. Although Deutsch pries these images loose from their original stories, one nonetheless senses them as part of a larger whole, fragments of an absent story. As fragments they refer to unseen future moments of narrative or revelation. Even separated from their original context, these images still have a narrative valance and momentum, an energy Deutsch abstracts from them but does not dissipate.

Thus, not only does a different sort of time operate in this section, but it creates a different dialectic between the pastness of history and the immediacy of the action. These images seem older, that is, more historical: we see their antiquated style not only in clothing and furnishings but in filmmaking devices and performance. The historicity of cinema displays itself before us. And yet in the midst of this powerful sense of the past, we also see an intensity of emotion, a compelling presentation of dramatic situations that fill us with curiosity to see what follows—the basic momentum of narrative film—to ask: What comes next? Deutsch both exploits and subverts this energy, withholding the expected satisfaction of narrative outcome by interrupting the story, or diverting our curiosity into other images. Like Kuleshov, Deutsch redefines the meaning of a shot by the shot which follows, but rather than completing a sequence, he often creates a simile, an echo, or a dreamlike doppelganger for the narrative development we might expect. If traditional narrative operates like electrical wiring, sending current along determined pathways, Deutsch's *Film ist.* episodes 7–12 frays the insulation, short-circuiting expected operations with a shower of sparks. Drawing on archival footage, Deutsch cares less about simply making new connections than about awakening energies slumbering in old material. This energy comes from chain reactions, splitting the cinematic atom of original meanings. Beyond simply recycling images of the past, the editing of found footage triggers a truly new moment, not only a new sense of presence but a prophetic sense of future possibilities. While Kuleshov's lessons demonstrated how shots could be given meaning in relation to each other, finding their place in a logical order like links in a chain, Deutsch more frequently sets off a series of resonances that echo across shots rather than directing them to a specific end. Like ripples expanding a across a pond, one shot sets another vibrating. Kuleshov vectorized editing, but Deutsch seems rather to make it twine and untwine in a helix-like pattern.

If the first two sections of *Film ist.* invoke (without being limited to) science pedagogy and the narrative of history, respectively, the latest episode—bearing the sinister number 13—probes the secret forces of cosmology, sexuality, and the drive toward death. Its title, *A Girl and a Gun*, refers to a definition of cinema offered by Jean-Luc Godard. Godard's phrase identifies sexuality and violence as driving impulses behind the manufacture of moving images. But more than this, the phrase also invokes cinema's fundamental affinity with the dynamic that psychoanalysis calls *displacement*, in which one thing stands in for another. In the movies, sex is never simply sex and violence is rarely simply violence; indeed, one substitutes for the other. The gun exerts a phallic force, but sexual desire is also channeled into national fantasies of dominance and conquest. Movies not only combine sex and violence but fuse the energy of one with the other. But *Film ist.* episode 13, *A Girl and a Gun*, goes beyond a critique of film's exploitation of sex and violence, and fashions an overarching mythology from images of these primal energies. The episode extends from genesis to apocalypse, exposing the forces underlying modern history and perhaps the cosmos as well. Simultaneously a myth and an anti-myth, episode 13 stages the battle of Thanatos and Eros, using the imagery of cinema to create a new epic form with found footage drawn from pornography, historical documentary, fictional dramas, and images of nature. *A Girl and a Gun* blends

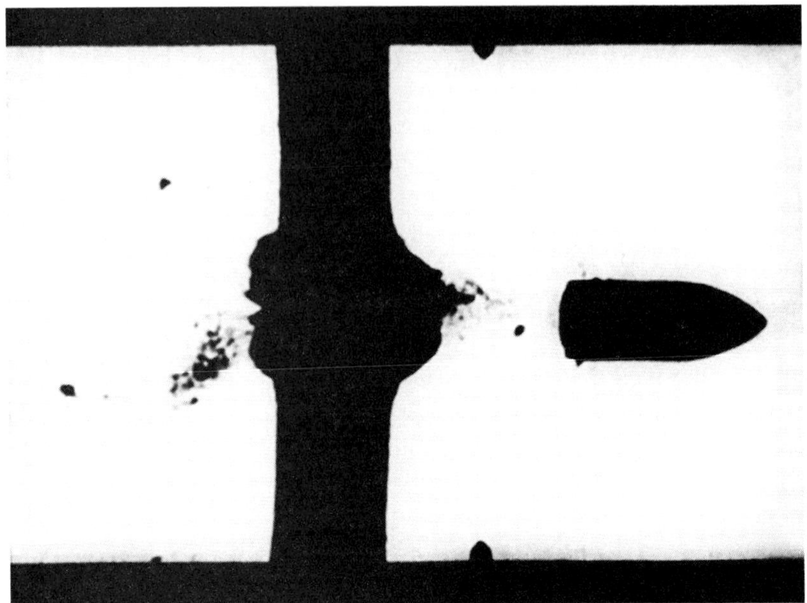

FIGURE 21.2. Gustav Deutsch, *Film ist. (1–6)* (1998).

these varied modes of filmmaking and their different temporalities in order to fashion a cinematic myth in which the full course of time and history unwinds within an eternal process of union and division.

Episodes 1–12 of *Film ist.* derived a new ambiguity and range of meanings from found footage. Episodes 1–6 loosened the images of scientific films from their intended pedagogic purposes, while episodes 7–12 liberated gestures, emotions, and incidents from the narratives to which they originally belonged. But in Episode 13 the images are impressed into a context that endows them with heavily symbolic roles and meanings. Images that may have originally demonstrated the patterns of smoke or the flow of molten magma become embodiments of the titanic forces of world creation, the energies of growth and genesis. Pornographic films evoke copulating deities. These images become the vehicles of metaphor, cogs within a cosmic mechanism. Sexuality does not appear here as the erotic gags or double meanings that enlivened the previous sections, but rather as the force that moves the sun and all the other stars, the momentum that fuses images into metaphors, triggering explosions and transformations. The cultural weight of the intertitles that quote religious and philosophical texts in this episode (as contrasted with the laconic section titles of the previous episodes) gives this succession of images a profundity that contrasts with the light-hearted puns and random associations the previous section often reveled in. Repetition, formal similarities, and actions that seem to flow across the cuts create a tsunami of meaning that sweeps across the film. A series of twined bodies are intercut with the tale from Plato's *Symposium* of the primal separation of the original androgynous human into separate sexes (which then strive their entire lives to find their twin and reunite). This series of mirror images seem more to illustrate this mythic account of Eros than to document the primal desire to recover a primal wholeness. The struggle of these bodies to merge rehearses the film's logic of juxtaposition, portraying the energy of editing itself, making visible the rhythm of a fission both nuclear and cinematic. Deutsch forces Kuleshov's montage beyond the simple creation of meaning to reveal a primal desire of images to unite and generate new figures of significance. The archive of cinema supplies the matrix of a new mythology, as the process of editing becomes a process of mythopoesis, manifesting the struggle between contraries and the conjunction of opposites.

A Girl and a Gun may not be the final episode of *Film ist.*, but it does constitute its alpha and omega, as these orphaned images unite to form a new cosmology of cinema. In the Kabbalah of Isaac Luria, creation began with a disaster, as the vessels of the cosmos shattered when divine energy streamed into them. This divine tragedy caused fragments of the transcendent energy to fall into a world of matter, seeding it with sparks from the heavenly realm. Religious meditation and rituals seek to restore the divine unity and heal this breach, liberating the captive sparks from their earthly container and allowing them to reascend to their original source. I believe this process stands as an ideal metaphor for Deutsch's transformation of found footage, reworking archival material, seeking to release and gather the energy contained within it: from the scientific exploration of the laws of motion, to the enigmatic configurations of narrative and history, to the expansion and contraction of the energy of the universe itself in the rhythms of erotic union and deadly division. In *Film ist.*, the past knits together and unravels before our eyes, demonstrating the way energy emerges from fission, worlds are created from disasters. Images of the past are refined and transmuted to yield a range of temporal experience, as a new present arises from fossilized films and the conjunction of shots revitalizes slumbering meanings. The essence of film consists in endowing still images with movement and life. *Film ist.* awakes the archives of moving images into new discoveries.

22

Flaming Images: Burning through the Celluloid Closet

> In *Fireworks* are released all the explosive pyrotechnics of a dream. Inflammable desires dampened by day under the cold water of consciousness are ignited that night by the libertarian matches of sleep and burst forth in showers of shimmering incandescence. These imaginary displays provide a temporary release.
>
> SPOKEN IN VOICE-OVER BY KENNETH ANGER AS A PROLOGUE IN SOME VERSIONS OF *Fireworks*[1]

I confess that I am not a historian of queer culture or history, or even of gay cinema; this puts me in danger, not only of the honest mistakes of ignorance, but perhaps of more devious faults, of reinventing the wheel. But if I am, as Kenneth Anger might put it, rushing in where angels fear to tread, I also confess I have my own agenda, seeing queer cinema and the avant-garde as an extremely powerful means to open up an issue often dealt with too coldly by academic cinema studies: cinema as a vehicle of desire. Queer cinema announces itself as focused on desire, even when that desire has been marginalized, disguised, repressed, refused public expression, criminalized, and demonized.

Cinematic form has frequently been determined by Eros. Mainstream narrative cinema tends to follow a romance structure, with the formation of a

This essay, previously unpublished, was written in 2009 and revised in 2020. It is dedicated to Ron Gregg.

romantic couple serving as the sign of closure in by far the majority of such films, particular during the Classical era—sealed with a kiss.[2] A less frequent variation, but hardly a radically different form, is the "weepy," in which a romantic couple is not allowed to form, or at least not allowed to consummate their relation through a recognized marriage, due usually to social conventions, often appearing as a sort of fate (from *Back Street* through *Now Voyager* to *Brokeback Mountain*). But I am envisioning a different erotic form of cinema, in which desire slides in and out of stories and opens up its own pathways, often diverging from the dramatic unities of space and time and psychologically unified characters. These films move less often toward narrative closure and the establishment of a couple but, rather, envision an elusive image of the beloved and celebrate an ecstasy that goes beyond closure.

In *Flaming Creatures* (1963) Jack Smith created a film of the sort I am seeking, one that tried to escape from the commercial system of intertwined titillation and repression by which the action of desire and the act of censorship are made to support each other. Contrariwise, Smith staged an orgy of faked violence and real genitals set within a junk palace that served as an artificial Arabian Nights paradise. Legendary in the twined history of queer culture and avant-garde cinema, Jonas Mekas's exhibition of the film in New York City in 1963 led to a raid and a series of arrests by the vice squad. Filmmaker Ken Jacobs was projecting the film, and his wife-to-be, Flo Karpf, was selling tickets.[3] One of the vice cops befriended Flo, telling her that he couldn't believe a lovely, young Jewish girl like herself could be involved in showing such filth. When Flo responded that she thought the film was beautiful, the goon immediately put the handcuffs on and arrested her as well as Mekas and Jacobs. Desire and beauty are dangerous commodities in a repressive society.

It is hard for contemporary film historians to recall the extent to which postwar American alternative cinema movements were fueled by audiences hoping to see some flash of flesh or depiction of sexual behavior. The success of the foreign art house cinema (successively, Italian Neorealism, Ingmar Bergman, and the first French New wave films), as well as the surprising popularity the American avant-garde films enjoyed in the 1950s and 1960s at New York's Cinema 16 and the Film-Makers' Cooperative, depended to a large degree on the promise of sexual attractions.[4] While this may seem to undercut an aesthetically driven history of sixties cinema, I think that having the social roots of these alternative movements in erotic expectation does not trivialize them. If spectators went to *Naked Night* or *Scorpio Rising* for the brief views of breasts or genitals they contained, it indicates how great a hunger for erotic images the repressive society had fomented.

Smith called his masterful film *Flaming Creatures*. It is a complex title, and clearly "flaming" has a specific resonance ("flaming faggot" was American slang for a flamboyant homosexual). But the title is also a literal synonym for stars, burning, luminous bodies. And stars are the foundation of the commercial film industry, one means of controlling and channeling desire and assuring profit. We could certainly engage in a hermeneutics of suspicion of the calculated system of sublimated desire that the Hollywood star represents. Although a valuable and insightful critique, the puritanical reaction against cinema's visual pleasure seems to me less useful both analytically and politically than the more far-reaching and ironic discourse of camp, which derived from a homosexual reception of popular culture. Camp maintains a distance born of irony but simultaneously embraces popular images and redefines them, projecting on them a humor and a personally redefined desire that deviates from the inscribed dominant ideological intent. In her classic essay, Susan Sontag proclaimed, "Camp taste is, above all, a mode of enjoyment, of appreciation—not judgment. Camp is generous. It wants to enjoy."[5] Like most of Sontag's pronouncements on camp, this statement falls flat if not understood dialectically. Camp is an enjoyment that at the same time reflects a deeper pain of repression. The flames of the stars burn as much as they illuminate.

Camp spectatorship provides a complex and dialectical model for the devious paths erotic cathexis can take in the cinema. If camp filmmakers of the 1960s performed a parody of the Hollywood star system, they took seriously the incandescent embodiment of desire to which stars aspired. The extension of star status to anyone with the chutzpah to claim it that characterized the underground cinema of the 1960s represents the radicalization of the utopian promise of Hollywood mass popularity, what Laura Mulvey once described as the "democratization of glamour."[6] The Warhol Factory, production center for both images of stars and stars themselves, extends this parodic discourse into a serial production in which the erotic becomes diffused across a succession of images, based in the endless deferral of desire as the person becomes eclipsed in the manufacture of personality. Underground queer culture provided a model for the erotics of film viewing that redirected the energies of Hollywood film, redefining the attraction of certain Hollywood practices (such as stardom, costuming, genre conventions, performance styles), and ultimately refashioned the sometimes alienating images of mass culture into an image that could excite, and perhaps fulfill, desire.

But avant-garde modes of production and exhibition also allowed the possibility of creating for the screen a personal image of desire, by making

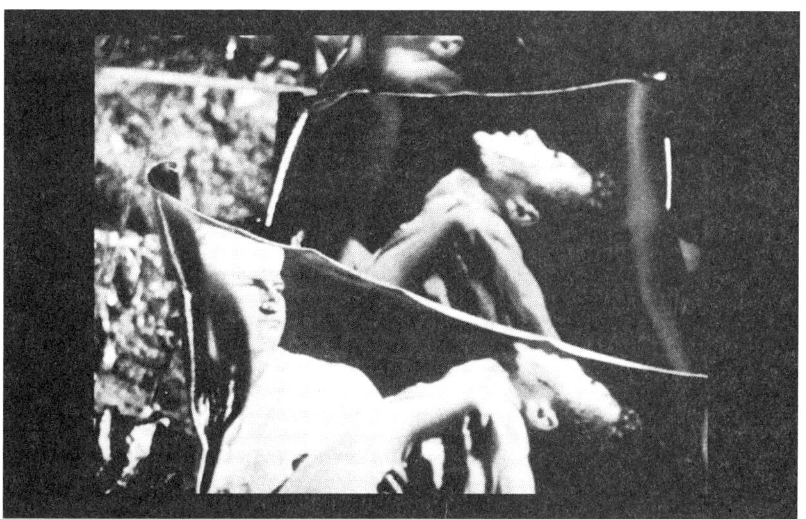

FIGURE 22.1. Kenneth Anger, *Fireworks* (1947).

one's own movie. Kenneth Anger's first extant film, *Fireworks*, stands as a beacon in this alternative metaphorical erotic cinema filled with camp irony but also cinematic ecstasy. The film offers a testament to the acting out and realization of an erotic fantasy that in 1947, the year of its making (and for decades after), would be officially declared not only deviant but criminal.[7]

The homegrown aesthetic of avant-garde film production, shot on smaller-gauge films with equipment designed for the amateur, valued, indeed flaunted, its poverty of means as part of an ironic critique of Hollywood glamour. Rather than using the tools of commercial cinema, the postwar American avant-garde film emerged from the noncommercial categories of the home movie and the amateur film.[8] This neglected earlier amateur tradition also often involved the ironic invocation of Hollywood, through an open and humorous acknowledgment of falling short of the very Hollywood glamour and genre conventions it evoked. Historian of American amateur film culture Charles Tepperman describes this mode as "a vernacular version of the fantasy produced by Hollywood."[9] These films occasionally smuggled in a camouflaged projection of a very personal desire.

The amateur film I will discuss, Theodore Huff's *Little Geezer: His Rise and Fall* (1932), may be unique in its anticipation of Anger's *Fireworks*, but the concept of a homemade film unites the avant-garde and the amateur movements, as does the fulfillment of personal fantasy. Huff was an early film scholar (author of the first serious book on Charlie Chaplin's films and of a detailed shot-by-shot analysis of D. W. Griffith's *Intolerance*), archivist, and amateur filmmaker, whose works have recently been seen as part of the first generation of American avant-garde cinema, a judgment based mainly on his collaboration on John Flory's Depression-era burlesque *Mr. Motorboat's Last Stand.*[10] But Huff's first films reflect the amateur film aesthetic and parody the key American action genres of the Western and the gangster film: *Hearts of the West* and *Little Geezer*, both reenacted by a cast of small boys and produced in the early 1930s, were praised by the amateur film journals, and *Little Geezer* won several prizes in amateur film competitions.

Little Geezer: His Rise and Fall relies on the viewer's familiarity with Hollywood genres, invoking the cycles of gangster films popular in the early 1930s through costumes and iconography—specifically Mervyn Leroy's *Little Caesar* (1931), whose last line it appropriates. It chronicles the attempt of bank robber Little Geezer to defy The Big Shot and his romance with streetwalker Greta Garbage, ending with The Big Shot's revenge on the romantic pair. The film is a wink-wink parody, as evident in The Big Shot's crocodile tears after shooting Little Geezer and Greta, then proclaiming to the camera (through an intertitle), "I'm sorry, folks, but all this is inevitable—the result of Prohibition and its attending evils." The film exemplifies an amateur practice that endures to this day: trying to approximate Hollywood commercial standards with limited means, while also guying those conventions in a lighthearted critique. One is impressed by the "tough" performances of the boy actors and the details of the costumes, props, and setting match their Hollywood models; but at the same time one realizes that the action is not to be taken seriously. Elements of obvious artificiality (such as the exaggerated makeup for the boy who portrays Greta Garbage) become intentional signs of parody, rather than failures of craft. Huff was very aware of the double address of his parodies, writing in an article he published in *Movie Makers*, a journal dedicated to amateur film, the same year he produced *Little Geezer*, "While it is difficult to compete with Hollywood producers on their own ground in a straight story since amateur actors are apt to suffer by comparison, in a burlesque, errors and crudities only add to the fun."[11]

Nonetheless, something else creeps into this parodic imitation and makes *Little Geezer* more than, as some commentators have called it, an early version of *Bugsy Malone* (1976), a big-budget Hollywood gangster parody with a preadolescent cast (including Scott Baio and Jodie Foster), or a parallel to the contemporaneous *Baby Burlesks* series of one-reelers, which cast toddlers in parodies of famous films, such as *Runt Page* (1932).[12] As Tepperman observes, "Huff's films point toward an alternative

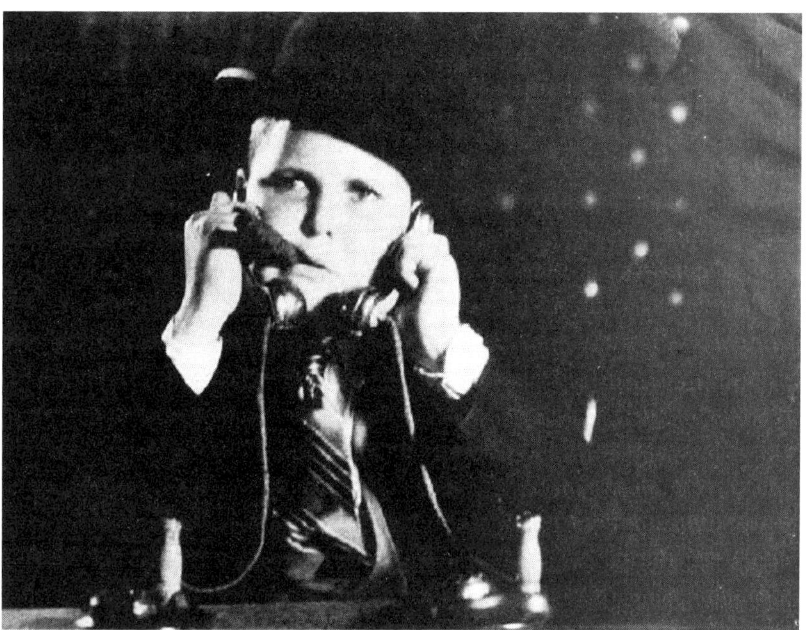

FIGURE 22.2. Theodore Huff, *Little Geezer* (1932).

film aesthetic."[13] Sophisticated editing and compositional style, and use of low angles, dramatic shadows, and Eisensteinian montages, exceed the stylistics of even the period's most radical gangster films and signal the filmmaker's avant-garde inspirations and aspirations. *Little Geezer*'s rapid and dynamic editing anticipates Anger's montage during the sailors' attack on the protagonist of *Fireworks*. Likewise, Garbage's exaggerated makeup and the boy actor's evocative—if awkward—vamping of Greta Garbo (especially her first talkie performance in the 1930 film *Anna Christie*) oddly recall the drag performances of Francis Francine or Joel Markman in *Flaming Creatures*, which also parodies a Hollywood genre (the 1940s Arabian Nights films of Maria Montez and Jon Hall).

An oddly subversive energy emerges from *Little Geezer*'s mixing of mainstream genre posturing, avant-garde stylistics, and preadolescent casting. It doesn't take much imagination to find within the boys' performances (particularly the images of Greta Garbage and the love scenes between Greta and the Geezer) an uncomfortable eroticism, which possibly even Huff could not acknowledge. Film historian Chuck Kleinhans, the only critic to discuss Huff at length, has described him as "a very closeted gay man."[14] Kleinhans cautions us against the temptation to "out" Huff, but I believe taking seriously these subterranean urges and atmospheres opens up a compelling dimension (personal, even private, even outwardly denied, but powerful).

In camp fashion, the irony of the parody provides just sufficient disguise for the erotic impulses to evade censorship. Even within a style based on absurdity, there are moments that feel excessive, partly because they anticipate gestures that will be fully developed by the underground queer cinema. The boy's exaggerated gestures as Greta offer one such moment, but also the flaming fireplace that casts its glow on Greta and Geezer as they make out in the film's extended erotic sequence. The shot of a fire blazing as a metaphoric substitution for sex had already entered mainstream filmmaking as a convenient displacement for censurable material. Although presented here as a cliché—and a parody of a cliché, thus twice removed from seriousness—the shot of the flames in the hearth that follows the two boys kissing nonetheless carries a freight of repressed desire. In *Fireworks* Anger takes this image even further, reworking it into a truly powerful metaphor, both erotic and subversive.

With *Fireworks* we enter an entirely different regime of personal desire and aesthetic achievement. But in terms of production values, modes of performance, and imagery, *Fireworks* resembles *Little Geezer* more than it does a Hollywood film. One can trace a continuity of practice and themes between the two films; the achievement of *Fireworks* begins in the foul rag-and-bone shop of a parody disguising a fantasy of attraction and denial, thus transforming Huff's repressions into an expression of transfiguration and acknowledgment, even celebration, of forbidden desire.

Legend has it that Anger shot *Fireworks* at the age of seventeen in his bedroom while still living with his parents.[15] This archetypal adolescent scenario of a secret creative and sexual life staged within the confines of one's own bedroom certainly corresponds to the film's claustrophobic sense of a private space of fantasy.[16] Anger himself plays the protagonist with some of the awkward charm of an amateur player. But instead of being intermittent and seemingly accidental, as in *Little Geezer*, the energy of personal revelation guides Anger's self-presentation, his combination of adolescent embarrassment and narcissistic display.

The title, *Fireworks*, announces the film's central image—fire—an image that goes through profound permutations. Anger uses fire as the image of desire, but rather than a simple one-off substitution, as in the conventional metaphor for sex, it provides an elemental structure to the whole work, blending associations of pleasure and pain. At one point during the encounter between Anger as the dreamer and the muscleman he tries to pick up, the backdrop suddenly changes from a bar to a blazing fireplace, almost as if Anger were referring to the hearth of *Little Geezer* (or, more likely, the many images of domestic seduction that Hollywood places in front of a blazing fireplace). But Anger lifts this image beyond cliché with a Looney Tunes–like exaggeration as the muscleman responds to the dreamer's request for a light for his cigarette by lifting a huge flaming brand from the hearth.

The film supplies a baseline of literal meanings for fire: the light for a cigarette, the fire in the fireplace, the burning of photographs of the sailor at the end of the film. The metaphoric dimension of fire emerges first in this fireplace scene: fire as sexual passion. But while Hollywood's fireplace imagery remains a dead metaphor, material for a joke in *Little Geezer*, Anger revives it through hyperbole. Instead of a domestic hearth, the anchor for homely contentment, the raging fire and the incendiary brand the muscleman plucks from it threaten to engulf the home in flames. The central spatial scenario of *Fireworks* explores the interpenetration of spaces of confinement and expansion, the explosion of privacy through fantasy, using flames to evoke danger and pain as well as blinding illumination, phoenixlike renewal, and even the transformation from flame to ash.

Early in the film Anger introduces the first of several visual jokes in which the dreamer's body seems to merge with alien but highly symbolic, if not magical objects. The dreamer wakes with a seemingly enormous boner poking up his sheets. He reaches under the sheets and brings out an African fetish. A sight gag worthy of Bob Clampett, the image not only provokes an obscene physical association but the ritualistic and Freudian relation of a fetish to a phallus. The double nature of this metaphor, as joke and ritual object, raises a central question of the film: are we simply in a realm of amusing substitutions and displacements, or on a voyage in which the pathways of desire lead to a realm of magical transformation? The dreamer's exit from his bedroom through the doorway initiates a sense of this voyage continuing its double nature.

The door as threshold served as a central image in the first group of American avant-garde films, the trance film psychodramas, from Maya Deren through Curtis Harrington and Stan Brakhage, and became a recurring image in Anger's films.[17] Most often in these films doors indicate a passage into a world of the imagination. The door in the bedroom in *Fireworks* bears a large homemade sign reading, GENTS. Anger raises the question of whether this passage leads outside or into a more private, more sequestered space. The sign also conjures the encounters in public restrooms that were part of the gay culture of the era, and that most likely form the film's autobiographical core (according to one account, Anger was arrested for homosexual activity in a public restroom not long before making the film).[18]

When Anger crosses through the door, however, he enters into a dark undefined space—certainly not a closet—where streetlights and passing car headlights, presented as the dreamer's point of view, seem to indicate a vast city of night. The passage through the GENTS door brings the dreamer into a space that is unpredictable, malleable, and highly symbolic, a space of encounters and ultimately of violent transformation. This moment of transition in both space and mode of representation would seem to correspond to Anger's description of his film in the *Filmmaker's Coop Catalogue*, where he declares that his protagonist "goes out in the night seeking a 'light' and is drawn through the needle's eye."[19] The overtone of possible threat escalates as the first character he encounters, the muscleman, not only offers the dreamer a much bigger light than he could have dreamed of but twists Anger's body into seemingly painful positions, albeit with both dancelike and erotic overtones, performing a twisted tango.

This single tormentor then gives way to a group of sailors who attack Anger, evoking both the supposed homosexual proclivities of sailors and the then-frequent incidents of gay-bashing by groups of servicemen that were frequent in this era, including, in 1943, the racist Zoot Suit Riots in Los Angeles.[20] While using montage techniques that show a mastery of both the suspense-building editing of the Hollywood genre film and the analysis of action of Soviet filmmakers, the attack moves increasingly into metaphorical and ritualistic territory, becoming, as P. Adams Sitney has pointed out, a *sparagmos*, the ritualistic dismembering of the god Dionysus.[21] Stripped bare, Anger is covered with white fluid while his body oozes something like blood. His orifices are probed, nostrils substituting for anus, fingers for phallus, until his very flesh is seemingly torn open.

This moment of extreme violence and extreme metaphor forms one of the cores of the film's erotic imagery. A broken milk bottle juxtaposed with a bare chest sets up the image of penetrating the flesh as surely as Buñuel posing the razor over the lady's eye in *Un Chien Andalou*. While less horrifying than the sliced donkey eye that follows in Buñuel's film, the shot of organs being torn open that follows in *Fireworks* conveys a visceral sense of violation. That we recognize the substitution of meat for living body, the trick of Anger's editing being very visible, only underscores the action's symbolic nature. To prevent us from smirking, thinking we have seen through Anger's trick effect, he pulls a joke on us. The bloody flesh parts to the probing fingers and reveals a ticking meter at the heart of things. A laugh of discovery accompanies our recognition that Anger is after more than just staging a snuff film, as this mechanical object replaces one of the protagonist's essential organs. A lyrical milk bath follows, the flow covering Anger's chest, both a sublimating image of baptism and a desublimating reference to hyperbolic ejaculation and water sports. Anger follows this climax in the metaphorical realm with a brief sequence that shocks us with its realism: a pan across a bank of public urinals, followed by a flash cut to a shot of Anger nude next to a urinal, apparently in an actual men's room. The realism of the scene surprises us, not only in contrast to the preceding highly dramatic, artificially lit and staged scenes, but because one imagines the filming of it must have involved some risk, a violation of public space with a highly private act, a blatant allusion to the pickup and sex acts in gents' rooms around the world.

The dreamer's venture out into the city of night in search of a light has reached its climax, and Anger now follows it with an apotheosis. The door to the GENTS opens slowly, but no one enters or exits. A cut to the undefined space of the opening shows the sailor seen in the film's prologue. The camera tracks forward. He opens his fly and reveals (through a jump cut) a Roman candle emerging from his crotch, which ejaculates in a torrent of sparks, literalizing the pyrotechnics promised by the title of the film. The magical body has undergone another transformation and absorption of an object. From African fetish, the phallus has become less an object than a spectacle, a dispenser of light and flames.

Anger's play of metaphor and bodily metamorphosis continues but takes on simultaneously a more absurd nature and a greater ritualistic logic. The Roman candle orgasm triggers a flash of the film's opening image of a torch plunging into water. The resulting splash seems solidified by a cut to the dreamer, his head now surmounted by (or replaced by) a Christmas tree bedecked with sparkling bulbs and tinsel whose scintillating form recalls the splash. The dreamer sways in ecstasy, a bandage presumably covering the wound from which his heart was removed (or rearranged). As the dreamer lowers his tree-topped head to cross the threshold of his room, the tip of the tree is shown to be aflame.

The image of the flaming Christmas tree head is as absurdist as a Magritte painting, a climactic merging of symbolic objects and Anger's body, a condensation of the American holidays of light and fireworks, a true Christmas in July. The dreamer returns from his encounter in the dark labyrinth of night, in which he was beset by demons and his body violated and transformed, like an archetypal shaman's journey of initiation, in which the head is often separated from the body and internal organs replaced by crystals that endow the shaman with magical powers.[22] A myth of transformation through ritualistic ordeal is invoked—whether that of the Classical mysteries or the occult Masonic initiation—but it is also parodied, expressed in pop terms, and relentlessly sexualized.

If this glorious image of a body made of light, shimmering and crowned by flames, supplies the film's climax, the remainder of the film forms an extraordinary diminuendo. Returning home, the transmogrified dreamer and his flaming tree crown bow before the fireplace and seem to ignite the photographs piled there at the film's opening. As the flames consume the images, revealing other nearly identical poses, we think not only of photographs but of the frames of a film, and the way cinema animates still frames by rapidly and briefly exposing them to intense light (a sort of premonition of Hollis Frampton's film *(nostalgia)*). Rather than supplying a dynamic source of phallic fire, the sailor now seems to surrender to the flames, to vanish into the work of fire, emphasizing what Anger has called the film's "temporary relief," passion now turned to ashes. The dreamer appears asleep on his bed in a pose nearly identical to our first view of him. It seems for a moment that the film has come full cycle, that we have simply witnessed the climax of a masturbation fantasy, the images of desire turned to ash by the brilliance of their illumination, the dreamer left surrounded by the detritus of his fantasy life, his spirit expended in a waste of shame.

But a coda contradicts this cycle of disillusioned desire. While the framing and location recall the opening—the dreamer lying in his bed—a slow camera movement reveals a series of differences: the fireplace remains ablaze, and the dreamer is no longer alone. A lover lies beside him, but if we look to find the features of the sailors or the muscleman, our identification is thwarted. The lover bears the face of the sun itself, a halo of glittering sunbeams wreathing his head and obscuring his face. The film transforms the body into an impossible amalgam for the final and most significant time. Instead of an ironic approximation of a magical being, relying on the distance supplied by camp humor, the aura of the sun-face introduces another layer of representation, scratching through the physical and material body of the film emulsion to let the unstained light of the projector through. In its drive to metaphor, the film does more than defeat conventional narrative logic: it displays the material conditions of film itself, celluloid exposed to light, and defaces the film's emulsion to create an image of desire so intense it bores through the surface to originating light.

Like all powerful images of desire, Anger's scratching of the sun into the surface of the film carries an overtone of violence beneath its glory. Physically attacking celluloid by scratching on film has long been an avant-garde technique, from the Dadaist films of Man Ray through the work

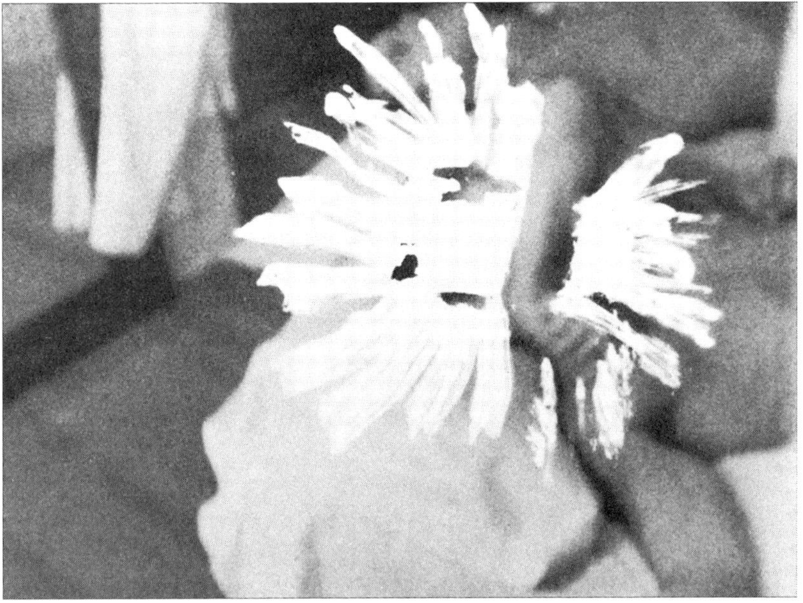

FIGURE 22.3. Kenneth Anger, *Fireworks* (1947).

of Stan Brakhage (whose signature for many years was scratched on the black leader that ended the film). In *Reflections on Black*, Brakhage used scratches on the film to express a sort of Tiresean blindness, gouging out the eyes of the protagonist. Scratching off emulsion can also be a gesture of effacing (according to one source, Anger scratched away his genitals in the restroom sequence of *Fireworks*), and preserving anonymity may have been one motivation for scratching out the lover's face here.[23] But here I believe Anger truly sublimates the violence inherent in the gesture, releasing the flames contained by the process of cinematic projection itself into a burst of metaphor, desire, and illumination, creating a star, a flaming creature rubbed raw from the body of the film itself.

23

Abigail Child: The Pulse of the Last Machine

1. MONTAGE, MON BON SOUCI (J.-L. G.)

> I envision the pulse of the last machine.
>
> ABIGAIL CHILD

For more than a decade I taught in a filmmaking program at the State University of New York, College at Purchase, a film historian/theorist/critic cast into the daily practical and aesthetic problems of students trying to learn the craft and the art of filmmaking. (In fact, it was there that I first met Abigail Child some time in the early 1980s when Dick Rogers brought her in to do a workshop on the optical printer.) I often thought my role there was to make sure the students questioned the conventions of filmmaking and directed them toward alternative films and filmmakers (not that the many unconventional filmmakers who taught there weren't doing the same thing, albeit in a different way). For the most part the students responded, and a number of edgy films became models for them. One of these was Jim Jarmusch's 1984 *Stranger than Paradise* (still my favorite of his films), which consisted of long takes joined (or separated) by sections of black leader. Almost immediately a number of students inserted black leader between shots in their films and raised the ire of the department's chair, an

This essay first appeared in *Is This What You Were Born For? Strategies of Appropriation and Audio-Visual Collage*, ed. F. Bovier (Geneva: Metis Presses, 2011), 13–34.

extraordinary filmmaker (both director and editor) in his own right, Aram Avakian, who promptly forbade the practice in his classes. Representing, I thought, the right to be unconventional, I confronted him, citing the technique's success in Jarmusch's film. Aram did not debate Jarmusch's style with me, but indicated that by inserting black leader, instead of learning how to edit, the students were avoiding dealing with the juxtaposition of one shot against another, precisely what he wanted them to face. His opposition was not aesthetic, but pedagogical. I was chastened and convinced.

Whether working in the tradition of Sergei Eisenstein and the Soviets; the postwar Americans Maya Deren, Kenneth Anger, and Stan Brakhage; Hollywood; or the New Wave, editing transforms time, space, rhythm, and movement and gives control of tempo and meaning. Although I am a great admirer of André Bazin, who pointed out the limitations of editing and championed styles of long takes and deep focus which permitted the unity of space and/or time, I confess I find the pervasive avoidance of editing in much of recent art cinema (even including the long takes of Hou Hsiao-Hsien, Abbas Kiarostami, or Béla Tarr, to name some of the strongest directors working in narrative cinema today) a bit academic and possibly a pernicious influence on younger filmmakers. Montage, while hardly the definition of cinema that the Soviets claimed, remains, I feel, possibly the most powerful voice film has, the tool by which it probes and questions reality. Few filmmakers today have maintained and expanded this tradition as Abigail Child has, and the series of films that make up *Is This What You Were Born For?* provide explorations and demonstration of the art of editing in an era where it may seem to be being abandoned and forgotten.

Child could be described as a didactic filmmaker. She has for decades been an inspiring teacher, and I feel the same energy drives her films. The very title of the series—"Is this what you were born for?"—captures the tone of her pedagogy: asking questions, not instilling answers, demanding a personal address from filmmaker to viewer, probing the very foundations of one's existence. The phrase comes from one of the etchings that makes up Goya's series *The Disasters of War*, chronicling the effects of the Napoleonic invasion of Spain in 1809. A standing figure wanders amid a heap of dead bodies. As he bends over them, his eyes wide and his arms outstretched, vomit sprays from his mouth. Goya's title (or comment) printed at the bottom of the etching, "*Para eso hobies nocido,*" has been translated into English both as a statement and as a question: "Is this what you were born for?" (the version Child adopts) and "This is what you were born for," which Spanish-speaking friends tell me is more accurate. But it is clear that the etching as a whole has the force of a question, even if the caption is a statement. The image itself confronts and unsettles the viewer; it hardly illustrates the words. Rather, caption and image offer a sort of vertical montage, each unsettling on its own, and even more unsettling together. The complexity of Child's pedagogy relies on such juxtapositions and transformations in meaning between image and sound, image and image, language and noise, as well as image and language. I will return to Child's question/title at the end of this essay, but I want this question to echo through this essay, in a number of ways, none of them reducible to a simple query that could be easily answered.

In my preface to Child's book *This Is Called Moving*, I described her as a neo-Constructivist, returning to the inspirations of the Soviet avant-garde.[1] Child showed allegiance to montage in an era when, in the wake of Warhol, many structural filmmakers sought out more minimal forms. Child's montage draws on many traditions, not limited to film: e.g., modern poetics based in Poundian juxtapositions; music concrète with its juxtapositions of sources, tonalities, and rhythms; and post-Graham dance with its sense of broken gestures and actions. This variety of sources (and Child herself works in all these forms) calls for serious comparative essays, but I will not attempt this task here. Instead I will focus on Child's film editing. Primarily, my analysis will be visual, which, too, is an arbitrary limitation. Child ranks as one of the strongest masters of sound editing and composition. However, I do not feel I have the knowledge of either the techniques of sound composition or its history to do an adequate job with this dimension of her works, although I acknowledge its overwhelming importance. Inevitably, however, sound enters into the montage of images (what Eisenstein called vertical montage), so I will not neglect it entirely. While deeply aware of the work and theories of montage from the Soviets, and their elaboration by the later avant-garde filmmakers (from Peter Kubelka and Bruce Conner to Arthur Lipsett), Child also draws on earlier editing styles that inspired the Soviets, from serial melodramas to the films of D. W. Griffith. Child addresses all these traditions, sometimes critically, probing their power and their calculations.

I want to offer a close analysis of some brief montage sequences from films in this series. This poses a bit of dilemma for a number of reasons. First, translating images and their juxtapositions into words dooms the writer to a prolix form of betrayal of the brevity, the wit, the ambiguity, and the pure physical sensation of actually viewing them. But I believe the task is worth it, because hopefully it directs our attention to the actual means by which Child raises her questions on every level. Brief sequences that open four of the films from this series will be central to my analyses. I feel that, rather than simply setting the stage or giving expositional information, the first moments of strong films frequently cue the viewer to the film's style and preoccupations.

Child keeps the challenge of montage alive and employs and redefines its power. While I place her within a tradition, she also explodes and reworks it, and leaves it alive and kicking. If I have described Child as a didactic filmmaker, the last thing I want this to indicate is that she has a message to deliver. Rather, Child's filmmaking, its sensual form, probes fundamentally how film speaks; nothing in her work splits the forms she uses from the issues she explores. Thus, to explore the role editing plays in her style means not only thinking through the history and affect of editing, but rediscovering (reinventing?) this medium which Hollis Frampton called "the last machine" in order to explore both its past and its future.[2] Child returns significance to the term "experimental film."

2. MOVEMENT AS STRUCTURE: "THIS IS CALLED MOVING"

> Movement can stretch to infinity.
>
> ABIGAIL CHILD

Film emerged from a desire to analyze motion. The experiments in chronophotography of Marey and Muybridge in the late nineteenth century sought less to capture movement than to break down action into separate phases: whether of a galloping horse, marching soldiers, or the crashing of waves. This analysis was founded upon interrupting movement, converting it into a series of still images. With the invention of motion pictures, Edison and the Lumières returned motion to these frozen images, but perhaps thereby lost a tool of analysis. But film editing articulates space and time in motion pictures, and analyzes motion without freezing it. Editing can extend motion beyond the end of the shot, bridging two shots by continuing a motion over the cut. For example, in a Hollywood film a person stands up, and during this action a cut switches from a medium shot to a long shot. The natural unfolding of the action covers the change in camera distance and hides the cut. But while editing of action may link motion into a seeming continuity, it can also break it down and transform it.

Griffith already understood this in his early Biograph films from 1908 and 1909. Instead of simply following one line of action, his editing would cut between two lines, interrupting one with the other. Such alternation became known as "parallel editing," and most famously Griffith used it to create suspense, as in his famous chase and last-minute rescue sequences, cutting back and forth between the plight of a victim and rescuers on the way. But Griffith never limited parallel editing to this narrative task. With parallel editing Griffith could interrupt the progression of an action, often interrupting a gesture in its unfolding in order to switch to another line of action. As his film *Intolerance* (1916) shows, alternation between lines of action enabled Griffith to play with space and time and create a new formal structure for a film.

In one of my earliest essays, entitled "Weaving a Narrative: Style and Economic Background in Griffith's Biograph Films,"[3] I compared Griffith's use of parallel editing to the primal cultural form of weaving, in which textiles are formed through a pattern of intercrossing threads. During the limited time I spent at a loom in my adolescence, I became mesmerized by the way the loom held the warp thread, while the shuttle pulled the weft thread in and out of the warp, forming a fabric from this interlacing. As in a game of hide-and-seek, a weft thread would dive beneath the warp, and then reappear. Years later in graduate school, studying with Peter Kubelka, I recognized a similar process when he described the logic of his film *Schwechater* (1958). As I recall his lecture, the film consists of a number of threads of images (one of the action of pouring from a bottle of beer, one of foaming beer, one of a couple at a table, one of a model drinking, etc.) presented in both positive and negative. Kubelka edited these actions together as if each thread was continuously playing but emerged on the screen only at moments, frames from one thread disappearing when frames from another appeared. (Thus frame 1 of the film might be frame 1 of the thread showing the foam; frame 2, frame 2 of the couple at table; frame 3, frame 3 of the foam; frame 4, frame 4 of the pouring bottle; frame 5, frame 5 of model drinking; frame 6, frame 6 of the couple at table, etc.).[4] I realized that such a pattern also underlay Griffith's parallel editing—less numerically precise, of course, but with one line of action continuing even when it was not shown on the screen. As in weaving, the interlacing of threads alternated between visibility and invisibility, and the sense of hidden action gave force to the sequence as much as the action literally displayed on the screen.

I do not believe Child uses a mathematical pattern such as Kubelka employed, but her editing employs patterns of alternation, of disappearance and reappearance, of continuing threads of action playing hide-and-seek. *Mutiny*, part 2 in the series *Is This What You Were Born For?*, recreates movement in relation to the art of editing and the structure of interruption and interlacing. In fact, the film ends with a black screen and we hear a voice say (rather offhandedly), "This is called moving"—a phrase Child later adopted for a collection of her writings. Although I snatch at this fragment of language for its multiple meanings, it also eludes me. Let me play with it a bit. Child seems to bury it here in the darkness that ends her film. The voice that speaks it is far from sounding authoritative or even overtly pedagogical. Yet I can't help thinking the phrase declares the film ("this") is called *moving* (even though it is really called *Mutiny*). What we have just seen is an encyclopedia of movement, gesture, and expression, but never simply a dictionary consisting of definitions. Rather the film is a *combinatoire*, a kaleidoscope in which movements jumble and tumble together in a wild yet calculated choreography. If I can wax Heideggerian, it is as though the film has called on movement, or has itself answered the call of the moving image. The phrase might also declare, "*This* (as opposed to something else) is what is properly called moving" (like "That's entertainment!" or "This is what I call living!"). The term *moving* itself has many resonances. Combined with the call to revolt made by the title, *Mutiny*—and (as the concentration on women in the film also leads us to think) the film could be said to be moving a mutiny along: it forms part of a movement, political and social. But also the phrase reminds us that the film is "moving" in another sense: i.e., that it moves us emotionally.

It is perhaps easier to capture in writing the to-and-fro of language that Child enacts than the flow of her images. Since analysis of the moving image involves the treacherous translation into words I mentioned earlier, I fear to dissect this dynamic and cinematic motion in static terms. But Child herself dissects movement throughout the film without ever reducing it to stasis. That is what film can do. This film cuts into motion in order to duplicate, liberate, and multiply it. And yet *Mutiny* also coheres to an astonishing degree, precisely through its interweaving of diverse threads, which move continuously through the film, emerging or hiding as the editing allows. Let me try to describe this pattern and process of interweaving in detail with a brief sequence that opens the film.

The first image of the film, a long shot, shows a young woman diving into a pool (actually, sliding into it), providing not only a powerful kinetic opening image, but an invitation for the viewer to plunge into this sea of images. In the next image, a medium close-up, a young woman standing on a street corner bows a violin with a toothbrush. This cut moves us from full-body motion to smaller hand movements, a type of transition found frequently in the film. However, the transition in shot scale enlarges the smaller movement and makes the two movements equivalent visually. The sync sound of the violin renders the second image very palpable. The next cut brings on a brief shot of a woman's torso wearing a red sweater bouncing through the frame. We return then to the violinist.

The interruption of the violinist's action with the shot of the bouncing woman, and then the return to the violinist introduces the pattern of alternation so basic to film editing: the weaving in and out, the A B A schema. The violinist takes on a central role in the film, marked both by the resonance of her performance as a musician using a traditional instrument in a nontraditional manner, and by her formal role of introducing the film's pattern of alternation. I see her as a "directing" figure, almost a surrogate for the filmmaker—a bit like the figures of the traffic cop and the film editor (not to mention the cameraman) who recur in Dziga Vertov's 1929 *Man with a Movie Camera*. These figures manage the traffic between images and allow them to intersect. Like them, the violinist threads throughout the film, interacting with many other threads, but also invoking a guiding hand. In the next shot a woman stands ironing; then we cut back to the woman in the red sweater, now seen in full figure, bouncing in an office space. This dancer also plays a nodal role in the film, carrying out her choreography in an everyday space, embodying one of the film's themes: the interpenetration of art and everyday life.

The pattern of interwoven threads gathers strength and begins to show its complexity, adding new elements and returning to ones already shown. We could schematize it like this: **A** (diving girl) / **B** (violinist) / **C** (bouncing woman) / **B** / **D** (woman ironing) / **C**. New threads are added in brief shots: a man performing in a darkened environment cuts to a female athlete (or ballet dancer in training) leaping in a brightly lit gym; cut to another girl leaping in the same location; return to the bouncing dancer in the red sweater; cut to a black-and-white image of a woman speaking earnestly and gesturing with her hands in front of a wall covered with photographs. A series of shots of this woman are given with slight gaps and sometimes frames of black leader, which break her gestures and make them more frenetic. We then return to two very brief shots of the violinist. The pattern thus far is **A, B, C, B, D, C, E, F, F, C, G** (multiple), **B, B**. Each of these images represents a thread that will be carried through the film, and dozens more threads are gathered and interwoven as the film progresses.

The interweaving creates unity out of this diversity. Although not all the threads portray the action of women, women predominate. These women are all moving, and movements of many different sorts and in many different environments are gathered together. We see overtly athletic movement (diving girl, gymnast, bouncing woman), artistic movement (violinist, bouncing dancer, male performer, ballerinas), everyday tasks (ironing), and intellectual discussion (woman in front of photographs). The cutting not only accents the movement that underlies all of these ways of behaving, but marks their rhythms and interrelates each of them with the other actions. The cuts interrupting actions in several cases make the action of one shot seem to trigger the next. The cut from the male performer suddenly lifting something (a microphone cord?) bumps the girl gymnast, as then her *jeté* triggers an *entrechat* in the next shot, a movement responded to in turn by the bouncing dancer in the office. The hand gestures of the speaking woman chime with the hand movement of the violinist at the end of this sequence. A complex choreography of interrelated movements ripples through these shots, the brevity of each cut rendering them almost continual. I stop my analysis arbitrarily at this point, after about a dozen shots. But lest the complexity of the description be deceiving, let me emphasize that this sequence lasts *less than twenty seconds on the screen*, less time than the opening shot of most films. The strong sense of order coexists with a sense of speed and rush. Can the viewer keep up? Intellect has a physical dimension, and viewing is an activity: the mind is a muscle, and here, it gets a workout. This is called moving!

3. TELL ME A STORY . . .

> There's a sense of humor with all this action and nothing happening.
>
> ABIGAIL CHILD

The dominance of dramatic filmmaking over both the commercial market and the field of film studies has led some critics, including myself, to stress polemically the nonnarrative aspects of cinema (as in my discussion of early cinema as a "cinema of attractions").[5] However, even in the case of early cinema, I maintain, a dialectic between spectacle and drama can be more engaging than purist demarcations of one form from the other. Narrative itself is a polyvalent term (although to my mind it can best be defined as telling a story). Not only are there many avant-garde narrative films (Christopher McLaine's *The End*, Cocteau's *Blood of a Poet*), there are many experimental films in which narrative played a deciding role for the filmmakers that is not necessarily evident to viewers. Brakhage has indicated all his films could be interpreted as narratives (to my mind a dismaying prospect), while filmmaker Lewis Klahr evokes narratives without making the story explicit (I have referred to these as "submerged narratives").[6] No absolute distinction between narrative and its alternatives (lyricism? rhetoric? absurdity?) exists. Film scholar Ben Brewster has described narrative as

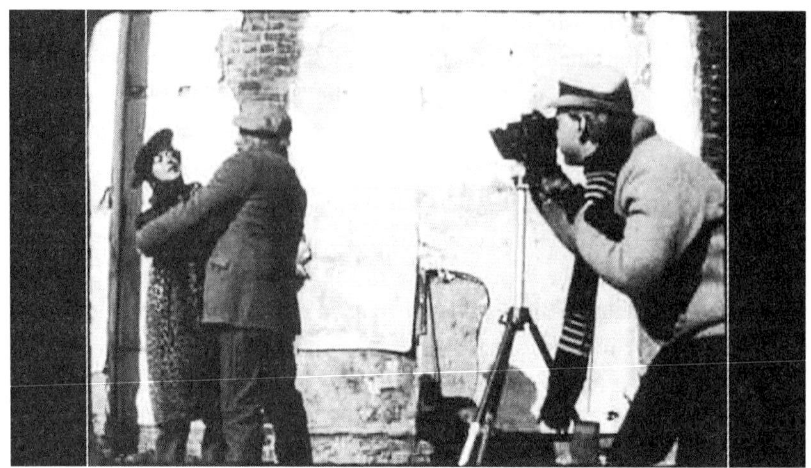

FIGURE 23.1. Abigail Child, *Perils* (1986).

an integrative form, which can absorb other material (songs, gags, didactic speeches, lyrical sequences—all these appear in films that are thought of as classical Hollywood films).[7] I call the narrative cinema that emerged around 1907 a "cinema of narrative integration" precisely to emphasize that narrative holds diverse elements together. However, in some films the narrative fails to actually keep everything together, even if it tries to. I believe that Child explores the disintegration of narrative, breaking it up into fragments, which nonetheless still bear the trace of narrative desire. I would even say she breaks up narratives in order to discover the desires that underlie them—their undercurrents.

Perils and *Mayhem* invoke narrative precisely to pick it apart, to literally deconstruct it, to probe what holds it together and to undermine this sense of wholeness and completion. This involves more than a narrative that fails to resolve itself (like, for instance, Michelangelo Antonioni's 1966 *Blow-Up*). Rather, Child's narrative seems to have trouble getting started. *Perils* seems to delight in the idea of a film which would be all introduction, opening with close-ups of the main characters, the sort of prologue to a film which began in the silent era and continued into the 1930s (when it vanished like the last trace of silent cinema), with its last gasp in kids' adventures serials. These close-ups are followed by titles and a series of posed tableaux of action. Importantly, we watch the actors assuming these poses (sometimes in front of a still camera). The tableaux invoke strong action, mainly fights, that never break into dramatic action, but simply relax and dissolve the tension. They seem like previews of action to come, or even stills to hang in the lobby of a movie theater and beckon the audience in with promises of fantasy and adventure.

Child's editing traces the fault line between stillness and motion, inverting the usual associations. Narrative is supposed to move us along with action and its consequences (as in Gilles Deleuze's concept of the movement image as an action image), while lyrical or abstract modes invoke a suspended time (Deren's vertical axis).[8] But *Mutiny*, which makes little use of narrative, moves constantly, while the narrative energies of *Perils* and *Mayhem* freeze into immobile tableaux. This is more than a perverse avant-garde reversal. Probing deeply into dominant forms of narrative, especially melodrama, Child uncovers the role stasis plays in these popular forms. Whether or not she would see it as an influence, I know she has read Peter Brooks's groundbreaking study of melodrama, *The Melodramatic Imagination*.[9] Brooks discussed the use of the tableaux in melodrama more thoroughly than any critic before him. The nineteenth-century melodramatic stage marked moments of extreme dramatic tension or significance by freezing the action into a "picture" (often using the French term *tableau*). Holding the action in a static pose intensified audience involvement, creating a moment of literal suspense. In *Perils* and *Mayhem*, Child restages the situations and film styles of two dominant forms of film melodrama: the action serial (Louis Feuillade, Pearl White) of the 1910s, and film noir of the 1940s and 1950s. The silent films employed literal tableaux, while film noir often collapsed into a state of hysterical paralysis (think of the endings of *Lady from Shanghai*, *Gun Crazy*, *Detour*, or *Criss Cross*).

Child's interest in stilling an action-based narrative compares curiously with the criticism of Roland Barthes, who wrote essays on both tableaux and film stills. I find Child's engagement with these forms in some ways more complex than Barthes's, at least in terms of their relation to motion. Barthes seems uncomfortable with motion. In his brilliant essay "The Third Meaning," he analyzed Eisenstein based on stills, rather than the actual projected films.[10] Child, as we have seen, lives and breathes movement, moves within it with confidence and joy. Approaching the tableau as used by Brecht and Eisenstein, Barthes sees it primarily as the cutting out of a fragment from a flow of action, the frozen moment of a fetish. Child is closer to Brooks (although she actually works between these positions), exploiting the dramatic tension generated by the tableau.

But Child's tableaux offer more than historical reference to melodramatic films. They also recall the absurdist and complexly erotic tableaux that appear in "underground" films from the 1960s, especially those of Jack Smith and Ken Jacobs. Like those earlier films, *Perils* and *Mayhem* parody Hollywood melodramas in order to appropriate their energies of fantasy and role-playing while detouring away from narrative conventions. Lurking behind these films lie pornographic tableaux that suspend the moment of arousal. Pornography poses the elements of sexual fantasy: the body postures, the costumes (or lack thereof), the props and settings within a composition designed to generate fantasy. These frozen images suspend the promise of desire in a state unsustainable in real life, a peak of excitement with no aftermath, a timeless ecstasy. As Deleuze shows in his analysis of the novels of Sacher-Masoch (whose name was inscribed in masochism), the eroticism of such scenarios finds its fulfillment in the construction of tableaux rather than action, the artistically controlled staging of desire in a frozen scene.[11]

Mayhem blends such erotic tableaux with film noir compositions. In their polymorphous perversity, Child's noir stagings undermine the heterosexual (and frequently misogynist and homophobic) scenarios that contain the energies of noir films. Child links "genre and gender," probing narrative patterns' dependence on conceptions of gender. Child parodies the gender stereotypes from these films (woman as threat, woman as victim), but also mines them for the erotic energy they try to hold in control. In traditional films, sexual energy drives the narrative, but into predictable scenarios. Child brakes that drive, blocking it into ambiguous tableaux (as in Sacher-Masoch, we wonder, who is the victim and who the aggressor; who is in control?). Further, she asks us: What do the figures in this image want? What do you, the viewer, want? Is this what you were born for?

In *Perils* and *Mayhem*, stillness does not appear as the opposite of motion—the traditional concept of repose—but as the blocking of motion, freezing it at a moment of intensity. Here she moves closer to Barthes, but even closer to Walter Benjamin's discussion of Brecht's use of the tableau as an alienation effect.[12] Suspending narrative action deflects our attention from what will happen next, and we are left wondering what caused all this in the first place. While Child understands the intensity generated by melodramatic tableaux, she sees it as revelatory rather than simply dramatic. Placing obstacles in the well-worn paths of narrative desire and fulfillment, Child sows tension and frustration, releasing an undefined anxiety that pervades these films.

After the opening darkness and credits, *Mayhem* presents a close-up of a woman's face (head and shoulders), crossed by the striated pattern of dark and light cast by a Venetian blind off-screen. This image, with its juxtaposition of opposites, shadow and light, projecting a hash pattern of confinement onto characters and space, has become a visual icon of film

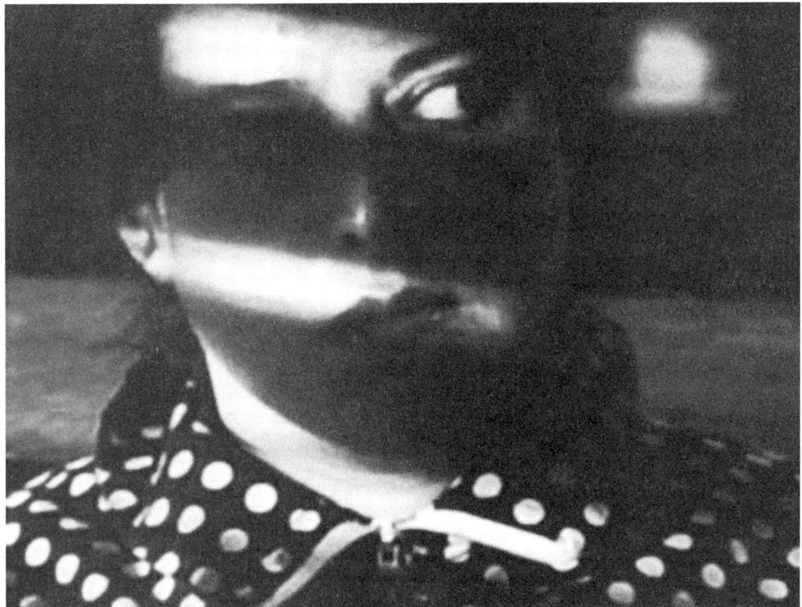

FIGURE 23.2. Abigail Child, *Mayhem* (1987).

noir. For Child the image not only carries a genre reference, or invokes a gendered gaze, but composes an attitude toward space and the viewer. She writes, "She's looking out of the picture. The bars across her face hold her in the picture and hold her from us."[13] Child actually comments here on a still from her film, but I think it refers to the actual film as well. Instead of seeing the shadow pattern as an aspect of the film's diegetic world (a Venetian blind, somewhere off-screen) or its emotional tone (entrapment), Child notes the alienation of the shot from the viewer, its isolation within the cinema frame. The next shot is a perfectly continuous, almost classical, cut back to a wider view of the same scene, but Child only hints at creating a fictional setting. This film takes place on the screen and in our memory of other films, imprisoned there (or perhaps liberated, freed from the continuities of narrative action).

These opening shots of *Mayhem* affect us dramatically. The lighting, the staging, and especially the performance of the woman (whose expression and roving eye give a sense of some unknown threat lurking off screen and make us hear the soundtrack as a door rattling, almost opening . . .). But none of these dramatic expectations become defined, fulfilled, satisfied. Rather the anxiety, the confinement, the sense of threat unchanneled, invade the entire film and perhaps even cross the barrier of the screen to infect the audience/viewer. Where *Mutiny* interweaves a logic of alternation and contrast of actions in a nonnarrative space, *Mayhem* works against the expectations instilled in us by years of film watching. In classical editing and narrative, an off-screen look opens an off-screen space, soon to be revealed. *Mayhem* blocks these connections, invoking and then stalling (or exploding) the conventional syntax of narrative editing. The basic suture between glance and object that holds much of the thriller genre together (and in Laura Mulvey's analysis fixes the woman as spectacle) is refused here. Child has written:

> I had long conceived of a film composed only of reaction shots in which all causality was erased. The isolation and dramatization of emotions through the isolation (camera) and dramatization (editing) of gesture. What would be left would be the resonant voluptuous suggestions of history and the human face.[14]

Child neither refuses or defuses narrative, genre, or drama. Rather she sets it off, then experiments with it: what would happen if . . . Instead of being simply absorbed into the melodrama, we watch the process of absorption and attraction. We are moved and blocked—and we think about why and how.

4. MERCY, MERCY, ME

> Held together by the wires of its exhilaration. . . . The mind itself is a network of channels.
>
> ABIGAIL CHILD

Mercy, which ends the series *Is This What You Were Born For?* (following directly from the two films discussed in the last section), seems to me Child's most beautiful and enigmatic film. The first image again offers what I could call a tutor image, teaching the viewer how to enter the film. *Mercy* begins in darkness with sound (a rhythmic snapping) before the first image appears: an Asian woman in close-up wearing headphones and seeming intent on what she is hearing. It is followed by four shots in AB alternation, a upside-down tracking shot over a table framing a number of masculine hands pointing and shuffling papers, intercut with black-and-white footage, rather vague, of women in their underpants. There follows a color close-up of a young girl, her head resting on the edge of a chair or couch as a hand comes into the frame and touches her; a brief black-and-white shot of a foot on the brake petal of a car, and a shot that rapidly approaches a tree until its darkness fills the frame. A voice cries out "No!" and then the title appears: *Mercy*.

This opening shows Child's unique appropriation of Soviet-influenced montage. It introduces a pattern of alternation which carries a strong formal and ideological contrast: male/female, color/black and white, etc., while the masculine hands cuffed in business suits and commandingly grabbing papers contrast with the women, seminude and full-bodied. The young girl evokes empathy and vulnerability (perhaps the recipient of the question "Is this what you were born for?"). The foot on the brake pedal and the rapid movement toward the tree until it blots out the screen, combined with a shriek of "No!," works like a textbook illustration of Eisensteinian montage: foot on brake plus camera movement into tree = car crash or, as Eisenstein would put it: montage as collision![15] But if the sequence seems very legible at first, ambiguities emerge. Are the hands that touch the girl's head a caring parent's, or a sinister threat? On the language level, the spoken "No!" followed by the printed "Mercy"—does it transform the title into its opposite: "No Mercy"? All of Child's work allows a penumbra of ambiguity to fall across our attempts to make meaning. The woman with headphones recurs throughout the film, setting up a key theme and central ambiguity: the interaction of people with technology. In many ways the woman parallels the violinist and the dancer in *Mutiny*: a nodal point between images. I called the dancer and violinist "directing figures" because of their performances, and saw them as stand-ins for the filmmaker. In contrast, this woman acts as a receiver. Intercut with the enormous range of images in this film, she listens to messages from beyond, trying to understand them. She could also parallel the filmmaker, gathering diverse material together. Rather than the traffic cop in Vertov's *Man with a Movie Camera*, she recalls—very directly, perhaps even intentionally—the woman with radio headphones who opens Vertov's first sound film, *Enthusiasm: Symphony of the Don Basin* (1931). She introduces the film, serving as a figure for his montage of both sound and image. Vertov, as a Soviet Constructivist, celebrated the progress of technology, the modernization and industrialization of the Soviet Union (which we now know was achieved at a great cost of human life and suffering). Child's film takes a more ambiguous view of the human/technology interface, but neither simply condemns nor celebrates it.

Enthusiasm celebrates the labor of miners and factory workers rhythmically and broadly struggling with their tools and raw material. Rather than this "athletic" labor, Child primarily shows technicians or subjects of experiments. They are receptive (I avoid saying passive) more than active: peering into microscopes, cameras, and other viewing devices, they take their place within the organized workplaces of laboratories or classrooms. Many of the human figures remain unmoving but under a watchful eye, partly identified with the camera (a series of sleeping children, subjects of experiments, medical patients). They seem inserted into a complex network, like the woman with her earphones. When we see machines they are large (steam shovels, ships, factory transports). Coils of wire or cables spooling or unspooling onto large reels thread through the film—the means of connecting the flow of information and energy, the visual form of networks. Child compares her style of montage, which connects everything with everything else, with the nature of the modern world, in which networks predominate and people find their place within them (weaving and networks have obvious similarities). Sections of *Mercy* intercut the actions of people (or the camera) from shot to shot as deftly as *Mutiny*, with leaps by one character completed by another, or the movement of the camera over one shot complexly mirrored in the movement of the shots that follow. This ripple of action and gesture across shots, however, seems less the product of the physical and emotional energy of figures engaged in an act of artistic expression, joyful communication, or political mutiny, than a coordinated network into which they all fit. The recurring image of the cable coiling or uncoiling provides an organizing rhythm.

When Child introduces language in her films, it serves less to define or clarify something than to allow her to explore the ambiguity of words. This is true of her exploration of the language of montage as well. Child reverses the ambition of early montage directors such as Lev Kuleshov (and in a way Vertov and Eisenstein) to create a syntax of editing whose meaning would be legible and unambiguous. Child too pursues the legibility of montage, but simultaneously uses it to shake up the apparent meaning of an image, expression, or gesture. Thus one sequence begins with a woman taking a photograph while a male voice-over says ". . . was ever worth a thousand words, this is it." Child counts on the viewer recognizing the cliché "a picture is worth a thousand words." As the male narrator continues, we see a mother hugging her son to congratulate him for having become a soldier (or, as the voice-over intones, "become a man"). This sentimental scene is repeated twice. But on its replay, Child cuts from the mother/son embrace to a rodeo image where a man "bulldogs" a steer, wrestling it to the ground. This is followed by television wrestlers seizing each other's heads in a hammerlock. In its original context, the embrace camouflaged

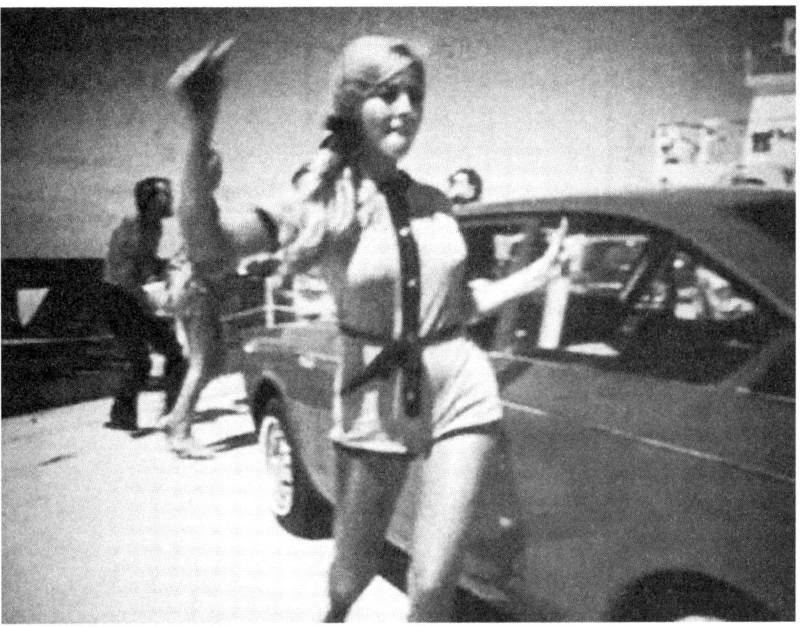

FIGURE 23.3. Abigail Child, *Mercy* (1989).

the action of a mother preparing her son to kill or be killed in the military with a sentimental message of family love and pride. Child's montage associates the loving embrace with images of overt aggression and violence, all using the same apparent gesture.

Such transformation of tone and meaning invokes the traditional meaning of ambiguity: an oscillation between two very different alternatives. Child also produces images in which the meanings cannot be separated and opposed, but remain fused in a complexity of ambivalent associations. For instance, after the relentless black and white of the two previous films in the series, the appearance of color in *Mercy* creates a very different tone. Shot at a time when black and white began to disappear from commercial film and television and was becoming a signifier for the "past," the lack of color in *Perils* and *Mayhem* also makes references to film history. The color in *Mercy*, especially when faded to magenta, accents a historical period, albeit more recent, evoking the 1950s and 1960s and the culture of postwar American consumerism and imperialism. Black and white appears in *Mercy* as well and establishes another device of formal contrast/alternation. But beyond the historical and formal references, color also carries a sensual address, as in the touristic images traveling through a swamp, which, in spite of their kitsch aspect, provide intense visual delight. (Child has written,

"Colors seem to say *kiss me*," and the color shots of the swamp in *Mercy* are literally intercut with images of couples kissing passionately.)

I connect these often-beautiful images of nature and color with the ambiguity of the film's title. After *Perils* and *Mayhem*, is *Mercy* a state the filmmaker achieves, or is it a plea for the violence to cease? I read it more often as the latter, but I also think Child envisions the former. The previous two films enact fantasies of desire and retribution, through the conventions of popular film narrative. In *Mercy* the forces of repression do not appear as the clichéd (yet dreamlike and evocative) figures of forbidden desire and dire punishment, but rather as the organized forces of technology and science. Which is more threatening: the glowering tough in the striped shirt, or the calm scientist at her microscope? If Child comes after the era of Vertov's enthusiasm for the possibilities of technology and industry—and after the collapse of that utopian vision—she nonetheless seems to maintain some faith in the possibility of turning that Leviathan around, of refashioning the technosphere in human terms. If humanizing technology seems almost impossible today, we might point to Child's own use of cinema as an attempt to divert its power and domination into other networks, a deliberate mutiny on the ship of "state of the art."

Mercy ends with a time-lapse image that I take to be a root, sprouting white filaments that spin a network of eerie beauty. Is this an image of mercy, of growth—or of decay? In nature, there is no absolute difference, of course; organic growth and decomposition depend on each other. I think here of the end of Heidegger's essay on the question of technology, where he quotes Holderlin's line from "Patmos": *Wo aber Gefahr ist, wächst / Das Rettende auch* (Where danger is, there grows / salvation also).[16] Child's concluding image of the growth of nature recalls the time-lapse films of bean sprouts and plants growing that so inspired two women of the French avant-garde in the 1920s, filmmaker Germaine Dulac and writer Colette (who described in one of her film reviews how children, watching the tendrils of a plant snake across the screen, spontaneously got up from their seats and danced in imitation).[17] This is a vision only cinema, as the daughter of technology, as the microscope of time, could give. Cinema makes a picture out of nature, a moving image. As I claimed earlier, the cinema was invented to present motion under new aspects, ones that allowed it to be studied and rearranged. We could imagine Child addressing her medium of cinema, asking it: "Is this what you were born for?"

24

The Secret Language of the Traces of Light: David Gatten's *Dividing Line*

1. WORD IMAGE TRACE

> This was handwritten then it was typeset then filmed and now it is light reading.
>
> MICHAEL SNOW, *So Is This*

My first viewing of films by David Gatten left me puzzled: intrigued certainly, and even attracted, but uncertain if these challenging and thought-provoking films could truly be considered cinema—even avant-garde or experimental cinema. The films I saw about a decade ago were from his ongoing series *Secret History of the Dividing Line: A True Account in Nine Parts*. The series focuses on the Byrd family of colonial Virginia, especially William Byrd II and his daughter Evelyn, key figures in the foundation of American culture, whose family melodrama paralleled their deep involvement in the pursuit of knowledge. These films consisted predominantly of words, especially typographical excerpts from Byrd family documents. This reliance on the printed word presented a provocation in a medium usually defined by its visual nature. Few images appear in these films, at least as the term *image* is usually understood—a picture or representation of something or someone.

This essay first appeared in *Texts of Light: A Mid-Career Retrospective of Fourteen Films by David Gatten* (Columbus: Wexner Center for the Arts, Ohio State University, 2011), with the following dedication: "For Erin Espelie who writes on Nature."

Presented visually, the word, of course, plays a role in most films (e.g., intertitles during the silent era; signs, letters, or telegrams that appear within shots; credits or end titles). More relevant to Gatten, a number of avant-garde films have foregrounded written words over images, such as Michael Snow's *So Is This* (1982), Hollis Frampton's *Poetic Justice* (1972), or Ernie Marrero and Susan Kouguell's *One Day Franz Came to My House* (1981, an unfortunately little-known film, although included in the Museum of Modern Art film archives). But in these and other experimental films, imagistic aspects of the words play a greater role than in some of Gatten's films (Frampton's film includes a tableau of a desktop, complete with coffee cup and cactus plant on which rests a written script; Snow uses a rhythmic pattern of editing, presenting one word at a time; *Franz* uses animation and other techniques to give the words an imagistic quality.) The way the words appear on the screen in these films highlights the temporal and visual aspects of cinema; further, these words ask you to imagine another scene that is described or referred to by the words on-screen. Gatten's texts also play visual games with us, moving into abstract close-up and seeming to fly by, often at great speed, but they primarily seem to force us to stick with the words as printed marks, as quotes, as documents, as letters somehow impressed on the surface of a medium. We experience them as flattened elements in a two-dimensional world from which we can never entirely escape.

Why are images nearly excluded from these films, especially the first film of the *Secret History* series (which bears the same title as the series as a whole)? Gatten has mused that his films might reflect "a gentle iconoclasm," referring to the tradition of forbidding representations and images on religious grounds. The phrase may be an oxymoron, since the struggle over iconoclasm, from the Byzantine Empire in the ninth century to the Islamic reaction to portrayals of Mohammed today, has generally been remarkably violent. The iconoclasts felt that images, especially images of holy subjects, such as Christ or Mary, functioned as idols and as such were forbidden by the Bible (the Islamic and Jewish traditions sometimes went so far as to forbid the portrayal of the human figure, since man was the image of God). However, the defenders of icons claimed such resemblances could put one in contact with the divine without claiming in any way to be identical (or consubstantial) with the divine. Marie-José Mondzain in her brilliant study of the icon, *Image, Icon, Economy*, shows how this sense of the image as a medium of exchange has deeply penetrated modern culture, especially our concept of photography. Contrary to the claims by iconoclasts that icons aspired to become idols and be worshipped, Mondzain claims that the icon enacts a play of presence and absence and not simply a realistic pursuit of representation. Unlike the iconoclasts, who were rarely gentle, Gatten remains true to the spirit of the iconophiles, seeking in his films to convey a sense of profound relation across an acknowledged gulf of separation and difference, meditating on the nature of the image in an era where visual technology surrounds us and pictures proliferate and multiply. By withholding, or at least attenuating, the cinematic image, what does Gatten give us? Certainly a sense of distance, and given the historical references of these fragments, his films evoke the elusiveness of the past and the memories it depends on. A conventional historical film tries to bring the past to life with images and reenactments; Gatten sees this process of resurrection as almost unholy, a violation of the way the past has vanished and cannot be simply recovered. But if the past vanished entirely, it could have no claim or attraction for us. Instead of disappearing, the past leaves traces, a memory that exists outside us in archives, in documents, in writing, and in other impressions it has left behind. Beyond these remains of history, Gatten's sparing use of images engages a basic interrelation between the representational and the abstract, picture and writing, and the roots of the image in the seemingly nonrepresentational, in the mark and the line.

Film and photography can also be understood as traces left by the past. Roland Barthes claims in his book *Camera Lucida* that every photograph carries the message "this has been," indicating that photographs preserve a record of something existing in the past. The word "photography" means "light writing"—as cinematography means "motion writing." As these terms indicate, the photographic and cinematographic processes, while usually thought of as making images, preserve a link with writing in their role of recording an impression of light and/or movement. Thus, on a truly basic level, Gatten's use of cinema as a means to record and project writing does not seem contradictory to its nature, simply unusual in its practice. Even when cinema records/presents an image of the world, one could say that it is capturing the trace of light and motion, writing down the impressions of the world. Semiotic film theorists call this the "indexical" aspect of film and photography, referring to one of philosopher Charles Peirce's categories of signs. An index, according to Peirce, signifies something through its actual relation to that thing or action. Thus smoke signifies fire, because the fire engenders the smoke; a fingerprint refers to the person whose imprint left it; a weathervane shows the wind direction because the wind actually moves it; and a photographic image is indexical because it was caused by light bouncing off the objects it records.

Although the concept of the index provides an important insight into film and photography, I feel, as a film historian and theorist, that its role has often been misunderstood. An indexical relation certainly exists in photographs, but all too often theorists have made it the source of the realism of the medium. Indexicality can establish a photograph as sort of witness, present at the event it records, but this fact does not in itself explain photography as perhaps the most realistic form of visual images. The visual accuracy of photography comes from its optical mechanics, its combination of lenses, shutter, and film stock, all elements that we know can *also* be used unrealistically (and of course in an era of digital manipulation, even more distorting manipulations become available). Indexicality by itself does not create a realistic or even a recognizable image. Smoke does not resemble fire, nor does a fingerprint look like the person it identifies. A photograph commonly resembles its subject, but that depends on how its optics are used, which could equally well distort it. Because most photographs (and perhaps most films) attempt to present a recognizable and familiar image, this aspect of resemblance (what Peirce calls the iconic aspect of a sign) has become confused with its indexicality, but these are actually different aspects and can be separated.

Gatten's films often capture the traces of things but less frequently present their images (at least in the sense of resemblance). But this attenuation of imagery does not simply make them abstract, or even iconoclastic. Rather, Gatten explores another aesthetic, that of the trace, the impressions things leave behind, often outside of representation or imagery. Instead his films focus on other types of signs, such as writing and diagrams in their various forms, marks and lines. In the completed films of the *Secret History* series, images remain subordinate to the abstraction and two-dimensional space of writing and printing. These films work systematically through the relation between image and writing, trace and sign, letter and picture.

2. DRAWING THE LINE

> Does whatever exists within the line, ringed by it, therefore have meaning, or a hollowed-out meaning? Does the line engender a full and differentiated space, or with its raw wound, its graphic fissure, does it mark the visible limits of the void itself?
>
> MARIE-JOSÉ MONDZAIN, *Icon, Image, Economy*

The initial film of the series, *Secret History of the Dividing Line* (2002), offers a theoretical starting point. Resolutely limited to sharply contrasting black and white, the film migrates through three primary forms: writing (as printed words); the line, as a two-dimensional mark that divides space; and finally, what we might call "blotches"—random and seeming aleatory forms of amorphous black and white, resembling stains. One could contrast these three modes in terms of their relation to form and matter. The blotches seem formless, swirls of darkness and light, the tohu-bohu of the chaos before creation, before the word of God divided day and night and introduced order and form. The line introduces form as the act of division, primal separation: this here, that over there (in its opening appearance, the line also acts as a "time-line" tracing a succession of dates and the progression of history). In the printed words, lines become shaped and contrasted and thus give specific forms to letters and ultimately to language, as words give way to meaning. These printed sections refer to bits of history, and especially geography, the setting of borders and the carving out of space and measurement of distances. The fragments of narrative they offer describe less the simple divisions of space than the contentions of politics: claims and counterclaims about where the dividing line belongs and who owns what, as well as the division between public history and secret history. (The film takes its title from rival accounts of a border dispute between North Carolina and Virginia, before the American Revolution, over where the border between the colonies belonged, and the fact that Byrd, who headed an expedition to settle the location, produced both a public and a secret account of his trek.)

But although I can divide what appears on the screen in this film into three contrasting modes, the actual experience of watching the film seems to confound as much as separate them. The line that appears first in the film does not resemble an abstract Euclidean vector joining two points, but rather a rough scratch, a torn edge, where matter separates absolutely but violently. It recalls the edge of dawn breaking on the horizon, or the beautiful diagram linguist Ferdinand de Saussure provides of the way sound and meaning relate in language. This line arises from the separation of matter, splitting darkness from light, a sloppy process of genesis, rather than the ideal differentiations of geometry. The fine distinctions of letters and language, and of geography and politics, arise from such material conflicts, bleeding across the borders. Gatten literally records this process cinematically, since the most material of his modes—the blotches of black and white—result from the interaction of splicing tape and emulsion, the black smut being the dark emulsion and the white appearing where the emulsion has been scraped or torn away and light penetrates. Within this matrix, left as the physical trace of editing, the transparent splicing tape has enclosed bubbles and bits of adhesive. These random patterns at points recall

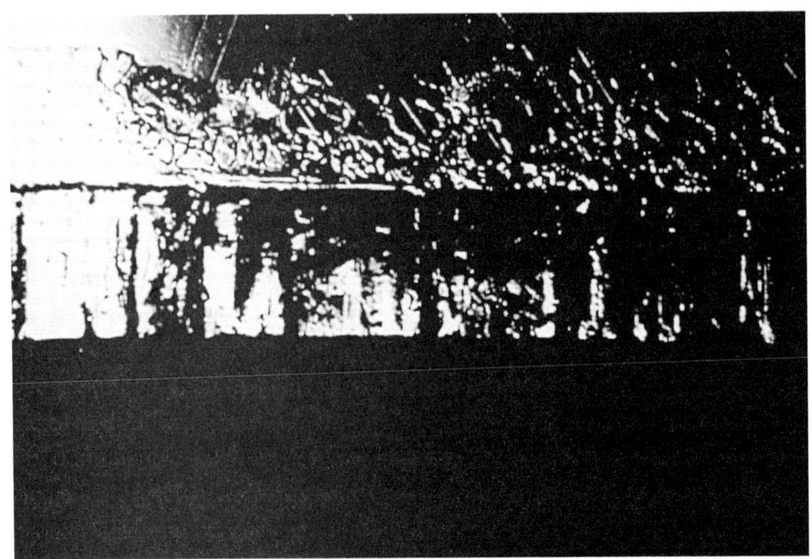

FIGURE 24.1. David Gatten, *Secret History of the Dividing Line* (1996–2002).

Chinese ink-painting landscapes, the charcoal drawings of Georges Seurat, or the materiality of abstract expressionism. But imagistic and evocative as these visual patterns are, they also serve as the means of cutting and joining the filmstrip together, the splice of film editing, which both separates and unites shots and endows cinema with the pulse of montage. The process of A/B printing in most films erases the messy trace of this mechanical process from the screen, so editing appears seamless. Revealed to the viewer by Gatten, this "secret dividing line" provides the film's most dramatic visual imagery.

As the first film in the series, *Secret History* sets up the premise of the whole, which becomes elaborated and complicated in subsequent films. Instead of directly dramatizing the intriguing and often moving story of the Byrd family (especially the gothic and ghostly story of William's daughter Evelyn and her tragic love affair, which becomes increasingly central in *The Enjoyment of Reading*, 2001, and *The Great Art of Knowing*, 2004), Gatten gives us only material (yet poignant) fragments of this story in the form of citations from documents, both public and private. The order Gatten gives to his four completed films (of a series he announces as ultimately having nine parts) does not correspond to their order of production, and I confess I have my own sense of their order. The first film completed, *Moxon's Mechanick Exercises or the Doctrine of Handy-Works Applied to the Art of Printing* (1999), which in Gatten's order comes third in the series, seems to me to respond directly to *Secret History of the Dividing Line* (first in Gatten's sequence but the third film completed). If *Secret History* displays the movement from the amorphous to the order of language, *Moxon's Mechanick Exercises* traces the formal development of letters in the casting and compositing of printing: not only the size and order of type but the spaces between letters and words. The drama of the Byrd family recedes in this film in favor of a bibliography: the inventory of William Byrd's extensive library, to which Joseph Moxon's 1683 book detailing the craft of printing belonged. Whereas Byrd left his histories of the dividing line expedition in manuscript, this film deals with the publicly circulated and technologically elaborated form of writing, the printed book. The texts excerpted in this film from Moxon's volume detail the art of the placing and spacing of letters, especially when printing the Bible, and we see both pages of print and printed illustrations of the printer's craft. If *Secret History* seems overwhelmed by the abstract and amorphous nature of the splice-produced blotches, Moxon's craft produces order and legibility, a mechanical process from which chance has been excluded by technical mastery. Gatten displays this careful craftsmanship of the printed page, but his extreme close-ups of printed letters and the rapidity with which they pass on the screen seem eventually to dissolve this order into a frenetic energy, never as abstract or formless as the blotches, yet similarly primal and dynamic. In their massive white forms against black backgrounds, the impressions of print resemble dinosaur bones excavated from the earth, rather than carefully placed bits of type.

Thus in *Moxon's Mechanick Exercises*, Gatten continues to reveal the dynamic between form and matter, between pure graphic energy and the clarity of printed language and image (since, in contrast to *Secret History*, several printed pictures appear in this film). However, the process of writing becomes more public, less secret, the order more firmly established than in the first film. The letters become difficult to read or recognize, yet we still sense them as letters rather than blotches. The craft described in the texts reproduced from Moxon deals less with measuring and sectioning nature and wilderness space and more with arrangement, order, and—especially—reproduction. Printing, after all, marks the beginning of mechanical reproduction, and this technical innovation complicates the idea of the trace or the index. Whereas the fingerprint or signature provides an index of individual identity because of its unique impression, printing endeavors through mechanics to make each impression identical, to proliferate rather than differentiate. It introduces standardization, an ideal of consistent reproduction: orthography—truth and accuracy in writing. In effect, this technical ideal announces the mode of photography as accurate iconic reproduction. Printing shares this technical ability to reproduce exactly with modern photography, whose negative can make multiple identical copies (as opposed to the daguerreotype, an early form of photography that produced only a single unique image). Contemporary digital reproduction of both sound and image pushes this ideal even further, eliminating any degeneration in the copy. One could claim that such abolition of difference between original and copy constitutes one of the drives of modern consciousness and that much of modern technology responds to it. If alphabetic letters constitute the first triumph of this ideal of linear communication without loss, and printing offers its technical realization, then cinema and sound recording push this destruction of the aura of the unique original beyond abstraction into a realm were images and sound become as reproducible and interchangeable as printed words.

In this film on the standardization of the handicraft of printing, Gatten both contemplates and undoes this process as he undermines the orthographic legibility of printed letters through photographic enlargement and brief cinematic cuts. He used a form of anti-printing in the film, in which the form of letters were stripped off the printed page with an adhesive tape, in effect reversing the act of printing by lifting ink off paper rather than impressing it. This process of transferring the ink onto a transparent base dominates the film, invoking a liberation of letter into spirit as if releasing the creative power of the word and letter from its technological framework and linear clarity. Various mystical traditions, the Kabbalah most gloriously, have assigned a creative role not only to language but to letters themselves. While *Secret History* seems to me to contemplate the act of genesis in the primal act of separating and drawing the line, *Moxon's Mechanick Exercises* envisions another process of creation, born of the word ordered and impressed into matter, going forth fruitfully to multiply into many editions. But Gatten's ambivalence comes through here as well. His violence against the letter announces its reversal, the apocalypse, when the inscribed scroll of revelation is unrolled and the affixed letters are freed as the text itself dissolves.

The two remaining completed films from this series allude more frequently to the personal history of the Byrd family, especially the conflict between William and Evelyn, his elder daughter, who was separated from her lover by her father due to religious differences and died soon after the young man's death at sea. Although the Byrd library and its inventory (and sale by auction after William's death to pay his son's gambling debts) remain central in these films, the fragility and tragedy of human lives haunt in the gaps between texts, taken from diaries and letters, as much as the words. Photographic imagery plays a more varied role in these films, as carefully composed close-ups of books reveal their materiality, not only the surface of the paper but the edges of the pages and the leather of the binding. The ideal space of signification becomes undercut by the material nature of the

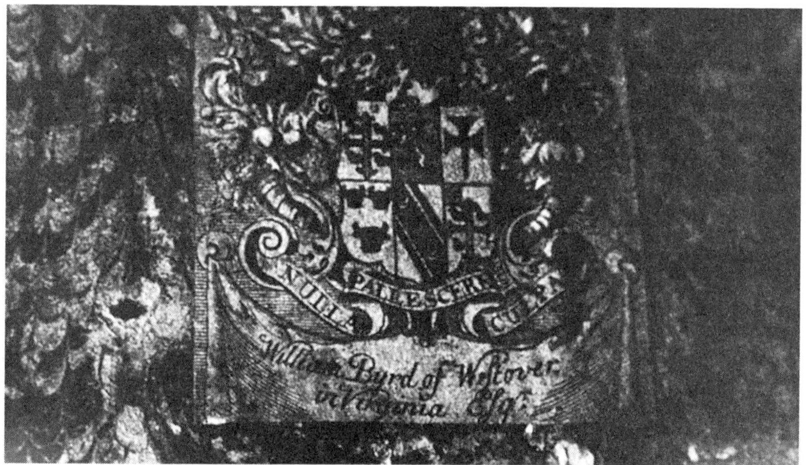

FIGURE 24.2. David Gatten, *The Great Art of Knowing* (2004).

sign itself, its historical and embodied nature, subject to decay and neglect. The realm of representation remains limited to these books and printed pages, along with a few objects and bits of nature. *The Enjoyment of Reading* portrays either books or patterns of light and its sources. Rather than illuminating objects, light in these shots is often refracted and out of focus, forming immaterial and abstract patterns. At other points light plays on the surface of a page, revealing its kinetic power more than just rendering the text legible. *The Great Art of Knowing*, to my mind the most powerful of Gatten's films, takes its title from an encyclopedic work by Athanasius Kircher, a seventeenth-century Jesuit described by recent scholars as "the last man to know everything," and author as well of *The Great Art of Light and Shadow*, a compendium of optical devices and effects often cited at the beginning of histories of the cinema, whose title-page illustration we see in the film. As Kircher sought in *The Great Art of Light and Shadow* to offer an epitome of all human knowledge, and as Byrd sought in his library and in the garden of his Virginia estate to contain the essence of both culture and of nature, Gatten's series of films uses abstraction not to reduce the world but to compress its essence and render it visible.

As I indicated at the opening of this essay, it seemed to me at first that the reliance on writing in Gatten's films neglected the visual aspect of cinema, eschewing film's imagistic possibilities for a more abstract and perhaps cerebral mode. However, dwelling for some time on these films, I now see how limited my initial view was. Although images, in the form of pictures, remain rare, Gatten has restricted his range in order to deepen the insight. Writing need not be restricted to significance, although that may be its ultimate purpose. Gatten shows the origin of writing not merely in the pursuit of abstract meaning, but in the visual line that marks and delineates, separates. Writing will always allow abstract signification (Peirce's third category of sign, which he called the symbol, indicates a sign whose nature is fixed by convention not based in resemblance, as the icon is, or in an actual relation, as in the index). But Gatten affirms that, as a mark, writing remains deeply incised in a material base, not only ink and paper but light and dark, celluloid and glue, and—ultimately space and time, geography and history. The act both of leaving a trace (writing and drawing) and of leaving an impression (printing) laid the foundation for human history and memory. Yet if writing embodies human power, it also reveals the fragility and mortality not only of human culture but of all of matter; books, which hold the art of knowing, are subject to the tragedies of existence: dispersal and decay. Libraries suffer separation as much as lovers do. Objects bear the destructive wear of time and history, along with the intentional imprint of the compositor's craft or the insubstantial play of light and shade. Far from simply cerebral, the mark of inscription reveals human and natural history, the chronicles of flesh and matter, as well as heart and mind.

The Great Art of Knowing remains subject to all these intentions and accidents, dependent on the handiwork of the art of printing and ascertaining the line of divisions and categories. The enjoyment of reading leads inevitably (and perhaps even tragically) to acknowledging this art of knowing. All these words ultimately lead through language and beyond it, just as the line that delineates leads us not only to words and their meanings but back to drawing and its material trace. A lovely quote from Evelyn's letters appears in *The Great Art of Knowing*: "I am learning to live inside fewer words. I do more drawings now than letters, though they seem still to go hand with glove." Writing and drawing share a common root in the trace, and if each developed toward a dematerialized form of representation and significance, through the technology of the cinema Gatten reveals the power of the material trace that lurks within them still.

3. WRITTEN ON THE WIND

> To translate the invisible wind by the water it sculpts in passing . . .
>
> ROBERT BRESSON, "NOTES ON CINEMATOGRAPHY"

Gatten ultimately makes us rethink the separation between writing and image, revealing that each mode reaches out toward the other, discovering a realm of expression that allows for more than either simple representation or signification. Writing and drawing both have their origins in the gesture of the trace. Both submit to technological development that takes them to new thresholds. Cinema is one of those developments, where the picture can be seen as the writing of light and movement, and writing can reveal the fragility of form and matter beyond fixed meaning. Although still rare in comparison to text, the filmed images in *The Great Art of Knowing* present the cinema as an art of writing and delineation. Composed of light and shadow, cinema could be seen as an immaterial art. Yet as filmmakers and theorists from Étienne-Jules Marey to Jean Epstein to André Bazin have claimed, cinema's union of photographic detail and acuity with motion allows it to penetrate uniquely into the drama of material life. As Antonin Artaud put it in his 1927 essay "Cinema and Reality," "Out of this pure play of appearances, out of this so to speak transubstantiation of elements is born an inorganic language that moves the mind by osmosis and without any kind of transposition into words. Because it works with matter itself, cinema creates situations that arise from the mere collision of objects, forms, repulsions, attractions. It does not detach itself from life but rediscovers the original order of things."

Gatten's images do not simply capture this moiling collision of material elements but transmute its forms into a sort of inscription. His crisp and intimate close-ups capture the linear patterns of the feathers of a dead bird, the edges of leaves, and the shapes of twigs or flowers. In their defining lines, these natural objects recall the images of the sharp cut of pages, the diagrams of mechanical forces, scientific instruments. Through Gatten's highly graphic shots, these images appear less composed of volumetric objects than configured by lines. A phrase that appears in the film twice stresses this process of abstraction: "instead of volume, lines." The act of delineation draws lines out of the manifold stuff of nature. In Gatten's photographic images, as in the linear graphs of movement that the physiologist Marey invented cinema in order to plot accurately, the world thus reveals its structure and complexity. Guided by the endless echo between sound and meaning that language sets off, I feel I must point out that this film bibliography also displays bound volumes composed of endless lines of words. As sound, as figure, as meaning, words evade and beckon us, marking our fate and perhaps mocking us. Evelyn Byrd, prevented by her father from joining her lover, perhaps dreamed of flying away with the birds that frequented her father's garden. Rarely has a pun on a name seemed so poignantly bitter. Evelyn seeks to enjoy the reading of nature in order to decipher its lines of flight. Does nature in response simply write her epitaph? Time and nature inscribe all of us within spaces of separation, as well as linear characters.

Gatten arranges his films in series, and most of them are still in progress. But if *Secret History of the Dividing Line* seems to me (thus far) to provide the spine of his oeuvre and perhaps its key, I find it revealing to think of it in relation to his first series of films, *What the Water Said* (begun in 1998). The two series seem initially at antipodes. Images and even color predominate in *What the Water Said*, as opposed to the dominance of text and black and white in *Secret History*. Rather than human characters engaged in historical and cultural projects, nature overflows *What the Water Said* and even takes charge—with nearly immediate results. The six different films that now make up this series are made from unexposed film stock that Gatten put into crabtraps and tossed into the ocean off the coast of South Carolina where salt water from the sea meets the fresh water of the Edisto River. Retrieving the film stock from the water, he then developed it. The resulting film, both visually and aurally, consists of footage exposed to this seawater sojourn, and whatever abrasions the traps and surf caused (I find Gatten's claim that crabs and other sea creatures made some of the marks by nibbling on the film a bit fanciful—but perhaps it's true!). The film was never passed through a camera, and in that sense is not at all photographic (it circumvents the optics of the camera entirely), but the film did undergo a chemical reaction due to its immersion and handling and the subsequent process of development, printing, and ultimately projection.

The result is stunning and delightful, abstract animation at its most frenetic and varied. We see a kaleidoscopic succession of scratches, abrasions, and blotches of a variety of colors, transforming at the rapid speed of 24 film frames a second, while a cacophony of white noise crashes and crackles on the soundtrack. Sometimes the backgrounds are black, sometimes white, pinkish, magenta, or salmon-colored. Some scratches are very linear, while other seem curved and circular; some lines are dark, others white or reddish. The blotches blossom like flowers in a spectrum of colors, or burst on the screen like white snowflakes or multicolored popcorn. Any verbal account only indicates the inadequacy of describing this visual experience in words. It is the kinetic energy of color and form, the dance between figures and backgrounds that delights the eye and mind. And, yes, there is something to think about there, even if you don't have to. The title, for one thing (there are also a series of literary quotes from Edgar Allan Poe, Herman Melville, Nathaniel Hawthorne, Daniel Defoe, T. S. Eliot, and Fernando Pessoa, which I find a bit unnecessary, although appropriate—perhaps unnecessary because *so* appropriate). Thinking of these images as "what the

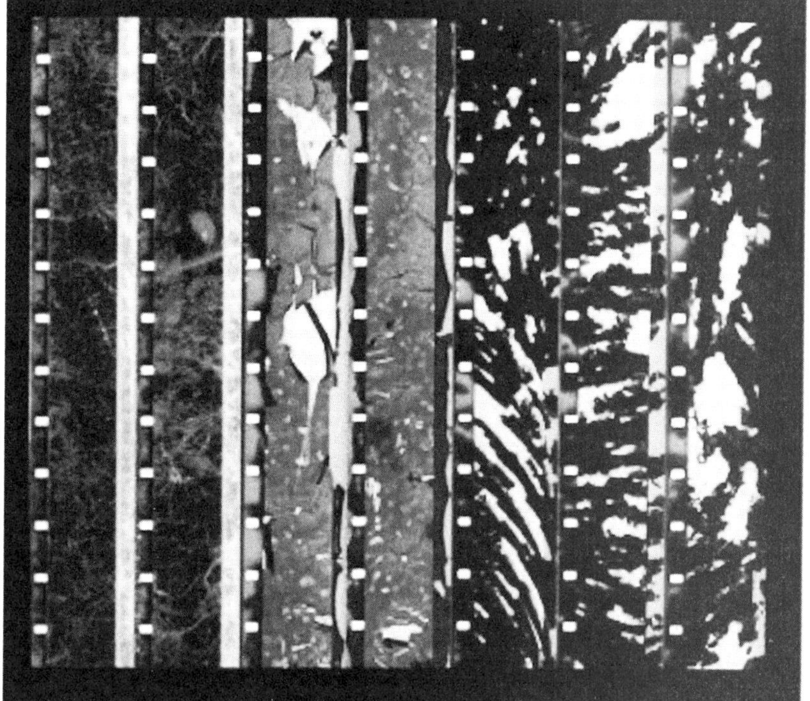

FIGURE 24.3. David Gatten, *What the Water Said, Nos. 1–3* (1998).

water said" enriches the film and relates strongly to themes from Gatten's other series. These films, like the others I have discussed, while utterly noniconic and nonrepresentational, are clearly indexical, the visual record of the interaction of the sea and the film stock. The visual and sound patterns are the result of the film's immersion in the sea, its subjection to natural forces, and Gatten refers to them as "oceanic inscription written directly into the emulsion of the film." They are in this sense another example of the writing of nature, the collision of elements Artaud found in cinema. The sea has left its mark on celluloid. The ocean made a film. This can only be said with some irony and humor, of course. Gatten threw the film into the ocean, and selected and developed the film. (Both Gatten and critic Scott McDonald refer to the series as collaborations between Gatten and the sea.)

The film is an artifact, of course. It remains mediated by the cinematic processes of developing, printing, and projection, even if it eliminates the usually essential mediation of the optics of the camera. But nothing human composed the images or sound; Gatten merely allowed and preserved them. They correspond to that ideal of religious art to which icons aspired, according to Mondzain, the *acheiropoietic* image, made without the intervention of human hands through the direct imprint of the divine, like the image of the face of Jesus imprinted on Veronica's veil.

The title *What the Water Said* constitutes the culminating act of authorship, and it is both serious and playful. It even involves, as Gatten confessed, a mistake on his part. He thought he was citing a subtitle from Eliot's *The Wasteland*, whose fifth and final section is actually called "What the Thunder Said." In the Brihadaranyaka Upanishad of Hinduism, the sound of thunder—"Da!"—recalls the words for the basic duties creatures owe; the sound of nature, through divine interpretation, becomes the words of divine commands. Gatten does not dare to translate what the water said, and the marks appearing on the film evoke the visual signs of saying, as much as sound roaring on the track. We not only hear the sounds the water left, but see its writing. A paradox appears here, of course, as the phrase "what is written on water" refers to what cannot last, be retrieved, or ultimately be read. Gatten aspires to capture what is written in the water, and yet within that daring act of appropriation lies a humble acknowledgment that nothing is ever written permanently. The images and sound we hear are neither words nor pictures; they remain, however, traces of delight, and we can read them as we wish. Cinema displays here a new form of imagery and language, which we could describe as blending trace, writing, and image but circumscribed or limited by none of these.

25

The Grain of the Scratch: The Precarity of Transparency in Cinema

The term "precarity," applied to media itself, remains for me, well, a bit precarious. It is a concept still in gestation, valuable for the debates it gives birth to, and I hope this essay contributes to that process. Originally generated within the radical Catholic Workers movement, it became defined as "a precarious existence, lacking in predictability, job security, material or psychological welfare."[1] But it has also come to be related to the material nature of specific media. Although the extension of this social term to media aesthetics gives me some pause, I think the issue of precarity in the moving image poses vital questions.

Let me begin by making my claim to what I think this term can mean and what it can open up. Precarity in a media context deals primarily with the issue of mediation, how things are mediated, and what a medium is. The call for papers for one of the conferences that led to this essay, at Berkeley, makes this clear:

> In spite of technological advances striving for greater clarity and resolution, visuals that counteract such perfection may never have been more appreciated. Feature films, photography, documentaries, televisual images, music videos and artists' films are currently saturated with images that, in various ways, are blurred, noisy and non-transparent. They invite

This essay, previously unpublished, was written in 2015. It grew out of a conference organized at the University of California at Berkeley by Arild Fetveit, which in turn developed from a conference at Lysebu near Oslo, Norway, overseen by Vivian Sobchack.

> us to see the world, yet at the same time, they obstruct our view, often to dazzling effect. By operating at the mercy of bodies and/or technologies that are unstable and liable to fail, mediation is here rendered precarious.[2]

I embrace this claim, but I am also bothered by it. It implies that in some (many?) cases of mediation there might be bodies or technologies that are *not* "unstable and liable to fail." In contrast to such a position, I would claim, rather, that mediation *always* includes the possibility of failure. This indeed is the nature of mediation: something is mediated by something. The shadow that passes between the sender and receiver of the message (to use Jakobson's model of communication) is mediation.

At an earlier conference in Norway, at Lysebu, Anna Catherina Dalmasso presented an essential and clarifying paper focusing on the concept of mediation in the work of Maurice Merleau-Ponty.[3] She described what she called the "myth of transparency," the ideal of a medium that poses no opposition or imposes no texture on the act of communication. In this mythical state, as Dalmasso puts it, "mediation seems to complete itself *as if there had not been* any medium."[4] To counter this myth of transparency, she reminds us of a beautiful passage in Merleau-Ponty's essay "Eye and Mind," which describes the act of seeing the bottom of a pool through the water it contains:

> When through the water's thickness I see the tiled bottom of the pool, I do not see it *despite* the water and the reflections; I see it through them and because of them. If there were no distortions, no ripples of sunlight, if it were without that flesh that I saw the geometry of the tiles, then I would cease to see it *as* it is and where it is—which is to say, beyond any identical, specific place.[5]

We must be careful, then, to be true to our experience of perception. We should not claim that it is impossible to eliminate the distortion media carry in the act of seeing, as if this distortion were some ineradicable blot of original sin that cannot be erased however much we desire to do so. Rather, as Merleau-Ponty claims, to eliminate all distortion would be to eliminate the act of seeing itself, especially seeing understood as an act of perception, an encounter with the world, rather than an ideal visual plotting of verifiable and quantifiable data. The act of seeing with our own eyes is constituted by the variety of media that, far from vitiating sight, constitute it. Seeing merges with all these varieties of filters, screens, and interventions; they form the flesh of vision, as opposed to sight's ideal mathematical reconstruction as a series of geometrical points plotted in an airless, contentless space. Mind you, the ideal of a mediumless display has its uses and practical applications, but it constitutes a realm of abstraction; while vision, which swims through an inhabited world, opens us to an understanding of the way the world intertwines with our perception. Perception dwells in a world defined by its precarity.

Therefore, when I said that all mediation must include the possibility of failure, I was in a sense in error, since this statement presents a false, or at least limited, view of how mediation operates. The invocation of "failure" implies a definite purpose. Such an instrumental model of mediation *can* be constructed, and indeed it plays a role in information and communication theory. Successful mediation in this context means relaying a message without distortion. But as Dalmasso comments, this is mediation with no mediation. In contrast, lived experience, and especially that construction of intense experience that we call art or aesthetics, glories in mediation. The textures, detours, and sensual games a medium allows, instead of being conducive to failure, are in fact its raison d'être.

As a historian of cinema and what I have called "cultural optics," I am preoccupied with visual mediation. Dalmasso claimed that the myth of transparency "underpins all relations to optical devices."[6] It is not hard to follow her point. Telescopes, microscopes, indeed most lenses, not only carry out their tasks of magnification or focusing, but strive to eliminate optical interferences, such as chromatic distortion, circles of confusion, or other artifacts such as distortions in rectilinear perspective by barrel or pincushion effects, and many others. But I must immediately claim that the work performed by optical devices hardly offers examples of transparency. An optical device alters vision, or it would lose its purpose. Lenses reveal how limited any concept of transparency can be in optical technology. Of course, one could differentiate between alterations that serve the purposes of the device (e.g., magnification) and those that are accidental and thus interfere with that purpose. To some extent this reveals an unspoken assumption about precarious mediation in relation to "the possibility of failure": mediation only fails by interfering with or degrading an intended effect. Thus, the blurring of focus or distortion of straight lines in a lens must be adjusted or corrected when the purpose of a lens is to replicate a certain geometric ideal of vision.

Within a purposeful project, the concept of a transparent medium makes sense. But the claim that art always has a purpose, a *telos* that must be accomplished, has been questioned at least since Kant's Third Critique. While communication theory must differentiate between message and noise, in the realm of aesthetics, this distinction not only becomes, well, precarious, but may even be inverted. Not only is an art of noise possible, as Futurist Luigi Russolo claimed, one might even claim that, at least in contrast to a model of transparent communication, art *is* noise.[7] The key modernist aesthetic theory of the Russian Formalists, as defined by Viktor Shklovsky, radicalized Kant's sense of art as nonpurposeful and characterized the aesthetic as precisely those elements that "roughened" rather than eased communication.[8] Shklovsky described the artistic as that which impedes and slows down our perception or understanding; we could perhaps describe it as the precarious. Thus, precarious aesthetics, far from being a new strategy in art-making, might define art-making in the modern era. But "the operational logics of precarious mediation," especially with regard to optical media, still needs to be described, not only theoretically but historically and technically.

Cinema has sometimes been said to exemplify an art of transparency, on several levels. First, there has been the belief that, as an outgrowth of photography, cinema shares with the photograph a sort of visual tautology, recording the world with absolute objectivity, as if the medium of photography were itself transparent. I think it would be hard to find someone to defend this theoretically, at least in its strong form, even if it haunts many people's approach to photographs. Then there was the claim that certain forms of cinema, for instance, (negatively) the Classical Hollywood Cinema or (positively) forms of Direct Cinema, strove to eliminate the marks of enunciation or the distortions of subjectivity in order to create either a complicit ideological illusion or an unbiased record of reality. Whether seeking to praise or to blame, these positions have also encountered strong criticism. But the transparency I want to examine is more literal and technological: the transparency of the now nearly vanished strip of celluloid.

In histories of the invention of cinema, the filmstrip has played a secondary role to the hardware of the motion picture camera and projector. The pioneering work on celluloid film by Deac Rossell, and Paul Spehr's detailed research into William K. L. Dickson's struggle to move Edison's invention from microphotographs embedded in a cylinder to transparent flexible rolls of celluloid have made scholars more aware of the onetime defining physical medium of *film*, vanishing as we speak.[9] By definition, transparency means allowing light to shine through. But in a media context, "transparent" indicates that appearances become manifest through something. While the idea of a transparent medium may theoretically imply a medium that absents itself in favor of what is seen or carried through it, transparency as a physical quality is not an ethereal state but a material quality that can be difficult to obtain. Moving from the semiotic neutrality of the concept to the material history of our first transparent manufactured item—glass—the technical skill needed to render glass transparent moves us away from simple neutrality or absence. The history of glass, not only as the covering for windows but as the material for scientific instruments, both containers and lenses, offers rich and complex material for thinking about the nature of a medium.

The long history of projected images originated with glass, as the archetypal visual instrument of image projection, the magic lantern, used glass both in the focusing lenses of its apparatus and in the manufacture of its glass slides on which images were painted. Indeed the earliest versions of motion pictures, taking the magic lantern as their model, employed glass as the carrier of images: Ducos du Hauron, Auguste LePrince, Oscar Anschutz, and even the Skladanowsky brothers used fragile and inflexible glass as the basis for their motion picture devices.[10] The importance of a flexible roll of transparent material was first hit upon by that too often neglected inventor of motion pictures Émile Reynaud, with his Pantomimes Lumineuses, which used gelatin squares carried through the projecting apparatus by leather belts.[11] The switch in the 1880s from glass plates to celluloid roll film in amateur cameras, popularized especially by Eastman's Kodak, cued Dickson to use it in Edison's motion picture inventions. However, manufacturing a reliable and consistent celluloid strip with enough durability, flexibility, and transparency posed a problem for Dickson as he perfected on Edison's Kinetograph. The success of celluloid in the Kinetoscope led to the abandonment of glass as the transparent medium of the cinema in almost all subsequent motion picture devices.

Projection of images relies, as if to allegorize Merleau-Ponty's understanding of vision, on an interplay between transparency and opacity or, to put it in terms of effects, light and shadow. But the dichotomy of darkness and light poses too simple a contrast, since the projection of color images also transforms light—paraphrasing Shelly, like "a many-colored glass stains the white radiance of eternity." The effect of coloring light has, of course, existed at least since stained-glass windows. Filmmaker and theorist Hollis Frampton demonstrated this play of light and shadow in his famous "A Lecture." After projecting a simple rectangle of white light, he explained:

> Our white rectangle is not "nothing at all." In fact, it is, in the end, all we have. That is one of the limits of the art of film.

> So, if we want to see what we call *more*, which is actually *less*, we must devise ways of subtracting, of removing, one thing and another, more or less, from our white rectangle.[12]

This led Frampton to a simple definition of film, based more in its opacity than in its transparency:

> It seems that a film is anything that may be put in a projector that will modulate the emerging beam of light.

The patterns of transparency, opacity and color on the filmstrip make a movie, or as Frampton puts it:

> Now, preserving a faithful record of where that light was, and was not, it modulates our light beam, subtracts from it, makes a vacancy, a hole, that looks to us like, say, Lana Turner.

But while celluloid may be able to be transparent, it cannot be incorporeal. In contrast to the electronic image, film is a thing: it can be grasped, and its surface eventually shows the wear of time. Therefore, that truly precarious, if not yet quite dead, medium, the filmstrip, most frequently exhibited two examples of visual precarity: scratch and grain.

Frampton, ever alert to the material of mediation, anticipated one of these issues:

> Suppose further that we take an instrument and scratch the ribbon of film along its whole length.
>
> Then the scratch is more often visible than Miss Turner, and the film is about the scratch.

"The film is *about* the scratch." This statement opens a can of worms. Is a film about something? I declared with some confidence earlier, with Kant and Shklovsky to back me up, that art was not purposeful, that it was not "about" communicating. Perhaps, therefore, art itself is not "about" anything. But we know that art does involve purposeful decisions, at the very least on the practical level of craft and style.

But is Frampton talking about this? Perhaps, since he describes deliberately making a scratch and thereby changing what the film is about. The scratch that slides along the screen and scarifies Lana Turner demands our attention and sets up issues of intention and interpretation. But, of course, most scratches in films do not occur intentionally but are produced by the process of projection, as dirt particles lodge in the projector gate (or occasionally at the shooting stage in the camera) and scratch the film as it runs through. Cameramen take pains to clean the gate and avoid damaging the film (which is usually discarded if a scratch inadvertently occurs), as do good projectionists (although my projectionist friends tell me that certain platter systems almost always ended up scratching films). One of the advantages (for elimination of a precarity) of digital electronic projection is that scratches cannot occur, since the images are electronic impulses with no physical medium; no emulsion to scratch off, no celluloid to dig a groove through. Indeed there are video programs that will endow an electronic image with artifacts that *look* like scratches to make an image appear old or just give it a desired texture. In fact, I find my awareness of scratches when watching older prints of films has increased in recent years (and my tolerance of them perhaps decreased). John Belton told me that when he recently screened a vintage print of John Ford's *Stagecoach* for his class, some students asked him if it had been a B-film. Surprised, he asked what made them think that. "All those scratches!" Now I can't technically reconstruct why a lower budget might produce scratches on celluloid, but the comment tells me two things: first, that scratches seem unusual to a contemporary viewer and, second, that although viewers may not know what produced them, scratches seem to indicate reduced care or quality in the making of the film.

Scratches indicate vulnerability, the precarity of the filmstrip, and recall the original mechanical (as opposed to electronic) process of film projection. Although I would much prefer a newly restored archival print of a film to a battered and scratched one (and I regret the scratches embedded in the newly found material of *Metropolis*), the sense of history and use that scratches convey nonetheless has some resonance for me as a viewer. A badly scratched print makes the idea of the failure of mediation caused by elements that "obstruct our view" sound less simplistic. If we want the film to be about Lana Turner, scratches certainly interfere. But if we wanted images of Lana to reinforce their historical or archival nature, scratches might serve a purpose.

But what of Frampton's declaration that the film might be *about* the scratch? In an era when a materialist, anti-illusionist aesthetic ruled within some avant-garde circles, the display of the materiality underlying pictorial representation was not only valorized but could be seen as a political act. Scratching Lana Turner may not really be about the scratch. It may be about destroying the hold the society of the spectacle has on its passive viewers, exposing the vacancy beneath their icons. This is certainly one use of precarity: releasing an iconoclastic energy that aggressively intends failure. Perhaps defacing the surface of a film will reveal something behind it, even if (especially if?) the something is only—nothing.

Thus, a seemingly simple scratch brings issues of intention, illusion, and materiality to the surface. It raises the question of the purposes of precarity in media. But besides the use of scratches as an overt gesture of defacing, we also find, especially within the avant-garde, complex strategies that, while engaging the materiality of the filmstrip, can intend more than simply proving a materialist tautology or inscribing a deliberate strategy of disillusionment.

It is hard to deny that scratching celluloid evokes aggression. But I would claim that whatever signification a scratch on film may assume, its material gesture, its attack (almost in the musical sense) on the film surface, carries a force that both evokes and evades any single meaning. I will explore this in some detail through two instances of scratches and their precarious dances with meaning and materiality.

My first example comes from Stan Brakhage's 1955 film *Reflections on Black*, one of the expressionistic trance films that preceded his later lyrical style, which abandoned the intermediaries of actors or staged narrative action. Blending influences from the trance films of Maya Deren, Kenneth Anger, and Curtis Harrington with German Expressionist and film noir imagery and tones, *Reflections on Black* follows a protagonist, apparently blind, as he walks along a city street and then climbs the stairs of a slum tenement. The scratches appear over the blind man's eyes, which are scratched out with a vigorous, even violent, starlike pattern. The attack on the image can be seen as indicating his blindness: with eyes scratched out, vision is not possible. But as scenes focused on sexual frustration and potential violence seem to be triggered within the tenement apartments as he passes by, we wonder if the blind man, following the Western tradition from Tiresias on, is actually a visionary. The scratched-out eyes appear as bright tears in the image, but they also allow the pure light of projection to pass through transparently. The represented image is sacrificed, possibly to another form of vision, and yet the violence of the act also shines through. This truly ambivalent approach to the fragility and precarity of image and the medium itself reflects Brakhage's pursuit at this early point in his career of a different mode of seeing that could replace a visual mastery rooted in the domination of sight by recognizable concepts and cliché images. Abandoning, soon after this film, dramatic structure, Brakhage transformed his later use of scratches into metaphors of a more expanded sense of vision. Thus, a scratch on film may be about more than the physical scratch, as effacing the image calls attention to the paradox of transparency and vision. The scratch does more than render the image precarious or lay bare the material of cinema. The immaterial light of the projector leaks through the scratch, as if revealing a power beyond figuration.

I am not attempting in this brief presentation to survey the uses of scratches in film, but I do want to convey something of the richness a scratch on celluloid can engender. This need not be restricted to the practices of the avant-garde, as an amazing instance of the scratch from a classic of narrative filmmaking, Fritz Lang's *Metropolis* (1927), reveals. The complex weave of allegories and symbols this film offers converge dramatically as Lang intercuts between the public unveiling of the robot Maria by Joh Fredersen and the inventor Rotwang and Joh's son, Freder, at home in his sickbed recovering from his shock of seeing what he took for his beloved Maria in the arms of his father.[13] Lang's intercutting implies a visionary witnessing of the public event on the part of Freder. As the dance of the robot Maria, the focus of the lustful eyes of a crowd of men, become more frenzied and sexual, Freder's fever dream becomes visionary and a series of allegorical tableaux appear. The first vision images the robot as the Whore of Babylon described in the book of Revelation, seated on the Great Beast with seven heads and ten horns. Then statues of the Seven Deadly Sins become animated, led by a skeletal figure of Death as the Grim Reaper, complete with scythe. Freder stares in terror as Death advances, swiping his huge scythe in the direction of camera (and, through editing, toward Freder). Freder's horrified reaction shot is cut across by the feathery stokes of an arcing scratch, as if the scythe had scored not only Freder but the surface of the film, inscribing its mark on the very medium of visibility. As the sweeping scratch travels off-screen, Freder screams and loses consci`ousness, and the shot fades out.

The sequence shows that even a super-production (*Metropolis* was the most expensive production ever mounted in Germany and bankrupted its production company, UFA) may exploit the precarity of film. An act of symbolic violence conveyed across distant spaces through the device of point-of-view editing carries as well an attack on the filmstrip as the medium of vision. As in *Reflections on Black*, loss of vision or consciousness is figured as an iconoclastic effacing of the film image. Both films unleash a primal violence and evoke a psychoanalytic equation of the loss of sight with castration (the figure of the Grim Reaper is a medieval version of Cronus, the god of time who castrated his father with his sickle). A revelation of the deeply rooted materiality of mediation exceeds an ideological critique and evokes primal fantasies and fears.

But scratching the surface of celluloid need not be an act of vandalism, or a threat of blinding or castration, just as precarity evokes more than the possibility of failure. Kenneth Anger scratched the magically appearing lover in his 1949 film *Fireworks*, remaking the actor's face as a halo of projected light promising erotic fulfillment.[14] In an essay on color in film I referred to *Coreopsis* (1998), a beautiful short film by Pat O'Neil that combines his signature optical printing with the handwrought process of scratching directly on film. He described his process to me in an email:

> The film was made by scratching through the emulsion of exposed 35mm leader such as appears on the head and tail of daily rolls of work print. This was reproduced in the optical printer on camera negative. The recursive nature of the imagery is obtained by progressive repetition (for instance, shooting 5 frames, rewinding the projector 4, shooting 5, rewinding 4, and so on, so that each repetition is 1 frame ahead of the last and a new frame appears).[15]

As O'Neil scratched black leader with sharp etching tools, color appeared, especially a striking yellow that recalls the bright hue of the flower for which the film is named. We experience the film less as a process of effacing than as a process of excavation, of revealing, as the range of emulsions contained within the black leader are literally brought to light by scraping away the surface. To play with Frampton's terms, this film starts with less and ends with more, but we realize that "more" comes from less as color emerges from darkness.

Coreopsis comes with a backstory. O'Neil had discovered some seeds in an envelope labeled "Helen's Coreopsis 1935" while going through his mother's effects after her death. He planted them and found that one of them actually bloomed, producing the vivid yellow, daisylike flower named coreopsis. Thus, the film's title refers to flowers blooming (imaged in the colors emerging from the black matrix). This backstory, of course, does not appear in the film—and the film certainly is not "about" O'Neil's mother—but the mysterious title nonetheless hints at the way mourning, survival, and renewal can participate in the cinematic process of color emerging through the process of scratching away the surface.

To describe artworks as having a purpose that the medium can fail in accomplishing distorts how art operates. I do not mean that art doesn't do something to us, but I question describing this effect in terms of a clear purpose, or of success or failure. Rather, the games artworks play, the gambles they take, recall O'Neil's act of planting old, desiccated seeds just to see what comes up, or scratching at the surface and being somewhat surprised by the result. Rather than calculating success or failure, precarity in aesthetics means allowing the medium itself to participate in the outcome, its materiality serving neither as an obstacle nor as a simple neutral channel, but as a matrix for the generation of unexpected effects.

I had originally intended in this essay to also discuss the use of grain in cinema—another material aspect of the chemical, as opposed to digital, cinema. That there are now programs that add the appearance of scratches and grain to digital footage is intriguing, but I wonder whether they represent a transitional phase based in maintaining familiarity, or are swiftly becoming an exercise in nostalgia, like the rather silly (and inaccurate) evocation of silent film past by undercranking, thereby speeding up the image. But grain, as a microelement of chemically produced photography, presents a significant opposition to the digital microelement, the pixel, and I want at least to touch on that as I conclude. Wikipedia defines grain thus:

> **Film grain** or **film granularity** is the random optical texture of processed photographic film due to the presence of small particles of a metallic silver, or dye clouds, developed from silver halide that have received enough photons.[16]

Grain results from a chemical process of the photographic image and, as the definition notes, its patterns are random. A contrast with the digital pixel is useful:

> . . . while film grains are randomly distributed and have size variation, image sensor cells [pixels] are of same size and are arranged in a grid. . . .
>
> In general, as the pixels form a digital image sensor cells set in straight lines, they irritate the eye of the viewer more than the randomly arranged film grains. Most people will reject an enlargement that show pixels, whereas a grained film enlargement with lower resolution will be acceptable, and perceived as "sharper."[17]

The pixel is truly a unit of the digital image, systematically arranged and uniform. A mobile "dance of film grain" occurs in photographic film because every frame has a somewhat different arrangement of silver particles. This, I believe, explains why some cinephiles refer to the digital image as dead, while claiming the older cinema images breathes (I might add, however, that digital copies of older films seem to pick up grain, often with an increased saliency).

Reaction to grain in photography runs a gamut, including a frequent perception of it as interference and noise, something to be eliminated in order to achieve a more effective, transparent image. Eastman Kodak produced stocks with ever-finer grain that lessened the textured feel of the image and were generally considered advances in photographic technology. But a counteraesthetic was equally evident, summarized in a directive I found recently in an online photography blog and podcast: "embrace the grain."[18]

But in thinking about precarity in media and whether it might be a new phenomenon (perhaps brought on by the rise of new media), I consider my own experience as a young (but already self-conscious) film viewer during the 1960s. I recall the impact John Cassavetes's *Faces* had on me when I first saw it in 1968. *Faces* was shot on a variety of film stocks, but primarily 16mm high-contrast, black-and-white stock, in an era where feature films were shot almost entirely on 35mm, generally using stocks that avoided the high-contrast effects Cassavetes courted. And blowing his smaller-gauge film up to 35mm greatly increased the grain.

Faces thus shows how complex the association of realism and transparency can be. The techniques Cassavetes used increase our sense of mediation, drawing attention to the filming process—to graininess, handheld camera movements, lens flare, echoey sound recording, even a hair caught in the camera gate. But most receptions of the film spoke of its "realism" and quasi-documentary style. I think this indicates that realism, at least in the 1960s, was primarily seen as in opposition to the rigid control of image and shooting that characterized most Hollywood productions. Documentary production, in contrast, was open to contingency, and Direct Cinema attempted to minimize the ways filming interfered with unfolding events by using lighter handheld cameras, direct sound, and film that was more light-sensitive (which tended to have more pronounced grain). The visual look of these practices, while secondary to the intentions of the filmmakers, created a visual style that became associated with realism. Realism in this case does not equal transparency.

But there is more to *Faces*'s use of these techniques than simulating a documentary look. As with Cassavetes's approach to performance, taking risks to avoid the predetermined means relinquishing, to some degree, the artist's control, delivering the film partly to the medium—whether this is understood as the material nature of film technology, the discoveries possible in improvisation, or the accidents that might occur. And this reveals the value of precarity as a strategy. "Transparency" and "realism" are tricky terms, basically ideological rather than descriptive. By contrast, the concept of precarity, avoiding any focus on the success or failure of an undistorted communication, should indicate an openness to contingency, to those elements of filmmaking that are not strictly controlled.

Perhaps this offers the strongest way to understand precarious mediation—not in opposition to an ideal of undistorted transmission, nor in terms of distortion, but in terms of openness and an understanding that the materialities of media have their own"agendas" or, rather, exist outside of the intentions that converge in the making of any work of art, which the artwork itself, as a mediated entity encountering human perception, cannot absolutely program or control.

26

Transport of Joy: A Meditation on the Medium of Stan Brakhage

This essay endeavors to grasp the medium of filmmaker Stan Brakhage. To do this I grapple with his films as a process, with the stuff of which his films are made and with the way he took this material and shaped it into a unique medium, creating a unique relation to film through handling its various possibilities.

What is a medium: what can this word mean? It means a *means*, a way to accomplish something. For this reason, a medium may seem to be defined by its purpose—providing a means to an end. In our instrumental society, the medium is therefore understood as secondary to a purpose—a way to get there, not the all-important goal. But in dealing with modernist art, the means looms before us, often overwhelming our lust for the end. Marshall McLuhan intoned that the medium is the message, and modern art, for a variety of reasons, located its essential difference from traditional representational art in a tendency to short-circuit the instrumental attitude and foreground the medium itself.

Focus on the artist's medium defined modern art for Clement Greenberg in his influential essay "Avant-Garde and Kitsch," differentiating it from commercial popular art. "In turning his attention away from subject matter of common experience," Greenberg claimed, "the poet or artist turns it in upon the medium of his own craft."[1] Modern art does not serve some purpose, such as accurate representation, political persuasion, or moral

This essay, previously unpublished, was written in 2013 and revised in 2021.

reform, but focuses on its means, its material—in a word, its medium. For Greenberg, the medium equals "the very processes and disciplines" of art-making. His essay has been widely and strongly criticized in recent years, as has the conflation of modern art with the avant-garde or drawing an absolute dichotomy between avant-garde and popular art. But I am less interested in entering these critical debates than in exploring what "medium" can mean in the experience of the beholder, especially in a medium like film, which has only a short history and whose disciplines remain in many ways undefined.

In the late 1970s and 1980s, the Materialist Film or Structuralist movement in Britain adopted Greenbergian principles as an artistic credo that claimed a political and even a moral basis. It aspired to be materialist and "anti-illusionist," attacking what it called "the illusionism of spurious pictorial or narrative involvement."[2] This focus on the medium of the artist's craft came to be understood as a logic of purging, of seeking to define the essence of an artwork through the elimination of everything else—a puritan aesthetic.

Malcolm Le Grice, in his polemic critical work *Abstract Film and Beyond*, indicates that initially the films of Stan Brakhage influenced the British Structuralist Film movement, but largely through a misunderstanding of his intentions. According to Le Grice, Brakhage, like other American avant-garde filmmakers, "is embedded in a Romantic, Symbolist, Expressionist tradition, with the roots of its cinematic form in Surrealist cinema."[3] Although praising Brakhage's distance from commercial cinema, Le Grice finds that his work fails to follow through the logic of an exclusive focus on the medium: "Brakhage never develops his initial innovation in attitude to the camera toward more precise limitations of its mode of functioning."[4] For Le Grice and Peter Gidal, the major theorists of the materialist film, the modernist artist must abandon subjectivity as its center, thereby, Gidal says, "escaping the cinematic solipsism exemplified by the films of Brakhage."[5] But we might ask if this stripped-down understanding of the primacy of the medium simply reduces the modernist attitude toward the medium to a calculatable formula.

I would claim that we need not think about this focus on the medium strictly, as Greenberg seems to do, on terms of abstract art or the aesthetics of material limitation Le Grice and Gidal derive from it. Exploration of the medium as an issue in itself stems especially from the transformation of the aesthetic that begins toward the end of the eighteenth century, precisely the Romantic tradition Le Grice wishes to escape. Literary theorist Tzvetan Todorov puts this in historical perspective: with the

Romantics, art became "intransitive," no longer a means but an end in itself. As Karl Phillip Moritz claimed already in 1785, "true beauty consists in the fact that a thing signifies nothing but itself, designates only itself, that it is a whole realized in itself."[6] For the Romantics, the artwork no longer simply represented the world of nature, but instead sought to imitate nature's processes, to grow organically, its end contained within itself and guiding its growth, not determining it from the outside. Instead of being an invisible instrumental means, the Romantic medium became opaque; not striving to get to something else, it became intransitive, self-contained. The modern medium therefore calls attention to itself: its process becomes its motivation; it does not allow one to simply pass through it without notice.

It may seem counterintuitive to describe attention to the medium as a hallmark of Romanticism, since a common view of Romanticism stresses its immediacy, its direct access to emotion and attempt to express it. I take Brakhage as an artist whose work demonstrates the complexity of the artistic dialectic of mediation/immediacy. What is gained by making a medium more difficult to pass through? And what sort of attention does a medium desire from us? What does it demand we attend to? I believe that thinking of a medium materially may indeed provide the thread we should follow in specifying Brakhage's medium, but taking a rather different course than Le Grice and Gidal.

Brakhage's 1963 film *Mothlight* penetrates to the core of the dialectic of the medium and the desire for immediacy. I have often felt that this seemingly simple film, four minutes in length, without plot or characters yet not truly abstract, might be the perfect movie, the ultimate film, the movie that shows us where movies come from and what they can do. I claim it renders the film medium, as Brakhage engaged it, visible as a process occurring before our eyes. As Fred Camper has put it, "Avant-garde films . . . often try to call attention to their materials, to reveal the conditions of their making. In *Mothlight*, Brakhage reveals those conditions in a very particular way."[7] Even Le Grice valued *Mothlight* as a contribution to the aesthetic he approves, "towards an awareness of the material aspects of film as the basis of 'content.'"[8] But rather than simply speaking of "material," I believe that exploring the way technology functions in this film reveals the dialectic inherent in Brakhage's engagement with his medium.

Mothlight can arguably be seen as the most material of films since Brakhage created it out of bits he collected of natural objects: the bodies of dead insects, especially the wings of moths, and fragments of plants—flower petals, seed pods, leaves of grass. These elements were placed between

FIGURE 26.1. Stan Brakhage, *Mothlight* (1963).

layers of transparent Mylar splicing tape that had the width and perforations of 16mm film. The collaged material was then sent to a laboratory to be contact-printed. Although we can certainly describe contact printing as photographic, no camera was used to capture the images placed by hand on the Mylar strips; the contact printer registered a direct visual imprint of material objects. Brakhage's experimental process required that the materials he placed within the splicing tape be translucent enough that light could pass through them and thin enough to be fed into a contact printer. Brakhage described his agony as the printer reacted to his handmade strips, slipping them out of alignment, punching unwanted sprocket holes into the strips or otherwise mangling them. Nonetheless, the process generated enough material for him to edit into the carefully structured four-minute film he ultimately titled *Mothlight.*[9]

What role does this technological process play in our experience of the film? Can we sense its complexity without its being explained beforehand? The process of contact printing is complex enough that few people viewing the film will fully grasp it (and indeed, Mark Toscano, master archivist of the avant-garde film for the American Academy of Motion Picture Arts and Sciences, cleared up some of my misconceptions). Le Grice experiences *Mothlight* as a sort of allegory of the materialist film:

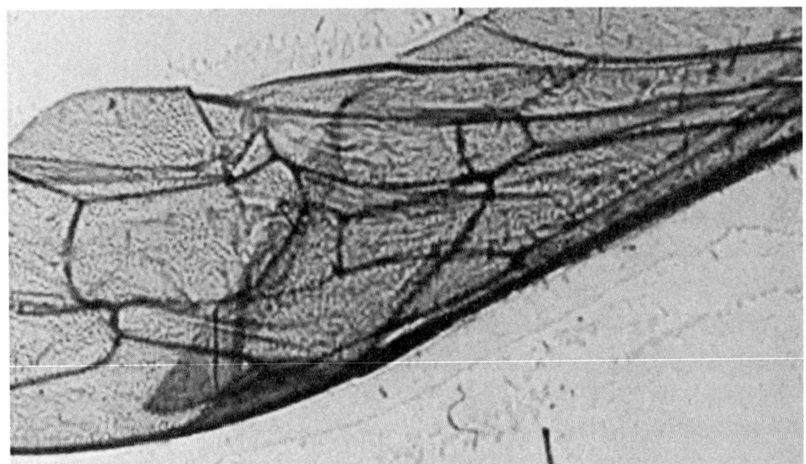

FIGURE 26.2. Stan Brakhage, *Mothlight* (1963).

> The physical problem of making a printable collage, which also allowed the passage of light through the surface, determined that the objects used should be thin or translucent. This makes them a metaphor for the nature of the celluloid on which they are supported, the implied depth of the image being the material depth of the object and the celluloid.[10]

Apparently Le Grice would allow metaphors, as long as they are metaphors of materiality. But is the tangible and recognizable nature of these objects immaterial to our experience of the film?

In contrast to that of commercial studio filmmakers, Brakhage's process has been described as artisanal. This suggests it is in some sense archaic, like the craftsmen who preceded the factory system. His films have been thought about as handicraft (Le Grice refers to them as "handmade films").[11] Artisanal, handicraft—such terms are often posed in opposition to technology, to the machine and the automatic, which replace the human hand in many processes. *Mothlight* might be seen as Brakhage's attempt to circumvent the technological, to triumph over it, most especially by avoiding the camera and its technological process of image-making and going directly to the things of nature. It is in a sense a cameraless film: the light projected through the screen of the contact printer was filtered, not through a photographic image of a moth, but through the diaphanous wing of the moth itself. The grass as it appears on-screen seems to perform a sort of reverse photosynthesis: its green, chlorophyll-based pigment, rather than absorbing the energy of light, lets light radiate throughthe plant's fibers in the contact printer, generating the print that will stain the screen. I believe we experience the images as being made by the objects we see—grass, mothwings, seeds—as if the process of representation had somehow been short-circuited. Are we in the realm of nature or of *techne*? It would seem this film was grown rather than made. And yet the process of its making was deeply technological, and thus we are confronted by a sort of material paradox in which metaphor and material seem to fuse.

All of this becomes a wonderful game, even a magic trick, that conjures up nature through a hidden technology. Brakhage does not avoid the camera so much as reinvent it, remaking it by hand. Further, he redefines the place of the photographic in the process, rendering it literal and making the process of making the film as much the subject of the film as any representation of flowers and bugs. Brakhage's camera did not shoot the bits of dead nature that flutter through his film; a contact printer transferred his collages onto film stock. In a letter to Robert Kelly, Brakhage describes the printer as a figure of demonic technology, looking like something out of 1920s German science fiction film (perhaps the Moloch machine in *Metropolis* swallowing the sacrificial slaves?). He dramatically describes the film's manufacture as a demon ingesting his handiwork into its photographic maw and spitting it out as a film material.[12] All of Brakhage's handmade films, collaged, painted, or scratched, entail and foresee a process of printing and transformation, in the later work most often using an optical printer—in some ways, a more complex technology than photographing the things of the world with a movie camera. What seems so pure and direct on the screen in *Mothlight* actually results from an agonistic process of collaging *and* printing. In effect, though, this process of printing remains invisible to us; we seem to be viewing the collages directly, as if the printer were a traditional nonmodernist medium that disappears in favor of what it shows.

If few films mirror the processes of nature more faithfully than *Mothlight*, it is technology (and indeed, a particularly mechanical and automatic technology, the printer) that allows this to happen. *Mothlight* certainly invokes its medium and joins the legacy of modernist practices in which an artwork becomes self-reflexive, exposing the process of its own making. In the critical tradition identified with Greenberg, modern art is intransitive because it takes itself as its subject. It explores and displays the laws of its own medium. Brakhage belongs to this tradition, and *Mothlight* shows how. But he also exceeds this tradition (rather than failing to follow it to its inevitable conclusion). *Mothlight* both provides a way into a self-reflexive experience of the film medium and opens horizons beyond it. Rather than remaining within the modernist opacity, an overt display of the process

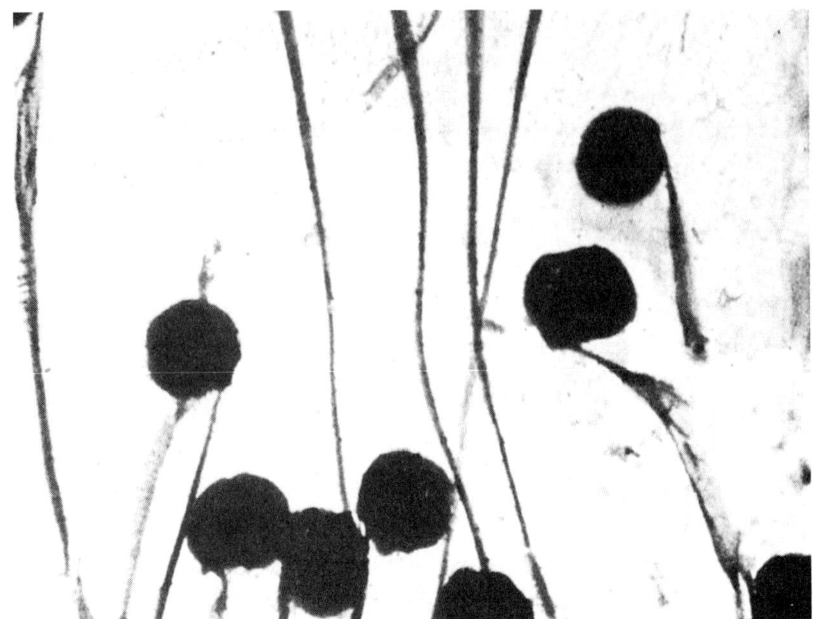

FIGURE 26.3. Stan Brakhage, *Mothlight* (1963).

that exposes the film as celluloid and thereby destroys cinema's illusionist aspect (which is how the British Structuralists, such as Le Grice, read the film), *Mothlight* exceeds a pedagogic demonstration and becomes playful.[13] More precisely, *Mothlight* plays hide-and-seek with technology. And perhaps this is its greatest affinity with nature, its most profound mimesis of nature's processes, this game of hiding. Fragment 123 by Heraclitus tells us, "Nature loves to hide" or "Nature loves concealment" (Φύσις κρύπτεσθαι φιλεῖ). Concealment rules the inner principle by which natural growth takes place, out of our eyesight, buried in the darkness of the soil. This mysterious power of genesis, of coming into visibility, forms the aspect of nature that the German Romantic poet who called himself Novalis, following Moritz, claimed the artist imitates, seeking not to copy the forms of nature but rather to rival her power and process.

Does the medium in *Mothlight* really remain hidden? Of course, we never see the demonic expressionist printer with its sprocket-grasping claws into which Brakhage's Mylar strips were fed. But what does it mean for a medium to remain invisible, hidden? Is it like keeping the lenses of your glasses clean, wiping away the smudges that would blur your sight? Is transparency really the opposite of the intransitive? Or is hiding just one phase of the game of hide-and-seek? In *Mothlight* we seem to see the things themselves, plants and insect parts. But is that all we see: an inventory of bits of nature, as if displayed in a botany sample case or textbook? By no means.

First, and most obviously, we also see the Mylar strip. This transparent strip makes such an impression on our viewing that I believe meditating on it leads us into the essence of Brakhage's medium. The plastic strip appears to us as an undefined background against which stuff comes and goes. Whereas the bits of nature dance, in a rhythm of constant change, set to the pulse of the frame-by-frame animation achieved by (first) the printer and (now) the projector, this strip remains constant; at points it may be obscured by the larger bits, but it is always revealed again as a white blank of light. The natural elements rush past us, appearing and disappearing, but the strip maintains its flow, a continuum that bears the stuff, like a current carrying flotsam and jetsam. Even when a leaf or petal covers the entire frame, this ground remains in our sensibility as the source of the light that passes through, illuminates, the diaphanous surfaces of nature.

Thus it is wrong to call it a "ground," for several reasons. It appears totally different from the opaque surfaces that usually provide the backing for a collage. The Mylar does not simply constitute the background of the images we see, providing a solid surface for them to cling to. It serves as a bank of light, the source of its illumination providing the light-infused surface that forms the film's condition of visibility. Rather than a ground (with its earthly connotations), the Mylar forms a light field, with associations that are ethereal and immaterial. It constitutes the invisible (in the sense of unfigured) source of visibility. It *is* light. Brakhage often quoted a statement by the medieval philosopher Scottus Eriugena (as quoted by Ezra Pound): "all things that are, are by light." But if light seems to be absorbed and reflected by the things of the world, it also seems to abdicate in favor of them (unless it glares brilliantly and makes us close our eyes lest it dazzle us). Milton spoke of Satan's Hell as "darkness made visible." In *Mothlight* we could speak of light made viewable. The transparent medium presents the dance of nature to us, but it also reveals itself as light.

But Brakhage teaches us that the light projected through film is far from immaterial. We sense this film light in a material fashion. It is visible, perceptible, even if it remains imageless. (Indeed, this neutral field on Mylar now has a yellowish tint—a product of aging?—which I don't recall being as strong in my early viewings of the film.) More importantly, this light field doesn't simply illuminate the images; it holds them and suspends them before us. We see it, but it also seems to have a physical, even a tactile dimension. The film not only projects the forms of nature's bodies but holds pulverized dust flaking off the moth wings, as well as bubbles of the adhesive stuff that holds them to the Mylar surface. Thus it literally renders visible the strip of film, the transparent coil of plastic that is now vanishing from our moving image culture. It recalls the conception of light in Robert Grosseteste's thirteenth treatise, *On Light* (the text spoken in the last segment of Hollis Frampton's *Zorns Lemma*), which argues that light is the first corporeal form. Even without recourse to Neoplatonic metaphysics, we can see how much work this invisible medium performs. It is by no means abstract. The Mylar strip presents to us bits of nature, illuminating them, holding them before us, giving them a place which is a non-place, serving as the condition for their existence in a self-effacing manner.

This may all sound quite abstract, but our sense of the Mylar strip as the medium underlying the film remains very material. We see it and we almost feel it. The Mylar strip endows these images with the tactile dimension that some recent film theorists have attributed to our experience of cinema.[14] But beyond being the condition for the display of what we see, it visuality, this strip is also the basis of its movement, its rapid flow before us. Even more than a medium of visibility, this strip is the medium of time and part of the mechanism of its passing as movement. *Mothlight* could never be mistaken for a set of botanical or entomological samples. Its specimens are not offered to our studious gaze; rather, they run past us in hurried procession, a ritual dance at breakneck speed that tests the thresholds of our perception and recognition. More than observing individual bits, we sense the speed of their succession. The motion depends on this strip, propelled by the action of the projector, which converts individual images into a rapid flow. What it produces is a stream of light, a flow of visibility.

Brakhage considered giving this film the title "Dead Spring." "Spring" refers not only to the season when nature comes out of hiding but also to the literal mechanics of the projector, "the eventual unwinding of the film," which he compared to a coil relaxing. The ultimate motive force of the film (of all film, of course) lies in the mechanics of the projector, but few films make us conscious of this prime mover. Brakhage's unchosen title refers as much to his medium as to his subject. Nature is a process of death and birth, as demonstrated by the insect husks and the fading remnants of plants severed from their sustaining earth that this film projects before us. The light toward which moths gravitate causes their death (Brakhage makes the point that the dead moths that star in his film were gathered from "light boxes and lamp bowls," and he constantly refers to his botanical elements as "dead plants"). The motion supplied by the film's unwinding may give these dead things an animate appearance, a "simulation of life," but can the mechanical ever serve as a source of resurrection?

Brakhage lets the question hover before us in this flow of images. The "dead spring" that moves the strip of Mylar and its flow of the once-alive rotates us from death to life and possibly back again.

Let me sum up what I think we learn about Brakhage's medium from *Mothlight*. Certainly his medium is film. But film, as Brakhage's medium, is not just inert material, the remnant of a modernist unmasking of our cinematic illusions, achieved by making us aware of the material and mechanics that underlie cinema. As a medium, film *does something*, though it recalls playing a game more than accomplishing a practical purpose. Film takes us on a ride. In *Mothlight* film becomes defined by its action as a corporeal medium that bears other things in its flow, like a river's current carrying detritus from the shore. The medium also conveys light, rendering things visible; it is therefore a flow of light. Its flow is measured through an abstract dimension of time, the ticking of a clock, but also experienced through the material process of movement and its continuity, as one thing flows into the next.

The medium itself may be transparent, allowing light to penetrate and other things (or their images) to be seen through it. But although this transparency means the medium itself often hides, it never truly disappears. It bows out for a moment to let other things be seen, and then either reemerges or, rather than overtly displaying itself, simply lets us feel its presence, its pulse of motion, through the effects it causes. *Mothlight* ends by reminding us of this field of light and semi-tactile material, revealing it alone on the screen as the moth wings seem to flit away, disappearing from our frame of view. The screen may seem to remain itself, but it also fills itself with light. Thus *Mothlight* presents us with a visible flow of light and movement, transparent to let the light shine through, but strong enough to carry other things in its current. Transparency blends with transport, a sense of being carried that refers both to the moving images themselves and the viewer who is swept up by the medium and taken somewhere. And yet that somewhere is not a goal outside itself, but a penetration and a participation in the very form and process of the film, its energy and its power. This is the nature of the medium as we learn it from *Mothlight*.

MEDIATION, MEDITATION

What then do I mean by Brakhage's medium? The question is not answered by simply saying "film," a technical medium based on images arranged systematically on a flexible transparent base and employing centrally the dual apparatus of projectors and cameras as well as a less often recalled variety of printers. Brakhage's work was made in this technical medium in a variety of gages: 16mm most often, but also 8mm (both super and regular 8), with a few limited forays into 35mm and even an experiment with IMAX. Brakhage did not work in video formats and at points proclaimed an explicit preference for film over video. He did, however, approve the DVD edition of his film work issued by Criterion in 2003—although he did not see the results before his death. (Fred Camper, one of the finest critics of Brakhage and an advisor on the Criterion edition, has also voiced his strong preference for seeing films on film, but nonetheless deems the Criterion video transfers acceptable as conveyors of Brakhage's work.[15]) Although I feel the specific technical medium of film certainly inspired Brakhage's work, I equate what I am calling his medium, not with film in this technical sense, but with a broader understanding of what I call "light-borne moving images." Further, I am trying in this essay to specify the way Brakhage redefined the film medium through his work and created a medium uniquely his own. This redefinition of medium recalls the way first the Romantics and then the avant-garde poets of the twentieth century redefined the role of language, going beyond treating it as simply a means of communication. This redefinition by the artist is essential to the modernist avant-garde medium, as I understand it. But I would claim that only a few filmmakers have actually redefined their medium in a unique manner. Brakhage is one of these.

Mothlight reveals essentials aspects of Brakhage's use of his medium, but it remains technically a rather singular film within his oeuvre.[16] Up until the 1980s, Brakhage's films primarily employed motion picture photography, occasionally including painting and scratching on the film. From the mid-1980s on, films whose imagery was not achieved by initial photography become increasingly dominant in his work. Although this change indicates a major stylistic transformation, I believe that a consistent attitude to his medium pervades Brakhage's corpus. This consistency defines what I am calling his medium, even if it allows, even encourages, changes and variations in style. In his photographic images, light is made to flow, the world is rendered transparent, and both the world and the viewer are put through a process of transport toward renewed perception of space, motion, and light.

Brakhage shaped his medium to lead his viewers through unique experiences: to convey less a message or representation than a viewer's trajectory. But can a medium be self-sufficient, self-contained? Does it really mean nothing other than itself? Doesn't such a tautology deny the nature of medium, its active force? Does this understanding of the "means" of modernist art restrict it to a rejection of meaning? Brakhage has riffed eloquently on this accusation of "meaninglessness," saying, "I do *not* deliberately empty meaning from the filmic shapes of my making . . . *my* meaninglessness is simply in the service of new means, making room, as it were, for what is felt as tender shoots, so to speak, pushing up through the human-earth old, impact of history."[17]

This issue has often been debated. In viewing art as something other than purposeful, the Romantics aspired to liberate it, rather than limiting it to a static reiteration of its own identity. The most profound of the early German Romantics, Novalis, argued that by eschewing simple communication, language became poetic and therefore raised itself to what he called its second power. Here is Novalis's somewhat difficult prose:

> Language to the second power, for example the fable, is the expression of an entire thought—and it belongs to the hieroglyphics of the second power—to the *language of sounds and of pictograms* of the second power. It has poetic qualities and it is not *rhetorical*—subordinated—when it is the perfect expression—when it is *euphonic* to the second power—correct and precise—when it is, so to speak, an *expression* for expression—when at least it does not appear as a means—but as being in itself a perfect production of the *higher linguistic power*.[18]

To untangle a bit (at my peril) this train of thought: poetic language does not convey a meaning but rather, through its sound (euphony) and its imagistic qualities (pictograms and hieroglyphics), embodies a unity, becoming an expression of expression. The very act of expression is art, and art comprises all its meaning. Can we understand this without simply being paradoxical? Yes, I think, if we consider how the medium of art, rather than serving as a vehicle for conveying a meaning, *carries us as viewers/readers*. What happens as we're carried along? That is what I am calling "transport." A process of being taken out of our selves somewhere.

Brakhage's medium offers an alternative to the dilemma of, on the one hand, an instrumental use of art as a practical tool and, on the other, an indolent assumption of tautological uselessness. His third path lies in redefining cinema such that it induces meditation in its viewer. Avoiding the abyss of defining either the meaning and technics of meditation, I favor its common sense—a removal from immediate purposes, distinct from practical concerns (*Ora et labora*, "pray and work," the monks used to say, stressing that both were needed for a spiritual life, but also that they were essentially different). Meditation appears in the titles of two series of films by Brakhage, *Sexual Meditations* (1970–1972) and *Visions in Meditation* (1989–1990). Religious overtones may be present in these reference (perhaps oxymoronic in the first series, arguably more direct in the second). As Brakhage pointed out in an essay (and P. Adams Sitney has wonderfully explicated), a major reference is Gertrude Stein's long poem *Stanzas in Meditation*—a secular, determinately modernist source.[19] Brakhage's understanding of what he calls Stein's "meditative art" involves the romantic/modernist practice of releasing the art form (in Stein's case, language) from the task of reference, description, and narrative, rendering it intransitive, to use Todorov's term. This liberates art for a different endeavor, which Brakhage calls "meditative inner formation" or, more emphatically, "the Transformative."[20] Far from inert, this noninstrumental act of transformation (holding, as Sitney points out, a punning reference to "trance") involves, Brakhage tells us, "a complex spiritual matter of author and reader, or filmmaker and viewer."[21] This is why I call Brakhage's medium a mode of transport, referring less to traveling to a destination than with being carried away, as in the phrase "transports of joy." *Mothlight* is a transport of joy as the filmmaker invites us for a ride in his sweet machine. Brakhage makes clear that this transformative exchange, at least in cinema, depends on "moving visual thinking," a succinct if somewhat abstract description of his medium. He adds, toward the end of this discussion of meditative art, "Keep it moving!"[22]

Brakhage's debt to Stein has been well acknowledged by the filmmaker himself and deftly analyzed by critics, especially Sitney and H. Bruce Elder.[23] Brakhage defined this debt in modernist terms, saying, "Gertrude Stein sensed paint and writ as freed from an obligation to re-present."[24] Stein's *Stanzas in Meditation* inspired Brakhage most primordially in his *Visions in Meditation* films, even though, as Sitney puts it, the series "bears no superficial similarities to that source."[25] In an interview with Saranjan Ganguly, Brakhage described the impact of *Stanzas* on his film series somewhat more directly: "The basic inspiration is from the poem in which Stein tries to free words from reference and allows them to exist, each with a life of their own, within the jostling of all the words across the length of the poem."[26] Beyond the materialist approach to the word, it is these aspects of Stein's poetics—the liberation of the word and the "jostling" of meaning this implies—that propel Brakhage's meditative cinema. Commentaries on Brakhage and Stein, as well as his own exegesis of her influence, stress the role of repetition in both their corpuses. Stein's repeating of words does more than de-automatize verbal reference by stuttering and rendering the words maddeningly perceptible. As Sitney puts it, "The primary lesson Brakhage had learned from Stein was that there was no such thing as repetition. Every recurrence has a new meaning."[27] Thus Brakhage's celebration of Stein's circular charm, "A rose is a rose is a rose . . .", stressed the puns and new meanings that arise from this echolalia. Such repetition, Bruce Elder points out, "emphasizes sound over meaning and allows for radical shifts of thought and reference even while the linguistic texture of the verbal construct remains unaltered."[28] Rather than a simple reiteration, with its potential tautological boredom, repetition triggers what Elder felicitously calls "Brakhage's use of perpetually regenerating forms."[29]

This flow of regeneration constitutes the well of inspiration that Brakhage drew from Stein in his own *Visions in Meditation.* In *Stanzas*, Stein continually recycles a number of simple words, new meanings emerging with each iteration as she rings the changes on these well-worn terms. I am particularly fascinated by the recurrent "well"—which turns to "welcome" and renews many common phrases: "well of meaning," "well meant," "well known," "well said," "think well," "tell well," "leave well alone," "spell well," "not only well but very well," "well to do," "gather well," "well caught," "happened well"—and the incantatory stringing together of "well" and "wish," as in, "who adds well to a wish / who adds a wish to well."

Brakhage understood—guided, of course, by Stein—that repetition does not put a stop to meaning but opens words up to a potentially infinite but always renewed flow. Elder describes it this way: "It is a movement that returns to where it started, a movement that goes nowhere and so, in a sense, is not movement. And since this is movement that is not real movement (in the sense that it does not progress toward an outcome), it is ceaseless."[30] Here again Brakhage's medium transports us. The movement of his film defines his medium, but this cinematic movement goes beyond simple visual kinesis, although seeing movement on the screen remains its basis. It is, as Brakhage increasingly calls it in his late writings, "moving visual thinking."[31] But this is not thought: it is *shown* by his medium, and it is seen by us.

Visions in Meditation # 2: Mesa Verde is one of Brakhage's most complex later films. It has been commented on brilliantly by P. Adams Sitney, and I will restrict myself to observing what it tells us about the mutual implication of medium and meditation.[32] Nothing in the film literally resembles the translucent Mylar matrix of *Mothlight*; no light field holds together the rush of nature's detritus. The film involves no hand-painting or scratching. Yet its nearly constant use of superimposition, in which we see through layers of images, sometime three of them at a time, recalls the underlying transparency of the film medium and renders material things

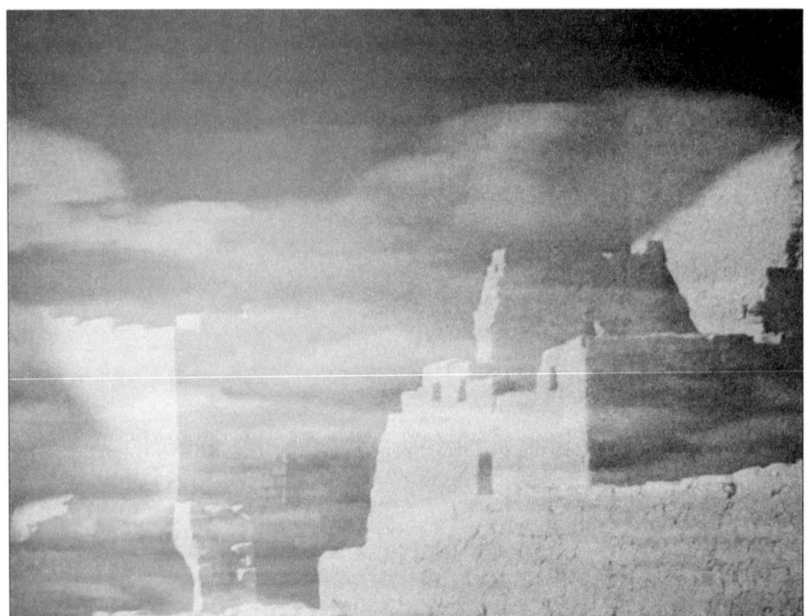

FIGURE 26.4. Stan Brakhage, *Visions in Meditation #2: Mesa Verde* (1989).

as surfaces that vision and light pass through. As in most of Brakhage's cinema, these photographed shots function as veils of light, picturing a diaphanous world rather than a solid, opaque one. At points, very similar images are superimposed, then seem to lift off and separate, like specters rising from earthly bodies. The images evoke Lucretius's Epicurean theory of vision, in which little films, lifting off from the surface of things, are conveyed by light to our eyes. In spite of the seeming solidity of cliffs, canyon walls, and stone houses, Brakhage renders them as transparent surfaces. But it is not just transparency that liberates them from the weight and resistance of matter; it is, rather, a continual sense of flow, as they are caught by an almost constantly moving handheld camera. Nearly every shot contains camera movement. The film's opening images, shot from some means of rapid transportation, most likely a car, give us the feel of a desperate journey rushing us along through a moving landscape. But lest we get caught up in anticipating an arrival, the journey seems to mark time, to stutter and never get anywhere, to go forward and backward, both alternatively (from shot to shot) and even at the same time (as superimposed shots move in different directions). Instead of the literal materiality of the bits of nature collaged onto Mylar in *Mothlight*, here the forms of nature reach us as images through photography.

Brakhage escapes any easily recognizable reference, a technique he claimed to have learned from Stein, transforming identifiable things into constantly moving and changing forms, their solid outlines dissolved into a flow of motion. Brakhage mixes together contrasting tones, textures, and hues, creating an elemental ballet of sky and earth, stone and water through a choreography of camera movement and montage. But if this dance expresses a transport of joy, it also evokes a trance of terror. Brakhage's camera twists and tortures these elements, subjecting them to a cinematic process of dematerialization, stretching their contours with anamorphic lenses, superimposing them into a palimpsest of rhythms, and making them streak across the screen with rapid camera movement. In the first third of the film especially, one feels nature itself convulsed in a violent process of transformation, as if undergoing a powerful inquisition, a torture determined to pry loose its hidden secrets, to make it reveal its sources and confess its past.

This natural landscape gives way to images of the remains of a human-built environment, the ancient dwellings of the Anasazi people tucked within the caves of the Mesa Verde canyon. This complex built environment was home to a community that constructed multistory and multi-room dwellings around 1200 CE but abandoned the site by the end of the century, an exodus that remains unexplained, although archaeologists now

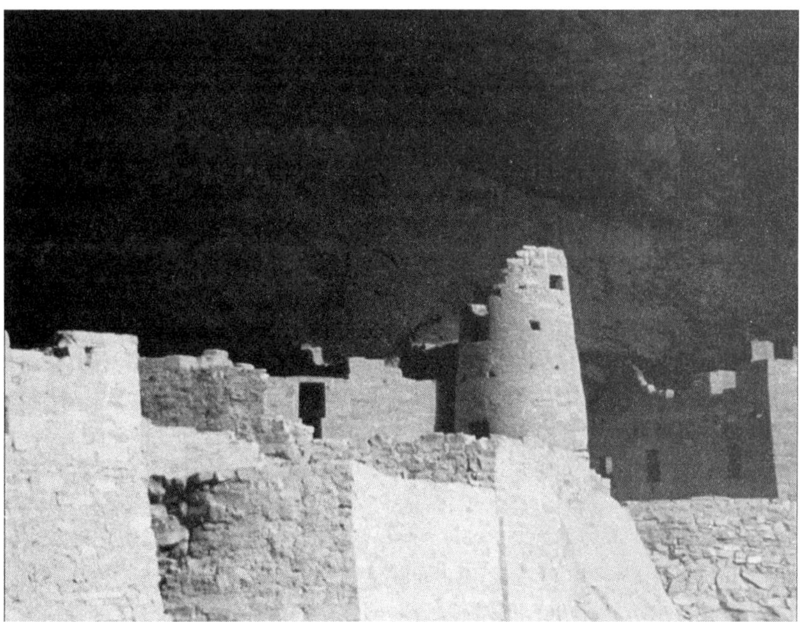

FIGURE 26.5. Stan Brakhage, *Visions in Meditation #2: Mesa Verde* (1989).

suspect environmental causes—drought or famine. On visiting the site, Brakhage had an impression that some great ancient trauma took place there, and his film partly envisions the apocalyptic energy of this past event.

In Brakhage's images the landscape of the Southwest, mountains and desert covered by scrub brush, seems invaded by a cancer that has caused the canyon walls and caves to become ulcerated with human dwellings that resemble tumors or boils. The camera changes the exposure of shots, alternatively overexposing the image to drain it of color or underexposing and thereby increasing its saturation. The hues of the canyon walls with their clinging ruins dim or overwhelm with brightness as we watch. These long abandoned ancient dwellings appear in the process of being swallowed back into the mineral forms from which they were wrenched. Brakhage undertakes an archaeological exploration, using his medium to excavate layers of the past, attempting to amplify what the rocks are saying. This ancient ruin holds the secret of a drama we will never fully learn, but by setting the space vibrating with his cinematic flow of motion Brakhage visually evokes an echoing scream that pervades his silent film. Everything may be dead or vanished here, but like the dead spring of *Mothlight*, Brakhage's medium channels its banshee spirit. This space remains haunted, and Brakhage releases its ghosts from their rockbound casements. Brakhage conjures a gradual process, taking time, like the hatching of an egg or the blooming of a flower. His medium works toward the moment when these revenants break through the surfaces of nature and the remnants of an abandoned human dwelling place. As in a ritual of invocation, during the first part of the film the frenzied energy of Brakhage's medium animates the inanimate—reveals the pulse hidden within rock and the forms fashioned by humans long dead and departed.

Recalling the sudden appearance of animals among the sleeping children in Brakhage's breakthrough 1958 film *Anticipation of the Night*, about midway through *Mesa Verde* we glimpse a small deer. At first this living presence seems at home in the wilderness, but despite its gentle appearance, its impassive gaze toward the camera gives it an uncanny power, even an affinity with the act of filming, as if mirroring the camera's look. Rather than simply being an element of this natural environment, the deer affects us as a visitation with a reflective power. It watches us as much as we watch it, regarding us steadily with its dark eyes, adding a living witness to this scene. But the deer also acts as a messenger, bringing a new level of imagery and presence to the ancient scene. Then, unexpectedly, the recumbent figure of a naked man appears, superimposed over the deer.

As Sitney points out, this rather ephemeral image, alien to the dominant tone of most of the film, comes from an early medical film of a man having an epileptic seizure, preserved in the Library of Congress Paper Print collection.[33] Even without this information it marks an intrusion into a scene of dead human culture bereft of living human presence. The quality of the image itself (black and white and oddly grainy within a color image), makes it feel like a rent in the fabric of the film, a foreign invasion into what had been a coherent, if frenzied, southwestern landscape, a gap through which another scene penetrates. The convulsed man is not rooted in this environment, but rather haunts it. The man appears, Sitney writes, like a vision summoned by the previous elemental cinematic frenzy, and I embrace his reading of the figure as an entranced shaman possessed by the spirit Brakhage has evoked from the rocks, or perhaps an exorcist compelling this energy to take on a human or animal form in order to banish it. If the figure's spastic movements recall the rhythm of the sensory overload that precedes it, it also seems to bring the frenzy to a releasing climax.

Brakhage's camera continues to prowl about the ruins with a weightless freedom, but its pace has slackened; the dead city gains more stability and weight. Then gradually images of water seep into the film through superimposition. Sometimes placid surfaces of blue, but just as frequently a scintillating liquid, mirrors sparking with light and agitated by the camera to create a violent calligraphy of lines of light scraping the screen, hypnotic in their patterns. As if welling up from a great depth, this wash of blue across the screen summons a deeper meditative experience, one derived from the previous convulsions of earth but flowing over it.

Superimposed or juxtaposed with the hot baked yellow and red of the stone dwellings, water eventually drowns this antediluvian space in sweet oblivion, perhaps cleansing it of trauma. In telephoto enlargement, some final rapid camera movements sweep over the close-up surfaces of the dead dwellings, seeming to dematerialize and banish the site, as a brief flash of the convulsing man almost subliminally submerges him in a field of blue. The final minutes of the film leave this cave of dreams behind and move to greener landscapes, showing flocks of birds gathered by water, mountain vistas, and the blue of sky mixed with clouds. Like the action of a ghostly Noh drama, which evokes the specters and sites of past tragedies, we have gone somewhere, transported by Brakhage's medium; we have meditated on a place and its past, penetrated into its spirits both calm and agitated. And left it more peaceful than when we came.

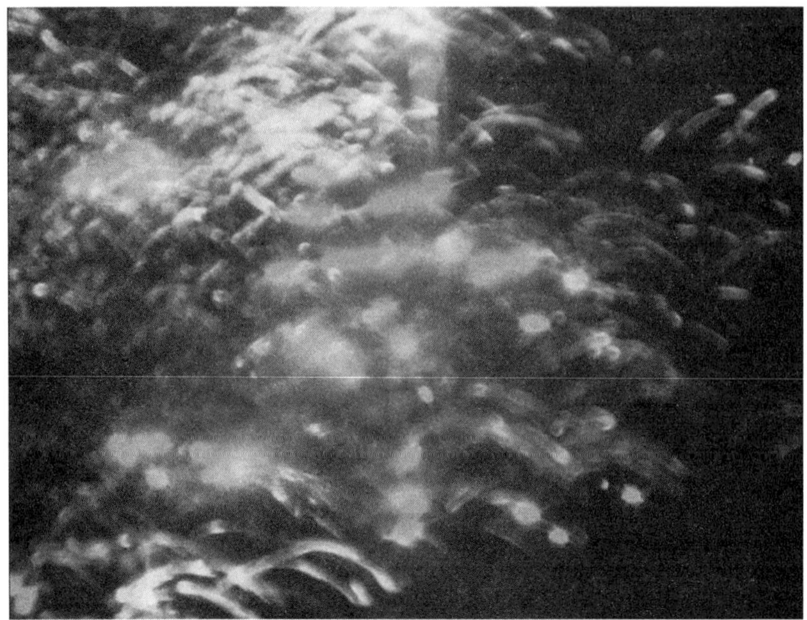

FIGURE 26.6. Stan Brakhage, *Visions in Meditation #2: Mesa Verde* (1989).

I recall this enigmatic passage toward the end of Stein's *Stanzas in Meditation*:

> I think well of landscape as a proof of another
> I wish well of having brought to think
> Which is why well at first.
> At first I did not know why well
> Why quite well as much as well
> Why it could be just as well
> That it is like or if and like
> This landscape this color.[34]

THE LANGUAGE OF NIGHT

What I am calling Brakhage's medium could be summed up by the cinematic realization of his phrase "the possibility of moving visual thinking."[35] I call it a medium rather than a style or a theme (though it relates to both) in order to emphasize how it defines and redefines the film medium through its use of the moving image. In some sense this medium implies simply the full unfolding of his call, in his manifesto at the opening of *Metaphors on Vision*, for "a pursuit of knowledge foreign to language and founded upon a visual communication demanding a development of the optical mind, and dependent on perception in the original and deepest sense of the word."[36] There is no question that Brakhage developed this sense of his medium consistently, at least from *Anticipation of the Night* and the films surrounding it made in 1958. But it is also clear to me and anyone who watches his films that his approach to his medium changed over the years, like any growing thing. His stated antipathy toward language was based, of course, on words being the dominant practical means of communicating information and commands—in other words, language's transitive instrumental role. But Brakhage became increasingly aware that ossified images could also serve practical purposes such as persuasion. Therefore it was too simple to just oppose the visual to the verbal. Through Brakhage's medium of transport and transformation everything can merge with its supposed opposite, and language itself can be liberated from any reduced role. Although present from the origins of his filmmaking, Brakhage's encounter with language, especially in the form of inscription, emerges as a looming specter in his later films. In one of his greatest late films, *First Hymn to the Night—Novalis* (1994), Brakhage directly confronts language in the form of writing or, perhaps more specifically, inscription. In this film it would seem he questioned his earlier opposition to the word and nonetheless ended up affirming his medium even more strongly by providing a place for the word and its inscription within it.

The hand-painted films that dominated Brakhage's late work achieve a certain climax in his articulation of his medium. These films have yet to be thoroughly studied, or analyzed as powerfully as P. Adams Sitney did for the earlier, more lyric and mythopoetic work, although increasingly cogent criticism is emerging.[37] While acknowledging the uniqueness of this late phase of Brakhage's work, I maintain that it extends rather than contradicts or ignores the medium he had established in the earlier work. The flow of motion, the constant modulation of transparency to light, and the ecstatic transport of the viewer becomes the exclusive focus of these rich yet rarified films. In John Powers's treatment of *Passage Through: A Ritual* (1990), a film he readily admits "stands out as an anomaly in Stan Brakhage's filmography," Powers describes how this often monochromatic film (as opposed to the colorful, hand-painted films that surround it) creates a "sensation of movement" that "detaches itself from apparatus and film and occupies a space between screen and viewer."[38] This, he says, has a potent effect: "By seeming to detach movement from the film, *Passage Through* emboldens its viewer to experience movement qua movement."[39] Although *Passage Through* is indeed a unique film, I believe that the movement Powers describes is at the center of what I am calling Brakhage's medium. This experience, Powers insists, "infuses the screen with a strong sensation of propulsion or driving or pushing forward."[40]

Powers's idea of "detached motion" indicates an experience that is more than the simple cinematic effect of the moving image; it becomes, I would claim, a meditation on motion, which causes the viewer to reflect on her own participation in the sense of movement not simply through a depicted space or within the confines of the film or even as a physiological/perception sensation. Rather, all of these a serve as a condition for the existence of the images on the screen—in short, their medium. Powers quotes Gertrude Stein to indicate the possibility of movement that is nonliteral: "If the movement, that is any movement, is lively enough, perhaps it is possible to know that it is moving even if it is not moving against anything."[41]

In *First Hymn to the Night—Novalis* Brakhage interweaves one of the most masterfully moderated visual voyages of hand-painting with those things one might think his medium excluded: language and writing, opacity and darkness. I have already referenced Novalis, discussing the Romantic attitude toward the artist's medium as a form, like nature, complete in itself. Novalis envisioned a form of expression in which there is no separation between means and end, but rather a process in which the artist enjoins us to accompany her, to move with her through the artwork. As Todorov comments, this double concept of language can appear to be a contradiction:

> The paradox of intransitive language is that the expressions that express only themselves may be—or better still, are—at the same time invested with the most profound meaning. It is even at the moment when one seems to be speaking about nothing at all that one says the most.[42]

Language doubles its power by turning in or around itself, becoming a sensual experience in place of an abstract sign or message. Novalis compared this rich sensual language to pictograms or hieroglyphics or the euphony of sound in language. This clue helps us move past the dead end of a simply irrational paradox in which language means nothing and everything simultaneously. The transparency or transitive nature of instrumental language tries to ferry us directly and swiftly to its meaning. The sound of the word, the images it might summon—these would only slow the act of comprehension and are therefore irrelevant. Aspects of Novalis's view of language appear as well in the poet who rivaled Stein as a model for Brakhage,

Ezra Pound, in his understanding of the Chinese ideogram. According to Pound and his mentor Ernest Fenollosa, forms of writing existed that had not abandoned imagistic power in favor of the practical facility of the phonetic alphabet. Based on different sources, paleontologist André Leroi-Gourhan offered a similar view of the evolution of writing and claimed that originally the role of the human hand in making inscriptions, which he calls "graphism," was as important to writing as phonetic transcription and allowed a different means of expressiveness: "The invention of writing, through the device of linearity, completely subordinated graphic to phonetic expression. . . . An image possesses a dimensional freedom which writing must always lack."[43] He adds:

> Language was placed on the same level as technics; and the technical efficacy of language today is proportional to the extent to which it has rid itself of the halo of associated images characteristic of archaic forms of writing. . . . Such unification of the process of expression entails the subordination of graphism to spoken language. . . . However, it also entails an impoverishment of the means of nonrational expression.[44]

The pictographs of ancient civilization could express domains of human experience that civilization moved away from and Novalis strove to recover. Brakhage's medium, too, belongs to this endeavor.

Brakhage's work in and on cinema developed this visual photographic technology into a means of modernist transformation of the sort Stein had taught him in her writing. This medium of motion and transformation, of illumination and merging, aspired to a reinvention of language. Instead of a conventional alphabet, Brakhage employed a constantly newly created system of juxtaposed images in motion. But if we could claim that Brakhage sought to overcome language by developing the optical mind and returning to a more original experience of perception, I would claim also that he returned, especially in his later films, to a primordial understanding of writing based in the expressive power of graphism and inscription. We could say that Brakhage rediscovered language, or the word, through painting—"(much as Paint, freed by The Photograph from representation, has reverted to its glyphic roots)," as he mentions parenthetically in his essay on Stein's use of language.[45] Late Brakhage reveals that his cinema, and that is to say, his medium, has been about the hand as much as the eye: the hand that marks and moves draws, writes, and gestures.

It is almost impossible to describe the film *First Hymn to the Night—Novalis* in words. Most of the film consists of colors painted on film. There is an incommensurability between language and color that triggers a philosophical conundrum—the silly anxiety over whether we all "see" the same green. But this unsolvable linguistic problem reveals that color exemplifies the realm of expression Novalis invokes; color means nothing but itself, yet it is hardly insignificant. We can make a scientific analysis of color, based in the rate of vibration of light and its place within the spectrum. But this data shows us only that color possesses its own order, which no language can translate. Admittedly, certain colors can be used instrumentally, such as red for a stop light. But while I believe such uses tell us something about how colors affect us, they do not explain why—because, again, color's expressiveness is contained in its sensual experience, and any attempt to abstract it simply distances us from this primary effect. I am not saying we can say nothing about color—or I would simply shut up. Its cultural uses and associations are manifold. But I am saying that color itself speaks by engaging our senses, and we will always find that verbal explanation differs radically from sensual experience.

While we might be able to discuss each hue individually, the complexity of color truly overwhelms us when we think of the ways colors interact. One of the world's greatest filmmakers invoked this aspect of painting as a way to explain the effect of film editing. In *Notes on Cinematography*, Robert Bresson wrote:

> An image must be transformed by contact with other images as is a color by contact with other colors. A blue is not the same blue beside a green, a yellow, a red. No art without transformation.

Brakhage could not have described the role color plays in his own medium better. It would be inadequate, however, to describe Brakhage's colors as being "beside" each other. Following in the wake of abstract expressionism, his colors defy edges or borders in viscous tides that mingle as they merge. Even when individual still frames are examined, these colors seem to roil with potential motion.

First Hymn to the Night—Novalis is far from a simple succession of colors or even color juxtapositions. The film extends the act of painting, as colors interact with pattern, shape, and the gestures of their formation. Brakhage's painting on film follows the modernist path, which, somewhat unfortunately, is usually called abstraction (as if these forms were not unreservedly and gloriously material!). There is no attempt at representation in any of his images, and they certainly relate strongly to the painting of Brakhage's formative era, the style of abstract expressionism, in which the

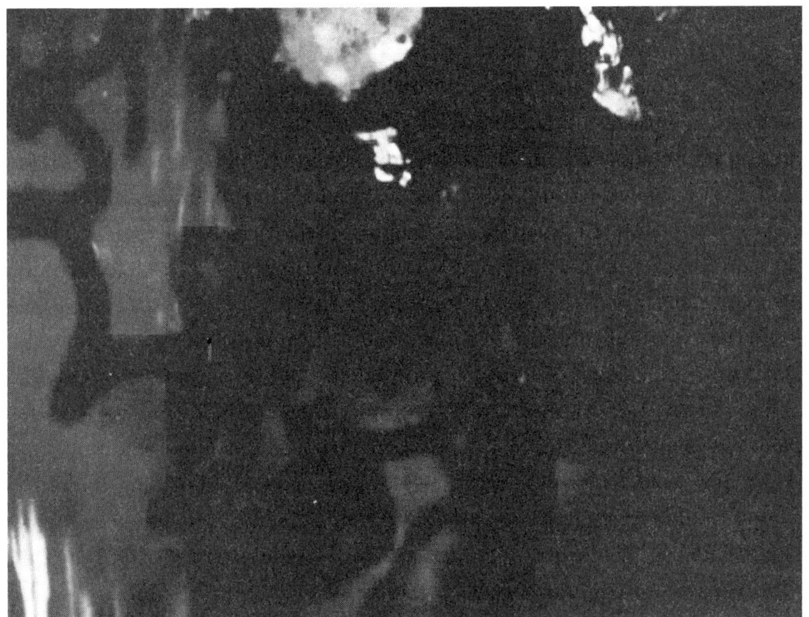

FIGURE 26.7. Stan Brakhage, *First Hymn to the Night—Novalis* (1994).

play of color, surface, and the gestural work of the artist's hand triumphed over recognizable images. Such painting relates back to the graphism Leroi-Gourhan saw as the common ground of art and ancient writing, from the first inscriptions by Homo sapiens on rocks and cave walls, for which the rhythm of the hand played as essential a role as the act of seeing. Primal human hand gestures left marks on surfaces even before any attempt to trace the outlines of things seen. Yet as powerful as Brakhage's debt to modern painting may be, his hand-painted films belong entirely to his medium and are transformed by being filmed. As *Mothlight* picked up and redefined the stuff of nature through its animation and projection, as *Mesa Verde* filmed landscapes and ancient ruins in order to transform them through a radical approach to motion picture photography and editing, so these hand-painted films absorb colors and painterly gestures into an ongoing, transparent, light-infused flow of motion.

It is not as though there is nothing to say about the painted sections of *Novalis*. They are highly structured in their patterns and in their transitions. In the first few seconds of the film, Brakhage shows us how many different ways he can fill the screen with moving color: the varying amount of saturation; the use of black; the areas of luminous white; brushstrokes that are hard-edged and aggressive contrasted to others that are watery and soft; places where the pigment seems like granular dust sprinkled across the frame and those where it appears thick and pasty. The recurrent use of dark lines intersecting with fields of color evokes the mosaic assembly of colored glass held by strips of lead in a stained-glass window, which undoubtedly served as an inspiration for the hand-painted films (thematized in Brakhage's magnificent *Chartres Series* of 1994). Freezing almost any single frame from these films yields extraordinary compositions, recalling not only the abstract expressionists but J. M. W. Turner, Franz Marc, or Wassily Kandinsky. Contemplating these images as stills is tempting, but it destroys our experience of the colors' seeming movement (impelled, of course, by the frame-by-frame process of the optical printer), the rhythms of their position within the frame, their disappearances and reappearances as frame succeeds frame. A stilled single-frame image captures something that might be expressed in the gestures of abstract expressionist painting, but the full expression of the film could be realized only through the transformative movement of Brakhage's medium, which is always much more than an animated painting. It is the transport of joy.

But in this film, another structure interacts with its choreography of color and pigment. The hand-painted sequences are punctuated by sections of black leader. I count twenty-five hand-painted sections, some of them very brief (a single frame), many more expansive (although none more than fifteen seconds). Most of the intervening sections of leader include inscriptions, words scratched into the film surface, appearing as white letters in a shaky script. About two-thirds of the way into the three-minute film, splitting the inscription "Night opens / infinite eyes," the color sequences alternate nine times with blank black leader bearing no inscription. The alternation between light-filled color footage in constant motion and the more static space of black and white, words written in scratches, is radical, as if two modes of expression were colliding, or perhaps were in passionate conversation. The section in which hand painting alternates with blank black leader sets up a contrast through a different, rapid rhythm, with most of the shots lasting under a second. It marks a contrast not simply between painting and writing, words and color, but more primarily between light and dark, alluding to the cosmic rhythm of the nocturnal and diurnal that Novalis describes in his series of poems *Hymns to the Night*; to the opening and closing of eyes in the passage scratched into the leader; and to the primal rhythm, the flicker of cinema, the shuttering alternation of the movie camera that makes the movement of Brakhage's medium possible.

Novalis wrote *Hymns to the Night* after the painful death of his fourteen-year-old fiancée Sophie von Kuhn. Brakhage inscribed fragments from the series' prose prologue, in which Novalis begins by praising light and day, then turns aside to "the holy, unspeakable, mysterious Night." With the departure of the light, which the poet at first mourns, Novalis discovers the infinity of night, which opens new eyes within him and initiates what he calls an eternal bridal night. The mystic theme of darkness opening us to a deeper vision, of the dark night of the soul, as painful as it may seem, leads to a deeper joy that resounds through Brakhage's work, especially of this later period. But if this forms an eternal theme, its ineffability and, indeed, invisibility pose a challenge for all known languages and even forms of art.[46] The traditional mystic response has been apophatic, describing religious experience and the nature of the divine only in the negative, realizing the limits of language.

If Brakhage's medium observes these limitations, it also expresses them by coming up against them. Brakhage's first manifestos and films seemed to champion light and vision over the limits of language. In *First Hymn to the Night—Novalis*, he confronts his alternative medium with the darkness of language and the obscurity of loss. He allows us to experience the transports of joy and color, but also their eclipse, the descent of veils of night over all things. Yet on this dark ground he also inscribes, with his own hand, the force of language through the inscription of writing. These words literally pierce the darkness of black leader and are formed in light. Yet one cannot lose a sense of them as meager shaky scratches etched against a broad expanse of blackness. Is the black the infinite, or does inscription open up the light of another world, which returns and departs in a constant rhythm? It is a question Brakhage's medium is capable of asking in all its fullness.

Brakhage's initial manifesto, *Metaphors on Vision*, proclaimed his opposition to language and his desire to discover in the moving image an alternative: "I suggest there is a pursuit of knowledge foreign to language and founded upon visual communication, demanding a development of the optical mind, and dependent upon perception in the original and deepest sense of the word."[47] But even a few pages into this early, unpaginated manifesto, Brakhage affirms his modernist understanding of medium, relating his own nonverbal visual experiences to modernist poetry attuned to sound and the possibilities of a "purely onomatopoeic art." Laying the foundation for his hand-painted cinema, he praised the abstract expressionist painters "who are fashioning the symbol-cuneiform-hieroglyphic letters for future communication."[48]

Perhaps nowhere is Brakhage's innovative commitment to a new understanding of the relation between the word and writing made more explicit than in his unique manner of titling his films, beginning with *Desistfilm* (1954) and continuing consistently from *Anticipation of the Night* (1958) on: hand-scratching the title and his final signature frame by frame into black leader. (*Mothlight* was instead written frame by frame with a marker on the transparent Mylar.) This tedious process yields writing that seems animated; the never-perfect registration from one frame to the next makes the letters jiggle, giving them a nervous rhythm. This jagged jitter is rendered even more abrasive by the visceral sense of scratches tearing through the dark emulsion of the film's surface. Rather than banishing the verbal from our consciousness, this novel approach to titling a film tends to highlight the words, while simultaneously rendering them intensely material. We sense the always highly significant words of Brakhage's titles not only as incisions into the film surface but as a process whose gestures we experience visually and tactilely. Brakhage used scratching on film in other contexts as well, most dramatically in his early psychodrama *Reflections on Black* (1955), where a blind man's eyes are scratched out and his "point of view" later given with scratches on the image. Brakhage films from the early 1960s, such as *Thigh Line Lyre Triangular* (1961) and parts of *Dog Star Man* (1961–1964), use scratches on images as essential elements of composition. But while these scratches are more akin to drawing or etching, linear and geometric, the titles and the scratches in *Novalis* and a few other late films—such as *I Dreaming* (1988) and *Untitled (For Marilyn)* (1992)—relate primary to writing and the shapes of letters.[49]

One could fruitfully discuss the role of inscription in terms of several Brakhage series that deal with numerals and writing systems: *The Roman Numeral Series* (1979–1980), *The Arabic Numeral Series* (1980–1982), and arguably *The Babylon Series* (1989–1990) and *Persian Series* (1999–2000). Brakhage has said of these films, "I'm working with the unnamable shapes that arise from human thinking, and how then those take shape as glyphs or script like the alphabet and numbers and symbols and pictures."[50] But I have not had the opportunity to study all of these films, so the light they would shed on my theme of Brakhage's medium and its relation to writing and language cannot be part of this essay. Let me clarify that my exploration of Brakhage's medium cannot be limited to such things as "film," "writing," "paint," "landscape," even "bits of nature," although the works we have looked at do use these elements. His medium is, rather, the moving image pierced through by light but defined in an immediately sensual manner, "moving visual thinking," in such a way that perception and thought are joined rather than separated, materialized rather then abstracted.

The writing in *Novalis* provides a rich instance. This is not simply writing, words whose meaning could be conveyed through a variety of media (handwriting, print, inscription, etc.). Writing becomes a physical gestural act leaving traces. We could call it calligraphy, although it does not resemble most examples of that tradition. Along with the words, we are impressed by the sense of the hand that shaped them and the material of which they are made. Perhaps more complexly, besides the sense of *a hand writing*, the technical, cinematic means of their presentation to the viewer forbids any transparent sense of communication. In contrast to the elegance and sense of grace found in most examples of calligraphy, both eastern and westen, these jagged, jittery words are difficult to read. They carry a sense of urgency (especially due to the speed with which they appear) and of precarity, as if the marks were difficult to make and their persistence fragile. Further, these materials are rather unfamiliar: neither pen nor ink brush inscribe them, neither paper nor canvas hold them; they are not formed by paint or ink, or printed in type. These words are scratched. Scratched into the emulsion that makes the dark field of the black leader, reversing, therefore, the dominant image of writing as dark marks on a white or light surface. But besides this negative reversal of light figures on a dark ground, the scratching carries a sense of desperation, as one were trying to grasp something with one's fingernails in an act of defense of clinging.

I have written elsewhere about the role of the scratch in film.[51] We know it mainly as a sign of wear and tear on the filmstrip from the pre-electronic era, but it has also been used intentionally, often as an avant-garde technique (as in Brakhage's *Reflections on Black* or the Lettrist films of Isidore Isou and Maurice Lemaître, whom Gregory Zinman points out Brakhage acknowledged as influences) or even as a compositional element, as in Fritz Lang's *Metropolis* (1927).[52] Most often, a scratched film carries the sense of a destructive energy (the blind man's vision in Brakhage's film, or the sweep to the Grim Reaper's scythe in *Metropolis*), stressing the precarity of the film medium. I believe the writing in Brakhage's *Novalis* carries some of the sense of fragility balancing on the edge—between life and death, night and day—that the original poem evokes. But beyond its aggression, the scratch makes the materials of cinema tangible: with emulsion scratched away, the transparency of the filmstrip is revealed—light penetrates, as if it had been lurking concealed and is now discovered. Cinema is based in the projection of light through a film, and that, we could say, allows Brakhage to write or carve letters made of light. This has resonance with the letter mysticism of the Kabballah, where the Creator forms the world through a combination of letters from the primal light.[53] This writing is not simply forms inscribed

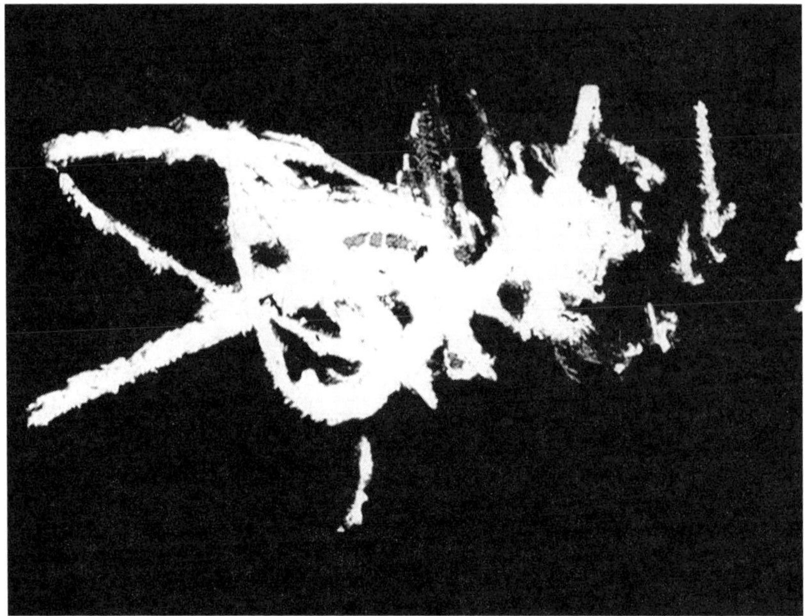

FIGURE 26.8. Stan Brakhage, *Chinese Series* (2003).

on the surface of a filmstrip, but a light image formed through the process of cinema.

The speed of the film and the brevity of their appearance on the screen makes these jittery words difficult to read. Especially when words first appear, they challenge our ability even to recognize them as words, much less to read what they say, their unsteady and brief nature causing a certain anxiety in the viewer about being able to grasp them. We struggle to make sense of them in their dynamic instability. This is moving writing—or to use a phrase I borrow from Walter Benjamin, "stirring writing" (*erregende Schrift*).[54] The energy of these marks denies any connotation of writing as static, past, inert ("for the letter killeth") and opens the way to a writing that is alive and renews itself in every frame. The jittering, so challenging to our eyes, demands "moving visual thinking" in the most literal sense. The word is animated, brought to life.

And yet we cannot deny the effect of the predominant darkness, the deep background of these works, especially in alternation with the brightly illuminated dance of colors that accompanies it. The surface of night with its poetry, the burst of day with its colors in motion—these provide the flesh to Novalis's prayer to love lost and yet hoped for.

On Brakhage's own deathbed he made his last cameraless film, working with the most primal of elements: a roll of 35mm black leader, his own saliva, with which he softened its emulsion, and his fingernails, with which he scratched patterns. Brakhage left instructions on how the scratched films should be printed, first repeating each frame and then printing each frame again singly, as Zinman nicely puts it, "Speeding up the imagery in a way that reads as a headlong rush to the ultimate end."[55] He called this final film *Chinese Series* (2003), relating it to his previous films dealing with "glyphs or script." Made directly with his own hand, these scratches do more than evoke the urgency of fingers trying to grasp and retain something—to leave their mark. They are the remnant of their maker's grasp on life in the presence of its termination—preserved and animated by Brakhage's medium.

Acknowledgments

Any book that suffers so many delays requires editors with patience and trust as well as skill. At the University of Chicago Press, I have been fortunate to work with three exceptional ones: Susan Bielstein, Dylan Montanari, and Karen Levine. James Whitman Toftness and Victoria Barry provided vital assistance in putting the essays and images together. Adrienne Meyers helped with promotions. And Joel Score provided superb copyediting of the previously unpublished material.

Outside the press, Maggie Sivit was vital in tracking down rights holders for out-of-print essays and securing permissions to republish them. Two reader reports provided excellent suggestions on essays to include, and good advice for the introduction. Sarah Osment compiled a wonderful index.

Most of all, I am grateful to Tom Gunning. Over the past twenty years, he moved from teacher to colleague, but whatever his official role, he has been, always, a mentor and friend. I hope this book does something to repay the debt I owe him.

Daniel Morgan

Notes

INTRODUCTION

1. See Tom Gunning, "The Non-Continuous Style of Early Film, 1900–1906," in *Cinema 1900–1906: An Analytical Study*, ed. Roger Holman (Brussels: FIAF, 1982), 219–30; Gunning, "Non-Continuity, Continuity, Discontinuity: A Theory of Genres in Early Films," *Iris* 2, no.1 (1984): 101–12; Gunning, "D. W. Griffith and the Narrator-System: Narrative Form and Industry Organization in Biograph Films, 1908–1909" (PhD diss., New York University, 1987).
2. See, e.g., Tom Gunning, "Dr. Jacobs' Dream Work," *Millennium Film Journal*, nos. 10–11 (Fall 1981–Winter 1982): 210–18, and "The Critique of Seeing with One's Own Eyes: Ernie Gehr's *Untitled (1976)*," *Millennium Film Journal*, no. 12 (Spring 1983): 134–36, reprinted in this volume as chapters 15 and 16.
3. Gunning has indicated that he read Jacques Aumont's *Montage Eisenstein*, published in French in 1979, to help think about the connection to Eisenstein. For his views on that text, see Tom Gunning, "Review of *Montage Eisenstein*," *Film Quarterly* 42, no. 1 (Autumn 1988): 53–56.
4. See, e.g., Manohla Dargis, "Jolt of Films and Crowds in Toronto," *New York Times*, September 13, 2013.
5. Tom Gunning, "The Cinema of Attraction: Early Film, Its Spectator and the Avant-Garde," *Wide Angle* 8, nos. 3–4 (Fall 1986), 63–70; Gunning, "The Cinema of Attractions: Early Cinema, Its Spectator, and the Avant-Garde," in *Early Cinema: Space, Frame, Narrative*, ed. Thomas Elsaesser (London: British Film Institute, 1990), 56–62. The latter, revised version is reprinted in this volume as chapter 1.
6. John Fell, ed., *Film before Griffith* (Berkeley: University of California Press, 1983); Noël Burch, "Porter, or Ambivalence," *Screen* 19, no. 4 (Winter 1978–1979): 91–105. See also Donald Crafton, "Pie and Chase: Gag, Spectacle and Narrative in Slapstick Comedy," in *The Slapstick Symposium*, ed. Eileen Bowser (Brussels: FIAF, 1988), 49–59; Charles Musser, "The Early Cinema of Edwin S. Porter," *Cinema Journal* 19, no. 1 (1979): 1–38; Musser, "The Nickelodeon Era Begins: Establishing the Framework for Hollywood's Mode of Representation," *Framework* 22/23 (1983): 4–11.
7. See Noël Burch, "Primitivism and the Avant-Gardes," in *In and Out of Synch: The Awakening of a Cine-Dreamer* (Aldershot, UK: Scolar Press, 1991), 157–86.

8. On the affinity between Gunning and Mulvey, see Scott Bukatman, "Spectacle, Attractions and Visual Pleasure," in *The Cinema of Attractions Reloaded*, ed. Wanda Strauven (Amsterdam: Amsterdam University Press, 2006): 71–82.
9. See, e.g., Jennifer M. Bean, "Technologies of Early Stardom and the Extraordinary Body," *Camera Obscura*, no. 48 (2001): 9–56; Maggie Hennefeld, *Specters of Slapstick and Silent Film Comediennes* (New York: Columbia University Press, 2018).
10. Tom Gunning, "Attractions: How They Came into the World," in Strauven, *Cinema of Attractions Reloaded*, 31–40; 33. The argument to which he is responding is Charles Musser, "Rethinking Early Cinema: Cinema of Attractions and Narrativity," *Yale Journal of Criticism* 7, no. 2 (1994): 203–32.
11. It is, we might say, a plea for the intersection of history and criticism. Gunning has argued that criticism remains the "least explored" aspect of the study of film but should be central to the work of both history and theory. Tom Gunning, "The Work of Film Analysis: Systems, Fragments, Alternation," *Semiotica*, no. 144 (2003): 343–57; 345, 352.
12. See Burch, "Primitivism and the Avant-Gardes." Also see P. Adams Sitney, "Structural Film," in *Film Culture Reader*, ed. P. Adams Sitney (New York: Cooper Square Press, 2000), 326–48; Bart Testa, *Back and Forth: Early Cinema and the Avant-Gardes* (Waterloo, ON: Wilfrid Laurier University Press, 1992).
13. Although, as Julie Turnock has detailed, the special effects in those films were done largely by experimental filmmakers who may have had stronger investments in film history. See Turnock, *Plastic Reality: Special Effects, Technology, and the Emergence of 1970s Blockbuster Aesthetics* (New York: Columbia University Press, 2015). On the explicit return to Méliès, see Annette Michelson, "Bodies in Space: Film as 'Carnal Knowledge,'" *Artforum* 7, no. 6 (February 1969): 53–64.
14. Stanley Cavell, *The World Viewed*, enlarged ed. (Cambridge, MA: Harvard University Press, 1979), 107.
15. See, e.g., the essays on Gustav Deutsch, David Gatten, and Stan Brakhage in this volume.
16. André Bazin, "The Ontology of the Photographic Image," in *What Is Cinema?*, ed. and trans. Hugh Gray (Berkeley: University of California Press, 1967), 1:9–16; 14 (translation modified).
17. Cavell, *World Viewed*, 212.
18. The automatic nature of this absorption is part of what led Michael Fried to say that films could never be modernist: in the cinema, absorption was guaranteed, not achieved. See Fried, "Art and Objecthood," in *Art and Objecthood: Essays and Reviews* (Chicago: University of Chicago Press, 1998), 148–72; 164.
19. Tom Gunning, "Animation and Alienation: Bergson's Critique of the Cinématographe and the Paradox of Mechanical Motion," *Moving Image* 14, no. 1 (Spring 2014): 1–9; 7.
20. Jean-Louis Baudry, "Ideological Effects of the Basic Apparatus," in *Narrative, Apparatus, Ideology: A Film Theory Reader*, ed. Phil Rosen (New York: Columbia University Press, 1986), 286–98.
21. Serge Daney, "The Therrorized (Godardian Pedagogy)" (1976), trans. Bill Krohn and Charles Cameron Ball, https://www.diagonalthoughts.com/?p=1620.
22. Eugenie Brinkema, *The Forms of the Affects* (Durham, NC: Duke University Press, 2014), 32.
23. Tom Gunning, "'Animated Pictures,' Tales of Cinema's Forgotten Future," *Michigan Quarterly Review* 34, no. 4 (Fall 1995): 465–85; 479.
24. This mode of thought moves away from teleological accounts of realism: "Instead of an image of the world, I have traced an image of energy. This new image seeks less to represent things, than to animate them, as the vibratory and transforming power of light creates a bond of fascination with the spectator." Tom Gunning, "Animating the Nineteenth Century: Bringing Pictures to Life (or Life to Pictures?)," *Nineteenth-Century Contexts* 36, no. 5 (2014): 459–72; 469.
25. Tom Gunning, "Weaving a Narrative: Style and Economic Background in Griffith's Biograph Films," *Quarterly Review of Film and Video* 6, no. 1 (Winter 1981): 11–25.
26. André Gaudreault and Tom Gunning, "Early Cinema as a Challenge to Film History," in Strauven, *Cinema of Attractions Reloaded*, 365–80; 374.

27. Gunning, "Animating the Nineteenth Century," 463.
28. A different way to track Gunning's career would be to look at his collaborations with other scholars. The work he did with André Gaudreault is perhaps most celebrated, precisely because it led to the formations of the conception of the "cinema of attractions." Subsequent collaborations may not have resulted in cowritten pieces, but Gunning's sustained dialogue with Yuri Tsivian and Miriam Hansen clearly shaped his understanding not only of how to think about the cultural context of early cinema but of how it could be understood to resonate with the broader energies released by the emergence of modernity, new urban spaces, and the new technologies of transportation and movement. Still later, Gunning would work with a younger generation—Joshua Yumibe and Giovanna Fossati, for example—as he broadened his work and sought to make early cinema available for different audiences. And then there are filmmakers and artists he has made work with or engaged in sustained dialogue with over the years, including Travis Preston, Lewis Klahr, Janie Geiser, Zoe Beloff, Ken Jacobs, Phil Solomon, and Ernie Gehr.
29. Tom Gunning, "A Little Light on a Dark Subject," *Critical Quarterly* 45, no. 4 (Winter 2003): 50–69.
30. Tom Gunning, "Review of Maureen Turim, *Flashbacks in Film: Memory and History*," *CiNéMaS* 2, nos. 2–3 (Spring 1992): 223–29; Gunning, "Nothing Will Have Taken Place—Except Place: The Unsettling Nature of Camera Movement," in *Screen Space Reconfigured*, ed. Susanne Saether and Synne Tollerud Bull (Amsterdam: Amsterdam University Press, 2020), 263–81.
31. Gunning, "Work of Film Analysis."
32. Tom Gunning, "One Way Street: Urban Chronotopes in Ruttmann's *Berlin: Symphony of a Great City* and Conrad's *Halsted Street*," in *Urban Images: Unruly Desire in Film and Architecture*, ed. Synne Bull and Marit Paasche (Oslo: Sternberg Press, 2011), 62–79.
33. Tom Gunning, "In and Out of the Frame: Paintings in Hitchcock," in *Casting a Shadow: Creating the Alfred Hitchcock Film*, ed. Will Schmenner and Corine Granof (Evanston, IL: Northwestern University Press, 2007), 29–47; Gunning, "The Desire and Pursuit of the Hole: Cinema's Obscure Object of Desire," in *Erotikon*, ed. Shadi Bartsch and Thomas Bartscherer (Chicago: University of Chicago Press, 2005), 261–77.
34. Tom Gunning, "Preface," in *Jean Epstein: Critical Essays and New Translations*, ed. Sarah Keller and Jason Paul (Amsterdam: Amsterdam University Press, 2012), 13–22; Gunning, "The World in Its Own Image: The Myth of Total Cinema," in *Opening Bazin: Postwar Film Theory and Its Afterlife*, ed. Dudley Andrew and Hervé Joubert-Laurencin (New York: Oxford University Press, 2011), 119–26.
35. Tom Gunning, "Invisible Cities, Visible Cinema: Illuminating Shadows in Late Film Noir," in *Comparative Critical Studies* 6, no. 3 (2009): 319–32. Also see the documentary film *The American Nightmare* (Adam Simon, 2000).
36. Tom Gunning, "On Knowing and Not Knowing, Going and Not Going, Loving and Not Loving: *I Know Where I Am Going* and Falling in Love Again," in *The Cinema of Michael Powell*, ed. Ian Christie and Andrew Moor (London: British Film Institute, 2005), 94–116.
37. Tom Gunning, "Loïe Fuller and the Art of Motion," in *Camera Obscura, Camera Lucida: Essays in Honor of Annette Michelson*, ed. Richard Allen and Malcolm Turvey (Amsterdam: University of Amsterdam Press, 2003), 75–90.
38. Tom Gunning, "Cinema and the New Spirit in Art within a Culture of Movement," in *Picasso, Braque, and Early Film in Cubism*, ed. Bernice Rose (New York: Pace Wildenstein, 2007), 17–33; Gunning, "In and Out of the Frame"; Gunning, "Landscape and the Fantasy of Moving Pictures: Early Cinema's Phantom Rides" (2010), reprinted in this volume as chapter 5.
39. Tom Gunning, "Gollum and Golem: Special Effects and the Technology of Artificial Bodies," in *From Hobbits to Hollywood: Essays on Peter Jackson's "Lord of the Rings,"* ed. Ernest Mathijs and Murray Pomerance (Amsterdam: Rodopi, 2006), 319–49.
40. See Tom Gunning, "Phantasmagoria and the Manufacturing of Illusions and Wonder: Towards a Cultural Optics of the Cinematic Apparatus," in *The Cinema, A New Technology for the 20th Century*, ed. André Gaudreault, Catherine Russell, and Pierre Veronneau (Lausanne: Editions Payot, 2004), 31–44.

41. Tom Gunning, "'Now You See it, Now You Don't': The Temporality of the Cinema of Attractions," *Velvet Light Trap* 32 (Fall 1993): 3–12; Gunning, "The Whole Town's Gawking: Early Cinema and the Visual Experience of Modernity," *Yale Journal of Criticism* 7, no. 2 (Fall 1994): 189–201.
42. Fred Camper, "The End of Avant-Garde Film," *Millennium Film Journal*, nos. 16–18 (1987): 99–124. On "major" work, see, for example, Michael Fried's claim that painting can no longer be minor (if it is to have any importance); it must be major or not at all.
43. See Scott MacDonald, *A Critical Cinema 5: Interviews with Independent Filmmakers* (Berkeley: University of California Press, 2006), 111–42.
44. See, e.g., Tom Gunning, "Tracing the Individual Body: Photography, Detectives, and Early Cinema," in *Cinema and the Invention of Modern Life*, ed. Leo Charney and Vanessa R. Schwartz (Berkeley: University of California Press, 1995), 15–45.
45. Leo Charney and Vanessa R. Schwartz, "Introduction," in Charney and Schwartz, *Cinema and the Invention of Modern Life*, 1–12; 1–2.
46. Miriam Hansen, "Fallen Women, Rising Stars, New Horizons: Shanghai Silent Film as Vernacular Modernism," *Film Quarterly* 54, no. 1 (2000): 10–22; 13.
47. Miriam Hansen, "The Mass Production of the Senses: Classical Cinema as Vernacular Modernism," in *Reinventing Film Studies*, ed. Christine Gledhill and Linda Williams (New York: Oxford University Press, 2000), 332–50; 341–42.
48. Hansen, "Mass Production," 343.
49. Gunning, "Whole Town's Gawking," 193.
50. Gunning, "Whole Town's Gawking," 194.
51. On these questions, see Ben Singer, *Melodrama and Modernity: Early Sensational Cinema and Its Contexts* (New York: Columbia University Press, 2001); John Rhym, "Historicizing Perception: Film Theory, Neuroscience, and the Philosophy of Mind," *Discourse* 40, no. 1 (2018): 83–109.
52. David Bordwell, *On the History of Film Style* (Cambridge, MA: Harvard University Press, 1997), 144–45.
53. See Charlie Keil, "'To Here from Modernity': Style, Historiography, and Transitional Cinema," in *American Cinema's Transitional Era: Audiences, Institutions, Practices*, ed. Charlie Keil and Shelley Stamp (Berkeley: University of California Press, 2004), 51–65.
54. Bordwell, *On the History of Film Style*, 301n100.
55. Gunning, "Animating the Nineteenth Century," 464.
56. See Tom Gunning, "An Unseen Energy Swallows Space: The Space in Early Film and Its Relation to American Avant-Garde Film," in Fell, *Film before Griffith*, 355–66.
57. For a model of Greek art that resonates with Gunning's arguments, especially the idea of wonder, see Richard Neer, *The Emergence of the Classical Style in Greek Sculpture* (Chicago: University of Chicago Press, 2013).
58. Quoted in Michael Cahn, "Subversive Mimesis: Theodor W. Adorno and the Modern Impasse of Critique," in *The Literary and Philosophical Debate*, vol. 1 of *Mimesis in Contemporary Theory*, ed. Mihai Spariosu (Philadelphia: Benjamins, 1984), 34.
59. Bukatman, "Spectacle, Attractions and Visual Pleasure," 72.
60. See Gunning, "Work of Film Analysis," 347.
61. Gunning, "Work of Film Analysis," 348.
62. For all Gunning's thoughts on montage, it is not the dominant focus of his theoretical work. In a late essay, he suggests that a preoccupation with editing as the transition out of a "primitive" cinema led theorists to overlook the importance of the *moving* image; see Gunning, "Animation and Alienation," 3.
63. Cavell, *World Viewed*, 168. Also see Ryan Pierson, "On Styles of Theorizing Animation Styles: Stanley Cavell at the Cartoon's Demise," *Velvet Light Trap* 69 (Spring 2012): 17–26.
64. For a polemical claim about the intersection of ethics, aesthetics, and ontology, see Dudley Andrew, *What Cinema Is!* (Malden, MA: Wiley-Blackwell, 2010).
65. See also Tom Gunning, "What's the Point of an Index? or, Faking Photographs" (2004), in *Still Moving: Between Cinema and Photography*, ed. Karen Beckman and Jean Ma (Durham, NC: Duke University Press, 2008), 23–40.

66. See Gunning, "Animation and Alienation"; Gunning, "The Transforming Image: The Roots of Animation in Metamorphosis and Motion," in *Pervasive Animation*, ed. Suzanne Buchan (New York: Routledge, 2013): 52–70; Gunning, "Animating the Instant: The Secret Symmetry between Animation and Photography," in *Animating Film Theory*, ed. Karen Beckman (Durham, NC: Duke University Press, 2014), 37–53.
67. Bazin, "Ontology of the Photographic Image," 1:10.
68. In this, Gunning is far more attuned to the theoretical promise of *Technics and Time, 1* than to the more critical account of the mass culture industry in Stiegler's treatment of cinema in the third volume.
69. Noël Carroll, "For God and Country," in *Interpreting the Moving Image* (Cambridge: Cambridge University Press, 1998), 80–91.
70. On desire, see also Gunning, "On Knowing and Not Knowing"; Gunning, "Desire and Pursuit of the Hole."
71. Stan Brakhage, "Metaphors on Vision," in *Essential Brakhage: Selected Writings on Filmmaking*, ed. Bruce R. McPherson (Kingston, NY: McPherson/Documentext, 2001), 12.
72. Annette Michelson picked up on this tendency in Brakhage but worried that his linking of the camera to "the body or its nervous system" would undermine the power of the "camera-eye" metaphor. See Michelson, "Film and the Radical Aspiration," in Sitney, *Film Culture Reader*, 404–21; 419.
73. Gunning, "Animated Pictures," 469, 479.
74. Gunning, "World in Its Own Image," 124.

1. THE CINEMA OF ATTRACTIONS

1. Fernand Léger, "A Critical Essay on the Plastic Qualities of Abel Gance's Film *The Wheel*," in *Functions of Painting*, ed. Edward Fry, trans. Alexandra Anderson (New York: Viking, 1973), 21.
2. See my articles "The Non-Continuous Style of Early Film, 1900–1906," in *Cinema 1900–1906: An Analytical Study*, ed. Roger Holman (Brussels: FIAF, 1982), and "An Unseen Energy Swallows Space: The Space in Early Film and Its Relation to American Avant-Garde Film," in *Film before Griffith*, ed. John Fell (Berkeley: University of California Press, 1983), 355–66, and our collaborative paper "Le cinéma des premiers temps: Un défi à l'histoire du cinéma?," delivered by A. Gaudreault at the conference at Cerisy on Film History (August 1985). I would also like to note the importance of my discussions with Adam Simon and our hope to investigate further the history and archaeology of the film spectator.
3. Robert C. Allen, *Vaudeville and Film: 1895–1915, A Study in Media Interaction* (New York: Arno Press, 1980), 159, 212–13.
4. Méliès, "Importance du scenario," in Georges Sadoul, *Georges Méliés* (Paris: Seghers, 1901), 118 (my translation).
5. Christian Metz, *The Imaginary Signifier: Psychoanalysis and the Cinema*, trans. Celia Britton, Annwyl Williams, Ben Brewster, and Alfred Guzzetti (Bloomington: Indiana University Press, 1982), esp. 58–80, 91–97.
6. Charles Musser, "American Viragraph 1897–1901," *Cinema Journal* 22, no. 3 (Spring 1983): 10.
7. Raymond Fielding, "Hale's Tours: Ultrarealism in the Pre-1910 Motion Picture," in Fell, *Film before Griffith*, 116–30.
8. I wish to thank Ben Brewster for his comments alter the original delivery of this paper, which pointed out the importance of including this aspect of the cinema of attractions here.
9. S. M. Eisenstein, "How I Became a Film Director," in *Notes of a Film Director* (Moscow: Foreign Language Publishing House, n.d.), 16.
10. S. M. Eisenstein, "The Montage of Attractions," in *Selected Works*, vol. 1, *Writings, 1922–1934*, ed. Richard Taylor (London: British Film Institute, 1988), 35.
11. Eisenstein, "Montage of Attractions," 35.

12. Yon Kama, *Eisenstein* (Bloomington: Indiana University Press, 1973), 59.
13. "The Variety Theater 1913," in *Futurist Manifestos*, ed. Umbro Apollonio (New York: Viking, 1973), 127.
14. Michael Davis, *The Exploitation of Pleasure* (pamphlet) (New York: Russell Sage Foundation, Dept. of Child Hygiene, 1911).
15. David Levy, "Edison Sales Policy and the Continuous Action Film, 1904–1906," in Fell, *Film before Griffith*, 207–22.
16. Laura Mulvey, "Visual Pleasure and Narrative Cinema," in *Visual and Other Pleasures* (London: Macmillan, 1989).
17. Paper delivered at the FIAF Conference on Slapstick, New York City, May 1985.
18. Nicholas Vardac, *From Stage to Screen: Theatrical Method from Garrick to Griffith* (New York: Benjamin Blom, 1968), 232.

2. WHAT I SAW FROM THE REAR WINDOW

1. Jacques Aumont, in his article "Le point de vue," lists four key meanings for point of view in cinema, each one more extensive, from "l'emplacement de la camera" to "le jugement du narrateur sur l'événement." *Communications* 38 (1983): 3–29; 4–5.
2. François Jost, *L'Oeil-caméra: Entre film et roman* (Lyon: Presses Universitaires de Lyon, 1987), 18.
3. Edward R. Branigan, *Point of View in the Cinema: A Theory of Narration in Classical Film*, in the series Approaches to Semiotics (Amsterdam: Mouton, 1984), 122–42.
4. Jost, *L'Oeil-caméra*, 21–22.
5. Branigan, *Point of View*, 19.
6. See André Gaudreault and Tom Gunning, "Le cinéma des premiers temps: Un défi à l'histoire du cinéma?" paper delivered at the colloquium "Nouvelles approches de l'histoire du cinéma" at Cerisy-la-Salle, 1985.
7. See Gaudreault and Gunning, "Cinéma des premiers temps"; Gunning, "The Cinema of Attractions: Early Film, Its Spectator and the Avant-Garde" (1986/1990), reprinted in this volume as chapter 1.
8. Branigan, *Point of View*, 103.
9. Branigan, *Point of View*, 103.
10. Branigan, *Point of View*, 134, for example.
11. Jost, *L'Oeil-caméra*, 63–64.
12. Branigan, *Point of View*, 180.
13. Roland Barthes, *S/Z*, trans. Richard Miller (New York: Hill and Wang, 1975).
14. Branigan, *Point of View*, 108.
15. In what is certainly the most insightful article written on point of view in early film, "A Scene at the Movies" (*Screen* 23, no. 2 [1982]), Ben Brewster indicates correctly that this classical figure of a POV shot appears rather rarely in Griffith's Biograph films. However, Brewster does not take account of what I call the "sight link" in Griffith's films, an edited relation between two spaces that is motivated by a character's glance. This differs from the classical point-of-view shot by eliminating the element Branigan describes as "from the point"—the location of the camera at the point previously occupied by the character (Branigan, *Point of View*, 103). Branigan describes such a shot as an "eyeline match" that "shows what a character sees and when, but not from where the character looks" (110). This corresponds precisely to what I am describing, but the term seems to me unfortunate since the eyelines do *not* match here. Sight links occur frequently in Griffith after 1909, and are conspicuous in *The Lonedale Operator*, for instance. Brewster's thesis that in Griffith's Biograph films actual point-of-view shots are less important than the development of "hierarchies of relative knowledge for characters and spectators" through narrative structure ("Scene," 7) needs some modification. The theoretical distinction between ocularization and focalization offered by Jost helps untangle this. Griffith does continue to use ocularization to convey character perception, through the sight link that is not identical

to the classical point-of-view shot. However, Brewster is quite right in pointing out that Griffith's use of focalization is often independent of ocularization, by which the relations of knowledge between narrator and spectator are managed. The importance of focalization in Griffith, compared to its relative absence in early cinema, is a clear mark of the cinema of narrative integration that Griffith represents, and the foundation of his use of suspense.

16. In some way this corresponds to what Jost calls "ocularisation interne primaire" (*L'Oeil-caméra*, 23–24), a shot that in itself bears some physical indication of being the viewpoint of an unseen character (e.g., the hair that blows across the image of the road in *Notorious*, indicating it as Alicia Hupperman's POV as she drives).
17. Aumont, "Le point de vue," 3. Branigan includes this possibility in his discussion of relations between narrators and readers, saying, "A personal address may also be aimed outside the narrative diegesis, for instance when a character stares at the camera and points a gun into the camera (*The Great Train Robbery*, Porter, 1903)" (*Point of View*, 44). What relation this bears to classical narration Branigan does not make clear.
18. Christian Metz, *The Imaginary Signifier: Psychoanalysis and the Cinema* (Bloomington: Indiana University Press, 1992).
19. Here I must signal my disagreement with Noël Burch, who in his article "Narrative/Diegesis: Thresholds/Limits" (*Screen* 23, no. 2 [1982]) declares that identification with the camera is "essential to the power of classical bourgeois narrative," and who sees *The Big Swallow* as basically in concert with the later classical style. Burch, I believe, underestimates the importance of the narrativization of this identification.
20. Quoted in Rachel Low and Roger Manvell, *The History of the British Film*, vol. 1, *1896–1906* (London: George Allen & Unwin, 1948), 75. It complicates my analysis of the film to note that (as was pointed out to me by André Gaudreault and Suzanne Richard) the apparatus wielded by the cannibalized cameraman is not actually a motion picture camera but a still camera. This might well indicate a prefilm model for this gag. However, I believe that the point of view of the photographer still functions in essentially the same way, even if pushed further toward paradox.
21. Quoted in Low and Manvell, *History of the British Film*, 1:83.
22. This assault on the camera/spectator is, of course, very different from the moments in *Lady in the Lake* (Montgomery, 1946), *Strangers on a Train* (Hitchcock, 1951), and *North by Northwest* (Hitchcock, 1959) when one character socks another and the blow in conveyed in POV shot by a fist invading the lens. In such shots the blow is received by a diegetic character whose point of view the camera represents. Burch, in "Narrative/Diegesis," makes some interesting points about the problematic nature of this use of a subjective camera in the Montgomery film (24–25).
23. Quoted in Low, 1:73.
24. Brewster, "Scene," 7.
25. The Pathé catalogue description for *Les Cartes lumineuses* describes the voyeur's pleasure this way: "Il est seul, aussi avec quelle joie va-t-il satisfaire sa curiosité mise en éveil" (Films et Cinématographes Pathé, 1907, 167).
26. The description of this film given in Pathé's 1905 London catalogue (which lists its title as *Scenes from My Balcony*) is very curious in this regard: "An old joker endeavors to pry into the secrets of his neighbors by means of a telescope, and gives his friends the benefits of his discoveries." Since neither the film as it exists nor its complete description in the Pathé Paris catalogue indicates any "friends" within the diegesis, I believe that this refers to us, the spectators, sharing this act of voyeurism with him.
27. Metz, *Imaginary Signifier*.
28. In the "peeping tom" series, these characters are joined by the scientist, who although supposedly a socially respectable character, undoubtedly joins the ranks as the embodiment of scopic curiosity. The Pathé catalogue describes a film nearly identical to *Ce que l'on voit de mon sixième* (if not the same film), *Ce que l'on voit de la Bastille*, in which the telescope wielding character is a "savant," initially observing the stars but then training his scientific instrument on his neighbors.

29. Noël Burch, "How We Got into Pictures: Notes Accompanying *Correction Please*," *Afterimage* 8/9 (Spring 1981): 36. The Pathé catalogue description of *Ce que l'on voit* . . . indicates that the film ends with the "savant" falling when his support collapses, an equivalent of the punishment ending, albeit not carried out by human agents. I suspect that the extant print of *Ce que l'on voit de mon sixième* is incomplete and contained a similar ending.
30. See Low and Manvell, *History of the British Film*, 1:60.
31. Reproduced in Kemp R. Niver, *Biograph Bulletins, 1896–1908* (Los Angeles: Locare Research Group, 1971), 102.
32. Laura Mulvey, "Visual Pleasure and Narrative Cinema," *Screen* 16, no. 3 (1975): 13–15.
33. Walter Benjamin, "The Paris of the Second Empire in Baudelaire," in *Charles Baudelaire: A Lyric Poet in the Era of High Capitalism*, trans. Harry Zohn (London: Verso, 1973), 48.
34. Stephen Bottomore, "Les thèmes du témoignage dans le cinéma primitif," in *Les premiers ans du cinéma français*, ed. Pierre Guibbert (Perpignan: Institut Jean Vigo, 1985). Sigmund Freud also made a contribution, in effect, to this literature with his essay "A Case of Paranoia Running Counter to the Psychoanalytic Theory of the Disease" (1915), in *The Standard Edition of the Complete Psychological Works of Sigmund Freud*, ed. and trans. James Strachey (London: Hogarth Press, 1957), in which a woman recounts to Freud that a man "had abused her confidence by getting an unseen witness to photograph them while they were making love, and that by exhibiting these pictures it was now in his power to bring disgrace on her" (14:263). Freud's analysis of the role of primal phantasies and paranoia in this delusion should provide an important basis for a psychoanalytical treatment of the constructions of narrative cinema, in addition to Mulvey's use of fetishism and sadism.
35. Including Louis Feuillade, whose *Erreur Tragique* (1913) gives the theme an interesting reworking, as the apparent evidence of guilt given by the cinema proves to be misinterpreted.
36. Original Biograph Bulletin, reproduced in Niver, *Biograph Bulletins*, 331.
37. Eileen Bowser, "Griffith's Film Career before *The Adventures of Dollie*," in *Film before Griffith*, ed. John Fell (Berkeley: University of California Press, 1983), 367.
38. Branigan, *Point of View*, 183.
39. Peter Brooks, *The Melodramatic Imagination: Balzac, Henry James, Melodrama and the Mode of Excess* (New Haven, CT: Yale University Press, 1976), esp. 2–5.

3. AN AESTHETIC OF ASTONISHMENT

1. Accounts of the first exhibitions can be read in most standard film histories. Georges Sadoul, in *Histoire generale du cinéma*, vol. 1, *L'Invention du cinéma 1832–1897* (Paris: Denoël, 1948), 288, describes the panic of the crowds before *The Arrival of a Train*, but, curiously, the testimony he cites refers to a Lumière street scene rather than the train film. Other testimomes sometimes cited, such us Maxim Gorky's article, discussed below, or the article Lynne Kirby quotes from *L'Illustration* (30 May 1896), describe the threat inscribed in the image itself but do not indicate actual panic in the audience. See Kirby, "Male Hysteria and Early Cinema," *Camera Obscura*, no. 17 (May 1988): 130. Recent histories are content to cite Sadoul or simply repeat the legend. However, Charles Musser tells me that his research on early traveling exhibitor Lyman H. Howe has uncovered a number of references to spectators screaming during early projections of train films, although not at the first Lumière screenings.

   I would like to recognize here the inspiration provided by Kirby's article and her ongoing work on early cinema and trains. I feel few writers have so well grasped the importance of shock in early cinema, even if I view its implications for early specratorship somewhat differently than she does. I would also like to acknowledge the conversations with NYU graduate student Richard Decroix, which stimulated my thinking about this essay.
2. Christian Metz, *The Imaginary Signifier: Psychoanalysis and the Cinema*, trans. Celia Britton, Annwyl Williams, Ben Brewster, and Alfred Guzzetti (Bloomington: Indiana University Press, 1982), 72–73. Ben Singer points out the limitations of Metz's application of Freud's concept

of the fetish to cinema in his article "Film, Photography and Fetish: The Analyses of Christian Metz," *Cinema Journal* 27, no. 4 (Summer 1988). However, my main problem with Metz's always-stimulating discussion lies in its ahistorical nature, which leads to an oversimplified view of cinema spectatorship. At the same time, I find that the lack Metz finds at the center of the cinematic image is a profound insight, worthy of more than a metapsychological treatment.

Charles Musser points out that in *Ars magna lucis et umbrae* (1671)—the first full treatment of the catoptric lamp, a forerunner of the magic lantern—Athanasius Kircher declares that demystifying illusion is essential to any display of the apparatus, absolutely forbidding any understanding of the spectacle as magic. The religious and social motivations for such demystification are obvious (Kircher was a Jesuit). Musser makes the provocative claim that this moment "suggests a decisive turning point for screen practice when the observer of projected/reflected images became the historically constituted subject we now call the spectator." Musser, *The Emergence of Cinema: The American Screen to 1907*, vol. 1 in the series History of the American Cinema, ed. Charles Harpole (Berkeley: University of California Press, 1994), 18. In other words, Musser sees demystification as essential to the existence of the spectator, and points out that a tradition of screen spectatorship preceded Lumière by centuries.

3. Metz, *Imaginary Signifier*, 72.
4. See my article "Primitive Cinema: A Frame Up? or, The Trick's on Us," *Cinema Journal* 29, no. 2 (Winter 1988–1989). Accounts of Méliès's theatrical illusions can be found in Madeliene Maltete-Méliès, ed., *Méliès et la naissance du spectacle cinématographique* (Paris: Klincksieck, 1984), esp. 53–58, and in Pierre Jenn, *Méliès: Cinéaste* (Paris: Albatros, 1984), 139–68. Paul Hammond's *Marvellous Méliès* (London: Gordon Fraser, 1974), 15–26, also includes a discussion of Méliès's stage work and an indication of his debt to Maskelyne.
5. Martin Battersby, *Trompe l'Oeil: The Eye Deceived* (London: Academy Editions, 1974), 19. I must signal here that my essay has been both inspired and provoked by Mary Ann Doane's fascinating essay "When the Direction of the Force Acting on the Body Is Changed: The Moving Image," *Wide Angle* 7, nos. 1–2 (1985): 42–57. There is a great deal of convergence in the topics covered by my essay and hers, as well as a great deal of divergence in method and conclusion.
6. The importance of the large scale of the original Lumière projections, particularly in competition with the Edison Kinetoscope, is pointed out by Jacques and Marie André in *Une saison Lumière à Montpellier* (Perpignan: Institut Jean Vigo, 1987), 64–65.
7. Gorky's account is included as an appendix in Jay Leyda, *Kino: A History of the Russian and Soviet Film* (London: Allen & Unwin, 1960), 407–9. The translation is by "Leda Swan."
8. Leyda, *Kino*, 407. I must add that it was Annette Michelson who first pointed out this fact to me when I was a graduate student years ago. Her discussion of the *frisson* of this instance of motion was a generative point for this essay. One might point out that a possibly equally rich projection trope can be found in Lumière's *Destruction of a Wall*, which was projected first forward and then in reverse, creating the magical effect of the wall reassembling and rising to its original height. A Montpellier journalist noted that this film "has always drawn applause from its admirers"; André and André, *Une saison Lumière*, 84 (my translation).
9. Quoted in Sadoul, *Histoire général du cinéma*, 271 (my translation).
10. Erik Barnouw, *The Magician and the Cinema* (New York: Oxford University Press, 1981), 75. The phrase is quoted from an 1899 article in the magical trade periodical *Mahatma*.
11. Albert E. Smith, with Phil A. Koury, *Two Reels and a Crank* (Garden City, NY: Doubleday, 1952), 39. Smith's book is notoriously inaccurate, as Charles Musser has shown. However, most of its errors seem to be misleading claims of fanciful achievements (e.g., filming in Cuba during the Spanish American War) and don't necessarily lessen the value of the description of his film shows.
12. Smith, *Two Reels*, 39–40.
13. See Tom Gunning, "The Cinema of Attractions: Early Film, Its Spectator and the Avant-Garde," first published in 1986 and reprinted in this volume as chapter 1. André Gaudreault and I introduced this term in a paper delivered to the colloquium "Nouvelles approches de l'histoire du cinéma" at Cerisy in 1985, called "Cinéma des premiers temps: Un défi à l'histoire du cinéma?"

Conversations with Adam Simon, a teaching assistant at Harvard University's Carpenter Center of Visual and Environmental Studies, 1984–1985, were influential in developing these ideas. The term *attractions* refers back to a popular tradition and forward to an avant-garde subversion. The tradition is that of the fairground and carnival, and particularly its development around the turn of the century in such modern amusement parks as Coney Island. The avant-garde radicalization of this term comes in the theoretical and practical work in theater and film of Sergei Eisenstein, whose theory of the montage of attractions intensified this popular energy into an aesthetic subversion, through a radical theoreticization of the power of attractions to undermine the conventions of bourgeois realism. For a clear account of this theory and a discussion of its roots in popular culture, sec Jacques Aumont's *Montage Eisenstein,* trans. Lee Hildreth, Constance Penley, and Andrew Ross (Bloomington: Indiana University Press, 1987), 41–48, as well as Eisenstein's own essays "The Montage of Attractions" and "The Montage of Film Attractions," in Eisenstein, *Selected Works,* vol. 1, *Writings, 1922–1934,* ed. and trans. Richard Taylor (Bloomington: University of Indiana Press, 1988).

14. Quoted in André and André, *Une saison Lumière,* 66.
15. John F. Kasson, *Amusing the Millions: Coney Island at the Turn of the Century* (New York: Hill and Wang, 1978), 77–78; Kirby, "Male Hysteria" (quoting *L'Illustration*), 119–120.
16. The role of the exhibitor showman in early American cinema has been brilliantly demonstrated in the work of Charles Musser, particularly in his article "The Nickelodeon Era Begins, Establishing the Framework for Hollywood's Mode of Representation," *Framework* 22/23 (1983), and in his volumes on Edwin S. Porter and Lyman Howe.
17. Gunning, "Cinema of Attractions." This issue is also discussed in my book *D. W. Griffith and the Origins of American Narrative Cinema* (Urbana: University of Illinois Press, 1991).
18. On the surrealist love of disorienting images in the cinema, see Paul Hammond, ed., *The Shadow and Its Shadow: Surrealist Writings on the Cinema* (London: British Film Institute, 1978), particularly Breton's essay "As in a Wood" (14).
19. Michael Fried, *Absorption and Theatricality: Painting and Beholder in the Age of Diderot* (Berkeley: University of Calitorma Press, 1980), e.g., 64, 104. A similar exclusion of the spectator is evident in the stenography and style of the nineteenth-century naturalist theater, embodied in the idea of the fourth wall.
20. St. Augustine, *The Confessions,* trans. Rex Warner (New York: New American Library, 1963), 245–47.
21. This satirical drawing is reproduced in Richard D. Altick, *The Shows of London* (Cambridge, MA: Harvard University Press, 1978), 254. As Miriam Hansen has pointed out to me, Michael Fried's discussion of Thomas Eakins's painting *The Gross Clinic* raises issues relevant to the aesthetic of attractions and its relation to repulsion. Although Fried convincingly places the painting within a tradition of absorption, the foci of Gross's bloodstained fingers and scalpel and the patient's open wound seem to provide another experience, which "mixes pain and pleasure, violence and voluptuousness, repulsion and fascination." Fried, "Realism, Writing and Disfiguration in Thomas Eakins' Gross Clinic," *Representations* 9 (Winter 1985): 71. As Fried says, "It is above all the conflictedness of that situation that grips and excruciates and in the end stupefies us before the picture" (73). This seems to me to describe the essential experience of the aesthetic of attractions; however, it is somewhat unclear to me how Fried sees this in relation to the experience of absorption. Fried does not relate this conflict to the tradition of the sublime, which clearly represents the acceptable form of the aesthetic of attractions (recall that Burke defines astonishment as the effect of the sublime in the highest degree). The relation of popular entertainment to the sublime is a basically unexplored and potentially fascinating topic, beyond the confines of this essay. But it is not irrelevant to point out that Fried follows Thomas Weiskel in associating the effect of the sublime with a Freudian understanding of the terror of castration. Although I am not inclined at the moment to pursue it, speculation in this direction about the trauma produced by the first projections could provide a new way of approaching the issue of fetishism in early cinema, locating the trauma that Metz did little to isolate. The interest of this speculation could be considerable if approached from a historical point of view, as in Benjamin's and Schivelbusch's

understanding (which I will discuss later in this essay) of the Freudian concept of the stimulus shield as a response to modern experience, rather than a biological principle.

22. Urban's series of films is described in Rachel Low and Roger Manvell, *The History of the British Film*, vol. 1, *1896–1906* (London: Allen & Unwin, 1948), 60.
23. Harry Fumiss, *Our Lady Cinema* (1914; New York: Garland Publishing, 1978), 41.
24. Wolfgang Schivelbusch, *The Railway Journey: Trains and Travel in the Nineteenth Century* (New York: Urizen, 1979), 66.
25. From the *New York Mail and Express* (25 September 1897), reprinted in Kemp R. Niver, *Biograph Bulletins, 1896–1908* (Los Angeles: Locare Research Group, 1971), 27. The journalist was commenting on a Biograph film shot from a locomotive going through the Haverstraw Tunnel.
26. Maxim Gorky, "Boredom," *The Independent* (8 August 1907), 311–12.
27. The key essays are, of course, "The Work of Art in the Age of Mechanical Reproduction" (in *Illuminations*, ed. Hannah Arendt, trans Harry Zohn [New York: Schocken, 1969]) and the two drafts of the essay on Baudelaire (in *Charles Baudelaire: A Lyric Poet in the Era of High Capitalism*, trans. Harry Zohn [London: Verso, 1973]). My understanding of Benjamin's work has been shaped by Miriam Hansen's masterful essay "Benjamin, Cinema and Experience: 'The Blue Flower in the Land of Technology,'" *New German Critique*, no. 40 (Winter 1987). This essay and Hansen's work on the spectator of American silent film in *Babel and Babylon* provide an essential background to my own essay. Her influence has been pervasive, and I see my ideas as developing out of a dialogue with her, without in any way implicating her in their final formulation. I also wish to thank her for her comments on a draft of this essay.
28. Siegfried Kracauer, "The Cult of Distraction," *New German Critique*, no. 40 (Winter 1987). I would also like to indicate my debt to Heide Schlüpmann's penetrating essay on Kracauer's early film theory, "Phenomenology of Film: On Siegfried Kracauer's Writings of the 1920s," as well as the valuable discussions of Kracauer contained in the essays by Thomas Elsaesser, Patrice Petro, and Sabine Hake—all in *New German Critique*, no. 40, an extraordinary issue on Weimar Film Theory.
29. Kracauer, "Cult of Distraction," 94.
30. Kracauer, "Cult of Distraction," 94.
31. Kracauer, "Cult of Distraction," 92.
32. Kracauer, "Cult of Distraction," 96.
33. Kracauer, "Cult of Distraction," 93.
34. Schivelbusch, *Railway Journey*, 156–57.
35. Hansen, "Benjamin, Cinema and Experience," 184. Lynne Kirby observes about the popularity of staged railroad smash-ups: "As a spectacularisation of technological destruction based on an equation of pleasure with terror, the 'imagination of disaster' says volumes about the kinds of violent spectacle demanded by a modern public, and the transformation of 'shock' into eagerly expected, digestible spectacle" (Kirby, "Male Hysteria," quoting *L'Illustration*, 120).
36. Kracauer, "Cult of Distraction," 96.
37. Hansen, "Benjamin, Cinema and Experience," 210–11.

4. IN YOUR FACE

1. Béla Balázs, *Theory of Film: Character and Growth of a New Art*, trans. Edith Boone (New York: Dover, 1970), 40. For insightful treatments of Balázs's concept of physiognomy in cinema, see Gertrud Koch, "Béla Balázs: The Physiognomy of Things," *New German Critique*, no. 40 (Winter 1987): 167–78; Sabine Hake, *The Cinema's Third Machine: Writing on Film in Germany, 1907–1933* (Lincoln: University of Nebraska Press, 1993), 212–46; and especially Jacques Aumont, *Du visage au cinéma* (Paris: Éditions de l'Étoile, 1992), 77–110. Aumont's brilliant treatment of the face in silent film brings the concerns of this essay into the context of European film culture in the 1920s, especially in the work of Balázs and Jean Epstein.

2. Balázs, *Theory of Film*, 76.
3. Dziga Vertov, "The Writings of Dziga Vertov," in *Film Culture Reader*, ed. P. Adams Sitney (New York: Praeger, 1970), 367; Jean Epstein, "The Soul in Slow Motion," *Paris Midi Ciné*, 11 May 1928.
4. On these issues, see my *D. W. Griffith and the Origins of American Narrative Film: The Early Years at Biograph* (Urbana: University of Illinois Press, 1991).
5. Marta Braun, *Picturing Time: The Work of Etienne-Jules Marey (1830–1904)* (Chicago: University of Chicago Press, 1992), 176–80.
6. Good accounts of physiognomy can be found in Patrizia Magli, "The Face and the Soul," in *Fragments for a History of the Human Body: Part Two*, ed. Michael Feher (New York: Zone, 1989), 86–127; Jurgis Baltrusaitis, "Animal Physiognomy," in *Aberrations: An Essay on the Legend of Forms*, trans. Richard Miller (Cambridge, MA: MIT Press, 1989), 1–57; Graeme Tytler, *Physiognomy in the European Novel* (Princeton, NJ: Princeton University Press, 1982); and Lynn Thorndike, *A History of Magic and Experimental Science*, vol. 8 (New York: Columbia University Press, 1958), 448–75.
7. Michel Foucault, *The Order of Things: An Archaeology of the Human Sciences* (New York: Random House, 1970), 26.
8. Charles Le Brun, *A Method to Learn to Design the Passions* (Los Angeles: University of California Press, 1980), 13. This reprint of a 1734 translation includes an abridgement of *Treatment of Physiognomy* by John Williams.
9. René Descartes, "Passions of the Soul," in *The Philosophical Writings of Descartes* (Cambridge: Cambridge University Press, 1985), 1:325–404.
10. Magli, "Face and the Soul," 119; see her entire study, together with Baltrusaitis, "Animal Physiognomy," for treatments of animal imagery in Le Brun and reproductions of his illustrations.
11. See Tytler, *Physiognomy*, 35–81.
12. Tytler, *Physiognomy*, 102.
13. See Tytler, *Physiognomy*, 57–59.
14. See Tytler, *Physiognomy*, 70.
15. Quoted in Judith Wechsler, *A Human Comedy: Physiognomy and Caricature in Nineteenth-Century Paris* (Chicago: University of Chicago Press, 1982), 25–26.
16. Vachel Lindsay, *The Art of the Moving Picture* (New York: Macmillan, 1922), "Hieroglyphics," 199–216.
17. See Wechsler, *Human Comedy*, 11–17, 20–31, 69–79, 93–95.
18. Wechsler, *Human Comedy*, 31–39.
19. Walter Benjamin, *Charles Baudelaire: A Lyric Poet in the Era of High Capitalism*, trans. Harry Read (London: Verso, 1973), 32.
20. Wechsler, *Human Comedy*, 29–30.
21. Alfred Binet, *La psychologie du raisonnement: Recherches experimentales sur l'hypnotisme* (Paris: Alcan, 1886), 56; quoted in Denis Bernard and André Gunthert, *L'Instant rêvé: Albert Londe* (Nimes: Jacqueline Chambron-Trois, 1993), 131.
22. Quoted in Sander Gilman, ed., *The Face of Madness: Hugh Diamond and the Origins of Psychiatric Photography*, 15–16.
23. On the concept of the medical gaze, see Michel Foucault, *The Birth of the Clinic: An Archaeology of Medical Perception*, trans. A. M. Sheridan Smith (New York: Vintage, 1975), 107–73.
24. G. B. Duchenne de Boulogne, *The Mechanism of Human Facial Expression*, ed. and trans. R. Andrew Cuthbertson (Cambridge: Cambridge University Press, 1990).
25. Duchenne, *Mechanism*, 4. Of course Duchenne was not the first to consider the mobile aspect of the face, even if he was the first to use technological means (photography) to capture it—hence his crucial importance to my argument. Le Brun's distinction between the Passions and Physiognomy accented the difference between structure and expression and Lavater's great critic Lichtenberg based himself in this distinction as well (Tytler, *Physiognomy*, 77). I thank Mikhail Yampolski for pointing this out to me, along with other oversimplifications of an earlier draft. Although Duchenne speaks of having taken some of the photographs himself, they were taken by Adrien Toumachon, the brother of Felix Tournachon, the famed photographer known

by his pseudonym, Nadar. See Maria Morris Hombourg et al., *Nadar* (New York: Metropolitan Museum of Art, 1995), 223.

26. Duchenne, *Mechanism*, 36.
27. Duchenne, *Mechanism*, 1.
28. Duchenne, *Mechanism*, 1.
29. Duchenne, *Mechanism*, 19.
30. See Duchenne, *Mechanism*, 102–3. It is interesting to note that this is part of a long tradition of French physiologists who write works applying their discoveries to artistic practice, such as Charcot's *Les démoniaques dans l'art* (1887) and Marey and Demenÿ's *Du mouvement de l'homme* (1893), intended, as Marta Braun reports, to be "an artist's handbook" (*Picturing Time*, 268).
31. Duchenne, *Mechanism*, 118.
32. See Duchenne, *Mechanism*, 101, 105.
33. Duchenne, *Mechanism*, 102.
34. Duchenne, *Mechanism*, 104–5.
35. Duchenne, *Mechanism*, 111–12.
36. Duchenne, *Mechanism*, 17.
37. Charles Darwin, *The Expression of the Emotions in Man and Animals* (Chicago: University of Chicago Press, 1965), 147.
38. Darwin, *Expression*, 12.
39. Darwin, *Expression*, 13.
40. Gilman, *Face of Madness*, 21.
41. Gilman, *Face of Madness*, 25–72.
42. The importance of the construction of the individual body and identity for modern conception is traced in Foucault, *Birth of the Clinic*, esp. 170; Alan Sekula's important article, "The Body and the Archive," *October*, no. 39 (Winter 1986): 3–64; and my essay, "Tracing the Individual Body: Photography, Detectives, and Early Cinema," in *Cinema and the Invention of Modern Life*, ed. Leo Charney and Vanessa R. Schwartz (Berkeley: University of California Press), 15–45.
43. Gilman, *Face of Madness*, 37.
44. Georges Didi-Huberman, *L'Invention de l'hystérie: Charcot et l'iconographie photographique de la Salpétrière* (Paris: Macula, 1982), 276.
45. Didi-Huberman, *L'Invention de l'hystérie*, 47. Sander Gilman quotes a contemporary review of the *Iconographie photographique de la Salpétrière* that appeared in *Progrès médical* in 1879, declaring the camera as necessary to the study of hysteria as the microscope to histology. "The Image of the Hysteric," in Gilman et al., *Hysteria beyond Freud* (Berkeley: University of California Press, 1993), 352.
46. Didi-Huberman, *L'Invention de l'hystérie*, 35.
47. Didi-Huberman, *L'Invention de l'hystérie*, 36, 39. See also Ruth Harris, *Murder and Madness: Medicine, Law, and Society in the Fin-de-Siècle* (Oxford: Clarendon, 1989), 165.
48. Quoted in Ulrich Baer, "Photography and Hysteria: Toward a Poetics of the Flash," *Yale Journal of Criticism* 7 (Spring 1994): 48.
49. Didi-Huberman, *L'Invention de l'hystérie*, 51. I might note here that photographic scientists have not fared well in recent discussions of hysteria by literary scholars. Felicia McCarren, in "The 'Symptomatic Act' circa 1900: Hysteria, Hypnosis, Electricity, Dance," *Critical Inquiry* 21 (Summer 1995): 769, describes Duchenne as Charcot's laboratory technician; Baer, in "Photography and Hysteria," 48, 53, 64, gives Londe's first name as Alfred; and Sander Gilman, in "Image of the Hysteric," 44, reproduces a cropped version of André Brouillet's famous painting, *Une Leçon clinique à la Salpêtrière* (1886)—a copy of which hung in Freud's office—but a version that omits Londe. (The error is presumably unintentional, since Gilman discusses other details of the painting which are also omitted in the cropped version.) In the complete painting, Londe sits in the foreground on the far left, his white apron and arms akimbo, differentiating him from the other auditors. See the engraving based on Brouillet's painting in Bernard and Gunthert, *L'Instant rêvé*, 44.
50. Martha Noel Evans, *Fits and Starts: A Geneaology of Hysteria in Modern France* (Ithaca, NY: Cornell University Press, 1991), 21.

51. See Baer, "Photography and Hysteria," 63–66.
52. Didi-Huberman, *L'Invention de l'hystérie*, 228.
53. See Didi-Huberman, *L'Invention de l'hystérie*, 197–200.
54. Harris, *Murder and Madness*, 58.
55. Didi-Huberman, *L'Invention de l'hystérie*, 52.
56. On Bertillon, see Sekula, "Body and the Archive"; Gunning, "Tracing the Individual Body."
57. See Bernard and Gunthert, *L'Instant rêvé*, 100.
58. See Bernard and Gunthert, *L'Instant rêvé*, 112–13.
59. Bernard and Gunthert, *L'Instant rêvé*, 111, 62.
60. Albert Londe, *La Photograpie médicale: Applications aux sciences médicales et physiologiques* (Paris: Gauthier-Villars, 1893).
61. See Bernard and Gunthert, *L'Instant rêvé*, 125–27.
62. See Bernard and Gunthert, *L'Instant rêvé*, 125–27. On the role of instantaneous photography in the development of the cinema, see my "'Animated Pictures,' Tales of Cinema's Forgotten Future," *Michigan Quarterly Review* 34, no. 4 (Fall 1995): 465–85.
63. See Bernard and Gunthert, *L'Instant rêvé*, 121–35.
64. See Bernard and Gunthert, *L'Instant rêvé*, 153–54.
65. See Wechsler, *Human Comedy*, 153–54.
66. See Bernard and Gunthert, *L'Instant rêvé*, 144–45, 160.
67. Georges Demenÿ, "Deboires d'un inventeur," in Marcel L'Herbier, ed., *Intelligence du Cinématographe* (Paris: Correa, 1946), 46.
68. See Braun, *Picturing Time*, 68–70.
69. See Braun, *Picturing Time*, 175.
70. Braun, *Picturing Time*, 176.
71. Braun, *Picturing Time*, 180.
72. Wechsler, *Human Comedy*, 168.
73. See Braun, *Picturing Time*, 182–83. For Marey's attitude toward the Cinématographe and projected motion pictures generally, see Braun, *Picturing Time*, 195–96; Wechsler, *Human Comedy*, 144. I discuss his lack of enthusiasm more extensively in "Animated Pictures," 476–79.
74. See Braun, *Picturing Time*, 182–86. Demenÿ's work as a chronophotographer, including his apparatuses and business deals, have been detailed by the exemplary scholar Laurent Mannoni in "Glissements progressifs vers la plaisir: remarques sur l'oeuvre chronographique de Marey et Demenÿ," *1895* 18 (Summer 1995): 11–52. Mannoni launches the audacious and fascinating theory that Demenÿ's negotiation with the Lumières may have culminated in the theft of certain of his technical ideas by the Lumières for the perfection of the Cinématographe (35).
75. Mannoni, "Glissements progressifs," 41. In his major work on early cinema, *Le grand art de la lumière et de l'ombre: Archéologie du cinéma* (Paris: Nathan Université, 1994), 311, Mannoni reveals that Georges Demenÿ's brother was Paul Demenÿ, the friend of Arthur Rimbaud to whom the famous "Lettre au voyant" was addressed in 1871.
76. Barnet Philips, "The Record of a Sneeze," *Harper's Weekly*, 24 March 1894.
77. St. Augustine, *The Confessions*, trans. Rex Warner (New York: New American Library, 1963), 246.
78. Hans Blumenberg, *The Legitimacy of the Modern Age*, trans. Robert M. Wallace (Cambridge, MA: MIT Press, 1985), esp. parts III and IV.
79. See Bernard and Gunthert, *L'Instant rêvé*, 114.
80. Neil Harris, *Humbug: The Art of P. T. Barnum* (Chicago: University of Chicago Press, 1973), 57.
81. On the relation between the tradition of *curiositas* and the early film style that I term "the cinema of attractions," see my essay, "An Aesthetic of Astonishment: Early Cinema and the (In)Credulous Spectator," first published in 1989 and reprinted in this volume as chapter 3.
82. Rachel Low and Roger Manvell, *The History of the British Film*, vol. 1, *1896–1906* (London: George Allen & Unwin, 1948), 76.
83. *The Chap Book*, 15 June 1896, quoted in Terry Ramsaye, *A Million and One Nights: A History of the Motion Picture* (New York: Simon and Schuster, 1926), 259.

84. André de Lorde and Alfred Binet, *Une leçon à la Salpétrière*, in André de Lorde, *Théâtre d'épouvante* (Paris: Charpentier et Fasquelle, 1909), 1–81. The coauthor, Binet, is the famous neurologist who also recounts Londe's anecdote about photographing Blanche Witman; see the epigraph to part two of this essay.
85. Rae Beth Gordon, "Le caf conc' et l'hystérie," *Romantisme* 64 (January–March 1989): 53–66.
86. Didi-Huberman, *L'Invention de l'hystérie*, 247–48. That the performer dressed as a woman in *Goo Goo Eyes* has sometimes been identified as a man only increases our sense of the carnivalesque in these films, the ambiguous physiognomy of gender found in both popular entertainment and hysteria.
87. On these utopian dimensions in Benjamin, see Susan Buck-Morss, "Mythic Nature: Wish Image," in *The Dialectics of Seeing: Walter Benjamin and the Arcades Project* (Cambridge, MA: MIT Press, 1989), 110–58.
88. Roland Barthes, "The Face of Garbo," in *Mythologies*, ed. and trans. Annette Laver (New York: Hill and Wang, 1977), 56–57.

5. LANDSCAPE AND THE FANTASY OF MOVING PICTURES

1. Renzo Dubbini, *Geography of the Gaze: Urban and Rural Vision in Early Modern Europe*, trans. Lydia G. Cochrane (Chicago: University of Chicago Press, 2002), 3.
2. Edgar Allan Poe, "The Domain of Arnheim," in *Poe: Poetry and Tales* (New York: Library of America, 1984), 859.
3. Descriptions of Claude's influential composition can be found in Kenneth Clark, *Landscape into Art* (New York: Harper and Row, 1976), 128, 139; Barbara Novak, *Nature and Culture: American Landscape and Painting 1825–1875*, revised ed. (New York: Oxford University Press, 1995), 228; and Andrew Wilton and Tim Barringer, *American Sublime: Landscape Painting in the United States 1820–1880* (Princeton, NJ: Princeton University Press, 2002), 13. A useful summary of the way these conventions were understood in nineteenth-century America is offered by Rachael Ziady DeLue in *George Inness and the Science of Landscape* (Chicago: University of Chicago Press, 2005), 97–103, and Stephan Oettermann describes the Ideal Landscape in *The Panorama: History of a Mass Medium*, trans. Deborah Lucas Schneider (New York: Zone, 1997), 25–30.
4. Quoted in John Dixon Hunt, *Gardens and the Picturesque* (Cambridge, MA: MIT Press, 1997), 106.
5. Allen S. Weiss, *Mirrors of Infinity: The French Formal Garden and Seventeenth-Century Metaphysics* (Princeton, NJ: Princeton Architectural Press, 1995), 16.
6. Dubbini, *Geography*, 118–20; Hunt, *Gardens*, 179.
7. Hunt, *Gardens*, 174–79.
8. Hunt, *Gardens*, 175.
9. Hunt, *Gardens*, 178.
10. Arnaud Maillet, *The Claude Glass: Use and Meaning of the Black Mirror in Western Art*, trans. Jeff Fort (New York: Zone, 2004), 86.
11. Maillet, *Claude Glass*, 110.
12. Maillet, *Claude Glass*, 88.
13. Maillet, *Claude Glass*, 96.
14. Scott McDonald, *The Garden in the Machine; A Field Guide to Independent Films about Place* (Berkeley: University of California Press, 2001), 429n36.
15. DeLue, *George Inness*, 102.
16. Leo Marx, *The Machine in the Garden: Technology and the Pastoral Ideal in America* (New York: Oxford University Press, 1964), 29.
17. Richard Grusin, *Culture, Technology and America's National Parks* (Cambridge: Cambridge University Press, 2004), 9–10.
18. Marx, *Machine*, 225.

19. Quoted in Marx, *Machine*, 249.
20. Marx, *Machine*, 195 ("technological sublime"), 252 (Thoreau). See also Allen S. Weiss's insightful essay "No Man's Garden," in *Unnatural Horizons: Paradox and Contradiction in Landscape Architecture* (Princeton, NJ: Princeton Architectural Press, 1998), 84–107.
21. Diderot, quoted in Bernard Comment, *The Painted Panorama* (New York: Harry Abrams, 1999), 78.
22. DeLue, *George Inness*, 127.
23. This political aspect of American landscape painting as embodying manifest destiny and the drive toward expansion has been treated in depth and with insight by Novak, *Nature and Culture*; Angela Miller, *The Empire of the Eye: Landscape Representation and American Cultural Politics, 1825–1875* (Ithaca, NY: Cornell University Press, 1993); and Albert Boime, *The Magisterial Gaze: Manifest Destiny and American Landscape Painting 1830–1865* (Washington, DC: Smithsonian Institution Press, 1991). See also W. J. T. Mitchell's important essay "Imperial Landscape," in *Landscape and Power*, ed. Mitchell (Chicago: University of Chicago Press, 2002), 5–34.
24. Boime, *Magisterial Gaze*, 75–76.
25. Novak, *Nature and Culture*, 165. A similar point is made by Susan Danly in her introduction to *The Railway in American Art: Representations of Technological Change*, ed. Susan Danly and Leo Marx (Cambridge, MA: MIT Press, 1988), 13.
26. Novak, *Nature and Culture*, 170.
27. Leo Marx, "The Railroad-in-the-Landscape: An Iconological Reading of a Theme in American Art," in Danly and Marx, *Railway in American Art*.
28. Detailed reading of Cole's *Course of Empire* can be found in Novak, *Nature and Culture*, 10–14; Miller, *Empire of the Eye*, 21–37; and Wilton and Barringer, *American Sublime*, 95–109.
29. Novak, *Nature and Culture*, 172–74, contrasts this expanse of stumps to the more limited and symbolic use of tree stumps in such clearly celebratory paintings as Asher B. Durand's *Progress* (1853). However, one could compare the stumps here to Sanford Robinson Gifford's *Hunter Mountain, Twilight* (1866), whose meaning is equally debated; see Wilton and Barringer, *American Sublime*, 120–21.
30. Inness, quoted in DeLue, *George Inness*, 117. See also the discussion of this painting in Boime, *Magisterial Gaze*, 125–27.
31. Boime, *Magisterial Gaze*, 128.
32. See Danly, introduction to Danly and Marx, *Railway in American Art*, 1–50; Novak, *Nature and Culture*, 175–77.
33. See, for instance, the chromolithograph published by Rand McNally and Company of the Rock Island Route and reproduced in Danly and Marx, *Railway in American Art*, 31. The importance of guidebooks and their illustrations in the American landscape tradition is carefully developed in the fine dissertation by Matt Johnson, "Surveying the Nation in Time: Landscape in Nineteenth-Century Print Culture" (University of Chicago, Department of Art History, 2004), with great insight into the symbiosis between railway travel and landscape culture.
34. Danly, introduction, 13.
35. Novak, *Nature and Culture*, 176.
36. Wolfgang Schivelbusch, *The Railway Journey: Trains and Travel in the Nineteenth Century* (New York: Urizen, 1979), 62.
37. Schivelbusch, *Railway Journey*, 66.
38. Quoted in Dubbini, *Geography*, 135. Although dealing mainly with formal French gardens, Allen S. Weiss's discussion of Le Nôtres seventeenth-century gardens at Vaux-le-Vicomte and Versailles provides a brilliant presentation of these gardens as a dramatic succession of views, *Mirrors of Infinity*, 39–61.
39. Quoted in Hunt, *Gardens*, 179.
40. Oettermann, *Panorama*, 7.
41. Oettermann, *Panorama*, 15.
42. Comment, *Painted Panorama*, 100.
43. Comment, *Painted Panorama*, 77.
44. Comment, *Painted Panorama*, 161.

45. Oettermann, *Panorama*, 21.
46. Quoted in Comment, *Painted Panorama*, 97.
47. Oettermann, *Panorama*, 22.
48. Oettermann, *Panorama*, 31.
49. Quoted in Novak, *Nature and Culture*, 71.
50. Oettermann, *Panorama*, 105.
51. Oettermann, *Panorama*, 110.
52. On audiences for the panorama, see Oettermann, *Panorama*, 30–31; Comment, *Painted Panorama*, 115–19.
53. See Comment's discussion of this debate in *Painted Panorama*, 84–88.
54. Quoted in Angela Miller, "The Panorama, the Cinema and the Emergence of the Spectacular," *Wide Angle* 18, no. 2 (1996): 35–69; 44.
55. Oettermann, *Panorama*, 244. Emily Godbey's dissertation, "Rubbernecking and the Business of Disaster" (University of Chicago, Department of Art History, Summer, 2005), presents an original and insightful discussion of the relation between the spectacle of sensation and the nineteenth-century sublime.
56. Gunning, "Animated Pictures: Tales of Cinema's Forgotten Future after 100 Years of Films," in *Re-inventing Film Studies*, ed. Christine Geldhill and Linda Williams (London: Arnold Press, 2000).
57. On the moving panorama, see Oettermann, *Panorama*, 323–42; Comment, *Painted Panorama*, 62–65.
58. Oettermann, *Panorama*, 323.
59. Miller, *Empire of the Eye*, 87.
60. Iris Cahn, "The Changing Landscape of Modernity," *Wide Angle* 18, no. 3 (1996): 85–100; 89.
61. Quoted in Wilton and Barringer, *American Sublime*, 13.
62. Quoted in Wilton and Barringer, *American Sublime*, 22.
63. McDonald, *Garden in the Machine*, 23–30.
64. Wilton, "The Sublime in the Old World and the New," in Wilton and Barringer, *American Sublime*, 17.
65. Quoted in Novak, *Nature and Culture*, 24.
66. Quoted in Novak, *Nature and Culture*, 27.
67. See, for instance, the comments of Heinrich von Kleist about a panorama of Rome and the description of the Mareorama in Comment, *Painted Panorama*, 104.
68. Kenneth Clark repeats this anecdote in *Landscape into Art* (187), without vouching for its reliability.
69. Godbey, "Rubbernecking."
70. Schivelbusch, *Railway Journey*, 66.
71. Quoted in Miller, *Empire of the Eye*, 163.
72. Jules Verne, *Around the World in Eighty Days*, trans. George Makepeace Towle (New York: William Morrow & Company, 1988), 52.
73. Peter Galassi, *Before Photography: Painting and the Invention of Photography* (New York: Museum of Modern Art, 1981), 29.
74. Quoted in Comment, *Painted Panorama*, 99–100.
75. Galassi, *Before Photography*, 19.
76. *Cosmos: A Sketch of the Physical Description of the Universe* was the title of Alexander von Humboldt's magnum opus, published in five volumes between 1845 and 1862. (See the two-volume reprint edition from Johns Hopkins University Press, 1997.) It greatly influenced American landscapists, especially Frederic Church.
77. Comment, *Painted Panorama*, 86.
78. On Muybridge's panorama, see David Harris with Eric Sandweiss, *Eadweard Muybridge and the Photographic Panorama of San Francisco, 1850–1880* (Montreal: Centre Canadien d'Architecture, 1993).
79. Evelyn Onnes-Fruiterma, "Of Panoramas Old and New," in *The Magical Panorama* (The Hague: BV Panorama Mesdag, 1996), 32–35; Comment, *Painted Panorama*, 242–45.

80. Comment, *Painted Panorama*, 138.
81. Comment, *Painted Panorama*, 144.
82. Emmanuelle Toulet, "Cinema at the Universal Exposition, Paris 1900," *Persistence of Vision* 9 (1991), 10–36.
83. Novak, *Nature and Culture*, 29.
84. Comment, *Painted Panorama*, 145.
85. Tom Gunning, "The Cinema of Attractions: Early Film, Its Spectator, and the Avant-Garde," first published in 1986 and reprinted in this volume as chapter 1.
86. Tom Gunning, "Before Documentary: Early Non-Fiction Films and the 'View' Aesthetic," in *Uncharted Territory: Essays on Early Nonfiction Film*, ed. Daan Hertogs and Nico De Klerk (Amsterdam: Nederlands Filmmuseum, 1997).
87. On early travel cinema, see Charles Musser's classic essay "The Travel Genre," *Iris* 2, no. 1 (1984): 47–60; Jennifer Peterson's *Education in the School of Dreams: Travelogues and Early Nonfiction Film* (Durham, NC: Duke University Press, 2013); and my own essay "Before Documentary."
88. The classic pioneering work on the train and the cinema is Lynne Kirby's *Parallel Tracks: The Railroad and Silent Cinema* (Durham, NC: Duke University Press, 1997). My own essays on the relation between cinema and the railroad include "Systematizing the Electric Message," first published in 2004 and reprinted in this volume as chapter 8; "The Whole World within Reach: Travel Images without Borders," in *Cinema sans frontières 1896–1918/Images across Borders: Internationality in World Cinema: Representations, Markets, Influences and Reception*, ed. Roland Cosandey and François Albera (Lausanne: Éditions Payot, 1995); and "An Unseen Energy Swallows Space: The Space in Early Film and Its Relation to American Avant-Garde Film," in *Film before Griffith*, ed. John Fell (Berkeley: University of California Press, 1983).
89. Charles Musser points out this double rivalry of motion picture companies and railroads in *Edison Motion Pictures, 1890–1900: An Annotated Filmography* (Washington, DC: Smithsonian Institution Press, 1997), 260.
90. See my "An Aesthetic of Astonishment: Early Film and the (In)Credulous Spectator," first published in 1995 and reprinted in this volume as chapter 3. An argument for the possibility of such a confusion is made by Stephen Bottomore in "The Panicking Audience? Early Cinema and the Train Effect," *Historical Journal of Film Radio and Television* 19, no. 2 (1999): 189–90.
91. The reviews from the *New York Telegraph* for 15 October and 17 October 1896 are reprinted in Kemp R. Niver, *Biograph Bulletins, 1896–1908* (Los Angeles: Locare Research Group, 1971), 14.
92. Comment, *Painted Panorama*, 103. Yuri Tsivian supplies a masterful reading of films of the "arrival of a train" genre in Russia, in *Early Cinema in Russia and its Cultural Reception* (Chicago: University of Chicago Press, 1998), 135–47.
93. Klaus-Jurgen Sembach, *Art Nouveau: Utopia: Reconciling the Irreconcilable* (Köln: Taschen, 1996), 9.
94. O. Winter, *New Review*, February 1896, reprinted in Colin Harding and Simon Popple, *In the Kingdom of Shadows: A Companion to Early Cinema* (London: Cygnus Arts, 1996). 13.
95. Maxim Gorky, reprinted in Jay Leyda, *Kino: A History of the Russian and Soviet Film* (London: Allen & `Unwin, 1960), 407–9.
96. Tsivian, *Early Cinema in Russia*, 146–47.
97. Review from *New York Mail and Express*, 13 October 1896, reprinted in Niver, *Biograph Bulletins*, 2.
98. As I have indicated elsewhere, this experience of startling emergence of figures from a screen had also appeared in a visual entertainment of the early nineteenth century, although one rarely associated with landscape painting, the Phantasmagoria of Philipstahl and Robertson. See Gunning, "Phantasmagoria and the Manufacturing of Illusions and Wonder: Towards a Cultural Optics of the Cinematic Apparatus," in *The Cinema, A New Technology for the 20th Century*, ed. André Gaudreault, Catherine Russell, and Pierre Veronneau (Lausanne: Éditions Payot, 2004), 31–44.
99. Barry Salt, *Film Style and Technology History and Analysis* (London: Starwood, 1983), 42.
100. Cahn, "Changing Landscape," 98.

101. Quoted in Musser, *Edison Motion Pictures*, 208.
102. Charles Musser, "Travel Film Genre," in *The Emergence of Cinema: The American Screen to 1907* (New York: Scribner's, 1990), 429.
103. Edison catalogue 1903.
104. Toulet, "Cinema at the Universal Exposition."
105. Reprinted in Musser, *Edison Motion Pictures*, 511.
106. Edison catalogue 1902.
107. See my discussion of such thrills in relation to early cinema in "An Aesthetic of Astonishment."
108. Novak, *Nature and Culture*, 175; Danly, 7.
109. Hales Tours are described in Musser, *Emergence of Cinema*, 429–31. Raymond Fielding's pioneering essay "Hale's Tours: Ultrarealism in the Pre-1910 Motion Picture," *Cinema Journal* 10, no. 1 (Autumn 1970): 34–47, provided the first scholarly account of this phenomenon, although Fielding errs is claiming it began at the 1903 St. Louis Fair.
110. Comment, *Painted Panorama*, 130.
111. Gunning, "Unseen Energy Swallows Space"; Gunning, "The Whole Town's Gawking: Early Cinema and the Visual Experience of Modernity," *Yale Journal of Criticism* 7, no. 2 (Fall 1994). Charles Musser cites another account of the same film written around the same time, published in *The Phonoscope*. It reads, in part: "He was a passenger on a phantom train ride that whirled him through space at nearly a mile a minute. . . . There was nothing to indicate motion save that shining vista of track that was eaten up irresistibly, rapidly, and the disappearing panorama of banks and fences. The train was invisible . . . and far away . . . was the mouth of the tunnel, and toward it the spectator was hurled as if a fate was behind him. . . . The darkness closed around and the spectator was being flung through that cavern with the demoniac energy behind him. The shadows, the rush of invisible force and the uncertainty of the issues made one instinctively hold his breath as when on the edge of a crisis that might become a catastrophe" (Musser, "Travel Genre," 53–54). The similarities between the two descriptions are striking and indicate either a broadly common mode of experiencing this film or, less excitingly, a single author. I suspect the former but can't rule out the latter.
112. *New York Mail and Express*, 25 September 1897, reprinted in Niver, 29.
113. Christian Metz, *The Imaginary Signifier: Psychoanalysis and the Cinema* (Bloomington: Indiana University Press, 1982), 96.
114. Ralph Waldo Emerson, "Nature," in *Nature: Addresses and Lectures* (Philadelphia: David McKay Publisher, n.d), 14. See Novak, *Nature and Culture*, 197.
115. Walter Benjamin, "On Some Motifs in Baudelaire," in *Selected Writings*, vol. 4, *1938–1940*, ed. Howard Eiland and Michael Jennings (Cambridge, MA: Harvard University Press, 2003), 341.
116. Noël Burch, *Life to Those Shadows* (Berkeley: University of California Press, 1990).
117. This thought, besides being prompted by the anonymous journalist and by Kant's concept of the sublime as an experience that makes us reflect ultimately on perception itself, is inspired by Annette Michelson's pioneering essay "Towards Snow," *Art Forum* 9, no. 10 (1971): 30–37, in which Michael Snow's extraordinary film *Wavelength* is seen as a phenomenological reflection of consciousness. Thinking about Snow's film in relation to Poe's painting could be a fascinating exercise. It is no coincidence that Snow has also made perhaps the greatest of all landscape films, *La Région Centrale*.
118. "On Beginning the Treatment (Further Recommendations on the Technique of Psycho-Analysis)," in *The Standard Edition of the Complete Psychological Works of Sigmund Freud*, ed. and trans. James Strachey (London: Hogarth Press, 1958), 12:135.
119. Edgar Allan Poe, "The Fall of the House of Usher," in *Poe: Poetry and Tales*, 325.
120. Charles Olson, *Call Me Ishmael: A Study of Melville* (San Francisco: City Lights Books, 1947), 12.
121. Olson, *Call Me Ishmael*, 12.
122. Benjamin, "Paris of the Second Empire," 27.
123. Inness's criticism of the Impressionists is quoted in DeLue, *George Inness*, 205.
124. DeLue, *George Inness*, 32.
125. DeLue, *George Inness*, 11.

126. DeLue, *George Inness*, 55.
127. DeLue, *George Inness*, 79.
128. DeLue, *George Inness*, 116, 193.
129. DeLue, *George Inness*, 108.
130. DeLue, *George Inness*, 82.
131. DeLue, *George Inness*, 215.
132. The major accounts of Ralph Blakelock's life and painting are Abraham A. Davidson, *Ralph Albert Blakelock* (University Park: Pennsylvania State Press, 1996), and Glyn Vincent, *The Unknown Night: The Genius and Madness of R. A. Blakelock, an American Painter* (New York: Grove Press, 2003).
133. Davidson discusses Blakelock's Indian paintings in *Ralph Albert Blakelock*, 43–80.
134. Description of Blakelock's technique can be found in Davidson, *Ralph Albert Blakelock*, 202–5.
135. Davidson, *Ralph Albert Blakelock*, 79.
136. See Davidson, *Ralph Albert Blakelock*, 77–78. The classic account of the Ghost Dance is James Mooney, *The Ghost-Dance Religion and the Sioux Outbreak of 1890* (Chicago: University of Chicago Press, 1965).
137. Vincent has done important research on Blakelock's Swedenborgian background and his relation to Inness (*Unknown Night*, 150–54, 161, 195–96); see also Davidson, *Ralph Albert Blakelock*, 130–33. Inness's Swedenborgian background forms an important theme in DeLue, *George Inness*, esp. 42–50.
138. DeLue, *George Inness*, 21.
139. Jean-Louis Comolli, "The Frenzy of the Visible," in *The Cinematic Apparatus*, ed. Teresa de Lauretis and Stephen Heath (New York: St. Martins Press, 1980).

6. THE PLAY BETWEEN STILL AND MOVING IMAGES

1. Jonathan Crary, *Techniques of the Observer: On Vision and Modernity in the Nineteenth Century* (Cambridge, MA: MIT Press, 1990). 70.
2. Crary, *Techniques*, 97.
3. R. L. Gregory, *Eye and Brain: The Psychology of Seeing* (London: World University Library, 1997) 49.
4. Nicholas J. Wade, ed., *A Natural History of Vision* (Cambridge, MA: MIT Press 1998), 159–66.
5. Crary, *Techniques*, 104.
6. Joseph Anderson and Barbara Fisher Anderson, "The Myth of Persistence of Vision," *Journal of the University Film Association* 4 (Fall 1978): 3–8.
7. Mary Ann Doane, "Movement and Scale: Vom Daumenkino zur Filmprojektion," in *Apparaturen bewegter Bilder, Kulture und Technik*, vol. 2, ed. Daniel Gethmann (Munster: LIT, 2006), 123–37 (German translation of "Movement and Scale: From the Flip-book to the Cinema"). I have used a manuscript kindly supplied by the author of the original English version and cite the page numbers from that manuscript.
8. Frederick Talbot, *Moving Pictures: How They Are Made and Worked* (London: J. B. Lippincott Co., 1912), 6.
9. Hugo Munsterberg, *The Photoplay: A Psychological Study* (New York: Appleton and Company, 1916), 60.
10. Munsterberg, *Photoplay*, 61.
11. Munsterberg, *Photoplay*, 69.
12. Anderson and Anderson, "Myth," 3.
13. Anderson and Anderson, "Myth," 4.
14. Gregory, *Eye and Brain*, 109.
15. Crary, *Techniques*, 106.
16. John Ayrton Paris, *Philosophy in Sport Made Science in Earnest: An Attempt to Illustrate the First Principles of Natural Philosophy by the Aid of Popular Toys and Sports*, 5th ed. (London:

John Murray, 1849), 337. Unless otherwise noted, all quotes are from this fifth edition. The reference to Cartesians does not appear in the book's first edition, which I also consulted.

17. Paris, *Philosophy in Sport*, 339.
18. Talbot, *Moving Pictures*, 2.
19. C. W. Ceram, *Archeology of the Cinema* (London: Thames and Hudson, 1963), 18; Talbot, *Moving Pictures*, 2.
20. Doane, "Movement and Scale," 11–12.
21. Doane, "Movement and Scale," 12.
22. Laurent Mannoni, *The Great Art of Light and Shadow: Archaeology of the Cinema*, trans. Richard Crangle (Exeter: University of Exeter Press, 2000), 206–7.
23. Wade, *Natural History of Vision*, 209.
24. Paris, *Philosophy in Sport*, 337.
25. Wade, *Natural History of Vision*, 207.
26. Mannoni, *Great Art of Light and Shadow*, 211. See also Stephen Herbert, *A History of Pre-Cinema* (London: Routledge, 2002), 303–21.
27. Mannoni, *Great Art of Light and Shadow*, 219.
28. Wade, *Natural History of Vision*, 208.
29. Herbert, *History of Pre-Cinema*, 293.
30. Jacques Deslandes reproduces a drawn version, which he identifies as "the first Phenakistiscope drawn by Plateau." Deslandes, *Histoire comparitif du cinema* (Paris: Casterman, 1966), 1:36.
31. Plateau, quoted in Wade, *Natural History of Vision*, 209.
32. Paris, *Philosophy in Sport*, 339.
33. Herbert, *History of Pre-Cinema*, 297–98.
34. Crary, *Techniques*, 132.
35. Theodor Adorno, *In Search of Wagner* (London:New Left Books, 1981), 83–96.
36. Doane, "Movement and Scale," 11.
37. Herbert, *History of Pre-Cinema*, 301.
38. Doane, "Movement and Scale," 23.
39. Doane, "Movement and Scale," 24.
40. David Bordwell and Kristin Thompson, *Film Art: An Introduction*, 9th ed. (New York: McGraw Hill, 2010), 8.

7. THE EXTERIOR AS *INTÉRIEUR*

1. These oneiric objects are described in Andre Breton, *Communicating Vessels*, trans. Mary Ann Caws and Geoffrey T. Harris (Lincoln: University of Nebraska Press, 1990), 39–40, and Breton, *Mad Love*, trans. Mary Ann Caws (Lincoln: University of Nebraska Press, 1987), 32–37.
2. Walter Benjamin, *The Arcades Project*, trans. Howard Eiland and Kevin McLaughlin (Cambridge, MA: Harvard University Press, 1999), L1a,1. Hereafter, this work is cited parenthetically as *AP*, by page or by numbered "Convolutes" (e.g., I4,5; L1a,1), "First Sketches" (F°,24; O°,10), or "Early Drafts" (d°,1; e°,1).
3. Wolfgang Schivelbusch, *The Railway Journey: Trains and Travel in the Nineteenth Century*, trans. Anselm Hollo (New York: Urizen, 1977), 123–25.
4. Theodor W. Adorno, *Kierkegaard: The Construction of the Aesthetic*, trans. and ed. Robert Hullot-Kentor (Minneapolis: University of Minnesota Press, 1989), 42.
5. See *AP*, K 1,1–5; N 4,3–4; G°,26–27; H°,1–2; p. 912.
6. Marcel Proust, *Swann's Way*, trans. C. K. Scott Moncrieff, vol. 1 of *Remembrance of Things Past* (New York: Vintage, 1982), 10–11.
7. Walter Benjamin, "Experience and Poverty," trans. Rodney Livingstone, in *Selected Writings* (Cambridge, MA: Harvard University Press, 1996–2003), 2:734.
8. Benjamin, "Experience and Poverty," 2:734.

9. Walter Benjamin, "The Paris of the Second Empire in Baudelaire," in *Charles Baudelaire: A Lyric Poet in the Era of High Capitalism*, trans. Harry Zohn (London: Verso, 1983), 69; also *AP*, M13a,2.
10. Benjamin, "Paris of the Second Empire," 48–54. See, as well, my essay "From Kaleidoscope to X-Ray: Urban Spectatorship, Poe, Benjamin and *Traffic in Souls* (1913)," *Wide Angle* 19, no. 4 (1999): 25–63.
11. Carlo Ginsburg, "Clues: Roots of an Evidential Paradigm," in *Clues, Myths, and the Historical Method*, trans. John and Anne Tedeschi (Baltimore: Johns Hopkins University Press, 1989), 96–125.
12. This culminating scene appears in scene 14 of the Charles Laughton translation. Bertolt Brecht, *Collected Plays*, ed. Ralph Mannheim and John Willett (New York: Vintage, 1972), 5:465–67.
13. G. W. Leibniz, "Monadology," in *Philosophical Texts*, ed. and trans. R. S. Woolhouse and Richard Francks (Oxford: Oxford University Press, 1998), 268.
14. Leibniz, "Monadology," 275.
15. *MacGuffin* is the term Alfred Hitchcock used to describe the pretext or device of a mystery text, the thing the detectives are searching for. He explains the term in an interview in François Truffaut, *Hitchcock* (New York: Simon and Schuster, 1967), 98.
16. Benjamin, *One Way Street*, in *Selected Works*, 1:447.
17. See, for instance, the insightful treatment of Green by Catherine Ross Nickerson, in *The Web of Iniquity: Early Detective Fiction by American Women* (Durham, NC: Duke University Press, 1998), 59–116.
18. This is the conclusion of traditional historians of the detective story, as well, such as A. E. Murch, *The Development of the Detective Novel* (London: Peter Owen, 1958), 158–64.
19. Gaston Leroux, *The Phantom of the Opera* (London: W. H. Allen, 1985). 225, 259–60.
20. Miriam Hansen has pointed out to me the resonance that this discussion of mirrors has with Siegfried Kracauer's essay "Photography." One might recall, in particular, the phrase "Nothing of these contains us, and the photograph gathers fragments around a nothing," in *The Mass Ornament: Weimar Essays*, trans. and ed. Thomas Y. Levin (Princeton, NJ: Princeton University Press, 1995), 56. Again, this raises the issues of the optics of modernity.
21. Leroux, *Phantom*, 246 (emphasis in original).
22. Examples can be found in numerous stories in Arthur Conan Doyle, *The Complete Sherlock Holmes* (Garden City, NY: Doubleday, 1930): "The Reigate Puzzle," 401, 410; "The Naval Treaty," 451; "The Adventure of the Dancing Men," 512, 515, 516, 526; "The Adventure of the Priory School," 545; "The Adventure of the Golden Pince-Nez," 610; and "The Adventure of the Missing Three-Quarter," 625–26. The original *Strand* illustrations by Sidney Paget are reproduced in *The Original Illustrated Sherlock Holmes* (Edison, NJ: Castle Books, 1976).
23. Anna Katharine Green, *The Leavenworth Case* (New York: Dover, 1981), 6, 166–67, 210, 220.
24. Nickerson, *Web of Iniquity*, 77.
25. Gaston Leroux, *The Mystery of the Yellow Room* (New York: Dover, 1977), 32, 90; Leroux, *The Perfume of the Lady in Black* (Sawry: Dedalus, 1998), 56, 59.
26. Anna Katharine Green, *The Woman in the Alcove* (Indianapolis: Bobbs-Merrill Co., 1906), 19.
27. Green, *Woman in the Alcove*, 54.
28. Green, *Woman in the Alcove*, 54–55.
29. Green, *Woman in the Alcove*, 62.
30. Leroux, *Perfume*, 45.
31. Sigmund Freud, "The 'Uncanny,'" in *The Standard Edition of the Complete Psychological Works of Sigmund Freud*, ed. and trans. James Strachey (London: Hogarth Press, 1964), 17:248.
32. Walter Benjamin, "The Work of Art in the Age of Mechanical Reproduction," in *Illuminations*, ed. Hannah Arendt, trans. Harry Zohn (New York: Schocken, 1969), 236–37.
33. Benjamin, "Surrealism: The Last Snapshot of the European Intelligentsia," in *Selected Works*, 2:217.
34. Strachey's translation of Freud's *unheimlich* as "uncanny," which he admits "is not, of course, an exact equivalent," has both virtues and limitations (Freud, "Uncanny," 17:219n1). Most obviously the association of the root *heim*—"home"—and *heimlich*—"homely" or "familiar"—are lost and

must be supplied by Strachey in his footnotes. However, *uncanny* does share the curious virtue with the German word of having an opposite that converges into a near synonym. *Canny* and *uncanny* derive from the root *can*, meaning "to know, to be able." Thus, an "uncanny" ability with a knife indicates an intensification of a "canny" ability with a knife, rather than its reversal. Further, *canny* takes on the idea of craft in both the sense of skill and the sense of being wily, or artful. The term can even take on the occult connotations usually attributed to *uncanny*—for example, calling a midwife or a "wisewoman" a "canny wife" or "canny woman" (*Oxford English Dictionary*, s.v. "canny"). Thus the word preserves an understanding of knowledge that exceeds the rational but is founded in craft and praxis.

35. See Regis Messac, *Le "Detective Novel" et l'influence de la pensée scientifique* (Paris: Librarie Ancienne Honore Champion, 1929); Siegfried Kracauer, *Der Detektiv-Roman*, in *Schriften*, vol. 1 (Frankfurt am Main: Suhrkamp, 1971). The primary application of Foucault to the detective novel has been made in D. A. Miller, *The Novel and the Police* (Berkeley: University of California Press, 1988).
36. Clearly, what I have described in this essay as the uncanny or dialectical optic of the detective relates to what Benjamin describes as the "optical unconscious" in both his "Work of Art" essay and "A Short History of Photography." But I claim that, in pondering the detective and the arcade, Benjamin finds in the optic not simply an experience but the basis of a method of analysis embodied in *The Arcades Project* itself. Clearly this method bears a profound relation to what he describes as "the mimetic faculty" and the concept Miriam Hansen has isolated in his work of "innervation"; see Hansen, "Benjamin and Cinema: Not a One-Way Street," *Critical Inquiry* 25, no. 2 (Winter 1999): 306–43. However, I believe that this uncanny optics represents a method intimately related to these other terms and yet not strictly identical to them.

8. SYSTEMATIZING THE ELECTRIC MESSAGE

1. Kristin Thompson, "*The Lonedale Operator*," in *The Griffith Project*, vol. 5, *Films Produced in 1911*, ed. Paolo Cherchi Usai (London: British Film Institute, 2002), 18; D. W. Griffith, advertisement, *New York Dramatic Mirror*, 13 December 1913, 36.
2. Charlie Keil, *Early American Cinema in Transition: Story, Style, and Filmmaking, 1907–1913* (Madison: University of Wisconsin Press, 2001).
3. David Bordwell, Janet Staiger, and Kristin Thompson, *The Classical Hollywood Cinema: Film Style and Mode of Production to 1960* (New York: Columbia University Press, 1985).
4. Keil, *Early American Cinema*; Tom Gunning, *D. W. Griffith and the Origins of American Narrative Film: The Early Years at Biograph* (Urbana: University of Illinois Press, 1985).
5. Bordwell, Staiger, and Thompson, *Classical Hollywood Cinema*, 163–66.
6. Keil, *Early American Cinema*, 43, 45, notes the conflicts within the transitional period in similar terms.
7. Although this standardization was first formalized by the MPPC, it was widely adopted by the Independent production companies and exchanges that grew up in opposition to the Trust.
8. Gunning, *D. W. Griffith*.
9. Ben Singer, *Melodrama and Modernity: Early Sensational Cinema and Its Contexts* (New York: Columbia University Press, 2001), 281–87.
10. Ben Brewster, "A Bunch of Violets," paper presented at the Society for Cinema Studies Conference, Los Angeles, 1991. Brewster's discussion of other Vitagraph films shows their systematic use of alternation, an element I have explored as well; see Tom Gunning, "Il film Vitagraph e il cinema dell'integrazione narrative," in *Vitagraph Co. of America*, ed. Paolo Cherchi Usai (Pordenone: Studio Tesi, 1987), 225–40. Keil, *Early American Cinema*, 57, also discusses recurring objects.
11. Raymond Bellour, *The Analysis of Film*, ed. Constance Penley (Bloomington: Indiana University Press, 2000); Christian Metz, *Language and Cinema* (The Hague: Mouton, 1974).
12. Bellour, *Analysis of Film*, 262.
13. Keil, *Early American Cinema*, 173.

14. The Blackhawk print that I analyzed at the Library of Congress has ninety-seven shots. Raymond Bellour's analysis, illustrated by photograms of each shot, also has ninety-seven shots and seems to correspond to the Blackhawk print. The MoMA restoration has ninety-eight shots and has some minor differences in shot position from the Blackhawk print. Kristin Thompson seems to indicate that the Blackhawk print she viewed had ninety-two shots, since she numbers the penultimate shot (the close-up of the wrench) as shot ninety-one.
15. Bellour, in his analysis, resolves most of these figures into alternation. Although his analysis is brilliant, I feel it tends to privilege polar and dichotomous relations, which Griffith likes to complicate into triadic relations. I don't think, however, that my change in emphasis undermines or contradicts Bellour's analysis.
16. This shot occurs only once in the Blackhawk version but twice in the MoMA restoration.
17. *New York Dramatic Mirror*, 29 March 1911, 31.
18. Thompson, "*Lonedale Operator*," 20.
19. This aspect of classical narration is described in Bordwell, Staiger, and Thompson, *Classical Hollywood Cinema*, 27–36.
20. In the MoMA restoration there is one exception: the first two long shots of the train are actually filmed from the same setup, splitting the action of the train moving toward the camera into two shots. Likewise, in the MoMA restoration the wider shot of the engine taken from the tender appears twice, whereas it appears only once in the Blackhawk print.
21. For a discussion of money and modernity, see Georg Simmel, *The Philosophy of Money*, ed. David Frisby, trans. Tom Bottomore and David Frisby (London: Routledge, 1990).
22. Tom Standage, *The Victorian Internet* (New York: Walker, 1998), 119–20.
23. Alfred Hitchcock introduced the term *MacGuffin* in numerous interviews. See François Truffaut, *Hitchcock* (New York: Simon and Schuster, 1967), 98–100.
24. Singer introduces the weenie via Pearl White; see Singer, *Melodrama and Modernity*, 208.
25. Bordwell, Staiger, and Thompson, *Classical Hollywood Cinema*, 31.
26. Gunning, *D. W. Griffith*, 139–41.
27. Stephen Kern, *The Culture of Space and Time, 1880–1918* (Cambridge, MA: Harvard University Press, 1983), 12–14; Wolfgang Schivelbusch, *The Railway Journey: Trains and Travel in the Nineteenth Century* (New York: Urizen, 1979), 41–49; Lynne Kirby, *Parallel Tracks: The Railroad and Silent Cinema* (Durham, NC: Duke University Press, 1997), 48–57.
28. Michael O'Malley, *Keeping Watch: A History of American Time* (Washington, DC: Smithsonian Institution Press, 1990), 141–42.
29. Kern, *Culture of Space*, 12–14. Lynne Kirby brilliant discusses the relation between time and both the railway and early cinema; see Kirby, *Parallel Tracks*, 48–57.
30. Keil, *Early American Cinema*, 16.
31. Keil, *Early American Cinema*, 84.
32. One could argue that the cuts between different views of the locomotive engine exemplify cutting within a single space, especially the cuts between the engineer climbing onto the engine and settling in the cab and, later, the engine coming into Lonedale station and the shot of the engineer leaping from the cab. I think, however, that any viewer would agree that the examples I give form the only indisputable examples of spatially overlapping cuts.
33. In the MoMA restoration an insert of the telegraph message intervenes here that is not present in the Blackhawk print. Thus, one could deny this is an example of a spatial overlap.
34. See David Bordwell's analysis of this sequence in *On the History of Film Style* (Cambridge, MA: Harvard University Press, 1997), 131.
35. Thompson, "*Lonedale Operator*," 22, quotes a reviewer in the trade journal *Motography* who complains that the wrench is made too obvious early in the film. This may indicate a greater degree of perspicacity on the part of contemporaneous audiences. I suspect, however, that this was not the majority's viewing experience and indicates carping by one critic.
36. David Bordwell discusses the withholding of narrative information and incommunicative narration, especially in terms of the mystery genre, in *Narration in the Fiction Film* (Madison: University of Wisconsin Press, 1985), 64–70.

37. Biograph Bulletin, "*The Lonedale Operator*," in *The Biograph Bulletins*, ed. Eileen Bowser (New York: Farrar, Straus and Giroux, 1973), 284.
38. Bellour, *Analysis of Film*, 277.
39. *Moving Picture World*, 8 April 1911, 780. Edison had released a film in 1910, apparently now lost, entitled *The Engineer's Romance*, whose plot *Moving Picture World* summarizes as follows: "A girl station agent in a lonely station is beset by thieves. She wires to a distance for help. Her sweetheart jumps on his locomotive and goes to her assistance. The last part of the film, showing alternately the progress of the locomotive and the steady retreat of the girl as the robbers force door after door is thrilling" (22 January 1910, 91). Clearly Mack Sennett, the author of the film story for *The Lonedale Operator*, took careful notes of the films he viewed! The wrench seems to be *Lonedale*'s contribution to the Edison plot. The indication of alternation makes one wish the Edison film were available for a detailed comparison, but it also indicates the commonality of narrative structures as well as plots during the single-reel era.
40. Keil, *Early American Cinema*, 81–82.
41. Bellour, *Analysis of Film*, 277.
42. Bellour, *Analysis of Film*, 277.
43. Bellour, *Analysis of Film*, 262.
44. See the various essays included in Bellour, *Analysis of Film*.
45. Kirby, *Parallel Tracks*.
46. Exemplary works—especially Shelley Stamp's *Movie-Struck Girls: Women and Motion Picture Culture after the Nickelodeon* (Princeton, NJ: Princeton University Press, 2000); Lauren Rabinovitz's *For the Love of Pleasure: Women, Movies, and Culture in Turn-of-the-Century Chicago* (New Brunswick, NJ: Rutgers University Press, 1998); and Miriam Hansen's pioneering *Babel and Babylon: Spectatorship in American Silent Film* (Cambridge, MA: Harvard University Press, 1991)—have tried to understand the development of early cinema in relation to female audiences well-known to have flocked to the movies, especially during the single-reel film era.
47. Singer, *Melodrama and Modernity*, 221–62; Kirby, *Parallel Tracks*.
48. Jennifer M. Bean, "Technologies of Early Stardom and the Extraordinary Body," *Camera Obscura*, no 48 (2001): 9–56; Vicki Callahan, "Screening Musidora, Inscribing Indeterminacy in Film History," *Camera Obscura*, no 48 (2001): 57–81. These and other extremely relevant essays also appear in the anthology *A Feminist Reader in Early Cinema*, ed. Jennifer M. Bean and Diane Negra (Durham, NC: Duke University Press, 2002).
49. I note here that both Bellour, *Analysis of Film*, 277, and Kirby, *Parallel Tracks*, 107, indicate the film ends with a kiss, but I see only this shy embrace. Am I missing something?
50. This term, which was only retained for the telephone, was widely used at the turn of the century for skilled manipulators of technology. It was, for instance, the early term for both film projectionists and those running the cameras.
51. See Edwin Gabler, *The American Telegrapher: A Social History, 1860–1900* (New Brunswick, NJ: Rutgers University Press, 1988); also Katherine Stubbs, "Telegraphy's Corporeal Fictions," in *New Media, 1740–1914*, ed. Lisa Gitelman and Geoffrey B. Pingree (Cambridge, MA: MIT Press, 2002), 91–111.
52. Gabler, *American Telegrapher*, estimates women were paid 50 percent of male wages, and average wages for operators declined steadily (134–35). One of the demands of the 1883 strike was equal pay regardless of gender.
53. Stubbs, "Telegraphy's Corporeal Fictions," 95–96. The wholehearted support by women operators of the Great Strike belies this, but there are other indications that women operators frequently did not support more local strikes and were used as scabs; see Gabler, *American Telegrapher*, 38.
54. Gabler, *American Telegrapher*, 135.
55. Gabler, *American Telegrapher*, 136–37.
56. Stubbs, "Telegraphy's Corporeal Fictions," 103.

57. Gabler, *American Telegrapher*, 106, cites a *Boston Globe* report that four operators at Western Union's main office fainted at the commencement of the Great Strike, which he points out may have had more to do with the July weather and the constricting clothing required of women in the 1880s than with any lack of fortitude. However, like the report that women fainted on seeing the Biograph film of an oncoming locomotive in 1896, this account indicates a myth about female consciousness worth exploring further.
58. Bellour, *Analysis of Film*, 270.
59. Eileen Bowser, "Le coup de téléphone dans le primitifs du cinéma," in *Les premiers ans du cinéma français*, ed. Pierre Guibbert (Perpignan: Institute Jean Vigo, 1985), 218–24; Gunning, "Heard over the 'Phone: *The Lonely Villa* and the De Lorde Tradition of the Terrors of Technology," *Screen* 32, no. 2 (Summer 1991): 184–96; Jan Olsson, "Framing Silent Calls: Coming to Cinematographic Terms with Telephony," in *Allegories of Communication: Intermedial Concerns from Cinema to the Digital*, ed. Jan Olsson (London: John Libbey, 2004), 157–92. Yuri Tsivian's work on telephone films remains unpublished.
60. Paul Young, "Media on Display: A Telegraphic History of Early American Cinema," in *New Media, 1740–1915*, ed. Lisa Gitelman and Geoffrey B. Pingree (Cambridge, MA: MIT Press, 2003), 229–64.
61. Young, "Media on Display," 230–31.
62. Stubbs, "Telegraphy's Corporeal Fictions," 98–99.
63. Shelley Stamp [Lindsey], "Screening Spaces: Women and Motion Pictures in America, 1908–1917" (PhD diss., New York University, 1994), 59–62.
64. Gunning, "Heard over the 'Phone."
65. That this retreat into successive rooms appears in the description of Edison's *The Engineer's Romance*, the apparent prototype of *The Lonedale Operator*, marks it as a device of the single-reel era rather than simply one of Griffith's inventions.
66. Friedrich A. Kittler, *Gramophone, Film, Typewriter*, trans. Geoffrey Winthrop-Young and Michael Wutz (Stanford, CA: Stanford University Press, 1999), 183. Kittler states oracularly: "The convergence of a profession, a machine, and a sex speak [*sic*] the truth."
67. Kittler, *Gramophone, Film, Typewriter*, 183–263.
68. Kittler, *Gramophone, Film, Typewriter*, 196–200.
69. Kittler, *Gramophone, Film, Typewriter*, 216; Richard Menke, "Telegraphic Realism: Henry James: *In the Cage*," *PMLA* 115, no. 5 (October 2000): 977.
70. Henry James, *Eight Tales from the Major Phase* (New York: Norton, 1958). *The Chapbook*'s denunciation of the Vitascope is quoted in Terry Ramsaye's *A Million and One Nights: A History of the Motion Picture* (London: Cass, 1926), 259–60. I want to thank Jonathan Auerbach for drawing my attention to James's novella and to Menke's article.
71. James, *Eight Tales*, 187.
72. Quoted in Standage, *Victorian Internet*, 110.
73. On telegraph codes, see Standage, *Victorian Internet*, 105–26. Commercial codes whose main purpose was to save money by shortening word counts were a common part of business. The telegraphic code for exchanges wishing to order prints of *The Lonedale Operator*, for instance, was "Rhinastre"; see Bowser, *Biograph Bulletins*, 284.
74. Menke, "Telegraphic Realism," 975–90.
75. Menke, "Telegraphic Realism," 985–86.
76. Menke, "Telegraphic Realism," 976.
77. James, *Eight Tales*, 251.
78. James, *Eight Tales*, 265–66.
79. Kirby, *Parallel Tracks*, 105–16.
80. Young, "Media on Display," 254, quoting an address by Lindsay reprinted and commented on in *Moving Picture World*, 10 March 1917, 1583.
81. Vachel Lindsay, "Photoplay Progress," originally published in *The New Republic*, 17 February 1917, 76–77; reprinted in *Spellbound in Darkness*, ed. George C. Pratt (Greenwich: New York Graphic Society, 1970), 225. Curiously, this article is a review of *The Photoplay: A Photographic*

Study by Hugo Münsterberg, the other pioneering American film theorist—and associate of Henry James's brother, William, as well as a teacher of Gertrude Stein.

82. Young, "Media on Display," 255.
83. Bean, "Technologies of Early Stardom," 12; see also Jennifer M. Bean, "Towards a Feminist Historiography of Early Cinema," in Bean and Negra, *Feminist Reader*, esp. 6–9.
84. The term "modernity thesis" appears simultaneously in Charlie Keil, "'Visualised Narratives,' Transitional Cinema, and the Modernity Thesis," in *Le Cinéma au tournant du siècle/Cinema at the Turn of the Century*, ed. Claure Dupré la Tour, André Gaudreault, and Roberta Pearson (Lausanne: Éditions Payot, 1998), 123–37, and in Bordwell, *On the History of Film Style*. The latter supplies an intriguing critique largely directed against my work (142–47). To some extent Keil continues this in *Early American Cinema in Transition*. Ben Singer has responded to many of the arguments offered by Bordwell and Keil in defending his own version of the modernity thesis in *Melodrama and Modernity*.
85. Don Crafton, "Pie and Chase: Gag, Spectacle, and Narrative in Slapstick Comedy," in *Classical Hollywood Comedy*, ed. Kristine Brunovska Karnick and Henry Jenkins (New York: Routledge, 1994), 106–19. Linda Williams's groundbreaking discussion of melodrama as the major dramatic mode of American cinema provides an important related argument; see *Playing the Race Card: Melodramas of Black and White from Uncle Tom to O. J. Simpson* (Princeton, NJ: Princeton University Press, 2001), esp. 16–23.

9. MOVING AWAY FROM THE INDEX

1. Charles Sanders Peirce, "Prolegomena to an Apology for Pragmaticism," in *Peirce on Signs*, ed. James Hoopes (Chapel Hill: University of North Carolina Press, 1991), 251.
2. Charles Sanders Peirce, *Philosophical Writings of Peirce*, ed. Justus Buchler (New York: Dover, 1955), 106–11.
3. Peirce, *Philosophical Writings*, 108.
4. In a series of carefully argued and provocative articles, historian and theorist Joel Snyder has questioned the usefulness of the index argument in describing photography. See Joel Snyder and Neil Walsh Allen, "Photography, Vision, and Representation," *Critical Inquiry* 2 (1975): 143–69; Snyder, "Picturing Vision," *Critical Inquiry* 6 (1980): 499–526; Snyder, "Visualization and Visibility," in *Picturing Science, Producing Art*, ed. Peter Galison and Caroline Jones (London: Reaktion, 1998), 279–400; Snyder, "Res Ipsa Books Loquitur," in *Things That Talk: Object Lessons from Art and Science*, ed. Lorraine Daston (New York: Zone, 2004), 195–222; Snyder, "Pointless," in *Photographic Theory*, ed. James Elkins (New York: Routledge, 2006), 369–400.
5. See Peter Wollen, "The Semiology of Cinema," in *Signs and Meaning in the Cinema* (Bloomington: Indiana University Press, 1969), 116–54, esp. 125–26.
6. For a recent reevaluation of Bazin, once dismissed as a naïve realist, one could cite Philip Rosen, *Change Mummified: Cinema, Historicity, Theory* (Minneapolis: University of Minnesota Press, 2001), esp. 1–42.
7. I use here the translation proposed by Daniel Morgan, who revises the widely available one by Hugh Gray, which renders this as "a decal or transfer." Morgan, "Rethinking Bazin: Ontology and Realist Aesthetics," *Critical Inquiry* 32 (2006): 441–81; André Bazin, "The Ontology of the Photographic Image," in *What Is Cinema?*, ed. and trans. Hugh Gray (Berkeley: University of California Press, 1967), 1:14. The original French is "transfert de réalité de la chose sur la reproduction" and "un décalique approximatif" André Bazin, "Ontologie de l'image photographique," in *Qu'est-ce que le cinema?* vol. 1, *Ontologie et langage* (Paris: Cerf, 1958), 16. Except as noted, other translations are Gray's.
8. Again, this is Morgan's revised translation ("Rethinking Bazin," 450). Gray has it thus: "The photographic image is the object itself, the object freed from the conditions of time and space that govern it. No matter how fuzzy, distorted, or discolored, no matter how lacking in documentary value the image may be, it shares, by virtue of the very process of its becoming, the being

of the model of which it is the reproduction; it is the model" (Bazin, "Ontology," 14). Morgan discusses the misinterpretation inherent in Gray's addition of the phrase "and space" (absent in Bazin). The original French reads "cet objet lui-même, mais libéré des contingences temporelles. L'image peut être floue, déformée, décolorée, sans valeur documentaire, elle procède par sa genèse de l'ontologie du modèle; elle est le modèle" (Bazin, "Ontologie," 1:16).

9. Bazin, "Ontology," 15.
10. André Bazin, "Theater and Cinema," in *What Is Cinema?* 1:91.
11. Wollen, "Semiology of Cinema," 125–26.
12. Wollen, "Semiolgy of Cinema," 126.
13. See Tom Gunning, "What's the Point of an Index? or Faking Photographs," in *Still Moving*, ed. Karen Beckman and Jean Ma (Durham, NC: Duke University Press, 2008).
14. See Morgan, "Rethinking Bazin."
15. Bazin, "Ontology," 1:14.
16. Noël Carroll, *Philosophical Problems of Classical Film Theory* (Princeton, NJ: Princeton University Press, 1988), 10–15.
17. Quoted in Bernard Chardère, *Le roman des lumières* (Paris : Gallimard, 1995), 313.
18. Key essays by Dulac and Epstein can be found in Richard Abel, *French Film Theory and Criticism: A History/Anthology, 1907–1939*, 2 vols. (Princeton, NJ: Princeton University Press, 1988). An excellent selection of Eisenstein's essays is *Film Form: Essays in Film Theory*, ed. and trans. Jay Leyda (New York: Harcourt, 1949).
19. Germaine Dulac, "Aesthetics, Obstacles, Integral Cinegraphie," trans. Stuart Liebman, in Abel, *French Film Theory and Criticism*, 394. The French original appears in Dulac, *Écrits sur le cinema, 1919–1937*, ed. Prosper Hillairet (Paris: Paris Expérimental, 1994), 98–105.
20. The recuperation of motion in contemporary film theory will immediately evoke Gilles Deleuze's two-volume philosophical work *Cinema I: The Movement Image* and *Cinema II: The Time Image*, trans. Hugh Tomlinson and Barbara Habberjam (Minneapolis: University of Minnesota Press, 1986/1989). There is much to learn from this work, although its background in and understanding of itself as an essay in philosophy, rather than film theory or history, should be taken seriously. I do not want to undertake a full-scale discussion of Deleuze's work here, since I feel that would pull us away from the issue of movement to a consideration of his methods, terms, and assumptions. As Deleuze announces about his work in his preface, "This is not a history of the cinema. It is a taxonomy, an attempt at the classification of images and signs" (1: xiv). Although a number of Deleuze's taxonomic distinctions provide insights into cinematic motion, discussion of them would lead us astray. Instead, I want to consider the discussion of cinematic motion that preceded Deleuze, emerging primarily from film practice and theory. Most of the issues I raise here, while having a relation to Deleuze, remain marginal to his discussions, while they are central to the earlier theorists I refer to. The best treatment of Deleuze's book, fully informed of the history and theory of film, is by D. N. Rodowick, *Gilles Deleuze's Time Machine* (Durham, NC: Duke University Press, 1997).
21. Notably, Deleuze devotes no real discussion to animation.
22. Lev Manovich, *The Language of New Media* (Cambridge, MA: MIT Press, 2001).
23. A key essay in this regard by Eisenstein would be "Methods of Montage," in *Film Form*, 72–83.
24. See also *Essential Deren: Collected Writings on Film*, ed. Bruce R. McPherson (Kingston: Documentext, 2005).
25. A fine collection of Brakhage's writing is *Essential Brakhage: Selected Writings on Filmmaking*, ed. Bruce R. McPherson (Kingston, NY: McPherson/Documentext, 2001). See also the discussion of Brakhage in P. Adams Sitney, *Visionary Film: The American Avant-Garde, 1943–2000* (New York: Oxford University Press, 2002), and Sitney, *Eyes Upside Down: Visionary Filmmakers and the Heritage of Emerson* (New York: Oxford University Press, 2008).
26. Abigail Child, *This Is Called Moving: A Critical Poetics of Film* (Tuscaloosa: University of Alabama Press, 2005).
27. Siegfried Kracauer, *Theory of Film: The Redemption of Physical Reality* (Princeton, NJ: Princeton University Press, 1960), 41–45.

28. André Bazin, *Jean Renoir* (New York: Da Capo, 1992), 43–46.
29. André Bazin, "Evolution," in *What Is Cinema?* 1:27. Morgan's detailed discussion of the camera movement in Rossellini's *Voyage to Italy* in "Rethinking Bazin," 465–68, shows one way camera movement can function within Bazin's realist aesthetic.
30. Christian Metz, "On the Impression of Reality in the Cinema," in *Film Language: A Semiotics of the Cinema,* trans. Michael Taylor (New York: Oxford University Press, 1974), 4–5.
31. Metz, "On the Impression," 6.
32. Bazin, "Evolution," 36.
33. Metz, "On the Impression," 4.
34. Metz, "On the Impression," 5, 7, 8.
35. Metz, "On the Impression," 9.
36. Henri Bergson, *Creative Evolution*, trans. Arthur Mitchell (Lanham, MD: University Press of America, 1983), 308. The discussion of motion extends over pages 297–314.
37. Metz, "On the Impression," 13.
38. Jean-Louis Baudry, "The Apparatus: Metapsychological Approaches to the Impression of Reality in the Cinema," in *Narrative, Apparatus, Ideology*, ed. Philip Rosen (New York: Columbia University Press, 1986), 690–707; Christian Metz, *The Imaginary Signifier: Psychoanalysis and Cinema*, trans. Celia Britton, Annwyl Williams, Ben Brewster, and Alfred Guzzetti (Bloomington: University of Indiana Press, 1982).
39. Metz, "On the Impression," 8.
40. Would a focus on movement entail a proscriptive definition that all films must include motion? Insofar as we are referring to the movement of the apparatus, the film traveling through the projector gate, this might be tautological. Duration as a measure of this motion of the film certainly provides the sine qua non for cinematic motion and all cinema, technically defined. However, I think we can certainly conceive of films that exclude motion, made entirely of still images. Interestingly, many films that use still images seem to do so to comment on movement. Clearly, the dialectical relation between stillness and movement provides one of the richest uses of motion in film. But I think it would be an essentialist mistake to assume a film could not avoid cinematic motion, even if the examples of such are very rare and possibly debatable.
41. Metz, "On the Impression," 15.
42. Sergei Eisenstein, *Eisenstein on Disney*, ed. and trans. Jay Leyda (London: Metheun, 1988), 27.
43. See my discussion of Gollum and CGI-generated characters in "Gollum and Golem: Special Effects and the Technology of Artificial Bodies," in *From Hobbits to Hollywood: Essays on Peter Jackson's "Lord of the Rings,"* ed. Ernest Mathijs and Murray Pomerance (Amsterdam: Rodopi, 2006).
44. Danto discussed this more than a decade ago at the Columbia Film Seminar in New York City. He specifically referred, as I recall, to the way Mickey Mouse and other cartoon characters often have fewer than five fingers but cogently convey the role of the hand in grasping. If my memory is faulty, I apologize to Mr. Danto (with humble admiration).
45. Eisenstein, *Eisenstein on Disney*, 21.
46. Metz, "On the Impression," 14.
47. Laura Mulvey, *Death 24× a Second: Stillness and the Moving Image* (London: Reaktion, 2006), esp. 54–66.
48. Metz, "On the Impression," 6.
49. Kracauer's argument for the realist mission of cinema, although also based in its photographic legacy, most certainly exceeds, if it implies at all, the index.

10. TO SCAN A GHOST

1. For a fine discussion contrasting Murnau's editing in this film with Griffith's editing, see Gilberto Perez, "The Deadly Space Between," in *The Material Ghost: Films and Their Medium* (Baltimore: Johns Hopkins University Press, 1989), 133–35. However, Griffith uses such metaphorical

cutting, a likely inspiration for Murnau's use of scientific images, in his adaptation of Poe, *The Avenging Conscience* (1914).

2. Microscopic cinema appears as early as 1899. For a detailed discussion of early scientific cinema and of the integration of such images into nonscientific films such as Luis Buñuel's *L'age d'or* (1931), see Oliver Gaycken, "Devices of Curiosity: Cinema and the Scientific Vernacular" (PhD diss., University of Chicago, 2005). A popular series of early scientific films specializing in microcinematography, offered by the Anglo-American filmmaker Charles Urban, was known as "The Unseen World"; Gaycken, "Devices," 30–64.
3. Thanks to Karen Beckman for drawing my attention to this specter of the voice.
4. The best discussions of *Nosferatu* are M. Bouvier and J. L. Letraut, *Nosferatu* (Paris: Cahiers du Cinéma, Gallimard, 1981), and Loy Arnold, Michael Farier, and Hans Schimd, *Nosferatu: Ein Symphonie des Grauen* (Munich: Belleville, 2000).
5. Walter D. Wetzels, "Johann Wilhelm Ritter and Romantic Physics in Germany," in *Romanticism and the Sciences*, ed. Andrew Cunningham and Nicholas Jardine (Cambridge: Cambridge University Press, 1990), 203. This excellent anthology provides a strong overview of Romantic science. See, as well, Dietrich von Engelhardt, "Natural Science in the Age of Romanticism," in *Modern Esoteric Spirituality*, ed. Antoine Faivre and Jacob Needleman (London: SCM Press, 1992), 101–31.
6. Johann Wilhelm Ritter, "Natural Philosophy of Femininity," in *Theory as Practice: A Critical Anthology of Early German Romantic Writings*, ed. Jochen Schulte-Sasse et al. (Minneapolis: University of Minnesota Press, 1997), 391.
7. See Griffith's description of film's objectivity as a medium of historical portrayal in "Five Dollar Movies Prophesied." Excerpted in Harry Geduld, ed., *Focus on D. W. Griffith* (Englewood Cliffs, NJ: Prentice Hall, 1971), 35.
8. The classic account of the pictorial deep staging style of the 1910s is given by Yuri Tsivian, "The Voyeur at Wilhelm's Court: Franz Hofer," in *A Second Life: German Cinema's First Decades*, ed. Thomas Elsaesser (Amsterdam: Amsterdam University Press, 1996).
9. Giorgio Agamben, *Stanzas: Word and Phantasm in Western Culture* (Minneapolis: University of Minnesota Press, 1993).
10. See the catalogues for this exhibition, *The Perfect Medium: Photography and the Occult* (New Haven, CT: Yale University Press, 2005), and for an earlier exhibit, arranged by Alison Ferris at the Bowdoin College Museum of Art: *The Disembodied Spirit* (Brunswick: Bowdoin College, 2003).
11. See my "Phantom Images and Modern Manifestations: Spirit Photography, Magic Theater, Trick Films and Photography's Uncanny," in *Fugitive Images from Photography to Video*, ed. Patrice Petro (Bloomington: Indiana University Press, 1995). See more recently, Tom Gunning, "Ghosts, Photography and the Modern Body," in Ferris, *Disembodied Spirit*, 8–19. In addition to *The Perfect Medium*, recent scholarship on spirit photography includes Martyn Joly, *Faces of the Living Dead: The Belief in Spirit Photography* (London: British Library, 2005).
12. See Tom Gunning, "Re-Newing Old Technologies: Astonishment, Second Nature, and the Uncanny in Technology from the Previous Turn-of-the-Century," in *Rethinking Media Change: The Aesthetics of Transition*, ed. David Thornburg and Henry Jenkins (Cambridge, MA: MIT Press, 2003), 39–59; Gunning, "Doing for the Eye What the Phonograph Does for the Ear," in *The Sounds of Early Cinema*, ed. Rick Altman and Richard Abel (Bloomington: University of Indiana Press, 2001), 13–31; Gunning, "Re-Animation: The Invention of Cinema: Living Pictures or the Embalming of the Image of Death?" in *Untot/Undead: Relations between the Living and the Lifeless*, ed. Peter Geimer (preprint 250; Berlin: Max-Planck-Institut für Wissenschaftsgeschichte, n.d.), 19–30; Gunning, "The Ghost in the Machine: Animated Pictures at the Haunted House of Early Cinema," *Living Pictures: The Journal of the Popular and Projected Images before 1914*, Issue 1 (Summer 2001), 3–17; Gunning, "'Animated Pictures,' Tales of Cinema's Forgotten Future," *Michigan Quarterly Review* 34, no. 4 (Fall 1995): 465–85.
13. "Modern media fire up magical or animist perceptions by technologically stretching and folding the boundaries of the self; these perceptions are then rountinized, commercialized, exploited, and swallowed up into business as usual." Erik Davis, *TechGnosis* (New York: Three Rivers

Press, 1998), 68. (The pop style and New Age ideology of Davis's book should not cause serious readers to neglect its many insights.)

14. See Giambattista della Porta, *Natural Magick* (New York: Basic Books, 1957); Athanasius Kircher, *Ars magna lucis et umbrae* (Amsterdam, 1671); David Brewster, *Letters on Natural Magic Addressed to Sir Walter Scott 1832* (New York: J. J. Harper, 1832).
15. See the discussion of such devices in Barbara Stafford and Frances Terpak, *Devices of Wonder: From the World in a Box to Images on a Screen* (Los Angeles: Getty Research Institute Publications, 2001).
16. See the discussion of such controversies in Catherine Wilson, *The Invisible World: Early Modern Philosophy and the Invention of the Microscope* (Princeton, NJ: Princeton University Press, 1995), 215–18.
17. For a powerful account of the tradition of natural magic and its relation to scientific instruments, see Thomas Hankins and Robert Silverman, *Instruments and Imagination* (Princeton, NJ: Princeton University Press, 1995).
18. See Schulte-Sasse et al., *Theory as Practice*; von Engelhardt, "Natural Science"; Cunningham and Jardine, *Romanticism and the Sciences.*
19. The best accounts of nineteenth-century Spiritualism are Ann Braude, *Radical Spirits: Spiritualism and Women's Rights in Nineteenth-Century America* (Boston: Beacon Press, 1989); R. Laurence Moore, *In Search of White Crows* (New York: Oxford University Press, 1977); and Alex Owen, *The Darkened Room* (London: Virago, 1989).
20. See Davis, *TechGnosis*, 63–68.
21. Jeffrey Sconce, *Haunted Media: Electronic Presence from Telegraphy to Television* (Durham, NC: Duke University Press, 2000), 24.
22. This account is described in Jean-Claude Schmitt, *Ghosts in the Middle Ages: The Living and the Dead in Medieval Society* (Chicago: University of Chicago Press, 1998), 39.
23. On the nature and existence of ghosts and spirits, see R. C. Finucane, *Ghosts: Appearances of the Dead and Cultural Transformation* (Amherst: Prometheus, 1996); Keith Thomas, *Religion and the Decline of Magic* (Oxford: University of Oxford Press, 1971), 589–606.
24. Schmitt, *Ghosts*, 211.
25. Schmitt, *Ghosts*, 212.
26. Aristotle, *On the Soul (De Anima)*, in *The Basic Works of Aristotle*, ed. Richard McKeon (New York: Random House, 1966), 595 (432a), 589 (429a). See also the entry for *phantasía* in F. E. Peters, *Greek Philosophical Terms: A Historical Lexicon* (New York: New York University Press, 1967), 156.
27. See Julia E. Annas, *Hellenistic Philosophy of Mind* (Berkeley: University of California Press, 1992), esp. 72–78, 81–83, 168–70. Annas translates *phantasia* as "appearance."
28. For a summary of Augustine's system, see Schmitt, *Ghosts*, 22–23.
29. Schmitt, *Ghosts*, 23.
30. The most useful summary of this tradition is David C. Lindberg, *Theories of Vision from Al Kindi to Kepler* (Chicago: University of Chicago Press, 1976).
31. Lucretius, *On the Nature of the Universe*, trans. Ronald Latham (London: Penguin, 1994), 95.
32. Lucretius, *On the Nature*, 101.
33. Lindberg, *Theories of Vision*, 58.
34. Lindberg, *Theories of Vision*, 113.
35. Lucretius, *On the Nature*, 99.
36. Schmitt, *Ghosts*, 23.
37. Ioan P. Couliano, *Eros and Magic in the Renaissance* (Chicago: University of Chicago Press, 1987).
38. Agamben, *Stanzas*, 23.
39. Couliano attributes what he calls the "abolition of the phantasmatic" to the move by the Roman Catholic Church against the magical culture of the Renaissance as embodied in the persecution of Giordano Bruno, one of the great explicators of the system of erotic phantasms, and continued by the Reformation, with the Jesuits reveling in the phantasmatic culture "in all its power for the last time." Couliano, *Eros and Magic*, 192–95.
40. Kepler's theory of vision is discussed in Lindberg, *Theories of Vision*, 185–208.

41. Terry Castle, *The Female Thermometer: Eighteenth-Century Culture and the Invention of the Uncanny* (Oxford: Oxford University Press, 1995), esp. 135. Castle's important discussion of the role of the phantasmatic after the Enlightenment as not only explainable by psychological causes but a metaphor for psychological processes, a displacement of the supernatural into ordinary mental processes of memory, describes an important element of the survival of the phantasmatic tradition. However, she underestimates how much what she sees as a Romantic innovation maintains earlier, pre-Enlightenment attitudes (*Female Thermometer*, 120–89).
42. Barbara Stafford, *Artful Science: Enlightenment Entertainment and the Eclipse of Visual Education* (Cambridge, MA: MIT Press, 1994), 5–6.
43. See Thomas, *Religion*; Finucane, *Ghosts*, 49–114.
44. Thomas, *Religion*, 596.
45. Reginald Scot, *The Discoverie of Witches* (New York: Dover, 1972).
46. Charles Musser, *The Emergence of Cinema: The American Screen to 1907* (New York: Scribner's, 1990), 17–27.
47. Castle's discussion of Anne Radcliffe emphasizes the interiorization or psychologization of the ghostly;. Castle, *Female Thermometer*, 120–39.
48. J. F. von Schiller, "The Ghost-Seer or The Apparitionist," in *Gothic Tales of Terror*, vol. 2, ed. Peter Haining (Baltimore: Penguin, 1973).
49. The literature on phantasmagoria is extensive. I discuss the phenomenon in "Phantasmagoria and the Manufacturing of Illusions and Wonder: Towards a Cultural Optics of the Cinematic Apparatus," in *The Cinema, A New Technology for the 20th Century*, ed. Andre Gaudreault, Catherine Russell, and Pierre Veronneau (Lausanne: Editions Payot, 2004), 31–44.
50. Laurent Mannoni, *The Great Art of Light and Shadow*, trans. Richard Crangle (Exeter: University of Exeter Press, 2000), 144.
51. Mannoni, *Great Art of Light and Shadow*, 148.
52. Castle offers a detailed discussion of the contradictory aspects of the phantasmagoria in *Female Thermometer*, 140–55.
53. Brewster, *Letters on Natural Magic*, 17.
54. Brewster, *Letters on Natural Magic*, 53.
55. Nadar, "Balzac and the Daguerreotype," in *Literature and Photography Interactions 1840–1990*, ed. Jane M. Rabb (Albuquerque: University of New Mexico Press, 1995), 8.
56. Nadar, "Balzac," 8.
57. Nadar, "Balzac," 8.
58. Honoré de Balzac, *Cousin Pons* (Harmondsworth, UK: Penguin, 1968), 140–141.
59. Castle, *Female Thermometer*, 167.
60. Castle, *Female Thermometer*, 137–38.
61. See the excellent essay on this transformation by Clément Chéroux, "Ghost Dialectics: Spirit Photography in Entertainment and Belief," in *Perfect Medium*, 45–71.
62. Sir David Brewster, *The Stereoscope: Its History, Theory, and Construction with Its Application to the Fine and Useful Arts and to Education* (London: John Murray, 1856), 204–10.
63. See the excellent account of Mumler by Crista Coutier, "Mumler's Ghost," in *Perfect Medium*, 20–28.
64. The best account of the Pepper's Ghost illusion is Jim Steinmeyer, *Hiding the Elephant* (New York: Carroll and Graf, 2003), 19–43. Martin Harries discusses the controversy over the "authorship" of the illusion and its dialectics of belief in *Scare Quotes from Shakespeare: Marx, Keynes and the Language of Reenchantment* (Stanford, CA: Stanford University Press, 2000), 23–53.
65. On display windows and the new commercial visual culture of nineteenth-century metropolises, see William Leach, *Land of Desire: Merchants, Power and the Rise of a New American Culture* (New York: Pantheon, 1993), esp. 39–70.
66. M. V. Pogorelsky, "Pisma o zhivontom magnetizme" (Letters on animal magnetism), *Rebus* (St. Petersburg), no. 20 (1899): 183–84 (emphasis in original). Translation by Yuri Tsivian.
67. Alex Owen's important recent study of occult and magical systems in turn-of-the-century Britain makes a compelling case for the occult as a peculiarly modernist sensibility rather than a purely

reactionary one. See Owen, *The Place of Enchantment: British Occultism and the Culture of the Modern* (Chicago: University of Chicago Press, 2004).

68. For a brilliant description of the blending of science and occult beliefs available to an avant-garde artist at the turn of the century, see Linda Dalrymple Henderson, *Duchamp in Context: Science and Technology in the Large Glass and Related Works* (Princeton, NJ: Princeton University Press, 1998).
69. Camille Flammarion, *Lumen* (Middletown, CT: Wesleyan University Press, 2002), 66.
70. Flammarion, *Lumen*, 69.
71. Marta Braun, *Picturing Time: The Work of Etienne-Jules Marey 1830–1904* (Chicago: University of Chicago Press, 1992), 264–318. See also Henderson, *Duchamp in Context.*
72. For accounts of Theosophy, see Emily B. Sellon and Renée Weber, "Theosophy and the Theosophical Society," in Faivre and Needleman, *Modern Esoteric Spirituality*, 311–29; Bruce F. Campbell, *Ancient Wisdom Revived: A History of the Theosophical Movement* (Berkeley: University of California Press, 1980).
73. For a concise, illustrated account of these bodies, see C. W. Ledbetter, *Man Visible and Invisible* (Madras: Theosophical Publishing House, 1964).
74. Schmitt, *Ghosts*, 5–7.
75. Jacques Derrida, *Specters of Marx* (New York: Routledge, 1994).
76. Roland Barthes, *Camera Obscura* (New York: Hill and Wang, 1981).
77. Garrett Stewart, *Between Film and Screen: Photosynthesis* (Chicago: University of Chicago Press, 1999).
78. Schmitt, *Ghosts*, 211.
79. J.-K. Huysmans, *Là bas [Down There]*, trans. Keene Wallace (New York: Dover, 1972), 132.
80. André Breton, *Nadja* (New York: Grove Press, 1960). He is describing the climax of the serial he knew as *The Grip of the Octopus*, which was originally released in the United States as *The Trail of the Octopus* (1919).
81. Sigmund Freud, "Mourning and Melancholia," in *The Standard Edition of the Complete Psychological Works of Sigmund Freud*, ed. and trans. James Strachey (London: Hogarth Press, 1957), 14:244.
82. See the description of the heroic malady in Couliano, *Eros and Magic*, 16–84.
83. Agamben, *Stanzas*, 129.
84. I discuss the often bizarre explanations by spiritualists of what and how and spirit photography represents in "Phantom Images and Modern Manifestations," 42–71. See also *Perfect Medium*, 50–52.

11. THE LONG AND THE SHORT OF IT

1. The description provided here comes from a number of sources, primarily Laurent Mannoni, *The Great Art of Light and Shadow: Archaeology of the Cinema*, trans. Richard Crangle (Exeter: University of Exeter Press, 2000), 136–75; Françoise Levie, *Étienne-Gaspard Robertson: La vie d'un fantasmagore* (Brussels: Éditions du Préambule, 1990).
2. Maurice Merleau-Ponty, *Phenomenology of Perception*, trans. Colin Smith (London and New York: Routledge, 2002), 330.
3. Levie, *Étienne-Gaspard Robertson*, 79.
4. Thomas Bloch, "The Glass Harmonica," music notes for the CD *Glass Harmonica* (NAXOS 8.555295, 2001).
5. The phrase "Un'armonia celeste" occurs in the mad scene in Donizetti's opera *Lucia di Lammermoor*, which is scored for glass harmonica. Mesmer's theories also involved a cosmology of celestial harmonies. See the description of the mesmeric treatment, including the glass harmonica, and its relation to the society of prerevolutionary France in Robert Darnton, *Mesmerism and the End of the Enlightenment in France* (New York: Schocken, 1970), esp. 8.
6. *Courrier des Spectacles*, 23 February 1800, cited in Mannoni, *Great Art of Light and Shadow*, 161.

7. Primarily speaking of effects in early cinema, Stephen Bottomore has applied "the looming effect," a term from perceptual psychology, to the two-dimensional image seemingly invading the audience's space. Bottomore, "The Panicking Audience? Early Cinema and the Train Effect," *Historical Journal of Film, Radio and Television* 19, no. 2 (June 1999): 189–90.
8. Announcement for a phantasmagoria show in London by Philipstahl, reproduced in Mervyn Heard, "Paul Philipstahl and the Phantasmagoria in England, Scotland and Ireland, Part One: They Seek Him Here They Seek Him There," *New Magic Lantern Journal* 8, no. 1 (October 1996): 4.
9. Prospero in *The Tempest.*
10. Cited in Mannoni, *Great Art of Light and Shadow*, 14.
11. Grimod de la Reynière, *Courrier des Spectacles*, 7 March 1800, cited in Mannoni, *Great Art of Light and Shadow*, 162.
12. Giacomo Leopardi, *Pensieri*, trans. W. S. Di Piero (Baton Rouge: Louisiana State University Press, 1981), 38–39.
13. Bertolt Brecht, "Galileo, by Bertolt Brecht, translated by Charles Laughton" (appendix), in *Collected Plays*, ed. Ralph Mannheim and John Willett (New York: Bloomsbury, 1972), 5:466–67.
14. Mannoni, in *Great Art of Light and Shadow*, discusses the camera obscura (3–27) and describes Della Porta's spectacle (9).
15. Karl Marx, *The German Ideology* (New York: International Publishers, 1970).
16. Karl Marx, *Capital: A Critique of Political Economy*, trans. Samuel Moore and Edward Aveling (New York: International Publishers, 1967), 1:72.
17. Walter Benjamin, "The Study Begins with Some Reflection on the Influence of *Les Fleurs du mal*," in *Selected Writings*, vol. 4, *1938–1940*, ed. Howard Eiland and Michael W. Jennings, trans. Edmund Jephcott et al. (Cambridge, MA: Harvard University Press, 2003), 96.
18. Arthur Rimbaud, "A Season in Hell," in Rimbaud, *Complete Works, Selected Letters*, trans. Wallace Fowlie (Chicago: University of Chicago Press, 1966), 184. Fowlie translates *fantasmagories* as "hallucinations"; see, in the same volume, "Letter to Paul Demenÿ," 307.
19. Rimbaud, "Season in Hell," 193.
20. Charles Baudelaire, "Richard Wagner and Tannhäuser in Paris," in *The Painter of Modern Life and Other Essays*, trans. and ed. Jonathan Mayne (London: Phaidon, 1970), 117.
21. Teodor Wyzéwa, "Notes sur la peinture wagnerienne et le Salon 1886," reprinted in Henri Dorra, ed., *Symbolist Art Theories: A Critical Anthology* (Berkeley: University of California Press, 1994), 149.
22. Maurice Maeterlinck, "Menus prepos sur le théâtre," *La Jeune Belgique* (September 1890), 331–36.
23. Cited in Frantisek Deak, *Symbolist Theater: The Formation of an Avant-Garde* (Baltimore: Johns Hopkins University Press, 1993), 167.
24. "Interrogating the Ideologies of Technology: An Interview with Judith Barry by Jim Drobnick," *Parachute* 84 (October–December 1996): 20.
25. See my essay "Phantom Images and Modern Manifestations: Spirit Photography, Magic Theater, Trick Films and Photography's Uncanny," in *Fugitive Images from Photography to Video*, ed. Patrice Petro (Bloomington: Indiana University Press, 1995), 42–71.

12. CHAPLIN AND THE BODY OF MODERNITY

1. James Agee, *A Death in the Family* (London: Penguin, 1998), 11.
2. "Hands Off Love," in *Second Surrealist Manifesto*, ed. Eugène Jolas (Paris: Transition, 1927).
3. Agee, *Death in the Family*, 12.
4. Agee, *Death in the Family*, 13.
5. William Paul, "Charles Chaplin and the Annals of Anality," in *Comedy/Cinema/Theory*, ed. Andrew S. Horton (Berkeley: University of California Press, 1991), 111.
6. Mikhail Bakhtin, *Rabelais and His World* (1941/1965), trans. Hélène Iswolsky (Bloomington: Indiana University Press, 1993), 353.

7. Julia Kristeva, *Powers of Horror: An Essay on Abjection* (New York: Columbia University Press, 1982), 8.
8. Aby Warburg, *Images from the Region of the Pueblo Indians of North America* (1923), trans. Michael P. Steinberg (Ithaca, NY: Cornell University Press, 1995), 34.
9. R. B. Gordon, "From Charcot to Charlot: Unconscious Imitation and Spectatorship in French Cabaret and Early Cinema," *Critical Inquiry* 27, no. 3 (2001): 515–49.
10. Jean Epstein, "Groississement" (1921), trans. Stuart Liebman, *October*, no. 3 (1977): 13.
11. Agee, *Death in the Family*, 14.

13. THE LANGUAGE OF MOTION

1. See André Gaudreault, "Les *vues cinématographiques* selon Georges Méliès; ou, Comment Mitry et Sadoul avaient peut-être raison d'avoir tort (même si c'est surtout Deslandes qu'il faut lire et relire)," in *Georges Méliès, l'illusionniste fin de siècle?*, ed. Jacques Malthête and Michel Marie (Paris: Presses de la Sorbonne Nouvelle/Colloque de Cerisy, 1997), 111–31.
2. Paul Spehr, *The Man Who Made Movies: W. K. L. Dickson* (New Barnet: John Libbey, 2008), 41–42.
3. Bernard Stiegler, *Technics and Time, 1: The Fault of Epimetheus* (Stanford, CA: Stanford University Press, 1998), 9.
4. Stiegler, *Technics and Time, 1*, 68.
5. Martin Heidegger, *The Question Concerning Technology and Other Essays*, trans. William Lovitt (New York: Harper and Row, 1977).
6. André Leroi-Gorhan, *Gesture and Speech*, trans. Anna Bostock Berger (Cambridge, MA: MIT Press, 1993), esp. 132–44.
7. Leroi-Gorhan, *Gesture and Speech*, 251.
8. Stiegler, *Technics and Time, 1*, 17.
9. Stiegler, *Technics and Time, 1*, 163.
10. Bernard Stiegler, *Technics and Time, 3: Cinematic Time and the Question of Malaise* (Stanford, CA: Stanford University Press, 2011).
11. Sergei Eisenstein, "Dickens, Griffith, and the Film Today," trans. Jay Leyda, in *Film Form: Essays in Film Theory* (New York: Harcourt , 1949), 240–55.
12. Gilles Deleuze, *Cinema 1: The Movement-Image*, trans. Hugh Tomlinson and Barbara Habberjam; *Cinema 2: The Time-Image*, trans. Hugh Tomlinson and Robert Galeta (Minneapolis: University of Minnesota Press, 1986, 1989).
13. Christian Metz, *Film Language: A Semiotics of the Cinema*, trans. Michael Taylor (Chicago: University of Chicago Press, 1991); Jurij Lotman, *Semiotics of the Cinema*, trans. Mark E. Suino (Ann Arbor: Michigan Slavic Contributions, 1976).
14. Metz, *Film Language*, 61–66, 114–16.
15. Metz, *Film Language*, 66–70.
16. Metz, *Film Language*, 115–17.
17. Lotman, *Semiotics of the Cinema*, 5–7.
18. Metz, *Film Language*, 121–33, 145–46.
19. Leroi-Gourhan, *Gesture and Speech*, 188.
20. Leroi-Gourhan, *Gesture and Speech*, 188.
21. Leroi-Gourhan, *Gesture and Speech*, 190.
22. Leroi-Gourhan, *Gesture and Speech*, 191, 196.
23. Leroi-Gourhan, *Gesture and Speech*, 192.
24. Leroi-Gourhan, *Gesture and Speech*, 195.
25. Leroi-Gourhan, *Gesture and Speech*, 195.
26. Leroi-Gourhan, *Gesture and Speech*, 195.
27. Leroi-Gourhan, *Gesture and Speech*, 209.
28. Leroi-Gourhan, *Gesture and Speech*, 211–12.

29. Descriptions of this experiment in editing vary. For one, see Lev Kuleshov, *Kuleshov on Film*, trans. Ronald Levaco (Berkeley: University of California Press, 1974), 200.
30. Eisenstein's essay "Film Form: New Problems," in *Film Form* (122–49) discusses the turn toward myths. His work *Non-Indifferent Nature*, trans. Herbert Marshall (Cambridge: Cambridge University Press, 1988), shows Eisenstein's desire to find other sources of communication.
31. See Ronald Levaco, "Eikhenbaum, Inner Speech and Film Stylistics," *Screen* 15, no. 4 (Winter 1974): 47–58.
32. Leroi-Gourhan, *Gesture and Speech*, 213.
33. Leroi-Gourhan, *Gesture and Speech*, 216.
34. Metz, *Film Language*, 31.
35. Gunning, "The Whole World within Reach: Travel Images without Borders," in *Cinéma sans frontières 1896–1918/Images across Borders: Internationality in World Cinema: Representations, Markets, Influences and Reception*, ed. Roland Cosandey and François Albera (Lausanne: Éditions Payot, 1995).
36. Heidegger, "The Age of the World Picture," in *Question Concerning Technology*, 115–54.
37. Paul Ricoeur, *Freud and Philosophy: An Essay on Interpretation* (New Haven, CT: Yale University Press, 1970), 27.
38. On the Archives of the Planet, see Paula Amad, *Counter-Archive: Film, the Everyday, and Albert Kahn's Archives de la Planète* (New York: Columbia University Press, 2010).
39. Stiegler, *Technics and Time, 1*, 204–72.
40. Stiegler, *Technics and Time, 1*, 236.

14. MOVING THROUGH FRIEDBERG'S VIRTUAL WINDOW

1. Saki (H. H. Munro), "The Open Window," in *The Short Stories of Saki* (New York: Modern Library, 1930), 290.
2. Anne Friedberg, *Window Shopping: Cinema and the Postmodern* (Berkeley: University of California Press, 1993); Friedberg, *The Virtual Window: From Alberti to Microsoft* (Cambridge, MA: MIT Press, 2006).
3. Friedberg, *Virtual Window*, 20.
4. Giambattista della Porta, *Natural Magick* (New York: Basic Books, 1957), 6.
5. Friedberg, *Virtual Window*, 7.
6. Friedberg, *Virtual Window*, 8.
7. Pierre Levy, *Becoming Virtual: Reality in the Digital Age* (New York: Plenum Trade, 1998), 23.
8. Rob Shields, *The Virtual* (London: Routledge, 2005), 3.
9. Donna Haraway, "The Politics of Monsters: A Regenerative Politics for Inappropriate/d Others," in *Cultural Studies*, ed. Larry Grossberg, Cary Nelson, and Paula Treichler (New York: Routledge, 1992), 325, quoted in Shields, *Virtual*, 4.
10. Friedberg, *Virtual Window*, 8.
11. Friedberg, *Virtual Window*; see 254n23.
12. Della Porta, *Natural Magick*, 202.
13. Friedberg, *Virtual Window*, 8.
14. Friedberg, *Virtual Window*, 10.
15. Disembodiment plays a major role in Katherine Hayles's critique of virtual culture in *How We Became Posthuman: Virtual Bodies in Cybernetics, Literature and Informatics* (Chicago: University of Chicago Press, 1999).
16. Johannes Kepler, *Optics: Paralipomena to Witelo and Optical Part of Astronomy*, trans. William Donahue (Santa Fe: Green Lion Press, 2000), 77.
17. Hayles, *How We Became Posthuman*; Oliver Grau, *Virtual Art: From Illusion to Immersion* (Cambridge, MA: MIT Press, 2003).

18. See David C. Lindberg, *Theories of Vision from Al-Kindi to Kepler* (Chicago: University of Chicago Press, 1976), 178–208; Kepler, *Optics*, esp. 172–226.
19. See Kepler, *Optics*.
20. Nicholas J. Wade and Michael T. Swanston, *Visual Perception: An Introduction*, 2nd ed. (Hove: Psychology Press, 2001), 39.
21. Alan E. Shapiro, "Images: Real and Virtual, Projected and Perceived, from Kepler to Deschales," in *Inside the Camera Obscura: Optics and Art under the Spell of the Projected Image*, ed. Wolfgang Lefèvre (Berlin: Max Planck Institute for the History of Science, 2007), 75.
22. For Kepler's relation to the camera obscura, see Sven Dupré, "Playing with Images in a Dark Room: Kepler's Ludi inside the Camera Obscura," and Isabelle Pantin, "'Res Aspectabilis Cujus Forma Luminis Beneficio per Foramen Transparet'—Simulachrum, Species, Forma, Imago: What Was Transported by Light Through the Pinhole?"—both in Lefèvre, *Inside the Camera Obscura*, 59–73, 95–96. See also Martine Bubb, *La camera obscura: Philosophie d'un appareil* (Paris: L'Harmattan, 2010), 119–44.
23. Shapiro, "Images," in Lefèvre, *Inside the Camera Obscura*, 88.
24. Shapiro, "Images," 75.
25. Randall D. Knight, *Five Easy Lessons: Strategies for Successful Physics Teaching* (Boston: Addison Wesley, 2002), 276–77.
26. A video posted by Khan Academy explains it clearly with the aid of diagrams: https://www.khanacademy.org/science/physics/geometric-optics/mirrors/v/virtual-image.
27. Friedberg, *Virtual Window*, 9.
28. Friedberg, *Virtual Window*, 9.
29. Friedberg, *Virtual Window*, 9.
30. Friedberg, *Virtual Window*, 9.
31. Friedberg, *Virtual Window*, 11.
32. Svetlana Alpers, *The Art of Describing: Dutch Art in the Seventeenth Century* (Chicago: University of Chicago Press, 1983), 35–36.
33. Rainer Maria Rilke, *Sonnets to Orpheus*, trans. C. F. MacIntyre (Berkeley: University of California Press, 1960), 60–61. In tribute to Anne's multilingual abilities, the original German is:

    Spiegel: noch nie hat man wissen beschrieben,
    Was ihr in euerem Wesen seid.
    Ihr, wie mit lauter Löchern von Sieben
    Erfüllten Zwischenräume der Zeit.

34. Friedberg, *Virtual Window*, 141.
35. Henri Bergson, *Matter and Memory* (New York: Zone, 1991), 37.
36. Keith Ansell Pearson, *Philosophy and the Adventure of the Virtual: Bergson and the Time of Life* (New York: Routledge, 2002), 148.
37. Friedberg, "Bergson's Virtual," in *Virtual Window*, 140–46.
38. Bergson, *Matter and Memory*, 9.
39. Ansell Pearson, *Philosophy*, 144.
40. Bergson, *Matter and Memory*, 30.
41. Bergson, "The Possible and the Real," in *The Creative Mind: An Introduction to Metaphysics* (Mineola: Dover, 2007), 74.
42. Ansell Pearson, *Philosophy*, 150.
43. Bergson, *Matter and Memory*, 36.
44. Bergson, *Matter and Memory*, 36.
45. Bergson, *Matter and Memory*, 37.
46. Bergson, *Matter and Memory*, 37.
47. Bergson, *Matter and Memory*, 37.
48. Bergson, "Possible and the Real," 75.
49. Jorge Luis Borges, *The Aleph and Other Stories, 1933–1969* (New York: E. P. Dutton, 1978), 23.
50. Levy, *Becoming Virtual*, 27.
51. Levy, *Becoming Virtual*, 27, 29.

52. Gilles Deleuze, *Bergsonism* (New York: Zone, 1988), 96–97; and Bergson, "Possible and the Real."
53. Gilles Deleuze, *Difference and Repetition* (New York: Columbia University Press, 1994), 211–12; Deleuze, *Bergsonism*, 97.
54. Bergson, "Possible and the Real," 82.
55. Deleuze, *Difference and Repetition*, 212; Ansell Pearson, *Philosophy*, 105.
56. Friedberg, *Virtual Window*, 141.
57. Deleuze, *Bergsonism*, 16–17.
58. Deleuze, *Difference and Repetition*, 212; Deleuze, *Bergsonism*, 97.
59. Levy, *Becoming Virtual*, 24.
60. Levy, *Becoming Virtual*, 16.
61. Shields, *Virtual*, 18.
62. Bergson, "Possible and the Real," 83.
63. Bergson, "Possible and the Real," 75.
64. Henri Bergson, *Creative Evolution* (Lanham, MD: University Press of America, 1983), 304–47; Gilles Deleuze, *Cinema 1: The Movement Image*, trans. Hugh Tomlinson and Barbara Habberjam (Minneapolis: University of Minnesota Press, 1986), 2; Friedberg, *Virtual Window*, 144.
65. Bergson, *Creative Evolution*, 305.
66. Bergson, *Creative Evolution*, 308–14; Bergson, "Possible and the Real," 85.
67. Bergson, "Possible and the Real," 75.
68. Maya Deren, "Letter to James Card," *Film Culture*, no. 39 (Winter 1965): 30.
69. Levy, *Becoming Virtual*, 93.
70. Shields, *Virtual*, 42.
71. Levy, *Becoming Virtual*, 94–95; Bernard Stiegler, *Technics and Time*, esp. vol. 1, *The Fault of Epimetheus*, trans. Richard Beardsworth and George Collins (Stanford, CA: Stanford University Press, 1998).

15. DR. JACOBS'S DREAM WORK

1. *Ken Jacobs: Interview by Lindley Hanlon*, Filmmakers Filming Monographs (Minneapolis: Walker Arts Center, 1979), 6.
2. Michael Kirby, "Structuralist Film," *Drama Review* 23, no. 3 (1979): 99–100.
3. Jacobs has pointed out to me that I misread this character. The doctor's housemate is his sister. When I was incredulous, he quoted me her line, "If our father hadn't left us this house . . ."
4. Another correction. Jacobs tells me he never actually worked for Cornell, only carried on a month-long job interview with endless trips to Utopia Parkway. It was during these meetings that he borrowed *Rose Hobart*.
5. Ken Jacobs, unpublished interview in his filmmaker file at Anthology Film Archives.
6. André Breton, "As in a Wood," in *The Shadow and Its Shadow: Surrealist Writings on the Cinema*, ed. Paul Hammond (London: British Film Institute), 42–43.
7. See Joseph Cornell, "Enchanted Wanderer: Excerpts from a Journey Album for Hedy Lamarr," in Hammond, *Shadow and Its Shadow*.
8. Hanlon, *Ken Jacobs*, 6–7.
9. Sigmund Freud, *The Interpretation of Dreams* (Avon ed., 1965), 136.

22. FLAMING IMAGES

1. Alice L. Hutchison, *Kenneth Anger* (London: Black Dog Press, 2004), 25.
2. Virginia Wright Wexman, *Creating the Couple: Love, Marriage, and Hollywood Performance* (Princeton, NJ: Princeton University Press, 1993).

3. The arrest and subsequent reaction and legal action is described in J. Hoberman, *On Jack Smith's Flaming Creatures and Other Secret-Flix of Cinemaroc* (New York: Granary Press, 2001), 36–51.
4. See the analysis of gay and queer culture and underground film in Juan A. Suárez, *Bike Boys, Drag Queens and Superstars: Avant-Garde, Mass Culture and Gay Identities in the 1960s Underground Cinema* (Bloomington: University of Indiana Press, 1996).
5. Susan Sontag, "Notes on Camp," in *Against Interpretation and Other Essays* (New York: Picador, 2004), 291.
6. Laura Mulvey, "Unmasking the Gaze: Some Thoughts on New Feminist Film Theory and History," *Lectora: Revista de dones i textualitat* 7 (2001): 5–14. See also Richard Dyer, *Heavenly Bodies: Film Stars and Society* (Oxon: Routledge, 2004).
7. *Fireworks* was also apparently confiscated by the Los Angeles police in 1957. See "Letter to Amos Vogel from Kenneth Anger 10/29/1957," in *Cinema 16: Documents towards a History of the Film Society*, ed. Scott Mc Donald (Philadelphia: Temple University Press, 2002). 311.
8. Charles Tepperman's *Amateur Cinema: The Rise of North American Moviemaking, 1923–1960* (Berkeley: University of California Press, 2104), provides the best history of the amateur filmmaking movement, with a clear treatment of its relation to the avant-garde.
9. Tepperman, *Amateur Cinema*, 261.
10. Chuck Kleinhans, "Theodore Huff: Historian and Filmmaker," in *Lovers of Cinema: The First American Film Avant-garde, 1919–1945*, ed. Jan-Christopher Horak (Madison: University of Wisconsin Press, 1995).
11. Quoted in Tepperman, *Amateur Cinema*, 266.
12. Although the best-known performer in the *Baby Burlesks* films was Shirley Temple, who made her screen debut in *Runt Page*, it has been claimed that Kenneth Anger also appeared in them; see Hutchison, *Kenneth Anger*, 22.
13. Tepperman, *Amateur Cinema*, 266.
14. Kleinhans, "Theodore Huff," 201.
15. The location has been disputed. See Bill Landis, *Anger: The Unauthorized Biography of Kenneth Anger* (New York: Harper Collins Publishers,1995), 44.
16. Beautifully expressed in the Beach Boys 1963 song "In My Room":

    There's a world where I can go
    And tell my secrets to
    In my room, in my room
    In this world I lock out
    All my worries and my fears
    In my room, in my room
    Do my dreaming and my scheming
    Lie awake and pray
    Do my crying and my sighing
    Laugh at yesterday

17. On the trance film, see P. Adams Sitney, *Visionary Film: The American Avant-Garde, 1943–2000* (New York: Oxford University Press, 2002), 20–23; 100.
18. Landis, *Anger*, 37.
19. Hutchison, *Kenneth Anger*, 25.
20. Ara Osterweil's insightful essay on *Fireworks* details the potential violence surrounding the gay culture of Los Angeles after World War II. See Osterweil, "Close Up: America Year Zero," *ArtForum* 55, no. 5 (January 2017): 191–94.
21. Sitney, *Visionary Film*, 213. Sitney actually applies *sparagmos* to Anger's film *Inauguration of the Pleasure Dome*.
22. Mircea Eliade, *Shamanism: Archaic Techniques of Ecstasy* (Princeton, NJ: Princeton University Press, 1964).
23. Landis, *Anger*, 46.

23. ABIGAIL CHILD

1. Tom Gunning, "Poetry in Motion," in Abigail Child, *This Is Called Moving: A Critical Poetics of Film* (Tuscaloosa: University of Alabama Press, 2005), xi–xx.
2. Hollis Frampton, "For a Metahistory of Film: Commonplace Notes and Hypotheses," in *Circles of Confusion* (Rochester: Visual Studies Workshop Press, 1983), 114.
3. Tom Gunning, "Weaving a Narrative: Style and Economic Background in Griffith's Biograph Films," *Quarterly Review of Film and Video* 6, no. 1 (Winter 1981): 11–25.
4. Peter Kubelka, "The Theory of Metrical Film," in *The Avant-Garde Film: A Reader of Theory and Criticism*, ed. P. Adams Sitney (New York: New York University Press, 1978), 139–59.
5. Tom Gunning, "The Cinema of Attractions: Early Film, Its Spectator, and the Avant-Garde," in *Early Cinema: Space, Frame, Narrative*, ed. Thomas Elsaesser (London: British Film Institute, 1990), 56–62, reprinted here as chapter 1.
6. Tom Gunning, "Towards a Minor Cinema: Fonoroff, Herwitz, Ahwesh, Lapore, Klahr and Solomon," *Motion Picture* 3, nos. 1–2 (Winter 1989–1990): 2–5; reprinted here as chapter 18.
7. Ben Brewster, "A Scene at the 'Movies,'" *Screen* 23, no. 2 (July–August 1982): 4–15.
8. Gilles Deleuze, *Cinema 1: The Movement-Image*, trans. Hugh Tomlinson and Barbara Habberjam (Minneapolis: University of Minnesota Press, 1986); Maya Deren, "Poetry and the Film: a Symposium," in *Film Culture Reader*, ed. P. Adams Sitney (New York: Praeger, 1970), 171–87.
9. Peter Brooks, *The Melodramatic Imagination: Balzac, Henry James, Melodrama, and the Mode of Excess* (New Haven, CT: Yale University Press, 1976).
10. Roland Barthes, "The Third Meaning: Research Notes on Some Eisenstein Stills," *Artforum* 9, no. 5 (January 1973): 46–50.
11. Gilles Deleuze, *Masochism: An Interpretation of Coldness and Cruelty* (New York: Georges Braziller, 1971).
12. Walter Benjamin, *Understanding Brecht* (London: New Left Books, 1973).
13. Abigail Child, "A Motive for Mayhem," in *This Is Called Moving*, 231.
14. Child, "Motive for Mayhem," 235.
15. S. M. Eisenstein, "The Dramaturgy of Film Form," in *Selected Works*, vol. 1, *Writings, 1922–1934* (Bloomington: Indiana University Press, 1988), 161–80.
16. Martin Heidegger, *The Question Concerning Technology, and Other Essays* (New York: Harper and Row, 1977).
17. See Antonia Lant and Ingrid Periz, eds., *Red Velvet Seat: Women's Writings on the First Fifty Years of Cinema* (London: Verso, 2006).

25. THE GRAIN OF THE SCRATCH

1. See Wikipedia, "Precarity," https://en.wikipedia.org/wiki/Precarity.
2. Call for papers for the Berkeley Conference on Precarious Aesthetics, UC, Berkeley, October 15–17, 2015.
3. Anna Catherina Dalmasso, "The Visible Medium: Merleau-Ponty and Precarious Mediation," circulated paper.
4. Dalmasso, "Visible Medium," typescript page 3.
5. Maurice Merleau-Ponty, "Eye and Mind," in *The Primacy of Perception* (Evanston, IL: Northwestern University Press, 1964), 182.
6. Dalmasso, "Visible Medium," 3.
7. Luigi Russolo, "The Art of Noises," in *The Art of Noise: Destruction of Music by Futurist Machines*, ed. Candice Black (Sun Vision Press, 2012), 55–66.
8. Victor Shklovsky, "Art as Technique," in *Russian Formalist Criticism: Four Essays*, ed. and trans. Lee T. Lemon and Marion J. Reis (Lincoln: University of Nebraska Press, 1965), 3–24.

9. Deac Rossell, *Living Pictures: The Origins of the Movies* (Albany: State University of New York Press, 1998), 57–87; Paul Spehr, *The Man Who Made Movies: W. K. L. Dickson* (New Barnet: John Libbey, 2008), 125–77.
10. See Rossell, *Living Pictures*, 151–67, for some uses of glass in cinematography.
11. See Dominique Auzel, *Emile Reynaud et l'image s'anima* (Paris: Editions Du Mai, 1992): Laurent Mannoni, *The Great Art of Light and Shadow: Archaeology of the Cinema*, trans. Richard Crangle (Exeter: University of Exeter Press, 2000).
12. Hollis Frampton, "A Lecture," in *On the Camera Arts and Consecutive Matters: The Writings of Hollis Frampton*, ed. Bruce Jenkins (Cambridge, MA: MIT Press, 2009), 125–30.
13. See my discussion of this sequence in Tom Gunning, *Fritz Lang: Allegories of Vision and Modernity* (London: BFI Press, 2000), 71–76.
14. I discuss this in my essay "Flaming Images: Burning through the Celluloid Closet," chapter 22 in this volume.
15. Letter from Pat O'Neil, 2009.
16. See Wikipedia, "Film grain," https://en.wikipedia.org/wiki/Film_grain.
17. Wikipedia, "Film grain."
18. "Embrace the Grain" podcast, https://podcasts.apple.com/us/podcast/embrace-the-grain-photography-podcast/id1459043812.

26. TRANSPORT OF JOY

1. Clement Greenberg, "Avant-Garde and Kitsch" in *Art and Culture* (Boston: Beacon Press, 1961), 6.
2. Malcom Le Grice, *Abstract Film and Beyond* (Cambridge, MA: MIT Press, 1979), 108.
3. Le Grice, *Abstract Film*, 87.
4. Le Grice, *Abstract Film*, 89.
5. Peter Gidal, *Materialist Film* (London: Routledge, 1989), 99.
6. Quoted in Tzvetan Todorov, *Theories of the Symbol*, trans. Catherine Porter (Ithaca, NY: Cornell University Press, 1982), 161.
7. Fred Camper, "Mothlight and Beyond," *La Furia Umana*, 30 September 2011.
8. Le Grice, *Abstract Film*, 90.
9. Brakhage, *Metaphors on Vision*, special issue of *Film Culture*, no. 30 (Fall 1963), ed. P. Adams Sitney, n.p.
10. Le Grice, *Abstract Film*, 90.
11. Le Grice, *Abstract Film*, 89.
12. Brakhage, *Metaphors on Vision.*
13. Brakhage, *Metaphors on Vision.*
14. See, e.g., Jennifer M. Barker, *The Tactile Eye: Touch and the Cinematic Experience* (Berkeley: University of California Press, 2009).
15. Fred Camper, comments on the Criterion DVD set *By Brakhage*, https://www.fredcamper.com/Brakhage/CriterionDVD.html.
16. *The Garden of Earthly Delights* (1981) revived *Mothlight*'s collage of plant fragments, but the role of the optical printer in the later film gives it a very different feel.
17. Stan Brakhage, "Exultations of Bruce Elder," in *Telling Time: Essays of a Visionary Filmmaker* (Kingston: Documentext, 2003), 126.
18. Quoted in Todorov, *Theories*, 174.
19. P. Adams Sitney, *Eyes Upside Down: Visionary Filmmakers and the Heritage of Emerson* (New York: Oxford University Press, 2008), 326; Gertrude Stein, *Stanzas in Meditation*, corrected edition, ed. Susannah Hollister and Emily Setina (New Haven, CT: Yale University Press, 2010).
20. Stan Brakhage, "Gertrude Stein: Meditative Literature and Film," in *Essential Brakhage: Selected Writings on Filmmaking*, ed. Bruce R. McPherson (Kingston, NY: McPherson/Documentext, 2001), 201–2.
21. Brakhage, "Stein," 202.

22. Brakhage, “Stein,” 202.
23. Sitney, *Eyes Upside Down*; Sitney, *The Cinema of Poetry* (New York: Oxford University Press, 2015); R. Bruce Elder, *The Films of Stan Brakhage in the American Tradition of Ezra Pound, Gertrude Stein and Charles Olson* (Waterloo, ON: Wilfrid Laurier University Press, 1998).
24. Brakhage, “Stein,” 195.
25. Sitney, *Eyes Upside Down*, 326.
26. Saranjan Ganguly, “Stan Brakhage—the 60th Birthday Interview,” *Film Culture*, no. 78 (Summer 1994): 2.
27. Sitney, *Cinema of Poetry*, 154.
28. Elder, *Brakhage*, 249.
29. Elder, *Brakhage*, 274.
30. Elder, *Brakhage*, 220.
31. Brakhage, “Painting Film,” in *Telling Time*, 79.
32. Sitney, *Eyes Upside Down*, 328–42.
33. Sitney, *Eyes Upside Down*, 338.
34. Gertrude Stein, Stanza XXXV, *Stanzas in Meditation*, 213.
35. Brakhage, “Stein,” 195.
36. Brakhage, *Metaphors on Vision*.
37. Recent discussions of Brakhage’s hand-painted films, in addition to the already cited essays by Camper and Sitney, include Victoria Young, “The Hand-Painted Films of Stan Brakhage: An Interdisciplinary and Phenomenological Exploration of Painted Moving Images” (PhD diss., University of Portsmouth, 2018); John Powers, an unpublished talk presented at the Ninth Brakhage Symposium 2013, University of Colorado, Boulder; and Gregory Zinman, in *Making Images Move: Handmade Cinema and the Other Arts* (Berkeley: University of California Press, 2020), 89–102.
38. John Powers, “Moving through Stasis in Stan Brakhage’s *Passing Through: A Ritual*,” *Screen* 60, no. 3 (Fall 2019): 410, 412.
39. Powers, “Moving,” 416.
40. Powers, “Moving,” 416.
41. Stein, *Lectures in America*, quoted in Powers, “Moving,” 416.
42. Todorov, *Theories*, 175.
43. André Leroi-Gourhan, *Gesture and Speech* (Cambridge, MA: MIT Press, 1993), 195.
44. Leroi-Gourhan, *Gesture and Speech*, 211–12.
45. Brakhage, “Stein,” 195.
46. Perhaps the best discussion of the apophatic tradition in religious writing is Michael A. Sells, *Mystical Languages of Unsaying* (Chicago: University of Chicago Press, 1994).
47. Brakhage, *Metaphors on Vision*.
48. Brakhage, *Metaphors on Vision*.
49. I thank Ken Eisenstein for checking this for me.
50. Brakhage, quoted in review by Fred Camper, “Glimpses of Greatness: New Films by Stan Brakhage” *Chicago Reader*, 10 September 1999, https://www.chicagoreader.com/chicago/glimpses-of-greatness/Content?oid=900139.
51. Tom Gunning, “The Grain of the Scratch: The Precarity of Transparency in Cinema,” 2015 talk, published here as chapter 25.
52. Zinman, *Making Images*, 89.
53. The relations between creation, light, and the letters of the Hebrew alphabet are integral to Jewish mysticism, from the Sepher Yetsirah through the Zohar and later Hasidism. See Gershom Scholem, *Major Trends in Jewish Mysticism* (New York: Schocken, 1961). See also Nicholas Hudson, *Writing and European Thought 1600–1830* (Cambridge: Cambridge University Press, 1994), 21–26.
54. Walter Benjamin, *The Origin of German Tragic Drama*, trans. John Osborne (New York: Verso, 1998), 176.
55. Zinman, *Making Images*, 99–100.

Index

Page numbers in italics refer to figures.

absorption, 8, 21, 76–77, 80, 108, 110, 113, 237, 417, 432, 498n18, 506n21; narrative, 26, 46, 52, 82

abstraction: in Stan Brakhage, 486; in Sergei Eisenstein, 310; in David Gatten, 440, 445, 447; in Maxim Gorky, 79; kinetic, 237; of language, 306, 308; in *The Lonedale Operator* (Griffith), 201–2; temporal, 402; and virtual image, 323; and vision, 453

actuality films, 42, 47, 62, 76, 77, 374, 404

Adorno, Theodor W., 25, 170, 176, 179, 287, 349

aesthetics: of astonishment, 47, 67, 69, 72–73, 81, 166, 169, 506n21; landscape, 15, 128; and realism, 227; romantic, 88; and mediation, 453; and modernism, 108; precarious, 454; as sense manipulation, 286; surrealist, 400; and technology, 133, 304

Agamben, Giorgio, 5, 257, 272

Agee, James: *A Death in the Family*, 289–90; *Let Us Now Praise Famous Men*, 290

Ahwesh, Peggy, 16, 364, 366, 368; *Martina's Playhouse*, 364

Alberti, Leon Battista, 115, 330

alienation, 304; in Abigail Child, 430–31; in Maxim Gorky, 79

Alighieri, Dante, 272; *Convivio*, 255; *Inferno*, 398

allegory: and face, 99; in landscape painting, 122; in *Metropolis* (Lang), 459; in *Moonlights* (Blakelock), 150–51; in *Mothlight* (Brakhage), 467; and phantom rides, 144, 147

Alpers, Svetlana, 322

amateur film, 33, 411–12

Anger, Kenneth, 16, 34, 408, 414, 458, 535n12; *Fireworks*, 408, 413, *411*, 414–19, 421, 460, 535n7

animation, 15, 28, 29, 232, 236, 242–43; in *Eureka* (Gehr), 375; in *Lost Camel Intentions* (Klahr), 369; in *Mothlight* (Brakhage), 487; in *One Day Franz Came to My House* (Marrero and Kouguell), 438; in *What the Water Said* (Gatten), 448

Anschutz, Oscar, 455

Ansell Pearson, Keith, 323, 324, 325

apparatus theory, 25, 171–72

Aristotle, 24, 86, 155, 256

Artaud, Antonin, "Cinema and Reality," 447, 449

Arthur, Paul, 365, 366

Arvidson, Linda, 193

astonishment, 47, 67, 69, 72–73, 81, 166, 169, 506n21. *See also* shock

attractions, 1–7, 9, 15, 18, 19–21, 25, 41–49, 61, 63–64, 77–78, 80–81, 105, 136, 142, 190, 233, 374, 375, 409, 506n13; aesthetic of, 47, 75; cinema of, 1–4, 6–7, 9, 14, 15, 18, 35, 42–43, 45–46, 47, 52–54, 58–63, 66, 69, 74–77, 79, 143, 225, 427; logic of, 1–3, 6–7, 9, 14–15, 20–21, 25, 35, 76; and repulsion, 77

Augustine, 21–22, 77, 254, 256; *curiositas*, 21, 77–78, 108; on vision, 256

Aumont, Jacques, 10, 54, 507n1

Auster, Paul, 147
Avakian, Aram, 421
avant-garde: anti-illusionist, 457; and cinematic time, 400–401; crisis of, 16, 346; doors in, 415; and dreams, 340, 343; and early cinema, 4, 10, 41, 43, 46, 49, 375, 401, 404, 427; energies of, 11, 36, 14, 363–67, 393; and found footage, 401–2; French, 436; immersion of Tom Gunning in, 12, 22; importance of, 15, 16; and language, 474; and materiality, 458, 491; and montage, 27, 422–23, 433–35, 479; motion in, 245; and narrative, 427; and New Narratives, 365, 367; poles of, 282; postwar American, 14, 36; and queer cinema, 408–13; and scientific photography, 267; Soviet, 422; and Structural Film, 365, 367

Bacon, Roger, 257
Baer, Ulrich, 100
Bakhtin, Mikhail, on carnivalesque, 291–92
Balázs, Béla, on human face, 83, 86, 89
Balzac, Honoré de, 89, 90, 261–62; *Cousin Pons*, 262; *The Human Comedy*, 262
Barnum, P. T., 109
Barry, Judith, 288
Barthes, Roland: *Camera Lucida*, 238, 252, 269, 439; on face of Garbo, 113; "The Third Meaning," 429–30
Battersby, Martin, 70
Baudelaire, Charles, 131, 285–86; "Salon of 1859," 130; on synesthesia, 286
Baudry, Jean-Louis, 8, 242, 321
Bazin, André, 25, 229, 237–39, 421, 447; on cinematic realism, 50, 229, 237, 242; on "the myth of total cinema," 37; on photographic image, 7, 25, 28, 230–32, 239, 244–45, 252, 351
Beach Boys, "In My Room," 535n16
Bean, Jennifer, 215, 225, 299
Belasco, David, 206
Bellour, Raymond, 26, 197, 203, 212, 214–15, 218, 220, 520n15; "To Alternate/To Narrate," 197; "The System of the Fragment," 197
Beloff, Zoe, 208
Belton, John, 457
Benjamin, Walter, 20, 79, 81, 235, 294, 430; *The Arcades Project*, 175, 178–79, 190, 192; on astonishment, 67; on city, 380; on commodity, 113, 285; on detective fiction, 64, 148, 179, 181, 187; on optical unconscious, 519n36; on panoramas, 125; on photography, 64; on physiologies, 90; on shock and perception, 74; on space, 175–78, 182, 184, 185, 189–92; "stirring writing," 492; "What Is Epic Theatre?," 67; "The Work of Art in the Age of Mechanical Reproduction," 78, 84, 331, 355
Benning, James, *Landscape Suicide*, 365
Bergson, Henri, 31, 100; on cinema, 329–30; *Creative Evolution*, 329; *Matter and Memory*, 323; on motion, 31, 239–41, 244; "The Possible and the Real," 325–27, 330; on virtual, 31, 324–28
Bernard, Denis, 102–3
Bierstadt, Albert, 119, 123, 131, 133; *The Rocky Mountain*, 131
Big Swallow, The (Williamson), 55–56, 58, 60, 503n19
Biograph (machine), 22, 305
Biograph Company, 1, 12, 76, 84, 137, 208; *Hooligan in Jail*, 45; *Personal*, 48; *Photographing a Female Crook*, 45, 76; *A Search for Evidence*, 58, 61–63, 65, 66; *The Story the Biograph Told*, 64
Bioscope, 305
Bioy Casares, Adolfo, *The Invention of Morel*, 258
Bitzer, Billy, *141*, 198, 204, 351
Black Diamond Express, The (Vitagraph), 44, 73–74, 75, 79
Blake, William, 196
Blakelock, Ralph, 147, 149–52; *Ghost Dance*, *152*; *Moonlights*, 150
Blumenberg, Hans, 108
body: in Kenneth Anger, 33, 415–18; and carnivalesque, 291–93; Cartesian, 88; cartoon, 2; and chronophotography, 105; and devolution, 297–301; female, 4; and gesture, 309; and machine, 170, 293, 295–96; and medical photography, 100–101, 103; and modernity, 290–301, 509n42; in motion, 166, 394, 425; and perception, 324–26; phantasmatic, 249, 251, 253, 257, 259, 261, 263, 267–68, 271; and photography, 22; in Marcel Proust, 177; and shock, 81; and visual devices, 154–55, 162, 169. *See also* Chaplin, Charlie: body of
Boime, Albert, 121, 123
Bordwell, David, 19–20, 171
Borges, Jorge Luis: "The Aleph," 327; *The Book of Imaginary Beings*, 388; "A New Refutation of Time," 359
Bottomore, Stephen, 64, 530n7
Bourneville, Désiré, 103
Bowser, Eileen, 3, 66, 218
Brakhage, Stan, 16, 22, 34–35, 237, 366–70, 389, 415, 419, 421, 427, 464–93; *Anticipation of the Night*, 483, 490; *The Arabic Numeral Series*, 490; *The Babylon Series*, 490; *Chinese Series*, 492, 493; color in works of, 17, 34, 370, 480–89, 492; *Desistfilm*, 490; *Dog Star Man*, 490; *First Hymn to Night—Novalis*, 22, 34, 483–87, 489; *I Dreaming*, 490; inscription in works of, 34, 483, 485–91; light in works of, 35, 366, 368, 389; mediation in works of, 370, 466, 473; *Meta-*

phors on Vision, 483, 489; *Mothlight*, 10, 34, 466–74, 476–78, 480, 487, 490; motion in works of, 34, 237, 367, 472–73, 479–80, 483–88, 492; *My Mountain*, 367; *Passage Through*, 34, 415–16, 483; *Persian Series*, 490; *Reflections on Black*, 419, 458–59, 490–91; repetition in works of, 476–77; *The Roman Numeral Series*, 490; *Sexual Meditations*, 476; *Thigh Line Lyre Triangular*, 490; *Twenty-Third Psalm Branch*, 367, 488; *Untitled (For Marilyn)*, 490; *Visions in Meditation*, 476–77; *Visions in Meditation # 2*, 478, 479, 482
Branigan, Edward, *Point of View*, 51–54, 59, 66, 502n15, 503n17
Brecht, Bertolt, 294, 429, 430; *The Life of Galileo*, 171, 283–84
Bresson, Robert, 373; "Notes on Cinematography," 446, 486
Breton, André, 175, 272, 341
Brewster, Ben, 59, 196, 427, 502n15
Brewster, David, 162, 252, 260–61, 264, 265, 319–20; *Letters on Natural Magic*, 260
British cinema, 13, 465, 470
Brooks, Peter, *The Melodramatic Imagination*, 66, 429
Bukatman, Scott, 25
Buñuel, Luis, *Un Chien Andalou*, 416
Burch, Noël, 3–6; on early cinema, 376; on exhibition and narrative, 43; on phantom rides spectatorship, 146; on punishment of "peeping toms," 60
Byrd, William, 437, 441–45

Cahn, Iris, 118, 128, 140
camera movement, 13, 139, 147, 235, 237, 241, 242, 347, 368, 377, 418, 433, 478–79
camera obscura, 133, 134, 179, 228, 259, 284–85, 315, 318–20, 322
Camper, Fred, 16, 22, 364, 466, 474
Candee, Helen Churchill, 213
Carus, Carl Gustav, 134
Cassavetes, John, *Faces*, 462
Castle, Terry, *The Female Thermometer*, 258, 259, 263, 528n41
Cavell, Stanley, 235; "automatism," 6; on cartoons, 28; on passive spectatorship, 7
Ceram, C. W., 161
Chagall, Marc, 298
Chaplin, Charlie, 289–301; body of, 290–301; *The Circus*, 296; *A Dog's Life*, 298–99; *The Gold Rush*, 298–300; *The Kid*, 290, 297; *Limelight*, 299; *Modern Times*, 292, 294–96; *One AM*, 296; *The Pawnshop*, 292; *Shoulder Arms*, 299, 300; walk of, 289–91, 294, 297–98
Charcot, Jean-Martin, 17, 21, 91, 95, 99–103, 108–12, 296
Charney, Leo, 18
chase films, 48
Child, Abigail, 10, 16, 27, 237, 367, 402, 420–36; editing in works of, 27, 421, 423, 429, 432; *Is This What You Were Born For?*, 421, 424; *Mayhem*, 428–32, 435–36; *Mercy*, 432–36; montage in works of, 10, 27–28, 237, 367, 420–23, 433–35; movement in works of, 423–27, 429, 433–34; *Mutiny*, 10, 424–25, 429, 432–34, 436; *Perils*, 428–30, 435–36; *This Is Called Moving*, 237, 422–23, 425, 427
chronophotography, 103–6, 267, 305, 349, 423
Church, Fredric, 118, 119, 123, 128, 131, 133, 134, 135; *The Heart of the Andes*, 128
Cinématographe, 22, 23, 42, 44, 70, 72, 73, 79, 104, 106, 109, 137, 138, 233, 305, 375
city symphonies, 13
classical Hollywood cinema, 197, 205, 305, 454
Claude glass, 24, 116–17, 124, 133–34
close-up; in Abigail Child, 425, 428, 430, 432; in *The Doctor's Dream* (Jacobs), 338; in early cinema, 21, 24, 44–45, 109, 211, 213; in David Gatten, 33, 438, 443–44, 447; in *The Gay Shoe Clerk* (Porter), 45; and human face, 83–84, 101, 109–11, 113, 211; ideology of, 109; information of, 306; in Ken Jacobs, 338, 353; in Mark LaPore, 369, 396; in *The Lonedale Operator* (Griffith), 27, 210–15; and narrative logic, 339; in *Nosferatu* (Murnau), 246, 247; in *Photographing a Female Crook* (Biograph), 76; and pleasure, 5; in *Visions in Meditation* (Brakhage), 481
Cocteau, Jean, 50; *Blood of a Poet*, 59, 427
Cohl, Emile, 243
Cole, Thomas, 119, 121–22, 129, 133, 148–49; *Course of Empire*, 130; *The Oxbow*, 122; *The Voyage of Life*, 129
comedy, 48, 61, 65, 76, 95, 290, 292
Comment, Bernard, 125–26, 135–36, 144, 146
Comolli, Jean-Louis, 152
computer generated images (CGI), 232
Conolly, John, 97
Conrad, Tony, 364
Constable, John, 127
Cooper, Merian, *This Is Cinerama*, 5
Cornell, Joseph, *Rose Hobart*, 340–42
Couliano, Iaon, 257, 527n39
Crafton, Donald, "Pie and Chase," 48
Crary, Jonathan, 154–55, 159, 169–70, 172
curiosities, 77, 108, 253, 315

Dalmasso, Anna Catherina, 452–53
dance, 13, 151, 165, 237, 243, 293, 300, 301, 422, 459, 472
Daney, Serge, 8
Danly, Susan, 123
Dante, 272; *Convivio*, 255; *Inferno*, 398
Danto, Arthur, 243, 525n44

Darwin, Charles, 297; *The Expression of the Emotions in Man and Animals*, 96–97
Daudet, Leon, 109, 111
David, Jacques-Louis, 127
death: in André Bazin, 230; in Stan Brakhage, 472–74, 491, 493; in Gustav Deutsch, 405; in Emily Dickinson, 270–73; in Thomas Edison, 76; in Nina Fonoroff, 368; in Ken Jacobs, 358; in *Metropolis* (Lang), 459; in Novalis, 488; of panorama, 135; and photography, 262, 269; in Bernard Steigler, 313; and virtual, 269. *See also* ghosts; haunting
Deleuze, Gilles, 8, 228, 240, 306, 324, 327–28, 363–64, 366, 371, 399, 430; on cinema, 306, 329; *Kafka*, 363–64, 366, 371; on movement image, 8, 429; on virtual, 327–28
della Porta, Giambattista, 86, 97, 107, 252, 284, 315, 317
Delluc, Louis, 235
DeLue, Rachael, 149–50, 152
Demenÿ, Georges, 84, 85, 86, 105–7, 109, 510n74
Deren, Maya, 237, 276, 331, 415, 421, 429, 458; *Choreography for the Camera*, 237; *Meditation on Violence*, 237; *Meshes of the Afternoon*, 276; *Ritual in Transferred Time*, 237; *The Very Eye of Night*, 237
Derrida, Jacques: "Edmond Jabès and the Question of the Book," 359; on haunting, 269
Descartes, René, *The Passions of the Soul*, 86, 88
desire: in Kenneth Anger, 408–11, 414–15, 418–19; in Stan Brakhage, 489; in Abigail Child, 428, 436; female, 94; for novelty, 6, 21, 77, 78; and phantasms, 272–73; queer, 33–34, 408–11, 414–15, 418–19; sexual, 405; signification of, 218; spectatorial, 113, 123, 385–86, 407; utopian, 112
detective stories, 64, 148, 178–81, 184, 187, 190
Deutsch, Gustav, 7, 16, 26, 36, 401–7; *Film ist.*, 16, 401–7; and found footage, 7, 16, 26; history in works of, 404
Diamond, Hugh W., 97; *Photograph of Patient*, *98*
Dickens, Charles, 193
Dickinson, Emily, 17, 269–73
Dickson, William K. L., 302–3, 454–55
Diderot, Denis, 121, 147
Didi-Huberman, Georges, 101, 112
digital media, 2, 13, 14, 15, 17, 28, 29–30, 35, 229, 232, 234, 236, 243, 318, 331, 440, 444, 457, 461; aesthetics of, 15
Direct Cinema, 454, 462
distraction, 21, 77, 79–81, 172, 353, 381
Doane, Mary Ann, 156, 161–62, 170
Doctor's Dream, The (Jacobs), 335–45, 351, 352, 355; dream work in, 343–44, 355; making of, 342; narrative logic of, 336–39
documentary, 2, 13, 45, 350, 351, 368–69, 398, 400, 405, 462
Dogma 95 movement, 242
Doyle, Arthur Conan, 179, 181, *186*
dream work, 343–44
Dubbini, Renzo, 115
Duchenne, G. B., 91–96, 100–101, 111, 112, 508n25
Dulac, Germaine, 235, 245

early cinema, 1–7, 10–11, 13–15, 19–20, 23–24, 27, 43–44, 46–47, 49, 52–54, 62, 69, 74, 76, 78–79, 84–86, 105, 107, 110, 113–14, 118–19, 136–37, 140, 143, 146, 148, 152, 194, 215, 218, 224–26, 304–5, 311, 374–75, 427; emergence of, 6, 13, 15, 23, 112, 158; gnostic potential of, 83; history of, 27, 42; myths of, 26, 67–69, 82, 138, 233
Eberhardt, J. A., 126
Edison, Thomas, 136, 140, 302, 303, 305, 394–96; devices of, 107, 109, 454–55; *Electrocuting an Elephant*, 76; *Facial Expressions*, 112; *Fred Ott's Sneeze*, 84, *85*, 109; *Goo Goo Eyes*, 112; *May Irwin Kiss*, 84, *111*; *Panorama of the Susquehanna River Taken from the Black Diamond Express*, 141; *Panoramic Scene, Susquehanna River*, 140; *Panoramic View, Kicking Horse Canyon*, 140; *Panoramic View of Lower Kicking Horse Canyon*, 142; *Panoramic View of Mt Tamalpias, Cal.*, 142; *Phantom Ride on the Canadian Pacific*, 141; *The Railroad Smash-Up*, 75; *View from Gorge Railroad*, 140. *See also* Edison Company; Kinetoscope
Edison Company, 48, 137, 140–42
editing, 16, 197, 421; in Kenneth Anger, 416; in Stan Brakhage, 367–68, 389, 486; in Robert Bresson, 486; in Abigail Child, 27, 421–24, 426, 429, 432; and continuity, 48; in Gustav Deutsch, 405, 407; and found footage, 16, 405; in David Gatten, 441–42; in D. W. Griffith, 198, 200, 202–3, 207–9, 211, 218, 219, 224, 423–24; hyper-, 198; in Ken Jacobs, 344, 351; and Kuleshov experiment, 339, 399–400, 402, 434; narrative, 42, 59, 76; in *Nosferatu* (Murnau), 247, 248, 459; parallel, 9, 194–95, 199; in Michael Snow, 438; Soviet theories of, 235, 306, 348, 434. *See also* montage
Eisenstein, Sergei, 2, 25, 28, 32, 46, 47, 49, 178, 235, 243–44, 300, 306, 309–10, 400, 421, 422, 429, 433, 434; on cinematic motion, 237, 243–44; on montage, 32, 237, 306, 310, 433; *October*, 33; *Strike*, 388
Elder, H. Bruce, 476–77
Eliot, T. S., 272, 448; *The Waste Land*, 313, 450
Elsaesser, Thomas, 3
Epstein, Jean, 25, 28, 84, 235, 294, 296, 447
Eriugena, Scottus, 471
erotic films, 43, 342. *See also* pornography
eroticism, 13, 413, 430

Esquirol, J. E. D., 97
exhibition, 137, 138, 148, 198, 276, 364
exhibitionism, 43, 45

face, 24, 84, 86, 88, 89, 91–95, 97–101, 103, 107, 110–13; and Georges Demenÿ, 84, 86, 105, 107; and physiognomy, 88, 89. *See also* close-up; physiognomy
facial expression films, 107, 109–10, 112
Fell, John, 3
film form, 12, 15, 42, 310, 340
film history, 1–2, 5–7, 10, 13, 14, 17, 20, 25, 27, 42, 49, 51–52, 54, 67, 84, 136, 194, 234, 364, 372, 435
film noir, 181, 367–68, 429–31, 458
film semiotics, 197, 307, 308
film theory, 3, 8, 26, 28, 83–84, 89, 228–30, 232, 234–38, 242, 305–6, 311; classical, 89, 234, 235, 242; and film history, 234; history of, 13, 15, 32; and indexicality, 228–30; origins of, 305
Fireworks (Anger), 33, 408, 411, 413–17, 419, 460, 535n7; desire in, 33, 408, 411, 414–15, 419; imagery in, 414–18; violence in, 416, 419
Flammarion, Camille, *Lumen*, 266–67
flashbacks, 13, 337
Fleischner, Bob, 351
Fonoroff, Nina, *A Knowledge We Can Not Lose*, 364, 366, 367, 368
found-footage film, 7, 16, 27, 250, 339–41, 351–54, 366, 370–71, 374, 383, 399–402, 405–7; and Gustav Deutsch, 399–402, 405–7
Frampton, Hollis, 5, 22, 337, 365, 399, 418, 438, 423, 455–57, 460, 472; *Gloria!*, 5; "A Lecture," 455–56; *nostalgia*, 337, 418; *Poetic Justice*, 438; *Zorns Lemma*, 22, 337, 338, 472
Freud, Sigmund, 81, 100, 147, 189–90, 271–72, 335, 343–45, 361, 362, 415, 504n34 (chap. 2), 504n2 (chap. 3), 506n21, 509n49, 518n34; on displacement, 343–45; *The Interpretation of Dreams*, 335; "Mourning and Melancholy," 271–72; "The Uncanny," 189–90, 518n34
Fried, Michael: on absorption, 76, 498n18; "Realism, Writing and Disfiguration in Thomas Eakins' Gross Clinic," 506n21
Friedberg, Anne, 31, 314–32; *The Virtual Window*, 22, 30, 314–15, 324, 330–31; *Window Shopping*, 314

Galassi, Peter, 133–34
galvanism, 276–77
Gance, Abel, *La Roue*, 41
gangster films, 412–13
Gatten, David, 16, 33, 34, 437–50; *The Enjoyment of Reading*, 442, 445; *The Great Art of Knowing*, 442, 445–47; *The Great Art of Light and Shadow*, 445; language in works of, 441, 443–44, 446, 447, 450; *Moxon's Mechanick Exercises or the Doctrine of Handy-Works Applied to the Art of Printing*, 442–43; *Secret History of the Dividing Line*, 437, 440, 442, 448; traces in works of, 439–40, 441, 442, 443; *What the Water Said, Nos. 1–3*, 34, 448–50
Gaudreault, André, 3, 9, 13, 42, 52, 302, 499n28
Gehr, Ernie, 1, 3, 8, 16, 36, 143, 337, 347–48, 365, 367, 372–91; *Eureka*, 347–48, 374–80, 382–83; *Field*, 376–77; *History*, 376–77; light in works of, 389–91; *Mirage*, 377, 389–90; movement in works of, 8, 347, 365, 367, 377, 383–85, 390; *Rear Window*, 383, 388–90; secrecy in works of, 373–76; *Serene Velocity*, 337, 346–48, 377–78, 384–85, 390; *Shift*, 348, 381–82, 384, 389; *Side/Walk/Shuttle*, 374, 381, 383–84, 386–89; *Signal—Germany on the Air*, 381–82, 386–87, 390; space in works of, 377–78, 385–86; *Still*, 378, 381–82; *This Side of Paradise*, 383, 387; time in works of, 378–79; *Untitled*, 347–48, 378, 382, 389; *Untitled, Part I*, 382, 287
gender, 94, 204, 213–18, 220, 221, 225–26, 430
genre, 2, 12, 57; and gender, 430–31; Hollywood, 416; in *Little Geezer* (Huff), 413; in *Mayhem* (Child), 430–31; "peeping tom" as, 57, 60; trompe l'oeil, 70. *See also* actuality films; attractions: cinema of; chase films; detective stories; facial expression films; found-footage film; horror; panorama films; travel films
ghosts, 15, 30, 151, 250–64, 268, 271, 282–83. *See also* haunting
Gidal, Peter, 465
Gilpin, James, 116–17, 124, 129, 134
Ginzburg, Carlo, 179
glass, projection on, 264–65, 455
Godard, Jean Luc, 5, 312, 399, 405; *Les Carabiniers*, 5, 312
Goethe, Johann Wolfgang von, "Amor as Landscape Painter," 114
Gordon, Bette, *Variety*, 368
Gordon, Rae Beth, 112, 296
Gorky, Maxim, 23, 70–71, 72, 79–80, 82, 138
grain (film), 348, 359, 370, 456, 461–62. *See also* materiality; scratch
Grau, Oliver, 318
Gravity (Cuarón), 2
Green, Anne Katharine, 181, 184–85; *The Leavenworth Case*, 185; *The Woman in the Alcove*, 187–88
Greenberg, Clement, "Avant-Garde and Kitsch," 464–65, 469
Griffith, D. W., 1, 3, 8, 10, 12, 13, 15, 19, 26–27, 42, 47, 54, 65–66, 84, 193–24, 247–48,

Griffith, D. W. (*cont.*)
411, 422, 423–24; *The Birth of a Nation*, 248; *Bobby's Kodak*, 65; *The Drive for Life*, 211; *Falsely Accused!*, 65; *The Girl and Her Trust*, 224; *Intolerance*, 248, 411, 424; *The Lonedale Operator*, 10, 15, 26, 193–225; narrative system of, 196; *The Red Man and the Child*, 54
Grosseteste, Robert, *On Light*, 22, 472
Grusin, Richard, *Culture, Technology and America's National Parks*, 119–20
Guattari, Félix, *Kafka*, 363–64, 366, 371
Gunthert, André, 103

Hale, George C., 44, 143
Hansen, Miriam, 18–19, 67, 81, 499n28, 506n21, 507n27, 518n20, 519n36
Harris, Neil, 109
haunting, 251, 259, 265, 268–69, 380
Hauron, Ducos du, 455
Hawthorne, Nathaniel, 117, 448; *The House of the Seven Gables*, 117
Hayles, N. Katherine, 318, 532n15
Heidegger, Martin: "The Age of the World Picture," 312–13, 394; "The Question Concerning Technology," 436
Hellzapoppin' (Potter), 62
Hepworth, Cecil, 54–55, 58, 61–63, 66, 110, 139; *How It Feels to Be Run Over*, 55, 139; *The Inquisitive Boots*, 58; *The Unclean World*, 58, 61–63; *The Unseen World*, 61
Herwitz, Peter, 16, 364, 366–68; *Musique de Ténèbres*, 364; *Mysterious Barricades*, 367
Hitchcock, Alfred, 13, 54, 237, 399, 518n15; *Rear Window*, 54
Hölderlin, Friedrich, 395, 436
Hollywood, 49, 119, 194, 197, 203, 221, 284, 287, 341, 344, 371, 410–16, 421, 423, 428, 430, 462. *See also* classical Hollywood cinema
horror, 13, 180, 184, 247, 269, 353, 382
Huff, Theodore, 411–15; *Little Geezer*, 411–15; *Mr. Motorboat's Last Stand*, 412
Hugo (Scorsese), 5
Humboldt, Alexander von, 127, 132, 134, 248
Hunt, John Dixon, 116
Huysmans, J. K., 271

ideology, 27, 109, 146, 218, 220, 253, 284–85, 342–44
immediacy, 8, 68, 79, 145, 239, 243, 370, 387, 466; desire for, 145
indexicality, 29, 32–33, 88, 103, 227–33, 236, 244–45, 267, 307, 439–40, 443, 446, 449, 525n49
Inness, George, 122–23, 134, 149–52; *The Lackawanna Valley*, 122
inscription, 32–34, 220, 305, 308, 446–49, 483, 485, 487–91

Jacobs, Ken, 1, 3, 16, 27, 36, 143, 335–45, 349–62, 365, 367, 375, 409, 429; apparatus in works of, 356–59; *Blonde Cobra*, 342, 350; *Camera Thrills of the War*, 43, 351; *The Doctor's Dream*, 335–45, 351, 352, 355; found footage in works of, 339–41, 351–52, 354, 362; *Lisa and Joey in Connecticut, January 1965*, 351; *Little Stabs at Happiness*, 350, 360; Nervous System performances, 351–52, 355–60, 367; *Nissan Ariana Window*, 350; *Orchard Street*, 350; *Perfect Film*, 36, 350–55, 359; *The Philippines Adventure*, 351, 359; *The Sky Socialist*, 350; *Soft Rain*, 350; *Star Spangled to Death*, 342, 351; time in works of, 359–62; *Tom, Tom, the Piper's Son*, 342, 350–52, 358, 360–61; *Urban Peasants*, 342, 350–51; *The Whole Shebang*, 351, 358; *XCXHXEXRXRXIXEXSX*, 351, 359
James, Henry, *In the Cage*, 221–23
Jarmusch, Jim, *Stranger than Paradise*, 420–21
Jarvies, James Jackson, 131
Jost, François, 51, 53
joy, 429, 434, 476, 479, 488–89

Kahn, Albert, *Archive of the Planet*, 312
Kant, Immanuel, 453–54, 456, 515n117
Kardec, Allan, *The Book on Mediums*, 252
Keaton, Buster, 2, 49, 293, 295–96
Keil, Charlie, 19, 194–95, 198, 208, 213, 523n84
Kepler, Johannes, 22, 255, 258, 261–63, 318–22, 330
kinesthesia, 236, 240–41
kinetograph, 302, 303, 305, 355
Kinetoscope, 73, 84, 106, 505n6
Kirby, Lynne, 75, 207, 214, 215, 223, 507n35
Kirby, Michael, 337–39
Klahr, Lewis, 366–70, 392, 427; *In the Month of Crickets*, 368; *Lost Camel Intentions*, 369–70; *Morning Films*, 367
Kleinhans, Chuck, 413
Kodak (Eastman), 65, 455, 462
Kracauer, Siegfried, 18, 20, 79–81, 192, 235, 237–38, 242, 262, 294, 525n49; "The Cult of Distraction," 79; "Photography," 518n20
Kubelka, Peter, *Schwechater*, 422, 424
Kuleshov, Lev, 28, 309–10, 339, 399–402, 405, 407, 434; experiment, 16, 310, 339, 399–402, 405, 407

landscape, 78–79, 114–37, 139–53, 176, 200, 374, 393; aesthetics, 15; in Stan Brakhage, 478–82, 487, 490; in Ernie Gehr, 374, 376; in Mark LaPore, 395; in *The Lonedale Operator* (Griffith), 202, 204–5; and technology. *See also* landscape painting; panorama; phantom rides
landscape painting, 24, 115–23, 130, 135, 137, 140, 147, 149, 153, 512n23, 514n98

Lang, Fritz, 12; *Metropolis*, 459, 491
language: in Stan Brakhage, 475, 476, 483–86, 489–90; in Abigail Child, 422, 425, 433–34; as film, 26, 83, 89, 197, 220, 235, 310, 366; in David Gatten, 441, 443–47, 450; as image, 32–35, 305–7, 368, 483–85
LaPore, Mark, 16, 17, 366–69, 392–98; *A Depression in the Bay of Bengal*, 394–96; everyday in, 394–95; *The Five Bad Elements*, 395; *The Glass System*, 395–97; *Kolkata*, 395, 397; labor in works of, 394–96; *Medina*, 367, 368; *The Sleepers*, 367, 369, 393; *Work and Play*, 368–69
laughter, 60, 94–95, 112, 287, 290–93, 297, 338
Lavater, Johann Caspar, *Physiognomische Fragmente*, 88–92, 97
Le Brun, Charles, *Conférence sur l'expression générale et particulière*, 86–88, 92–93, 97, 107
Lefebvre, Henri, *The Production of Space*, 203
Léger, Fernand, 41, 43; *Ballet Mécanique*, 293–94
Le Grice, Malcolm, *Abstract Film and Beyond*, 465–68, 470
Leopardi, Giacomo, *Pensieri*, 283–84
LePrince, Auguste, 455
Leroi-Gourhan, André, 32–34, 304–11, 485, 487; on "graphism," 32–34, 307–9, 485, 487; on technology, 32–33, 304–11
Leroux, Gaston, 181–85, 188; *The Mystery of the Yellow Room*, 185; *The Perfume of the Lady in Black*, 185, 188
Levy, Pierre, 327–28, 331
Lindberg, David, 257
Lindsay, Vachel, 89, 224
Lloyd, Harold, 293, 295–96
Londe, Albert, 86–90, 99–108; *Attaque d'hystérie chez l'homme*, 104
Lonedale Operator, The (Griffith), 10, 15, 26, 193–225; close-ups in, 209–13; editing of, 194, 197–203, 207–9, 211, 218–19; gender in, 215–18, 220–21, 225; narration of, 196–97, 203, 207–9, 211, 224–25
Lorrain, Claude, 115
Lucas, George, *Star Wars*, 6, 242
Lucretius, 256–57, 262–63: on vision, 478, 256–57
Lumière, Antoine, 233
Lumière brothers (Auguste and Louis), 3, 42, 104–5, 107, 233, 248, 302, 312, 394, 423, 504n1, 510n74; *The Arrival of a Train at La Ciotat*, 67, 70–77, 137–38, 375

Maeterlinck, Maurice, 287
magic films, 43–44
magic lantern, 78, 137, 168, 177, 259–60, 279, 281, 285, 287, 312, 319, 455, 505n2
Magli, Patrizia, 88
Maillet, Arnaud, 116–17
Mannoni, Laurent, 107, 162, 164–65, 510n74
Manovich, Lev, 236
Marey, Étienne-Jules, 21, 86, 103–7, 241, 267, 302, 305, 349, 356, 360, 394, 423, 447
Marinetti, F. T., 46–47, 49
Marx, Karl, 179; *Capital*, 285; *The German Ideology*, 284–85
Marx, Leo, *The Machine in the Garden*, 119–21
materialist film, 465, 467
materiality, 10, 30, 35, 113, 162, 170, 242, 249–50, 287, 315, 321–22, 442, 444, 457–61, 468. *See also* grain (film); mediation; scratch
Mayakovsky, Vladimir, "The Backbone Flute," 355
McDonald, Scott, 117–19, 129, 449
McLuhan, Marshall, 464
mediation, 20, 56, 124–25, 255, 321, 342, 370, 449, 441–59, 466
Méliès, Georges, 2, 3, 6, 42–44, 47, 49, 69–70, 72–74, 248, 288; *A Trip to the Moon*, 43
Melville, Herman, 246, 290, 448; *Moby Dick*, 246
Menke, Richard, 222–23
Merleau-Ponty, Maurice, 9, 275, 452, 455
Mesmer, Franz Anton, 278, 529n5
Metz, Christian, 26, 32, 43, 55, 68–69, 144, 197, 238–45, 306–7, 309, 311, 505n2, 506n21; on cinematic movement, 238–45; *Language and Cinema*, 197; "On the Impression of Reality in the Cinema," 238; on spectator credulity, 68–69; on voyeurism, 26
Michelson, Annette, 12, 22, 28, 314, 381, 501n72, 505n8, 515n117
Miller, Angela, 122, 128
Milton, John, 471
Minh-ha, Trinh, *Naked Spaces*, 369
minor cinema, 16, 23, 364, 366, 368–69, 371
Mitchell, Susan, "Bird, A Memoir," 175
Mitchell, W. J. T., "Imperial Landscape," 114
modernism, 19, 26–27, 29, 83, 108, 113
modernity, 15, 30, 82, 225; and Charlie Chaplin, 290, 298, 300; debates of, 17–20, 523n84; and detective fiction, 190, 192; and gender, 213–21; logic of, 14; and *The Lonedale Operator* (Griffith), 208; and phantasmagoria, 23, 190; and railway, 189
Mondzain, Marie-José, *Image, Icon, Economy*, 438, 440, 450
montage, 27–28, 32, 400, 421; in Kenneth Anger, 413, 416; in Stan Brakhage, 367–68, 479; in Charlie Chaplin, 298–300; in Abigail Child, 10, 421–23, 433–35; in Gustav Deutsch, 36, 407; in Sergei Eisenstein, 46, 235, 237, 300; in D. W. Griffith, 8, 10, 27; logic of, 35; power of, 400; Soviet, 27–28, 235, 306, 309–11, 400, 416, 421, 422, 433
Moran, Thomas, 123, 129, 131
Morgan, Daniel, 230–31
Moritz, Karl Phillip, 466, 470
Morris, Errol, *The Thin Blue Line*, 365

motion, 8, 9, 36, 73, 162–71, 235–45, 358, 423; in Stan Brakhage, 34, 472, 473, 474, 479, 480, 483–88; in Abigail Child, 237, 423, 425, 429–32; and cinema, 21–22, 236, 436; and Gilles Deleuze, 8, 429; and Guillaume-Benjamin Duchenne, 92; in Ernie Gehr, 374–81, 391; and human body, 394; as illusion, 78, 82, 110, 113, 155–59, 161, 170, 356–60; as landscape, 142–43, 145–46; and Albert Londe, 103–4; and Étienne-Jules Marey, 106–7, 356; slow, 45, 402; and spectatorial participation, 240; and stillness, 154, 160, 165, 237, 358, 429–30; and vitality, 77. *See also* camera movement; kinesthesia
Mozhukin, Ivan, 16, 310, 339, 399–400
Mulvey, Laura, 26; on glamour, 410; on indexicality, 244; on spectacle and narrative, 48, 63; "Visual Pleasure and Narrative Cinema," 1, 4, 432
Mumler, William, 264
Munsterberg, Hugo, 157–58
Murnau, Friedrich: *Nosferatu*, 246–50; *Tabu*, 238
musical, 5, 43, 76
Musser, Charles, 43, 141, 259, 504–5nn1–2, 515n111
Muybridge, Eadweard, 86, 103, 105, 106, 135, 137, 305, 356, 385, 394, 423

Nadar, Félix, 181, 261–62
narrative film, 12, 42, 59, 336–37, 339
narrative form, 195, 197, 198, 214
new media, 29, 123–24, 136, 172, 227–28, 233, 236, 245, 248–49, 274, 304, 307, 317, 330–31, 462. *See also* digital media
Nickerson, Catherine Ross, 184
Novak, Barbara, 121–23, 135
Novalis, 22, 35, 470, 475, 484–86, 488–89, 492; *Hymns to the Night*, 488; on physiognomy, 88
Nutty Professor, The (Lewis), 62

Oettermann, Stephan, 125, 126, 128
One Day Franz Came to My House (Marrero and Kouguell), 438
O'Neil, Pat, *Coreopsis*, 460
optical toys, 6, 14, 155–56, 159–72, 177, 179, 259–61, 264–67, 330
Osterweil, Ara, 535n20
Owen, Alex, 528n67

painting, 8, 13, 34, 54, 70, 76, 237, 390; cave, 308; and Stan Brakhage, 474, 484–88; and Ernie Gehr, 390; genre, 340; landscape, 24, 115–23, 130, 135, 137, 140, 147, 149, 153, 512n23, 514n98; modernist, 359
panorama, 24, 78–79, 125–44, 146, 153, 180, 182, 190, 318, 385. *See also* panorama films
panorama films, 143, 374
Paris, John Ayrton, 160–62
passivity, 7, 9, 68, 218, 311, 457–58
Pathé Company, 43, 57, 199, 292; *Ce que l'on voit de mon sixième*, 58; *La Fille de bain indiscrète*, 58; *La Loupe de Grand-Maman*, 57; *Le Déjeuner du sauvant*, 58, 61; *Les Cartes lumineuses*, 58; *Peeping Tom*, 58, 63; *Un coup d'oeil par étage*, 58, 59
Paul, William, 292
Peirce, Charles Sanders, 227–31, 439–40, 446
phantasmagoria, 7, 9, 15, 23, 30, 170, 176, 179, 190, 260–88 passim; history of, 276–85; ideology of, 282–85; logic of, 281
phantasms. *See* ghosts
phantom rides, 8, 24, 140–44, 146, 148–49
phenakistiscope, 106, 164–68, 170
Philips, Barnet, 107
Philipstahl, Paul de, 281
phonoscope, 106
photography, 21, 24, 64, 86, 133, 134, 259, 439; and face, 21, 24, 84, 86, 90–91, 93, 99, 101, 110, 113; and image of real, 273; and indexicality, 228–33, 236, 244–45; landscape, 137; medical, 91, 99–104; and memory, 311; ontology of, 252, 351, 400, 439–40, 443–44; reception of, 261–64; scientific, 21, 99–105, 110, 154, 246, 250, 252–53, 402; spirit, 13, 30, 93, 250–53, 255, 259, 263–66, 273; still, 86, 103, 104, 238, 244, 269
physiognomy, 22, 86, 88–91, 97, 101, 103, 106, 108, 394, 511n86; and mental illness, 101
Plateau, Joseph, 161, 164–66, 168
Plato: *Phaedrus*, 360; *Symposium*, 407
pleasure, scopic, 5, 18, 57, 59–60, 62–63, 65, 66, 75
Poe, Edgar Allan, 148, 178, 181, 184, 448; "The Domain of Arnheim," 115, 148; "The Fall of the House of Usher," 144, 147; "Landor's Cottage," 148; "The Man of the Crowd," 148, 178
Pogorelsky, M. V., 265–66, 380–81
Polidor, Philip, 281
Pope, Alexander, on gardening, 116
pornography, 401, 405–6, 430
Porter, Edwin S., 42; *The Gay Shoe Clerk*, 45; *The Great Train Robbery*, 48; *How a French Nobleman Got a Wife through the New York Herald "Personal" Columns*, 48
Pound, Ezra: on Chinese ideogram, 485; on light, 47; and montage, 422
Powers, John, 483–84
precarity, 451, 453, 456–63, 491. *See also* materiality; scratch
psychoanalysis, 4, 36, 101, 190, 232, 234, 344, 354–55, 405
Ptolemy, 155
Pudovkin, Vsevolod, 28, 309, 399
Pythagoras, 24, 86

queer cinema, 408–10, 414; and desire, 33, 408–10, 414; and refusal of closure, 409

railroad, 74–75, 117–24, 130, 132, 137, 140, 142, 355, 507n35
Rainer, Yvonne, 365
realism, 9, 21, 26–29, 68–72, 127–28, 134, 202, 243, 324; in Kenneth Anger, 417; bourgeois, 506n13; cinematic, 227, 229–33, 243; communicative, 27; diegetic, 6, 20, 76, 214, 224; in *Faces* (Cassevete), 462; indexical, 29, 227, 229–33, 238, 241, 440; and modernism, 26, 27; novelistic, 223; and transparency, 224, 462
Renoir, Jean, 242; *The Crime of M. Lange*, 238
Reynaud, Émile, 455
Richer, Paul, "Gonflement du cou chez un hystérique," *102*
Ricoeur, Paul, 312
Rilke, Rainer Maria, *Sonnets to Orpheus*, 323
Rimbaud, Arthur, *Season in Hell*, 286, 288
Ritter, J. W., 248
Robertson, Étienne-Gaspard, 260, 276–80, 285, 288
Rossell, Deac, 454
Russolo, Luigi, on noise, 454

Saki, "The Open Window," 314
Salt, Barry, 139
Saussure, Ferdinand de, 441
Schiller, J. F. von, "The Ghost-Seer," 260
Schivelbusch, Wolfgang: on panoramic perception, 78, 81, 124–25, 132, 139–40, 144; on railway, 176, 189
Schmitt, Jean-Claude, 255, 256, 268, 271
Schwartz, Vanessa, *Cinema and the Invention of Modern Life*, 18
scientific films, 61, 246–47, 401–3, 406
Sconce, Jeffrey, 253
scratch, 366, 456–59, 461, 469; in Kenneth Anger, 33–35, 418–19; in Stan Brakhage, 469, 474, 477, 488–91, 493; in David Gatten, 448; in Ernie Gehr, 378–79; in Ken Jacobs, 360
Sembach, Klaus-Jurgen, 138
semiotics, 197, 227–28, 231–32, 234, 306–8
sex: in *Fireworks* (Anger), 414, 417; and violence, 405
Shakespeare, William, *Hamlet*, 268, 281
Shapiro, Alan, 319
Shelley, Percy Bysshe, 455
Sherlock Jr. (Keaton), 62
Shields, Rob, 316–17, 328, 331
Shklovsky, Viktor, 454, 456
shock, 21, 52, 56, 69, 72, 74, 78, 81–82, 139, 142, 145, 176, 188, 277, 364–65, 395, 459. *See also* astonishment
Shub, Estir, *The Fall of the Romanov Dynasty*, 400
Simmel, Georg, 81
Singer, Ben, 196, 205, 215, 523n84
Sitney, P. Adams, 12, 341, 416, 476–77, 481, 483
Smith, Albert E., 73
Smith, G. A.: *As Seen through a Telescope*, 57, 60; *Grandma's Reading Glass*, 57
Smith, Jack, 2, 49, 341, 409, 429; *Flaming Creatures*, 409
Snow, Michael, 365; *So Is This*, 437, 438; *Wavelength*, 515n117
Snyder, Joel, 523n4
Solomon, Phil, 366; *Night of the Meek*, 401; *The Secret Garden*, 367, 370–71; *Walking Distance*, 401
Sontag, Susan, on camp, 410
spectacle, 45, 49, 52, 81, 505n2; cinema of, 54; destruction of, 457–58; in early cinema, 60, 72, 75–76; logic of, 6; and magic lantern, 260; and narrative, 48, 59, 62–63, 427; and panorama, 132; phallus as, 417; and phantasmagoria, 260, 276, 279, 281; and realism, 9; woman as, 432. *See also* attractions; exhibitionism
spectatorship, 25, 68, 119, 127, 129–31, 138, 144, 153, 171, 236, 242, 410, 505n2; and absorption, 8, 21, 26, 46, 59, 76–77, 127, 238, 244; and credulity, 68–70, 72; and distraction, 21, 77, 79; and terror, 68–70, 73–74, 82. *See also* attractions
Spehr, Paul, 302–3, 454
spirit photography, 13, 30, 93, 250–53, 255, 259, 263–66, 273
Spiritualism, 253–55, 266, 271
Stampfer, Simon, 163, 164, 166
Star Wars, 6, 242
Stein, Gertrude, *Stanzas in Meditation*, 476–77, 479, 482, 484–85
stereoscope, 78, 177, 182, 264, 265
Stewart, Garrett, 269
Stiegler, Bernard, *Technics and Time*, 32, 303–4, 311, 313, 331
Stoker, Bram, *Dracula*, 247
Structural Film, 350, 365–67, 422, 465, 470
Surrealism, 113, 191, 341
Symbolism 286, 287, 288

Talbot, Frederic, 134, 156, 161
Taylor, Bayard, 132
Tepperman, Charles, 411, 412
thaumatrope, 159–63, 165, 166, 168, 169
Thompson, Kristin, 171, 194, 202
Thoreau, Henry David, on locomotive, 119–21
Thornton, Leslie, 363, 402
3-D films, 356–58
Todorov, Tzvetan: on intransitivity of art, 465, 476; on language, 484
trace, 33, 35; and detective fiction, 179; in David Gatten, 439–43, 446–47, 450; photographic,

trace (*cont.*)
228, 232, 244, 400; in *Still* (Gehr), 379. *See also* inscription
train films, 70, 74, 78, 79, 119, 140, 143, 147
transparency: and film materiality, 454–56, 459, 473, 477–78, 491; myth of, 452–53; and realism, 462; as transitive, 470, 484
travel films, 17, 42, 137, 398
trick films, 43, 45, 47
trompe l'oeil, 70, 72
Tsivian, Yuri, 83, 139, 218, 265, 298, 499n28
Turner, J. M. W., 129, 131, 133, 135, 143, 160; *Rain, Steam, Speed*, 132
Turner, Lana, 456, 457

Untitled (1977) (Gehr), penetration of space in, 347–48
Urban, Charles, *Unseen World*, 27

Vertov, Dziga, 28, 84, 309, 348, 434, 436; *Enthusiasm*, 433; *Man with a Movie Camera*, 426, 433; *Symphony of the Don Basin*, 433
violence, 10, 78, 176, 217, 237, 290, 336, 371, 405, 409, 416, 418–19, 435–36, 444, 458–59
virtual, 30, 251, 271, 276, 315–31; image, 162, 163, 166, 169–70, 255–56, 259, 261, 263–69, 271–73, 312; reality, 9, 287. *See also* Friedberg, Anne
visibility, 10, 41, 43, 146, 188, 211–12, 234, 246, 250, 424, 470–72
vision: in antiquity, 37, 256–58; in Stan Brakhage, 34, 458–59, 478, 489, 491; Jonathan Crary on, 154–55; crisis of, 254, 268; in Emily Dickinson, 271, 273; fallibility of, 107, 171; and ghosts, 30, 254–58, 268, 273, 281; in Martin Heidegger, 312; in Cecil Hepworth, 61; and Johannes Kepler, 318–19, 322; loss of, 459; mediated, 249, 254–58; in Merleau-Ponty, 452–53, 455; and panorama, 126, 133, 140; persistence of, 156–61, 164, 166, 347; theory of, 21, 318; uncanny, 189, 190–92; in *The Woman in the Alcove* (Green), 188
Vitagraph company, 73, 196, 305, 519n10
Vitascope, 22, 44, 109, 305
voyeurism, 26, 43, 47, 57–60, 62–66, 80, 389, 503n26

Wagner, Richard, 286–87
Walpole, Horace, 124
Warburg, Aby, 293
Wees, William, 401
Welles, Orson, 242; *Don Quixote*, 5
Wertheimer, Max, 158
Wilton, Andrew, 131
Wollen, Peter, on semiology, 229–30
writing. *See* inscription; trace
Wyzewa, Teodor, 286

Young, Paul, 218, 224

Zentropa (von Trier), 147
Zinman, Gregory, 491, 493
zoetrope, 6, 156–57, 167, 170. *See also* optical toys